MEASUREMENT AND EVALUATION IN PSYCHOLOGY AND EDUCATION

FOURTH EDITION

ROBERT L. THORNDIKE
RICHARD MARCH HOE PROFESSOR
OF PSYCHOLOGY AND EDUCATION
TEACHERS COLLEGE
COLUMBIA UNIVERSITY

ELIZABETH P. HAGEN
PROFESSOR OF PSYCHOLOGY AND EDUCATION
TEACHERS COLLEGE
COLUMBIA UNIVERSITY

JOHN WILEY & SONS

New York • Chichester • Brisbane • Toronto • Singapore

Library of Congress Cataloging in Publication Data:

THORNDIKE, ROBERT LADD, 1910–
    MEASUREMENT AND EVALUATION IN PSYCHOLOGY AND EDUCATION.

INCLUDES BIBLIOGRAPHIES AND INDEX.
1. MENTAL TESTS. I. HAGEN, ELIZABETH P., 1915–
JOINT AUTHOR. II. TITLE.

LB1131.T59 1977   155.9   76-50630
ISBN 0-471-86366-1

PRINTED IN THE UNITED STATES OF AMERICA

20 19 18 17 16 15 14 13 12

PREFACE

When the first edition of this book appeared 22 years ago, the American public and American education were in a hectic push for excellence in response to Russian space exploits. A good many Sputniks have flown across the sky since then, and many winds of change have blown over education and educational and psychological measurement. Within society, pressure for integration, for equal rights and for fair employment have called in question the appropriateness of admissions, employment and licensure testing. Within the schools, revived proposals for individualizing instruction have led to a recognition that comparison of the pupil with a group of peers does not always provide the information that one needs for an educational decision. But the need for objective, dependable information as the basis on which to make decisions remains unaltered. Test and measurement procedures represent one important source of this information.

In this, our fourth edition we appraise recent emphases on fair testing, the rights of individuals and criterion-referenced tests, taking what is useful from the new without gulping it down whole, and blending it with the solid foundation in educational and psychological measurement developed over the past 70 years. Our purpose is to produce a balanced treatment that is sensitive to the concerns of the 1970s without losing the solid foundation of the past.

In this edition we have made a consideration of testing and measurement as an aid to decision making the central theme. We identify a wide range of educational and personal decisions, and ask how testing and measurement procedures can contribute to each. This seems to us to be the heart of the matter. Tests and measurements are of value to the extent that they permit, and are used for better decision making. If this end is kept always in view, a sound appraisal of testing as one means to that end seems possible.

We would also like to suggest that if your students seek further aid in the area of measurement and evaluation that they obtain PERSPECTIVES IN MEASUREMENT AND EVALUATION: A Study Guide prepared by Daniel J. Mueller of Indiana University, keyed to our text published by John Wiley & Sons, Inc. It contains master checklists of key concepts with page references to the text, study aids, supplementary reading, study exercises, and practice tests.

ROBERT L. THORNDIKE
ELIZABETH P. HAGEN

CONTENTS

MEASUREMENT
AND
EVALUATION
IN PSYCHOLOGY
AND
EDUCATION

CHAPTER ONE
ORIENTATION TO TESTING

This world is a world full of decisions. Some are decisions at the national and international level, having to do with policies concerning budgets and treaties, energy, and pollution—but these are not our present concern. Some are decisions about things—whether to buy a new car, and if so what kind—but these too are not our present concern. However, many are decisions about people, individually and in groups, and these are what psychological and educational evaluation and measurement are all about. The teacher, the counselor, the school administrator, the psychologist in business and industry are continuously involved in making decisions about people, or in helping people to come to decisions about their own lives. The role of measurement procedures is to provide the information that will permit these decisions to be informed and appropriate.

TYPES OF DECISION ABOUT PERSONS

Some decisions are *instructional* decisions; many that a teacher makes are of this sort. Some of these instructional decisions relate to the class as a whole; for example, should class time be spent in reviewing the concept of "borrowing" in subtraction, or does most of the class have adequate competency in this skill? Some instructional decisions relate to specific students in the class; for example, what reading materials are likely to be suitable for Mary, in view of her interests and level of reading skill? If such decisions are to be made wisely, it is important to know the level of skill that the class has in "borrowing" in the first instance; how competent a reader Mary is in the second.

Some decisions are *curricular* decisions. A school may be considering some curricular change, such as introduction of the Phonetic Initial Teaching Alphabet for the initial stages of reading instruction. Should the change be made? A wise decision on this point hinges upon finding out, either by research directly within the school itself or by assembling the voluminous results of prior research, how well children are found to progress in reading using this approach rather than the conventional one. And such research can be only as good as the measures of reading competence by which we assess the outcomes of the two alternative instructional procedures.

Some decisions are *selection* decisions made by an employer or by an educational institution. A popular college must decide, on some basis, which of the applicants to admit to its freshman class. Criteria for admission are likely to be multiple and complex, but one criterion will usually be that the admitted student is likely to be able to carry on successfully the academic work that the college provides. The college seeks information, in part through high school records, but in part through a uniform testing program, to permit it to judge which applicants are likely to succeed in its program. Selection decisions arise in employment as well as in education, and the employer, seeking to identify the potentially more effective employees, may also find that standard performances in a controlled testing situation provide information that can improve the accuracy and objectivity of his decisions.

Sometimes decisions are *placement* or *classification* decisions. A high school may have to decide whether a senior should be put in the rapid moving advanced placement section in mathematics, or in the regular section. Or the Army personnel technician may have to decide whether recruit Don Blessing should be assigned to the school for electronic technicians or the school for cooks and bakers. For placement and classification decisions the decision maker needs information to help him predict how much the individual will learn from or how successful he will be in each of the alternative programs. Measures of aptitude, interest, and previous achievement can provide some of this information.

Finally, there are many decisions that can best be called *personal* decisions. They are choices that the individual makes concerning himself at the many crossroads of life. Should he plan to go to college, or to some other type of post-high school training? Or should he seek a job at the end of high school? If a job, what kind of job? In the light of his decision, what sort of program should he take in high school? To answer questions of this sort he may ask: What sort of a person am I? How do I compare with other people? How do I stack up against the demands of this type of job? Can I do it? Will I like it? Measures of abilities, interests, and temperament can provide some of the evidence that will permit the person to give an informed answer.

THE ROLE OF MEASUREMENT IN DECISION MAKING

Throughout this book the central question will be: How can educational and psychological measurement techniques help people to make better decisions? All the other questions that are raised will grow out of and feed back into this central question. We will ask what properties measurement devices must have if they are to help us make sound decisions. We will ask in what form test results should be presented if they are to be most helpful to the decision maker. As we look at each type of evaluation technique that has been developed, we will ask for what types of decision that particular technique can contribute information of value. Throughout, we shall be concerned with the variety of factors, including poor motivation, emotional upset, inadequate schooling, or deviant cultural background, that may distort the information provided by a test, questionnaire, or other assessment procedure, and shall consider the precautions that need to be employed in using the information from each evaluation technique in decision making.

It is of course clear that measurement procedures do not make decisions; *people* make decisions. Measurement procedures can at most provide information on *some* of the factors that are relevant to a decision. A scholastic aptitude test can provide an indication of how well Peter is likely to do in college-level work. Combined with information about how academically demanding the engineering program is at Siwash, the test score may provide a specific estimate about how well Peter is likely to do in the engineering program at Siwash. But only Peter can decide whether he should go to Siwash and study engineering. Is he interested in engineering? Does he have any personal reason for wanting to go to Siwash rather than somewhere else? What are the economic factors in the decision? What type of role in life does Peter aspire to? Maybe he would like to be a farmer or a beachcomber. Maybe he has no motivation for or interest in higher education.

This illustration should make it clear that decisions on actions to be taken involve not only facts but also values. Should Peter try to go to Siwash or to Harvard? A scholastic aptitude test produces a score that is a *fact,* and that fact may permit a prediction that Peter has five chances in six of being admitted to Siwash and only one in six of being admitted to Harvard. But if Peter considers Harvard 10 times as desirable as Siwash, it might still be a sensible decision for him to apply to Harvard instead of Siwash in spite of his radically lower chance of gaining admission. The point is that the test provides no information about the domain of values. This information has to be supplied from other sources before a sensible decision can be made.

Again, an aptitude test may permit an estimate of the probability of success for a black or Hispanic student, compared to the probability for white students, in some type of professional training. However, a decision with respect to admission would have to include, explicitly or implicitly, some judgment as to the relative value to society of adding more white persons to that profession in comparison to the value of having increased black or Hispanic representation. Such issues of value are always complex, often controversial. But issues of value are usually deeply involved in decision making. It is important that this be recognized, and important that assessment procedures that can supply us with better facts not be blamed for the ambiguities or conflicts that may be found in our value systems.

The role of educational and psychological assessment procedures can be no more than to provide some of the information in terms of which decisions may be made. We hope they can provide useful information, and provide it better than can alternate approaches. The study of educational and psychological assessment should provide an acquaintance with the tools and techniques that are available for obtaining information about people. Beyond that, such study should provide criteria for evaluating the information that is provided by these tools, for judging what degree of confidence is to be placed in the information that they provide and for sensing the limitations inherent in that information.

So far we have considered practical decisions leading to action. Measurement is also important in providing information to guide theoretical decisions. In these cases the desired end result is not action but understanding. Do girls read better than boys? A reading test is needed to provide the information on which to base a decision. Do students who are anxious about tests do worse on them than students who take them in stride? A questionnaire on "test anxiety" and a test of academic achievement could be used to obtain information that would help to permit a decision on this question. Measurement is fundamental to answering practically all the questions that science asks, not only in the physical sciences, but also in the biological and social sciences.

ASPECTS OF THE INDIVIDUAL RELEVANT TO DECISIONS

Some decisions that we may be interested in call for information about what a person or group of persons *can now do*. Many instructional decisions in schools call for information of this sort. Walter is making a good many mistakes in his oral reading. Can he match words with their initial consonant sounds? A brief test focused on this specific skill can help us decide whether lack of this particular skill is part of Walter's difficulty. How many of the children in Walter's class have mastery of the rule on capitalizing proper names? A focused test can provide evidence to guide a decision as to whether further teaching of this skill is needed. Is the current program in mathematics in Centerville producing satisfactory achievement? A survey mathematics test with national and regional norms can permit comparisons of Centerville students with students in the rest of the country, and this comparison can be combined with other information about Centerville's pupils and its schools to reach a judgment as to whether progress is satisfactory.

The type of ability test that describes what a person *has learned to do* is called an *achievement* test. The achievement tests represented in the above illustrations are of two rather sharply contrasting types. The test of initial consonant sounds is concerned with mastery of one specific skill by one student, and no question is raised as to whether Walter is better or worse than any other student. The only question is, can he perform this task well enough so that it is adequate for his reading. Similarly, Walter's teacher is concerned with the level of mastery, *within* this class, of a specific skill of English usage. Tests concerned with mastery of such defined skills are often called *content-referenced* or *criterion-referenced* tests, because the focus is solely upon reaching a standard of performance on the specific skill called for by the test exercises. Many, perhaps most, assessments needed for instructional decisions are of this sort.

With these we may contrast the mathematics survey test given to appraise mathematics achievement in Centerville. Here the decision is whether Centerville is showing satisfactory achievement *when compared with other towns like Centerville.* The point of reference is not a task per se, but the performance in some more general reference group. A test used in this way may be spoken of as a *norm-referenced* test because the norm of acceptable performance is set by group comparison. A norm-referenced test may appropriately be used in many curricular decisions, many guidance decisions, and many research decisions. We shall have occasion from time to time throughout this book to compare and contrast criterion-referenced and norm-referenced achievement tests with respect to aspects of their construction, their desired characteristics, and their use.

Some decisions that we need to make call for information about what a person *can learn to do.* Will Helen be able to master the techniques of computer programming? How readily will Richard assimilate calculus? Selection and placement decisions typically involve predictions about future learning, based on present characteristics of the individual. A test that is used in this way as a predictor of some future performance is spoken of as an *aptitude test.*

It should be pointed out that some of the effective predictors of future learning are measures of past learning. Thus, for both computer programming and calculus, an effective predictor might be a test measuring competence in high school algebra. Such a test would measure previously learned knowledge and skill, but we would be using that measure to predict future learning. It must be recognized that any test, whatever it is called, assesses a person's present abilities. We cannot directly measure a person's hypothetical "native" or "inborn" ability. All we can measure is what that person can do in the here and now. That information may then be used to evaluate past learning, as when an algebra test is used to decide whether Richard should get an A in his algebra course, or to predict future learning, as when it is used to decide whether Richard has a reasonable probability of successfully completing calculus. The distinction between an aptitude and an achievement test lies more in the purpose for which the results are used than in the nature or content of the test itself.

Some decisions call for information on what a person *likes to do.* Here we are dealing with assessment of interests or values. In the decisions that an individual makes involving educational choices or career choices, it may be as important to be able to estimate whether a particular future will be one in which the person will find satisfaction and contentment as it is to judge whether he is likely to achieve a high level of success. Systematic procedures for getting from a person a catalogue of his or her likes and dislikes enable us to produce scores that indicate the probability that he or she will be interested in any of a number of occupations or types of activity.

Some decisions in relation to persons call for information on what each *typically does do*. In interaction with others, does Marian typically take the initiative and strive for a leadership role, or is she content to sit back and follow the lead of someone else? Under pressure of an examination or some other important event, does Sam "keep his cool," or does he "blow it"? Assessments of life style or temperament or personality constitute some of the most varied, some of the most interesting, and some of the trickiest of psychometric devices.

Finally, some decisions—especially theoretical decisions having to do with extending our understanding of human behavior—call for measures of *inner states* and *traits* of individuals. These are *constructs*—attributes of individuals that we literally construct in order to help us to explain or theorize about their behavior. Expressions like anxiety, internality, field dependence, authoritarianism, and many others refer to aspects of feeling and acting that have seemed to some to provide useful ways of gaining understanding of the organization and dynamics of behavior.

In the chapters that follow we will look at measures of ability, both achievement and aptitude, measures of interest and temperament and measures of constructs that may help to understand people. But first let us consider where information about people can come from, what is called for in good measurement procedures, and what some of the key current issues are in psychological and educational measurement.

SOURCES OF EVIDENCE
ABOUT A PERSON

Where does the evidence come from by which we assess the characteristics of a person? We may divide the sources into two main types: naturally occurring life situations and specially structured "test" situations.

It is important to remember, perhaps especially in a book on "tests and measurements," that much of the evidence by which we reach characterizations of a person comes from the naturally occurring events of life. A teacher observes students day by day in the classroom as they interact with their classmates and with the materials and tasks of the day. A supervisor sees the employees on the job. All of us see our family and friends as we work and play together. From all of these interactions, we form impressions of the observed person—impressions that are often rough and unsystematic, but that are based on a broad range of real-life situations.

We may try to systematize and use these real-life observations in various ways. When it is a matter of using accumulated observations that have already taken place in the past, we may try to organize and quantify these through some type of report or rating form. The problems and issues in using rating procedures are set forth in Chapter 12. We may try to observe behavior as it occurs—the classroom behavior of a teacher or the playgroup behavior of a preschooler. But natural behavior is a complex stream with many aspects, so it will be necessary to define carefully what is to be observed, to set up procedures for recording the desired features, and to train observers to follow the definitions and to use the procedures. The problems and the procedures for assessing aspects of a person through direct observation also are considered in detail in Chapter 12.

There are very real advantages in basing appraisals on naturally occurring behavior. Of course, the primary advantage is that the behavior *is* spontaneous and unrehearsed; it is the way individuals act when they are being themselves, and is free from unintended facade or intentional distortion. The individual being observed is not showing us the person that he would like to be, but rather the person that he is. But there are many disadvantages too. Observation is demanding and time consuming. Memory of past behavior is subject to all sorts of distortion. The kind of behavior that we are interested in may not occur spontaneously in a way that we can observe it, or sufficiently often to give us an adequate supply of observations. For these reasons we find a good many occasions when it is more effective to rely upon specially structured situations designed to elicit the behavior that we are interested in, in a form that we can observe conveniently.

One type of specially structured situation, and the type we are most likely to think of when we speak of psychological and educational measurement, is the paper-and-pencil test of aptitude or achievement. We shall consider the preparation of such tests in Chapter 7 and their application and use in Chapters 8, 9 and 10. However, we can also use the paper-and-pencil format to obtain a description of an individual's feelings and personal reactions. Self-report inventories are especially important in assessing interests, attitudes, values, and aspects of temperament and adjustment. Instruments of this type will be considered in Chapter 11.

Contrived "test" situations are not limited to those given in a test booklet in a classroom or similar setting. The test may require individuals to carry out a performance, demonstrating some skill, as in a typing test. Or it may place them in some interpersonal situation with a defined task to be performed by the group. Or, again, it may provide tools and a misbehaving television set and require the person to locate and correct the malfunction. Such performance measures are a good deal less convenient than are tasks that can be assembled in a test booklet, but they serve an important function in assessing performance skills that are important both in aspects of education and in life. Some problems peculiar to this type of testing are described in Chapter 13.

ESSENTIAL STEPS IN MEASUREMENT

In this book we speak of the measurement of human abilities, interests and personality traits. We need to pause for a moment and see what is implied by measurement and what requirements must be met if we are to legitimately speak of measurement. We need to ask further how well the techniques for measuring the aspects of people that we are interested in do in fact meet these requirements.

Measurement in any field always involves three common steps: (1) identifying and defining the quality or attribute that is to be measured, (2) determining a set of operations by which the attribute may be made manifest and perceivable, and (3) establishing a set of procedures or definitions for translating observations into quantitative statements of degree or amount. An understanding of each of these steps and of the difficulties that it presents provides a sound foundation for understanding the procedures and problems of measurement in psychology and education.

IDENTIFYING AND DEFINING THE ATTRIBUTE

We never measure a thing or a person. Measurement is always of a quality or attribute of the thing or person. We undertake to measure the *length* of the table, the *temperature* of the blast furnace, the *durability* of the auto tire, the *flavor* of the cigarette, the *intelligence* of the school child, the *emotional maturity* of the adolescent. When we deal with the simplest physical attributes, such as length, it rarely occurs to us to wonder about the meaning or definition of the attribute. A clear meaning for length was established long ago in the history of both the race and the individual. Though mastery of concepts of "long" and "short" may represent significant accomplishments in the life of a preschool child, the concepts are automatic and axiomatic in adult society. We all know what we mean by *length*. However, this is not true of all physical attributes. What do we mean by *durability* in an auto tire? Do we mean resistance to wear and abrasion from contact with the road? Do we mean resistance to puncture by pointed objects? Do we mean resistance to deterioration and decay with the passage of time? Or do we mean some combination of these three and possibly other elements? Until we can reach some agreement as to what we mean by *durability,* we can make no progress toward measuring it. To the extent that we disagree on what *durability* means, we will disagree on what procedures are appropriate for measuring it, and if we use different procedures, we will disagree in the value that we get as representing the durability of a particular brand of tire.

The problem of reaching agreement as to what a given concept means is even more acute when we start to consider those attributes with which the psychologist or educator is concerned. What do we mean by intelligence? What kinds of behavior shall we characterize as intelligent? Shall we define the concept primarily in terms of dealing with ideas and abstract concepts, or will it include dealing with things—with concrete objects? Will it refer primarily to behavior in novel situations, or will it include response in familiar and habitual settings? Will it refer to speed and fluency of response, or to level of complexity of reaction without regard to time? We all have a general idea as to what we mean when we characterize behavior as intelligent, but you can see that there are many specific points on which we may disagree as we try to make our definition precise. This is true of almost all psychological concepts— some more than others—and the first problem that the psychologist or educator faces as he tries to measure the attributes that he is interested in is that of arriving at a clear, precise, and generally accepted definition of the attribute that he proposes to measure.

Of course, we also face a prior question. We must decide which attributes are relevant and important to measure if our description is to be useful for our present needs. A description may fail to be useful for the need at hand because we choose irrelevant features to describe. Thus in describing a painting we might report its height, its breadth, and its weight. We might report these with great precision. If our concern were to crate the picture for shipment, these might be just the items of information we would need. On the other hand, if our purpose was that of characterizing the painting as a work of art, our description would be worthless. The attributes of the picture we had described would be essentially irrelevant to its quality as a work of art.

Similarly, a description of a person may be of little value for our purpose if we choose the wrong things to describe. Thus a company selecting employees to become truck drivers might test their verbal comprehension and ability to solve quantitative problems, getting very accurate measures of these functions. It is likely, however, that information on these factors would help little in identifying people who would have low accident records and be steady and dependable on the job. Other factors, such as eye-hand coordination, depth perception, and freedom from uncontrolled aggressive impulses might prove much more relevant to the tasks and pressures that a truck driver faces.

Again, we have known a high school music teacher who tested very thoroughly the pupils' knowledge of such facts as who wrote the Emperor Concerto and whether andante is faster than allegro, getting a very dependable appraisal of their information about music and musicians, without presenting them with a single note of actual music, a single theme or melody, a single interpretation or appraisal of living music. As an appraisal of musical appreciation the test seemed to us almost worthless because it was using bits of factual knowledge *about* music and composers in place of any indication of progress in the appreciation of music itself.

DETERMINING A SET OF OPERATIONS TO EXPOSE THE ATTRIBUTE TO VIEW

The second aspect of measurement is finding or inventing a set of operations that will isolate the attribute in which we are interested and display it to us. Once again, the operations for measuring the length of an object such as a table were laid down in the early history of mankind. We convey them to the child early in elementary school. The ruler, the yardstick, the tape measure are uniformly accepted as appropriate instruments, and laying them along the object as an appropriate procedure for displaying to our eye the length of the table, desk, or other object we are studying. But the operations for measuring length or distance are not always so simple. By what operations do we measure the distance from New York to Chicago? From the earth to the sun? From the solar system to the giant spiral nebula in Andromeda? How shall we measure the length of a tuberculosis bacillus or the diameter of a neuron? Physical science has progressed by developing instruments that extend the capabilities of our senses and indirect procedures that make accessible to us amounts too great or too small for the simple direct approach of laying a measuring stick along the object. The operations for measuring length or distance have become indirect, elaborate, and increasingly precise. And they are accepted because they give results that are consistent, verifiable, and useful.

Turning to the example of durability of an auto tire, we can see that the operations for eliciting or displaying that attribute will depend upon and interact with the definition that we have accepted for it. If our definition is in terms of resistance to abrasion, we need to develop some standard and uniform procedure for applying an abrasive force to a specimen and gauging the rate at which the rubber wears away—some standardized simulated road test. If we have indicated puncture resistance as the central concept, we need a way of applying graduated puncturing forces. If our definition has been in terms of deterioration from sun, oil, and other destructive agents, our procedure must expose the specimens to these agents and must provide some index of the loss of strength or resilience that results. If our definition incorporates more than one aspect, then each must be incorporated, with appropriate weight, in our assessment.

The definition of an attribute and the operations for eliciting it interact. On the one hand, the definition we have set up determines what we will accept as relevant and reasonable operations. Conversely, the operations we are able to devise to elicit or display the attribute constitute in a very practical sense the definition of the attribute. We speak of an *operational definition*. What we are saying is that the set of procedures we are willing to accept as showing the durability of an auto tire become the effective definition of durability so far as we are concerned.

The history of psychological and educational measurement during this century has been in large part the history of invention of instruments and procedures for eliciting, in a standard way and under uniform conditions, the behaviors that serve as indicators of the relevant attributes of persons. Thus the series of tasks devised by Binet and his successors constitute operations for eliciting behavior that is indicative of intelligence, and the Stanford-Binet and other tests have come to provide operational definitions of intelligence. The fact that there is no single universally accepted test, and that different tests vary somewhat in the tasks they include and in the order in which they rank people is evidence that we do not have complete consensus as to what intelligence is on the one hand, or what the appropriate procedures are for eliciting it on the other. And this lack of consensus is generally characteristic of the "state of the art" so far as psychological and educational measurement are concerned. There is enough ambiguity in our definitions on the one hand, and enough variety in the instruments we have devised to elicit the relevant behaviors on the other, that different measures of what is alleged to be the same trait may rank persons quite differently. Consider, for example, the rubric "citizenship," which appears as a trait to be rated on a number of school report cards. What does good citizenship mean in a school child? How well can we agree in defining it? And once we have had a try at defining it, what operations can we devise to assess its presence or absence?

QUANTIFYING THE ATTRIBUTE
IN UNITS OF DEGREE OR AMOUNT

The third step, once we have accepted a set of operations for eliciting an attribute, is to express the result of those operations in quantitative terms. We ask the question, "How many or how much?" In the case of the length of a table the question becomes "How many inches?" The inch represents a basic unit, and we can demonstrate that any inch equals any other by laying them side by side and seeing their equality. This is the direct and straightforward proof of equality for some of the simplest physical measures. For other measuring devices, such as the thermometer, equality of units rests upon a *definition*. Thus we define equal increases in temperature as corresponding to equal amounts of expansion of a volume of mercury. Long experience with this definition has shown it to be a useful one because it gives results that relate in an orderly and meaningful way to many other physical measures.

None of our psychological attributes have units whose equality can be demonstrated by direct comparison, in the way that the equality of inches or pounds can. How shall we demonstrate that arithmetic problem X is equal, in amount of arithmetical ability that it represents, to arithmetic problem Y?

How can we show that one symptom of anxiety is equal to another anxiety indicator? Thus, for the qualities with which the psychologist or educator is concerned, we always have to fall back upon some definition to provide units and quantification. Most frequently, we call one task successfully completed—a word defined, an arithmetic problem solved, or an analogy made—equal to any other task in the series successfully completed, and count the total number of successes for an individual. For a criterion-referenced test focused on a specific skill, we may set some percentage of successes—say 80 or 90— as our criterion of mastery, and base our decision for the individual on whether he does or does not reach the standard. For a norm-referenced test the raw score of tasks done correctly is converted into some statement about the age or grade group that a person matches, or about his standing within such a group, by procedures discussed more fully in Chapter 4. This count of tasks successfully completed or of choices of a certain type provides a plausible and manageable definition of amount, but we have no really adequate evidence of the equivalence of different test tasks or different questionnaire responses. By what right do we treat a number series item such as "1 3 6 10 15 __?__ __?__ " as showing the same amount of intellectual ability as, for example, a verbal analogies item such as "Hot is to cold as wet is to __?__"?

Thus the definition of equivalent tasks, and consequently of units for psychological tests, is rather shaky at best. When we have to deal with a teacher's rating of a child's cooperativeness or a supervisor's evaluation of an employee's initiative, for example, where some set of categories such as "superior," "very good," "good," "satisfactory," and "unsatisfactory" is used, the meaningfulness of the units in which these ratings are expressed is even more suspect.

In psychological and educational measurement we encounter problems in relation to all three of the steps that have just been set forth. First, we have problems in selecting the attributes with which to be concerned and in defining them clearly, unequivocally, and in terms upon which all can agree. Even for something as straightforward as "reading ability" we can get a range of interpretation. To what extent should a definition include each of the following?

1. Speed of reading.
2. Mechanics of converting visual symbols to sounds.
3. Getting direct literal meanings from a text.

4. Drawing inferences that go beyond what is directly stated.
5. Being aware of the author's bias or point of view.

As we deal with more complex and intangible concepts, such as cooperativeness, anxiety, adjustment, or rigidity, we may expect even more diversity in definition.

Second, we encounter problems in devising procedures to elicit the relevant attributes. For some psychological attributes, we have been fairly successful in setting up operations that call upon the individual to display the attribute, and permit us to observe it under uniform and standardized conditions. This holds true primarily for the domain of abilities, where standardized tests have been assembled through which the examinee is called upon, for instance, to read with understanding, to perceive quantitative relationships, or to identify correct forms of English expression. But there are many attributes with which we have been clearly less successful. By what standard operations can we elicit, in a form in which we can assess it, a potential employee's initiative, a school pupil's anxiety, or a soldier's suitability for combat duty? With continued research and with more ingenuity we may hope to devise improved operations for making certain of these qualities manifest. But one suspects that there are many psychological qualities for which the identification of suitable measurement operations will always remain a problem.

Finally, even our best psychological units of measure leave something to be desired. Units are set equal by definition. The definition may have a certain amount of plausibility, but the equality of units cannot be established in any fundamental sense. So the addition, subtraction, and comparison of scores will always be somewhat suspect. Furthermore, the precision with which the attribute is assessed—the reliability from one occasion to another or from one appraiser to another—is often discouragingly low.

QUALITIES DESIRED IN A MEASUREMENT PROCEDURE

The three steps that we have just considered for developing a measurement procedure focus our attention on the qualities crucial to a measurement procedure if it is to help people to make better decisions. Basically, there are two. The procedure must provide information that is relevant to the decision to be made, and it must provide information that is accurate.

For some types of decision it may be possible to determine relevance rather directly by examining the nature of the task that is set for the examinee or the kind of product that he produces. Thus, if we wish to hire a typist, and we know that a major part of the job will consist of typing neatly and accurately from rough copy, a test of typing from rough copy would appear to have obvious relevance for a decision on whether to hire. If we must decide whether a class needs instruction on placing the decimal point in multiplication, a set of problems like $11.33 \times 4.5 = 50985$, in which the examinee is required to insert the decimal point at the proper place, would seem to bear directly upon the decision about whether to provide further instruction.

In other cases the judgment of relevance is much more complex. Is a performance on a test based on the comprehension of reading passages relevant to a decision on whether Mary Kay should be accepted by Siwash Law School? Is an inventory assessing social ascendance relevant to Joe Myers' decision as to whether he should seek a job selling life insurance? Is a test of ability to pick out hidden figures in a complex of camouflage adequate to identify the "field dependent" individuals in a group, in order to study the relationship between "field dependence" and sociability? The answer is often not easy to come by, but that answer is central to a judgment of the usefulness of each of the measurement procedures that are offered for use in education and in psychology. The problems of assessing the relevance of test and measurement results to educational and psychological decisions will be considered in detail in Chapter 3, under the heading of test validity.

Evidence from a measurement procedure needs to be not only relevant but also accurate and representative. If a candidate for employment as a typist does 70 words per minute on a typing test, the personnel office wants some assurance that this figure is truly representative of the applicant's rate of work, and that a second testing wouldn't show a speed of 40 words per minute (or 100 wpm). If Vivian gets 9 out of 10 of a set of decimal point problems right on a mastery test on Monday, so that the teacher decides that she has mastery of that skill, we want to be reasonably confident that Vivian will get more than 5 or 6 right if she is given a comparable test on Friday. Of course no measure is absolutely accurate—even when we are measuring something as simple as length or weight. But we need to know how much variation we can expect in our measurement procedure, and consequently how much faith we can place in the scores that we get. These issues are also discussed more fully in Chapter 3, under the heading of reliability.

SOME CURRENT ISSUES IN MEASUREMENT

Educational and psychological assessments fall far short of perfection. Ever since the attempt was made to develop measurement techniques in a systematic way, the procedures have provided a target for a wide spectrum of critics. And a good deal of the criticism has been a justified response to some of the naive enthusiasms of measurement proponents and to some of the ill-conceived applications and interpretations of measurement results. In our discussion of test interpretation and use in subsequent chapters we shall try to be sensitive to earlier criticisms, and to the more technical questions that come up concerning the reliability and validity of test results. At this point we would like to identify and comment briefly on some of the issues that have been of special concern in the recent past.

TESTING OF MINORITY PERSONS

One issue that has received a great deal of attention in recent years is the use and interpretation of tests with minority groups and with other persons whose experiences and culture differ from what is typical of the general population of our country. There are, of course, all sorts of subgroups in our society, differing from one another in many ways. But the ethnic and linguistic minorities are probably the most clear-cut of these, and the ones for whom the appropriateness of tests and questionnaires built for the typical middle class white American are most open to question.

Some questions arise in relation to achievement tests that undertake to assess what a student *has learned* to do. In part these questions center around the degree to which the same educational objectives hold for groups from minority cultures. Is the ability to read standard English with understanding an important goal for black or Hispanic or Indian children? Is knowledge about the U.S. Constitution as relevant for these groups as for the middle class white eighth grader? One senses that so far as the basic skills of dealing with language and numbers are concerned, many of the same objectives would apply, but that as one moves into the content areas of history and literature there might be more divergence.

In part the questions focus on the specific materials through which basic skills are to be exhibited. Is the same reading passage about the life of the Eskimo appropriate in a reading test for a ghetto or reservation youngster, or should the material be specifically tailored to the life and experiences of each? We know all too little about the importance of factors of specific content in performance in areas such as reading comprehension, and need to do further research to determine how important such factors are.

In part the questions concern the motivation of minority groups to do well on tests in the school setting. Have unfortunate experiences with testing in school soured minority group members to the whole enterprise, so that they withdraw from the task and do not try? This is perhaps a challenge to the whole pattern of schooling, as well as to the choice of testing instruments, to provide a reasonable balance of satisfying and successful experiences in school and with all types of school task. Tasks and tests need to be adapted to the present capabilities and concerns of the individual student.

Many more, and more serious questions are raised when tests are used as a basis for deciding what an individual *can learn to do;* that is, as aptitude measures. An inference from a test score obtained at time T about what a person can learn to do at time T plus X is clearly a more "iffy" inference than an inference that merely states what he can do today. There are many intervening events that can throw the prediction off. And there are correspondingly more possibilities of biasing factors coming in to systematically distort the prediction for minority group members. Present facts that imply one prediction for the general majority may imply a different prediction for a minority group member whose experiences prior to the testing were far from typical.

Our problem is to learn what types of inference *can* appropriately be made for individuals with atypical backgrounds, and what types of adjustments or modifications of inferences need to be cranked into the system in order to permit the most accurate and equitable inferences and decisions for such persons.

INVASION OF PRIVACY

A second concern that has frequently been expressed in recent years involves invasion of privacy. What kinds of information is it reasonable to require an individual to give about himself, and under what circumstances? This issue arises not only in relation to testing, but in relation to all types of information from and about a person. What types of record should appropriately be kept, and to whom may they be made available? At one end of the scale, there are tests of job knowledge or skill, such as a typing test, to which no one is likely to object when the skill is clearly and directly relevant to the position for which the person is an applicant. At the other end of the scale are some self-descriptive instruments that lead to inferences about emotional stability, or a scattering of tests that try to assess honesty under temptation to lie or steal, in which the individual is led to give information about himself without awareness of what information he is giving or of how it will be used. In between are instruments that involve varying degrees of self-revelation and that appear to have varying degrees of immediate relevance to a decision.

At issue is not only what information is being obtained, but the purpose for which it is being obtained. Is the information being obtained at the individual's request to provide help with personal or vocational problems, or for use in a counseling relationship? The fact that the person has come for help implies a willingness to provide the information that is needed for help to be given, and a willingness to open himself up for inspection; invasion of privacy becomes a matter of relatively minor concern. However, when the information is being obtained to further institutional objectives, that is, those of an employer, an educational institution, or of "science," then concern for the individual's right to privacy mounts, and some equitable balance must be struck between individual values and social values. For example, more students were willing to allow use of a questionnaire designed to verify the emotional stability of an airline pilot than that of a bank clerk (75 vs. 34 percent). The rights of the individual are not absolute, but the feeling is often expressed that they have been too little considered in the past.

THE USE OF NORMATIVE COMPARISONS

A somewhat different type of issue has been raised concerning the emphasis, in test interpretation, on comparing the performance of one student with norms representing the typical performance of a national, or sometimes a local, sample of students. The point that has been made with increasing fervor is that many of the decisions for which tests are used, especially instructional decisions, do not call for and are only confused by comparisons with other persons. The essential information, it is urged, is whether the student can perform a specified task; this is the information that should guide decisions as to what should be taught or what tasks should be undertaken next. Of course there are settings in which comparison with others is essential to a sound judgment and decision. Is the latest applicant at the personnel office a good typist? How do we define "good typist" except in terms of the performance of other job applicants? A rate of 40 words per minute with 2 errors per minute is meaningless unless we know that the average graduate from a commercial school can type about 50 words per minute, with perhaps 1 error per minute. The employer wants an employee who comes up to a standard of typical performance, and that standard is set by the performance of others. In the same way, a school system that is trying to evaluate the reading achievement of its sixth graders as "good," "satisfactory," or "needing improvement" needs some bench mark against which to compare the performance in its own school. There is no absolute standard of reading performance. Whether it is reasonable to expect sixth graders in Centerville to read and understand a particular article in *Reader's Digest* can only be judged by knowing whether representative groups of sixth graders countrywide are able to read and understand the article.

In the past there have been many instances in which normative comparisons with an outside reference group have been used to guide decisions for which they had little or no relevance. Currently, a reaction has set in against misuses of normative data. Great emphasis is being given to content-referenced, criterion-referenced, or mastery tests. These do have an important place for some sorts of decision—but not for all. We need to know which type of comparison is useful for which situation. When should we ask if a student can satisfactorily perform some specific task, and when should we ask how he stands in relation to his fellows?

A POINT OF VIEW FOR TODAY

We conclude this introductory chapter by stating six propositions that seem to us to provide the foundation for a contemporary view of educational and psychological measurement procedures and of their role in our schools and our society. Each proposition is stated and briefly elaborated; finally, the purpose of this book is related to these propositions.

1. *Decisions have to be made.* They won't just go away. A teacher has to decide what is to be done during the reading period tomorrow. A medical school must decide which of the many applicants are to be admitted. A 17-year-old must decide whether to apply for college admission, and, if so, where to apply. These are illustrations of the myriad decisions that *must* be made, on some basis, day by day.

2. *The more relevant and more accurate the information, the better the decision.* To some extent this proposition rests on faith—the faith that the more we know about a situation, the better we can handle it. It says that ignorance is not bliss; it is folly. Of course information cannot be equated to wisdom. To know more about a situation, or to know more accurately, doesn't guarantee that a person will act wisely. Perhaps we could say that knowledge is a necessary but not a sufficient condition for wise decisions.

3. *Measurement instruments and procedures provide an important set of tools for improving the information available for decision making.* Much of the evidence upon which decisions have traditionally been based can be shown to be subjective, biased, and undependable. Though far from perfect, carefully planned and developed educational and psychological measurement devices permit significant gains in validity and reliability of the information available for decision making.

4. *The user of any type of information for decision making needs to know what that information signifies and how far it can be trusted.* When someone tells us that the road from Orford to Wentworth is "a little narrow and winding," we need to know whether that means merely that it is not an interstate highway or that it is a goat path. And we need to know whether our informant has traveled the road or has merely heard about it from a friend of a friend of a friend. Similarly, for any procedure for assessing persons, the user must know what inferences legitimately can be drawn from that procedure, under what conditions, and with what confidence.

5. *The facts and values involved in any decision are complex.* A measurement procedure can supply only *some* of the facts. Further facts, and a formulation of the values involved in the decision in question, must be supplied by the decision maker from other sources.

6. *The wisdom of the decider is crucial.* In the final analysis, though measurements can supply useful inputs of information, the enlightened user of that information fills the key role. The user must assemble and combine the information from tests and other sources, and must provide the value framework within which a final decision is made.

Our objective in this book is to improve the wisdom of deciders by giving them a better basis for evaluating different measurement procedures, for knowing what each signifies and how much confidence can be placed in each. To this end, we will describe the process of preparing test exercises, develop the general criteria of validity and reliability by which all types of measures are evaluated, provide a familiarity with different ways of reporting test scores, and describe and evaluate a number of the techniques and instruments commonly used for appraising human characteristics. Our success will be measured by the extent to which our readers use measurement results with wisdom and restraint in the decisions that they are called upon to make.

QUESTIONS AND EXERCISES

1. List some instances, preferably recent, of decisions you made about yourself or others made about you in which results from some kind of educational or psychological measurement played a part. Classify each as (1) instructional, (2) selection, (3) placement or classification, or (4) personal.

2. Describe one or more instances in your personal experience of a decision for which an educational or psychological measurement could have been helpful but was not available. On what basis was the decision actually made?

3. What are the alternatives to educational or psychological measures as guides to each of the following decisions.

(a) How much time should be spent on phonics in the first-grade reading program?

(b) Which 5 of these 15 applicants should be hired as statistical clerks?

(c) Should Peter Wylie be encouraged in his expressed desire to go to college and law school and become a lawyer?

4. What are the advantages of the alternatives that you have proposed in Question 3, as compared with some type of test or questionnaire? What are the disadvantages?

5. Considering the three decisions stated in Question 3, to what extent and in what way might *values* be involved in each case?

6. Give an example of each of the following types of test.

(a) A criterion-referenced achievement test.

(b) A norm-referenced achievement test.

(c) An aptitude test.

(d) A measure of likes and preferences.

(e) A measure of a trait or construct.

7. For one of the attributes named below, indicate how you might go about (1) defining the attribute, (2) setting up procedures to make it observable, and (3) quantifying it.

    (*a*) Scientific thinking.

    (*b*) "Good citizenship" in a fourth-grade pupil.

    (*c*) Sociability.

    (*d*) Competence as an automobile driver.

8. The usefulness of tests for decisions involving minority group members may well depend upon the type of decision involved. For what sorts of decision would a test be most defensible? For what sorts most questionable?

9. Which of the following would you consider acceptable, and which would you consider to be an offensive invasion of privacy? What factors influenced your decision?

    (*a*) Requiring medical school applicants to take (1) an achievement test in biology, (2) a questionnaire designed to evaluate emotional stability, or (3) an attitude scale on attitudes toward socialized medicine.

    (*b*) Requiring applicants for a secretarial job to take (1) a test of general intelligence, (2) a test of typing speed and accuracy, or (3) a questionnaire designed to appraise dependability.

    (*c*) Giving to a 10-year-old who is two years retarded in reading (1) a nonverbal test of intellectual ability, (2) an interview focused on his home conditions, or (3) a series of diagnostic tests of specific reading skills.

SUGGESTED ADDITIONAL READING

Airasian, Peter W. and George F. Madaus. Functional types of student evaluation. *Measurement and Evaluation in Guidance,* 1972, 4, 221-233.

Barclay, James R. *Controversial Issues in Testing.* Guidance Monograph Series. Series III: Testing. Boston: Houghton Mifflin, 1968.

Buchwald, A. M. Values and the use of tests. *Journal of Consulting Psychology,* 1965, 29, 49-54.

Coffman, William E. Concepts of achievement and proficiency. In David A. Payne and Robert F. McMorris (Eds.), *Educational and psychological measurement.* (2nd Ed.) Morristown, N.J.: General Learning Press, 1975.

Cronbach, Lee J., and Goldine C. Gleser. *Psychological tests and personnel decisions.* (2nd Ed.) Urbana, Ill.: University of Illinois Press, 1965.

DuBois, P. H. *A history of psychological testing.* Boston: Allyn and Bacon, 1970.

Ebel, Robert L. The social consequences of educational testing. *Proceedings of the 1963 Invitational Conference on Testing Problems.* Princeton, N.J.: Educational Testing Service, 1964.

Glaser, Robert and Anthony J. Nitko. Measurement in learning and instruction. In R. L. Thorndike (Ed.), *Educational Measurement.* (2nd Ed.) Washington, D.C.: American Council on Education, 1971.

Linden, James D. and Kathryn W. Linden. *Tests on trial.* Guidance Monograph Series. Series III: Testing. Boston: Houghton Mifflin, 1968.

Linden, Kathryn W., James D. Linden, Robert L. Bodine. Test bias: Fuss n' facts. *Measurement and Evaluation in Guidance,* 1974, 7, 163-168.

Miller, L. P. (Ed.) *The testing of black students: A symposium.* Englewood Cliffs, N.J.: Prentice-Hall, 1974.

Sarason, Seymour B. The unfortunate fate of Alfred Binet and school psychology. *Teachers College Record,* 1976, 77, 579-592.

The responsible use of tests: A position paper of AMEG, APGA, and NCME. *Measurement and Evaluation in Guidance,* 1972, 5, 385-388.

Thorndike, R. L. Educational decisions and human assessments. *Teachers College Record,* 1964, 66, 103-112.

Tittle, Carol Kehr. Sex bias in educational measurement: Fact or fiction. *Measurement and Evaluation in Guidance,* 1974, 6, 219-226.

Wolf, Theta H. *Alfred Binet.* Chicago: University of Chicago Press, 1973.

CHAPTER TWO
MEASUREMENT AND NUMBERS

Catherine Johnson and Peter Cordero wanted to find out about their two sixth grade classes, so they decided to give a reading test that was provided with the reader series, a review test from the arithmetic book, and a dictation spelling test based on the words their classes had been studying during the past six weeks. They marked the papers, counted the number of right answers on each, and wrote down the score. Then they made up a joint class list that showed the three scores for each child. At this point they realized that they had a flock of numbers, and wondered what they should do with them.

Tests *do* produce scores, and scores *are* numbers. So if we are to think about and use test scores, we must think with and work with numbers. The numbers that represent test scores can be organized to provide the answers to quite a range of questions, but first we must know what kinds of questions to ask. Once we have the questions in mind, we can begin to ask how the numbers can be arranged to provide the answers.

Look at the numbers (scores) for the sixth graders in the two classes. These are shown in Table 2.1 as they might have been written down. What kinds of question might Ms. Johnson and Mr. Cordero have addressed to this set of numbers? What questions can *you* ask? Before reading further, suppose you study the sets of scores and jot down on a piece of scrap paper the questions that come to *your* mind in connection with these scores. See how many of the question types you can anticipate.

A first, rather general question you might ask is: What is the general pattern of the set of scores? How do they "run"? What do they "look like"? How can we picture the set of reading scores, for example, so that we can get an impression of the

Table 2.1

RECORD SHEET FOR SIXTH GRADES AT SCHOOL X

Name	Test Scores		
	Reading	Arithmetic	Spelling
1. Carol A.	32	3	27
2. Mary B.	27	27	26
3. Ruby C.	31	9	23
4. Alice D.	36	18	32
5. Theresa E.	47	21	38
6. Ida F.	42	24	38
7. Vivian G.	22	4	13
8. Grace H.	50	42	46
9. Opal I.	20	18	12
10. Ursula J.	37	2	36
11. Beatrice K.	25	10	21
12. Karen L.	37	13	30
13. Susan M.	28	20	18
14. Jane N.	34	15	32
15. Dorothy O.	31	19	28
16. Frances P.	21	2	17
17. Elizabeth Q.	35	48	30
18. Pearl R.	59	41	54
19. Joan S.	44	41	39
20. Nancy T.	32	40	28
21. Judith U.	56	24	54
22. Edith V.	38	24	37
23. Louise W.	38	18	30
24. Helen X.	29	12	24
25. Martha Y.	24	26	22
26. Doris Z.	36	12	28
27. James A.	36	29	33
28. Albert B.	21	16	13
29. Donald C.	27	7	24
30. Peter D.	37	29	31
31. Samuel E.	46	36	37
32. George F.	33	10	31
33. Roger G.	17	14	14
34. Newton H.	35	18	30
35. Karl I.	30	12	25
36. Isidore J.	22	30	17
37. John K.	43	9	37
38. Benjamin L.	31	15	29
39. Theodore M.	50	38	48
40. Michael N.	34	20	27
41. Herman O.	30	15	29.
42. Charles P.	52	39	47
43. Patrick Q.	40	33	33
44. William R.	42	6	33
45. Martin S.	17	26	17

Table 2.1 (*Continued*)

27
measurement
and numbers

RECORD SHEET FOR SIXTH GRADES AT SCHOOL X

Name	Test Scores		
	Reading	Arithmetic	Spelling
46. Frank T.	32	20	23
47. Ralph U.	38	20	30
48. Thomas V.	29	29	33
49. Henry W.	36	25	44
50. Oscar X.	43	19	45
51. Edward Y.	27	19	35
52. Leonard Z.	39	19	44

group as a whole? To answer this question we will need to consider simple ways of tabulating and graphing a set of scores.

A second question that will almost certainly arise is: What is this group like, on the average? In general, have they done as well on the test as some other sixth grade group? What is the typical level of performance in the group? All these questions call for some single score to represent the group as a whole, some measure of the middle of the group. To answer this question we shall need to become acquainted with statistics developed to represent the average or typical score.

Third, in order to describe the group you might feel a need to describe the extent to which the scores spread out away from the average value. Have all the children in the group made about the same progress, or do they show a wide range of achievement? Do they look as though you would expect them to progress at about the same rate, or does it seem that different progress should be anticipated? How does this group compare with other classes with respect to the *spread* of scores? This calls for a study of measures of variability.

Fourth, you might ask how a particular individual stands on some one test. Thus you might want to know whether James A. has done well or poorly on the arithmetic test, and if you decide that his score is a good score you might want some way of saying just how good it is. You might ask whether James A. has done better in reading or in arithmetic. To answer this question you would need a common yardstick in terms of which to express performance in two quite different areas. One need, then, is for some uniform way of expressing and interpreting the performance of an individual. How does he stand, relative to his group?

A fifth query is of this type: To what extent do those who excel in reading also excel in arithmetic? To what extent do these two abilities tend to go together in the same individuals? Is the individual who is superior in one likely also to be superior in the other? To measure this, we shall need to become acquainted with measures of correlation.

There are many other questions that may arise with respect to a set of scores. The most important ones concern the drawing of general conclusions from data on a limited group. For example, the 26 girls in this group have an average reading score of 35.0, while the 26 boys have an average score of 34.1. This is a descriptive fact true of this testing of these particular girls and boys. We might want to know whether we can safely conclude that the *total population of girls* from which this sample is drawn would surpass the *total population of boys* on this same test. This is a problem of *inference*. Problems of statistical inference make up the bulk of advanced statistical work, but we shall not be concerned with them. They do not enter into the basic interpretation of test scores for an individual or a group.

The routines that have been developed for organizing numbers to answer these and other questions constitute the field called *statistics*. This name and, in fact, the very prospect of working with numbers seem a bit scary to some people—people who have never quite recovered from an encounter with long division in the fifth grade. Fortunately, much of the mechanics of working with numbers can now be turned over to a pocket calculator that can be bought almost anywhere for the price of a good book; so we can concentrate on the questions, and on the ways in which the numbers will be arranged so as to answer them.

In practice, a great deal of statistical work is now done on electronic calculators and computers. For analyses of any size hand calculation is rarely used, and the skill of calculating means, standard deviations, and correlation coefficients is becoming somewhat obsolete, just as arithmetic in the home is. In a day when most people have a pocket calculator on hand to check their income tax or the per pound price of groceries in the supermarket, it may seem unnecessary to learn hand procedures for calculating basic statistics. However, it *is* important for the embryo statistician to know what he is doing and why he is doing it. And there still are situations in which no computer or calculator is available. For these reasons we continue to display the long-established computational routines.

WAYS OF TABULATING
AND PICTURING A SET
OF SCORES

29
ways of
tabulating and
picturing a set
of scores

In Table 2.1 we show a record sheet on which test scores for 52 sixth grade pupils are recorded. Let us look at the scores in the column headed Reading and consider how they can be rearranged to give us a clearer picture of how the pupils have done on the reading test.

The simplest rearrangement is merely to arrange them in order from highest to lowest. We then have something that looks like this:

59	43	37	34	30	22
56	42	37	33	29	22
52	42	36	32	29	21
50	40	36	32	28	21
50	39	36	32	27	20
47	38	36	31	27	17
46	38	35	31	27	17
44	38	35	31	25	
43	37	34	30	24	

This arrangement gives a somewhat better picture of the way the scores fall. We can see the highest and lowest scores at a glance: 59 and 17. It is also easy to see that the middle person in the group falls somewhere in the mid-30s. We can see by inspection that roughly half the scores fall between 30 and 40. But this simple rearrangement of scores still has too much detail for us to see the general pattern clearly. It is also not a convenient form to use for calculations; it would be quite impractical if data were available, for example, for 500 pupils. We need to condense the data into a more compact form.

PREPARING A FREQUENCY DISTRIBUTION

A further step in organizing scores for presentation is to prepare what is termed a *frequency distribution*. This is a table showing how often each score has occurred. Each score value is listed, and the number of times it occurs is shown. A portion of the frequency distribution for the reading test is shown in Table 2.2. However, Table 2.2 is still not a very good form for reporting the facts. The table is too long and spread out. We have shown only part of it: the whole table would take 43 lines. It would have a number of zero entries, and there would be

Table 2.2

FREQUENCY DISTRIBUTION OF READING SCORES

(Ungrouped Data)

Test Score	Frequency
59	1
58	0
57	0
56	1
55	0
54	0
53	0
52	1
51	0
50	2
.	.
.	.
.	.
20	1
19	0
18	0
17	2

marked variations in the "Frequency" column from one score to the next.

In order to improve the form of presentation further, scores are often *grouped* together into broader categories. In our example we group together three adjacent scores, so that each grouping includes three points of score. When this is done, the set of scores is represented as shown in Table 2.3, a fairly compact table showing how many persons there are in each group, or *class interval*. Thus we have eight persons in the interval 34–36. We do not know how many of them got 34s, how many 35s, and how many 36s; we have lost this information in the grouping. We assume that they are evenly divided. In most cases there is no reason to anticipate that any one score will occur more often than any other and this assumption is a sound one, so the gains in compactness and convenience of presentation more than make up for any slight inaccuracy introduced by this grouping.*

In a practical situation we always face the problem of deciding how broad the groupings should be, that is, whether to

* In some special types of social statistics, such as reports of income, certain values are more likely than others, i.e., $2,000, $3,000, $5,000, etc. Special precautions are necessary in grouping material of this type. In particular, one should strive to get popular values near the *middle* of a class interval.

Table 2.3
FREQUENCY DISTRIBUTION OF READING SCORES

(Grouped Data)

Score Interval	Tallies	Frequency
58–60	/	1
55–57	/	1
52–54	/	1
49–51	//	2
46–48	//	2
43–45	///	3
40–42	///	3
37–39	//// //	7
34–36	//// ///	8
31–33	//// //	7
28–30	////	5
25–27	////	4
22–24	///	3
19–21	///	3
16–18	//	2

group by 3s, 5s, 10s, or some other number of points of score. The decision is a compromise between losing detail from our data, on the one hand, and obtaining a convenient, compact, and smooth representation of the results, on the other. A broader interval loses more detail but condenses the data into a more compact picture. A practical rule of thumb is to choose a class interval that will divide the total score range into roughly 15 groups. Thus in our example the highest score is 59 and the lowest is 17. The range of scores is $59 - 17 = 42$. Dividing 42 by 15, we get 2.8. The nearest whole number is 3, and so we group our data by 3s. In addition to the "rule of 15," we also find that intervals of 5, 10, and multiples of 10 make convenient groupings. Since the purpose of grouping scores is to make a convenient representation, factors of convenience enter as a major consideration.

It should be noted that sometimes there is no need to group data into broader categories. If the original scores cover a range of no more than, say, 20 points, grouping may not be called for.

In practice, when we are tabulating a set of data, deciding on the size of the score interval is the *first* step. Next we set up the score intervals, as shown in the left-hand column of Table 2.3. Each individual is then represented by a tally mark, as shown in the middle column. (It is easier to keep track of the tallies if every fifth tally is a diagonal line across the preceding four.) The column headed Frequency is obtained by counting the number of tallies in each score interval.

GRAPHIC REPRESENTATION

It is often helpful to translate the facts of Table 2.3 into a pictorial representation. A common type of graphic representation, called a *histogram,* is shown in Fig. 2.1. This can be thought of, somewhat grimly, as "piling up the bodies." The score intervals are shown along the horizontal base line (abscissa). The vertical height of the pile (ordinate) represents the number of cases. The diagram indicates that there are two "bodies" piled up in the interval 16–18, three in the interval 19–21, and so forth. This figure gives a clear picture of how the cases pile up, with most of them in the 30s and a long low "tail" running up to the high scores.

Another way of picturing the same data is by preparing a *frequency polygon.* This is shown in Fig. 2.2. Here we have plotted a point at the midpoint of each of the score intervals. The height at which we have plotted the point corresponds to the number of cases, or frequency (f), in the interval. These points have been connected, and the jagged line provides a somewhat different picture of the same set of data illustrated in Fig. 2.1. The polygon permits the data to be seen more clearly when two different groups are included in a single chart. Otherwise, the choice between the two is a matter of personal esthetics, since they are interchangeable ways of showing the same facts.

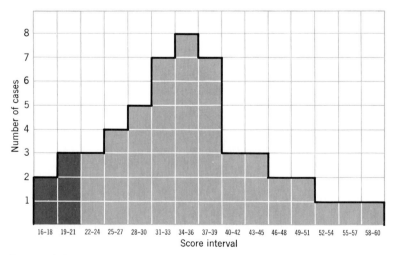

Figure 2.1
Histogram of reading scores.

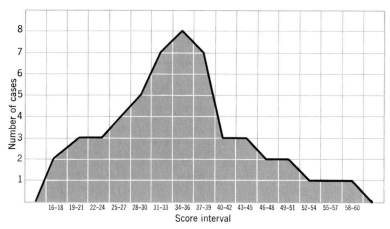

Figure 2.2
Frequency polygon of reading scores.

MEASURES OF CENTRAL TENDENCY

We often need a statistic to represent the typical, or average, or middle score of a group of scores. A very simple way of identifying the typical score is to pick out the score that occurs most frequently. This is called the *mode.* If you examine the array of scores on p. 29, you will find that the score 36 occurs 4 times and is the mode for this set of data. You may also note another fact. The score values 38, 37, 32, 31, and 27 occur 3 times each. If there were 1 less 36 and 1 more 27, for example, the mode would shift by 9 points. The mode is sensitive to such minor changes in the data and is therefore a crude and not very useful indicator of the typical score. In Table 2.3, where we have the grouped frequency distribution, the *modal interval* is the interval 34–36. This is as closely as we can identify the mode for data presented in this way.

MEDIAN

A much more useful way of representing the typical or average score is to find the value on the score scale that separates the top half of the group from the bottom half. This is called the *median.* In our example, in which there are 52 cases, this means separating the top 26 from the bottom 26 pupils. The required value can be estimated from the scores shown in Table 2.3. Starting with the lowest score, we count up until we have the necessary 26 cases. The "counting up" is best done in a systematic way, as shown in Table 2.4. Table 2.4 shows the *cumulative*

Table 2.4

FREQUENCY DISTRIBUTION AND CUMULATIVE FREQUENCIES FOR READING SCORES

Score Interval	Frequency	Cumulative Frequency
58–60	1	52
55–57	1	51
52–54	1	50
49–51	2	49
46–48	2	47
43–45	3	45
40–42	3	42
37–39	7	39
34–36	8	32
31–33	7	24
28–30	5	17
25–27	4	12
22–24	3	8
19–21	3	5
16–18	2	2

frequencies as well as the frequency in each interval. Each entry in the column labeled Cumulative Frequency shows the total number having a score equal to or less than the highest score in that interval. That is, there are 5 cases scoring at or below 21, 8 scoring at or below 24, 12 scoring at or below 27, and so forth. As indicated, we wish to identify the point below which 50 percent of the cases fall. Since 50 percent of 52 = 26, we must identify the point below which 26 pupils fall.

Table 2.4 shows that 24 individuals have scores of 33 or below. We need to include 2 more cases to obtain the required 26 cases. Note that in the next score interval (34–36) there are 8 individuals. We require only $\frac{2}{8}$, or $\frac{1}{4}$, of these individuals. Now how shall we think of these cases being spread out over the score interval 34–36? As indicated on p. 30, a reasonable assumption is that they are spread out evenly over the interval. Then to include $\frac{1}{4}$ of the scores, we would have to go $\frac{1}{4}$ of the way up from the bottom of the interval toward the top.

At this point, we must define what we mean by a score of 34. First, let us note that although test scores go by jumps of 1 unit (34, 35, 36), we consider the underlying ability to have a continuous distribution taking all intermediate values. We might liken the situation to a digital clock. Though time is continuous, the recording instrument goes by jumps, with one jump every time the basic unit of a minute has passed.

This is illustrated in Fig. 2.3. The heavy line represents the continuum of ability. We will define "34" as meaning closer to

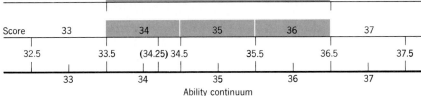

Figure 2.3
Relation between scores and ability continuum.

34 than to either 33 or 35. Thus in Fig. 2.3, 34 is represented as a slice extending from 33.5 to 34.5. Although somewhat arbitrary, this definition of a score is a reasonable one, and is accepted by most statistics textbooks. The class interval 34–36 is really to be thought of as extending from 33.5 to 36.5, as shown in the figure. We do not get scores lying *between* 33 and 34—not because those levels of ability do not exist, but just because our measuring instrument does not register any values between 33 and 34.

Since we require $\frac{1}{4}$ of the cases in the interval 34–36, we must go $\frac{1}{4}$ of the way from 33.5 to 36.5; that is, we have $\frac{1}{4}(36.5 - 33.5) = \frac{1}{4} \times 3 = \frac{3}{4} = 0.75$. We must add 0.75 to the value 33.5, which is the borderline between the 2 intervals. The median for this set of scores is $33.5 + 0.75 = 34.25$.

To Compute the Median	*In Our Example*
1. Calculate the number of cases that represents 50 percent of the total group.	**1.** 50 percent of 52 is 26.
2. Starting with the lowest score interval, accumulate the scores up through each score interval.	**2.** The cumulative frequencies, as shown in Table 2.4, are 2, 5, 8, 12, 17, etc.
3. Find the interval for which the cumulative frequency is just less than the required number of cases.	**3.** In our example, the cumulation through the 31–33 interval is 24.
4. Find the score distance to be added to the top of this interval, in order to include the required number of cases, by the following operation: $\left(\dfrac{\text{No. of added cases needed}}{\text{No. of cases in next interval}}\right)\left(\begin{array}{c}\text{No. of points}\\ \text{in interval}\end{array}\right)$	**4.** $(\frac{2}{8})(3) = 0.75$
5. Add this amount to the upper limit of the interval identified in 3 to give the median.	**5.** $33.5 + 0.75 = 34.25$

PERCENTILES

The same procedure may be used to find the score below which any other percentage of the group falls. These values are all called *percentiles*. The median is the 50th percentile, that is, the score below which 50 percent of individuals fall. If we want to find the 25th percentile, we must find the score below which 25 percent of the cases fall. Twenty-five percent of 52 is 13. Thirteen cases take us through the interval 25–27, and include 1 of the 5 cases in the 28–30 interval. So the 25th percentile is computed to be $27.5 + (\frac{1}{5})3 = 27.5 + 0.6 = 28.1$.

As another illustration, consider the 85th percentile. We have $(.85)(52) = 44.2$. Since 42 cases carry us to the top of the 40–42 interval, and there are 3 cases in the next interval, we have for the 85th percentile $42.5 + [(44.2 - 42)/3](3) = 44.7$. Other percentiles can be found in the same way. Percentiles have many uses, especially in connection with test norms and the interpretation of scores.

ARITHMETIC MEAN

Another frequently used statistic for representing the middle of a group is the familiar "average" of everyday experience. Since the statistician speaks of all measures of central tendency as averages, he identifies this one as the *arithmetic mean*. This is simply the sum of a series of scores divided by the number of scores. Thus the arithmetic mean of 4, 6, and 7 is

$$\frac{4 + 6 + 7}{3} = 5.67$$

In our example we can add together the scores of all 52 individuals in the group. This gives us 1,798. Dividing by 52, we get 34.58 for the average, or arithmetic mean, for this group. This is the way a computer does it, and if the group is small it may be the most efficient routine for hand calculation—especially if an adding machine or calculator is available. However, for hand calculation with large groups, more efficient procedures are available, based on the frequency distribution given in Table 2.3.

These calculations are based on a type of "trial balance." Picking a score interval that looks to be about in the middle of the group, we sum the plus and minus deviations from this starting place. An adjustment based on the excess of plus or minus deviations is applied to this starting place to give the value for the mean. The application of this procedure to the reading test data is shown in Table 2.5, and the steps are outlined below.

Table 2.5

FREQUENCY DISTRIBUTION OF READING SCORES SHOWING STEPS IN CALCULATING ARITHMETIC MEAN AND STANDARD DEVIATION

Score Interval	Frequency f	x'	fx'	$f(x')^2$
58–60	1	8	8	64
55–57	1	7	7	49
52–54	1	6	6	36
49–51	2	5	10	50
46–48	2	4	8	32
43–45	3	3	9	27
40–42	3	2	6	12
37–39	7	1	7	7
			+61	
34–36	8	0	0	0
31–33	7	−1	−7	7
28–30	5	−2	−10	20
25–27	4	−3	−12	36
22–24	3	−4	−12	48
19–21	3	−5	−15	75
16–18	2	−6	−12	72
			−68	
Sum 52			−7	535

Sequence of Steps	Symbolism*	Illustrative Example
1. Choose some interval for the arbitrary starting place, or *origin*. The midpoint of this arbitrarily chosen interval (A) is called "zero" in our calculations.	A	$A = 35$ For $X = 34\text{–}36$, $x' = 0$
2. Call the next higher interval $+1$, the one above that $+2$, etc., and the ones below -1, -2, etc.	x'	Thus, 37–39 is called $+1$, 40–42 is called $+2$, etc., as shown in the column headed x' in Table 2.5.

* A list of common statistical symbols and their meanings is given at the end of the chapter. Reference to these definitions may help in reading the remainder of the chapter.

Sequence of Steps	Symbolism	Illustrative Example
3. For each row, multiply the number of cases (frequency) by the number of steps (x') above or below the chosen origin.	fx'	Thus $1 \times 8 = 8$, $1 \times 7 = 7$, etc., as shown in the column headed fx' in Table 2.5
4. Sum the values in the fx' column, taking account of the plus and minus signs. (Mistakes will be avoided if the plus entries are summed separately, the minus entries summed, and the two part sums combined to give the final total.)	$\Sigma fx'$	$\Sigma f(x')^{+} = +61$ $\Sigma f(x')^{-} = -68$ $\Sigma f(x') = -7$
5. Sum the frequencies in the column headed Frequency (or f) to give the total number of cases in the group. This is usually labeled N.	$\Sigma f = N$	$\Sigma f = 52$
6. Divide the sum of fx' values by N to get the average of the deviations from the arbitrary origin (in interval units).	$\dfrac{\Sigma fx'}{N}$	$\dfrac{-7}{52} = -0.135$
7. Multiply by the size of the interval to express the deviation in score units.	$i\left(\dfrac{\Sigma fx'}{N}\right)$	$3\left(\dfrac{-7}{52}\right) = 3(-0.135)$ $= -0.405$
8. Add the result to the value of the arbitrary origin.	$A + i\left(\dfrac{\Sigma fx'}{N}\right)$	$35 + (-0.405) =$ 34.595 or 34.60

Summarizing all the steps, we may say:

$$\text{Mean} = (\text{Interval})\left(\frac{\text{Sum of } fx'}{N}\right) + \text{Arbitrary Origin}$$

or in our example:

$$\text{Mean} = 3\left(\frac{-7}{52}\right) + 35 = 34.60$$

Starting where we did, the minus deviations slightly over-balanced the plus ones. There was an excess of 7 on the minus side. Our starting point was a little too high. We had to shift it down $\frac{7}{52}$ of 1 interval or $\frac{7}{52} \times 3$ points of score to find a true balance point. Since the middle of our zero interval corresponded to a score of 35, we had to move down $\frac{21}{52}$ points below 35 to get the true balance point, the correct arithmetic mean.

The value 34.60 that we got in this way is almost the same as the 34.58 that resulted from adding all the scores together and dividing by the number of cases. The correspondence is usually not perfect, because of slight inaccuracies resulting from grouping the scores into classes in the frequency distribution, but the values obtained by the two methods will always agree closely. When we work with the frequency distribution it makes no difference which interval we use for a starting point. Barring mistakes in arithmetic, the result will be identical for any starting interval.

The arithmetic mean and the median do not correspond

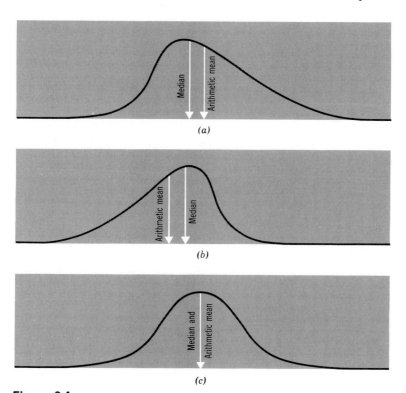

Figure 2.4

Frequency distributions differing in skewness. (a) Positively skewed; (b) negatively skewed; (c) symmetrical.

exactly, but usually they will not differ greatly. In this example, the values are 34.60 and 34.25, respectively. The mean and median will differ substantially only when the set of scores is very "skewed," that is, when there is a piling up of scores at one end and a long tail at the other. Figure 2.4 shows three distributions differing in amount and direction of skewness. The top figure is positively skewed, that is, has a tail running up into the high scores. We get a distribution like this for income in the United States, since there are many people with small and moderate incomes and only a few with very large incomes. The center figure is negatively skewed. A distribution like this would result if a class were given a very easy test that resulted in a piling up of perfect and near-perfect scores. The bottom figure is symmetrical and is not skewed in either direction. Many physical and psychological variables give such a symmetrical distribution. In the many distributions that are approximately symmetrical either mean or median will serve equally well to represent the average of the group, but with skewed distributions the median generally seems preferable. It is less affected by a few cases out in the long tail.

MEASURES
OF VARIABILITY

When describing a set of scores, it is often significant to report how *variable* the scores are, how much they spread out from high to low scores. For example, two groups of children, both with a median age of 10 years, would represent quite different educational situations if one had a spread of ages from 9 to 11 while the other ranged from 6 to 14. A measure of this spread is an important statistic for describing a group.

A very simple measure of variability is the *range* of scores in the group. This is simply the difference between the highest and the lowest score. In our reading test example it is $59 - 17 = 42$. However, the range depends only upon the two extreme cases in the total group. This makes it very undependable, since it can be changed a good bit by the addition or omission of a single extreme case.

SEMI-INTERQUARTILE RANGE

A better measure of variability is the range of scores that includes a specified part of the total group—usually the middle 50 percent. The middle 50 percent of the cases in a group are the cases lying between the 25th and 75th percentiles. We can compute these two percentiles, following the procedures out-lined on pp. 33–36. For our example, the 25th percentile was computed to be 28.1. If you calculate the 75th percentile, you will find that it is 39.5. The distance between the 25th and 75th percentiles is thus seen to be 11.4 points of score.

The 25th and 75th percentiles are called *quartiles,* since they cut off the bottom quarter and the top quarter of the group respectively. The score distance between them is called the *interquartile range.* A statistic that is often reported as a measure of variability is the *semi-interquartile range* (Q). This is half of the interquartile range. It is the average distance from the median to the 2 quartiles; that is, it tells how far the quartile points lie from the median, on the average. In our example the semi-interquartile range is

$$Q = \frac{39.5 - 28.1}{2} = 5.7$$

If the scores spread out twice as far, Q would be twice as great; if they spread out only half as far, Q would be half as large. Two distributions that have the same mean, same total number of cases, and same general form, and that differ only in that one has a variability twice as large as the other are shown in Fig. 2.5.

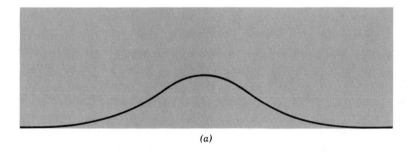

(a)

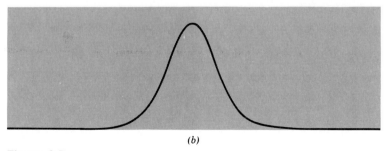

(b)

Figure 2.5
Two distributions differing only in variability. (a) Large variability; (b) small variability.

STANDARD DEVIATION

The semi-interquartile range belongs to the same family of statistics as the median. Its computation is based upon percentiles. There are also measures of variability that belong to the family of the arithmetic mean and are based upon score deviations. Suppose we had four scores of 4, 5, 6, and 7 respectively. Adding these together and dividing by the number of scores, we get

$$\frac{4 + 5 + 6 + 7}{4} = \frac{22}{4} = 5.5$$

This gives us the arithmetic mean. But now we ask how widely these scores spread out around that mean value. Suppose we find the difference between each score and the mean; that is, we subtract 5.5 from each score. We then have -1.5, -0.5, 0.5, and 1.5. These represent *deviations* of the scores from the mean. The bigger the deviations, the more variable the set of scores. What we require is some type of average of these deviations to give us an overall measure of variability.

If we simply sum the above four deviation values, we find that they add up to zero. This is necessarily so. We defined the arithmetic mean as the point around which the plus and minus deviations exactly balance. We shall have to do something else. The procedure that statisticians have devised for handling the plus and the minus signs is to square all the deviations, thus getting only plus values. (A minus times a minus is a plus.) An average of these squared deviations is obtained by summing them and dividing by the number of cases. To compensate for squaring the individual deviations, the square root of this average value is computed. The resulting statistic is called the *standard deviation* (*SD* or *s*). It is the square root* of the average of the squared deviations from the mean. For our little example of 4 cases, the calculations are as follows:

$$SD = \sqrt{\frac{(-1.5)^2 + (-0.5)^2 + (0.5)^2 + (1.5)^2}{4}}$$

$$= \sqrt{\frac{2.25 + 0.25 + 0.25 + 2.25}{4}} = \sqrt{\frac{5.00}{4}}$$

$$= \sqrt{1.25} = 1.12$$

* With many modern calculators one need only press the designated key to get the square root of a number.

The standard deviation also may be computed from the grouped frequency distribution. The necessary steps have been carried out in Table 2.5. Take special note of the column headed $f(x')^2$. Each entry in this column represents the number of cases (f) multiplied by the square of the deviation (x') of that score interval from the arbitrary origin. The sum of the values in this column gives a sum of squared deviations, but these deviations are around the arbitrary origin and are expressed in interval units. Several adjustments are necessary to express the deviations in *score* units and in terms of the *true* arithmetic mean. The steps are outlined below.

1. Carry out the operations for computing the arithmetic mean, as described on pp. 36–38.

2. In addition, prepare the column headed $f(x')^2$. Each entry in this column is the frequency (f) times the square of the deviation value (x'). However, this last column can be computed most simply by multiplying together the entries in the two preceding columns, i.e., x' times fx'. Note that all the signs in this column are positive, since a minus times a minus gives a plus.

	Symbolism	*Illustrative Example*
3. Get the sum of the $f(x')^2$ column.	$\Sigma f(x')^2$	535
4. Divide this sum by the number of cases.	$\dfrac{\Sigma f(x')^2}{N}$	$\dfrac{535}{52} = 10.288$
5. Divide the sum of the fx' column by the number of cases.	$\dfrac{\Sigma fx'}{N}$	$\dfrac{-7}{52} = -0.135$
6. Square the value obtained in 5 above.	$\left(\dfrac{\Sigma fx'}{N}\right)^2$	$\left(\dfrac{-7}{52}\right)^2 = (-0.135)^2$ $= 0.018$
7. Subtract the value in 6 from that in 4.	$\dfrac{\Sigma f(x')^2}{N} - \left(\dfrac{\Sigma fx'}{N}\right)^2$	$\dfrac{535}{52} - \left(\dfrac{-7}{52}\right)^2 = 10.288$ $- 0.018$ $= 10.270$
8. Take the square root of the value in 7.	$\sqrt{\dfrac{\Sigma f(x')^2}{N} - \left(\dfrac{\Sigma fx'}{N}\right)^2}$	$\sqrt{10.270} = 3.20$
9. Multiply by the number of score points in each class interval.	$i\sqrt{\dfrac{\Sigma f(x')^2}{N} - \left(\dfrac{\Sigma fx'}{N}\right)^2}$	$3(3.20) = 9.60$

Presenting all the computations* for our example in summary form, using the formula given in step 9 above, we have

$$SD = 3\sqrt{\frac{535}{52} - \left(\frac{-7}{52}\right)^2} = 9.60$$

INTERPRETING THE STANDARD DEVIATION

It is almost impossible to say in any simple words what the standard deviation *is* or what it corresponds to in pictorial or geometric terms. Primarily, it is a statistic that characterizes a distribution of scores. It increases in direct proportion as the scores spread out more widely. The larger the standard deviation, the wider the spread of scores. A student sometimes asks: But what is a small standard deviation? What is a large one? There is really no answer to this question. Suppose that for some group the standard deviation of weights is 10. Is this large or small? It depends on whether we are talking about ounces, or pounds, or kilograms. It depends upon whether we are dealing with the weights of mice, or men, or mammoths.

The standard deviation gets its most clear-cut meaning for one particular type of distribution of scores. This distribution is called the *normal* distribution. It is defined by a particular mathematical equation, but to the everyday user it is defined approximately by its pictorial qualities. The normal curve is a symmetrical curve having a bell-like shape. That is, most of the cases pile up in the middle score values; as one goes away from the middle in either direction the pile drops off, first slowly and then more rapidly, and the cases tail out to relatively long tails on each end. An illustration of a typical normal curve is shown in Fig. 2.6 on page 45. This curve is the normal curve that best fits the reading test data we have been using as an illustration. It has the same mean, standard deviation, and total area (number of cases) as the reading test data. The histogram of reading test scores appears in light dotted lines, so one can see how closely the curve fits the actual test scores.

For the normal curve there is an exact mathematical relationship between the standard deviation and the proportion of

---

* For a person using an electronic calculator or computer, the efficient calculation procedures would be somewhat different. He would accumulate in the calculator the sum of squares of the individual scores and divide this sum by N. From this value he would subtract the square of the mean. The square root of the resulting value would give him the standard deviation.

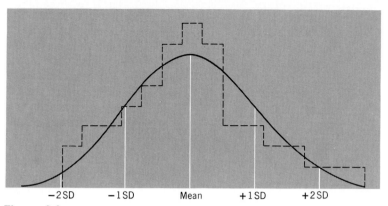

−2SD −1SD Mean +1SD +2SD

Figure 2.6
Example of a normal curve (fitted to reading test data).

cases. The same proportion of cases will always be found within the same standard deviation limits. This relationship is shown in Table 2.6. Thus in *any* normal curve about two-thirds (68.2 percent) of the cases will fall between +1 and −1 standard deviation from the mean. Approximately 95 percent will fall between +2 and −2 standard deviations from the mean, and very nearly all the cases will fall between +3 and −3 standard deviations from the mean. An individual who gets a score 1 standard deviation above the mean will surpass 84 percent of the group, that is, he will surpass the 50 percent who fall below the mean and the 34 percent who fall between the mean and +1 standard deviation.

This unvarying relationship of the standard deviation unit to the arrangement of scores in the normal distribution gives the standard deviation a type of *standard* meaning. It becomes a yardstick in terms of which different groups may be compared or the status of a given individual may be evaluated. Although the relationship of the standard deviation unit to the score

Table 2.6
PROPORTION OF CASES FALLING WITHIN CERTAIN SPECIFIED STANDARD DEVIATION LIMITS FOR A NORMAL DISTRIBUTION

Limits within Which Cases Lie	Percentage of Cases
Between the mean and *either* +1.0 *SD* or −1.0 *SD*	34.1
Between the mean and *either* +2.0 *SD* or −2.0 *SD*	47.7
Between the mean and *either* +3.0 *SD* or −3.0 *SD*	49.9
Between +1.0 and −1.0 *SD*	68.2
Between +2.0 and −2.0 *SD*	95.4
Between +3.0 and −3.0 *SD*	99.8

distribution does not hold *exactly* in distributions other than the normal distribution, frequently the distribution of test scores or other measures approaches the normal curve closely enough so that the standard deviation continues to have very nearly the same meaning.

The meaning of being a given number of standard deviations above or below the mean may be expressed in terms of the percentage of cases in the group whom the individual surpasses. A short table showing the percentage of cases falling below different standard deviation values on the normal curve is given in Appendix One. This table makes it easy to translate any score, expressed in standard deviation units, into the equivalent percentile on a normal curve. Thus, consider the set of reading test scores for which we computed the mean and standard deviation to be 34.6 and 9.6 respectively. Suppose a person has a score of 48. Since the mean of the group is 34.6, he falls $48 - 34.6 = 13.4$ points above the mean of the group. The 13.4 points by which he surpasses the mean is equal to $13.4/9.6 = 1.4$ standard deviations. Since he is 1.4 standard deviations above the mean, we might expect him to surpass approximately 92 percent of the cases in our group. (An actual count shows that this score is better than $^{47}/_{52} = 90.4$ percent of the scores in our set of data.)

A score expressed in standard deviation units has much the same meaning from one set of scores to another. Thus, if a boy falls half a standard deviation above the mean of his group in arithmetic and three-fourths of a standard deviation above in reading, we can describe him as better in reading than in arithmetic. If he was half a standard deviation above the group mean in arithmetic when he was in grade 3, but is only a quarter of a standard deviation above now in grade 6, we may say that he has dropped back in his arithmetic performance relative to his group. The standard deviation provides a unit in terms of which scores can be directly compared from one test to another or from one time to another.

In summary, the statistics most used for describing the variability of a set of scores are the semi-interquartile range and the standard deviation. The semi-interquartile range is based upon percentiles, that is, the 25th and 75th percentiles, and is commonly used when the median is being used as a measure of the middle of the group. The standard deviation is a measure of variability that goes with the arithmetic mean. It is useful in the field of tests and measurements primarily as providing a standard unit of measure having comparable meaning from one test to another.

The problems of interpreting the score of an individual will be treated more fully in Chapter 4, when we turn to test norms and units of measure. It will suffice now to indicate that the two sorts of measures we have just been considering, that is, percentiles and standard deviation units, give us a framework in which we can view the performance of a specific person. Thus, referring to the example we worked out, if a new boy in the class got a score of 48 on the reading test we could say either

1. That he surpassed 90 percent of the group, that is, that he fell at the 90th percentile, or
2. That he fell 1.4 standard deviations above the mean.

Either statement gives his score meaning in relation to his group; he is well above average, being surpassed by only about a tenth of the group. Since they are based on the same score, they are two ways of saying the same thing. Each has certain advantages, which we will examine more carefully in Chapter 4.

MEASURES
OF RELATIONSHIP

We look now for a statistic to express the relationship between two sets of scores. Thus in our illustration we have a reading score and an arithmetic score for each pupil. To what extent did those pupils who did well in arithmetic also do well on the reading test? In this case, we have two scores for each individual. We can picture these scores by a plot in two dimensions. This is shown in Fig. 2.7. The first person in our group, Carol A., had a score on the reading test of 32 and a score on the arithmetic test of 3. Her scores are represented by the X in Fig. 2.7, plotted at 32 on the vertical or reading scale and at 3 on the horizontal or arithmetic scale. There is a dot to represent each other child's scores.

When a child who does well in reading also does well in arithmetic, his scores will be represented by a dot in the upper right-hand part of our picture. A child who does poorly on both tests will fall at the lower left. Where good score on one test goes with poor score on the other, we will find the points falling in the other corners, that is, upper left and lower right. Inspection of Fig. 2.7 reveals some tendency for the scores to splatter out in the lower-left to upper-right direction, that is, from low-low to high-high. But there are many exceptions. The relationship is far from perfect. It is a matter of degree. We need some type of statistical index to express this degree of relationship.

As an index of this degree of relationship, a statistic known as the *correlation coefficient* can be computed. (The symbol r is used to designate this coefficient.) This coefficient can take values ranging from $+1$ through zero to -1. A correlation of $+1$ signifies that the person who had the highest score on one test also had the highest score on the other, the next highest on one was the next highest on the other, and so on, exactly in parallel through the whole group. A correlation of -1 means that the scores go in exactly the reverse direction, that is, the person highest on one is lowest on the other, next highest on one is next lowest on the other, and so on. A zero correlation represents a complete lack of relationship. In-between values of r

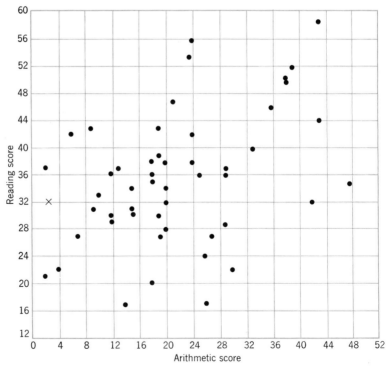

Figure 2.7
Plot of reading versus arithmetic scores.

represent tendencies for relationship to exist, but with many discrepancies.

Figure 2.8 below illustrates four different levels of relationship. In box (a) the correlation is zero, and the points scatter out in a pattern that is just about circular. All combinations are found—high-high, low-low, high-low, and low-high. Box (b) corresponds to a correlation of +.30. You can see a barely perceptible trend for the points to group in the low-low and high-high direction. The tendency is more marked in box (c), which represents a correlation of +.60. In box (d), which portrays a correlation of +.90, the trend is much more marked. Note that if the correlation were −.90 the scattering of the points would be just the same, but the swarm of dots would fall along the other diagonal—from lower right-hand corner to upper left-hand corner. But even with as high a correlation as this, the scores spread out quite a bit and do not lie directly on

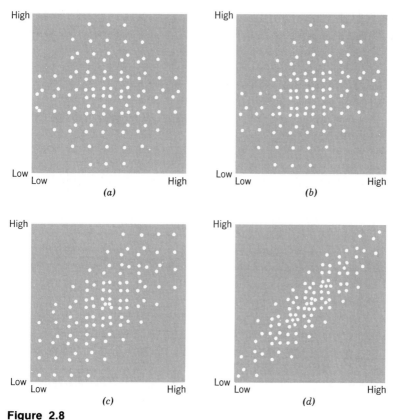

Figure 2.8
Distribution of scores for representative values of correlation coefficient.
(a) Correlation of .00; (b) Correlation of +.30; (c) Correlation of +.60;
(d) Correlation of +.90.

the line from low-low to high-high. We may note in passing that the scores plotted in Fig. 2.7 correspond to a correlation coefficient of +.46. Procedures for computing the correlation coefficient are outlined in Appendix Two for those readers who wish to carry out the calculations with a numerical example.

There are three important settings in which correlation coefficients will be encountered in connection with tests and measurements. The first situation is one in which we are trying to determine how precise and consistent a measurement procedure is. Thus, if we wanted to know how consistent a measure of speed we should expect to get from a 50-yard dash, we could have each child run the distance twice, perhaps on successive days. Correlating the two sets of scores would give us information on the precision or reliability of this measure of running speed. The second situation is one in which we are studying the relationship between two different measures in order to evaluate one as a predictor of the other. Thus we might want to study a scholastic aptitude test as a predictor of college grades. The correlation of test with grades would give an indication of the test's usefulness as a predictor.

The third situation is more purely descriptive. We often are interested in the relationships between variables just in order to understand better how behavior is organized. What correlations do we find between measures of verbal and of spatial abilities? How close is the relationship between interest in mechanical jobs and comprehension of mechanical devices? Is rate of physical development related to rate of intellectual development? Many research problems in human behavior can only, or best, be studied by observing relationships as they develop in a natural setting.

We face the problem, in each case, of evaluating the correlation we obtain. Suppose the two sets of 50-yard dash scores yield a correlation of .80. Is this satisfactory or not? Suppose the aptitude test correlates .60 with college grades. Shall we be pleased* or discouraged?

The answer lies in part in the plots of Fig. 2.8. Clearly, the higher the correlation, the more closely one variable goes with

---

* The wording of this statement implies that we want correlations to be high. When a correlation expresses the reliability or consistency of a test, or its accuracy in predicting an outcome of interest to us, it is certainly true that the higher the correlation is, the more pleased we are. In other contexts, however, "bigness" need not correspond to "goodness," and we may not have any preference as to the size of a correlation or may even prefer a low one.

the other. If we think of discrepancies away from the diagonal line from low-low to high-high as "errors," the errors become smaller as the correlation becomes larger. But, these discrepancies are still discouragingly large for even a rather substantial correlation coefficient, for example, box (c) in Fig. 2.8. We must always be aware of these discrepancies and realize that with a correlation such as .60 between an aptitude test and school grades there will be a number of children whose school performance differs a good deal from what we have predicted from the test.

However, everything is relative, and any given correlation coefficient must be interpreted in comparison to values that are commonly obtained. Table 2.7 below contains a number of correlations that have been reported for different types of variable. The nature of the scores being correlated is described and the coefficient reported. An examination of this table will provide some initial background for interpreting correlation coefficients. The coefficient will gradually take on added meaning as the reader encounters coefficients of different sizes in his reading about and work with tests.

Table 2.7
CORRELATION COEFFICIENTS FOR SELECTED VARIABLES

Variables	Correlation Coefficient
Heights of identical twins	.95
Intelligence test scores of identical twins	.88
Reading test scores grade 3 versus grade 6	.80
Rank in high school class versus teachers' rating of work habits	.73
Height versus weight of 10-year-olds	.60
Arithmetic computation test versus nonverbal intelligence test (grade 8)	.54
Height of brothers, adjusted for age	.50
Intelligence test score versus parental occupational level	.30
Strength of grip versus speed of running	.16
Height versus Binet IQ	.06
Ratio of head length to width versus intelligence	.01
Armed Forces Qualification Test scores of recruits versus number of school grades repeated	− .27
Artist interest versus banker interest	− .64

SUMMARY STATEMENT

We opened this chapter by pointing out the various kinds of question we might wish to answer by referring to a set of test scores. Let us look at these questions again and see what answers we have offered for them.

1. *How do our scores "run"; what do they "look like"?* To answer this question, we can arrange our scores into a frequency distribution (Table 2.3) or plot them in a histogram (Fig. 2.1).

2. *What score is typical of the group; represents the middle of the group?* To represent the middle of the group we may calculate the median—the 50th percentile (pp. 33–36), or the arithmetic mean—the common average (pp. 36–39).

3. *How widely spread out are the scores; how much do they scatter?* To represent the spread of scores statisticians have developed (1) the semi-interquartile range, half the distance between the 25th and 75th percentile (pp. 40-41), and (2) the standard deviation (pp. 42-44), a type of average of the deviations of the scores away from the average.

4. *How are we to determine what the score of an individual means— whether it is high or low?* Though this problem is left for fuller discussion in Chapter 4, we have seen that the individual score takes on meaning as it is translated into a percentile rank, the percentage of the group he beat, or into a standard score, how many standard deviations above or below the mean he fell (p. 47).

5. *To what extent do two sets of scores go together; to what extent are the same individuals high or low on both?* A measure of relationship is given by the correlation coefficient, a numerical index of "going-togetherness" (pp. 47-51). This index is important as describing the precision or reliability of a test, as describing the accuracy with which a test score predicts some other factor, such as school grades or job success, and as describing the relationships of traits in a group of individuals.

STATISTICAL SYMBOLS

The student who reads test manuals, books dealing with tests, or articles about testing in the educational journals will encounter a number of conventional symbols to refer to statistical concepts or operations. Some of the commonest are defined below. This table of definitions should help in reading later chapters of this book, as well as outside references.

Symbol	Definition
N	The total number of cases in the group.
f	Frequency. The number of cases with a specific score or in a particular class interval.
X	A raw score on some measure.
x	A deviation score, indicating how far the individual falls above or below the mean of the group.
x'	A deviation score from some arbitrary reference point, often expressed in interval units.
i	The number of points of score in one class interval.
$\bar{X}$ or M	The mean of the group.
Md	The median of the group.
Q_1	The lower quartile, the 25th percentile.
Q_3	The upper quartile, the 75th percentile.
Q	The semi-interquartile range. Half the difference between Q_3 and Q_1.
P	A percentile.
A subscript	Modifies a symbol and tells which specific individual or value is referred to, e.g., P_{10} is the 10th percentile, X_j is the raw score of person j.
SD or s	Standard deviation of a set of scores.
σ	Standard deviation in the *population*, though sometimes used to refer to the particular sample.
p	Percent of persons getting a test item correct.
q	Percent of persons getting a test item wrong ($p + q = 100$).
r	A coefficient of correlation.
r_{11}	A reliability coefficient. The correlation between two equivalent test forms or two administrations of a test.
Σ	"Take the sum of."

QUESTIONS AND EXERCISES

1. For each of the sets of scores indicated below, select what appears to you to be the most suitable class interval, and set up a form for tallying the scores:

Test	Number of Cases	Range of Scores
Arithmetic	84	8 to 53
Reading comprehension	57	15 to 75
Interest inventory	563	68 to 224

2. In each of the following distributions, indicate (1) the size of the class interval, (2) the midpoint of the intervals shown, and (3) the real limits of the intervals (i.e., the dividing lines between them).

(a) 4–7	(b) 17–19	(c) 50–59
8–11	20–22	60–69
12–15	23–25	70–79
.	.	.
.	.	.
.	.	.

3. Using the spelling scores given in Table 2.1 on pp. 26–27, make a frequency distribution and a histogram. Compute the median and the upper and lower quartiles. Compute the arithmetic mean and standard deviation.

4. In the Bureau of Census reports the *median* is used in reporting average income. Why is it used, rather than the arithmetic mean?

5. A 50-item vocabulary test given to 150 pupils yielded scores ranging from 18 to 50. Ninety-seven fell between 40 and 50. What would this distribution of scores look like? What could you say about the suitability of the test for the group? What measure of central tendency would be most suitable? Why? What measure of variability would you probably use?

6. A high school teacher gave two sections of a mathematics class the same test. Results were as follows:

	Section A	Section B
Median	64.6	64.3
Mean	65.0	63.2
75th percentile	69.0	70.0
25th percentile	61.0	54.0
Standard deviation	6.0	10.5

From these data, what can you say about the two classes? What implications do the data have for teaching the two groups?

7. A test in biology given to 2500 10th- and 11th-grade students had a mean of 52 and a standard deviation of 10.5. How many standard deviations above or below the mean would the following pupils fall?

Alice	48	Henry	60	John	31
Willard	56	Jane	36	Oscar	84

8. If the distribution in the previous example was approximately normal, about what percentage of the group would each of these pupils surpass?

9. Assuming that the scores are normally distributed, what proportion of cases would fall below each of the following scores for a test that has a mean of 72 and a standard deviation of 12?

(a) 64	(b) 75	(c) 89

10. Explain the meaning of each of the following correlation coefficients:

(*a*) The correlation between scores on a reading test and on a group intelligence test is +.78.

(*b*) Ratings of pupils on "good citizenship" and on "aggressiveness" show a correlation of −.56.

(*c*) The correlation between height and score on an achievement test is .02.

SUGGESTED
ADDITIONAL READING

Downie, N. M. and R. W. Heath. *Basic statistical methods.* (4th Ed.) New York: Harper and Row, 1974.

Gillman, E. S. *Statistics for teachers.* New York: Harper and Row, 1973.

Guilford, J. P. and B. Fruchter. *Fundamental statistics in psychology and education.* New York: McGraw-Hill, 1973.

Koosis, Donald J. *Statistics.* New York: John Wiley & Sons, Inc., 1972.

CHAPTER THREE
QUALITIES DESIRED IN ANY MEASUREMENT PROCEDURE

Whenever we would like to use a test to provide information to help in some decision, we face the problem of which test to use, or whether there is any test that will really help in the decision. Usually there are several tests that have been designed to help, or that seem at least to have the possibility of helping with the decision. We would like to know whether any one will indeed provide useful information, and if so, which is the best one to use. How shall we make the choice?

There are many specific considerations entering into the evaluation of a test, but we shall consider them here under three main headings. These are, respectively, validity, reliability, and practicality. *Validity* refers to the degree to which a test provides information that is relevant to the decision that is to be made. Thus a judgment of validity is always in relation to a specific decision or use. *Reliability* has to do with accuracy and precision of a measurement procedure. Indices of reliability give an indication of the extent to which a particular measurement is consistent and reproducible. *Practicality* is concerned with a wide range of factors of economy, convenience, and interpretability that determine whether a test is practical for widespread use. These three aspects of test evaluation will be considered in detail in the following sections.

VALIDITY

The first and foremost question to be asked with respect to any testing procedure is: How valid is it? When we ask this question, we are inquiring whether the test measures what we want it to measure, all of what we want it to measure, and nothing but what we want it to measure.

When we apply a steel tape measure to the top of a desk to determine its length, we have no doubt that the tape does in fact measure the length of the desk and will give information directly related to our decision, which may be to decide whether we can put the desk between two windows in our room. Long experience with this type of measuring instrument has confirmed beyond a shadow of doubt its validity as a tool for measuring length.

Suppose now that we give a test of reading achievement to a group of children. This test requires the children to select certain answers to a series of questions based on reading passages and to make little pencil marks on an answer sheet. We count the number of pencil marks made in the predetermined right places and give the child as a score the number of his right answers. We call this score a measure of his reading comprehension. But the score itself is not the comprehension. It is the *record* of a *sample* of behavior. Any judgment regarding comprehension is an inference from this number of allegedly correct answers. The validity of the score is not self-evident but is something we must establish on the basis of adequate evidence.

Consider again the typical personality inventory that endeavors to provide an appraisal of "emotional adjustment." In this type of inventory the respondent marks a series of statements about feeling or behavior as being characteristic of him or not characteristic of him. On the basis of various types of procedure, which we shall consider in detail in Chapter 11, certain responses are keyed as indicative of emotional maladjustment. A score is obtained by seeing how many of these responses an individual selects. But making certain marks on a piece of paper is a good many steps removed from actually exhibiting emotional disturbance. We must find some way of establishing the extent to which the performance on the test actually corresponds to the quality of behavior in which we are directly interested. How can we determine the validity of such a measurement procedure?

TYPES OF EVIDENCE OF VALIDITY

A test may be thought of as corresponding to some aspect of human behavior in any one of three senses. The terms that have been adopted to designate these senses are (1) content validity, (2) criterion-related validity, and (3) construct validity. Let us explore each of these three, so that we may understand clearly what is involved in each case, and for what kinds of tests each of the three is relevant.

Content validity.   Consider a test that has been designed to measure competence in using the English language. How can we tell how well the test does in fact measure that achievement? First, we must reach some agreement as to the skills and knowledge that comprise correct and effective use of English, and that have been the objectives of language instruction. Then we must examine the test to see what skills, knowledge, and understanding it calls for. Finally, we must match the analysis of *test content* against the analysis of *course content* and instructional objectives and see how well the former represents the latter. To the extent that our objectives, which we have accepted as goals for our course, are represented in the test, the test is valid for use in our school.

Since the analysis is essentially a rational and judgmental one, this is sometimes spoken of as *rational* or *logical validity*. The term *content validity* is also used, since the analysis is largely in terms of the test content. However, we should not think of content too narrowly, because we may be interested in *process* as much as in simple content. Thus in the field of English expression we might be concerned on the one hand with such "content" elements as the rules and principles for capitalization, use of commas, or spelling words with "ei" and "ie" combinations. But we might also be interested in such "process" skills as arranging ideas in a logical order, writing sentences that present a single unified thought, or picking the most appropriate word to convey the desired meaning. In a sense, *content* is what the pupil works with; *process* is what he does with it.

The problem of appraising content validity is closely parallel to the problem of preparing the blueprint for a test, to be discussed in Chapter 7, and then building a test to match the blueprint. A teacher's own test has content validity to the extent that a wise and thoughtful analysis of course objectives has been made in the blueprint, and care, skill, and ingenuity have been exercised in building test items to match that blueprint. A standardized test may be shown to have validity for a particular school or a particular curriculum insofar as the content of that test corresponds to and represents the objectives accepted in that school or that curriculum.

It should be clear that rational or content validity, is important primarily for measures of achievement. In particular, validity of a formative test concerned with mastery of one or more specific educational objectives, the type of test that has been called content- or criterion-referenced, will be judged on how well the test tasks represent the defined objective. But for the summative, norm-referenced achievement test, too, we will be primarily concerned with how well the tests represent what the best and most expert judgment would consider to be important knowledge and skill. If the correspondence is good, the test will be judged to have high validity; if poor, the validity must be deemed to be low.

The responsible maker of a test for publication and widespread use goes to considerable pains to determine the widely accepted goals of instruction in the field in which his test is to be built. There are many types of source to which he may, and often does, resort. These include, among others: (1) the more widely used textbooks in the field, (2) recent courses of study for the large school units, that is, states, counties, and city systems, (3) reports of special study groups, often appearing in yearbooks of one or another of the educational societies, (4) groups of teachers giving instruction in the course, (5) specialists in university, city, and state departments concerned with the training or supervision of teachers in the field.

Gathering information from these sources the test maker develops the blueprint for his test, and in terms of this blueprint he prepares the test items. Because of variations from community to community, no test published for national distribution can be made to fit exactly the content or objectives of every local course of study. In this sense a test developed on a national basis is always less valid for a specific community than an equally workmanlike test tailored specifically to the local situation. However, the well-made commercial test can take the common components that appear repeatedly in different textbooks and courses of study and build a test around them. It represents the common core that is central in the different specific local patterns.

It should be clear from what has just been said that the relationship between teaching and testing is typically intimate. Test content is drawn from what has been taught, or what is proposed to be taught. The instructional program is the original source of test materials. Sometimes the thinking in a test may lead the thinking underlying a local course of study, as when a group of specialists have been brought together to design a test corresponding to some emerging trend in education. Sometimes the test may lag behind, as when the test is based on the relatively conventional objectives emphasized in established textbooks. But usually test content and classroom instruction are in close relationship to one another, and the test may be appraised by how faithfully it corresponds to the significant goals of instruction.

To appraise the validity of a test as representing curricular objectives, there is no substitute for a careful and detailed examination of the actual test tasks. A test may be labeled "Mathematical Concepts," but call for nothing but knowledge of the definitions of terms. A test of reading comprehension may only call for answers to questions concerning specific details that appear in the passage. It is the tasks presented by the items that really define what a test is measuring, and one who would judge the validity of its content for *his* curriculum must take a hard look at the individual items.

Criterion-related validity. Frequently, we are interested in using a test in connection with a decision that implies predicting some specific future outcome. We give a scholastic aptitude test to predict how likely the high school student is to be successful in college X, where success is represented at least approximately by grade-point average. We give an employment test in order to pick machine operators who are likely to be successful employees, as represented by some such criterion as high production with little spoilage and low personnel turnover. For this purpose, we care very little what a test looks like.* We are interested almost entirely in the degree to which it correlates with some chosen criterion measure of job success. Thus some other measure (often, but not necessarily, one maturing at a later point in time) is taken as the criterion of "success," and we judge a test in terms of its relationship to that criterion measure. The higher the correlation, the better the test.

Evaluation of a test as predicting is primarily an empirical and statistical evaluation, and this aspect of validity has sometimes been spoken of as *empirical* or *statistical validity*. The basic procedure is to give the test to a group who are entering some job or training program, to follow them up later, get for each one a specified criterion measure of success on the job or in the training program, and then to compute the correlation be-

---

* This is not entirely true. What a test "looks like" may be of importance in determining its acceptability and reasonableness to those who will be tested. Thus a group of would-be pilots may be more ready to accept an arithmetic test dealing with wind drift and fuel consumption than they would the same essential problems phrased in terms of costs of crops or of recipes for baking cakes. This appearance of reasonableness is sometimes spoken of as *face validity*.

tween test score and criterion measure of success. The higher the correlation, the more effective the test as a predictor.

This relationship can be pictured in various ways. For example, the bar chart in Fig. 3.1 shows the percentage of persons failing Air Force pilot training at each of nine score levels on a predictor-test battery. The chart shows a steady increase in the percentage failing training as we go from the high to the low scores, so successful completion of training is related to aptitude level. The relationship pictured in this chart corresponds to a correlation coefficient of .49.

The problem of the criterion. We said above that predictive validity can be estimated by determining the correlation between test scores and a suitable criterion measure of success on the job. The joker here is the phrase "suitable criterion measure." One of the most difficult problems that the investigator of selection tests faces is that of locating or creating a satisfactory measure of job success to be used as a criterion measure for

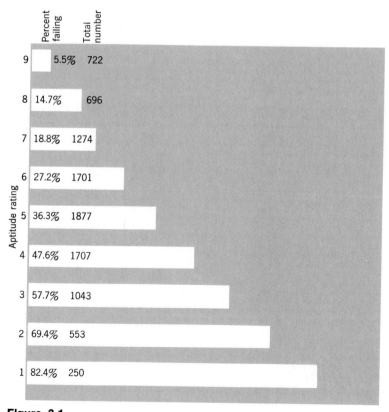

Figure 3.1
Percent of cadets eliminated from pilot training at each aptitude level.
The correlation coefficient for these data is .49.

test validation. It might appear that it should be a simple matter to decide upon some measure of rate of production or some type of rating by superiors to serve as a criterion measure. It might also seem that this measure, once decided upon, should be obtainable in an easy and straightforward fashion. Unfortunately, this is not the case. Finding or developing acceptable criterion measures usually involves the research worker in the field of tests and measurements in a host of troublesome problems.

Each possible type of criterion measure presents its problems. A record of actual performance has a good deal of appeal—number of widgets made, freedom from errors as a cashier, amount of insurance sold. But there are many jobs, such as physician, teacher, secretary, or receptionist, that yield no objective record of performance or production. And when such records do exist, the production is often influenced by an array of factors that are outside the worker's control. The production record of a weaver may depend not only upon his own skill in threading or adjusting the loom, but also on the condition of the equipment, the adequacy of the lighting where he must work, or the color of the thread he must weave. The sales of an insurance agent are a function not only of his own effectiveness as a salesman but also of the territory in which he must work and the supervision and assistance he receives.

Because of the absence or the shortcomings of performance records, the personnel psychologist has often depended on some type of rating by a supervisor as a criterion measure. Such ratings may be a part of the routine personnel procedures in a company, as when each employee receives a semiannual efficiency report, or the ratings may have to be gathered especially for the selection research. In either event they will typically be found to depend as much upon the person giving the rating as upon the person being rated. Ratings tend to be erratic and influenced by many factors other than job performance. The problems in using rating procedures to describe and evaluate people are discussed in more detail in Chapter 12.

There are always many criterion measures that might be obtained and used for validating a selection test. In addition to quantitative performance records and subjective ratings, which have already been mentioned, we might use later tests of proficiency. This is the type of procedure that is involved when a college entrance mathematics test is validated in terms of its ability to predict later performance on a comprehensive examination on college mathematics. Here the comprehensive examination serves as the criterion measure. Another common type of criterion measure is the average of grades in some type of educational or training program. Thus tests for the selection of engineers may be validated against course grades in engineering school.

All criterion measures are only partial in that they measure only a part of success on the job or only the preliminaries to actual job performance. This last is true of the engineering school grades mentioned above, which represent a relatively immediate but partial criterion of success as an engineer. The ultimate criterion would be some appraisal of the man's lifetime success in his profession. In the very nature of things such an ultimate criterion is inaccessible, and the investigator must be satisfied with substitutes for it. These substitutes are only partial and are never completely satisfactory. His problem is always to choose the most satisfactory measure or combination of measures from among those that it appears feasible to obtain. He is faced, then, with the problem of deciding which of several criterion measures is most satisfactory. How shall he decide?

Qualities desired in a criterion measure. There are four qualities desired in a criterion measure. In order of their importance they are (1) relevance, (2) freedom from bias, (3) reliability, and (4) availability.

We judge a criterion to be relevant to the extent that standing on the criterion measure corresponds to or exemplifies success on the job. In appraising the relevance of a criterion, we are thrown back once again upon rational considerations. There is no empirical evidence that will tell how relevant freshman grade-point average is, for example, as an indicator of having achieved the objectives of Supercolossal University. For achievement tests we have found it necessary to rely upon the best available professional judgment to determine whether the content of the test accurately represents sound educational objectives. In the same way, with respect to a criterion measure it is also necessary to rely upon professional judgment to provide the appraisal of the degree to which some available partial criterion measure is relevant to the ultimate criterion of success in an educational program or in a job.

A second factor important in the criterion measure is freedom from bias. By this we mean that the measure should be one on which each person has the same opportunity to make a good score. Examples of biasing factors are such things as variation in wealth from one district to another, for our previous example of the insurance salesman; variation in the quality of equipment and conditions of work, for a factory worker; variation in "generosity" of the bosses rating private secretaries; or variation in the quality of teaching received by students in different classes. To the extent that the score depends upon factors in the conditions of work or in the evaluation of work, rather than upon competence in the job, there is no real meaning to the correlation between test results and a criterion score.

The third factor, reliability, will be discussed in general terms later in this chapter. As it applies to criterion scores, the problem is merely this: A measure of success on the job must be stable or reproducible if it is to be predicted by any type of test device. If the criterion score is one that jumps around from day to day, so that the person who shows high job performance one week may show low job performance the next or who receives a high rating from one supervisor gets a low rating from another, then there is no possibility of finding a test that will predict that score. A measure that is completely unstable itself cannot be predicted by anything else.

Finally, in the choice of a criterion measure we always encounter practical problems of convenience and availability. How long will we have to wait to get a criterion score for each individual? How much is it going to cost—in dollars or in disruption of normal activities? Though a personnel research program can often afford to spend a substantial part of its effort in getting good criterion data, there is always a practical limit. Any choice of a criterion measure must take this practical limit into account.

The interpretation of validity coefficients.   Suppose that we have gathered test and criterion scores for a group of individuals and computed the correlation between them. Perhaps the predictor is a scholastic aptitude test, and the criterion is an average of college freshman grades. How shall we now decide whether the test is a good predictor?

Obviously, other things being equal, the higher the correlation, the better. In one sense, our basis for evaluating any one predictor is in relation to other possible prediction procedures. Does Peter's Perfect Personnel Predictor yield a higher or lower validity coefficient than other tests that are available? Than other types of information, such as high school grades or rating by school principal? We will look with favor on any measure whose validity for a particular criterion is higher than that of measures previously available to us, even though the measure may fall far short of perfection.

A few representative validity coefficients are exhibited in Table 3.1 on p. 66. These give some picture of the size of correlation that has been obtained in previous work of different kinds. The investigator concerned with a particular course of study or a particular job will, of course, need to become intimately acquainted with validities previously found for the particular criterion measure he is using.

The usefulness of a test as a predictor depends not only on how well it correlates with a criterion measure, but also on how much *new* information it gives. Thus, the *Differential Aptitude Tests' Verbal Reasoning Test* was found to correlate on the average .48 with high school English grades, and the test of sentence usage to correlate .51 with the same grades. But the two tests have an intercorrelation of .62. They overlap and, in part at least, the information either test provides is the same as that provided by the other test. The net result is that pooling information from the two tests can give a validity coefficient of no more than .55. If the two tests had been uncorrelated, each giving evidence completely independent of the other, the combination of the two tests would have provided a validity coefficient of .70.*

Clearly, the higher the correlation between a test or other predictor and a criterion measure, the more pleased we shall be. But in addition to this relative standard, we should like some absolute one. How high must the validity coefficient be for the test to be useful? What is a "satisfactory" validity? This is a little bit like asking, "How high is up?" However, we can try to give some sort of answer.

To an organization using a test as a basis for deciding whether to hire a particular job applicant or admit a particular student, the significant question is: How much more often will we make the right decision on whom to hire or admit if we use this test than if we operate on a purely chance basis or on the basis of some already available but less valid measure? The answer to this question depends in considerable measure on the proportion of individuals who must be accepted. A selection procedure can do much more for us if we need to accept only the individual who appears to be the best one in every 10

---

* Statistical procedures have been developed that enable us to determine the best weighting to give the two or more predictors and to calculate the correlation that will result from this combination. The procedures for computing the weights for the separate components (called *regression weights*) and the correlation (*multiple correlation*) resulting from the combination are beyond the scope of this discussion but will be found in standard statistics texts.

Table 3.1
VALIDITY OF SELECTED TESTS AS PREDICTORS OF CERTAIN EDUCATIONAL AND VOCATIONAL CRITERIA

Predictor Test	Criterion Variable	Validity Coefficient
Lorge-Thorndike Intelligence Test (Verbal)	*Iowa Tests of Basic Skills (Total Score—Gr. 4)*	.78
American College Testing Program Test Index	College Grades—English	.54
	College Grades—Math	.44
Seashore Tonal Memory Test	Performance test on stringed instrument	.28
Short Employment Test		
Word Knowledge Score	Production index—80 bookkeeping machine operators	.10
Word Knowledge Score	Job grade—106 stenographers	.53
Arithmetic Skill Score	Production index—80 bookkeeping machine operators	.26
Arithmetic Skill Score	Job grade—106 stenographers	.60
Differential Aptitude Tests (Grade 8)		
Verbal Reasoning	English grades 3½ years later	.57
Space Relations	English grades 3½ years later	.01
Mechanical Reasoning	English grades 3½ years later	.17

applicants than if we must accept 9 out of 10. However, to provide a specific example, let us assume that we will accept half of the applicants. Let us examine Table 3.2.

The model is set up to show 200 persons in all, 100 in the top half on the test and 100 in the top half on the job. If there were absolutely no relationship between test and job, there would be 50 persons in each of the four cells of the table. Defining "success" as being in the top half on the job, the success ratio would be 50 in 100 for those accepted, and also for those rejected. There would be no difference between the two and the correlation would be zero.

Table 3.2
TWO-BY-TWO TABLE OF TEST AND JOB SUCCESS

		Performance on the Job		
		Bottom Half "Failures"	Top Half "Successes"	
Score on Selection Test	Top Half (Accepted)			100
	Bottom Half (Rejected)			100
		100	100	200

Table 3.3

**PERCENTAGE OF CORRECT ASSIGNMENTS WHEN
50 PERCENT OF GROUP MUST BE SELECTED**

Validity of Selection Procedure	Percent of Correct Choices
.00	50.0
.20	56.4
.40	63.1
.50	66.7
.60	70.5
.70	74.7
.80	79.5
.90	85.6

Table 3.3 above shows the percentage of correct choices (that is, "successes") among those accepted for correlations of different sizes. The improvement in our "batting average" as the correlation goes up is shown in the table. Thus, for a correlation of .40, we will pick right 63.1 percent of the time; with a correlation of .80 the percentage of right decisions will be 79.5, and so forth.

The table shows not only the accuracy for any given correlation but the gain in accuracy if we improve the validity of the predictor. Thus, if we were able to replace a predictor with a validity of .40 by one with a validity of .60, we would increase the percentage of correct decisions from 63.1 to 70.5. All these percentages refer, of course, to the ground rules set in the previous paragraph. However, Table 3.3 gives a fairly representative basis for understanding the effects of a selection program from the point of view of the employing or certifying agency.

In many selection situations the gain can be crudely translated into a dollars-and-cents saving. Thus, if it costs a company $500 to employ and train a new worker up to the point of useful productivity, a selection procedure that raised the percentage of successes from 56.4 to 63.1 would yield a saving in wasted training expenses alone of $3,350 per 100 persons employed. This takes no account of the possibility that the test-selected workers might also be *better* workers after they had completed their training. This dollar saving would have to be balanced, of course, against any increase of cost in applying the new selection procedure.

Another way of appraising the practical significance of a correlation coefficient, and one that is perhaps more meaningful from the point of view of the person being tested, is shown in Table 3.4 on page 68. The rows in the little tables represent the fourths of a group of applicants, potential students or employees, with respect to a predictor test. The columns indicate the number of cases falling in each fourth on the criterion score. Look at the little table in Table 3.4 corresponding to a validity coefficient of .50. Note that of those who fall in the lowest fourth on the predictor 480 out of 1,000, or 48.0 percent, fall in the lowest fourth on the criterion score, 27.9 percent in the next lowest fourth, 16.8 percent in the next to highest fourth, and 7.3 percent in the highest fourth. The diagonal entries in dark print represent cases that fall in the same fourth on both predictor and criterion. The further we get from the diagonal, the greater the discrepancy between prediction and outcome. Cases on or near the diagonal represent instances in which the predictor has been right; cases falling far from the diagonal represent instances in which the predictor has been decidedly wrong.

Table 3.4

ACCURACY OF PREDICTION FOR DIFFERENT VALUES OF THE CORRELATION COEFFICIENT (1,000 CASES IN EACH ROW OR COLUMN)

r = .00

Quarter on Predictor	Quarter on Criterion			
	4th	3rd	2nd	1st
1st	250	250	250	**250**
2nd	250	250	**250**	250
3rd	250	**250**	250	250
4th	**250**	250	250	250

r = .40

Quarter on Predictor	Quarter on Criterion			
	4th	3rd	2nd	1st
1st	104	191	277	**428**
2nd	191	255	**277**	277
3rd	277	**277**	255	191
4th	**428**	277	191	104

r = .50

Quarter on Predictor	Quarter on Criterion			
	4th	3rd	2nd	1st
1st	73	168	279	**480**
2nd	168	258	**295**	279
3rd	279	**295**	258	168
4th	**480**	279	168	73

r = .60

Quarter on Predictor	Quarter on Criterion			
	4th	3rd	2nd	1st
1st	45	141	277	**537**
2nd	141	264	**318**	277
3rd	277	**318**	264	141
4th	**537**	277	141	45

r = .70

Quarter on Predictor	Quarter on Criterion			
	4th	3rd	2nd	1st
1st	22	107	270	**601**
2nd	107	270	**353**	270
3rd	270	**353**	270	107
4th	**601**	270	107	22

r = .80

Quarter on Predictor	Quarter on Criterion			
	4th	3rd	2nd	1st
1st	6	66	253	**675**
2nd	66	271	**410**	253
3rd	253	**410**	271	66
4th	**675**	253	66	6

This table emphasizes not so much the gain from using the predictor test as the variation in job success still remaining for those who are similar in predictor scores. From the point of view of schools or employers, the important thing is the improved percentage of "correct" decisions illustrated in Table 3.3. Dealing in large numbers, they can count on gaining from any predictor that is more valid than the procedure currently in use. From the point of view of the single individual, the many marked discrepancies between predicted and actual success shown in Table 3.4 may seem at least as important. If he has done poorly on the test, an applicant may be less impressed by the fact that the *probability* is that he will be below average on the job than by the fact that he *may* do very well. He may always be the exception.

There are several factors that tend to distort validity coefficients and complicate their interpretation. One is unreliability of the predictor and of the criterion that is being predicted. The effect of this is discussed on p. 101. The other is restriction of the range of ability in the group by some type of preselection. This effect will be discussed further in Chapter 10. Low reliability on the one hand or preselection on the other will tend to lower the values that are obtained for validity coefficients.

One further point can well be emphasized in conclusion. Validity is always specific to a particular curriculum or a particular job. When an author or publisher claims that his test is valid, it is always appropriate to ask: Valid for what? An achievement test in social studies that accurately represents the content and objectives of one program of instruction may be quite inappropriate for the program in a different community. An achievement test must always be evaluated against the objectives of a specific program of instruction. Again, an aptitude test battery quite valid for picking department store sales clerks who will be pleasant to customers, informed about their stock, and accurate in financial transactions may be entirely useless in identifying insurance salesmen who will be effective in going out and finding or creating new business. Validity must always be evaluated in relation to a situation as similar as possible to the one in which the measure is to be used.

For what kinds of test is criterion-related validity important? Clearly, this kind of validity is most important for a test that is to be used to predict outcomes that are represented by clear-cut criterion measures. The more readily we can identify a performance criterion that unquestionably represents the end results that we are interested in, the more we will be prepared to rely upon the evidence from correlations between a test and measures of that criterion to guide our decision on whether to use the test. There are two elements in this statement—prediction and clear-cut criterion measures. The main limitation to using criterion-related validity within the prediction context lies in the adequacy of the available criterion measures.

Construct validity. Sometimes we ask, with respect to a psychological test, neither "How well does this test predict job success?" nor "How well does this test represent our curriculum?", but rather "What do scores on this test *mean* or *signify?*" What does the score tell us about an individual? Does it correspond to some meaningful trait or construct* that will help us in understanding him? For this question of whether the test tells us something meaningful about people the term *construct validity* has been used.

Let us examine one specific testing procedure and see how its validity as a measure of a useful psychological quality or construct was studied. McClelland (1953) developed a testing procedure to appraise the individual's need or motivation to achieve—to succeed and do well. The test used pictures like those in the Thematic Apperception Test (see Chapter 13). The individual was called upon to make up a story about each picture, telling what was happening and how it turned out. A scoring system was developed for these stories, based on counting the frequency with which themes of accomplishment, mastery, success, and achievement appeared in the story material. Thus each individual received a score representing the strength of his motivation to achieve. Now, how are we to determine whether this measure has validity in the sense of truthfully describing a meaningful aspect of the individual's makeup? Let us see how McClelland and his co-workers proceeded.

In essence the investigators proceeded to ask: "With what should a measure of achievement motivation be related?" They made a series of predictions. Some of the predictions were as follows:

1. Those high on achievement motivation should do well in college, in relation to their scholastic aptitude.

* The term *construct* is used in psychology to refer to something that is not observable, but is literally *constructed* by the investigator to summarize or account for the regularities or relationships that he observes in behavior. Thus most names of traits refer to constructs. We speak of a person's "sociability" as a way of summarizing observed consistency in his past behavior in relation to people and of organizing a prediction of how he will act on future occasions.

2. Achievement motivation should be higher for students just after they have been taking tests described to them as measuring their intelligence.

3. Those high on achievement motivation should complete more items on a motivated speeded test.

4. Achievement motivation should be higher for children of families emphasizing early independence.

Each of these predictions was based on a sort of "theory of human behavior." Thus academic achievement is seen as a combination of ability and effort. Presumably those with higher motivation to achieve will exert more effort and will, ability being equal, achieve higher grades. A similar chain of reasoning lies back of each of the other predictions.

In general McClelland found that most of his predictions were supported by the experimental results. The fact that the test scores were related to a number of other events in the way that was predicted from a rational analysis of the trait that the test was presumably measuring lent support to the validity of the test procedure as measuring a meaningful trait or construct, whose essential characteristics are fairly well summarized by the label "achievement motivation."

A great many psychological tests, and, to a lesser extent, some educational tests, are intended to measure general traits or qualities of the individual. Verbal reasoning, spatial visualizing, sociability, introversion, mechanical interest are all designations of traits or constructs. Tests of these functions are valid insofar as they behave in the way that such a trait should reasonably be expected to behave.

A theory about a trait will lead to predictions of the following types that can be tested to see if they hold up.

1. *Predictions about correlations.* The nature of the trait, and therefore of valid measures of it, will indicate that it should be related to certain other measures. These other measures may be already accepted measures of the function in question. Thus many subsequent group intelligence tests have been validated in part by their correlations with earlier tests, especially with the individually administered Stanford-Binet. Or the other measures may be ones with which the trait should logically be related. Thus intelligence tests have been validated, in part, through their correlation with success in school; measures of mechanical aptitude, by their correlation with rated proficiency in mechanical jobs.

One way of studying the constructs or attributes that a test measures is to study jointly the intercorrelations of this test and a number of others. The patterning of these correlations makes it possible to see which tests are measuring some common factor. An examination of the tests clustering together in a single factor may serve to clarify the nature and meaning of the factor and of the tests that measure it. However, this internal, or "factorial," validity still seems to need evidence of relationship to life events outside the tests themselves if the factor is to have much substance and vitality.

It may also be appropriate to predict that the measure of Construct X will show low or vanishing correlations with measures of certain other attributes, that is, that the construct is different from them. Thus a test designed to measure mechanical comprehension should show only a modest correlation with a test of verbal ability. A measure of sociability should not show too high a correlation with a measure of assertiveness, if the two assess genuinely different constructs.

2. *Predictions about group differences.* A theory will often suggest that certain kinds of group should score especially high or low on the trait, and consequently on a test of it. Thus it seems reasonable that a group of salesmen should be high on a measure of ascendance, or assertiveness, and that a group of librarians should be low. We would probably predict that children of professional and business parents would be more ascendant than those whose parents were in clerical or semiskilled occupations. For any given trait, our general knowledge of our society and the groups within it will suggest an array of group differences that seem to make sense. Applying a test to these groups, the investigator finds out how consistently his predictions are borne out.

3. *Predictions about response to experimental treatments or interventions.* A theory may imply that the expression of a human characteristic will be modified as a result of certain experimental conditions or treatments. Thus one could reasonably predict that anxiety would increase just before a person was to undergo a minor operation. Rate of flicker fusion* has been proposed as an indicator of anxiety level. In one study (Buhler, 1953) it was found that, as predicted, the flicker fusion threshold was lower before the operation than after when the anxiety had presumably relaxed.

For any test that presumes to measure a trait or quality, we can formulate a network of theory, leading to definite predic-

---

* The rate at which alternation of black and white stimulation fuses into a steady gray.

tions. These predictions can be tested. Insofar as they are borne out, the validity of the test as a measure of the trait or construct is supported. Insofar as the predictions fail to be verified, we are led to doubt the validity of the test, or our theorizing, or both.

Evidence of validity is, as we have seen, partly rational and partly empirical. Rational consideration of what is measured takes the center of the stage when we are considering an end product—either a test that is serving to describe an individual's past learning or some indicator that we are accepting as a criterion measure. Again, the elaboration of a theory by which we decide how to test out the validity of a measure of a psychological construct is a rational exercise. By contrast, when we use a test as a selection device to predict some accepted criterion measure, validation becomes primarily statistical. And checking out the theory that we have built up for a measure of some construct is also an empirical undertaking. Judgment and evidence join together in the validation enterprise.

RELIABILITY

The second question we raise with respect to a measurement procedure is: How reliable is it? We are now asking not what it measures, but how accurately it measures whatever it does measure. What is the precision of our resulting score? How accurately will it be reproduced if we measure the individual again?

Suppose we were to test all the boys in a school class today and again tomorrow to see how far each can throw a football. We mark a starting line on the field, give each boy one of the old footballs that the physical education department has for team practice, send an assistant out to mark where the ball hits, and tell each boy to throw the ball as far as he can. With a steel tape, we measure the distance from the starting line to where our assistant marked the fall of the ball. We have each boy make a throw today and then make a throw again tomorrow.

When we compare the two scores for a boy, we will find they are almost never exactly the same. The two throws differ. Most of the differences will be fairly small, but some will be moderately large, and a few will be quite large. These differences show that one throw is not perfectly reliable as a measure of the boy's throwing ability. Results are, to some degree, inconsistent from one day's throw to the next. Why?

We can identify three classes of reasons for inconsistency between a throw today and a throw tomorrow.

1. *The person may actually have changed* from one day to the next. On one day he may be more rested than he was on the other. On one day he may have been motivated to try harder on the task. He may even have gotten some special coaching from his father between the two tests. If the interval between the two tests is months rather than days, there may have been very real physical growth, and growth that differed from boy to boy between the two testings. Our example has been of changes affecting physical performance, but it is easy to think of similar categories of change that would apply to a test of mental ability or to a self-report inventory dealing with mood or with interests.

2. *The task may have been different* for the two measurements. For example, the ball used one day may have been tightly inflated, whereas the other day it may have been a squashy one that permitted a somewhat different grip. Or one day the examiner may have permitted the boys to take a run up to the release line, whereas the examiner on the second day may have allowed only a couple of steps. And these variations may have helped some boys more than others. In paper-and-pencil tests we often use one form of the test upon one occasion and a parallel form on the second occasion. The specific items are then different, and some pupils may happen to be better able to handle one sampling of tasks, while others are better at the second sampling.

3. *The limited sample of behavior* will have resulted in an unstable and undependable score. Even if we had each boy make two throws with the same ball and same instructions, with only a five-minute rest in between, the two distances would rarely come out to be exactly the same. A single throw is a meager sample of behavior. That sample, and the evaluation of it, are subject to all sorts of chance influences. Maybe the boy's finger slipped. Maybe he got mixed up in the coordination of his legs and arm. Maybe the ball was held a little too far forward or a little too far back. Maybe the scorer was looking the other way when the ball landed. Maybe there was a gust of wind just as he threw. Maybe any one of a hundred things—some favorable, some unfavorable. These all add up to the end result that a small sample of behavior does not provide a stable and dependable characterization of the individual—whether the sample be of footballs thrown for distance or of sentences read for understanding.

There are two ways in which we can express the reliability or precision of a set of measurements, or, from the reverse point of view, the variation within the set. One approach indicates directly the amount of variation to be expected within a set of repeated measurements of a single individual. If it were possible to have Johnny throw the football 200 times (assuming for the present that this could be done without introducing effects of fatigue or practice), we would produce a frequency distribution of distances thrown. This frequency distribution has an average value, which we can think of as approximating the "true" distance that Johnny can throw a football. It also has a standard deviation, describing the spread or scatter of these distances. We shall call this variation the *standard error of measurement*, since it is the standard deviation of the "errors" of measuring the distance of throw for one person.

With psychological data we usually cannot make a whole series of measurements on each individual. There *are* practice and fatigue effects; besides, time does not permit giving 200 reading tests or 200 interest inventories. Often we are fortunate if we can get *two* scores for each individual. But if we have a pair of measurements for each individual we can make an estimate (see p. 85) of what the scattering of scores would have been for the average person if we had made the measurements again and again.

Reliable measurement also implies that the individual stays in about the same place in his group. The boy who scores highest on the football throwing test the first time should also be one of the highest the next time, and each person in the group should stay in about the same position. We have already seen in Chapter 2 that the correlation coefficient provides us with a statistical index of the extent to which two things go together, high with high and low with low. If the two things we are correlating happen to be two applications of the same measure, the resulting correlation provides an indicator of reliability. We can designate it a *reliability coefficient*. The characteristics of the correlation coefficient are those that we have already seen in Chapter 2 and in our discussion of validity. But the relationship now before us is that of two measurements with the same measuring instrument. The more nearly individuals are ranked in the same order the second time, the higher the correlation and the more reliable the test.

A measure is reliable, then, to the extent that an individual remains nearly the same in repeated measurements—nearly the same as represented by a low standard error of measurement or by a high reliability coefficient. But what exact type of data do we need in order to get an appropriate estimate of this degree of stability or precision in measurement? We shall consider three distinct possibilities, noticing their similarities and differences and evaluating the advantages and disadvantages of each.

1. Repetition of the same test or measure.
2. Administration of a second "equivalent" form of the test.
3. Subdivision of the test into two or more equivalent fractions.

Let us examine each of these in turn.

RETEST WITH THE SAME TEST

If we wish to find how reliably we can evaluate an individual's football throw, we can have him tested twice. It may be a reasonable precaution to have the two measures taken independently by two persons. We don't want the experimenter's recollection of the first score to color the second score. It may be desirable to have the two testings done on different days. That depends on what we are interested in. If we want to know how accurately a single throw (or possibly a single set of throws) characterizes a person at one specific point in time, the two measurements should be carried out one right after the other. Then we know that the *person* has stayed the same and that the only source of variation or "error" is in the operation of measuring him. If we want to know how precisely a given measurement characterizes a person from day to day—how closely we can predict his score next week from what he does today—it would be appropriate to measure him on two separate occasions. Now we are interested in *variation of the individual from one time to another* as well as *variation due to the operation of measurement.*

Sometimes we are interested in variation of the individual from day to day; sometimes we are not. We may ask: How accurately does our measurement characterize S at this moment of time? Or we may ask: How accurately does our measure of S today describe him as he will be tomorrow, or next week, or next month? Both are sensible questions. But they are not the same question. The data we must gather to answer one are different from the data we need to answer the other.

To study the reliability of measurement of such a physical characteristic of a person as height or weight, repetition of the measurement is a straightforward and satisfactory operation. It appears satisfactory and applicable also with some simple aspects of behavior, such as speed of reaction or the type of motor skill that is exemplified by the football throw. But suppose now we are interested in the reliability of a test of reading comprehension. Let us assume that the test is made up of 6 reading passages with 5 questions on each. We administer the test once and then immediately administer it again. What happens? Certainly, the child is not going to have to reread all the material he has just read. He may do so in part, but to a considerable extent his answers the second time will involve merely remembering what answer he had chosen the time before and marking it again. If he had not been able to finish the first time, he will now be able to work ahead and spend most of his time on new material. These same effects will hold true to some degree even over a longer period of time. Clearly, a test like this given a second time does not present the same task that it did the first time.

There is a second consideration entering into the repetition of such a test as a reading comprehension test. Suppose that one of the five passages in the test was about baseball and that a particular boy was an expert on baseball. The passage would then be especially easy for him, and he would in effect get a bonus of several points. The test would overestimate his general level of reading ability. But note that it would do it consistently on both testings if the material remained the same. The error for individual S would be a *constant error* in the two testings. Since it would affect both his scores in the same way, it would make the test look reliable rather than unreliable.

In such an area of ability as reading, we must recognize the possibility that an individual does not perform uniformly well throughout the whole area. His specific interests, experiences, and background give him strengths and weaknesses. A particular test is *one sample* from the whole area. How well individual S does on the test, relative to other persons, is likely to depend in some degree upon the particular sample of tasks chosen to represent the domain of ability or personality we are trying to appraise. If the sample remains the same for both measurements, his behavior will stay more nearly the same than if the sample of tasks is varied.

Note that so far we have identified three main sources of variation in performance that will tend to reduce the precision of a particular score as a description of an individual:

1. Variation from trial to trial in response to the task at a particular moment in time.

2. Variation in the individual from one time to another.

3. Variation arising out of the particular sample of tasks chosen to represent a domain of behavior.

Retesting the individual with identically the same test can be arranged to reflect the first two types of "error," but this procedure cannot evaluate the effects of the third type. In addition, there may be the memory and practice effects to which we referred above.

PARALLEL TEST FORMS

Concern about this third source of variation, variation due to the particular sample of tasks chosen to represent a domain of behavior, leads us to another set of procedures for evaluating reliability. If the sampling of items may be a significant source of "error," and if, as is usually the case, we want to know with what accuracy we may generalize from the specific score based on one sample of tasks to the broader domain that sample is supposed to represent, we must develop some procedures that take account of variation due to the sample of tasks. We may do this by correlating two equivalent forms of a test.

Equivalent forms of a test should be thought of as forms built according to the same specifications but composed of separate samples from the defined behavior domain. Thus two equivalent reading tests should contain reading passages and questions of the same difficulty. The same sorts of question should be asked, that is, the same balance of specific fact and general idea questions. The same types of passage should be represented, that is, expository, argumentative, aesthetic. But the specific passages and questions should be different.

If we have two forms of a test, we may give each pupil first one form and then the other. They may follow each other immediately if we are not interested in stability over time, or may be separated by an interval if we are. The correlation between the two forms will provide an appropriate reliability coefficient. If a time interval has been allowed between the testings, all three sources of variation will have had a chance to get in their effects—variation arising from the measurement itself, variation in the individual over time, and variation due to the sample of tasks.

To ask that a test yield consistent results under these conditions is the most rigorous standard we can set for it. And if we want to use test results to generalize about what Johnny will do on other tasks of this general sort next week and next month, then this is the appropriate standard by which to evaluate a test. For most educational situations, this *is* the way we want to use test results, and so evidence based on equivalent test forms should usually be given the most weight in evaluating the reliability of a test.

The use of two parallel test forms provides a very sound basis for estimating the precision of a psychological or educational test. This procedure does, however, raise some practical problems. It demands that two parallel forms of a test be available and that time be allowed for testing each person twice. Sometimes no second form of a test exists, or no time can be found for a second testing. To administer a second, separate test is often likely to represent a somewhat burdensome demand upon available resources. These practical considerations of convenience and expediency have made test makers receptive to procedures that extract an estimate of reliability from administration of only one form of a test. However, such procedures are compromises at best. The correlation between two parallel forms, usually administered with a lapse of several days or weeks in between, represents the preferred procedure for estimating reliability.

SUBDIVIDED TEST

Practical considerations often dictate that a reliability estimate be obtained from a single testing. A widely used procedure for doing this divides the existing test up into two presumably equivalent halves. The half-tests may be assembled on the basis of careful examination of the content and difficulty of each item, making a systematic effort to balance out the content and difficulty level of the two halves. A simpler procedure, often relied upon to give equivalent halves, is to put alternate items into the two half-tests, that is, to put all the odd-numbered items in one half-test and all the even-numbered items in the other. This is usually a sensible procedure, since items of similar form, content, or difficulty are likely to be grouped together in a test. For a reasonably long test, say, of 60 items or more, splitting the test up in this way will tend to balance out factors of item form, content covered, and difficulty level. The two half-tests will have a good probability of constituting "equivalent" tests, as these were defined in the preceding section.

The procedures we are discussing now divide the test in half only for scoring, not for administration. That is, a single test is given at a single sitting and with a single time limit. However, two separate scores are derived—one by scoring the odd-numbered items and one by scoring the even-numbered items. The correlation between these two scores provides a measure of the accuracy with which the test is measuring the individual.

However, it must be noted that the computed correlation is between two half-length tests. This value is not directly applicable to the full-length test, which is the actual instrument prepared for use. In general, the larger the sample of a person's behavior we have, the more reliable the measure will be. The more behavior we record, the less our measure will depend upon chance elements in the behavior of the individual or in the particular sampling of tasks. Single lucky answers or momentary lapses of attention will be more nearly evened out.

Where the two halves of the test, which gave the scores actually correlated, are equivalent, we can get an unbiased estimate of total-test reliability from the correlation between the two half-tests. This estimate is given by the formula

$$r_{11} = \frac{2r_{\frac{1}{2}\frac{1}{2}}}{1 + r_{\frac{1}{2}\frac{1}{2}}} \tag{1}$$

where r_{11} is the estimated reliability of the full-length test, $r_{\frac{1}{2}\frac{1}{2}}$ is the actual correlation between two half-length tests.

Thus, if the correlation between the two halves of a test is .60, formula (1) would give

$$r_{11} = \frac{2(0.60)}{1 + 0.60} = \frac{1.20}{1.60} = .75$$

This formula, referred to generally as the Spearman-Brown Prophecy Formula from its function and the names of its originators, makes it possible for us to compute an estimate of reliability from a single administration of a single test.

The appealing convenience of the split-half procedure has led to its wide use. Many test manuals will be found to report this type of reliability coefficient and no other. Unfortunately, this coefficient has several types of limitations, which we must now examine.

First, when we have extracted two scores from a single testing, both scores necessarily represent the individual as he is at the same moment of time. Even events lasting only a few minutes will affect both scores about equally. In other words, variation of the individual from day to day cannot be reflected in this type of reliability coefficient. It can only give evidence as to the precision with which we can appraise him at a specific moment in time.

A second factor will sometimes make two half-tests more alike than would be true of separate parallel forms. If the test includes groups of items based on common reference material, that is, reading items based on a single passage, science items referring to a single described experiment, etc., performance on all of these items will depend to some extent on the common act of comprehending the reference materials. Thus the examinee who succeeds on one item of the set is likely to succeed on the others. The items are not experimentally independent. If we divide such sets of items between the two half-tests, as would happen in an odd-even reliability coefficient, we will produce a spurious and inflated resemblance between the two halves. With such materials the appropriate procedure, rarely used, is to assign alternate *sets* of items to the two half-length tests. If correlation between two half-length tests is to provide an appropriate estimate of the reliability of the full test, the two halves should be experimentally independent and equivalent. That is, there should be no undue overlap of items in one test with items in the other, and each half-test should be built to the same specifications as the whole test.

Third, a split-half reliability coefficient becomes meaningless when a test is highly speeded. Suppose we had a test of simple arithmetic, made up of 100 problems like $3 + 5 = ?$, and that the test were being used with adults with a 2-minute time limit. We would get wide differences in score on such a test, but the differences would be primarily differences in speed. Errors would be a minor factor. The person who got a score of 50 would very probably have attempted just 50 items, *and of these 25 would be odd and 25 would be even.* In other words, the two halves of the test would appear perfectly consistent, because opportunity to attempt items automatically would be balanced out for the two half-tests.

Few tests depend as completely upon speed as does the one chosen to illustrate this point. However, many involve some degree of speeding. This speed factor tends to inflate estimates of reliability based on the split-half procedure. The amount of overestimation depends upon the degree to which the test is speeded, being greater for those tests in which speed plays a greater role. However, speed enters in sufficiently generally so that split-half estimates of reliability should always be discounted somewhat. Test users should demand that commercial publishers provide reliability estimates based on parallel forms of the test.

The teacher or investigator who makes much use of tests and who reads extensively in test manuals will encounter one other type of procedure for estimating test reliability from a single test administration. This procedure depends upon the consistency of the individual's performance from item to item, and is based on the standard deviation of the test and the standard deviations of the separate items. In its most general form, it is called *coefficient alpha,* and is given by the formula

$$\alpha = \left(\frac{n}{n-1}\right)\left(\frac{s_t^2 - \Sigma s_i^2}{s_t^2}\right) .$$ (2)

where α is the estimate of reliability,

n is the number of items in the test,

s_t is the standard deviation of the test,

Σ means "take the sum of" and covers the n items,

s_i is the standard deviation of an item.

When each item is scored as either 1 or 0, that is, as either passed or failed,

$$s_i^2 = pq$$

where p is the proportion passing the item, and

q is the proportion failing the item.

The formula then becomes

$$r_{11} = \left(\frac{n}{n-1}\right)\left(\frac{s_t^2 - \Sigma pq}{s_t^2}\right)$$ (3)

This formula, called Kuder-Richardson Formula 20 after the names of the originators and the numbering in their original article, provides an estimate of what is called the *internal consistency* of a test—the degree to which all of the items measure a common characteristic of the person. When the test is homogeneous, in the sense that every item measures the same general factors of ability or personality as every other item, coefficient alpha and the Kuder-Richardson estimates have essentially the same interpretation as the odd-even coefficient we have just considered. The Kuder-Richardson estimate likewise (1) takes no account of variation in the individual from time to time, and (2) is inappropriate for speeded tests. Within these two limitations, it provides a conservative estimate of the split-half type of reliability.*

COMPARISON OF METHODS

A summary comparison of the different procedures for estimating reliability is given in Table 3.5. This shows four factors that may make a single test score an inaccurate picture of the individual's usual performance. The table shows which of the sources of error are reflected in each of the procedures for estimating reliability we have discussed. In general, the more Xs there are in a column, the more conservative (that is, lower)

Table 3.5
SOURCES OF VARIATION REPRESENTED IN DIFFERENT PROCEDURES FOR ESTIMATING RELIABILITY

Sources of Variation	Experimental Procedure for Estimating Reliability					
	Immediate Retest, Same Test	Retest after Interval, Same Test	Parallel Test Form without Time Interval	Parallel Test Form with Time Interval	Odd-Even Halves of Single Test	Coefficient Alpha for Single Test
How much the score can be expected to fluctuate owing to:						
Variations arising within the measurement procedure itself	X	X	X	X	X	X
Changes in the individual from day to day		X		X		
Changes in the specific sample of tasks			X	X	X	X
Changes in the individual's speed of work	X	X	X	X		

* A formula involving simpler calculations (Kuder-Richardson Formula 21), which yields a reasonably close but conservative approximation to Formula 20, is

$$r_{11} = \frac{n}{n-1}\left[1 - \frac{M_t\left(1 - \frac{M_t}{n}\right)}{s_t^2}\right]$$

where M_t is the mean score of the group and the other symbols have the same meaning as given above.

estimate of a test's reliability we will get. It can be seen that the different procedures are not equivalent. Only administration of parallel test forms with a time interval between permits all sources of variation to have their effects. Each of the other methods masks some source of variation that may be significant in the actual use of tests. Retesting with the same identical test neglects variation arising out of the sample of items. Whenever all the testing is done at one point in time, variation of the individual from day to day is neglected. When the testing is done as a unit with a single time limit, variation in speed of responding is neglected. The facts brought out in this table should be borne in mind in evaluating reliability data found in a test manual or in the report of a research study.

OVERLAP OF RELIABILITY AND VALIDITY

One way of thinking about the usefulness of a test is to ask to what extent one may safely generalize from a test score. If two forms of the test are given on the same day, the correlation between them tells us with what degree of confidence we can generalize from one set of test tasks to another set built to the same specifications, and by implication, with what degree of confidence we can generalize from the score to the whole domain of tasks sampled by the test. If testing is done on different days, we get evidence over a domain of occasions. And if the testing on different days is also with different test forms, evidence is provided on the degree of generalizability over both tasks and occasions. If two different but similar tests are given, each intended by its author to measure the same trait or construct, one gets evidence of the generalizability from test to test. One is now considering a still broader domain that includes not merely samples of tasks chosen according to a common blueprint or design, but also the range of blueprints and designs prepared by different authors. One is moving beyond what is ordinarily thought of as reliability into what is considered *construct validity*. And, of course, it is possible to consider generalizability from a test to other indicators of the same attribute, such as self-description or ratings by peers, supervisors, or teachers. The notion of generalizability encompasses both reliability and construct validity, indicating that they differ only in the breadth of the domain to which generalization is undertaken. As indicated in Fig. 3.2, we can view the situation as resembling the layers of an onion, and can ask for any test how well it enables us to generalize to situations at successive levels of remoteness from the central core.

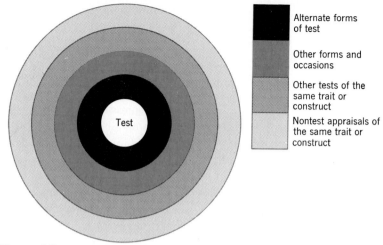

Alternate forms
of test

Other forms and
occasions

Other tests of the
same trait or
construct

Nontest appraisals of
the same trait or
construct

Test

Figure 3.2
Layers of generalization from a test score

INTERPRETATION OF RELIABILITY DATA

Suppose that analysis of data obtained from an elementary
school test of academic aptitude has yielded a reliability coefficient of .85. How shall we interpret this result? What does it
mean concerning the precision of an individual's score? Should
we be pleased or dissatisfied to get a coefficient of this size?

We have already tried to give some content and meaning to
correlation coefficients in Fig. 2.8 and in Tables 2.7, 3.1, 3.3
and 3.4. These have shown typical values of the correlation
coefficient, the scatter of scores for representative correlations,
and the accuracy of prediction with correlations of different
sizes. A further contribution to the interpretation of test reliability is found in the relationship between the reliability coefficient and the standard error of measurement.

It will be remembered that the standard error of measurement is an estimate of the standard deviation that would be
obtained for a series of measurements of the same individual.
(It is assumed that he is not changed by being measured.) The
standard error of measurement can be calculated from the reliability coefficient by the formula

$$s_m = s_t \sqrt{1 - r_{11}} \qquad (4)$$

where s_m is the standard error of measurement,
s_t is the standard deviation of test scores,
r_{11} is the reliability coefficient.

Suppose that the test has a reliability of .85 and a standard deviation of 15 points. Then we have

$$s_m = 15 \sqrt{1 - .85} = 15 \sqrt{.15} = 15(.387) = 5.8$$

In this instance a set of measures of some one person would have a standard deviation of 5.8 points. Remember that a fairly uniform proportion of observations falls within any given number of standard deviation units from the mean. Certain values for this relationship were given in Table 2.6. That table shows that for a normal curve, 31.8 percent of cases, or about 1 in 3, differ from the mean by more than 1 standard deviation; 4.6 percent by more than 2 standard deviations. Applying this to the case in which the standard error of measurement is 5.8 points, one could say that there is about 1 chance in 3 that a score gotten for an individual differs from his "true" score by as much as 5.8 points (1 standard error of measurement), about 1 chance in 20 that it differs by as much as 11.6 points (2 standard errors of measurement).

The numerical values of .85 and 15 are fairly representative of what might be found for standard scores from one of the commercially distributed group academic aptitude tests applied to children in the upper elementary grades. Note that even with this relatively high reliability coefficient, appreciable errors of measurement are possible in at least a minority of cases. With a standard deviation of 15 or 16, shifts of 5 or 10 points from one testing to another can be expected fairly frequently just because of errors of measurement. Anyone who is impressed by and tries to interpret a score difference of 5 points between two persons or two testings of the same person has been fooled into thinking the test has a precision that it simply does not possess. Further testing could perfectly well reverse the result. Any interpretation of a test score or comparison of test scores must be made with acute awareness of the standard error of measurement.

The manner in which the standard error of measurement is related to the reliability coefficient is shown in Table 3.6. Note that the magnitude of errors decreases as the reliability increases, but also that errors of appreciable size can still be found even with reliability coefficients of .90 or .95. In interpreting the score of an individual, it is the standard error of measurement that must be kept in mind. A range extending from 2 standard errors of measurement above the obtained score to 2 below will produce a band within which we can be

Table 3.6
STANDARD ERROR OF MEASUREMENT FOR DIFFERENT VALUES OF RELIABILITY COEFFICIENT

| Reliability Coefficient | Standard Error of Measurement | |
	General Expression	When S_t^* = 10
.50	.71 S_t^*	7.1
.60	.63 S_t	6.3
.70	.55 S_t	5.5
.80	.45 S_t	4.5
.85	.39 S_t	3.9
.90	.32 S_t	3.2
.95	.22 S_t	2.2
.98	.14 S_t	1.4

* S_t signifies the standard deviation of the test.

reasonably sure (19 chances in 20) that the individual's true score lies. Thus, in the case of the aptitude test described in previous paragraphs, we can think of a test standard score of 90 as meaning rather surely a score lying between about 80 and 100. If we think in those terms, we shall be much more discreet in interpreting and using test results.

When interpreting the test score of an individual, it is desirable to think in terms of the standard error of measurement and to be somewhat humble and tentative in drawing conclusions from that test score. But for making comparisons between tests and for a number of types of test analysis, the reliability coefficient will be more useful. Where measures are expressed in different units, as height in inches and weight in pounds, the reliability coefficient provides the only possible basis for comparing precision. Since the competing tests in a given field, such as primary reading, are likely to use types of scores that are not really comparable, the reliability coefficient will usually represent the only satisfactory basis for test comparison. *Other things being equal,* the test with the higher reliability coefficient is to be preferred, that is, the test that provides a more consistent ranking of the individual within his group.

The other things that may not be equal are primarily considerations of validity and practicality. Validity, insofar as we can appraise it, is the crucial requirement in a measurement procedure. Reliability is important only as a necessary condition for a measure to have validity. The ceiling for the possible validity of a test is set by its reliability. A test must measure *something* before it can measure what we want it to measure. A measuring device with a reliability of .00 is reflecting nothing but chance factors. It does not correlate with itself and cannot correlate with anything else.

The theoretical ceiling for the correlation between any two measures is the square root of the product of their reliabilities. Thus, if a selection test has a reliability of .80 and a set of supervisory ratings has a reliability of .50, the theoretical maximum for the correlation between the two is $\sqrt{(.80)(.50)} = \sqrt{.40} = .63$. Clearly, here the limit on prediction is set more by the low reliability of the criterion measure than of the predictor test—and this is often the situation that we face. But if the reliability of the test had been only .40, by contrast, the ceiling on the prediction would now be a correlation of .45. Often there is not too much that we can do about the reliability of a criterion variable, except to get information about it, but we can take steps to assure reasonable reliability in predictor tests.

The converse of the relationship we have just presented does not follow. A test may measure with the greatest precision and still have no validity for our purposes. Thus we can measure head size with a good deal of accuracy, but the measure is still useless as an indicator of intelligence. Validity is something over and beyond mere accuracy of measurement.

Considerations of cost, convenience, and so on, may also sometimes lead to a decision to use a less reliable test. We may accept a less reliable 40-minute test in preference to a more reliable 3-hour one because the 3 hours of testing time is too much of a burden in view of the purpose the test is designed to serve.

Within the limitations discussed in the preceding paragraphs, we prefer the more reliable test. There are several factors that must be taken into account, however, before we can fairly compare the reliability coefficients of two or more different tests. These will be discussed in the paragraphs that follow.

1. *Range of the group.* The reliability coefficient indicates how consistently a test places each individual relative to the others in the group. When there is little shifting from test to retest or form A to form B, the reliability coefficient is high and vice versa. But the extent to which individuals will switch places depends on how closely similar they are. It does not take very accurate testing to differentiate the reading ability of second graders from that of seventh graders. But to place each second grader accurately within his own class is much more demanding.

If children from several different grades are pooled together, we may expect a much higher reliability coefficient. For example, the manual for the Otis Quick-Scoring Mental Ability Test—Beta reported alternate-forms reliabilities for single grade groups ranging from .65 to .87, with an average value of .78. But for a pooling of the complete range of grades (4–9), the reliability coefficient was reported as .96. These data are all for the same test. They reflect the same precision. Yet the coefficient for the combined groups is strikingly higher.

In evaluating a reported reliability coefficient, the range of ability in the group tested must be taken into account. If the reliability coefficient is based upon a combination of age or grade groups, it must usually be sharply discounted, as can be seen above. But even in less extreme cases, account must be taken of the variability of talent. Reliability coefficients for age groups will tend to be somewhat higher than for grade groups, because an age group will usually contain a greater spread of talent than a single grade. A sample made up of children from a wide range of socioeconomic levels will tend to yield higher reliability coefficients than a very homogeneous one. In comparing different tests we must take account of the type of sample on which the reliability data were based, insofar as this can be determined from the reported facts, and judge more severely the test whose estimated reliability is based on data from the more heterogeneous group.

2. *Level of ability in the group.* Precision of measurement by a test may be related to the ability level of the persons being measured. However, no simple rule can be formulated for stating the nature of this relationship. It depends upon the way in which the particular test was built. For those people for whom the test is very hard, so that they are doing a large amount of guessing, accuracy is likely to be low. At the other extreme, if a test is very easy for a group, so that all of them can do most of the items very easily, that test may be expected to be ineffective in discriminating among the group members. When everyone can do the easy items, it is as if one had shortened the test, since all differentiation is based on just those harder items that some can do and some cannot.

It is possible, also, that a test may vary in accuracy at different intermediate difficulty levels. The meticulous test constructor will report the standard error of measurement for his test at different score levels. When separate values of the standard error of measurement are reported in the manual, they provide a basis for evaluating the precision of the test for different types of groups, and permit a more appropriate estimate of the accuracy of a particular individual's score. Each individual's score can be interpreted in relation to the standard error of measurement for scores of that level. For example, the *Cognitive Abilities Test, Verbal Level A,* for which results are expressed as "standard age scores" with a standard deviation of 16 points, reports the standard error of measurement at different raw score levels as follows:

Raw Score	Standard Error in SAS Units
15	4.3
25	3.6
35	3.1
45	2.1
55	2.3
65	2.8
75	4.8

This test measures a good deal more accurately (when the measures are expressed in equal-sized standard deviation units) those pupils who get about half of the 100 items right than those who succeed with only a few items or with almost all. This result was produced intentionally, by including many items of moderate difficulty that discriminate degrees of ability in the middle range and relatively few very easy or very hard items. In effect, a longer test is operating for pupils in the middle range than at the extremes, and the result is more accurate measurement of this large middle group.

3. *Length of test.* As we saw on p. 80 in discussing the split-half reliability coefficient, test reliability depends on the length of the test. If we can assume that the quality of the test items and the nature of the examinees remain the same, then the relationship of reliability to length can be expressed by the simple formula

$$r_{nn} = \frac{nr_{11}}{1 + (n-1)r_{11}} \tag{5}$$

where r_{nn} is the reliability of a test n times as long as the original test,

r_{11} is the reliability of the original test,

n is, as indicated, the factor by which the length of the test is increased.

This is a more general form of formula (1) found on p. 80. Suppose we have a spelling test made up of 20 items that has a reliability of .50. We want to know how reliable the test will be if it is lengthened to contain 100 items comparable to the original 20. The answer is

$$r_{nn} = \frac{5(.50)}{1 + 4(.50)} = \frac{2.50}{3.00} = .83$$

As the length of the test is increased, the chance errors of measurement more or less cancel out; the score comes to depend more and more completely upon the characteristics of the person being measured; and a more accurate appraisal of him is obtained.

Of course, how much we can lengthen a test is limited by a number of practical considerations. It is limited by the amount of time available for testing. It is limited by factors of fatigue and boredom on the part of examinees. It is sometimes limited by our inability to construct more equally good test items. But within these limits, reliability can be increased as needed by lengthening the test.

One special type of lengthening is represented by increasing the number of raters who rate an individual or a product he has produced. To the extent that the unreliability of an assessment is due to the inconsistency with which a sample of behavior is judged, this source of unreliability can usually be reduced by increasing the number of judges. If several judges are available who have equal competence with the materials to be rated or equal familiarity with the ratee if the ratings are of a person, then a pooling of their ratings will produce a composite that is more reliable; the increase is found to be described approximately by formula (5) above. For example, if a typical pair of judges evaluating samples of writing show a correlation of .40, then the pooled rating of three judges could be expected to correlate with three others as follows:

$$\frac{3(.40)}{1 + 2(.40)} = \frac{1.20}{1.80} = .67$$

4. *Operations used for estimating.* How high a value will be obtained for the reliability coefficient depends also upon which of the several sets of experimental operations is used to estimate the reliability. We saw in Table 3.5 that the different procedures treat different sources of variation in different ways, and that it is only the use of parallel forms of a test with a period intervening that includes all four sources of variation in "error." That is, this procedure of estimating reliability represents

Table 3.7

COMPARISON OF RELIABILITY COEFFICIENTS OBTAINED FROM EQUIVALENT FORMS AND FROM FRACTIONS OF A SINGLE TEST

Test	Equivalent Forms	Single Test
Lorge-Thorndike Intelligence Tests		
Verbal test—Level C	.91	.94
Nonverbal test—Level C	.87	.94
Iowa Tests of Basic Skills		
Arithmetic test—Grade 5	.87	.90
Spelling—Grade 5	.86	.90
Gates-MacGinitie Reading Test—Survey D		
Vocabulary—Grade 4	.85	.88
Comprehension—Grade 4	.83	.94

a more exacting definition of the test's ability to reproduce the same score. The individual must then show consistency both from one sample of tasks to another and from one day to another. We have gathered together a few examples that show reliability coefficients for the same test when these have been computed by two different procedures. These are shown in Table 3.7.

The two procedures compared in Table 3.7 are correlation of alternate forms and correlation of half-tests made up from a single form. It will be noted that the alternate-forms correlation is lower in every case. This is consistent with the earlier discussion, in which we pointed out that the alternate-forms procedure constitutes a more demanding test of an instrument's precision. The difference between the two procedures varies from test to test, being as small as .03 in one instance and as large as .11 in another. But in every instance, it is necessary to discount the odd-even correlation.

HOW HIGH MUST THE RELIABILITY OF A MEASUREMENT BE?

Obviously, other things being equal, the more reliable a measuring procedure is, the better satisfied we are with it. A question that is often raised is: What is the *minimum* reliability that is acceptable? Actually, there is no general answer to this question. If we *must* make some decision or take some course of action with respect to an individual, we will do so in terms of the best information we have, however unreliable it may be, provided only that the reliability is better than zero. (Of course, here as always the crucial consideration is the validity of the measure.) The appraisal of any new procedure must always be in terms of other procedures with which it is in competition. Thus a high school mathematics test with a reliability coefficient of .80 would look relatively unattractive if tests with reliabilities of .85 to .90 were already available. On the other hand, a procedure for judging "leadership" that had a reliability of no more than .60 might look very attractive if the alternative were a set of uncontrolled ratings having a reliability of .45 to .50.

Although we cannot set an absolute minimum for the reliability of a measurement procedure, we can indicate the level of reliability that is required to enable us to achieve specified levels of accuracy in describing an individual or a group. Suppose that we have given a test to two individuals, and that individual A fell at the 75th percentile of the group while individual B fell at the 50th percentile. What is the probability that A would still surpass B if they were tested again? In Table 3.8 the probability is shown for different values of the reliability coefficient. Thus, where the correlation is .00, there is exactly a 50-50 chance that the order of the two individuals will be reversed. When the correlation is .50, the probability of a reversal is more than 1 in 3. For a correlation of .90, there is still 1 chance in 12 that we will get a reversal on repetition of

Table 3.8
PERCENTAGE OF TIMES DIRECTION OF DIFFERENCE WILL BE REVERSED IN SUBSEQUENT TESTING FOR SCORES FALLING AT 75TH AND 50TH PERCENTILE

	Percent of Reversals with Repeated Test		
Reliability Coefficient	Scores of Single Individuals	Means of Groups of 25	Means of Groups of 100
.00	50.0	50.0	50.0
.40	40.3	10.9	0.7
.50	36.8	4.6	0.04
.60	32.5	1.2	
.70	27.1	0.1	
.80	19.7		
.90	8.7		
.95	2.2		
.98	0.05		

the testing. To have 4 chances in 5 that our difference will stay in the same direction, we require a reliability of about .80.

Table 3.8 also shows the situation when we are comparing two groups—for groups of 25 or of 100. For example, if in class A, of 25 pupils, the average fell at the 75th percentile of some larger reference group, whereas in class B the average fell at the 50th percentile, what is the probability that we would get a reversal if the testing were repeated? Here we still have a 50-50 chance in the extreme case in which the reliability coefficient is .00. However, the security of our conclusion increases much more rapidly with groups than with individuals as the reliability of the test becomes greater. With a reliability of .50 the probability of a reversal is already down to 1 in 20 for groups of 25, to 1 in 2,500 for groups of 100. With a correlation of .70 the probability is only 1 in 1,000 for groups of 25 and is vanishingly small for groups of 100. Thus a test with relatively low reliability will permit us to make useful studies of and draw accurate conclusions about groups, especially groups of substantial size, but quite high reliability is required if we are to speak with confidence about individuals.

THE CONCEPT OF RELIABILITY APPLIED TO THE FORMATIVE MASTERY TEST

All of the discussion of reliability up to this point has assumed measurement of a continuous variable that has no limit, or "ceiling." We have excluded the idea of a "perfect" performance. However, in sharply focused formative evaluations, when a test is designed to measure some specific skill, it is reasonable to expect that a good proportion of students may get perfect scores on the test.

Consider a test that was designed for use with foreign students studying English, to assess their mastery of certain specific English constructions. In this test Blatchford (1970) assessed mastery of each of 10 English constructions, using 4 items for each construction. Two forms of the test were developed and administered to groups of students with an interval of about a week between the two testings. Multiple-choice items illustrating two of the constructions are shown below. The student was required to choose the one that was correct English usage. Each item is followed by a table showing the percentage of the students getting 0, 1, 2, 3, or 4 items right on each of the testings. That is, the entry in the top row and first column for Set 6 shows that 2 percent of the group got 0 right on Form *A* and 4 right on Form *B*.

Set 6.   The use of "but" after an "although" clause

   (1) Because he was late, he still attended the meeting.
*(2) Although he was late, he still attended the meeting.
   (3) Although he was late, but he still attended the meeting.
   (4) Because he was late, but he still attended the meeting.

| Number Right—Form B | Number Right—Form A | | | | | |
	0	1	2	3	4	Total
4	2	1	2	6	36	47
3	1	1	1	4	7	14
2	1	1	1	1	1	5
1	3	1	1	1	1	7
0	21	3	1	1	1	27
Total	28	7	6	13	46	

Set 10.   The use of "most" with plural nouns.

   (1) The most of the students must study three hours every night.
*(2) Most students must study three hours every night.
   (3) Most student must study three hours every night.
   (4) Most of student must study three hours every night.

| Number Right—Form B | Number Right—Form A | | | | | |
	0	1	2	3	4	Total
4	1	3	4	12	18	38
3	1	2	3	5	5	16
2	2	2	1	3	2	10
1	4	4	1	1	1	11
0	15	5	1	3	1	25
Total	23	16	10	24	27	

Let us turn our attention first to Set 6. Note that 36 percent of the students got perfect scores on *both* testings and 21 percent got zero scores on *both* testings. For this 57 percent of the group the little 4-item test gave perfectly consistent and unequivocal information. One group appeared to have completely mastered the correct usage and the other group appeared to be completely in the dark. The other 43 percent showed some inconsistency either within a test or between the two tests. How shall we express the degree of inconsistency or unreliability?

The important thing to remember is that a test such as this is being used to decide whether each student has mastery of a specific skill. We might set a severe standard and accept only a perfect performance—4 right out of 4—as indicating mastery. Or we might be willing to accept a more relaxed standard of 3

* Correct answers are marked with an asterisk.

out of 4 as satisfactory performance, recognizing that lowered vigilance or some extraneous factor might have been responsible for a single error. Whichever standard is set, the question we ask is: How often would the decision have been reversed on the other testing? How often would we have switched from "pass" to "fail" or the reverse?

The results from Set 6 are shown below for the two standards.

Form B	Severe Standard (all 4 correct) Form A		Form B	Lenient Standard (3 of 4 correct) Form A	
	Fail	Pass		Fail	Pass
Pass	11	36	Pass	8	53
Fail	43	10	Fail	33	6

Using the severe standard, we would reach the same decision for both forms for 79 percent of students and opposite decisions for 21 percent. With the more relaxed standard the corresponding percentages are 86 and 14.

The decisions for Set 10 can be expressed in the same way.

Form B	Severe Standard (all 4 correct) Form A		Form B	Lenient Standard (3 of 4 correct) Form A	
	Fail	Pass		Fail	Pass
Pass	20	18	Pass	14	40
Fail	53	9	Fail	35	11

Clearly, the percentage of reversals is greater for Set 10 than for Set 6. There are 29 and 25 percent reversals by the severe and lenient standards. This set provides a less reliable basis for the central decision: Has the student mastered the skill?

For a test that is being used for the single go–no go decision of "mastery" versus "nonmastery," the percentage of consistent decisions is perhaps the best index of reliability. Unfortunately this index is a function of the characteristics of the group as well as the test. If many students are close to the threshold of mastery, having learned a certain skill but just barely learned it, there are likely to be numerous reversals from one testing to another. If, on the other hand, there are many who have considerably overlearned the skill, or many who have never learned it at all, reversals will be relatively infrequent. It will be important, therefore, to evaluate the reliability of a formative mastery test with groups of students who have reached just about the same degree of assurance in their mastery of the skill as those with whom the test will eventually be used.

We now need some way to decide what percentage of consistent decisions represents a satisfactory test. At one extreme, with two choices (i.e., "pass" or "fail"), pure chance should produce agreement 50 percent of the time. If the test yields no more consistent results than flipping a coin, it is obviously worthless. At the other extreme, if there were 100 percent agreement between two forms in the decision to which they led, the reliability of that decision is clearly perfect. It is the intermediate percentages, which almost always occur, that require evaluation. Are the agreement percentages of 79, 86, 71, and 75 that were found for the two 4-item tests by two standards of mastery good, just tolerable, or unsatisfactory?

It is hard to give a general answer to the above question. The answer depends on the length of the test, on the one hand, and on the seriousness and irreversibility of the decision on the other. The shorter the test, the more reversals we must expect, and the less crucial the decision, the more reversals we can tolerate. Considering that the tests that we analyzed were composed of only 4 items, consistencies ranging from 70 to 85 percent are probably as good as can be expected. If the test results were to be used merely to guide review and remedial instruction, this level of consistency might be quite tolerable, because errors in the initial decision would usually be corrected in later testing. Test makers have not done much systematic work studying the properties of short, sharply focused tests. Consequently, there is little available doctrine as to what percentage of consistency can be expected with 5- or 10- or 20-item tests, or how the consistency relates to the narrowness of definition of the objectives.

The illustration that we have discussed used data from alternate test forms given about a week apart. Of course it would be possible to subdivide a test and get two scores from a single testing. These could be tabulated to determine the frequency of reversals of the decision of "pass." However, it seems likely that with students who are just on the threshold of mastery, changes from one testing to another will be much more common than those from one subscore to another at a single point in time. Thus Blatchford found median reliability coefficients for a 4-item test at a single moment in time to be .80, while the median correlation between forms given a week apart was only .61. Such a result suggests that two very short tests given on different days may provide a good deal more conservative, and probably a sounder basis for a decision on mastery than a longer test at one specific point in time.

RELIABILITY OF DIFFERENCE SCORES

Sometimes we are less interested in single scores than we are in the relationship between scores taken in pairs. Thus we may be concerned with the differences between scholastic aptitude and reading achievement in a group of pupils, or we may wish to study gains in reading from an initial test given in October to a later test given the following May. In these illustrations the significant fact for each individual is the difference between two scores. We must inquire how reliable our estimates of these differences are, knowing the characteristics of the two component tests.

It is unfortunately true that the appraisal of the difference between two tests usually has substantially lower reliability than the reliabilities of the two tests taken separately. This is due to two factors: (1) the errors of measurement in both separate tests accumulate in the difference score, and (2) whatever is common to both measures is canceled out in the difference score. We can illustrate the situation by a diagram (see Fig. 3.3).

Each bar in Fig. 3.3 represents performance* on a test, broken up into a number of parts to represent the factors producing this performance. The first bar represents a scholastic aptitude test, and the second a reading test. Notice that we have divided reading performance into three parts. One part, labeled "common factors," is a complex of general intellectual abilities that operate both in the reading and the scholastic aptitude test. A second part, labeled "specific reading factors," is abilities that appear only in the reading test. The third part, labeled "error," is chance error of measurement. Three similar parts are indicated for the aptitude test.

Now examine the third bar, representing the difference score—that is, reading score expressed in some type of standard-score units minus aptitude test score expressed in those same units. In this bar the common factor has disappeared. It appeared with one sign in the reading test and the reverse sign in the aptitude test, and thus canceled out. Only the specific factors and the errors of measurement remain. These are the factors that determine the difference score. And the errors of measurement bulk relatively much larger in this third bar. If two tests measured exactly the same common factors, only the

---

* More precisely, variance in performance.

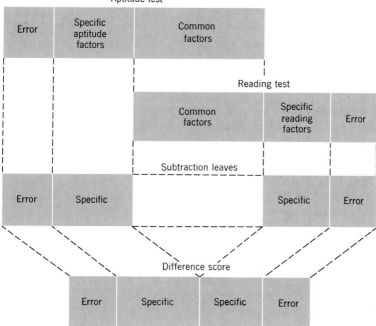

Figure 3.3
Nature of a difference score.

errors of measurement would remain in the difference scores, and the differences would have exactly zero reliability.

The reliability of the difference between two measures expressed in standard scores can be obtained by a fairly simple formula, which reads

$$r_{Diff.} = \frac{\frac{1}{2}(r_{11} + r_{22}) - r_{12}}{1 - r_{12}} \tag{6}$$

where r_{11} is the reliability of one measure,
   r_{22} is the reliability of the other measure,
   r_{12} is the correlation between the two measures.

Thus, if the reliability of test A is .80, the reliability of test B is .90, and the correlation of A and B is .60, for the reliability of the difference score we have

$$r_{Diff.} = \frac{\frac{1}{2}(.80 + .90) - .60}{1 - .60}$$

$$= \frac{.25}{.40} = .62$$

Table 3.9
RELIABILITY OF A DIFFERENCE SCORE

Correlation between Two Tests (r_{12})	Average of Reliability of Two Tests $\frac{1}{2}(r_{11} + r_{22})$					
	.50	.60	.70	.80	.90	.95
.00	.50	.60	.70	.80	.90	.95
.40	.17	.33	.50	.67	.83	.92
.50	.00	.20	.40	.60	.80	.90
.60		.00	.25	.50	.75	.88
.70			.00	.33	.67	.83
.80				.00	.50	.75
.90					.00	.50
.95						.00

In Table 3.9 the value of $r_{Diff.}$ is shown for various combinations of values of $\frac{1}{2}(r_{11} + r_{22})$ and r_{12}. Thus, if the average of the reliabilities of two tests is .80, the reliability of the difference score is .80 when the two tests have .00 intercorrelation, is .60 when the intercorrelation is .50, and is .00 when the intercorrelation is .80. It is clear that as soon as the correlation between the two tests begins to approach the average of their separate reliability coefficients, the reliability of the difference score drops very rapidly.

The low reliability that tends to characterize difference scores is something to which the psychologist and educator must always be sensitive. It becomes a problem whenever we wish to use test patterns for diagnosis. Thus the judgment that Herbert's reading lags behind his scholastic aptitude is a judgment that must be made a good deal more tentatively than a judgment about either his scholastic aptitude or his reading grade taken separately. The conclusion that Mary has improved in reading more than Jane must usually be a more tentative judgment than that Mary is now a better reader than Jane. Any difference needs to be interpreted in the light of the standard error of measurement of that difference.*

Many differences will be found to be quite small relative to their standard error, and consequently quite undependable. The interpretation of profiles and of gain scores are places where this caution especially applies.

* The standard error of measurement of a difference is roughly equal to

$$\sqrt{S^2_{m_1} + S^2_{m_2}}$$

where S_{m_1} is the standard error of measurement on one test and S_{m_2} is the standard error of measurement of the other.

There is one further effect of unreliability that merits brief attention here because it affects our interpretation of the correlations between different measures. Let us think of a measure of reading comprehension and one of arithmetic reasoning. In each of these tests the individual differences in score are due in part to "true" ability and in part to chance "errors of measurement." But if the errors of measurement are really chance matters, the reading test errors and the arithmetic test errors must be uncorrelated. There is no relationship between one toss of a coin and a later toss of a coin. So we have these uncorrelated errors in the total scores. This means that they must water down any correlation that exists between the true scores. That is, the actual scores are a combination of true score and error, so the correlation between actual scores is a compromise between the correlation of the underlying true scores and the .00 correlation that characterizes the errors.

We would often like to extract an estimate of the correlation between the underlying true scores from our obtained data in order to understand better how much the functions involved have in common. Fortunately, we can do this quite simply. Such an estimate is provided by the formula

$$r_{1\infty2\infty} = \frac{r_{12}}{\sqrt{r_{11}r_{22}}} \tag{7}$$

where $r_{1\infty2\infty}$ is the correlation of the underlying "true" scores,

r_{12} is the correlation of the obtained scores,

r_{11} and r_{22} are the reliabilities of the two measures in question.

Thus, if the correlation between the reading test and arithmetic test were found to be .56, and the reliability coefficients of the tests were respectively .71 and .90, we would have

$$r_{1\infty2\infty} = \frac{.56}{\sqrt{(.71)\ (.90)}} = .70$$

Our estimate is that the correlation between error-free measures of arithmetic and reading would be .70. In thinking of these two *functions*, it would be appropriate to think of the correlation as .70 rather than .56, though the *tests* correlate only .56.

FACTORS MAKING
FOR PRACTICALITY
IN ROUTINE USE

Though validity and reliability may be all-important in measures that are to be used for special research purposes, when a test is to be used in classrooms throughout a school or school system a number of down-to-earth practical considerations must also be taken into account. It is easy for the administrator to pay too much attention to small financial savings or to economies of time that make it possible to fit a test into the standard class period with no shifting of schedules; nevertheless these factors of economy and convenience are real considerations. Furthermore, there are other factors relating to the readiness with which the tests may be given, scored, and interpreted that bear more importantly on the use that will be made of the tests and the soundness of the conclusions that will be drawn from them.

ECONOMY

The practical significance of dollar savings does not need to be emphasized. Dollars are of very real significance for any educational or industrial enterprise. Economy in the case of tests depends in part on cost per copy. It depends in part on the possibility of using the test booklets over again. In the upper elementary grades and beyond, it is feasible to administer a test using a separate answer sheet and then to use test booklets for a number of testings. If a test will be used in successive years or if testing can be scheduled so that different classes or schools can be tested on different days, an important economy can be effected by using the same test booklet a number of times.

A second aspect of economy is saving of time in test administration. However, this is often false economy. We saw in the previous section that the reliability of a test depends on its length. As far as testing time is concerned, we get about what we give. Some tests may be a little more efficiently designed, so that they give a little more reliable measure per minute of testing time, but, by and large, any reduction in testing time will be accomplished at the price of loss in the precision or the breadth of our appraisal.

A third, and quite significant aspect of economy is ease of scoring. The clerical work of scoring a battery of tests by hand can become either burdensome if it is done by the already busy teacher, or expensive if it is carried out by clerical help hired especially for the purpose. As a result, test users are relying more and more upon mechanized scoring, and test publishers are producing tests that can be processed by the more and more sophisticated equipment that is being developed. The test user has the option of hand scoring his own tests, of setting up his own mechanized scoring unit, or of sending tests to one of the test-scoring services that specialize in high-speed test processing.

There are several test-scoring services that provide very efficient test scoring and reporting. The basic equipment consists of a photoelectric document reader combined with a digital computer. The document reader responds to marks on an answer sheet, or even on an actual test booklet. The use of a separate answer sheet is familiar to most American college graduates, who have taken a variety of tests during their educational careers. But separate answer sheets are not satisfactory for young children. The complications of finding an answer in the test booklet, keeping the code letter of the chosen answer in mind while the proper place is located on the answer sheet, and then marking in the proper spot on the answer sheet are too much for children in the primary grades. However, current equipment makes it possible to use a booklet for these levels and either to slice the bound edge off the test booklet and run the separate pages through the scanner, or to print the test in a fanfold booklet that can be unfolded and run through the scanner as a unit.

In large-volume scoring services, the information from the optical scanner is fed into a digital computer where it is compared with a key that has been recorded in the computer's memory. One or more scores are determined and printed out on a record form or pressure-sensitive label. The computer can also be programmed to produce various statistics such as class means, school system means and standard deviations, and local percentiles. Thus the scoring service provides not only test scores for individuals, but the complete range of statistical information about the test results that are of interest to the local school system.

Most local school systems cannot support the elaborate equipment that we have just been describing. However, there are several optical scanner-scorer devices available for rent or purchase by city or state school systems that will handle quite a large volume of scoring. These will scan an answer sheet (not a booklet), and will either print a score upon it or prepare a punched-card record that can be processed subsequently in data processing equipment.

Thus a test that is to be economical for use in large-scale

testing programs will be produced in format for scoring by the different types of scanning and scoring equipment. Almost any type of separate answer sheet can be hand-scored relatively efficiently by using an overlay stencil. Some test publishers supply plastic overlay stencils for this purpose. Others use a special type of answer sheet made up of two sheets fastened together, the back one carbon-covered. The key is printed on the back of the first sheet, and as the examinee marks the front, the carbon-backing transfers his marks to the back of the sheet, where the number falling in the printed key spaces can be counted. In some special types of tests the answers are marked by pushing a pin through the answer sheet at the locations corresponding to the choices that are to be marked. Again, the key is printed on the inside of a complex answer form, and the test is scored by counting the number of pinpricks falling within circles printed on the answer form.

The potential test purchaser will want to determine what types of answer forms and what scoring services are available for any test that he is considering using.

FEATURES FACILITATING TEST ADMINISTRATION

In evaluating the practical usability of a test, one factor to be taken into account is the ease of administration. A test that can be handled adequately by the regular classroom teacher with no more than a session or so of special briefing is much more readily fitted into a testing program than a test requiring specially trained administrators. Several factors contribute to the ease of giving and taking a test.

1. A test is easy to give if it has clear, full instructions. The instructions for the administrator should be written out substantially word for word, so that all the examiner must do is read them and follow them. Instructions for the examinee should also be complete and should provide appropriate practice exercises. The amount of practice that should be provided depends upon how novel the test task is likely to be for those being tested. When it is a familiar type of task or a simple and straightforward instruction, no more than a single example will be needed. However, for an unusual item format or test task more practice will be desirable.

2. A test is easy to give if the number of units to be separately timed is few, and close timing is not critical. Timing a number of brief subtests to a fraction of a minute is a bothersome undertaking, and the timing is likely to be inaccurate unless a stop watch is available for each tester. Some tests have as many as eight or ten parts, each taking only 2 or 3 minutes. A test made up of three or four parts, with time limits of 5, 10, or more minutes for each, will be easier to use.

3. The layout of the test items on the page has a good deal to do with the ease of taking the test. Items in which response options are all run together on the same line, items with small or illegible pictures or diagrams, items that are crowded together, and items that run over from one page to the next all make difficulty for the examinee. Print and pictures should be large and clear. Response options should be well separated from one another. All parts of an item and all items referring to a single figure, problem, or reading passage should appear on the same page or double-page spread. Shortcomings on any of these points represent black marks against a test as far as ease of taking it is concerned.

FEATURES FACILITATING INTERPRETATION AND USE OF SCORES

It seems axiomatic, though the point is sometimes overlooked, that a test is given to be used. If the score is to be used, it must be interpreted and given meaning. The author and publisher of the test have the responsibility of providing the user with information that permits him to make a sound appraisal of the test in relation to his needs and to give appropriate meaning to the score of each individual. This they do primarily through the *test manual* and other collateral materials that are prepared to accompany the test. What may the test user reasonably expect to find in the manual for a test, together with its supporting materials? We have outlined below the aids we believe the test user should expect.

1. *A statement of the functions the test was designed to measure and of the general procedures by which it was developed.* This is the author's statement of what he considers the test to be valid for and the evidence that proper steps have been taken to achieve that validity. Particularly for achievement tests, in which we are concerned primarily with content and process validity, the author should tell the procedures by which he arrived at his choice of content or his analysis of the functions being measured. If he is unwilling to expose his thinking to our critical scrutiny, we may perhaps be skeptical of the thoroughness or profundity of that thinking.

Procedures involve not only the rational procedures by which range of content or types of objective were selected, but also the empirical procedures by which items were reviewed, tried out, and screened for final inclusion in the test.

2. *Detailed instructions for administering the test.* We have discussed in an earlier section the need for this aid to uniform and easy administration by the teachers or others who will have to use the test.

3. *Scoring keys and specific instructions for scoring the test.* The problems of scoring have also been discussed, under the heading of economy. The manual and supporting materials should provide detailed instructions as to how the score is to be computed, how errors are to be treated, and how part scores are to be combined into a total score. Scoring keys and stencils should be planned to facilitate as much as possible the onerous task of scoring, when scoring is to be done by the local user.

4. *Norms for appropriate reference groups,* together with information as to how they were obtained and instructions for their use. Chapter 4 will be devoted to a full consideration of types of test norms and their use. It is therefore sufficient at this time to point out the responsibility of the test producer to develop suitable norms for the groups with which the test is to be used. General norms are a necessity, and norms suitable for special types of communities, special occupational groups, and other more limited subgroups will add to the usefulness of a test in many cases.

5. *Evidence as to the reliability of the test.* This evidence should indicate not only the bald reliability statistics but also the operations used to obtain the reliability estimates and the descriptive and statistical characteristics of each group on which reliability data are based. If a test is available in more than one form, it is highly desirable that the producers report the correlation between the two forms, in addition to any data that were derived from a single testing. If the test yields part scores, and particularly if it is proposed that any use be made of these part scores, reliability data should be reported for the separate part scores. It is good procedure for the author to report standard errors of measurement as well as reliability coefficients. An author who indicates what the standard error of measurement is at each of a number of score levels is particularly to be commended, since this information shows over what range of scores the test maintains its accuracy.

6. *Evidence on the intercorrelations of subscores.* If the test provides several subscores, the manual should provide evidence on the intercorrelations of these. This is important in guiding the interpretation of the subscores and particularly in judging how much confidence to place in *differences* between the subscores. If the scores are correlated to a substantial degree, measuring much the same things, the differences between them will be largely meaningless and uninterpretable.

7. *Evidence on the relationships of the test to other factors.* Insofar as the test is to be used as a predictive device, correlations with criterion measures constitute the essential evidence on how well it does in fact predict. Full information should be provided on the nature of the criterion variables, the groups for which data are available, and the conditions under which the data were obtained. Only then can the reader fairly judge the validity of the test as a predictor.

It will often be desirable to report correlations with other measures of the same function as collateral evidence bearing on the validity of the test. Thus correlations with individual intelligence test score are relevant in the case of a group intelligence measure.

Finally, indications of the relationship of test score to age, sex, type of community, socioeconomic level, and similar facts about the individual or the group are often helpful. They provide a basis for judging how sensitive the measure is to the background of the group and to circumstances of their life and of their education.

8. *Guides for using the test and for interpreting results obtained with it.* The developers of a test presumably know how it is reasonable for the test to be used and the results from it to be evaluated. They are specialists in that test. For the test to be most useful for others, especially the teacher with limited specialized training, suggestions should be given of ways in which the test results may be used for diagnosing individual and group weaknesses, forming class groupings, organizing remedial instruction, counseling with the individual, or whatever other activities may appropriately be based on that particular type of instrument.

GUIDE FOR EVALUATING A TEST

As a help to the potential test user, we end this chapter with a guide for evaluating a test. The guide consists of a series of questions, based in large part on the *Standards for Educational and Psychological Tests and Manuals* prepared by a joint committee from the American Psychological Association (1974), together with the American Educational Research Association and the National Council on Measurement in Education. The complete *Standards* will well repay careful study by the journeyman test user.

You will note that many of the questions in the guide relate to the availability and adequacy of reporting of information about the test. There is an implied, though not explicitly stated, second question as a sequel to many sections of the guide, especially those relating to validity and reliability. This is: "Given that the information is provided, how satisfactory does the test appear to be, in comparison with others as well as by absolute standards, for the use that I want to make of it?" A number of the questions refer to the adequacy of norms and converted scores. These are matters that are considered in the following chapter. You will find it profitable to review this portion of the guide after reading Chapter 4.

GENERAL IDENTIFYING INFORMATION

1. What is the name of the test?

2. Who are its authors—by name and position if that information is available.

3. Who publishes the test, and when was it published?

4. How many alternative forms are available?

5. What does it cost?

6. How long does it take to administer?

INFORMATION ABOUT THE TEST

1. Is there a manual for the test (or other similar source) that is designed to provide the information that a potential user needs?

2. How recently has the test been revised? How recently has the test manual been revised? Has as much as 10 years elapsed since revision in either case?

AIDS TO INTERPRETING
TEST RESULTS

1. Does the manual provide a clear statement of the purposes and applications for which the test is intended?

2. Does the manual provide a clear statement of the qualifications needed to administer the test and interpret it properly?

3. Do the test, manual, record forms, and accompanying materials guide users toward sound and correct interpretation of the test results?

4. Are the statements in the manual that express relationships presented in quantitative terms, so that the reader can tell how much precision or confidence to attach to them?

1. Does the manual report evidence on the validity of the test for each type of inference for which the test is recommended?

2. Does the manual *avoid* referring to correlations between item and total test score as evidence of validity?

3. If the test is designed to be a sample of a specified domain of behaviors (that is, an achievement test), does the manual define the domain clearly and indicate the procedures for sampling from that domain?

4. When criterion-related validity is involved, does the manual describe criterion variables clearly, comment on their adequacy, and indicate what aspects of the criterion performance are *not* adequately reflected in these measures?

5. Are the samples used for estimating criterion-related validity adequately described, and are they appropriate to the purpose?

6. Are statistical analyses for criterion-related validity presented in a form that permits the reader to judge the degree of confidence that can be placed in inferences about individuals?

7. If the test is designed to measure a theoretical construct (that is, trait of ability, temperament, or attitude), is the proposed interpretation clearly stated, and differentiated from alternate theoretical interpretations? Is the evidence to support this interpretation clearly and fully presented?

In summary, to what extent does the evidence with respect to validity justify the uses of the test suggested in the manual, or the use that you would want to make of the test results?

RELIABILITY

1. Does the manual present data adequate to permit the reader to judge whether scores are sufficiently dependable for the recommended uses?

2. Are the samples on which reliability data were obtained sufficiently well described so that the user can judge whether the data apply to his situation?

3. Are the reliability data presented in the conventional statistics of product-moment reliability coefficients and standard errors of measurement?

4. If more than one form of the test was produced, are data provided to establish comparability of the several forms?

5. If the test purports to measure a generalized homogeneous trait, is evidence reported on the internal consistency (interitem or interpart correlations) of the parts that make up the test?

6. Does the test manual provide data on the stability of test performance over a period of time?

In summary, to what extent do the reliability data provided in the manual justify the uses for the results suggested by the authors or the use that you would want to make of the test results?

ADMINISTRATION AND SCORING

1. Are the directions for administration sufficiently full and clear so that the administrator will be able to duplicate the conditions under which the norms were established and reliability and validity data were obtained?

2. Are the procedures for scoring set forth clearly and in detail, in such a way as to maximize scoring efficiency and minimize the likelihood of scoring error?

SCALES AND NORMS

1. Are the scales used for reporting scores clearly and carefully described, so that the test interpreter will fully understand them and be able to communicate the interpretation to an examinee?

2. Are norms reported in the manual that are in appropriate form, usually standard scores or percentile ranks in appropriate reference groups?

3. Are the populations to which the norms refer clearly defined and described, and are they populations with which most users can appropriately compare their data?

4. If more than one form is available, including revised forms, are tables available showing equivalent scores on the different forms?

5. Does the manual discuss the possible value of local norms, and provide any help in preparing local norms?

QUESTIONS AND EXERCISES

1. If the Educational Testing Service were developing a general survey test in science for high school seniors, what might they do to establish the validity of the test?

2. What type of validity is indicated by each of the following statements that might be found in a test manual?

(*a*) Scores on Personality Test X correlated +.43 with teachers' ratings of adjustment.

(*b*) The objectives to be appraised by Reading Test Y were rated for importance by 150 classroom teachers.

(*c*) Scores on Clerical Aptitude Test Z correlated +.57 with supervisors' ratings after 6 months on the job.

(*d*) Intelligence Test W gives scores that correlate +.69 with Stanford-Binet IQ.

(*e*) Achievement Battery V is based on an analysis of 50 widely used texts and 100 courses of study from all parts of the U.S.

3. Comment on the statement "The classroom teacher is the only one who can judge the validity of a standardized achievement test for his class."

4. Look at the manuals of two or three tests of different types. What evidence on validity is presented? How adequate is it for each test?

5. Using Table 3.4 on p. 68, determine what percentage of those selected would be above average on the job if a selection procedure with a validity of .40 were used and only the top quarter were accepted for the job. What percentage would be above average if the top three-quarters were selected? What would the two percentages be if the validity were .50? What does a comparison of the four percentages bring out?

6. If Air Force personnel psychologists were doing research on tests for the selection of jet engine mechanic trainees, what might they use as criterion measures of success as a mechanic? What are the advantages and limitations of each possible measure?

7. What advantages and disadvantages does freshman Grade Point Average have as a criterion measure for validating a college admissions test?

8. A test manual contains the following statement: "The validity of test X is shown by the fact that it correlates .80 with the Stanford-Binet." What additional information is needed to evaluate this assertion?

9. Look at the evidence presented on reliability in the manuals of two or three tests. How adequate is it? What are its shortcomings?

10. The manual for test T presents reliability data based on (1) retesting with the same test form a week later, (2) correlating odd with even items, and (3) correlating form A with form B, the two forms being given a week apart. Which procedure may be expected to yield the *lowest* coefficient? Why? Which to yield the most *useful* estimate of reliability? Why?

11. A student has been given the Stanford-Binet Intelligence Test four different times during his school career, and his cumulative record card shows the following IQs: 98, 107, 101, and 95. What significance should be attached to the fluctuations in IQ?

12. A school plans to give form A of a reading test in October and form B in May, in order to study individual differences in improvement during the year. The reliability of each form of the test is known to be about .85 for a grade group. The correlation between the two forms turned out to be .80. How much confidence can be placed in the individual differences in amount gained? What factors other than real differences in learning can account for individual differences in gain?

13. You are considering three reading tests for use in your school. As far as you can judge, the three are equally valid. The reliability of each is reported to be .90. What else would you need to know to make a choice among the tests?

14. Examine several tests of aptitude or of achievement that would be suitable for a class you are teaching or might teach. Write an evaluation of one of these tests, following the guide on pp. 108-110.

SUGGESTED ADDITIONAL READING

American Psychological Association. *Standards for educational and psychological tests.* Washington, D.C.: American Psychological Association, 1974.

Bauer, David H. Error sources in aptitude and achievement test scores: A review and recommendation. *Measurement and Evaluation in Guidance,* 1973, 6, 28-34.

Cronbach, Lee J. Test validation. In R. L. Thorndike (Ed.), *Educational measurement.* (2nd Ed.) Washington, D.C.: American Council on Education, 1971.

Equal Employment Opportunity Commission (EEOC). Guidelines on employee selection procedures. *Federal Register,* 1970, 35(149), 12333-12336.

Farver, Albert S., William E. Sedlacek, and Glenwood C. Brooks, Jr. Longitudinal predictions of university grades for blacks and whites. *Measurement and Evaluation in Guidance,* 1975, 7, 243-250.

Fincher, Cameron. Differential validity and test bias. *Personnel Psychology,* 1975, 28, 481-500.

Stanley, Julian C. Reliability. In R. L. Thorndike (Ed.), *Educational measurement.* (2nd Ed.) Washington, D.C.: American Council on Education, 1971.

CHAPTER FOUR
NORMS AND UNITS FOR MEASUREMENT

THE NATURE OF A SCORE

Johnny got a score of 15 on his spelling test. What does that mean, and how should we interpret it?

Actually, standing by itself it has no meaning at all and is completely uninterpretable. At the most superficial level, we don't even know whether this represents a perfect score, that is, 15 out of 15, or a very low percentage of the possible, that is, 15 out of 50. But even supposing we do know that it is 15 out of 20, or 75 percent, what then?

Look at Table 4.1. This shows two 20-word spelling tests. A score of 15 on Test A would have vastly different meaning from that same score on Test B. A person who got only 15 right on Test A would not be outstanding in a second or third grade class. Try Test B out on some friends or classmates. You will probably not find many of them who can spell 15 of these words correctly. When this test was given to a class of graduate students, only 22 percent of them spelled 15 or more of the words correctly. A score of 15 on Test B is a good score among graduate students of education.

As it stands, then, a score of 15 words right, or even of 75 percent of the words right, has no direct meaning or significance. It gets meaning only as we have some standard with which to compare it.

For one group of tests that we have called content-referenced, or criterion-referenced, the standard is provided by the definition of the specific objective that the test is designed to measure, and by a level of performance that the teacher,

Table 4.1

TWO 20-WORD DICTATION SPELLING TESTS

Test A	Test B
bar	baroque
cat	catarrh
form	formaldehyde
jar	jardiniere
nap	naphtha
dish	discernible
fat	fatiguing
sack	sacrilegious
rich	ricochet
sit	citrus
feet	feasible
act	accommodation
rate	inaugurate
inch	insignia
rent	deterrent
lip	eucalyptus
air	questionnaire
rim	rhythm
must	ignoramus
red	accrued

school, or school system has agreed upon as representing an acceptable level of mastery of that objective. Thus the illustrative content-referenced test of capitalizing place names on p. 168 is presumed to provide a representative sample of tasks calling for this specific competence. If we accept the sample of tasks as representative, and if we agree that 80 percent accuracy in performing this task is the minimum acceptable, then a score of 10 of 12 words correctly underlined defines the standard in an absolute sense.

In the usual classroom test for summative evaluation such a standard operates indirectly and imperfectly, partly through the teacher's choice of tasks to make up the test and partly through his standards for evaluating the responses. Thus the teacher picks tasks to make up the test that he considers appropriate to represent the learnings of his group. No teacher in his right mind would give spelling test A to a high school group or test B to third graders. When the responses vary in quality, as in essay examinations, the teacher sets a standard for grading that corresponds to what he considers it reasonable to expect from a group like his. Quite different answers to the question "What were the causes of the War of 1812?" would be expected from a ninth grader and from a college history major.

However, the inner standard of the individual teacher is very subjective, inaccurate, and unstable. Furthermore, it provides no basis for comparing different classes or different areas of ability. Such a yardstick can give no answers to such questions as: Are the children in school A better in reading than those in school B? Is Mary better in reading than in arithmetic? Is Johnny doing as well in algebra as we would expect? We need some broader, more uniform, objective, and stable standard of reference if we are to be able to interpret those psychological and educational measurements that undertake to appraise some trait or to survey competence in some broad area of the school curriculum. The bulk of this chapter is devoted to describing and evaluating several reference frames that have been used to give a standard meaning to test scores.

TYPES OF NORM

We can approach the problem of a frame of reference for interpreting test results from two rather different points of view. One focuses on the tasks themselves, the other on the typical performance of people. Consider the 20 spelling words in Test A. If we knew that these had been chosen at random from the words taught in a third grade spelling program, and if we had agreed on some grounds (at this point unspecified) that 80 percent correct represented an acceptable standard for performance in spelling when words are presented by dictation with illustrative sentences, then we could interpret Ellen's score of 18 right on the test as indicating that she had reached the criterion of mastery in third grade spelling and Peter's score of 12 right as indicating that he had not. We have here a criterion-referenced test and test interpretation. The test is criterion referenced in that (1) the tasks are drawn from and related to a specific instruction objective, (2) the form of presentation of the tasks and response to them is set in accordance with the defined objective, and (3) a level of acceptable mastery is defined in advance, with which the performance of each student is compared.

For some types of instructional decision, this "mastery" frame of reference may be an appropriate one. Thus decisions on what material and methods should be used for further instruction in spelling with Ellen and Peter might turn on the question of whether they had or had not reached the specified criterion of mastery of the third grade spelling words. More crucially, in a sequential subject such as arithmetic, the decision on whether to begin a unit involving "borrowing" in subtraction might depend on whether the student had reached a criterion of mastery on a test of two-place subtraction that did not require borrowing.

You may ask: Where does the criterion level representing satisfactory mastery come from? Ideally the level should be based on empirical studies showing that the specified level of mastery is required if the student is to make satisfactory progress on the next instructional unit. The evidence should indicate that students who have reached the specified standard do typically make satisfactory progress on the next unit, and that those who fall below the criterion level do not. However, it must be admitted that in a good deal of the current use of so-called criterion-referenced tests this empirical evidence is weak or lacking. The criterion level of mastery seems often to be set quite arbitrarily on the basis of someone's "professional judgment," and to have little empirical justification.

The other frame of reference for interpreting test performance is based not on a somewhat arbitrary standard defined as representing mastery, but rather on the typical performance of typical persons. This represents a norm-referenced interpretation. Thus the scores of third graders Ellen and Peter can be viewed in relation to the performance of a large reference group of third graders, or of students in different school grades. Their performance is viewed not in terms of mastery versus nonmastery, but as above average, average, or below average; and ways are sought to refine that scale of relative performance so that all degrees of excellence can be expressed in quantitative terms.

In seeking a scale to represent degrees of excellence, we would like to report results in units that have the following properties:

1. Uniform meaning from test to test, so that a basis of comparison is provided through which we may compare different tests—for example, different reading tests, a reading test with an arithmetic test, or an achievement test with a scholastic aptitude test.

2. Units of uniform size, so that a gain of 10 points on one part of the scale signifies the same thing as a gain of 10 points on any other part of the scale.

3. A true zero point of "just none of" the quality in question, so that we can legitimately think of scores as representing "twice as much as" or "two-thirds as much as."

The different types of norm that have been developed for tests represent marked progress toward the first two of the above objectives. The third can probably never be reached for the traits with which psychological and educational measurement is concerned. We can put five 1-pound loaves of bread on one side of a pair of scales, and they will balance the contents of a 5-pound bag of flour placed on the other. "No weight" is *truly* "no weight," and units of weight can be added together. But we don't have that type of zero point or that way of adding together in the case of educational and psychological measurement. If you put together two morons, you will not get a genius, and a pair of bad spellers cannot jointly win a spelling bee.

Basically, a raw point score is given meaning only by referring it to some type of group or groups. A score on the typical test is not high or low, good or bad in any absolute sense; it is higher or lower, better or worse than other scores. There are two general ways in which we may relate one person's score to a more general framework. One way is to compare him with a graded series of groups and see which one he matches. Each group in the series usually represents a particular school grade or a particular chronological age. The other way is to find where in a particular group he falls in terms of the percentage of the group he surpasses or in terms of the group's mean and standard deviation. Thus we find four main patterns for interpreting the score of an individual. These are shown schematically in Table 4.2. We shall consider each in turn, evaluating its advantages and disadvantages.

Table 4.2
MAIN TYPES OF NORM FOR EDUCATIONAL AND PSYCHOLOGICAL TESTS

Type of Norm	Type of Comparison	Type of Group
Grade norms	Individual matched to group whose performance he equals	Successive grade groups
Age norms	Same as above	Successive age groups
Percentile norms	Percentage of group surpassed by individual	Single age or grade group to which individual belongs
Standard score norms	Number of standard deviations individual falls above or below average of group	Same as above

For any trait that shows a progressive and relatively uniform increase from one school grade to the next, we can prepare a set of grade norms. The norm for any grade, in this sense, is the average score obtained by individuals in that grade. In simplest outline, the process of establishing grade norms involves giving the test to a representative sample of pupils in each of a number of consecutive grades, calculating the average score at each level, and then estimating grade equivalents for the in-between scores. Thus a *Paragraph Meaning Test*, such as that from the *Stanford Achievement Test, Intermediate I*, might be given in October to pupils in grades 3, 4, 5, and 6, with results as shown below.

Average Raw Score	Grade Level
19	3.2*
27	4.2
35	5.2
43	6.2

* Grade level is shown as 3.2, etc., because testing was done in the second month of a 10-month school year. Sometimes the level will be seen written without the decimal point; i.e., as 32, 42, etc.

The testing establishes grade equivalents for raw scores of 19, 27, 35, and 43. However, grade equivalents are also needed for the in-between scores. These are usually determined arithmetically by interpolation, though sometimes intermediate points may be established by actually testing at other times during the school year. After interpolation, we have a table that looks like this.

Raw Score	Grade Equivalent	Raw Score	Grade Equivalent
19	3.2	31	4.7
20	3.4	32	4.8
21	3.6	33	4.9
22	3.7	34	5.0
23	3.8	35	5.2
24	3.9	36	5.3
25	4.0	37	5.4
26	4.1	38	5.6
27	4.2	39	5.7
28	4.3	40	5.9
29	4.4	41	6.0
30	4.6	42	6.1
		43	6.2

Since raw scores on this particular test can range from 0 to 60, some way is needed to establish grade equivalents for the more extreme scores. This is often done by equating scores on the level of the test on which we are working with scores from lower level and higher level tests of the same series, forms that have been given in earlier and later grades. In this way grade equivalents are extended down as low as 2.0 and as high as 9.5, and a complete table of raw scores to grade equivalents is prepared.

If Jennifer got a raw score of 38 on this test, it would give her a grade equivalent of 5.6, and this could be translated as "performing as well as the average child who has completed 6 months of the fifth grade." This is a seductively simple interpretation of a child's performance, but it has a number of drawbacks, as we shall see presently.

A first major question about grade norms is whether we can think of them as providing precisely or even approximately equal units. In what sense is the growth in ability in paragraph reading from grade 3.2 to grade 4.2 equal to the growth from grade 6.2 to grade 7.2? Grounds for assuming equality are clearly tenuous. When the skill is one that has been taught throughout the school years, there may be some reason to expect a year's learning at one grade level to be about equal to a year's learning at some other. And there is some evidence that during the elementary school (and possibly the junior high) grade-score units are near enough to equal to be quite serviceable. However, even in this range and for areas where instruction has been continuous the equality is only approximate. If we are concerned with something like Spanish, in which instruction typically does not begin until secondary school, or something like biology, for which instruction is concentrated in a single grade, grade equivalents become almost completely meaningless. In addition, instruction in many skills, such as basic skills in reading and in arithmetic computation, tapers off and largely stops by high school, so grade units have little or no meaning at this level. For this reason many achievement batteries show a grade equivalent of 10.0+ or 11.0+ as representing the whole upper range of raw scores. When grade equivalents such as 12.5 are reported, these do not really represent the average performance of students tested in the middle of the twelfth grade, but rather an artificial and fictitious extrapolation of the score scale so as to provide some converted score to be reported for the most capable eighth and ninth graders.

A further caution must be introduced with respect to the

interpretation of grade norms. Consider a bright and educationally advanced child in the third grade. Suppose we find that on a standardized arithmetic test he gets a score for which the grade equivalent is 5.9. This does *not* mean that this child has a mastery of the arithmetic taught in the fifth grade. He has a *score* as high as that gotten by the average child at the end of the fifth grade, but this higher score almost certainly has been obtained in part by superior mastery of third grade work. The average child falls well short of a perfect score on the topics that have been taught at his own grade level. Thus the able child can get a number of additional points of score (and consequently a higher grade equivalent) merely by complete mastery of this material. This is worth remembering. The fact that a child has a grade equivalent of 5.9 need not mean that the child is ready to move ahead into sixth grade work. It is only the reflection of a score and does not tell in what way that score was attained.

Finally, there is reason to question the comparability of grade equivalents from one school subject to another. Does being a year ahead of (or behind) one's grade level in language usage represent the same amount of advancement (or retardation) as the same deviation in arithmetic concepts? There is a good deal of evidence, which we consider on p. 135, that it doesn't. Growth in different subjects proceeds at different rates, depending upon in-school emphasis and out-of-school learning. For this reason, the glib comparison of a pupil's grade equivalents in different school subjects can result in quite misleading conclusions.

Grade norms are relatively easy to determine, since they are based on the administrative groups already established in the school organization. In the directly academic areas of achievement, the concept of grade level is perhaps a more meaningful one than age level. It is in relation to his grade placement that a child's performance in these areas is likely to be interpreted and acted upon. Outside of the school setting, grade norms have little meaning.

To summarize, grade norms, which relate the performance of an individual to that of the average child at each grade level, are useful primarily in providing a framework for interpreting the academic accomplishment of children in the elementary school. For this purpose they are relatively convenient and meaningful, even though we cannot place great confidence in the equality of grade units or their exact equivalence from one subject to another.

If a trait is one that may be expected to show continuous and relatively uniform growth with increasing age, it may be appropriate to convert a score into an age equivalent as a type of common score scale. During childhood we can observe continuous growth in height and weight, in various indices of anatomical maturity, and in a wide range of perceptual, motor, and cognitive performances. It makes a crude type of sense to describe an 8-year-old as being as tall as a 10-year-old, having the strength of grip of a 9-year-old, and the speaking vocabulary of a 6-year-old. In the early development of intelligence and aptitude tests, raw scores were typically converted into age equivalents, and the term "mental age" was added to the vocabulary of mental tester and layman alike.

An age equivalent is, of course, the average score of individuals of a given age, and is obtained by testing representative samples of 8-year-olds, 9-year-olds, 10-year-olds, and so forth. In this respect it parallels the grade equivalent described in the previous section. And as in the case of grade equivalents, a major issue is whether we can reasonably think of a year's growth as representing a standard and uniform unit. Is the growth from age 5 to age 6 equal to the growth from age 10 to age 11, and similarly for each age on our scale? As we push up the age scale, we soon reach a point where we see that the year's growth unit is clearly not appropriate. There comes a point, some time in the teens or early 20s, when growth in almost any trait that we can measure slows down and finally stops. In Fig. 4.1 the slowdown takes place quite abruptly after age 14. A year's growth after 14 seems clearly to be much less than a year's growth earlier on the scale. After about 14 or 15, the concept of height–age ceases to have any meaning. The same problem of a flattening growth curve is found, varying only in the age at which it occurs and in abruptness, for any trait that we can measure. The failure of the unit "1 year's growth" to have uniform meaning is most apparent as we consider the extremes of age, but there is no guarantee that this unit has uniform meaning even in the intermediate range.

The problem introduced by the flattening growth curve is most apparent when we consider the individual who falls far above the average. What age equivalent shall we assign to a girl who is 5 feet 10 (70 inches) tall? The average woman *never* gets that tall at any age. If we are to assign any age value, we must invent some hypothetical extension of our growth curve such as the lightly dotted line in Fig. 4.1. This line assumes

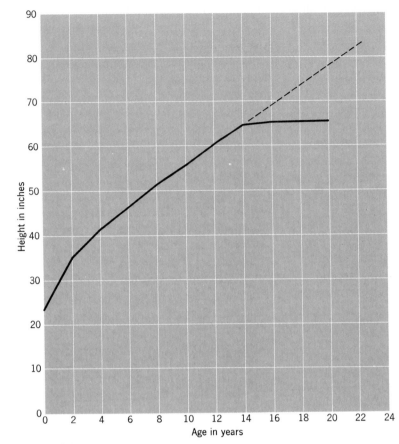

Figure 4.1
Girls' age norms for height. (Adapted from Boynton, 1936.)

that growth after 14 continues at about the same rate that was typical up to age 14. On this extrapolated curve, the height of 5 feet 10 is assigned a height–age of about 16 years, 6 months. But this is a completely artificial and arbitrary age equivalent. It does *not* correspond to the average height of 16½-year-olds. It does not correspond to average height at *any* age. It merely signifies "taller than average."

This same type of artificial age equivalent must be used for ability or achievement tests to express the performance of superior pupils in their teens. Mental growth curves also show a leveling off similar to that illustrated in Fig. 4.1. After the age of 14 or 15, increases become smaller and gradually disappear. The increase from age 15 to 18 may be no more than that from age 11 to 12, and after 18 there may be little or no further rise. Thus, when we report a mental age of 18 or 20 on a test such as the Stanford-Binet, we do *not* mean that this individual is performing like an average 18-year-old or 20-year-old. These age equivalents represent an arbitrary extension of the score-to-age conversion, like that shown by the dotted line of Fig. 4.1. Such arbitrary and artificial values are required if we are to have some way of representing the performance of the upper half of our teenage and adult population, just as artificial grade equivalents are required in order to represent the achievement of the most able eighth or ninth grade student.

It is also true that growth curves are not entirely comparable for different functions. From test to test, rate of growth and time of reaching a maximum differ substantially. How shall we compare age scores on a vocabulary test and a maze-tracing test, for example, if the first continues to rise up to and into the 20s, while the second reaches a maximum in the early teens? For a 10-year-old to have reached the 12-year-old level may represent appreciably different degrees of superiority for different traits.

Of course, age norms are primarily appropriate for traits that depend on general normal growth. A trait showing no continuous improvement over an age range (such as acuity of vision) cannot possibly be expressed in terms of a scale of age units. One that depends primarily upon specific educational experiences, such as facility in arithmetical operations, seems to be more reasonably related to the educational framework of school grades than to the biological framework of years of growth.

Finally, though it does not directly concern the consumer of tests, it is worth noting that from the viewpoint of the test producer age norms present some serious practical problems. It is often difficult to get together a truly representative sample of individuals of a given age. Thus if we wanted a cross section of 12-year-olds we would have to look for some of them in the elementary school and some in the junior high school. They would have to be assembled from quite a range of school grades. Toward the older ages, the sample we need to reach is widely scattered—some in school, some at college, some in the military establishment, and some in the world of work. To reach a truly representative sample of 18-year-olds, for example, is a very forbidding task. This is one more reason why the usual age norms for tests become suspect as one moves up into the teens.

In summary, age norms, which are based on the performance of the average person at each age level, provide a readily comprehended framework for interpreting the status of a particular individual. However, the equality of age units is open to serious question, and as one goes up to adolescence and adulthood age ceases to have any meaning as a unit in terms of which to express level of performance. Age norms are most appropriate for the elementary school years and for abilities that grow as a part of the general development of the individual. Physical and physiological characteristics such as height, weight, and dentition, and psychological traits such as general intelligence appear to be ones for which this type of norm is most acceptable.

PERCENTILE NOR

We have just seen that in the case of age and grade norms meaning is given to an individual's score by determining the age or grade group in which he would be just average. But it often makes more sense to compare him to his own age or grade group—to a group of which he may legitimately be considered a member. This is the type of comparison made in using percentile norms.

We saw in Chapter 2 how we could compute, for any set of scores, the median, quartiles, and any percentile. For each score value, we can compute the percentage of cases, p, falling below that score. Any person getting that score then surpasses p percent of the group on which the percentile values were computed. We say that he falls at the pth percentile, or has a percentile rank of p.

Fig. 4.2 shows percentile norms of boys in the first semester of the ninth grade tested on each of the subtests (and one combination of two subtests) of the *Differential Aptitude Test Battery, Form L.* Look at the column headed *Verb. Reas.* (Verbal Reasoning). The entries in this column are raw scores. Thus a score of 30 or 31 corresponds to the 75th percentile on this test. On the *Abstract Reasoning Test (Abst. Reas.)*, a score of 31 corresponds to the 50th percentile. This score represents the same degree of excellence as a raw score of 21 on the *Verbal Reasoning Test.*

Note that not every percentile is given in Fig. 4.2. For most of the range the percentiles are tabled in steps of 5, and sometimes several score points are listed opposite a given percentile value. If more detailed tables were given, these scores would correspond to different percentiles. However, no score is precisely accurate (see Chapter 3), so over most of the score range locating an individual to the nearest 5 percentiles is as close as is usually justified and certainly close enough for all practical decisions.

BOYS

Percentile	Verb. Reas.	Num. Abil.	VR+NA	Abst. Reas.	Clerical S and A*	Mech. Reas.	Space Rela.	LU-I: Spell.	LU-II: Gram.	N=2400+ Percentile
99	44-50	38-40	77-90	44-50	75-100	61-68	54-60	93-100	48-60	99
97	42-43	36-37	73-76	43	67-74	60	51-53	89-92	45-47	97
95	39-41	34-35	68-72	42	62-66	58-59	48-50	85-88	41-44	95
90	36-38	32-33	64-67	41	59-61	56-57	44-47	81-84	37-40	90
85	34-35	30-31	61-63	39-40	56-58	54-55	41-43	77-80	35-36	85
80	32-33	28-29	58-60	38	54-55	53	38-40	74-76	33-34	80
75	30-31	26-27	54-57	37	53	51-52	36-37	72-73	31-32	75
70	28-29	25	51-53	36	51-52	50	34-35	69-71	30	70
65	26-27	24	49-50	35	50	49	32-33	67-68	28-29	65
60	24-25	23	47-48	33-34	48-49	48	30-31	64-66	27	60
55	22-23	22	44-46	32	46-47	47	28-29	62-63	26	55
50	21	20-21	41-43	31	45	45-46	26-27	60-61	25	50
45	20	19	38-40	30	44	44	24-25	58-59	23-24	45
40	18-19	18	36-37	28-29	43	43	22-23	56-57	21-22	40
35	17	17	34-35	26-27	42	42	20-21	54-55	20	35
30	15-16	15-16	32-33	24-25	40-41	40-41	19	52-53	19	30
25	14	14	29-31	22-23	38-39	38-39	17-18	50-51	18	25
20	13	13	27-28	19-21	36-37	36-37	15-16	47-49	15-17	20
15	11-12	12	25-26	14-18	34-35	33-35	13-14	44-46	13-14	15
10	9-10	10-11	22-24	11-13	31-33	30-32	12	41-43	11-12	10
5	8	8-9	18-21	8-10	25-30	27-29	11	36-40	9-10	5
3	6-7	6-7	15-17	5-7	17-24	23-26	10	30-35	7-8	3
1	0-5	0-5	0-14	0-4	0-16	0-22	0-9	0-29	0-6	1
Mean	22.4	20.9	43.3	29.3	45.6	44.8	27.9	61.3	25.2	Mean
SD	9.9	8.0	16.6	10.6	11.9	9.5	11.7	15.2	9.6	SD

Figure 4.2

Percentile norms for *Differential Aptitude Tests. Reproduced by permission of The Psychological Corporation*

Percentile norms are very widely adaptable and applicable. They can be used wherever an appropriate normative group can be obtained to serve as a yardstick. They are appropriate for young or old, for educational or industrial situations. To surpass 90 percent of a reference comparison group signifies a comparable degree of excellence whether the function being measured is how rapidly one can solve simultaneous equations or how far one can spit. Percentile norms are widely used. Were it not for the two points that we must now consider, they would provide a framework very nearly ideal for interpreting test scores.

The first problem that faces us in the case of percentile norms is specifying the norming group. On what type of group should the norms be based? Clearly, we will need different norm groups for different ages and grades in the population. A 9-year-old must be evaluated in terms of 9-year-old norms; a sixth grader, in terms of sixth grade norms; an applicant for a job as stock clerk, in terms of stock clerk applicant norms. The appropriate norm group is in every case the group to which the individual belongs and in terms of which his status is to be evaluated. It makes no sense, for example, to evaluate the performance of a medical school applicant on a biology test by comparing his score with norms based on high school seniors. If the test is to be used by a medical school, the user must find or develop medical school applicant norms.

If percentile norms are to be used, then, multiple sets of norms are usually needed. There must be norms appropriate for each distinct type of group or situation with which the test is to be used. This is recognized by the better test publishers, and they provide norms not only for age and grade groups but also for special types of educational or occupational population. However, there are limits to the number of distinct groups for which a test publisher can produce norms, so published percentile norms will often need to be supplemented by the test user, who can build up norm groups particularly suited to his individual needs. Thus a given school system will often find it valuable to develop local percentile norms for its own pupils. This will permit individual scores to be interpreted in relation to the local group, a comparison that may be more significant for local decisions than comparison with national norms. Again, an employer who uses a test with a particular category of job applicants may well find it useful to accumulate results and prepare norms for this particular group of people. Evaluating a new applicant will be much facilitated by these strictly local norms.

The second problem in relation to percentile norms has to do with the question of equality of units. Can we think of 5 percentile points as representing the same amount throughout the percentile scale? Is the difference between the 50th and 55th percentile equivalent to the difference between the 90th and 95th? To answer this, we must notice the way in which test scores for a group of individuals usually pile up. We saw one histogram of scores in Chapter 2 (p. 32). This picture is fairly representative of the way the scores fall in many cases. There is a piling up of cases around the middle score values and a tailing off at either end. The ideal model of this type of score distribution, which is called the *normal curve,* was also considered in Chapter 2 (pp. 44-46) and is shown in Fig. 4.3. The exact normal curve is an idealized mathematical model, but many types of test and measure distribute themselves in a manner that approximates a normal curve. You will notice the piling up of most of the cases in the middle, the tailing off at both ends, and the symmetrical pattern.

In Fig. 4.3, 4 score points have been marked. These are, in order, the 50th, 55th, 90th, and 95th percentiles. Note that near the median 5 percent of cases (the 5 percent lying between the 50th and 55th percentile) fall in a tall narrow pile. Toward the tail of the distribution 5 percent of cases (the 5

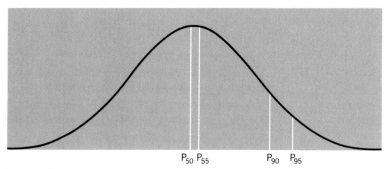

P₅₀ P₅₅   P₉₀ P₉₅

Figure 4.3
Normal curve, showing selected percentile points.

percent between the 90th and 95th percentile) make a relatively broad low bar. Five percent of the cases spread out over
a considerably wider range of the trait in the second case than
in the first. The same number of percentile points corresponds
to about three times as much of the trait when we are around
the 90th to 95th percentile as when we are near the median.
The further out on the tail we go, the more extreme the situation becomes.

Thus percentile units are typically and systematically un-
equal. The difference between being first or second in a group
of 100 is many times as great as the difference between being
50th and 51st. Equal percentile differences do not, in general,
represent equal differences in amount. Any interpretation of
percentile ranks must take into account the fact that such a
scale has been pulled out at both ends and squeezed in the
middle. Mary, who falls at the 50th percentile in arithmetic
and the 55th in reading, shows a trifling difference in these two
abilities, whereas Alice, with percentiles of 90 and 95, shows a
fairly marked difference.

Percentile bands. Any measurement provides only an estimate of the true level of ability of an individual. This matter
was discussed more fully in the section of Chapter 3 dealing
with reliability. Bearing in mind the error of measurement
characterizing a test score, some publishers have prepared
norms tables in the form of *percentile bands.* For each raw score
the manual reports, instead of a specific percentile corresponding to that score, a range of percentile values within which the
true ability of the examinee may be presumed to lie. A section
of such a table for the *STEP Reading Test* is shown in Table 4.3.
The table would be read as follows: An end-of-fifth-grade pupil with a raw score of 50 may be presumed to have ability

Table 4.3

PERCENTILE BANDS CORRESPONDING TO RAW SCORES ON *STEP READING TEST 4A*

Raw Score	Grade Level		
	Spring 3 Fall 4	Spring 4 Fall 5	Spring 5 Fall 6
60	99–99+	99–99+	99–99+
59	99–99+	99–99+	99–99+
58	99–99+	99–99+	98–99+
57	99–99+	99–99+	98–99+
56	99–99+	98–99+	96–99
55	99–99+	98–99+	93–98
54	99–99+	97–99	91–96
53	99–99+	95–99	86–96
52	98–99+	93–98	82–94
51	98–99+	91–97	78–92
50	97–99+	89–97	76–91
.	.	.	.
.	.	.	.
.	.	.	.
18	5–40	2–23	1–12
17	3–36	1–20	(1−)–11
16	2–32	1–17	(1−)–10
15	1–28	(1−)–15	(1−)–8
14	1–24	(1−)–13	(1−)–7
13	(1−)–21	(1−)–10	(1−)–6
12	(1−)–13	(1−)–6	(1−)–4
11	(1−)–10	(1−)–5	(1−)–3
10	(1−)–7	(1−)–3	(1−)–2
9	(1−)–3	(1−)–1	(1−)–1
0–8	(1−)–2	(1−)–1	(1−)–1

* Adapted from *Teacher's Manual* for *STEP Series II, Form 4A* and *4B*, pp. 4–25. Copyright ©1971 by Educational Testing Service. All rights reserved. Reprinted by permission.

falling somewhere in the range from the 76th to the 91st percentile of the reference group.

The objective in using percentile bands is to keep the test user from attaching unwarranted precision to a test score, and to encourage awareness of the variability of pupil performance from day to day and from one form to another of a test. The band that is usually reported extends 1 standard error of measurement on either side of the obtained score, so if we were to interpret the raw score of 50 fully we should say something like: "There are about 2 chances in 3 that this examinee's true level of ability falls between the 76th and 91st percentile." Thinking in terms of a band rather than a point helps in seeing which differences between subject areas for a single pupil, or between pupils in a given subject, are large enough so that we can have some confidence in their reality and feel a need to pay some attention to them.

To conclude, percentile norms provide a basis for interpreting the score of an individual in terms of his standing in some particular group. If the percentile is to be meaningful, the group must be one with which it is reasonable and appropriate to compare him. It is usually necessary to have a number of tables of percentile norms based on different groups, if we are to use a test with different ages, grades, or occupations. As long as percentiles for appropriate groups are supplied, this type of norm is widely applicable. But interpretation of percentile values is made more difficult by the fact that they constitute a systematically "rubber" scale whose units are small in the middle range and large at the extremes.

STANDARD SCORES

Because the units of a score system based on percentiles are so clearly not equal, we are led to look for some other unit that does have the same meaning throughout its whole range of values. *Standard-score scales* have been developed to serve this purpose.

In Chapter 2 we became acquainted with the standard deviation as a measure of the spread or scatter of a group of scores. The standard deviation was a type of average of the deviations of scores away from the mean—the root mean squared deviation. Any score may be expressed in standard deviations away from the mean. Thus in Fig. 4.2 the mean *Numerical Ability* score is 20.9 and the standard deviation is 8.0, so a person who got a score of 25 falls

$$\frac{25 - 20.9}{8.0} = 0.51$$

standard deviation units above the mean. A score of 15 would be 0.73 standard deviation units *below* the mean. In standard deviation units, we would call these scores $+0.51$ and -0.73 respectively.

Suppose we have given the *Differential Aptitude Test* to the pupils in a ninth grade class and two pupils have the following scores on *Numerical Ability* and *Spelling*.

	Numerical Ability	Spelling
Henry	25	75
Joe	32	70

Let us see how we can use standard scores to compare performance of an individual on the two tests, or performance of the
two individuals on a single test.

The mean and standard deviation for *Numerical Ability* and
spelling are as follows.

	Numerical Ability	**Spelling**
Mean	20.9	61.3
S.D.	8.0	15.2

On *Numerical Ability* Henry is 4.1 points above the mean or
4.1/8.0 = 0.51 standard deviations above the mean. On *Spelling* he is 13.7 points or 13.7/15.2 = 0.90 standard deviations
above the mean. Henry is about four-tenths of a standard deviation better in spelling than in numerical ability. For Joe the
corresponding calculations give

$$\text{Numerical } \frac{32 - 20.9}{8.0} = 1.39 \qquad \text{Spelling } \frac{70 - 61.3}{15.2} = 0.57$$

Thus Henry has done about as well on *Numerical Ability* as Joe
has done on *Spelling*, while Joe's *Numerical Ability* score is about
half a standard deviation better than Henry's *Spelling*.

Each pupil's level of excellence is expressed as so many standard deviation units above or below the mean of the comparison group. This is a standard unit of measure having essentially
the same meaning from one test to another. For aid in interpreting the degree of excellence represented by a standard
score, see Table 2.6 (p. 45).

The type of score in standard deviation units that we have
just presented is satisfactory except for two matters of convenience: (1) it requires use of plus and minus signs which may
be miscopied or overlooked, and (2) it gets us involved with
decimal points which may be misplaced. We can get rid of the
need to use decimal points by multiplying every standard deviation score by some constant, such as 10. We can get rid of
minus signs by adding to every score a convenient constant
amount such as 50. Then, for Henry's scores on *Numerical Ability*
and *Spelling*, we would have:

	Numerical Ability	**Spelling**
Mean of distribution of scores	20.9	61.3
Standard deviation of distribution	8.0	15.2
Henry's raw score	25	75
Henry's score in standard deviation units	+0.51	+0.90
Standard deviation score × 10	+5	+9
Plus a constant amount (50)	55	59

Table 4.4

STANDARD SCORE EQUIVALENTS FOR _NUMERICAL ABILITY TEST,_ NINTH GRADE—BOYS. (STANDARD SCORE MEAN = 50, _S.D._= 10)

Raw Score	Standard Score	Raw Score	Standard Score	Raw Score	Standard Score	Raw Score	Standard Score
49	85	37	70	24	54	12	39
48	84	36	69	23	53	11	38
47	83	35	68	22	51	10	36
46	81	34	66	21	50	9	35
45	80	33	65	20	49	8	34
44	79	32	64	19	48	7	33
43	78	31	63	18	46	6	31
42	76	30	61	17	45	5	30
41	75	29	60	16	44	4	29
40	74	28	59	15	43	3	28
39	73	27	58	14	41	2	26
38	71	26	56	13	40	1	25
		25	55			0	24

A table of standard scores for _Numerical Ability_ based on this conversion, in which the mean is set equal to 50 and the standard deviation to 10, is shown in Table 4.4.

The standard scores in Table 4.4 are based on a simple equation that changes the size of the units and the location of group mean. In symbolic form the equation is

$$Z = 10 \left(\frac{X - \bar{X}}{S.D.} \right) + 50$$

where Z is the standard score,
X is the raw score,
$\bar{X}$ is the mean of the raw scores,
$S.D.$ is the standard deviation of raw scores.

The scale of scores in a table such as this is stretched out or squeezed together (depending on whether the original standard deviation is smaller or larger than 10), but the stretching or squeezing is uniform all along the scale of scores. The _size_ of the units is changed, but it is changed uniformly throughout the score scale. If the score scale represented equal units to begin with, it still does, but nothing has been done to _make_ the units more equal. Since the above equation is the equation of a straight line, this type of transformation of scores is called a _linear conversion_ or _transformation_.

Frequently, standard score scales are developed via the percentiles corresponding to the raw scores, making the assumption that the trait that is being measured has a normal distribution. This is called an _area conversion_ of scores. Thus in the

Numerical Ability Test it is found that 35 percent of ninth grade boys fall below a score of 17. In a table of the normal curve, the base line value in a normal curve below which 35 percent of cases fall is -0.39 standard deviations. Consequently we would assign to a raw score of 17 a standard score of -0.39. Expressing this result on a scale in which the standard deviation is to be 10 and the mean 50, we have

$$T = 10(-0.39) + 50 = -4 + 50 = 46.$$

The designation *T*-score and the symbol T have often been used to identify this particular type of normalized standard score scale.

Normalized standard scores make sense whenever it seems likely that the group is a complete one that has not been curtailed by systematic elimination at the upper or lower ends. Furthermore, they make sense whenever it seems likely that the original raw score scale does not represent a scale of equal units. Many test makers systematically plan to include in their tests many items of medium difficulty and few easy or hard items. The effect of this is to produce tests that spread out and make fine discriminations among the middle 80 or 90 percent of pupils, while making coarser discriminations at the extremes. That is, the raw score units in the middle range correspond to smaller true increments in the ability being measured than do raw score units at the extremes. The "true" distribution of ability is pulled out into a flat-topped distribution of scores. The operation of normalizing the distribution reverses this process.

We could have used values other than 50 and 10 in setting up the conversion into convenient standard scores. The Army has used a standard score scale with mean of 100 and standard deviation of 20 for reporting its test results. The College Entrance Examination Board has long used a scale with mean of 500 and standard deviation of 100. The Navy has used the 50 and 10 system.

A type of normalized standard score that has become quite popular for educational tests in recent years is the so-called stanine* score. Stanine units each represent ½ a standard deviation on the basic trait dimension. The relationship of stanine units to standard deviation units and to percentiles is shown on the following page.

Stanines, like percentile bands, tend to play down small differences in score and to express performance in broader categories so that attention tends to be focused on differences that are big enough to make a difference.

* A condensation of the phrase, "standard nine-point scale."

Stanine	Standard Deviation Range	Percentile Range
9	+1.75 & up	96–99
8	+1.25 to +1.75	89–95
7	+0.75 to +1.25	77–88
6	+0.25 to +0.75	60–76
5	−0.25 to +0.25	41–59
4	−0.75 to −0.25	24–40
3	−1.25 to −0.75	12–23
2	−1.75 to −1.25	5–11
1	up to −1.75	1–4

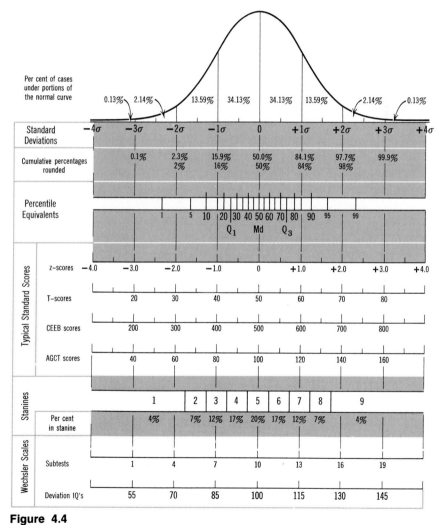

Figure 4.4

Various types of standard score scales in relation to percentiles and the normal curve. (Reproduced by permission of the Psychological Corporation.)

The relationships among a number of the different standard score scales and the relationship of each to percentiles and to the normal curve are shown in Fig. 4.4. The model of the normal curve is shown, and beneath it are a scale of percentiles and several of the common standard score scales. This figure illustrates the equivalence of scores in the different systems. Thus a College Board standard score of 600 would represent the same level of excellence (in relation to some common reference group) as an Army standard score of 120, a Navy standard score of 60, a stanine score of 7, or a percentile rank of 84. The particular choice of score scale is arbitrary and a matter of convenience. It is too bad that all testing agencies have not been able to agree upon a common score unit. However, the important thing is that the same score scale and comparable norming groups be used for all tests in a given organization, so that results from different tests may be directly comparable.

In summary, standard scores, like percentiles, base the interpretation of the individual's score on his performance in relation to a particular reference group. They differ from percentiles in that they are expressed in presumably equal units. The basic unit is the standard deviation of the reference group, and the individual's score is expressed as the number of standard deviation units above or below the mean of the group. Standard scores may be based on either a linear or an area (normalizing) conversion. Different numerical standard score scales have been used by different testing agencies.

INTERCHANGEABILITY OF DIFFERENT TYPES OF NORM

Whichever type of norm is used, a table of norms will be prepared by the test publisher. This will show the different possible raw scores on the test, together with the corresponding score equivalents in the system of norms being used. Many publishers provide tables giving more than one type of score equivalent. An example is given in Table 4.5 on p. 135. Here are shown the norms for the *Comprehension Test* of the *Gates-MacGinitie Reading Tests, Primary B.* Four types of norm are shown. The percentiles are based on a group tested early in the second grade. The standard score scale assigns a mean of 50 and a standard deviation of 10 to an early second grade group. Thus a boy with a score of 21 can be characterized as:

Table 4.5
COMPREHENSION NORMS FOR GATES-MACGINITE
READING TEST—PRIMARY B

Grade Level 2.1 (Oct.)

Raw Score	Standard Score	Percentile	Grade Score	Stanine
1	—	—	—	1
2	30	2	—	1
3	32	4	—	1
4	34	5	—	2
5	35	7	1.2	2
6	38	12	1.3	3
7	39	14	1.4	3
8	41	18	1.4	3
9	44	27	1.5	4
10	46	34	1.6	4
11	47	38	1.6	4
12	49	46	1.7	5
13	50	50	1.8	5
14	51	54	1.9	5
15	52	58	2.1	5
16	53	62	2.2	6
17	54	66	2.3	6
18	55	69	2.4	6
19	56	73	2.5	6
20	57	76	2.5	6
21	58	79	2.6	7
22	58	79	2.7	7
23	59	82	2.8	7
24	60	84	3.1	7
25	61	86	3.4	7
26	62	88	3.6	7
27	63	90	3.7	8
28	64	92	4.0	8
29	65	93	4.3	8
30	66	95	4.5	8
31	68	96	4.7	9
32	70	98	4.9	9
33	72	99	5.1	9
34	75	99	5.4	9

1. Having a grade equivalent of 2.6.
2. Falling at the 79th percentile in the second grade group.
3. Receiving a standard score of 58.
4. Receiving a stanine of 7.

From Table 4.5 it is easy to see that the different systems of norms are different ways of expressing the same thing. We can translate from one to the other, moving back and forth. Thus a child who falls at the 66th percentile in the second grade group has a grade equivalent of 2.3. A grade equivalent of 2.3 corresponds to a standard score of 54. The different systems of interpretation support one another for different purposes.

However, the different norm systems are not entirely consistent as we shift from one type of test to another. This is because some functions mature more rapidly from one year to the next, relative to the spread of scores at a given age or grade level.

This can be seen most dramatically by comparing reading comprehension and arithmetic computation. The phenomenon is illustrated by the pairs of scores shown in Table 4.6, based on the *Stanford Achievement Test Battery*. It is assumed that the three boys were tested at the end of 2 months in the fifth grade. John received scores on both tests that were just average. His grade equivalent was 5.2 and he was close to the 50th percentile for pupils tested after 2 months in the fifth grade. Henry shows superior performance, but how does he compare in the two subjects? From one point of view, he does equally well in both; he is just 1 full year ahead of his grade placement. But in terms of percentiles he is much better in arithmetic than in reading, that is, 89th percentile as compared with 74th percentile. Will, on the other hand, falls at just the same percentile for both reading and arithmetic. However, in his case the grade equivalent for reading is 7.3 and for arithmetic is 6.3.

The discrepancies that appear in the above example are due to differences in the variability of performance and rate of growth of reading and arithmetic. Reading shows a *wide* spread within a single grade group, relative to the change from grade to grade. Some fifth graders read better than the average eighth or ninth grader, so a reading grade equivalent of 8.0 or even 9.0 is not unheard of for fifth graders. In fact a grade equivalent of 8.0 corresponds to the 95th percentile for pupils at grade 5.2. By contrast, a fifth grader almost never does as well in arithmetic as an eighth or ninth grader—in part because he has not encountered or been taught many of the topics that will be presented in the fifth, sixth, seventh, and eighth grades and included in a test for those grade levels. Thus fifth

Table 4.6

137
quotients

COMPARISON OF GRADE EQUIVALENTS AND PERCENTILES

	Paragraph Meaning			Arithmetic Computation		
	John	Henry	Will	John	Henry	Will
Raw score	28	36	46	14	20	21
Grade equivalent	5.2	6.2	7.3	5.2	6.2	6.3
Grade 5.2 percentile	52	74	90	56	89	90

graders are more homogeneous with respect to arithmetic skills; or, looked at another way, arithmetic shows more rapid gains from fifth to eighth grade than does reading.

This point must always be borne in mind, especially in comparing grade equivalents for different subjects. A bright child will often appear most advanced in reading and language, least so in arithmetic and spelling, when the results are reported in grade equivalents. This difference may result, in whole or in part, simply from the differences in the growth functions for the subjects, and need not mean a genuinely uneven pattern of progress for the child.

For this reason most testing specialists are quite critical of grade equivalents, and express a strong preference for percentiles or some type of standard score.

QUOTIENTS

In the early days of mental testing, after age norms had been used for a few years, the need was felt to convert the age score into an index that would express rate of progress. The 8-year-old who had an age equivalent of $10\frac{1}{2}$ years was obviously better than average, but how much better? Some index was needed to take account of chronological age (actual time lived) as well as the age equivalent on the test (score level reached).

The expedient was hit upon of dividing test age by chronological age to yield a quotient. This procedure was applied most extensively with tests of intelligence, where the age equivalent on the test was called a *mental age* and the corresponding quotient was an *intelligence quotient*.

The formula for computing the intelligence quotient in this way is given below and is illustrated for the 8-year-old who reaches the $10\frac{1}{2}$-year level on the test.

$$IQ = \frac{100MA}{CA}$$

$$= \frac{100(10.5)}{8} = 131$$

How does an intelligence quotient come to have meaning? In the first place, it is obvious by the way in which the quotient was established that 100 should be average at every age group, since the average 10-year-old, for example, should fall exactly at the 10-year level on any test if the age equivalents are properly established. But how outstandingly good is 125? How poor is 80? Such questions as these can only be answered by becoming acquainted with the distribution of quotients that a particular test yields.

The intelligence quotient was originally developed in connection with the individual intelligence tests of the type represented by the *Stanford-Binet* (see Chapter 9). The circumstance that made intelligence quotients from such a test as the *Stanford-Binet* relatively interpretable was that their mean and standard deviation remained relatively uniform from age to age. For this reason an IQ of 125 signified about the same status, relative to a child's own age group, whether obtained for a 5-year-old or a 15-year-old. This situation would not necessarily be true and was not perfectly true even for this test, but in many instances quotients were found to maintain the same average and spread of values in different age groups sufficiently closely so that a common interpretation was appropriate at all age levels.

To all intents and purposes, such quotients represented a type of standard score. The 1937 revision of the *Stanford-Binet* produced a standard score with a mean of approximately 100 and standard deviation of approximately 16 in a general sample of American children. This relationship of quotients to standard scores is explicitly recognized in most recent intelligence tests. For these tests, tables of IQ equivalents have been set up at each age level, and have been built so as to give the same mean and standard deviation for all age groups. As a matter of fact, the current edition of the *Stanford-Binet* also uses standard scores designed so that the mean is 100 and the standard deviation 16 at each age level, rather than the MA/CA ratio that was the basis for the IQ when it first appeared.

The notion of the intelligence quotient, or IQ, is deeply imbedded in the history of the testing movement, and, in fact, in 20th-century American culture. The expression "IQ test" has become a part of our common speech. We are probably stuck with the term. But now and in the future IQs will in most cases really be standard scores, and this is how we should think of them and use them.

In a number of recent tests of intelligence the converted scores that are reported are, in fact, normalized standard scores, based on the type of normalizing area transformation that is discussed on page 132. These are sometimes referred to as Deviation Intelligence Quotients (DIQs), since they are basically standard scores expressed as a deviation above or below a mean of 100.

Unfortunately the score scale for reporting IQs does not have *exactly* the same meaning from test to test. The Wechsler test series (see Chapter 9) is based on a mean of 100 and standard deviation of 15, while the Binet and most group tests are based on a mean of 100 and a standard deviation of 16. Furthermore, tests are normed at different points in time and use different sampling procedures. This also leads to some variation in the norms, and consequently in the distribution of IQs they yield for any given school or community.

PROFILES

The various types of norm we have been considering provide a means of expressing scores on quite different tests in common units in such a way that they can be meaningfully compared. There is no direct way of comparing a score of 30 words correctly spelled with a score of 20 arithmetic problems solved. But if both are expressed in terms of the grade level to which they correspond or in terms of the percentage of some defined common group that gets scores below that point, then a meaningful comparison is possible. The set of different test scores for an individual, expressed in a common unit of measure, constitutes his *score profile*. The separate scores may be presented for comparison in tabular form by listing the converted score values. A record form showing the converted scores is given in Fig. 4.5. The comparison of different subareas of performance is made pictorially clearer by a graphic profile. Two ways of plotting profiles are shown in Figs. 4.6 and 4.7 on pages 141 and 142.

Figures 4.5 and 4.6 show a class record form and an individual profile chart for the *Iowa Tests of Basic Skills*. The class record illustrates the form in which data are reported back to schools by one of the large-scale computerized test scoring organizations. The upper left-hand scores reported here are grade equivalents, and since the tests were given after the pupils had spent 2 months in the seventh grade, the norm for the country as a whole would be 72.* The scores in the lower right

---

* The decimal point is omitted in the print-out, so the 66 in Vocabulary for Anthony G. (in Fig. 4.5) should be read as 6.6.

CLASS RECORD SHEET   Iowa Tests of Basic Skills

Grade __7__ Semester (1st or 2nd) __1st__ School Building __Shepard__ Date __11/6/66__ Form __B__

City, or District __Woodford__ County __Erie__ State __N.Y.__ Teacher __Mr. Peters__

Each value cell shows the raw score (top) and the percentile rank (bottom), written here as *score / percentile*.

Names of Pupils	SEX (Write B or G)	AGE — Age in Years at Last Birthday	AGE — Months Since Last Birthday	TEST V — Vocabulary (V)	TEST R — Reading Comprehension (R)	TEST L LANGUAGE SKILLS — Spelling (L-1)	Capitalization (L-2)	Punctuation (L-3)	Usage (L-4)	TOTAL TEST L (L)	TEST W WORK-STUDY SKILLS — Map Reading (W-1)	Reading Graphs and Tables (W-2)	Knowledge and Use of Reference Materials (W-3)	TOTAL TEST W (W)	TEST A ARITHMETIC SKILLS — Arithmetic Concepts (A-1)	Arithmetic Problem Solving (A-2)	TOTAL TEST A (A)	COMPOSITE V, R, L, W, A (C)
Anthony G.	M	12	8	66/39	64/36	75/57	95/84	37/7	78/60	71/51	58/26	68/43	60/29	62/33	77/63	83/80	80/73	69/46
Grant O.	M	12	4	92/89	101/97	80/65	90/78	87/76	88/76	86/77	105/98	98/94	102/98	102/98	102/98	88/88	95/95	95/91
Glenna O.	F	13	2	71/49	68/44	76/58	102/93	81/66	67/44	82/70	75/57	81/71	81/69	79/69	79/67	67/40	73/57	75/58
Janet G.	F	13	8	58/25	60/29	53/22	47/13	44/13	58/31	50/15	69/46	57/25	40/3	55/18	48/6	59/25	54/13	55/20
Gustav J.	M	12	10	78/65	76/61	80/65	105/96	104/96	78/60	92/87	90/87	51/17	67/42	69/48	79/67	77/66	78/69	78/67
Robert C.	M	13	3	56/22	63/34	69/47	55/24	44/13	54/29	55/23	72/52	73/54	60/29	68/46	68/42	63/32	66/39	62/33

Figure 4.5
Class record sheet for *Iowa Tests of Basic Skills*. (Reproduced by permission of Houghton Mifflin Co.)

of each box are percentile ranks for autumn testing in the seventh grade.

Fig. 4.6 shows data for five testings of a boy in grades 3.2, 4.2, 5.2, 6.2, and 8.2. The so-called "standard scale" referred to toward the left is actually a scale of grade equivalents. Thus this pupil had a vocabulary grade equivalent of 4.1 when he was tested in the third grade. In the fourth grade his grade equivalent was 4.8, and in the fifth grade it was 5.9.

The results show him to have been generally above the national average in his vocabulary score, though he fell below it at the sixth grade testing. Again, an examination of his profile for the eighth grade test indicates that he was strongest in language skills and weakest in arithmetic. Some of the hazards of paying a great deal of attention to small ups and downs of a profile can be seen in a comparison of his performance on successive testings. Thus spelling appears as the highest peak in the profile for third grade testing, but is just average a year later; reading graphs and tables is next to highest in grade 3, but shows an actual drop between grades 3 and 4 and is the

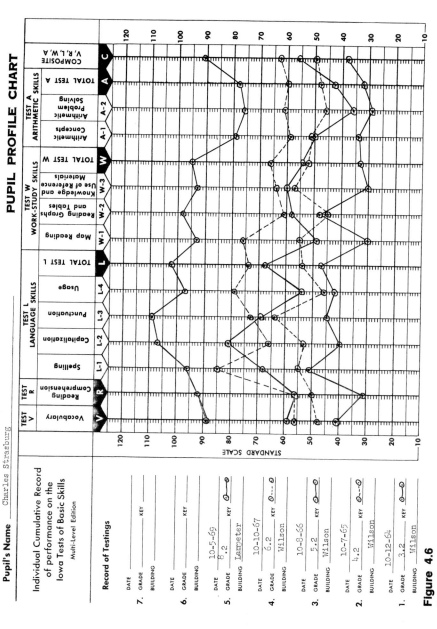

Figure 4.6
Pupil profile chart for *Iowa Tests of Basic Skills* (Reproduced by permission of Houghton Mifflin Co.)

lowest point in the grade 4 profile. There are a number of other inconsistencies from one testing to the following one. It is possible that some of these shifts are meaningful, but many of them stem from nothing more than the error of measurement in subtests that are rather short and not very reliable.

Fig. 4.7 shows a type of profile chart for the component tests

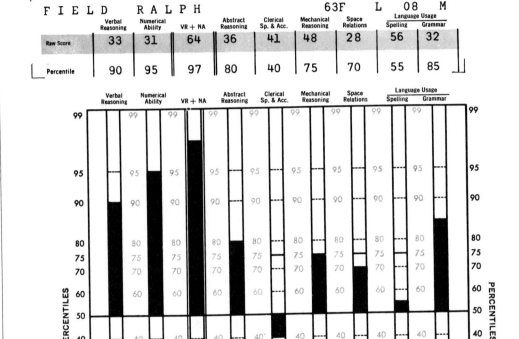

Figure 4.7
Pupil profile chart of *Differential Aptitude Tests* (Reproduced by permission of The Psychological Corporation.)

of the *Differential Aptitude Test Battery*. This battery appraises different aspects of ability that its authors considered important in a high school guidance program. Note that in this case the different tests are represented by separate bars, rather than points connected by a line. The scale used in this case is a percentile scale, but in plotting percentile values appropriate adjustments in the scale have been made to compensate for the inequality of percentile units. That is, percentile points have been spaced in the same way as they are in a normal curve, being more widely spaced at the upper and lower extremes than in the middle range. This percentile scale corresponds to the scale called percentile equivalents that is shown in Fig. 4.4 (p. 133). By this adjustment the percentile values for an individual are plotted on an equal unit scale. A given linear distance can reasonably be thought of as representing the same amount of ability whether it lies high, low, or near the middle of the scale. By the same token, the same distance can be considered equivalent from one test to another.

Note that in Fig. 4.7 the bars have been plotted up and down from the 50th percentile. For this type of norm the average of the group constitutes the anchor point of the scale, and individual scores can be referred to this base level. This type of figure brings out the individual's strengths and weaknesses very clearly.

The profile chart makes a very effective way of representing an individual's scores. But profiles must be interpreted with caution. In the first place, procedures for plotting profiles assume that the norms for the several tests are comparable. For this to be true, age, grade, or percentile scores must be based upon equivalent groups for all the tests. The best guarantee of equivalence is, of course, a common sample used for norming all the tests. We usually find this to be the case for the different subtests of a test battery. Norms for all are established at the same time on the basis of testing the same group. The guarantee of comparability of the norms for the different component tests is one of the most attractive features of an integrated battery. If separately developed tests are plotted in a profile, we can usually only hope that the groups on which norms were established were comparable and that the profile is an unbiased picture of relative achievement in the different fields. When it is necessary to use tests from several different sources, one way to be sure of having equivalent norm groups is to develop local norms on a common population and to plot individual profiles in terms of those local norms.

A second problem is that of deciding how much attention to pay to the ups and downs in a profile. Not all the differences that appear in a profile are meaningful, either in a statistical or a practical sense. We must decide which of the differences deserve some attention on our part and which should be ignored. This problem arises because no test score is completely exact. The problems of reliability and of the error of measurement in a test score were considered in Chapter 3. Reporting scores in percentile bands, as discussed on pp. 127–128, is one way of dealing with this problem. If the percentile band, rather than a specific percentile, were plotted in Fig. 4.7, we could see by inspection which bands overlapped and which were clearly separate. An alternative procedure is to calculate the approximate vertical distance on the standard score scale of the profile chart that corresponds to the standard error of measurement, and then use a ruler to help judge which differences are large enough to merit attention. (For Fig. 4.7 this vertical distance is approximately $\frac{1}{2}$ inch.) Of course, there is no magic size at which a score difference suddenly becomes worthy of attention, and any rule of thumb is at best a rough guide. But differences must be big enough so that (1) we can be reasonably sure that they would still be there if we tested the person again, and (2) they make a practical difference, before we start to interpret them and base actions on them.

Organizing the separate test scores of an individual into a graphic profile is, then, a very effective way of dramatizing the high and low points in a score pattern. Such a profile may be plotted whenever scores from several different tests are expressed in the same units. However, a profile must be interpreted with a good deal of caution, because even unreliable differences may look quite impressive.

NORMS FOR SCHOOL AVERAGES

When evaluating the achievement of a school in relation to other schools, it is sometimes useful to have norms for school averages. It should be clear that the variation from school to school in average ability or achievement is very much less than the variation from pupil to pupil. No school average comes even close to reaching the level of its ablest student, and no average drops to anywhere near the performance of the least able. Thus a single pupil at the beginning of the fifth grade who gets a reading grade equivalent of 6.2 falls at the 75th

Table 4.7

**INDIVIDUAL AND SCHOOL AVERAGE NORMS FOR *ITBS*
READING TEST AT BEGINNING OF FIFTH GRADE (5.2)**

Grade Equivalent	Percentile for Individual	Percentile for School Average
6.5	83	99
6.0	73	92
5.5	61	73
5.0	47	41
4.5	35	19
4.0	24	7
3.5	15	2

percentile, whereas a school whose *average* reading grade equivalent of beginning fifth graders is 6.2 falls at the 94th percentile of schools. The values in Table 4.7 illustrate the relationship more fully. When a school principal or an administrator in a central office is concerned with interpreting the average performance in a school, norms for school averages are the appropriate ones to use, and it is reasonable to expect the test publisher to provide them.

CAUTIONS IN USING NORMS

For a test that assesses standing upon some trait or competence in some area of knowledge, norms provide a basis for interpreting the scores of an individual or a group. Converting the score for any test taken singly into age or grade equivalent, percentile, or standard score, permits an interpretation of the level at which the individual is functioning on that particular test. Bringing together the set of scores for an individual in a common unit of measure, and perhaps exhibiting these scores in a profile, brings out the relative level of performance of the individual in different areas.

The average performance for a class, a grade group in a school, or the children in a grade throughout a school system may be reported similarly. We then see the average level of performance within the group on some single function or the relative performance of the group in each of several areas. Norms provide a frame within which the picture may be viewed and bring all parts of the picture into a common frame. Now what does the picture mean, and what should we do about it?

Obviously it is not possible, in a few pages, to provide a ready-made interpretation for each set of scores that may be obtained in a practical testing situation. However, we can lay out a few general guiding lines and principles that may help to forestall some unwise interpretations of test results.

The most general point is that test results, presented in terms of age or grade equivalents, percentiles, or standard scores are a *description of what is,* rather than a *prescription of what should be.* They make it possible to compare an individual or a class with other individuals and classes with respect to one or more aspects of accomplishment or personality, but they do not in any absolute sense tell us whether the individual or the group is doing "well" or "badly." They do not provide this information for several reasons that we shall now consider.

1. *Converted scores give relative rather than absolute information.* They tell whether a pupil has as high achievement as other pupils or whether a class scores as high as other classes. But they do not tell us whether the basic concepts of numbers are being mastered or whether pupils read well enough to comprehend the instructions for filling out an income tax return. Furthermore, they give us little guidance as to how much improvement we might expect from *all* pupils if our educational system operated throughout at 100 percent efficiency.

It must be remembered that, by the very nature of relative scores, there will be as many below average as above. When "the norm" means the average of a reference group, it is a statistical necessity that about half the group will be, to a greater or lesser degree, below average—unless all individual differences are to be eliminated. There has been an enormous amount of foolishness—both in single schools and in state-wide legislation—about bringing all pupils "up to the grade norm." Conceivably, this might be done temporarily if we had a sudden and enormous improvement in educational effectiveness; but then the next time new norms were established for the test it would take a higher absolute level of performance to "read at the sixth grade level," for example, so we would be back again with half the pupils falling at or below the average.

The relative nature of norms has been recognized in the recent emphasis on criterion-referenced tests. When a teacher or a school is concerned with appraising mastery of some *very specific* instructional objective, it will be more useful to develop test exercises that appraise that objective, to agree upon some standard as representing an acceptable level of mastery, and to determine which students do and which do not have mastery of that specific objective.

2. *Output must be evaluated in relation to input.* Test results typically give a picture of output—of the individual or group as it exists at the present time, after a period of exposure to educational effort. But what of the input? Where did the group start?

The notion of input is a complex and rather subtle one. Our conception of input should include not only earlier status on the particular ability being measured; not only individual potential for learning, so far as we are able to appraise this; but also the familial circumstances and environmental supports that make it easier for some children to learn than for others. Parental aspirations for the child, parental skills at tuition and guidance of learning, parental discipline and control, linguistic patterns and cultural resources in the home are part of the input just as truly as are the biological characteristics of the young organism. Furthermore, peer group and community attitudes are an additional real, though possibly modifiable, part of the input so far as the prospects for learning for a given child are concerned.

We still do not know too well how to measure input. Some of the overly simplified approaches to the problem will be discussed in Chapter 9, when we consider the use of "expectancy tables" to view a child's achievement in the light of his performance on an aptitude test. For the present we must be content to recognize that the adequate appraisal of input is no simple matter, and that, correspondingly, the appraisal of output as "satisfactory" or "unsatisfactory" is something we do with only modest confidence.

3. *Output must be evaluated in relation to objectives.* The design, content, and norms for published standardized tests are based on the authors' perception of common national curricular objectives. The topics included, their relative emphasis, and the levels at which they are introduced reflect that general national pattern. To the extent, then, that a given school system deviates in its objectives and curricular emphases from the national pattern, as interpreted by the test maker, its output at a given grade level can be expected to deviate from the national norms. If computational skills receive little emphasis, it is reasonable that computational facility will be underdeveloped. If map reading has been delayed beyond the grade level at which it is introduced into the test, it is reasonable that relative standing on that part of the test will suffer. Unevenness of the local profile, in relation to national norms, should always lead one to inquire whether the low spots represent failures of the local program to achieve its objectives or reflect a planned deviation of emphasis from what is typical in schools more generally.

If these considerations are borne in mind, and the test interpreter also maintains a healthy respect for the standard error of measurement when he is concerned with results for a single individual, test results, as they are reported to teacher, principal, superintendent or school board, will be interpreted and used with increased wisdom and restraint.

SUMMARY STATEMENT

A raw score, taken by itself, rarely has meaning. A score may be given meaning by comparing it with a standard of performance that is set before the test is given; for example, 90 percent of the items answered correctly. This method of giving a raw score meaning is called a criterion-referenced interpretation. Such an interpretation is appropriate for tests that are focused on a single objective and for which standards of performance can be either empirically or logically derived.

Since most tests are designed to appraise more than one objective and since meaningful absolute standards of performance are not available for most tests, a raw score is given meaning by comparison with some reference groups or groups. This method of giving a raw score meaning is called a normative-referenced interpretation. The comparison may be with

1. A series of grade groups (grade norms).
2. A series of age groups (age norms).
3. A single group, indicating what percentage of that group the score surpassed (percentile norms).
4. A single group, indicating standard deviations above or below the group mean (standard scores).

Each alternative has certain advantages and certain limitations, which we have considered.

To get a single index to express the degree to which individuals deviated from their age group, quotients such as the intelligence quotient (I.Q.) were developed. Because quotient type scores have all the limitations of age norms and grade norms plus others, they have been replaced by standard score norms. Strictly speaking the term, I.Q., should no longer be used to refer to general ability tests or to the scores from them.

If the norms available for a number of different tests are of the same kind and are based on comparable groups, all the tests can be expressed in comparable terms. The results can then be shown pictorially in the form of a profile. Profiles emphasize score differences within the individual. When profiles are used, care must be taken not to overinterpret their minor ups and downs.

Norms represent a descriptive framework for interpreting the score of an individual, a class group, or some large aggregation. However, before a judgment can be made as to whether an individual or group is doing well or poorly, allowance must be made for ability level, cultural background, and curricular emphases. The norm is merely an average, not a strait jacket into which all can be forced to fit.

QUESTIONS AND EXERCISES

1. A pupil in the seventh grade received a raw score of 13 on the *Metropolitan Reading Test, Intermediate Level*. What additional information would be needed to interpret this score?

2. Why do standardized tests designed for use with high school students almost never use age or grade norms?

3. What limitations would national norms have for use by a county school system in rural West Virginia? What might the local school system do about it?

4. What assumption or assumptions lie back of the development of age norms? Grade norms? Normalized standard scores?

5. In Fig. 4.4, p. 133, why are the standard scores evenly spaced whereas the percentile scores are unevenly spaced?

6. You are a guidance counselor and have given *Form L* of the *Differential Aptitude Battery* to a ninth grade in October. Using Fig. 4.2 prepare a summary report and interpretation for a boy with the following scores:

Verbal Reasoning	18	Mechanical Reasoning	54
Numerical Ability	23	Clerical Speed and Acc.	45
Abstract Reasoning	31	Spelling	48
Spatial Relations	39	Sentences	22

7. School A gives a battery of achievement tests each May in each grade from the third through the sixth. The median grade level in each subject in each teacher's class is reported to the superintendent. Should they be reported? If so, what else should be included in the report? In what ways might a superintendent use the results to advantage? What uses should he avoid?

8. Miss B prides herself that each year she has gotten at least 90 percent of her fifth grade group "up to the norm" in each subject. How desirable is this as an educational objective? What limitations or dangers do you see in it?

9. School C operates on a policy of assigning transfer students to a grade on the basis of their average grade standing on an achievement battery. Thus a boy with a grade score of 6.4 on the battery as a whole would be assigned to the sixth grade, no matter what his age or his grade in his previous school. What values do you see in this plan? What limitations?

10. The superintendent of schools in city D noted that school E fell consistently about ½ grade below national norms on an achievement battery. He was distressed because this was the lowest of any school in his city. How justified is his dissatisfaction? What more do you need to know to answer this?

11. The board of education in city F noted that the second and third grades in their community fell substantially below national norms in arithmetic, though coming up to the norms in other subjects. They propose to study this further. What additional information do they need?

12. The third grade teachers in school G have prepared a 20-item test to appraise mastery of the basic multiplication facts. What score should they accept as constituting "mastery" of these facts? How should such a score be determined?

13. What are the advantages of reporting test performance in terms of stanines? In terms of percentile bands? What problems arise from using each of these forms of normative report?

14. Look at the manual for some test and study the information that is given about the norms.

(*a*) How adequate is the norming population? Is adequate information given about this?

(*b*) Figure out the chance score (i.e., the score to be expected from blind guessing) for each test, and note its grade equivalent. What limitations does this suggest on use of the test?

(*c*) What limitations are there on the usefulness of the test at the upper end of its range?

(*d*) How many raw score points correspond to 1 full year on a grade equivalent scale?

SUGGESTED
ADDITIONAL READING

151
suggested
additional
reading

Angoff, William H. Scales, norms, and equivalent scores. In R. L. Thorndike (Ed.), *Educational measurement.* (2nd Ed.) Washington, D.C.: American Council on Education, 1971.

Angoff, William H. and Scarvia B. Anderson. The standardization of educational and psychological tests. In David A. Payne and Robert F. McMorris (Eds.), *Educational and psychological measurement.* (2nd Ed.) Morristown, N.J.: General Learning Press, 1975.

Bayless, D. L., J. W. Bergsten, L. H. Lewis, and R. J. North. *Considerations and procedures in national norming: An illustration using the ACT assessment of career development and ACT career planning program, Grades 8-11.* ACT Research Report No. 65. Iowa City, Iowa: The American College Testing Program, July 1974.

Beggs, Donald L. and A. N. Hieronymous. Uniformity of achievement growth. In G. H. Bracht, K. D. Hopkins, and J. C. Stanley (Eds.), *Perspectives in educational and psychological measurement.* Englewood Cliffs, N.J.: Prentice-Hall, 1972.

Loret, Peter G., Alan Seder, John C. Bianchini, and Carol A. Vale. *Anchor test study. Equivalence and norms tables for selected reading achievement tests (Grades 4, 5, 6).* National Center for Education Statistics. Washington, D.C.: U.S. Government Printing Office, 1975.

CHAPTER
FIVE
WHERE
TO FIND
INFORMATION
ABOUT
SPECIFIC
TESTS

The production of educational and psychological tests has been going on for little more than half a century, but during that time literally thousands of different tests have been produced. A comprehensive bibliography extending to about 1945 contained entries for 5,294 different tests. Buros (1974) produced a bibliography of tests for English-speaking examinees that were available in 1974 from commercial publishers, and the list contained 2,470 entries. Some of these have since become unavailable, but new ones have appeared to take their places, and the number of currently available tests is almost certainly still above 2,000, not counting those instruments that appear only in the research literature.

Not only is the total number of tests great. So also is the variety. Tests vary widely in testing procedures, in content, and in group for which designed. There are paper-and-pencil tests, individual performance tests, rating scales, self-report instruments, observational procedures, and projective techniques. There are measures of attitude, of interest, of temperament, of personal adjustment, of intellect, of special aptitudes, and of all aspects of school achievement. There are tests designed for infants, for preschool children, for school children and adolescents, and for adults.

No one book can hope to introduce you to even a representative sampling of tests of all types, covering all sorts of content for all age levels. The following chapters will introduce some of the most important and most widely known tests, discussing them as examples of many others. But this book cannnot give a complete treatment of any particular age group or subject area, and there are so many special situations in which some one of you may be interested or for which you may need a test that the tests discussed here may include not even one that fits your particular need.

Since it is impossible to list and evaluate all or even most of the tests that might be of concern to an audience with varied interests, we shall approach the problem at a different level. We shall try to guide you to sources in which you can find the available tests listed, and in some cases evaluated, and we shall try to guide you in evaluating the tests you locate. The present chapter discusses resource materials for finding tests and for finding out about them. Chapter 3 has given an orientation in the factors to be considered in evaluating the suitability of a particular test for a particular purpose.

The knowledge of where to go to find out about tests of a particular type and how to evaluate one when found is probably more important than predigested information about a particular test. Tests change and the purposes of the test user change. It is impossible to anticipate what type test will be required for some future need. The important thing is to know how to go about finding the tests available for that need when it arises, and how to evaluate their relative merits.

There are several different types of question about a test or an area of measurement for which you may seek answers. Some of the types of question are:

1. What tests have been developed that might serve my present need or purpose?

2. What are the *new* tests in my field of interest?

3. What is test A, of which I have heard, like? For what groups and purposes was it designed? Who made it? How long does it take and how much does it cost? What skills are needed to give and use it?

4. What do specialists in the field of measurement have to say about test A? How do they evaluate it, in comparison with competing techniques?

5. What basic factual material do we have on test A? What are its statistical attributes? What are its relationships to other measures?

6. What research has been been done studying or using test A?

Let us see what materials are available to us as we try to answer questions such as these. These resources include (1) text reference books in special areas of testing, (2) the *Mental Measurements Yearbooks* and their supplementary monographs, (3) test reviews in professional journals, (4) publishers' test catalogues, (5) each test itself together with its accompanying manual, (6) articles in professional journals reviewing a broad field of testing, and (7) educational and psychological abstract and index series. These will be considered in turn, the most useful items will be identified, and the information to be obtained from each type of source will be indicated.

TEXT AND REFERENCE BOOKS IN SPECIAL AREAS

There are a number of text and reference books covering specialized areas of testing. When the scope is limited to include only elementary school tests, tests for diagnosis of individual maladjustment, or tests for vocational placement, it becomes possible to cover the field in more detail. A book dealing with tests of a particular type provides a good general introduction to the materials of the field. Such a book usually acquaints the reader with a representative selection of established tests in the area—those that the author considers worthy of mention. In addition, some evaluation of each test is usually given, indicating the purposes for which it may well be used, and what the writer considers to be its strengths, weaknesses,and distinctive characteristics. The book usually also contains some discussion of the problems of testing in the field it covers, apart from discussion of specific tests.

It is not possible to list all the books that might prove useful to some reader. However, a brief list is included in the suggested readings at the end of the chapter. Criteria for including titles, when several alternatives existed, were recency and judged quality of treatment. In addition, an attempt has been made to cover a wide range of specialized interests.

One limitation of books such as those listed becomes apparent from an examination of the publication dates. At the time that these were selected (1975), each was judged to be the most recent good book in its field, and yet some were already a number of years old. When we add to this the time that has elapsed in the preparation and printing of this book, it is easy to see that a book reviewing a field cannot be relied upon for current materials. The typical textbook gives information about well-established and accepted tests, but recently published devices or techniques that are still in the experimental stages are not likely to be represented. There is a lag of several years between production of a device and reporting of it in books reviewing an area of testing.

Another feature of most books surveying a field, which may be in some cases an advantage and in others a disadvantage, is that they are selective. They must be. The author cannot discuss everything, so he must pick the items he wishes to present. He selects for discussion the tests he considers valuable. Insofar as his judgment is sound, he does a real service to the novice in the field, who is thus led directly to the more important and valuable material. However, this means that you cannot expect to use a textbook as a source to lead you to *all* the tests in an area and permit you to compare them. For a full listing of the tests of any particular type you will have to look elsewhere.

COMPILATIONS OR COMPENDIA OF INSTRUMENTS

Since the middle 1960s a number of compilations of measuring instruments have been produced. The format of these compilations varies considerably from one to another, but each of these compilations attempts to make available information on instruments, both commercially and noncommercially published, that have been developed to appraise various constructs or attributes of individuals. In some of the compilations, for example Robinson and Shaver's *Measures of Social Psychological Attitudes* (1973), actual instruments are presented as well as a critique of each instrument and a general discussion of the construct being appraised by the instrument. In other compilations, for example Chun, Cobb, and French's *Measures for Psychological Assessment* (1975), only a comprehensive bibliography of all measures of certain constructs is presented.

The primary value of these compilations is that each brings together in one book either all of the instruments that have been used to measure a certain construct, or exhaustive bibliographic references to all measures that have been used as of the date of preparation of the compilation. Frequently, these sources will lead you to unpublished instruments that would be difficult for a single individual to locate.

The major disadvantage of all of the compilations is that they become outdated unless continuous efforts are made to keep them current. However, if you would like to develop a complete list of instruments that have been used to appraise a particular construct you could combine one of these compilations with an ERIC search (see p. 162) to obtain an up-to-date list of instruments. A further disadvantage of some of the compilations is that they are noncritical. The authors' aim is to be comprehensive and all-inclusive, so that all instruments–good, bad, or indifferent–are listed. Fortunately, most of the authors in the introduction to the book explicitly tell the reader whether selective criteria have been applied, and if they have not, the reader is warned against assuming that each instrument has desirable psychometric properties.

Despite the limitations of the bibliographies and compilations, they are valuable resources, particularly for researchers and particularly in the area of attitude measurement, where commercially published instruments are few. A list of the most valuable ones is given at the end of the chapter.

THE MENTAL MEASUREMENTS YEARBOOKS

Probably the most important single resource for a person needing to make choices or plan programs in the field of testing is the series of *Mental Measurements Yearbooks* prepared by Buros (1938, 1941, 1949, 1953, 1959, 1965, 1972). The *Yearbooks* have been supplemented (Buros, 1975) by a number of more specialized monographs dealing with tests in specific delimited areas (reading, intelligence, personality, vocations, single school subjects).

The *Yearbooks* undertake to provide a listing and one or more frank and critical reviews of each new standardized test that is published. A large panel of reviewers has cooperated in the preparation of these volumes, each reviewer evaluating two or three tests in an area in which he is presumed to be competent. The tests considered to have more widespread interest are appraised by two and sometimes even more reviewers. The reviews are fairly full, pointing out strengths and weaknesses of a test, comparing it with others in the field, and indicating the purposes for which the reviewer considers it useful. A review does, of course, represent the opinion of a specific individual. It expresses his biases as well as his wisdom, and should be read with a recognition of human fallibility. However, the reviewer is a disinterested outsider who presumably does not stand to gain either from the test's success or its failure.

In addition to reviews of tests, the *Yearbooks* also include the factual items about each test that a potential user is likely to need—such items as author, publisher, publication date, cost, time to administer, grades for which suitable, and number of forms available. Finally, for each test the *Yearbooks* give a cumulative bibliography of books and articles that have appeared dealing with that particular test. These bibliographies are quite extensive, amounting in the case of one test to 4,580 titles.

The *Yearbooks* have two other features that add to their value to the test user. One is a section on books and monographs related to measurement problems. This section undertakes to list all the significant books on measurement for the period covered and in addition gives excerpts from the reviews of these books that have appeared in psychological and educational journals. The bibliography and reviews provide a guide to, and evaluation of, publications in the field.

Also valuable is a very complete index and directory section. This includes (1) a directory and index of the publishers of the tests and of the books on measurement reviewed in the volume, (2) a directory and index of the periodicals that have included reviews of test or books on testing, (3) an index of titles of books and tests, (4) an index of names occuring in any connection, and (5) a classified index of tests organized by content or type. These indices make it possible to locate any test or type of test, to locate the complete original of any excerpted test review, and to get in touch with the publisher of any test.

When a question arises about a test or a type of test, the *Mental Measurements Yearbooks* are the volumes for which one reaches almost automatically. They are a "must" for any individual or any office that must answer frequent questions about tests or testing.

There are two types of supplementary publication that extend the usefulness of the *Yearbooks*. One of these is *Tests in Print* (1961, 1974), which undertakes to list all commercially available tests using the English language. The current (1974) edition also updates the bibliographic and other information on each test. The other is a series of monographs bringing together information on such specialized areas as personality tests (1970, 1975), reading tests (1968, 1975), intelligence tests (1975), vocational tests (1975), and tests in five subject matter areas (1975). Within its field, each of these is complete, and obviates the need to check through the whole series of *Yearbooks* to make sure that you have complete information concerning a specific test or tests of some specific type.

A new test is ordinarily reviewed in the first *Yearbook* that came out after it was published, and reviews sometimes also may appear in subsequent volumes. Space limitations did not permit review in the 1938 *Yearbook* of all the older tests that were thought to merit review, and reviews of some of these first appeared in later volumes. Even the set of volumes taken together does not undertake to be *exhaustive* in its coverage of tests of a given type. However, if you bring together the material in the complete series, you will probably find an appraisal of any test that you are likely to consider using, published up to the time that planning for the last *Yearbook* was completed. The first two *Yearbooks* cover tests up to about 1939; the third covers the period from 1940 through 1947; the fourth deals with material from 1948 through 1951; the fifth brings us up to 1958, the sixth to 1964, and the seventh to 1971. For one of the fields covered by the specific monographs, a more efficient strategy is to use that monograph, since it brings together in one place the material appearing in all seven of the *Yearbooks*.

JOURNAL TEST REVIEWS

We still face the problem of getting information on the *latest* tests and testing developments. One way of keeping up with important new tests is through reviews in professional journals. At different times in their history, different educational and psychological journals have included test reviews. The most useful journal in 1975 is probably the *Journal of Educational Measurement,* though the *Journal of Counseling Psychology* also occasionally includes reviews of tests likely to be of interest to counselors. These sources should be of some help in keeping you up to date on the most significant new educational and psychological tests within a year or so of their appearance.

TEST PUBLISHERS

The most current information on what tests are available is probably to be obtained from the test publishers themselves, either through correspondence or through their catalogues. There are many publishers, too many to list here,* so that gathering information from all of them would be quite an undertaking. However, the number who publish *extensively* in the testing field is a good deal more limited. A number of the most important publishers are listed in Appendix III together with their addresses.

* They *are* listed in the *Mental Measurements Yearbooks.*

The limitations of a test publisher as an entirely unbiased source of information on the values and limitations of his own publications are, of course, obvious. Reversing Marc Antony, we may say he comes to praise his tests, not to bury them. However, as a source of information about, rather than evaluation of his tests, he can be very helpful. In Chapter 3 we have considered how you may go about appraising a new test for yourself in the light of the information you can get from the test producer and from other sources.

TEST AND MANUAL

If you are seriously considering using a particular test you will certainly need to examine the test itself and the manual the publisher has prepared to go with it. Each publisher's catalogue will indicate the price for which a specimen set of each test may be obtained. The specimen set contains a copy of the test itself, the instructions for administering and scoring, and part or all of the supplementary materials available to the user to help in interpreting the test.

The amount of supplementary materials included in a specimen set varies from one publisher to another. You can legitimately expect the publisher to include in a specimen set materials that will provide all the information you need in order to arrive at a decision as to the suitability of the test for your purposes. You should be skeptical of any test for which the information supplied is incomplete. However, you must recognize that when a test has been widely used, and a considerable research literature has developed dealing with it, research results can at best be sampled or summarized in the manual that accompanies the test.

To obtain specimen sets of tests from a publisher, you must ordinarily present some sort of credentials. A letter on the official letterhead of your school or institution will often suffice. A note from the university where you are studying may serve the function. The limitations that publishers place upon the distribution of their materials depend upon the nature of the materials. They will often refuse to distribute tests that require special skills to administer and interpret unless you can give evidence that you have the training and skills that qualify you to use those materials. If you wish to examine a number of different tests without buying specimen sets of each you may be able to find a test file in the library or the guidance department of your local university.

A detailed examination of the test itself will provide you with a basis for judging how well the content of the test and the form of test exercises correspond to the objectives and functions you wish to measure. The accompanying material, which we have collectively called the test manual, is a very important part of any test. It varies enormously in quality and comprehensiveness from one test to another. In some of the better current tests this collateral material becomes almost a book. It provides a great variety of important information to help in using and interpreting the test. We have indicated in Chapter 3 (pp. 105–108) the types of information a test user has a right to expect to find in the test manual. A manual that provides all this information becomes a very important source for information about the test.

Manuals differ greatly not only in comprehensiveness but also in impartiality and integrity. Probably no test manual is entirely free of a promotional element. However, sometimes the manual becomes to a very large extent a promotional device focused on increasing the sales of the test. You must always be aware of this aspect of the manual and must endeavor to discount appropriately claims made for the test. There often appears to be an inverse relationship between the grandeur of the claims that are made and the evidence on which they are based. You will do well to keep your attention focused on the evidence presented in the manual, to view claims in the light of this evidence, and to be extremely suspicious of the test whose manual makes sweeping claims but presents very little data.

JOURNAL REVIEW ARTICLES

It is sometimes useful to refer to summary articles covering recent developments in tests and testing. From 1932 to 1968 a review of research in tests and measurements appeared every three years in the *Review of Educational Research*. Since 1970, however, review articles in that journal have dealt with more specialized topics, as submitted by a reviewer. Some of these do deal with specialized measurement issues.

Since 1950 the *Annual Review of Psychology* has provided a yearly review and bibliography on selected psychological topics. Chapter headings such as Individual Differences and Theory and Techniques of Assessment suggest sources for material of possible interest to the psychological tester.

An annotated bibliography on reading has appeared in recent years in the *Journal of Educational Research.* This deals with reading tests, as well as with other reading problems.

An additional journal source that may be of interest to a test user who is especially concerned with predictive validities of different tests is a section entitled Validity Studies Section, which appears in alternate issues of *Educational and Psychological Measurement.* A somewhat similar section also appeared for a number of years in *Personnel Psychology* under the heading of Validity Information Exchange.

ABSTRACTS AND INDICES

Finally, the serious student will want to know about basic bibliographic sources. Three will be mentioned here: the *Psychological Abstracts,* the *Education Index* and the ERIC system.

The *Psychological Abstracts* undertakes to list, and usually to abstract, all current scientific and technical publications in psychology, including, of course, those related to psychological tests and testing. Some of the sections in each issue in which articles relating to tests and measurements are most likely to be found include

1. Psychometrics and Statistics.
2. Test Construction and Validation.
3. Educational Psychology—Counseling and Measurement.
4. Applied Psychology—Occupational Guidance and Personnel Selection and Training.

However, you must rely primarily on subject headings in the semi-annual subject index to find material on the topic in which you are interested. For recent years of the *Abstracts,* it is possible to get a computer search and printout of all material indexed under a set of key terms, but the effectiveness of this procedure is very dependent upon the applicability of one or two key phrases to the problem in which you are interested.

The *Education Index* covers a considerably wider range of material, since it deals with the whole broad area of education and includes popular and professional materials as well as those of a more technical and scientific nature. It gives references only, providing no information about the nature and content of the item. Material is topically organized, and if you look under such topics as ability tests, educational measurement, mental tests, or personality tests you will find most of the material relating to measurement in education.

A source that is especially useful for new material, and for material not appearing in journals or books, is the Educational Resources Information Center (ERIC), established under the auspices of the National Institute of Education. Each ERIC Center receives, abstracts and indexes material in a special field of educational research. There is currently (1975) an ERIC for tests and measurements at the Educational Testing Service, Princeton, New Jersey. This organization not only feeds abstracts of specific materials into the ERIC system, but undertakes to assemble and review the literature on selected measurement topics. The monthly and annual issues of *Research in Education* provide an index and abstracts of current materials. This index can be searched in person, or it is possible to supply selected key phrases from the "thesaurus" that accompanies the ERIC index and have the body of entries searched by computer.

SUMMARY STATEMENT

At the beginning of this chapter a number of questions were suggested to which a test user might wish answers. The important sources of information about tests and testing have now been discussed. By way of summary, we may try to relate the sources to the questions. An attempt has been made to do this in Table 5.1. At the top of this chart are listed various questions one might raise about a test, type of test, or testing problem. On the side are listed the most important types of source material referred to in this chapter. In each cell is a symbol to represent the extent to which the source should help in answering the question. The symbol ** is used to designate one of the sources that would probably be *most* helpful and to which one would turn first. Sources marked * are ones that would also be expected to contribute to the needed answer. Sources marked ? are ones that might perhaps provide some useful information. Where there is *no* entry at all, the source is not likely to be helpful in that connection. A critical study of this table, with analysis of the reasons for the various entries, should leave you well prepared to go out and get for yourself the information you need in order to select a test or as background for a specific testing problem.

Table 5.1

APPRAISAL OF SOURCES OF INFORMATION ABOUT TESTS AND TESTING

Sources	To Find Out, in Any Field					
	What Tests There Are	What *New* Tests There Are	What Test X Is Like	What Specialists Think of Test X	What Facts We Have about Test X	What Research Has Been Done on or with Testing Problem Y
Texts in special areas of measurement	*		*	?	*	*
Compilations of instruments	*	?	*		*	*
Mental Measurements Yearbooks	**	?	*	**	*	**
Tests in Print	**				*	*
Reviews in current professional journals		*	*	*		
Publishers' catalogues	*	**	*			
Test blank and manual			**		**	*
Review articles in *Review of Educ. Research,* etc.		?		?	?	**
Psychological Abstracts	*				*	**
Education Index	*					*

Key: ** Most helpful   * Somewhat helpful   ? Possibly helpful.

QUESTIONS AND EXERCISES

1. Using the sources indicated in the text, prepare as complete a list as you can of currently available standardized tests for a specific grade and purpose (i.e., tests in first year Spanish, reading readiness tests, tests in American history for the twelfth grade, etc.).

2. For some attribute that interests you (e.g., self-concept, attitude toward war, cognitive style, etc.) determine what research tests are available in the literature, using the compilations and bibliographic sources referred to in the chapter.

3. Using the *Mental Measurements Yearbooks,* find out what reviewers think of a particular test that you are interested in.

4. Using the *Seventh Mental Measurements Yearbook,* find out what reviewers have to say about one of the following titles that interests you:

(*a*) Allen, R.M. and Allen, S.P. *Intellectual evaluation of the mentally retarded child: A handbook.*

(*b*) Barrett, R. S. *Performance rating.*

(*c*) Bower, E. M. *Early identification of emotionally handicapped children in school.*

(*d*) Cattell, R. B., and Butcher, H. J. *The prediction of achievement and creativity.*

(*e*) Dennis, W. *Group values through children's drawings.*

(*f*) Fleishman, E. A. *The structure and measurement of physical fitness.*

(*g*) Guilford, J. P. *The nature of human intelligence.*

5. To what sources would you go to try to answer each of the following questions? To which would you go first? What would you expect to get from each?

(*a*) What test should I use to study the progress of two class groups in beginning French?

(*b*) What kinds of norms are available for the *Stanford Achievement Tests?*

(*c*) Is the *Rorschach Test* of any value as a predictor of academic success in college?

(*d*) Has a new revision of the *Wechsler Adult Intelligence Scale* been published yet?

(*e*) What intelligence tests have been developed for use with the blind?

(*f*) What are the significant differences between the *Metropolitan Achievement Tests* and the *Comprehensive Tests of Basic Skills?*

(*g*) How much does the *Otis-Lennon Mental Ability Test* cost?

(*h*) What do testing people think of the *Brainard Occupational Preference Inventory?*

6. Look at two or three publishers' catalogues. Compare the announcements of tests of the same type. How adequate is the information that is provided? How objective is the presentation of the tests' values and limitations?

SUGGESTED ADDITIONAL READING

Beatty, Walcott H. (Ed). *Improving educational assessment and an inventory of measures of affective behavior.* Washington, D.C.: National Education Association, Association for Supervision and Curriculum Development, 1969.

Bojean, Charles M., Richard J. Hill, and S. Dale McLemore. *Sociological measurement: An inventory of scales and indices.* San Francisco: Chandler Publishing, 1967.

Cattell, Raymond B. and Frank W. Warburton. *Objective personality and motivation tests: A theoretical introduction and practical compendium.* Urbana, Ill.: University of Illinois Press, 1967.

Chun, Ki-Taek, Sidney Cobb, and John R. P. French, Jr. *Measures for psychological assessment: A guide to 3,000 original sources and their applications.* Ann Arbor, Mich.: Institute for Social Research, University of Michigan, 1975.

Comrey, Andrew L., Thomas E. Backer, and Edward M. Glaser. *A sourcebook for mental health measures.* Los Angeles: Human Interaction Research Institute, 1973.

Johnson, Orval G. and James W. Bommarito. *Tests and measurements in child development: A handbook.* San Francisco: Jossey-Bass, 1971.

Lake, Dale G., Matthew B. Miles, and Ralph B. Earle, Jr. (Eds). *Measuring human behavior: Tools for the assessment of social functioning.* New York: Teachers College Press, 1973.

Miller, Delbert C. *Handbook of research design and social measurement.* New York: David McKay, 1970.

Robinson, John P., Robert Athanasion, and Kendra B. Head. *Measures of occupational attitudes and occupational characteristics.* Ann Arbor, Mich.: Univerisity of Michigan, Institute for Social Research, Survey Research Center, 1969.

Robinson, John P., Jerrold C. Rusk, and Kendra B. Head. *Measures of political attitudes.* Ann Arbor, Mich.: University of Michigan, Institute for Social Research, Center for Political Studies, 1968.

Robinson, John P. and Phillip R. Shaver. *Measures of social psychological attitudes.* Ann Arbor, Mich.: University of Michigan, Institute for Social Research, Survey Research Center, 1973.

Rosen, Pamela (Ed.) *Test collection bulletin: A quarterly digest of information on tests.* Princeton, N. J.: Educational Testing Serivce.

Shaw, Marvin E. and Jack M. Wright. *Scales for the measurement of attitudes.* New York: McGraw-Hill, 1967.

Wylie, Ruth C. *The self-concept: A review of methodological considerations and measuring instruments.* Volume One. Lincoln, Neb.: University of Nebraska Press, 1974.

CHAPTER SIX
ACHIEVEMENT TESTS AND EDUCATIONAL DECISIONS

For many types of decision by or about persons in and out of school, tests of achievement provide relevant information. In this chapter we will identify different types of decision and discuss for each the different types of achievement measure that might provide useful information to guide such a decision. In this connection we shall have occasion to contrast teacher-made tests and standardized tests, criterion-referenced tests and norm-referenced tests, diagnostic tests and survey tests, school-oriented tests and job-oriented tests. Each has distinctive characteristics and each has its own part to play in the total array of academic, vocational, and personal decisions.

DAY-BY-DAY INSTRUCTIONAL DECISIONS

One important role of assessments of achievement is to guide the day-by-day decisions of the classroom teacher as to what is to be taught, studied by, or practiced by child X, or to or by the class as a whole. The weekly spelling quiz, which determines what words will be reviewed—and perhaps written out 25 times—is a venerable and traditional classroom practice. Quizzes in spelling, grammar, or arithmetic have been prepared and used by teachers from time immemorial to guide their decisions on tomorrow's lesson or on the specific assignment for Jimmy or Marie.

Partly as a by-product of a renewed interest in individualization of instruction, which has been facilitated by the development of programmed instructional materials and by the availability of computers to handle some of the scoring and record keeping, there has been a burgeoning interest in tests to be used in guiding instructional decisions. If a pupil is working at an individual rate on a particular topic or skill, some procedure is needed to provide information on how well he has mastered the topic or skill, so that the teacher (or the student) can decide whether he needs to study it further or can move on advantageously to the next unit. This kind of information is especially relevant for subjects that are to some degree sequential—progress on Topic B being dependent upon an adequate understanding of Topic A. Of course mathematics is the prime example of such a subject, and it is for this reason that many illustrations of instructional tests of this type are drawn from the field of mathematics.

A test to measure competence in a specific topic or skill is clearly a very specific or focused test. It deals with the content of the specific topic, and the user generally sets some criterion—usually a pretty arbitrary one—as representing an adequate degree of competence. It is these properties that have led to the application of the terms content-referenced and criterion-referenced to tests of this kind. Such a test is designed to present a representative sample of tasks from a narrowly defined domain. Since the domain *is* relatively narrow, test items tend to be redundant, and it has seemed reasonable to expect that a person either will be able to answer all or almost all of the items, or else will perform not much better than at a chance level.

By way of illustration we show below two teacher-made criterion-referenced tests. The first is a test to see if the students in a fifth grade class know what a prime number is.* The second is a test of capitalization of proper names, designed to identify students who are having trouble with this writing skill.

TEST OF PRIME NUMBERS

Directions: Do you know what a prime number is? Look at the numbers shown below. Six of them are prime numbers. For each one, see if it is a *prime number*. If it is, draw a circle around it. If it is not, leave it unmarked.

31	47	143
33	49	293
35	51	415
38	59	763
41	97	942

* For those who have forgotten, or may have never known, a prime number is one that cannot be divided evenly by any number other than itself or unity. Examples are 11, 13, or 17.

TEST ON CAPITALIZATION

Read the paragraph. The punctuation is correct, and the words that begin a sentence have been capitalized. No other words have been capitalized. Some need to be. Draw a line under *each word* that should begin with a capital.

*   *   *

We saw mary yesterday. She said she had gone to chicago, illinois, to see her aunt helen. Her aunt took her for a drive along the shore of lake michigan. On the way they passed the conrad hilton hotel, where mary's uncle joseph works. Mary said that she had enjoyed the trip, but she was glad to be back home with her own friends.

You can see that each little test is quite short—there are 15 numbers in the first and 12 words that should be underlined in the second. Setting a criterion level of 90 percent correct on each test as constituting adequate competence permits the examinee to goof off on 1 item, but assumes that more frequent mistakes imply inadequate mastery of the concept or skill. These tests illustrate one extreme of breadth or scope for a test, and are clearly related to quite specific judgments about what a pupil has learned. They sample from narrowly and explicitly defined domains, and ones that are relatively easy to define.

In much of schooling, the domain that is represented by a unit of instruction is much fuzzier, and consequently the stock of admissible problems or questions is much less explicitly and clearly defined. Consider, for example, a unit of instruction on the Bill of Rights. We *could* test an individual's ability to *identify* or to *recall* each of the first 10 amendments to the Constitution. But if we were concerned with the meaning, the significance, and the application of these same 10 amendments in contemporary America, how could we meaningfully define and sample from that domain? In this instance the notion of "mastery" slips through our fingers. We may question whether even the Justices of the Supreme Court have really achieved complete mastery.

When it is impossible to define clearly the boundaries of a domain, it becomes simultaneously impossible to determine what constitutes a representative sample of exercises to assess degree of mastery of that domain. Different test makers may produce very different sorts of test exercises. At this point the concept of a content-referenced test with a specified criterion performance that represents a defined level of "mastery" loses much of its meaning. A teacher-made test may still provide some useful information to guide decisions about further teaching, but the information is not so sharp and focused as it is in the two illustrations shown on pp. 167–168. There is a good deal of ambiguity as to what any given score means so far as precisely what the student has learned and can do.

What guidelines can be set for the construction of criterion-referenced tests? We shall suggest three.

1. The test exercises should be broadly representative of the domain that is being sampled. Thus, if the domain is capitalization of proper names, the test should include the names of cities, rivers, mountains, and so forth, as well as the names of persons.

2. The test exercises should be free of irrelevant difficulties. Thus it probably would be inappropriate to include in the prime numbers test numbers such as 15017, 16541, and 17013, because the sheer computational burden of dividing these numbers by each prime number in turn would introduce difficulties that bore no real relationship to whether the student had the basic ability to define and identify prime numbers. The question should be asked for each test: Are the other aspects of the task simple enough *for the sort of pupils I am testing* so that the only probable cause of failure is inadequate mastery of the skill or concept that I wish to test for?

3. Tests for day-by-day instructional decisions should be short enough so that they are practical to prepare and to use in the classroom, but long enough so that a pupil is unlikely to achieve a qualifying score without having the required knowledge.

A number of tasks involving specific skills may really permit only two alternative responses, as in the two illustrations we provided. A number either is prime or can be factored; a word is capitalized or it isn't. We can ask in the case of tests of any specified length and number of response choices what the likelihood is that the pupil will get 80 percent or 90 percent of the items right by blind guessing. Results are shown in Table 6.1.

Table 6.1
PERCENTAGE DISPLAYING APPARENT MASTERY BY RANDOM GUESSING

	Percentage reaching 80%				Percentage reaching 90%			
	2-Choice	3-Choice	4-Choice	5-Choice	2-Choice	3-Choice	4-Choice	5-Choice
5 test items	18.8	4.5	1.5	0.5	3.1	0.4	0.1	0.03
10 test items	5.5	0.3	.04	0.01	1.1	0.03		
15 test items	1.8	.003			0.05			
20 test items	0.6				0.02			

Figure 6.1 shows for a 10-item test the percentage that could be expected to get each possible score in the case of a 2-choice and of a 4-choice item. From Table 6.1 and from Fig. 6.1 we can see that when the standard for performance is set at 80 or 90 percent right, a 10-item test with two-answer choices per item is barely adequate to differentiate between lucky guessers and those with some actual knowledge, but with 4-choice items, the 10-item test is quite adequate.

Of course it is an oversimplification to divide students into "guessers" and "knowers." Even in a domain as homogeneous as prime numbers, specific exercises differ markedly in diffi-

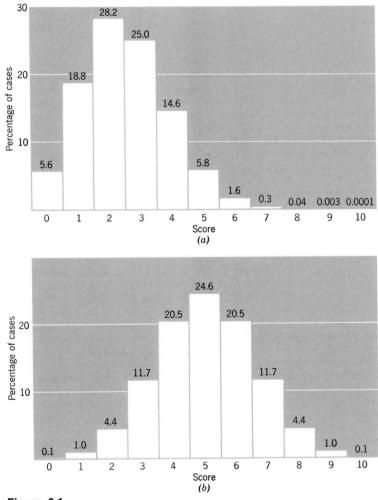

Figure 6.1
Score distributions resulting from random guessing for a 10-item test.
(a) 4-choice items; (b) 2-choice items.

culty. Thus when a student makes 1 or 2 errors in identifying numbers as prime, errors pile up on 51, 97, 143, and 293. Within the 1 or 2 error group, 56 percent of the responses to these 4 items were wrong, compared with 12 percent of the responses to the remaining 11 items. It appears, therefore, that whether a pupil will be judged to have satisfactory competence or not, even on these quite homogeneous exercises, depends very markedly on which tasks he is presented. If competence is being demanded for a *complete* skill, then it can only be tested efficiently by those test exercises involving the skill on which the less-than-perfect student is *likely* to make mistakes. The problem of selection of specific items becomes especially acute in schoolwide or statewide surveys in which only one or two exercises may be used to represent a complete skill area.

One of the issues that tends to be dealt with inadequately by the proponents of criterion-referenced tests is how to decide on an appropriate criterion level. When subsequent units build upon mastery of prior units, it is possible to determine, through rather time-consuming and painstaking research, what level of mastery on a test on Unit A is required to make it probable (at some specified level of probability) that the pupil will reach some criterion level on Unit B within the standard period of instruction. Research to provide this information is the exception, however, and in most cases criterion levels are set somewhat arbitrarily. It would be possible, of course, to set a criterion level of what children *should* achieve on the basis of previous experience of what most children *do* achieve. But as soon as we do this we introduce a comparative, or norm-referenced, interpretation, and the notion of an absolute criterion level is lost.

In the past, highly specific mini-tests to guide instructional decisions were produced primarily by teachers for their own use. However, in the last few years a number of test publishers have started to produce sets of such tests as aids to the classroom teacher. These are typically single-sheet tests with 10 to 20 items. Some use the relatively novel latent image printing process. The examinee is given a chemically impregnated crayon or felt-tipped pen to mark his answer choice. When the choice is marked, a printed letter appears (T or F; R or W) giving the examinee immediate feeback on whether he has made the correct choice. A count of the errors provides an immediate score, without any further work by the teacher. Some of the available test series of this type are listed and briefly described in Appendix IV.

STUDENT APPRAISAL DECISIONS

Classroom tests are needed not only for information about pupil or class level of mastery of highly specific skills, but also for a more general picture of progress in a segment of the school program. Each teacher has the responsibility to report, for the information of student and parent and for use in a variety of decisions within the school, how well each student is progressing in acquiring the broad range of skill, knowledge, and understanding that represents the objectives of a course or similar segment of the school program. In this assessment it is important to determine not merely that a student has mastered, but that for some period of time he has retained that mastery of the skills and concepts that represent specific objectives of a course. It is for this purpose that unit, semester, and comprehensive examinations are needed. Since such examinations typically have as their function to determine how well an individual has learned and retained the material taught in a *specific* course or program, they are usually most appropriately prepared by the teacher or group of teachers who have designed and presented the instruction. The planning of such tests of achievement, and the writing of exercises for them, will be considered in the following chapter. Published tests are rarely as appropriate for appraising how well a student has learned what has been taught in a specific course with specific content and objectives as are tests prepared with just that end in view. The relation of test results to the assignment of course grades is discussed in Chapter 15.

TESTING FOR DIAGNOSTIC AND REMEDIAL DECISIONS

Decisions relating to remedial instruction constitute one subset of instructional decisions. Diagnostic tests given for the purpose of helping with those decisions are in some ways very similar to content- or criterion-referenced tests: one tends to focus on specific competencies and the other tries to identify specific deficiencies. However, diagnostic testing is not ordinarily based on immediate past instruction; it grows out of a child's general educational problem, such as inadequate reading, and is directed toward understanding the dimensions and the roots of that present difficulty.

Like a content-referenced test, to be useful a diagnostic test needs to be sharply focused. Each test must give evidence on the strength or weakness of a very specific skill, and collectively a diagnostic test battery should cover most or all of the specific skills that underlie the more general skill that we call "reading," or "long division," or "expository writing." Whereas day-by-day instructional tests are primarily forward looking (asking, "Where do we go from here?"), diagnostic tests are primarily backward looking (asking, "How did the present difficulty develop?").

The foundation upon which any program of diagnostic testing is built is a thorough and precise analysis of the skills that are required if one is to perform the complex task currently under study. Thus a child who is to begin to move ahead in reading must have at least the following skills.

1. Maintain a left-to-right orientation as he decodes words and puts them together in sentences.

2. Recognize the visual forms of the letters of the alphabet.

3. Transform the visual forms of letters and of letter combinations into their auditory equivalents.

4. Recognize the spaces in a text as the boundaries that set off separate words.

5. Give proper phonetic values to the initial and final letters in a word unit.

6. Analyze and combine the visual elements that constitute a word and give them the proper phonetic values.

7. Assign meaning to the phonetic pattern that constitutes a word.

8. Assign meaning to the sequence of words that constitutes a sentence.

9. Recognize the role of punctuation and capitalization in organizing the words and sentences into a message.

This is a relatively brief and superficial analysis of the processes involved in beginning reading. Yet it already suggests some of the diagnostic tests that might be helpful in understanding the problems that some particular child is having with the early development of reading skills.

Does the child have difficulty in maintaining a consistent left-right orientation within and between words? Within-word orientation can be tested with a list of words that are meaningful read from either end, word pairs such as

pat	tap
was	saw
bad	dab

Evidence of difficulty in a between-word left-right orientation may appear in reversals of word sequence in oral reading, and can be assessed by an oral reading exercise.

Can the child recognize the visual forms of the letters of the alphabet? It is simple enough to show him the letters, one at a time, and ask him to name each one. For a test such as this we would want to be sure to include the easily confused letters, such as b, d, p, and q and check especially to see if the pupil mixed these up—which would, incidentally, be a form of letter reversal.

Can the child match the sounds of single letters or letter combinations with the visual forms of the letters? The examiner can sound the letter or letter combination and call upon the pupil to mark the proper choice from a set of alternatives that might look like the following:

Stimulus (Spoken)	*Choices (Printed)*			
b — be	d	p	b	g
bl — black	br	pl	cl	bl
tr — tr	fly	tie	try	pry

In the same way, tests may be designed for each other specific skill that is identified as a contributor to or prerequisite for the complex skill of reading. The relevance and effectiveness of the diagnostic battery will depend most critically upon shrewdness and thoroughness in analysis of the complex task and in breaking it into its component skills. They will depend secondarily on ingenuity in presenting these component skills in simple, efficient test exercises. In the case of reading, a number of authors have published batteries of diagnostic tests based upon their analyses of the reading task and their identification of important component skills. By way of illustration, the *Gates-McKillop Reading Diagnostic Test* includes the following subtests.

1. *Oral Reading:* Seven paragraphs of increasing difficulty are presented for the student to read orally. The words used provide many opportunities for the student both to make errors and to apply word attack skills. The more difficult passages are hard enough to challenge even fairly able elementary school pupils.

2. *Words: Flash Presentation:* Words of increasing difficulty are exposed to view for $\frac{1}{2}$ second and the examinee must identify the word.

3. *Words: Untimed Presentation:* Examinee reads words of increasing difficulty and complexity. The examiner keeps a record of the methods of word attack used.

4. *Phrases: Flash Presentation:* Examinee must read phrases of 2 to 4 words after ½ second of exposure.

5. *Knowledge of Word Parts:* Word Attack.

5-1. *Recognizing and Blending Common Word Parts:* Examinee is required to read a list of nonsense words that are made up of common word sounds.

5-2. *Giving Letter Sounds:* Examinee gives the sounds of the letters of the alphabet.

5-3. *Naming Capital Letters.*

5-4. *Naming Lowercase Letters.*

6. *Recognizing the Visual Form of Sounds.*

6-1. *Nonsense Words:* Examinee identifies the written form of the nonsense word pronounced by the examiner.

6-2. *Initial Letters:* Examinee identifies the written form of the first letter of a word pronounced by the examiner.

6-3. *Final Letters:* Examinee identifies last letter of a word pronounced by the examiner.

6-4. *Vowels:* Examinee identifies the vowel used in the middle of a nonsense word.

7. *Auditory Blending:* Examinee pronounces a word that the examiner has given in parts, for example, ch — ump.

In addition to the basic tests there are four supplementary tests: spelling, oral vocabulary, syllabication, and auditory discrimination.

Other diagnostic reading tests are listed and briefly described in Appendix IV.

Diagnostic tests for beginning reading have been rather extensively developed—in part because of the importance of this basic skill and in part because the skill has been analyzed in some detail. There is no comparable supply of tests for example, for effective writing skills, in part because the skills of effective (as distinct from grammatically correct) writing are not as readily identified by analysis and in part because it is more difficult to generate test formats through which single component skills can be displayed.

Some diagnostic tests are essentially criterion referenced, in that it is reasonable to expect perfect or near-perfect performance. Thus by the second or third grade we would expect the average pupil to recognize all of the letters of the alphabet, and failure to do so would indicate a deficiency in one basic skill. Other diagnostic tests assess skills that may exist at a considerable range of levels. Thus vocabulary or word-recognition skills are ones that vary widely in degree among elementary school pupils, and for these it hardly makes sense to inquire whether any given pupil has achieved "mastery" of that component of reading. The reasonable question is whether he is doing as well as we would expect for a person of his level—as represented by age, grade level, or level of mental maturity. What we would expect is established, of course, by what other children do in fact do, so for these tests we must fall back on what is essentially a normative interpretation. Though norms are frequently based on somewhat limited data, they are usually available for published diagnostic tests.

There are on the educational scene quite a variety of tests that bear the label "diagnostic" or that are promoted for their diagnostic potential. In one sense any test that yields more than a single score can claim to be considered a diagnostic test. When you encounter such a test, you should ask two kinds of questions.

1. Statistically, how distinguishable are the several scores that the test yields? Taking account of the unreliability of each score, are they really measuring anything different? For example, in the *Stanford Diagnostic Reading Test,* a test entitled *Beginning and Ending Sounds* shows a correlation of .81 with a test entitled *Blending.* Though each of the tests *is* quite reliable, both appear to measure so nearly the same skill that there would be few cases indeed in which we could feel with confidence that a child has done better on one of these tests than on the other.

2. How clearly do the subtests correspond to teachable skills, so that a test deficiency points the direction for remedial action? If we find that a child who is having difficulty with a math unit on factoring fails miserably on a test on prime numbers, we have both identified one likely source of his difficulty with the unit on factoring and spotted one lacking key concept that can be taught directly. By contrast, if we find that a child does poorly on a test of *Sentence Comprehension* (a subtest of the early *Iowa Silent Reading Test*), what guide does that give us for action? Do we have him read lots of sentences? Do we have him analyze the grammatical structure of sentences? Or what? A specific diagnostic test is useful to the degree that its difficulty lies within a single identified subskill, so that a deficiency on the test provides a direct cue for remedial teaching.

Though achievement tests focused on specific facets of skill are important aids in educational diagnosis, it is important to realize that they provide only a part of the needed information. One fairly obvious question, sometimes overlooked by educators, is whether a child has normal vision and hearing. Some "slow" children have been in school for years before it is discovered that they have a hearing loss.

A measure of general academic aptitude, preferably a non-reading measure, helps to indicate whether academic difficulty is specific to some school subject or is a reflection of a more general difficulty in abstract thinking. Information on home conditions, home resources, and home support for learning can help to provide a more rounded picture of an academic problem. Diagnostic study of an academic difficulty involves a wide-ranging study of the individual child, in which sharply focused tests of specific underlying academic skills provide *one* important part.

PLACEMENT DECISIONS

There are a number of occasions in education when alternative paths or programs are available and a decision must be made for or by each student as to which option that student is to pursue. At the college freshman level, for example, a number of colleges have different levels of courses in English or in math open to freshmen. Should Evelyn Johnson be placed in the remedial writing section, the regular section of freshman English, or a special class in creative writing? Should Julius Jurinski go into a section of the math course that assumes only minimal competence in high school algebra, into a course in the fundamentals of analytic geometry, or into a course that moves directly into differential and integral calculus? Other placement decisions arise at the high school level as different options in program and in sectioning become available. Admission to "advanced placement" sections of upper level courses to prepare and qualify for exemption from college freshman courses is a case in point. And the perennial problem of whether and how to provide for homogeneous grouping in the elementary school is another illustration. A somewhat different sort of placement problem arises whenever a program of individualized instruction is initiated or a transfer student must be fitted into an ongoing program. The problem then is: Where should each person enter into the programmed sequence of units and learning activities?

It is perhaps appropriate to ask: For whose benefit is the placement decision being made? The immediate and obvious answer is that the decision on the placement of Evelyn Johnson is being made in order to provide the best learning opportunities for Evelyn Johnson. And in part this is true—but it is an oversimplification. Placement decisions are made in some part with concern for the other students who would be in the class to which Evelyn might be assigned, and in some part with concern for the teacher of that class. To put Evelyn, who is a minimally competent writer, in a creative writing class might be bad for Evelyn, in that she would learn less and make less progress than if she were in a remedial program designed primarily to remedy basic deficiencies in writing skills—or it might not. But her presence in the class could very possibly constitute an irritation to the others in the class if her problems and questions were quite different from theirs and if class time were devoted to answering questions to which the rest of the group already knew the answer or to dealing with problems that the others had already solved. Her presence could be frustrating to the teacher, whose efforts to deal with the group more or less as a unit would be blocked by the need to provide special and very different instruction for this student. The point is that motivations for placement of deviant students in special groups are mixed motivations involving not only the welfare of the individual student but also the comfort of the other students and the convenience of the teacher. The mixed motives back of many placement decisions rule out any neat and elegant procedures for optimizing the decision.

Let us return to the specific student about whom a placement decision is being made. Assignment to treatment A (a particular course, section of the class, or entry point for instruction) rather than treatment B might seem advantageous either because the two treatments differ, in whole or in part, in the goals toward which they are directed or because they differ in the means or route to common goals. Thus the prime goal of a remedial college English section might be correctness and clarity in writing simple exposition, while the prime goal of the creative writing class might be originality and dramatic effectiveness in writing narrative prose or poetry. Different goals are seen as appropriate for the two groups. On the other hand, the goals of both a regular and an advanced placement section of high school mathematics might be progress toward and mastery of a domain that we designate "mathematical analysis," but with the expectation that the advance placement group would pursue topics in greater depth and at a faster tempo. It might then be that a common assessment procedure would indicate how far the members of each group had progressed toward their common goal.

In this last type of situation the question we ask is: In which type of section would a given student be likely to make the best progress? Suppose we gave each student a survey test of math achievement at the end of grade 10, at the time that the decision on placement was to be made. Suppose that we then assigned some students randomly to treatment A (the regular section) and some to treatment B (the enriched or accelerated section). Suppose, finally, at the end of grade 12 we gave a common comprehensive test based on the full range of objectives sought for either or both treatments. We would be likely to find a situation somewhat like that shown in Fig. 6.2.

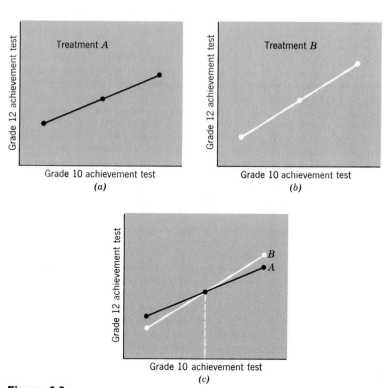

Figure 6.2

Average final achievement as a function of initial achievement and educational treatment.

The diagram shows that on the average the students who had better achievement in grade 10 still had better achievement at the end of grade 12. This will almost universally be the case. However, of more interest is the comparison of the lines relating final to initial achievement (called *regression lines*) for treatments A and B. These are shown plotted together in Fig. 6.2c. This chart shows that the relation of final to initial achievement was closer (the regression line is steeper) for treatment B than it was for treatment A. Those who were poor achievers in grade 10 did *relatively* better under treatment A than under treatment B, while those who were better achievers in grade 10 did *relatively* better under treatment B. The crossover point is indicated at score X on the tenth grade measure. If this situation prevailed, then students scoring below X in the tenth grade could be placed advantageously in treatment A, while those above X would be better off under treatment B. (This type of relationship is sometimes spoken of as *trait-treatment interaction.*)

Fig. 6.2 illustrates circumstances under which placement in different treatments can clearly contribute to better learning. However the situation is not always so clear as this. Fig. 6.3 shows several other models of what the outcome might be. In Model I (Fig. 6.3a) achievement is just the same for both treatments at all levels of initial ability. The initially abler students do better no matter where they are assigned, but placement in one or the other treatment makes no difference. Model II (Fig. 6.3b) illustrates the case in which one treatment (here designated as A) is better for all levels, and equally so at all levels. Model III illustrates a case in which the advantage of treatment A becomes greater at the higher ability levels, and Model IV a case where it becomes less—but in both of these models the soundest strategy would still be to place *all* students in treatment A, because all tend to learn more under this treatment. The purpose of showing these illustrations is to point out that it is only under the conditions illustrated in Fig. 6.2 that placement in different treatments makes sense, and to emphasize that we really need the kind of information that is displayed in these charts if we are to judge whether placement of some students in one and some in another treatment makes sense.

Over the years it has seemed reasonable to use some test of initial achievement as the basis or a part of the basis for placement decisions in which different students are placed in different treatments in order to facilitate their learning (and learning by the other members of each group). However, research

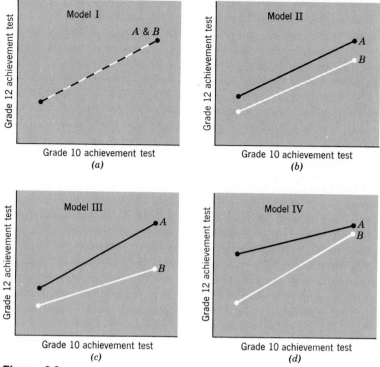

Figure 6.3
Various patterns of final achievement as a function of initial achievement and educational treatment. (a) Model I; (b) Model II; (c) Model III; (d) Model IV.

evidence on the gains from such placement is quite mixed. A number of factors contribute to ambiguity in the results. The bases on which grouping was carried out have varied from study to study. Grouping has often been on some general appraisal of academic performance or academic aptitude, rather than upon entry status in specific subject-oriented skills. It is often not clear how much or in what ways the treatment has varied for different groups—and if there is no noticeable adaptation of the treatment, there is no good reason to expect differences in outcomes. And we are not sure to what extent common objectives characterize the different treatments, or to what extent they really have different goals so that no common instrument to appraise learnings would be appropriate. Without being able to document the belief in any systematic way, it is our conviction that tests are most likely to permit constructive placement decisions when (1) the tests relate to very specific entry knowledge and skills for one particular subject area, and (2) the alternative instructional treatments will differ substantially in method and content as well as in tempo. This implies that the most useful placement tests are likely to be centered in an area of subject matter. Examination of published tests may identify one or more whose content focuses on the desired entry skills. Failing that, it may be necessary to develop a locally made test that has the desired focus.

COUNSELING AND GUIDANCE DECISIONS

The decision to place a student in one section of a class or in one course or program is a decision oriented primarily toward optimizing the learning opportunities for that student, and thus toward guiding the student into experiences that will be rewarding and productive. There are a number of other situations in which good measures of achievement can be helpful in contributing to counseling decisions by or for the student. These relate on the one hand to the acceptability of the student's current academic progress, and on the other to plans for the student's future.

ASSESSING ACCEPTABILITY OF ACADEMIC PROGRESS

It is important to the student, to the parents, and to the school to know whether a particular student is making satisfactory progress in school work. To the student, evidence of progress and accomplishment is a substantial motivating force, and evidence of specific difficulties provides a cue to seek help to overcome the difficulties. Focused tests of the sort discussed in the first section of this chapter provide an important form of feedback to guide student as well as teacher in identifying gaps in knowledge or skill that call for further study or practice.

Parents are in most cases vitally concerned with the progress of their children in school. Of course families do differ a good deal in the depth of this concern, and differ a good deal more in the resources that they provide for coaching in school skills and for supporting the child's efforts at learning. At one extreme, some parents can function as informed and knowledgeable teachers; at the other, they are able to offer the child little or nothing as tutors and rather inadequate physical and social conditions to support his own efforts at learning. But parents must certainly be considered partners with the school in the child's learning activities, and, if they are to be effective partners, they need to know both in general how their child is progressing and more specifically where he is in each school subject and in which he is encountering difficulties. Test results of all kinds provide a tangible basis for communication from school to parent, and for interpretation of the student's progress and difficulties. As we shall see, interpretations may be of two kinds. The teacher/school may provide a criterion-referenced interpretation that reports to a parent some specific competencies that the child has recently developed to a satisfactory level of mastery or some specific skills with which he is currently having difficulty. On the other hand, a norm-referenced interpretation may be given that compares the child's general level of performance in a subject area with that of his class, his school, or a broader regional or national reference group. His performance may also be compared with the level of performance to be expected in the light of what is known about his potential for school learning.

School personnel, too, need to judge whether a child's progress is acceptable in the light of what is known about his abilities in order to decide whether any special study needs to be made of the child. If progress falls well below what should be expected, more intensive diagnostic study may be indicated in order to try to pinpoint sources of difficulty and plan a program of corrective action.

These needs bring us face to face with the problem of determining whether a child is showing acceptable progress. This is a tricky problem, a controversial problem, a politically sensitive or even explosive problem. We shall explore three definitions of acceptable performance that we have labeled (1) performance in relation to perfection, (2) performance in relation to par, and (3) performance in relation to potential.

Performance in relation to perfection is the standard that is typically applied to criterion-referenced tests of the sort discussed on pp. 167–168. We ask: How close did the student come to exhibiting a perfect score on the quiz that we gave him? We are likely to interpret a perfect score as "complete mastery"— but this is dangerous interpretation even in the case of a narrowly focused test and is completely inappropriate for a test that covers a fairly broad domain. In the latter case there are always more difficult tasks that could have been set for the examinee, and we never can say that he knows *everything* there is to know about a subject. Even with tasks as specific as identifying prime numbers, some numbers turn out to be a good deal more difficult than others. So "perfection" is displayed only on the specific sample of tasks that is used to represent the domain. Interpreting "80 percent correct" on the usual teacher-made test as "knows 80 percent of the subject" is completely absurd, and at most the interpretation might be "knows 80 percent of the answers that the teacher thinks a pupil might be expected to know." On the other hand, this standard of "what the teacher expects" is a very real one, and can be important to both pupil and parent.

By *performance in relation to par* we have in mind the typical norm-referenced interpretation of a test score. In this case adequacy of performance is defined by the performance of others. For a teacher-made test it may be that student's standing in *his* class. For the published test it is a student's standing in relation to a broader reference group, such as all children at his age level or his grade level.

Even with criterion-referenced testing there can be a par. Par is then represented by the *rate* at which the individual reaches the criterion level in successive skills, or the number of skills "mastered" in a certain period of time. Some such interpretation *must* be available if a parent asks: "How is Ellen doing? Should I be pleased with her progress, or concerned?" Unfortunately, in much of the current enthusiasm for criterion-referenced tests, little recognition is given to this need and little provision is made for meeting it. At the least, a school or teacher needs some informal records of the rate of progress that is typical in individualized instruction and criterion-referenced testing, so that some type of par or standard can be established to define typical progress.

In Chapter 4, we discussed various sorts of converted scores, using different score scales and reference frames for reporting the score of an individual. We expressed a general preference for percentile rank, standard score, or stanine, as representing a student's performance in relation to performance of other members of a group in which he logically belongs. The one that probably conveys the most immediate meaning to a parent or other person not particularly sophisticated about measurement issues is the score reported in terms of relative position—"at the 15th percentile," "in the second tenth," "in the bottom quarter."

Two aspects of such a report are troubling. One is that it is possible (though perhaps not likely) that within a specific class the differences of performance are so small that the distinction between "top quarter" and "bottom quarter" is of no practical importance. That is, one may be forcing distinctions where no real differences exist. The other is that use of the group as a standard means that there must always be 50 percent of the total group who are "below the average," 25 percent who are "in the bottom quarter," with the implication that they have somehow "failed." We face a basic problem in our use of language, in which "average" means to the statistician, "middle of the group," but has come to have the connotation in everyday speech of "minimum acceptable," so that anything below the average carries the connotation of "unacceptable." Somehow, the two interpretations of "average" must be separated in our thinking, so that the student who falls at the 20th or 30th percentile of his group on some measure is not viewed as a failure.

With a published test the normative data supplied by the publisher permit "par" to be referred to some national or regional group, or the school system may develop system-wide norms. The use of national norms may ease the pressure on some fortunately situated schools that draw primarily from an advantaged community in which most children approach or exceed the national average. However, if this par is used, it serves to accentuate the sense of failure in schools from districts or communities that are at the low end of the scale in economic and cultural resources, where a very large proportion of the students will not reach the national or regional average. A blind application of national norms, whether to schools or individuals, cannot fail to lead to unreality and frustration.

It is recognition of the inequity of assessing performance in relation to a uniform and unvarying par that has led tests users and educational evaluators in general to try to express *performance in relation to potential.* This orientation rejects the notion that all persons are identical and interchangeable and that the same par is applicable to each. It tries to establish a par for each person. It asks: In the light of all we know about this child, what level of performance should we reasonably expect?

This is an easy question to phrase. When we start to explore it, however, we find that it becomes a tricky one to answer, with a wide range of technical and even ethical overtones. How do we decide what level of achievement we can reasonably expect of an individual?

That expectation must be tempered by what we know about a person is readily demonstrated if we consider the simple factor of age. We know that it is unreasonable to expect an 8-year-old to jump as far, run as fast, read as well, or do as wide a range of arithmetic problems as a 12-year-old. But 8-year-olds differ in size. Perhaps it is unreasonable to expect an undersize 8-year-old to jump as far as an oversize one. And, by the same token, 8-year-olds differ in their performance on tests

Table 6.2

IOWA TESTS OF BASIC SKILLS READING TEST GRADE EQUIVALENTS OF SELECTED PERCENTILES FOR SIXTH GRADERS, BY LEVEL OF NON-VERBAL STANDARD AGE SCORE COGNITIVE ABILITY TEST (C.A.T.)

Reading Percentile	CAT Non-Verbal SAS Band							
	Below 70	70–79	80–89	90–99	100–109	110–119	120–129	130+
99	6.1+	7.1+	7.6+	8.3+	9.0+	9.6+	10.1+	10.6+
95	5.7	6.5	7.0	7.7	8.4	8.9	9.4	10.0
90	5.4	6.1	6.6	7.3	8.0	8.5	9.0	9.6
75	4.9	5.3	5.9	6.6	7.3	7.9	8.4	9.0
50	4.2	4.7	5.1	5.8	6.5	7.1	7.7	8.2
25	3.6	4.0	4.4	5.1	5.7	6.3	6.9	7.5
10	3.1	3.4	3.8	4.4	4.9	5.5	6.1	6.7
5	2.8	3.1	3.5	3.9	4.5	5.1	5.7	6.2
1	2.5−	2.6−	3.1−	3.5−	3.8−	4.4−	5.2−	5.7−

designed to measure their general intellectual development. Perhaps it is unreasonable to expect the same level of reading or arithmetic performance from a child who scores low on a scholastic aptitude test as from one who scores high. As a matter of observed fact, there is no question that children who score low on a test designed to assess general scholastic aptitude *do* tend to perform less well on measures of reading, arithmetic, or other aspects of academic achievement. Our basic problem is to decide whether these children have less *potential* for academic achievement.

In a statistical sense, the answer is certainly: Yes. As a matter of statistical fact, there is a substantial correlation between measures designed to assess general intellectual ability and measures designed to assess academic achievement. Children with low IQs *tend* to be poor readers and those with high IQs to be good readers. We can prepare an *expectancy table* showing the probable level of achievement for individuals at different IQ levels. Part of such a table is shown in Table 6.2. This table shows the percentile ranks on the *Iowa Tests of Basic Skills Reading* for sixth grade pupils at different aptitude levels on the *Cognitive Ability Test, Non-Verbal.* The body of this table shows reading grade equivalent scores. Thus, for a sixth grader with a *Cognitive Ability Test* Standard Age Score* of 70 or less, a reading grade equivalent of 4.4 is a little above average. This same reading level falls at the 25th percentile of those in the 80–89 Standard Age Score band, and at the 10th percentile of those in the 90–99 SAS band. If we accept the *Cognitive Abilities Test*

* Standard scores with a mean of 100 and a standard deviation of 16.

as a measure of potential (and this remains a big "if"), then the reading grade equivalent of 4.4 is as good as we should expect for the sixth grader with SAS below 70, is somewhat below expectations for the child with SAS in the 80s, definitely below expectation when the SAS is in the 90s, and almost unbelievably bad for a child with SAS over 110. Similar tables are supplied by a number of the publishers of standardized tests, covering all subject areas and all grade levels.

"Expected achievement" can be determined not only for groups performing at different levels on tests of general cognitive abilities, but also for schools serving children of different demographic backgrounds. Table 6.3 shows percentile values for schools in several different settings. The first two columns show the extent of differences between two major regions in the USA. The differences are real, though not very large. The next column shows results obtained in large cities, and the lower performance is more noticeable. The final two columns compare a group of suburban schools with a group of schools from inner city deprived neighborhoods and here, of course, the differences are striking. A score that would be just average in the suburban schools would fall above the 99th percentile in the other set.

The basic questions are: How should we interpret and how should we use the information that shows how achievement does in fact differ as a function of measures of scholastic aptitude or as a function of demographic facts about the commu-

Table 6.3

ITBS READING TEST GRADE EQUIVALENTS OF SELECTED PERCENTILES FOR SIXTH GRADERS FROM SEVERAL DEMOGRAPHIC GROUPS

	Demographic Group				
Reading Percentile	**Region 1**	**Region 2**	**Large City**	**Suburb**	**Schools in Deprived Neighborhoods**
99	9.8+	9.8+	9.2+	10.6+	7.8+
95	9.0	9.2	8.7	9.9	7.5
90	8.5	8.7	8.2	9.5	7.3
75	7.6	7.8	7.3	8.7	6.2
50	6.4	6.7	6.2	8.0	4.9
25	5.4	5.6	5.1	7.3	4.0
10	4.6	4.6	4.3	6.7	3.3
5	3.9	4.2	3.9	6.4	3.0
1	3.4−	3.4−	3.4−	6.0−	2.2−

nity from which the school draws? Should we consider those variables that are related to score to be measures of potential in some fundamental, perhaps biological sense? Should we think of them as somehow setting a ceiling on what can be achieved? Should we think of measured aptitude as in some way a "cause" of later achievement? Or should we think of a "scholastic aptitude" test as just another, somewhat more general measure of achievement—a measure that is as much subject to improvement or decline as are measures of the specific academic skills? Should we set the same standard for all individuals and all groups? To deny the reality of individual and group differences in achievement seems to be to take flight from the world in which we live. But to accept the world in which we live as the inevitably given may be to deny the possibility that educational developments and social reforms can change our world for the better. It is not easy to maintain a balance between realism and hope.

What *is* a scientifically sound, educationally constructive, and ethically defensible approach to using those individual-to-individual and school-to-school differences in background variables in interpreting achievement? At the level of the individual child, the immediate practical decisions are of two types: (1) What message about school achievement should one communicate to the parent or a child when the child's aptitude appears to be clearly below (or above) that of the other children in the group? (2) How should plans for special diagnostic study or a special instructional program be modified by knowledge about the child's background or level of performance on an aptitude test? Some further consideration of this problem will be found in Chapter 9, after a review of the nature of tests of scholastic aptitude.

PLANNING EDUCATIONAL FUTURES

As children progress through the school system they move closer and closer to, and finally reach, points of decision concerning future educational plans. Past achievement is certainly one type of information that should influence such decisions. Present measured achievement is one of the best predictors we have of future achievement in the same field. General level of achievement is significant in a decision of how high to plan to aim in the educational scheme of things, and relative achievement in different fields can be a factor in the decision as to what specialization to pursue at a given level. School marks provide one indicator of achievement, and in some ways the most relevant indicator, but the variability of standards from teacher to teacher within a school and from school to school limit the value of marks as guides to planning academic futures. Marks are personal and local in their significance. For this reason, standardized tests, with broadly representative norms and norms that are comparable from one content area to another, provide a more uniform and universal basis for appraising overall level of achievement and specific strengths and weaknesses.

Two mistakes must be avoided in using test results for planning purposes. One is premature decision making. Individuals do change, and present performance predicts the future imperfectly. A counselor is ill advised to close out options—such as going to college—prematurely. The other is a predominately negative use of test results. Test scores are more constructive if they are used to open doors rather than to close them. It is as important that test results serve to identify talent and encourage its further development as that they redirect those for whom the typical college education seems an unrealistic goal.

SELECTION DECISIONS

Whereas placement decisions represent attempts to achieve the most for the individual who is being placed in one or another treatment (using treatment in the broad sense of educational programs, as well as the narrower sense of remedial treatment), selection decisions represent attempts to pick the persons who will have the greatest utility to an organization. The term *utility* is used in the general economic sense of value received, in whatever currency value can be expressed. Thus value for an employer hiring a typist might be expressed (crudely) as number of error-free lines of text typed in an average working day, whereas value for a college might be expressed (perhaps even more crudely and incompletely) as freshman grade-point average. In the simplest terms the purpose of a system for selection decisions is to hire or admit those individuals who will maximize the total value or utility to the institution.

It should be clear that the notion of utility or value is both fuzzy and complex. Any simple indicator, such as lines typed or GPA is at best a rough, pragmatic approximation to a person's true utility to an organization, be it employer or educational institution. The problems of criterion measures have already been discussed in some detail in Chapter 3, and will not be dealt with further here. The point that needs to be recognized is that past achievements, as represented by present performance, often have a good deal of validity as predictors of future utility. Thus high school grades consistently have been found to be among the best predictors of future college grades, and job skills at the time of employment provide a good indication of what those same skills will be on the job.

The rationale for using an objective test of achievement in one or more academic subjects to replace or supplement high school grades as a predictor of college success is that such a test provides a uniform set of tasks for all applicants, and thus provides a way of equating or calibrating the rather different marking standards of different secondary schools. However, this calibration can be done equally well by the measures of more generalized scholastic abilities found in scholastic aptitude tests. Furthermore, these measures tend to be rather less dependent on what has been specifically taught in each school. For this reason the widely used college admission tests (*College Board Scholastic Aptitude Test, American College Testing Program Tests*) have been based on rather general reading, verbal, and quantitative skills.

In the world of work academic achievement tests would appear to have relatively little role as selection devices. What *do* seem to have important potential are *proficiency* tests that test specific job skills. This is true especially of those jobs in which a person is employed on the basis of skills already possessed, rather than on the basis of potential for learning new skills. Examples would be found in almost any of the skilled trades— carpenter, machinist, electrician—as well as in office jobs such as typist, bookkeeper, or computer programmer.

A few published job proficiency tests exist, primarily for office skills. However, for most situations, a proficiency test will have to be developed locally. The steps in development of a proficiency test are essentially as follows.

1. A careful and critical study of the job, to determine what the person must know and what skills he must possess to carry out the duties of the job.

2. Selection of certain aspects of the job that are both important and susceptible to appraisal by a test.

3. Development of a test plan. To the extent that one is testing job *knowledge*, the plan can take the form of a blueprint similar to that for an achievement test, to be described in Chapter 7. When one is concerned with measuring a skill, such as typing or driving a vehicle, the plan should set forth in some

detail the nature of the task to be presented, the equipment to be used, the conditions under which the task is to be done, and the bases for scoring the performance or product.

4. Preparation of test exercises, directions for administration and scoring, and materials, in accordance with the plan.

5. Preliminary tryout, perhaps with a group of employees, to permit review, editing, and selection of test exercises, to clear up any problems of test administration and (especially for performance tests) of scoring the performance or product.

6. Administration of the test to a sample of persons employed in the job, to determine what level of performance represents a reasonable standard of competence.

CURRICULAR DECISIONS

One function for which measures of achievement are needed is for the evaluation of alternative curricular materials or instructional designs. In education there is a steady flow of proposals for change—change in curricular emphasis, change in instructional materials, change in instructional procedures. If innovations are to be introduced rationally rather than capriciously, and if education is to show any cumulative progress in effectiveness rather than an oscillation from one fad to another, systematic evaluation of the outcomes from any change is imperative. Carrying out adequate studies to evaluate any proposed change is admittedly difficult. Much educational research is inconclusive as a result of the technical complexities that are involved. But without evaluative research studies, decisions to change are made blindly, supported only by the eloquence of the proponent.

A first requirement of any evaluative research is clear specification of what a proposed innovation is designed to achieve. That is, we need a statement of the objectives of the program. The statement needs to be comprehensive, covering the full range of outcomes sought by the proposed new program, as well as those sought by the program that it is designed to replace. Thus if a revised math program is designed to produce improved understanding of the number system, and the program is replacing one that has emphasized computational skills, it is important that in the evaluation of the outcomes the two programs be compared *both* on understanding of the number system *and* on computational skills. A decision between the two systems can only be made on a rational basis if we know how well each program achieves not only its own focal objectives, but also the objectives focal to the other. We are then in a position to weight the importance of the several aspects of achievement in terms of a specified system of values, and come up with a composite decision as to which set of outcomes is to be preferred.

The form in which objectives can be expressed most suitably will be discussed in some detail in Chapter 7. The need to phrase objectives in terms of observable behavior will be emphasized. However, objectives may be phrased at quite different levels of generality. "Understanding of the number system" represents a very broad statement indeed. Such a statement may be useful in summarizing a major area of concern, but it must be much further specified if it is to guide the planning of either instructional or evaluation procedures. The general objective could include a number of explicit performances such as "Given a 4-digit number such as 7362, identifies the number of thousands, hundreds, tens, or units in the number." These more specific performances serve to define in terms of a reasonably complete array of illustrations what is meant by "understanding of the number system." The point is that in thinking about what a program is designed to achieve we tend to organize our thinking around a manageably small set of general categories. However, for the general categories to acquire real substance and meaning, each must be elaborated into an array of specifics that tell what is to be taught and what is to be assessed.

Once the objectives of an instructional program have been stated, with enough detail and explicitness to guide instruction and evaluation, we may ask whether some or all of those objectives can be assessed appropriately by use of existing published tests. There is, of course, a certain economy of time and effort in using an already existing test, as well as some gain in the availability of normative data. When the design for a published test is prepared, it involves a fairly thorough analysis of the content and objectives of the field that it is to cover. This analysis may have been made some years before publication, and it will have been made in terms of a general rather than a special or a local curriculum. But much of the content of education changes slowly, and there is much that is common in the objectives of educational programs that differ in form and in specific content. So it will pay to examine existing tests before trying to mobilize the resources of time, skill, and money to produce a new test specifically for the local evaluation project.

By way of illustration, consider the analysis of arithmetic concepts, shown in Table 6.4, that was used in planning the items for the *Iowa Tests of Basic Skills.* Each item in the test has been classified using this schema. A person interested in evaluating level of mastery of arithmetical concepts with children in some specific school grade can use this code to see what aspects of the area are included in the test at that grade level, and can determine whether these aspects correspond to the ones with which his school is concerned.

Table 6.4

ANALYSIS OF *TEST A-1, ARITHMETIC CONCEPTS,* IN *IOWA TESTS OF BASIC SKILLS*

Skills classification

C—Currency (Money)
   C-1 Reading and writing amounts
   C-2 Counting
   C-3 Relative values of coins
   C-4 Making change

D—Decimals
   D-1 Reading and writing
   D-2 Relative sizes
   D-3 Rounding
   D-4 Fraction, decimal, per cent equivalents
   D-5 Fundamental operations: ways to perform
   D-6 Fundamental operations: estimating results

E—Equations

F—Fractions
   F-1 Part of a whole and part of a group
   F-2 Relative sizes
   F-3 Reducing
   F-4 Terms
   F-5 Fundamental operations: ways to perform
   F-6 Fundamental operations: estimating results

G—Geometry
   G-1 Parallel and perpendicular lines
   G-2 Recognizing kinds of geometric figures
   G-3 Angles and triangles
   G-4 Dimensions, perimeters, and areas of polygons
   G-5 Parts and areas of circles
   G-6 Use of protractor and compass

M—Measurement
   M-1 Quantity
   M-2 Time (telling time, time zones, calendar)
   M-3 Temperature
   M-4 Weight
   M-5 Length (use of ruler, precision)
   M-6 Area and volume
   M-7 Liquid and dry capacity
   M-8 Fundamental operations with compound denominate numbers

N—Numerals and Number Systems
   N-1 Counting
   N-2 Ordinals
   N-3 Place value and zero as a place holder
   N-4 Roman numerals
   N-5 Odd and even numbers
   N-6 Positive and negative numbers

P—Percents: meaning and use

R—Ratio and Proportion

W—Whole Numbers
   W-1 Reading and writing
   W-2 Relative sizes
   W-3 Rounding
   W-4 Partition and measurement; average
   W-5 Fundamental operations: terms
   W-6 Fundamental operations: number facts
   W-7 Fundamental operations: ways to perform
   W-8 Fundamental operations: estimating results

The only dependable way to size up what a published test is measuring is to examine in detail the test booklet and the test manual. The manual (or supplementary material available from the publisher) will often state item by item what knowledge or skill each item is designed to assess. The reasonableness of that statement can be checked by examining the item itself. If the major objectives, and the representation of them in the tasks presented by specific items, agree reasonably well with the objectives as defined for the programs being compared, the published test may be the best choice for inclusion in the evaluation study. Of course, if one or more of the objectives is sufficiently distinctive so that no published test can be found that adequately represents it, then it will be necessary to construct a new instrument specifically tailored to represent that objective.

One feature of curricular evaluations, or any analysis that leads to a decision applied to a whole class, school, or school system is that it is not necessary that *every* pupil be tested with *every* test exercise. If, for example, there are enough different test exercises covering the various objectives of a school program that it would take 4 hours for a pupil to respond to all of them, and if only 30 minutes of testing time is available, then it may be possible to break the material up into eight test forms, and to have each pupil take some one of the test forms. If a school has, for example, 120 sixth grade pupils, each of the eight forms will be taken by approximately 15 pupils. For the school as a whole, it will be possible to determine average level of performance on the complete test, since all of the items will have been used and all of the pupils will have served as examinees. This procedure, which is designated *item sampling,* provides a practical way to cover a wide range of curricular objectives by using a large number of examinees each for a relatively short time. However, item sampling does require the assembly of tests specifically for the current occasion, either through local efforts or from the item files of commercial publishers. It should perhaps be repeated that with item sampling we do *not* get a meaningful or useful score for any single pupil.

PUBLIC
AND POLITICAL DECISIONS

Every community is interested in and concerned about its school system. Expenditures for education represent a major item in the budget of every community and every state. The citizens want to know whether they are getting good value for those expenditures. They want to know how their schools stack up against other schools in their state and throughout the country. They want to know how well the children in their community are learning the things that they as parents and citizens feel children should learn. The decisions about their schools that are available to citizens are fairly limited, and frequently negative. They may vote down a school budget or a school bond issue. They may organize to protest a person, program, or policy. Conversely, of course, they may decide to support the school with money, time, or approbation. Which of these things they do will depend upon how they feel about their schools, and this in turn will depend in part at least upon what they know about their schools.

Knowing about the schools is partly a matter of knowing what is going on in them—what activities are available for children to participate in, what resources are available to help children with their learning, what new ideas are being tried out. But to parents and to other concerned citizens it is at least in part knowing how much the children are learning. Thus, in its relations with its public, each school system faces the problem of presenting to that public some picture of student progress.

One approach to reporting school progress is in terms of very specific competencies. Thus the school might report: "78 percent of pupils at the end of grade 3 were able to identify the number of thousands, hundreds, tens, and units in a number such as 7562." But such a report conveys little meaning to even an informed citizen. The likely response is "So is that good or bad? What percentage should be expected to do this? How does this compare with last year? With Hohokus next door?" If specific accomplishments are reported, there must be so many of them that teacher and citizen alike get drowned in a mass of detail. Thus, in reporting to the public, some kind of summary seems to be necessary. And the summary will by the very nature of things involve comparison—comparison with last year's performance, comparison with national norms, or comparison with some group of similar schools or communities. It would be possible for a school system to develop its own set of assessment instruments, to use these in successive years, and to compare this year's performance with that of previous years. But this is a limited type of comparison, and one that may not prove very satisfying to the public. Some broader basis of comparison is usually wanted, and this can only be supplied by a test for which normative data are available. Thus one significant role for standardized tests is in providing the basis by which one community can compare itself with other communities and with the country as a whole or some defined slice of it.

An intermediate level of comparison is that made possible by some of the statewide assessment programs that have been in operation in recent years. These vary from state to state, but in a number of states the results are reported to local communities in a form that makes it possible for each community to compare itself with the state as a whole or with communities of a certain size or type within the state.

The test that forms the most appropriate basis for presenting a school's results to that school's public is the test that best represents the school's educational objectives. Thus there are no new or different criteria for selecting a test that is to provide public information; it will be the same test that is most useful for appraising the achievement level of single pupils.

Once the test has been given and scored, it is necessary to assemble the data and present them in a form that will fairly and clearly communicate the results to the public. "Fairly" relates to the proper comparison group; "clearly" relates to the form of presentation. Ways in which a school system may report its achievements to the public are considered in some detail in Chapter 14.

QUESTIONS AND EXERCISES

1. Prepare a brief criterion-referenced test to measure some specific skill in arithmetic, language usage, or some other field, following the guidelines given on p. 169.

2. What score on the above test will you accept as representing mastery of the skill? What is the basis for your decision?

3. Prepare a list of specific skills that go into effective writing. Design a procedure for testing one or two of these.

4. Why might a test that is very suitable as a measure of past achievement have limited value for a placement decision?

5. By what procedures might a community college section the entering freshmen for a required English course? What would be the objectives of such sectioning? What gains might be expected? What losses?

6. In April of the 6th grade, Helen has a reading grade equivalent on the *Iowa Tests of Basic Skills* of 6.2. How should this be interpreted if her *Cognitive Abilities Test Nonverbal* SAS is 85? If it is 115? If it is 135?

7. How does your answer to the above question change as you shift from "performance in relation to potential" to "performance in relation to par"?

8. What would be involved in preparing a *proficiency* test for television repairmen? What form might the test take?

9. In what ways might a testing program to evaluate a proposed modified mathematics curriculm differ from a program designed to place students in the appropriate mathematics section?

SUGGESTED ADDITIONAL READING

Bloom, B. S., J. T. Hastings, and C. F. Madaus. *Handbook on formative and summative evaluation of student learning.* New York: McGraw-Hill, 1971.

Dustin, D. Some effects of exam frequency. *The Psychological Report,* 1971, 21, 409–414.

Ebel, R. L. Some limitations of criterion-referenced measurement. In G. H. Bracht, K. D. Hopkins, and J. C. Stanley (Eds.), *Perspectives in educational and psychological measurement.* Englewood Cliffs, N.J.: Prentice-Hall, 1972, 144–149.

Gaynor, Jessica and Jim Milham. Student performance and evaluation under variant teaching and testing methods in a large college course. *Journal of Educational Psychology,* 1976, 68, 312–317.

Hambleton, R. K. and M. R. Novick. *Toward an integration of theory and method for criterion-referenced tests.* ACT Research Report No. 53. Iowa City, Iowa: The American College Testing Program, September 1972.

Klein, Stephen P., and Jacqueline Kosecoff. *Issues and procedures in the development of criterion-referenced tests. (TM Report 26.)* ERIC Clearinghouse on Tests, Measurement and Evaluation. Princeton, N. J.: Educational Testing Service, 1973.

Meskouskas, John A. Evaluation models for criterion-referenced testing: Views regarding mastery and standard-setting. *Review of Educational Research,* Winter 1976, 46, 133–158.

Millman, Jason. Criterion-referenced measurement. In W. James Popham (Ed.) *Evaluation in education.* Berkeley, Calif.: McCutchan, 1974.

Sax, Gilbert. The use of standardized tests in evaluation. In W. James Popham (Ed.) *Evaluation in education.* Berkeley, Calif.: McCutchan, 1974.

CHAPTER SEVEN
LOCALLY CONSTRUCTED TESTS

In the last chapter we considered the various types of educational and personnel decisions to which measures of academic achievement should be expected to contribute useful information. For some of these the most useful information would come from widely used, nationally standardized tests, carefully constructed, based on common objectives, and normed on broadly representative samples. For other decisions, however, locally constructed tests often seem more suitable. When the need is to assess degree of mastery of a specific unit that the teacher has been teaching, to evaluate competence in what has been taught in a specific course, or to appraise progress toward locally defined curricular goals, a test that is tailormade to fit the local purpose will often be more appropriate than any that can be found in test publishers' catalogues. But locally made tests, whether made by a single teacher for a single class, or by some cooperative group effort for more widespread use, need to be well-made tests. How is this to be achieved?

Better local tests can result from better planning of the test making enterprise and from better skills in the preparation of test exercises. It is to these two aspects of test making that we now address ourselves.

PLANNING THE TEST

Many locally made tests suffer from weakness, or even absence, of planning carried out before work is begun on writing the test exercises. Before a single question or problem is written, it is appropriate to raise and to provide the best answer to the following questions:

1. What function or functions is this test intended to serve? Is it to guide an immediate instructional decision as to what to teach or re-teach, and to whom? To assess general level of competence, and perhaps to assign a mark? To evaluate the effectiveness of some segment of the schools's program?

2. What objectives is the school or the teacher trying to achieve in the area covered by this test?

3. What content has been dealt with in the field covered by this test? How much emphasis has been given to each topic?

4. What types of test exercise will be both practical and effective in providing evidence on achievement of those objectives identified under (2)?

As indicated above, the first point to be clear on is the function that the test is to serve. If that function is to assess degree of mastery of some specific skill, in order to permit a decision on what to teach or study next, a sharply focused mini-test of the type illustrated by the prime numbers test (p. 167) and the capitalization test (p. 168) is called for. As stated in the previous discussion of criterion-referenced tests such as these, it is important to define precisely the skill that is being assessed, design a form of test exercise through which the skill can be simply and efficiently displayed, and agree upon the level that will be accepted as indicating satisfactory competence in that skill.

When the function of the test is to appraise general level of competence in some broad segment of the curriculum, planning becomes more complex. It then becomes important to develop a reasonably full statement of the objectives for that course or unit. A clear formulation of objectives serves as a guide both for teaching and for evaluation.

DEFINING OBJECTIVES

For a teacher, a group of teachers, or other local group designing a test, the first and most important step is to clarify in your own mind just what you hope a student will be able to do as a result of a segment of instruction. One of the best ways to be sure that you have a clear idea of what you are trying to accomplish is to write it down in a form that will be clear to others. If you can do this, you are pretty sure to have the matter clear in your own mind, and if you cannot, then it is unlikely that these ideas have the clarity needed to guide the later steps in preparing the test.

In almost all educational settings one finds statements of the aims and goals of the institution. These are usually very general and global statements, supposed to serve as an overall frame of reference for developing curricula, for organizing learning experiences, and for selecting teaching methods. They include such broad goals as "effective citizenship," "worthwhile use of leisure time," "ability to use the scientific method." Within this broad framework, the teacher is responsible for developing instructional objectives for a particular group of individuals in a particular area of study. Although a teacher can turn to curriculum guides, yearbooks of a national association, the taxonomies of educational objectives developed by Bloom (1956) and Krathwohl (1964), and many other sources for help in identifying appropriate objectives, the ultimate responsibility for selecting objectives suitable for the group of students that he or she is teaching and stating those objectives in such a way that they can guide instruction and evaluation rests with the classroom teacher.

The majority of statements of objectives written by teachers are too vague and global to be useful as a guide to evaluation or teaching. To serve this purpose, a set of objectives should have the following characteristics.

1. *Objectives should be stated in terms of student behavior,* not in terms of learning activities or purposes of the teacher. For example, "Observes bacteria through a microscope" is not a satisfactory statement of an objective. This describes a learning activity. Why does a teacher want the students to observe bacteria? An analysis of the activities and contents of the course of study in which the objective appears indicates that the teacher wants the student to know the characteristics of organisms that cause diseases, and that observation of bacteria is incidental to this objective. It might be better to state the objective as, "Recalls characteristics of organisms that cause diseases."

2. *Objectives should begin with an active verb that indicates the behavior that a student should show* in dealing with content. This format tends to guarantee a focus on the student and what he does. The objective should not consist of a list of content. For example, the statement "Scurvy, beriberi, rickets, and pellagra are caused by a lack of vitamins in the body" is a statement of content not a statement of an objective. The objective should be stated, "Identifies certain disease conditions that are caused by lack of vitamins."

3. *Objectives should be stated in terms of student behavior that is observable.* For example, an objective formulated as, "Always practices good health habits to prevent the spread of disease" is not stated in observable terms. The inclusion of "always" in the formulation means that it is impossible to gather the evidence needed to judge the achievement of the students. One cannot *always* observe a student. Another example is the statement, "Does his share to create good emotional atmosphere during meals at home." The behavior specified in this statement occurs in a situation outside of school in which the teacher would be unable to observe the student. It is unlikely that he is going to be able to get relevant evidence on the achievement of the objective. Another example is the statement, "Feels secure in making wise choices of food." In this statement "feels secure" is unobservable; it is a covert characteristic of a student. One cannot observe a feeling of security. One can only observe behavior and perhaps make inferences about the security of the student.

4. *Objectives should be stated precisely,* using terms that have uniform meaning. For example, in the objective, "Understands the responsibility of the community in control of communicable disease" the word "understands" means different things to different people. To one teacher it may mean that the students can name the different agencies in the community that have responsibility for controlling communicable disease. To another it may mean that the student given a novel problem concerning a communicable disease, can identify the appropriate community agency or agencies and indicate the services or actions to be expected from these agencies.

There are a number of terms that have been used by teachers that lead toward ambiguity in formulating objectives. Some of these are listed in the left-hand column of Table 7.1. By way of contrast, some of the active verbs that tend to focus attention on student behavior are shown, in no particular order, in the right-hand column. Test planners are encouraged to use the words in the right-hand column, and others like them, and steer clear of such ambiguous or unobservable terms as appear in the left-hand column.

5. *Objectives should be unitary;* each statement should relate to only one process. For instance, the objective, "Knows elementary principles of immunization and accepts immunization willingly," contains two processes, a cognitive process of recall of information and an affective process of acceptance of an action. The two processes are different and require different evaluative procedures to obtain relevant evidence on their achievement. If both are important instructional objectives, they should be stated as two separate objectives.

Table 7.1

SAMPLES OF POOR AND GOOD OPENINGS FOR STATEMENT OF AN OBJECTIVE

Do Not Use in Stating Objectives	Recommended for Use in Stating Objectives
Understands . . .	Defines . . .
Appreciates . . .	Gives examples of . . .
Thinks critically about . . .	Compares . . .
Is aware of . . .	Describes . . .
Feels the need for . . .	Classifies . . .
Is growing in ability to . . .	Summarizes . . .
Becomes familiar with . . .	Applies in a new situation . . .
Grasps the significance of . . .	Solves a problem in which . . .
Is interested in . . .	Expresses interest in . . .
Feels the need for . . .	States what he would do if . . .

6. *Objectives should be stated at an appropriate level of generality.* On the one hand, the statement of an objective should not be so general and global as to be meaningless, nor, on the other hand, should the statements be so narrow and specific that the educational process seems to be made up of isolated bits and pieces. In the latter case an adequate list of objectives becomes too long and too unwieldy to use effectively. For example, the objective, "Knows nutrition" is too vague to serve any useful purpose. On the other hand, a series of statements such as "Identifies the function of proteins in the body," "Identifies the function of fats in the body," "Identifies the function of carbohydrates in the body," "Identifies the function of vitamins in the body," not only becomes boring to read but is also unnecessarily specific. At an appropriate level of generality, all specific statements could be combined into one statement that reads, "Identifies the function of the five classes of nutrients in the body."

7. *Objectives should represent intended direct outcomes* of a planned series of learning experiences. For example, it is obvious that one would never write as an educational objective for eighth graders "Increases in height," simply because health instruction is not directed toward making eighth graders taller. However, it is common to find statements of objectives that deal with attitudes in programs in which no particular instructional effort is given to the development of attitudes.

In such a case either the objective concerned with attitudes should be omitted or the instruction should be redesigned so that some attention is devoted to attitude change. This brings out the point that clarification of objectives may influence not only the evaluation procedures, but also the form and content of instruction.

8. *Objectives should be realistic* in terms of the time available for teaching and the characteristics of the students. An example of an unrealistic objective would be, "Understands the reasons why people become drug addicts." This is unrealistic simply because no one knows why people become drug addicts; therefore it is impossible to teach toward this objective.

Another example of an objective that would be an unrealistic one for eighth graders reads, "Understands the principles of immunization." The principles of immunization are extremely complex, and understanding of the nature of immunization is probably beyond the experience level of the students in the eighth grade. The objective should be reexamined and probably recast in the form of knowing the different kinds of immunization or of knowing the methods that have been developed for immunizing against disease.

Let us look at an actual example of a set of objectives that were prepared for a 6-week unit in nutrition for an eighth grade class. In Table 7.2 column 1 gives the objectives as they appeared in the teacher's course outline, column 2 indicates the weakness, if any, of each objective, and column 3 suggests revisions for the objectives where they are needed.

As you can see, the objectives as originally written have many faults. The revised list of objectives provides a better guide both for teaching and evaluation. The revisions in the objectives were made after studying the detailed curriculum guide. Objectives that were eliminated were ones for which no specific learning experiences were provided in that curriculum guide.

SPECIFYING CONTENT TO BE COVERED

When the purpose of a test is to appraise what each student has learned from a major section of a course or a curriculum, a second step in planning the test is to specify the content to be covered. The content is important because it is the vehicle through which the process objectives are to be achieved. If a teacher has developed a detailed outline or set of lesson plans for a course, these materials could guide the specification of content. Otherwise, an outline of content could be prepared based on the appropriate sections of the textbook or curriculum guide, or the test maker could merely indicate the content to

Table 7.2

OBJECTIVES FOR UNIT ON NUTRITION FOR AN EIGHTH GRADE CLASS

Objective as Originally Written in Curriculum Guide	Comment	Suggested Revision
1. Knows terms and vocabulary used in nutrition.	1. "Knows" is vague. At what level is the student supposed to know these?	1. Recalls or recognizes definitions of terms and vocabulary.
2. Has a rudimentary knowledge of food nutrients and their functions.	2. What is a "rudimentary knowledge"? What kind of behavior does a student show who has a "rudimentary knowledge"?	2. Recalls or recognizes names of essential food nutrients and their functions in the body.
3. Values the health protection provided by good dietary habits.	3. "Value" is vague. How does this objective differ from (7), (9), (11), and (13)?	3. (a) Identifies good sources of various food nutrients. (b) Identifies effects of poor diets.
4. Understands the digestive process.	4. "Understands" is vague. How does a student show he understands?	4. (a) Identifies parts of digestive system and functions of each. (b) Identifies process of digestion for each nutrient. (c) Recognizes factors that interfere with digestion.
5. Plans meals and snacks using principles of good nutrition.	5. Well-stated objective. Desired student behavior is clear. Stated at an appropriate level of generality.	5. No revisions
6. Realizes that food patterns differ in various parts of U.S.A. and world.	6. "Realizes" is vague. Objective is too specific.	6. Identifies factors that influence kinds and amounts of food that people eat.
7. Is willing to choose an adequate diet.	7. Willingness to do something is covert. One can observe whether a student does something, but not his willingness to do it.	7. Chooses adequate lunch in school cafeteria.
8. Understands that the daily food guide is based on scientific research.	8. The last part of the objective is a specific fact. What is there to "understand"? Essential part of objective is included in 12.	8. Eliminate objective.
9. Uses information about nutrition every day.	9. Doesn't everyone? More of a fond hope than an objective. See comment on (3).	9. Eliminate objective.

Objective as Originally Written in Curriculum Guide	Comment	Suggested Revision
10. Persuades other members of his family to develop good nutritional habits.	**10.** Is this reasonable? How would one obtain evidence on the achievement of the objective? Is this a direct outcome of teaching?	**10.** Eliminate objective.
11. Recognizes flaws in his diet and desires to eliminate them.	**11.** Double objective. Contains two different behaviors. First part of objective is restatement of (2) and (5). Second part is stated in (7).	**11.** Eliminate objectives.
12. Is aware that advertisements and statements concerning food are not always based on facts.	**12.** "Is aware of" is vague. What behaviors should the student exhibit?	**12.** (a) Distinguishes statements about foods and diets that are based on good scientific evidence from those that are not. (b) Identifies authoritative sources of information about foods and diets.
13. Appreciates being healthy.	**13.** "Appreciates" is vague. What behavior is a student to show when he appreciates being healthy? How do you teach a student to appreciate being healthy?	**13.** Eliminate objective.

be covered by marking the appropriate sections in the textbook.

PREPARING THE TEST BLUEPRINT

The content and a statement of process objectives represent the two dimensions into which a test plan for a test covering some major section of a course or curriculum should be fitted. These two dimensions need to be put together to show which objectives especially relate to which segments of content and to provide a complete framework for the development of the test. In planning for the *total evaluation of a unit,* the teacher would be well advised to make a blueprint covering *all* objectives and to add a column to the blueprint indicating the method or methods to be used in evaluating student progress toward achieving each objective. However, in making a blueprint for a *test*, only those objectives that can be assessed either wholly or in part by a paper-and-pencil test should be included.

In a list of objectives, any objective that calls for only cognitive processes can be appraised by a paper-and-pencil test. These are objectives that specify such processes as recalling, recognizing, identifying, defining, applying, analyzing, synthesizing, generalizing, predicting, or evaluating. In the list of revised objectives in Table 7.2, all the revised objectives except (7) can be evaluated by a paper-and-pencil test. Objective (7) cannot be measured by a paper-and-pencil test because it involves the actual act of choosing food. The extent to which objective (7) has been achieved can be determined only by systematic observation of students in the school cafeteria. Examples of other types of objective that cannot be assessed by paper-and-pencil tests are those that involve affective behaviors, such as interests, and attitudes, that is, feelings of favorableness or unfavorableness toward an object, group, or institution. This type of objective would need to be evaluated through self-report or observation. The teacher should remember that no single test or evaluation device can measure all the objectives he is trying to achieve.

Fig. 7.1 (pp. 208–209) shows a blueprint for a final examination in health for an eighth grade class. As it has been prepared, with the specification calling for 60 items, this illustration is based on a decision that the test is to be a short-answer or objective test with a large number of separate items. It is especially for this type of test that a formal blueprint is useful. However, the choice of 5 or 6 questions for an essay test can also be improved by the kind of thinking that goes into the formulation of a blueprint. The issues that are involved in the decision about type of test exercise to use are considered later (p. 257).

In the blueprint the process objectives for the unit in nutrition as well as for the other units have been listed in the left-hand column. The titles of each of the 3 units have been entered as headings on the other columns. Each box, or cell, under the unit headings contains content entries that relate to the objective opposite the cell. The complete blueprint specifies the content deemed important and indicates what the student is supposed to be able to do with that content.

The preparation of such a two-dimensional outline is an exacting and time-consuming task. The busy classroom teacher may often fall short of achieving such a complete analysis. There is no question, however, that attempting the analysis will go far toward clarifying the objectives of a particular unit and toward guiding not only the preparation of a sound test but also the teaching of the unit itself. It is also true that once such a complete blueprint has been prepared it can be used until the curriculum or teaching emphasis is changed.

Examination of the blueprint at this point should make clear to the reader that any test can be only a sample of student behaviors related to the content covered in class. First, the objectives included in the blueprint represent only those objectives that are suitable for appraisal by a paper-and-pencil test. Second, the entries in the cells under each area of content are examples that illustrate, but do not exhaust the total content. Third, there is an unlimited number of questions that could be written for the material that is included in the blueprint. Time available for testing is always limited; one can ask only a relatively small number of all the possible questions. If the test is to reflect accurately and truly the emphasis and the goals of teaching, then the test maker must choose carefully the sample of items to represent the domain being assessed.

To complete the test plan so that it will be an adequate guide for constructing a test that will truly represent the teaching emphasis, the test maker must arrive at some answer to each of the following questions before starting to write the exercises for the test.

1. What relative emphasis should each of the content areas and each of the process objectives receive on the test? In other words, what proportion of all the items on the test should be written for each content area and, within each content area, for each process objective?

2. What type or types of items would be most appropriate to use on the test?

3. How long should the test be? How many questions or items should the total test have? How many items should be written for each cell of the blueprint?

4. What should the difficulty of the items be to achieve adequately the purpose of the test?

Determining relative emphasis of content areas and process objectives. The proportion of test questions on each content area should correspond to the instructional emphasis given to the topic, and the proportion of items calling for each process objective should correspond to the importance the test maker considers that process to have for the level of students to be tested. The decisions made in allocating the questions on a test are necessarily subjective ones. The basic principle underlying

Process Objectives	Content Areas			Number of Items
	A. Nutrition, 40%	B. Communicable Diseases, 40%	C. Noncommunicable Diseases, 20%	
1. Recognizes terms and vocabulary 20%	Nutrients Incomplete protein Vitamins Complete protein Enzymes Amino acids Metabolism Glycogen Oxidation Carbohydrate 4 or 5 items	Immunity Epidemic Virus Pathogenic Carrier Endemic Antibodies Protozoa Incubation period 4 or 5 items	Goiter Deficiency diseases Diabetes Cardiovascular diseases Caries 2 or 3 items	12
2. Identifies specific facts 30%	Nutrients essential to health Good sources of food nutrients Parts of digestive system Process of digestion of each nutrient Sources of information about foods and nutrition 7 or 8 items	Common communicable diseases Incidence of various diseases Methods of spreading disease Types of immunization Symptoms of common communicable diseases 7 or 8 items	Specific diseases caused by lack of vitamins Specific disorders resulting from imbalance in hormones Incidence of noncommunicable diseases Common noncommunicable diseases of adolescents and young adults 3 or 4 items	18
3. Identifies principles, concepts and generalizations 30%	Bases of well-balanced diet Enzyme reactions Transfer of materials between cells Cell metabolism Functions of nutrients in body 7 or 8 items	Basic principles underlying control of disease Actions of antibiotics Body defenses against disease Immune reactions in body 7 or 8 items	Pressure within cardiovascular system Control of diabetes Inheritance of abnormal conditions Abnormal growth of cells 3 or 4 items	18

			Number of items
4 Evaluates health information and advertisements 10%	Analyzes food and diet advertisements Interprets labels on foods Identifies good sources of information about foods and diets 2 or 3 items	Distinguishes between adequate and inadequate evidence for medicines Identifies misleading advertisements for medications 2 or 3 items	Identifies errors or misleading information in health material Identifies appropriate source of information for health problems 1 or 2 items	6
5 Applies principles and generalizations to novel situations 10%	Identifies well-balanced diet Computes calories needed for weight-gaining or weight-losing diet Predicts consequences of changes in enzymes on digestive system Identifies services and protection provided by the Federal Food and Drug Act 2 or 3 items	Recognizes conditions that are likely to result in increase of communicable disease Identifies appropriate methods for sterilizing objects Gives appropriate reasons for regulations, processes, or treatments 2 or 3 items	Predicts consequences of changes in secretion of certain hormones Predicts probability of inheriting abnormal conditions 1 or 2 items	6
Number of items	24	24	12	60
Total time for test—90 minutes			Total number of items—60	

Figure 7.1
Blueprint for final examination in health for eighth grade.

these decisions is that the test should maintain the same balance in relative emphasis on both content and mental process that the teacher has been trying to achieve through instruction. Allocation of differing numbers of items to different topics and process objectives is one way (and the most desirable way) of weighting topics and objectives differentially in the test.

Weighting of both the content areas and the process objectives is done initially by assigning percentages to each content area and to each process objective in such a way that the total of the percentages across the content areas adds up to 100 percent and the total of the percentages for the process objectives also adds up to 100 percent. In the blueprint shown in Fig. 7.1, the test maker decided that topic A, Nutrition, should receive a weight of 40 percent; topic B, Communicable Disease, should also receive a weight of 40 percent; topic C, Noncommunicable Disease, should receive a weight of 20 percent. Since 5 weeks of instructional time were spent on topic A and also on topic B and only 2 weeks were spent on topic C, the allocation of weights, corresponds roughly to teaching time.

For the process objectives in Fig. 7.1 the test maker decided that 20 percent of all the items should be allocated to objective (1), 30 percent each to (2) and (3), and 10 percent each to (4) and (5). These allocations imply that the teacher has emphasized in teaching those objectives that relate to remembering or recalling terms, specific facts, principles, concepts and generalizations. In other words, the concern has been primarily with increasing the student's fund of knowledge, and less attention has been given to the ability of the students to use the information in novel situations. If the allocation of items to the process objectives truly reflects the teacher's emphasis in teaching, then the allocation is appropriate. We might take issue with the teacher's emphasis in teaching but, given that emphasis, we cannot say that the allocation of test items is inappropriate.

Determining the type or types of items to be used. There are a number of different types of items that can be used on a teacher-made test. The different types of items can be placed in two major categories: (1) the type in which the student produces his own answer, and (2) the type in which the student selects his answer from answer choices supplied by the test maker. Examples of type 1 are the essay question requiring an extended answer from the student; the short-answer question requiring no more than 1 or 2 sentences for an answer; and the completion item requiring only a word or phrase for an answer. Examples of type 2 are the alternative response item such as the true-false statement; the multiple-choice item; and the matching item.

The decision as to which type of item to use depends to a large extent upon the process objective to be measured. Other factors that can influence the decision are the content and the skill of the teacher in constructing the different types.

Determining the total number of items for the test. The test maker must now decide upon the total number of items for the test. If the teacher decides to use the essay type of exercise calling for extended answers, there will be time for only a few questions. The more elaborate the answer, the fewer the questions, so that a 40-minute test in high school might have 3 or 4 questions each calling for an answer of a page or two, while a 3-hour examination in graduate school might still present no more than 3 or 4 questions, but call for extended answers. The balance of this section assumes that the test maker has decided to use short-answer or objective items, and considers the number of items within this context.

The total number of items included in a test should be large enough to provide an adequate sample of student behavior across content areas and across process objectives. The larger the number of content areas and process objectives to be measured by a test, the longer the test needs to be. A weekly quiz can be a short test because both the content and objectives to be tested are rather limited, whereas a 6-week test or final examination needs to have a larger number of items because there are more content areas and more objectives to be covered in the test.

The time available for testing is a practical factor that limits the number of items on a test. Most teacher-made tests should be power tests, not speed tests; that is, there should be enough time so that at least 80 percent of the students can attempt to answer every item. There are few subject areas in which speed of answering is a relevant aspect of achievement. The number of test items that can be asked in a given amount of time depends upon many different factors such as:

1. *The type of item used on the test.* A short-answer item in which a student has to write his answer is likely to require more time than a true-false or multiple-choice item in which a

student is only required to write or mark a number or letter to indicate his answer.

2. *The age and educational level of the student.* Students in the primary grades whose skills of reading and writing are just beginning to develop require more time per test item than do older students who have well-developed skills in these areas. Young children also do not have the ability to attend to the same task for very long periods of time. Therefore testing time should be less for them, and this further reduces the number of items.

3. *The ability level of students.* High-ability students not only have better developed reading and writing skills than low-ability students but also generally have better command of the subject matter and better skills of problem solving. As a rule, high-ability students can answer more questions per unit of testing time than low-ability students of the same age and grade.

4. *The length and complexity of the item.* If test items are based on a reading passage, tabular material, map, or graph, time must be allowed for reading and examining the stimulus material. The more stimulus material of this type that is used on a test, the fewer the number of items that can be asked in a given amount of time.

5. *The type of process objective being tested.* Items that require only the recall of knowledge can be answered more quickly than those that require the application of knowledge to a new situation.

6. *The amount of computation or quantitative thinking required by the item.* Most individuals work more slowly when dealing with quantitative materials than when dealing with verbal materials; therefore, if the items require mathematical computation the time allotted per item must be longer than for a purely verbal item.

It is impossible to give hard and fast rules about the number of items to be included in a test for a given amount of testing time. A teacher who becomes familiar with the kinds of students usually in a class will be able to judge the number of items that can be included in a given amount of time while still having a power test. As a rough rule of thumb, the typical student might require from 30 to 45 seconds to read and attempt to answer a simple factual type multiple-choice or true-false item and from 75 to 100 seconds to read and attempt a fairly complex multiple-choice item requiring problem solving.

The total amount of time required for a number of items sufficient to provide adequate coverage of the blueprint may sometimes be more than a single class period. The most satisfactory solution to this problem is to break the test up into two or more separate subtests that can be given on successive days.

For the illustrative final examination in health for the eighth grade, the teacher had 90 minutes of testing time. Keeping in mind all of the factors mentioned above, the teacher decided to have 60 questions on the test. Now we would go back to the blueprint to determine how many items should be written for each cell in the blueprint. The first thing to do is to determine the total number of items for each content area and for each process objective. The blueprint in Fig. 7.1 specifies that 40 percent of the items, or 24 items ($.40 \times 60$), should be on topic A, 40 percent, or 24 items, on topic B, and 20 percent, or 12 items, on topic C. These numbers are entered in the bottom row of the blueprint. The percentage assigned to each process objective is multiplied by the total number of items to determine the number of items that should be written to measure each process. When this is done, we get the numbers that are entered in the extreme right-hand column of the blueprint.

To determine the number of items in each cell of the blueprint, we multiply the total number of items in a content area by the percentage assigned to the objective in each row. For example, to determine the number of items for the first cell under topic A, Nutrition, we multiply 24 by 0.2 (20 percent), which gives 4.8 items. Since the number 4.8 is between 4 and 5, we can note that we should have either 4 or 5 items covering this content and this objective. The other cells in the blueprint are filled in by the same process. However, it must be recognized that certain process outcomes may be related primarily to certain aspects of content. Thus in a social studies examination an objective related to map reading might be testable primarily in a content unit on natural resources rather than one on human resources. This may lead the test maker to modify the cell entries so as to adjust to these particular congruences of content and process. Furthermore, it is probably desirable to indicate a range of items for each cell, as in our example, in order to provide flexibility if difficulty is encountered in writing acceptable items for certain cells. The number of items planned for each cell is to be thought of as a guide, not as a straitjacket.

When writing the items for a test, it is best to write each one on a separate 5×8 card or slip of paper. This will make it easier to revise, discard, or rearrange the items for the test. After all the items have been constructed, the teacher should make a final check by sorting the items according to the blueprint cells to make sure that the test matches the blueprint.

Determining the appropriate level of difficulty of the items. The final decision to be made in the preliminary planning for a test concerns the desired difficulty of the test items. Once again, difficulty implies something different for an essay test calling for an extended answer than for a short-answer or objective test. A question that is of appropriate difficulty for an essay examination, as such examinations are typically used, is one for which each member of the class can produce some kind of an answer showing at least minimal awareness of the issues, and one that elicits responses varying in completeness, thoughtfulness, and quality of organization of ideas. In the case of an objective item difficulty takes on a sharper definition, and may be defined as the percentage of examinees who get the item right. For example, if a particular item on a test is answered correctly by 40 percent of all the students who take the test, we say the item has a 40 percent difficulty.

The most suitable average difficulty and spread of difficulty of test items is dependent in large part upon the purpose of the test. When the test is being designed to measure *mastery* of the basic essentials in an area, the questions should be limited to those essentials. If a unit has been well taught, all the items may then turn out to be very easy for the group. On such a test a teacher may well expect to have perfect or near perfect scores for most of the students, with only a few of the students, or none, missing any given item. For this type of test a large number of perfect scores gives the desired information, that the students have indeed learned the essentials in the area. On a diagnostic test, the purpose of which is to locate isolated individuals who are having special difficulty, it is also reasonable to expect a large number of perfect scores or near perfect scores and very few relatively low scores. On the other hand, suppose that we want to give a test before starting instruction on a new topic, to find out how much our students already know about it. In this case, since the material has not yet been taught, we would not be surprised to get a large number of near-zero scores; in other words, we would expect such a test to be very difficult for our students.

On mastery tests, on diagnostic tests, or on pretests before instruction, we are not concerned about spreading people out. Even if everyone gets a perfect score or if everyone gets a zero score, these scores give us the information that we sought from the test. On the other hand, when the purpose of the test is to discriminate levels of achievement of different members of the group, that is, to serve as a basis for ranking or grading, then we want the test to yield a spread of scores. We want to be able to separate the really high achiever from the next highest achiever and the really low achiever from the next to the lowest achiever. We do not want anyone to get a perfect score on such a test because then we cannot be sure we have gotten an adequate measure of how much he can do. However, we would not want to get zero or chance level scores from any person because then we would not have gotten down to his level. On such a test, we would not want an item that everyone got right or an item that everyone got wrong simply because neither of these items contributes to making discriminations among students according to their level of achievement.

Usually when we talk about difficulty of a test, we talk about it in terms of average difficulty. For example, suppose we made up a test of 50 items and gave this test to a group of students. Assume that when we scored the papers we found that the average score for all the students who took the test was 25 items right. Since the average score for the group of students was 25 out of 50 we would say that the test had an average difficulty of 50 percent (25/50 = 50 percent). When one uses this method to express difficulty in operational terms, that is, the percentage of all students getting an item right, the following chart has been found to provide a good rule-of-thumb guide for the test maker to shoot at in preparing tests made up of different types of item (Lord, 1952).

Type of Item	Average Difficulty (Percent Correct)
Completion type items and short-answer items	50
5-choice multiple-choice	70
4-choice multiple-choice	74
3-choice multiple-choice	77
True-false or 2-choice items	85

These percentages allow for the possibility of getting right answers by guessing, and for the typical finding that very difficult items are often ambiguous and nondiscriminating as between the more and the less able students. To follow through our example, suppose the 60 items on the health test were all completion items. We would want the average score of the class to be .50 × 60 = 30 items right. If the 60 items had been 5-choice multiple-choice items, we would have wanted the average score to be about .70 × 60 = 42 items right.

The percentages shown in the table sometimes bother teachers who are accustomed to thinking of "passing" scores or "failing" scores in terms of the percentage of the items that a student gets right on a test. The above suggestions have nothing to do with passing or failing; assigning marks or grades to students is an entirely different problem and will be taken up in a later chapter. The percentages that are suggested here will tend to yield a set of test scores that will be maximally useful to a teacher who wants to discriminate levels of achievement among students.

In the process of achieving the average difficulty level that is wanted on a test, the teacher is likely to produce some hard items that are passed by as few as 30 or 40 percent of pupils (assuming a 4-choice item) and some easy ones that are passed by 85 to 90 percent. We would hope that many of the items would approach the desired average level of 74 percent, and they should be written with that goal in mind. However, it is much more important that the items provide a good coverage of content and objectives and that each item be one that is passed more often by able than by less able students (a matter that will be considered later) than that any particular spectrum of item difficulties be maintained.

In summary, then, the test plan at this stage includes:

1. An outline of content and process objectives.

2. Specific suggestions of what might be covered under each combination of content and process objective.

3. An allocation of percentages of the total test by content area and by process objective and an estimate of the total number of items.

4. A decision on the types of item format to be used, and an estimate of the number of such items needed for each cell of the blueprint.

5. Specifications for the spread of item difficulties.

WRITING TEST ITEMS

The next task is to prepare the actual test items. There are certain process objectives for which essay questions have distinctive advantages. However, for the present we shall assume that one or another of the formats for relatively objectively scored items will be used. Some of the guidelines for preparing such items will be discussed here, and at the end of the chapter brief consideration will be given to essay questions.

There are a few general admonitions that apply more or less equally to all kinds of test exercise, and these can be stated first. They represent practices that are followed quite automatically by professional test makers, and can be applied, though less formally and elaborately, to local test making activities.

1. *Keep the test plan or blueprint in mind, and probably in view, as test exercises are written.* The blueprint represents your master plan and should be readily available to guide the specific tasks of item writing and review.

2. *Draft the test exercises some time in advance,* put them on the back burner for a few days, and then review them. It is amazing how often a statement or question that seemed perfectly clear as it was written turns out to be ambiguous or to have alternative meanings when it is reexamined after a lapse of time.

3. *Have the test exercises examined and critiqued by one or more colleagues.* When this can be done it is preferable to a personal review. A completely fresh reading by another person will elicit a wide assortment of questions and suggestions. If possible the reviewer should select or provide answers to the questions (without seeing your key), so that you can check to be sure that there is agreement on the answer.

4. *Prepare a surplus of test exercises.* Then if some do not stand up under further scrutiny there will still be enough. Again, a surplus will give some freedom for adjusting the composition of the test to match the blueprint.

Let us turn our attention to the several formats of structured-response test items. These are items in which the possible responses are presented to the examinee and his task is to choose from among the available alternatives. The most familiar of these formats are true-false, multiple-choice, and matching items. Structured-response items, particularly multiple-choice items, can be used to appraise a wide variety of educational objectives. They are efficient and, minute for minute, yield scores that are more dependable than those from free-response questions. However, the advantages of objective items can be achieved only if they are well constructed. In the follow-ing sections we first will present suggestions that apply to al-most any type of objective item, and then consider different item types, indicating the specific virtues and limitations of that type of item and giving suggestions for writing and editing.

GENERAL SUGGESTIONS
FOR WRITING OBJECTIVE ITEMS

1. *Keep the reading difficulty and vocabulary level of the test item as simple as possible.* Ordinarily we do not want involved sentence structure or unnecessarily difficult words to interfere with a student's showing what he knows. When technical vocabulary has been taught in a course and knowledge of that vocabulary is one of the objectives of instruction, it may appropriately be used, but obscure general vocabulary should be avoided. In the poor example below, which was written for eighth graders, the sentence posing the question is unnecessarily wordy and com-plex, and the words "promiscuous," "pernicious," and "delete-rious" are unnecessarily difficult for this age level.

EXAMPLE

Poor: The promiscuous use of sprays, oils, and antiseptics in the nose during acute colds is a pernicious practice because it may have a deleterious effect on

    A. the sinuses.
    B. red blood cells.
    C. white blood cells.
    D. the olfactory nerve.

Better: Frequent use of sprays, oils, and antiseptics in the nose during acute colds may result in

    A. spreading the infection to the sinuses.
    B. damage to the olfactory nerve.
    C. destruction of white blood cells.
    D. congestion of the mucous membranes in the nose.

2. *Be sure the item has a correct or best answer on which experts would agree.* Ordinarily statements of a controversial nature do not make good objective items, though there are instances when knowledge of different viewpoints on controversial issues may be important. When this is the case the item should clearly state whose opinion or what authority is to be used as the basis for answering. The student should not be placed in the position of having to endorse a particular opinion or viewpoint as an indisputable fact.

EXAMPLE

Poor: T F   Alcoholism is a disease.
Better: T̲ F   According to your textbook, alcoholism is a disease.

3. *Be sure each item deals with an important aspect of the content area, and not with trivia.* Sometimes teachers try to increase the difficulty of a test by basing items on obscure or trivial detail such as the content of the third footnote on p. 90 in the textbook. The first poor example below, written for the eighth grade health test, asks for an utterly trivial, specific detail, knowledge of which could not possibly make any significant difference in an eighth grader's competence in health. Example 2 says nothing; it is an example of lifting a statement from the textbook, and the best answer to it is "Ho-hum, who cares?"

EXAMPLE 1

Poor: In 1967 the death rate from accidents of all types per 100,000 population in the age group 15–24 was

   A. 59.0
   B. 59.1
   C̲. 59.2
   D. 59.3

Better: In 1967 the leading cause of death in the age group 15–24 was

   A. respiratory diseases.
   B. cancer.
   C̲. accidents.
   D. rheumatic heart disease.

EXAMPLE 2

Poor: T̲ F   The manufacture of prescription drugs is a highly scientific industry.

4. *Be sure that each item is independent. The answer to one item should not be required as a condition for solving the next item.* Every individual should have a fair chance at each item as it comes. Thus, in the example shown below, the person who does not know the answer to the first question is in a very weak position in answering the second one.

EXAMPLE

Poor: 1. Scurvy is caused by the lack of

    A. vitamin A.
    B. vitamin B_1
    C. vitamin B_{12}
    D. vitamin C.

    2. A good source of this vitamin is

    A. orange juice.
    B. cod-liver oil.
    C. liver.
    D. whole rice.

It is also important to make sure that the statement of one question does not provide the answer to some other question.

    5. *Avoid trick and catch questions in an achievement test.* Objective items tend to be trick items when the student has to pick one word or number out of a sentence that appears to be focusing on an entirely different point. In the poor example below, the item is keyed false because the immunizing agent for diphtheria is either a toxoid or an antitoxin, not a vaccine. However, the statement conveys the idea that the student is to react to the effectiveness of immunization procedures against diphtheria. If the purpose of the item is to test whether a student knows the correct use of the word "vaccine," the item should be rephrased as indicated. Trick questions are likely to mislead the better student who attempts to focus on the meaning of the statement rather than checking each word.

EXAMPLE

Poor: T F   The use of diphtheria vaccine has contributed to the decline in death rate from this disease between 1900 and 1968.
Better: T F   The immunizing material used to prevent diphtheria is called a vaccine.

    6. *Be sure that the problem posed is clear and unambiguous.* This is a general admonition, somewhat like "Sin no more!" and it may be no more effective. However, it is certainly true that ambiguity of statement and meaning is the most pervasive fault in objective test items.

EXAMPLE 1

Poor: T F   Diabetes develops after 40.

The statement is keyed true, but what does it mean? Does it mean "only after 40 years of age" or does it mean "more frequently after 40"? What does "develop" mean in this context? One can obtain data on the relative frequency of diagnosis of diabetes in people of different ages, but the time of diagnosis and the time of development are not the same. What kind of diabetes is the item writer referring to—*diabetes mellitus* or *diabetes insipidus* or some other form? Items such as this are likely to trouble the student who knows the most and not the ill-informed student. The item cannot be revised to make it an adequate item and should be dropped from the test.

EXAMPLE 2

Poor: Which of the following substances is most essential to man?

   A. Protein
   B. Water
   C. Vitamins
   D. Minerals

The keyed answer to the question is B, but all of the substances are essential to man. In order to answer the question the examinee has to guess what the item writer meant by "most essential". In this question the item writer was trying to determine whether the students knew that healthy people could survive for a fairly long time without food but could survive only for a few days without replenishing water lost from the body. The revised question tests for this knowledge with greater clarity.

EXAMPLE

Better: A healthy person is marooned on a deserted island. To survive, the person needs to find *almost immediately* a source of

   A. protein to maintain body cells.
   B. water to drink.
   C. vitamins to maintain body metabolism.
   D. carbohydrates or fats to supply energy.

WRITING ALTERNATE-RESPONSE ITEMS

Any item or question for which a student is given two choices from which to select an answer is an alternate-response item. For example, the item frequently used on classroom tests to appraise knowledge of verb forms such as "Neither John nor Jim (a) has (b) have enough money to buy a ring," is an alternate-response item. However, the most widely used item of this type is the one that presents a declarative statement and requires the examinee to indicate whether it is true or false.

The true-false item has had wide popularity in teacher-made tests, probably in large part because it seems so easy to prepare. But this facility is misleading, because it is achieved at the cost of producing many bad items. The true-false item is best suited for assessing knowledge of facts that are unequivocally true or false. It is particularly well suited to situations in which there exist only two contrasting options, for example, bacteria that may be either pathogenic or nonpathogenic, diseases that may be either communicable or noncommunicable. But only a small fraction of the knowledge in a field is of this type, and much that fits the pattern is relatively unimportant. Consequently many of the items that appear in true-false tests either strain to cast a debatable matter into a format of universal truth or else deal with facts that, while unequivocal, are of marginal importance. Since the statement that constitutes an item typically appears in isolation, out of context, no frame of reference is provided within which the truth or falsity of the statement can be judged, and this aggravates the problem faced by the student, and perhaps especially the more able student.

A quite different type of problem arises from the large role that can be played by guessing and "luck" with two-choice items. Because the pupil has a 50 percent chance of getting the answer right by guessing on a true-false test, this format yields less accurate information about a student per item than do other forms of item, and many more items are needed to provide an equally precise appraisal of each student's competence. Thus true-false tests should have a relatively large number of questions, and there should be time enough for all pupils to read and respond to all of them.

In a later section we will discuss variations that have been used to make the item type more effective in appraising achievement, but the more immediate problem is the writing of good true-false items.

1. *Be sure that the item as written can be classified unequivocally as either true or false.* Each statement should be true enough or false enough that experts would unanimously agree on the answer. Many statements that are supposed to be true cause difficulty because the well-informed person can think of a number of exceptions or reasons why the statement is not universally true. Look at the poor example on p. 223. Although the statement is keyed true, the student with the most information knows that penicillin is effective against certain types of pneumonia but not other types. Such a student might well mark the statement false. The revised statement removes the ambiguity.

EXAMPLE

Poor: T F   Penicillin is an effective drug for the treatment of pneumonia.
Better: T F   Pencillin is an effective drug for the treatment of streptococcal pneumonia.

2. *Avoid the use of "specific determiners."* Statements that include such words as "all," "never," "no," "always," or other all-inclusive terms represent such broad generalizations that they are likely to be false. Qualified statements involving such terms as "usually," "sometimes," "under certain conditions," "may be," are likely to be true. The test-wise student knows this and will use such cues to get credit for knowledge he does not possess. "All" or "no" may sometimes be used to advantage in *true* statements because the guesser will tend to mark F, and so get the item wrong.

EXAMPLE

Poor: T F   All bacteria cause disease.
Better: T F   All pathogenic bacteria are parasites.

3. *Avoid ambiguous and indefinite terms of degree or amount.* Expressions such as "frequently," "greatly," "to a considerable degree," and "in most cases," are not interpreted in the same way by everyone who reads them. An item in which the answer depends on guessing what the item writer had in mind is likely to be unsatisfactory and frustrating to students. In the poor example the student may be troubled by "frequently" because the method is used extensively today only for fruits.

EXAMPLE

Poor: T F   Drying is frequently used to preserve foods.
Better: T F   Fruits can be preserved by drying.

4. *Avoid the use of negative statements, and particularly double negatives,* Wason (1961), working with adults, and Zern (1967), working with elementary school children, have both shown that time required to answer a negatively phrased item is longer than for an equivalent positively phrased item and that more errors are made to negatively phrased items. Both investigators used pairs of statements such as "36 is not an even number" and "36 is an odd number." The negative statement requires a rather involved, reverse process of reasoning to untangle its meaning and is semantically more difficult. In addition, students under time pressures of the examination can easily overlook the negative. Double negatives can be particularly difficult.

EXAMPLE

Poor: T F̲   Resistance to smallpox obtained through the use of smallpox vaccine is not called active immunity.

Better: T F   Resistance to smallpox obtained through the use of smallpox vaccine is called passive immunity.

EXAMPLE 2

Poor: T̲ F   Tuberculosis is not a noncommunicable disease.

Better: T̲ F   Tuberculosis is a communicable disease.

5. *As a rule, limit true-false statements to a single idea.* Complex statements that include more than one idea are frequently difficult to read and comprehend. A statement that contains one true idea and one false idea borders on the category of trick items. Such an item tends to be a measure of reading skills rather than knowledge of the content area. Complex statements may be used if the student's attention is directed toward the one part of the statement that he is to judge to be true or false.

EXAMPLE

Poor: T F̲   Bleeding of the gums is associated with gingivitis, which can be cured by the sufferer himself by brushing his teeth daily.

Better: T F̲   Daily brushing of the teeth will cure gingivitis.

6. *Keep true and false statements approximately equal in length.* On a locally made test there is a tendency for true statements to be longer than false ones. Generally, the greater length of true statements is due to the need to include qualifications and limitations to make the statement unequivocally true. An occasional long true statement is not serious if it is matched by an occasional long false one, and if there is no consistent difference in length between the two categories of statements.

Variations of true-false items.   Several variations have been introduced in an attempt to improve true-false items. Most of these try to accomplish one or more of the following: (1) reduce the ambiguity of the items; (2) reduce the effects of guessing on the scores; (3) provide more specific information as to how much a student knows. The three most frequently used variations are described below.

1. *Underlining a word or clause in the statement.* This is the simplest variation and is intended to reduce ambiguity by focusing the attention of the examinee on the important part of the statement.

EXAMPLE

1. T F   Malaria is transmitted by the Anopheles mosquito.
2. T F   If foods are frozen, then harmful bacteria in them
will be killed.

The instructions for such items should clearly indicate that the student is to judge the truth or falsity of the underlined portion in relation to the rest of the statement. Use of underlining permits the use of more complex statements.

2. *Requiring students to correct false statements.* A student who correctly marks a false statement as false may have made a lucky guess, but he may also have chosen the answer on the basis of misinformation. For example, in the item, "Insulin is secreted by the pituitary gland," a student could mark it false because he thinks insulin is secreted by the adrenal glands. In this case, his incorrect information leads him to a correct answer. To make sure that the student knows the true facts underlying a false statement and to reduce guessing, the student can be instructed to provide the correct answer whenever he marks a statement false. This works well when combined with the underlining described in the first variation, but is likely to be difficult to score if no constraints are introduced in the item. Our example can be corrected by changing insulin to one of the pituitary hormones, by changing "is secreted" to "is not secreted," by changing "the pituitary gland" to "an endocrine gland" or "the pancreas." It seems unnecessary to mention that, if this variation is used, all statements, true or false, must have underlined portions. The part of the statement that is underlined should be the specific content that the teacher is trying to appraise. Thus, in the example, if the teacher were trying to determine whether the student knew the name of a hormone secreted by the pituitary gland, he should underline the word "insulin." If the teacher were interested in determining whether the student knew the name of the gland that secretes insulin, he should underline "the pituitary gland."

3. *Basing true-false items on specific stimulus material provided for the student.* The true-false item tends to be most effective and most useful when it is based on some given stimulus material such as a chart, map, graph, table, or reading passage. In this situation the student is instructed to respond to the item only in terms of the given material; therefore he usually has a better defined frame of reference in terms of which to judge the truth or falsity of the statement. This type of true-false item can be effectively used to appraise comprehension, interpretation, extrapolation, and logical reasoning if appropriate stimulus material is used and items are written to elicit these abilities. An example of this item type is given below.

EXAMPLE

Directions: The pie graph below shows how each dollar for medical care is spent. Look at the graph carefully. Statements are given below the graph. Read each statement carefully.

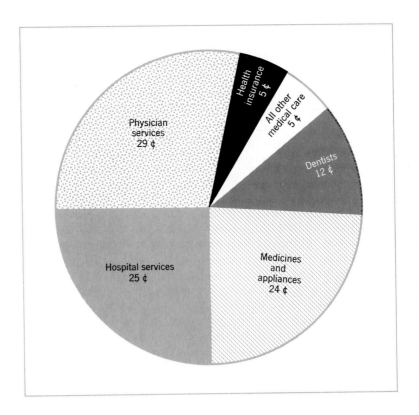

Mark T, if the data in the graph support the statement.

Mark F, if the data in the graph contradict the statement or no data are provided in the graph to either support or contradict the statement.

(T)   1. More of the medical care dollar is spent for physicians' services than for any other one category of expense.

(F)   2. Few Americans have health insurance.

(F)   3. Americans spend 24 cents out of every dollar they make on medicines and appliances

(T)   4. Hospital and physicians' services together account for slightly more than half of the money spent for medical care.

(T)   5. Less money is spent on dental care than on physicians' services.

(T)   6. About 25 percent of the medical care dollar is spent on nursing service in hospitals.

This form of item is sometimes made more complex by requiring the student to answer in four or five categories such as "definitely true"; "probably true"; "insufficient data to determine whether it is true or false"; "probably false"; and "definitely false." In this format the item becomes a multiple-choice item rather than a true-false item.

4. *Grouping short true-false items under a common question or statement heading.* Two examples of this variation are given below.

EXAMPLE

Directions: Place a T in front of each choice that is a correct answer to the question. Put an F in front of each choice that is NOT a correct answer to the question.

A. Which of the following diseases are caused by viruses?

(T) 1. Chicken pox		(T) 5. Measles
(F) 2. Diphtheria		(T) 6. Mumps
(T) 3. Influenza		(F) 7. Tuberculosis
(F) 4. Malaria		(F) 8. Typhoid fever

B. A girl, 14 years old, ate the following food during a 24-hour period.

Breakfast	*Lunch*	*Dinner*
Cup of black coffee	1 glass Coca-Cola (8 oz)	Roast rib of beef (9 oz)
	1 hamburger (4 oz) with bun	Mashed potatoes (½ cup)
	French fried potatoes— 20 pieces	Milk—1 glass (8 oz) Apple pie—1 piece

In which of the following was her diet deficient?

(T) 1. Calcium   (F) 5. Niacin
(F) 2. Calories   (F) 6. Protein
(F) 3. Carbohydrates (T) 7. Vitamin A
(T) 4. Iron   (T) 8. Vitamin C

The format of this variation looks like a multiple-choice item, but the task for the student is to judge whether each choice is true or false in relation to the original question; therefore it is basically a series of true-false items. The variation can be an efficient way to test for knowledge of categories, classifications or characteristics, and for simple applications. It is particularly effective for testing a particular part of a topic in depth. The format reduces the reading load for the student and the question serves as a frame of reference for judging truth or falsity, thus removing some of the ambiguity in true-false statements.

WRITING MULTIPLE-CHOICE ITEMS

The multiple-choice item is the most flexible of the objective item types. It can be used to appraise the achievement of any of the educational objectives that can be measured by a paper-and-pencil test except those relating to skill in written expression and originality. An ingenious and talented item writer can construct multiple-choice items that require not only the recall of knowledge but also the use of skills of comprehension, interpretation, application, analysis, or synthesis to arrive at the keyed answer.

The multiple-choice item consists of two parts: the stem, which presents the problem, and the list of possible answers or options. In the standard form of the item, one of the options is the correct or best answer and the others are misleads or foils or distractors. The stem of the item may be presented either as a question or as an incomplete statement. The form of the stem apparently makes no difference in the overall effectiveness of the item (Dunn and Goldstein, 1959) as long as the stem presents a clear and specific problem to the examinee.

The number of options used in the multiple-choice question differs on different tests, and there is no real reason why it cannot vary for items in the same test. An item must have at least 3 answer choices to be classified as a multiple-choice item and the typical pattern is to have 4 or 5 answer choices to reduce the probability of guessing the answer. A distinction should be made between the number of options presented for a multiple-choice item and the number of *effective* or *functioning* options that the item has. In the poor example below, written for that eighth grade test on health, the item will really function as a 2 choice item because no one is likely to choose option A or D. The revised item still presents 4 answer choices but is now likely to really function as a 4-choice question because options A and D have been made more reasonable.

EXAMPLE

Poor: About how many calories are recommended daily for a girl, age 14, height 62 in., weight 103 lb, moderately active?

   A. 0
   B. 2,000
   <u>C</u>. 2,500
   D. 30,000

Better: About how many calories are recommended daily for a girl, age 14, height 62 in., weight 103 lb, moderately active?

   A. 1,500
   B. 2,000
   <u>C</u>. 2,500
   D. 3,000

The revised item will probably be more difficult than the original one because the options are closer together in value. The difficulty of a multiple-choice item depends upon the process called for in the item as well as the closeness of the options. Consider the set of three items shown below all relating to the meaning of the term "fortified food." We can predict that version 1 will be relatively easy, version 2 somewhat more difficult, and version 3 still more difficult. In version 1 the stem is a direct copy of the definition of "fortified food" in the textbook and the misleads are not terms used to indicate the addition of nutrients to foods. The difference between 1 and 2 is that the stem of 2 recasts the text book definition into a novel form and calls for a different mental process than 1. The difference between 2 and 3 is in the closeness of the options.

EXAMPLE

1. When a nutrient has been added that is not present in the natural food, the food is said to be

   <u>A</u>. fortified.
   B. processed.
   C. pasteurized.
   D. refined.

2. In the processing of milk for sale, Vitamin D concentrate has been added to provide at least 400 U. S. P. units per quart. The carton can then legally state that the milk is

A. fortified.
B. processed
C. pasteurized.
D. refined.

3. In the processing of milk for sale, Vitamin D concentrate has been added to provide at least 400 U. S. P. units per quart. The carton can then legally state that the milk is

A. fortified.
B. enriched.
C. irradiated.
D. restored.

Good multiple-choice questions take time and skill to construct. One way to cut down on the time is to draw from existing pools of items; selected references to collections of items in different content areas are provided at the end of the chapter. A step-by-step analysis of the process of constructing multiple-choice items is provided in the booklet *Multiple-Choice Questions: A Close Look* (Educational Testing Service, 1963). In the following pages a series of suggestions are given for improving both the stem and the options of multiple-choice questions.

1. *Be sure the stem of the item clearly formulates a problem.* The stem should be worded so that the student clearly understands what problem or question is being asked before he reads the answer choices. Look at the poor example below. When you finish reading the stem you know only that the item is related to a part of the pancreas. You have no idea what the problem is until you read each of the options. The answer choices that are provided are heterogeneous in content; that is, one relates to structure, one to function, one to permanence, and one to location. The poor item is really nothing more than four true-false items with the words "The cell islets of the pancreas" in common. The revised item provides both a more clearly formulated problem in the stem and a more homogeneous set of answer choices.

EXAMPLE

Poor: The cell islets of the pancreas

A. contain ducts.
B. produce insulin
C. disappear as one grows older.
D. are located around the edge of the pancreas.

Better: The cell islets of the pancreas secrete the substance called

    A. trypsin.
    <u>B.</u> insulin.
    <u>C.</u> secretin.
    D. adrenalin.

2. *Include as much of the item as possible in the stem and keep options as short as possible.* In the interests of economy of space, economy of reading time, and clear statement of the problem, try to word and arrange the item so that the answer choices can be kept relatively short. If the same words and phrases are repeated in all or most of the options, as in the poor example below, rewrite the stem to include the repetitious material if it is needed to make the item clear. Answer choices that are long in relation to the stem frequently occur because of failure to formulate a problem clearly in the stem.

EXAMPLE

Poor: The term "empty-calorie" food designates

    <u>A.</u> a food that has few essential nutrients but high caloric value.
    B. a food that has neither essential nutrients nor caloric value.
    C. a food that has both high nutritive value and high caloric value.
    D. a food that has high nutritive value but low caloric value.

Better: The term "empty-calorie" is applied to foods that are

    <u>A.</u> low in nutrients, high in calories.
    B. low both in nutrients and calories.
    C. high both in nutrients and calories.
    D. high in nutrients, low in calories.

3. *Include in the stem only the material needed to make the problem clear and specific.* Items with long, wordy stems containing material that is irrelevant to the problem are likely to reduce the effectiveness and efficiency of the test. First, the added material increases the reading load of the test, thus making it more difficult to separate generalized skill in reading from compentence specific to the subject matter area. Second, it increases reading time at the expense of answering time, making the test inefficient. The practice of including irrelevant material in the stem, as in the poor example below, appears to be a result of the teacher's misinterpretation of the idea that tests should teach as well as test. Tests teach as well as test when they (1) reflect accurately the objectives of instruction; (2) pose clear and meaningful questions or problems; and (3) are commented on specifically and returned promptly to the students; not when new material or review material is introduced in the test item.

EXAMPLE

Poor: Cells of one kind belong to a particular group performing a specialized duty. We call this group of cells a tissue. All of us have different kinds of tissues in our bodies. Which of the following would be classified as epithelial tissue?

    A. Tendons
    B. Adenoids and tonsils
    C. Mucous membranes
    D. Cartilage

Better: Which of the following would be classified as epithelial tissue?

    A. Tendons
    B. Adenoids and tonsils
    C. Mucous membranes
    D. Cartilage

If the purpose of the test item is to appraise whether the examinee can differentiate data necessary to solve a problem or support an argument from those that are either unnecessary or irrelevant, then one would have to include extra data in posing the problem. In this instance, though, the extra material is central to the process being measured; therefore it would not be irrelevant.

    4. *Use the negative only sparingly in the stem of an item.* Negative stems when combined with the answer choices can present difficult reading problems to students. (See the example on p. 238 and material on negatives in true-false items on p. 223) Negative items also provide the teacher with little information concerning the positive knowledge that a student has.

    There are times when it is important for the student to know the exception or to be able to detect errors. For these purposes a few items with the words "not" or "except," in the stem may be justified, particularly when overinclusion is a common error for students. When a negative word is used in a stem, it should be underlined and/or capitalized to call the student's attention to it.

    The poor example below was written to measure whether students knew the function of the semicircular canals, but the item as written does not measure this aspect of the student's knowledge. The revised example measures more directly what the teacher wanted to test for. The second "better" example shows a more appropriate use of the negative stem because (1) the most common error made by students about the duties of the Food and Drug Administration is to include inspection of meat, which is the duty of the Department of Agriculture; and (2) it would be difficult to get three plausible misleads if the item were stated in positive form.

EXAMPLE

Poor: Which of the following structures of the ear is *NOT* concerned with hearing?

   A. Eardrum
   B. Oval window
   C. Semicircular canals
   D. Cochlea

Better: 1. Which one of the following structures of the ear helps to maintain balance?

   A. Eardrum
   B. Oval window
   C. Semicircular canals
   D. Cochlea

2. Which one of the following activities is *NOT* the responsibility of the Food and Drug Administration?

   A. Inspection of warehouses storing food for interstate shipment
   B. Inspection of slaughter houses that ship meat across state lines
   C. Initiation of court action to remove an adulterated food from the market
   D. Testing samples of foods for interstate sale

   5. *Use novel material in formulating problems to measure understanding or ability to apply principles.* Most locally made tests focus too closely on rote memory of the text or material presented in the classroom and neglect measurement of the ability to use information. The multiple-choice item is well adapted to measuring understanding, but a novel situation must be presented to the student if more than rote memory is to be required to answer the question. The second and third variations of the example on p. 230 illustrate an attempt to move away from the form in which the concept was stated in the eighth grade text on health. Two examples are given below to illustrate how an item can be structured to appraise ability to use information.

EXAMPLE

Rote memory: 1. Which of the following foods will yield the largest number of calories when metabolized in the body?

    A. 1 gram of fat
    B. 1 gram of sugar
    C. 1 gram of starch
    D. 1 gram of protein

Application: Which of the following would result in the greatest reduction of calories if it were eliminated from the daily diet?

    A. 1 tablespoon of butter
    B. 1 tablespoon of granulated sugar
    C. 1 slice of white, enriched bread
    D. 1 boiled egg

Rote memory: 2. Death from pneumonia and influenza is most frequent among

    A. infants and aged people.
    B. infants and elementary school children.
    C. teenagers and aged people.
    D. teenagers and young adults.

Interpretation. Look at the graph below, which shows the death rate from disease A by age group.

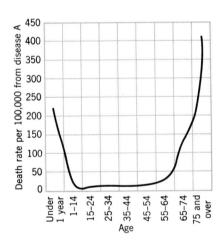

Which of the following diseases could be disease A?

    A. Pneumonia
    B. Cancer
    C. Tuberculosis
    D. Heart disease

6. *Be sure that there is one and only one correct or clearly best answer.* In the typical multiple-choice item the examinee is instructed to choose one and only one answer. Having instructed the examinee to choose *the* answer that is best, the test constructor is obligated to provide one and only one for each item. This seems obvious, but many items on classroom tests either have two or more equally good answers or no good answer. Thus in the following example B is keyed as the correct answer but there is also a large element of correctness for C and E. The revised version eliminates this fault but will probably be an easy item.

EXAMPLE

Poor: A color-blind boy inherits the trait from a

    A. male parent.
    B. female parent.
    C. maternal grandparent.
    D. paternal grandparent.
    E. remote ancestor.

Better: A color-blind boy most probably inherited the trait from his

    A. father.
    B. mother.
    C. paternal grandfather.
    D. paternal grandmother.

In addition to making sure that there is *only* one correct best answer, the item writer should see to it that the one answer is unequivocally best. It is his responsibilty to use his very best scholarship, as well as his skill in phrasing stem and answer choices, to produce a problem and answer with which experts in the field will agree.

7. *Be sure wrong answer choices are plausible.* One of the major advantages of the multiple-choice item is, that it can require the examinee to select his answer from among 3, 4, or 5 answer choices, thus reducing the chance of guessing the answer. However, the wrong answer choices must be ones that will attract examinees who have no or only partial information. To accomplish this, the wrong answer choices should be logically consistent with the stem and should represent common errors made by students at a particular grade or ability level. This is related to the point made on pp. 229–230 about difficulty.

In the first poor example options A and C are compounds, not elements, and thus not consistent with the stem. In the second poor example options C and D are very implausible.

EXAMPLE

Poor: 1. Which of the following elements is found in proteins but not in carbohydrates or fats?

    A. Carbon dioxide
    B. Oxygen
    C. Water
    D. Nitrogen

2. The gas that is formed in the cells after the oxidation of food and taken to the lungs and expelled is

    A. oxygen.
    B. carbon dioxide.
    C. helium.
    D. chlorine.

8. *Be sure no unintentional clues to the correct answer are given.* Inexperienced test constructors frequently give away the correct answer to an item or give clues that permit the examinee to eliminate one or more of the wrong answer choices from consideration. Dunn and Goldstein (1959) have shown that items containing irrelevant cues or specific determiners, correct answers consistently longer than incorrect answers, and grammatical inconsistencies between the stem and the options are easier than items without these faults. Chase (1964) demonstrated that examinees can learn to use length of option as a cue to the correct answer, and Wahlstrom and Boersma (1960) have shown that ninth graders can be taught to use various item writing faults to improve their scores on multiple-choice tests.

Examples of some types of unintentional cue are given below. Number 1 is an example of a *clang association*, that is, a repetition of a word or phrase or sound in the keyed answer and stem. Number 2 contains specific determiners that have the same effect in multiple-choice options as in true-false statements (see p. 223). In number 3 the keyed answer is much longer than the other options. Number 4 is an example of one kind of grammatical inconsistency in which the word "a" in the stem implies a singular word but options A and C are both plural.

The revised items show how each of these faults can be corrected to make the item potentially more effective in measuring knowledge rather than testwiseness.

EXAMPLE

237
writing test
items

Poor: Clang association
1. The function of the platelets in the blood is to help in

A. carrying oxygen to the cells.
B. carrying food to the cells.
C. clotting of the blood.
D. fighting disease.

Poor: Specific determiners
2. Which of the following is characteristic of anaerobic bacteria?

A. They never live in soil.
B. They can live without molecular oxygen.
C. They always cause disease.
D. They can carry on photosynthesis.

Poor: Length cues
3. The term "side effect" of a drug refers to

A. additional benefits from the drug.
B. the chain effect of drug action.
C. the influence of drugs on crime.
D. any action of the drug in the body other than the one the doctor wanted the drug to have.

Poor: Grammatical inconsistency
4. Penicillin is obtained from a

A. bacteria.
B. mold.
C. coal-tars.
D. tropical tree.

Better: 1. Which of the following structures in the blood help in forming blood clots?

A. Red blood cells
B. Lymphocytes
C. Platelets
D. Monocytes

2. The *one* characteristic that distinguishes *all* anaerobic bacteria is their ability to

A. withstand extreme variation in air temperature.
B. live without molecular oxygen.
C. live as either saprophytes or parasites.
D. reproduce either in living cells or nonliving culture media.

3. Which of the following, if it occurred, would be a side-effect of aspirin for a man who had been taking two aspirin tablets every three hours for a heavy cold and slight fever?

A. Normal body temperature
B. Reduction in frequency of coughing
C. Easier breathing
D. Ringing in the ears

4. Penicillin is obtained from

A. bacteria.
B. molds.
C. coal tars.
D. tropical trees.

9. *Use the option "none of these" or "none of the above" only when the keyed answer can be classified unequivocally as right or wrong.* This type of option has been used by experienced test writers on tests of spelling, mathematics, and study skills. In these types of test an absolutely correct answer can be given. On other types of test, where the student is to choose the best answer and where the keyed answer is the best answer but not necessarily absolutely correct, the use of "none of these" or "none of above" is inappropriate.

Teachers tend to use this type of option indiscriminately. On teacher-made tests the option frequently fails to make any sense because it does not complete the stem grammatically, as shown in the item below which appeared on a tenth grade biology test.

EXAMPLE

Poor: Of the following the one that is *never* a function of the stem of plants is

A. conduction.
B. food storage.
C. photosynthesis.
D. support.
E. none of the above.

Not only is the option "none of the above" grammatically inconsistent with the stem, but it is also logically inconsistent with the stem. Option E does not name a function of the plant, and the double negative effect of the option and the "never" in the stem makes comprehension of the meaning of the item difficult. There is no way of revising the item to make it better since any function of a plant is performed by the stem in some plant.

Some studies of the use of "none of these" as an option have indicated that use of the option makes items more difficult and more discriminating [Boynton (1950), Hughes and Trimble (1965)], but other studies have failed to confirm this finding [Wesman and Bennett (1946), Rimland (1960)].

If "none of these" or its equivalent is used as an option in items requiring quantitative solutions or in spelling tests, it should be used as frequently for the correct option as any other answer choice and the stem of the item should be phrased as a question. On such tests the option functions best if it is used as the correct answer on some of the easier items at the beginning of the test to reinforce the instructions that "none of the above" is sometimes the correct answer.

The poor example given below represents a poor use of the "none of the above" option in an item calling for a numerical answer because only approximations are given rather than exact quantities. Although option B is keyed as the correct answer, option E is the better answer since the estimates of the blood volume for an average adult range from a low of 10 pints to a high of 16 pints. One could raise the issue of the importance of a junior high school student's knowing this particular fact.

EXAMPLE

Poor: How many pints of blood does a normal human adult of average weight have?

   A. 3 pints
   B. 13 pints
   C. 30 pints
   D. 50 pints
   E. None of the above

Better: Approximately what percentage of the body weight of a healthy human adult is blood?

   A. 3 to 5 percent
   B. 8 to 9 percent
   C. 12 to 15 percent
   D. 20 to 25 percent

10. *Avoid the use of "all of these" or "all of the above" in the typical multiple-choice item.* Usually when the option "all of these" is used on teacher-made tests, it is the correct answer. Items using this option tend to be somewhat easy because the examinee can be led to the correct answer even though he has only partial information. Look at the poor example below. Assume that the student has been instructed to mark only one answer and that he knows that both age and weight are used to compute basal energy requirements. He must then mark D for his answer; thus he gets credit for having complete information even though he does not. In the revised version, he must have full information to arrive at the keyed answer.

The option "all of these," is much more effective if it is used in the variation of the complex multiple-choice item described in the next section.

EXAMPLE

Poor: Which of the following factors must be considered in computing basal energy requirements?

    A. Age
    B. Height
    C. Weight
    D. All of the above

Better: Which of the following factors must be considered in computing basal energy requirements?

    A. Weight only
    B. Age only
    C. Height and weight only
    D. Age and weight only
    E. Age, height, and weight

Variations of multiple-choice items.   A number of variations of the standard multiple-choice items have been used on tests. Gerberich (1956) gives illustrations of most of these variations. One commonly used variation is the matching item that will be discussed in a separate section. In this section we discuss two variations that are used frequently.

    1. *Complex multiple-choice item.* This variation gets its name from the format and the combinations of options that are used as answer choices. The variation is most effective when it is used to appraise knowledge of or ability to apply or interpret multiple causation, effects, functions, or uses. Example 1 illustrates an effective use of the item type because it requires the student to discriminate between both the kind of food and the kind of commerce that come under the jurisdiction of the Food and Drug Administration. Hughes and Trimble (1965) have

shown that this type of item is both more difficult and more discriminating than the typical form of multiple-choice item that tests for the same knowledge.

Example 2 represents a poor use of the complex multiple-choice item and several faults of item construction. Although there are multiple signs of impaired circulation, the options are short; therefore the knowledge could be tested more efficiently in the usual format as in the item on p. 240. The technical faults of the item are as follows: (1) no specific problem is presented to the examinee; (2) signs numbered 1, 2, and 3 are used in all the answer choices so that the student is required

EXAMPLE 1

Effective: 1. Look at each of the food processing or producing activities below.

1. A housewife makes jellies and sells them in her home town.
2. A butcher makes scrapple and pork sausage and sells them only in the state of Maryland.
3. A food processor makes jellies in California and sells them in New York.
4. A slaughterhouse in Chicago ships meats to all states.
5. A citrus grower produces oranges in Florida and ships them to all Eastern states.

Which of the above would be subject to the regulations and supervision of the federal Food and Drug Administration?

A. 2 and 4 only
B. 3 and 5 only
C. 3, 4, and 5 only
D. 1, 3, and 5 only
E. All of them

EXAMPLE 2

Poor: 1. If a bandage or cast on the arm is too tight, it may interfere with the circulation in the arm. Signs of interference with circulation include

1. cold.   3. numbness.   5. loss of motion.
2. blanching.   4. swelling.

A. All of these
B. 1, 2, 3 and 4
C. All except 5
D. 1, 2, 3 and 5

only to determine whether numbers 4 and 5 are correct; (3) the method of presenting choices (contrast between option C and options B and D) is varied, which creates unnecessary difficulty for the student.

The complex multiple-choice item should be used very sparingly on locally made tests.

2. *Use of paired statements as stimuli.* This variation is illustrated below.

EXAMPLE

Directions: Items 1 through 3 are based on pairs of statements. Read each statement carefully. On your answer sheet, mark:

    A. If the amount in statement I is greater than that in statement II.

    B. If the amount in statement II is greater than that in statement I.

    C. If the amount in statement I is equal to that in statement II.

(B)   1.   I Caloric value of 1 tablespoon of cane sugar.
            II Caloric value of 1 tablespoon of butter.

(A)   2.   I The daily requirement of calories for a male lumberjack, 73 inches tall, weight 190 lbs, age 25.
            II The daily requirement of calories for a male office clerk, 73 inches tall, weight 190 lbs, age 25.

(A)   3.   I The daily requirement of iron for a 16-year-old girl.
            II The daily requirement of iron for a 16-year-old boy.

The paired item format is an efficient and effective way of measuring judgment of relative amounts or quantities, relative effects of changing conditions, or relative chronology. This format preferably should be used for content having established quantitative values. For example, the use of the pair of statements: "(I) The number of hours of sleep needed by a 14-year-old boy and (II) The number of hours of sleep needed by a 30-year-old man," would be undesirable because there is no empirically determined value for the number of hours of sleep required for any age group.

WRITING MATCHING ITEMS

The characteristic that distinguishes the matching item from the ordinary multiple-choice item is that there are several problems whose answers must be drawn from a single list of possible answers. The matching item has most frequently been used to measure factual information such as meanings of terms, dates of events, the achievements of people, symbols for chemical elements, and authors of books. Effective matching items can be constructed by basing the set of items on a chart, map, diagram, or drawing. Features of the figure can be numbered and the examinee can be asked to match names, functions, and so on, with the numbers on the figure. This method of constructing matching items is particularly useful in tests dealing with study skills, science, or technology, for example, identification of cell structures on a biology test.

Matching items on locally made tests often have many technical faults and as a result tend to be relatively superficial measurement devices. Look at the sample matching exercise on the page below, which appeared on a test in health and hygiene for an eighth grade class.

This example illustrates most of the common mistakes made in preparing matching items. First, the directions are vague; they do not specify the basis for matching. Second, the set of stimuli is too miscellaneous for a good matching exercise. How

EXAMPLE

Poor: Directions: Place the correct letter to the left of each number. Use each letter only once.

Column I		Column II
(P)	1. Number of permanent teeth	A. Malocclusion
(I)	2. Vitamin D	B. Tear and rip food
(N)	3. Vitamin C	C. Trench mouth
(K)	4. Enamel	D. Straightening teeth
(O)	5. Bleeding gums	E. Jawbone socket
(C)	6. Vincent's Angina	F. Contains nerves and blood vessels
(D)	7. Orthodontia	G. Grind food
(E)	8. Alveolus	H. Crown
(A)	9. Lower jaw protruding	I. Sunshine
(F)	10. Pulp	J. Cleaning device
(M)	11. Acid	K. Hardest substance
(L)	12. Low percentage of decay	L. Primitives
(B)	13. Cuspids	M. Decay
(G)	14. Molars	N. Citrus fruits
(H)	15. Visible part of tooth	O. Gingivitis
(J)	16. Dental floss	P. 32

Note. The "correct" answers are those designated by the teacher who constructed the exercise.

many answer choices in Column II are logically possible answers for the first statement in Column I? For the second? The statements in Column I have very little in common except that they relate to teeth and dental health in general. Third, the set is too long and the answer choices in Column II are not arranged in any systematic order. Even if the examinee knows the answer to a statement, he has to search through the entire list in Column II to find it, which is time consuming. Fourth, some of the entries are vague; for example, 9, 11, and 12 in Column I and I, L, and M in Column II. The vagueness makes it difficult to justify the answer keyed as correct by the teacher; furthermore, the accuracy of number 12 can be questioned. Fifth, there are 16 statements in Column I and 16 answer choices in Column II. If the student knows 15, he automatically gets the sixteenth correct.

The guides for writing good matching items are given below.

1. *Keep the set of statements in a single matching exercise homogeneous.* In the illustration they should all be parts of a tooth or all be diseases of the teeth and gums or all methods of promoting good oral hygiene. A homogeneous set will require the student to make genuine discriminations to arrive at a correct answer.

2. *Keep the set of items relatively short.* One reason for keeping the set short is that the statements are more likely to be homogeneous in content. The second reason is that a short answer list puts less of a clerical burden on the examinee.

3. *If the two columns differ in length of statements, have the students choose answers from the column with the least reading load.* The reason for this suggestion is that the answer column will be read several times by the student and it takes less time to read short statements than long ones.

4. *Use a heading for each column that accurately describes its content.* A descriptive heading helps to define the task for the examinee. If the test constructor is unable to identify a heading that specifically defines the content then he probably has a heterogeneous collection of items.

5. *Have more answer choices than the number of statements to be answered unless answer choices can be used more than once.* The larger number of answer choices reduces the probability of guessing the answer or obtaining automatic credit as in the poor example.

6. *Arrange the answer choices in a logical order if one exists.* If a student knows the answer, he should be able to find it easily.

Arranging names in alphabetical order or dates in chronological order reduces the time required to find the answer.

7. *Specify in the directions the basis for matching and whether answer choices can be used more than once.* This will tend to reduce ambiguity and to result in a more uniform task for all examinees.

A variation of the matching exercise is the classification type or master list. This variation can be used quite effectively to appraise application, comprehension, or interpretation. It is an efficient way of exploring range of mastery of a concept or related set of concepts. An illustration of this type of exercise is given below.

EXAMPLE—MASTER MATCHING

Instructions: Below are given four kinds of appeals that advertisers of health and beauty products make.

A. Appeal to fear or a sense of insecurity.

B. Appeal to snobbery or identification with a particular, small group or individual.

C. Appeal to desire to be like others, to join the "bandwagon."

D. Appeal to authority.

Statements 1 to 6 are advertisements of imaginary products. Read each statement carefully. For each statement, mark the letter of the appeal that is being used. Answer choices may be used more than once.

(A) 1. Don't let iron-tired blood get you down. Keep your verve and vivacity. Take Infantol.

(D) 2. Research shows Lucy's Little Lethal Pills are 10 times more effective than ordinary pain-killers.

(B) 3. Dutchess Poorhouse, the international beauty, bathes her face twice a day with Myrtle's Turtle Oil.

(B) 4. Men, are you tired of a woman's deodorant? Be a man. Use No-Sweat. Leave the weaker stuff to the weaker sex.

(B) 5. At $1,629.21 the Inside Jogger is not for everyone. Only a select few can be proud owners of one! Are you one of these?

(C) 6. Be one of the crowd. Drink and serve Popsie's Cola.

PREPARING THE OBJECTIVE TEST FOR USE

Objective tests, particularly multiple-choice tests, should be reproduced in some way so that each examinee has his own copy. Oral administration of objective tests is not satisfactory. Many schools have a spirit duplicator or "Ditto" machine that is adequate for reproducing tests for groups of moderate size. For large groups, mimeographing or offset printing is preferable. More important than the process of duplication is the quality of work, both in organizing the layout of the test and in typing up the master copy. The most important points to consider in arranging the items of the test will be discussed in the paragraphs that follow.

1. *Arrange items on the test so that they are easy to read.* In the interest of the person taking the test, items should not be crowded together on the test paper. Multiple-choice questions are easier to read if each response is on a separate line. Having part of an item on one page and part on the next page should be avoided, since such an arrangement may confuse the examinees. If several items all refer to a single diagram or chart, try to arrange the test so that the diagram or chart and all of the items are on the same page.

2. *Plan the layout of the test so that a separate answer sheet can be used to record answers.* Consideration should be given to the convenience of the student in recording his answers and to the convenience of the person scoring the test. An objective test can be scored much more quickly and efficiently if the answers are recorded on a separate answer sheet. Many teachers feel that the use of a separate answer sheet makes the test taking task more difficult for students. However, even third grade students can be taught very quickly to use a separate answer sheet and usually have little or no difficulty in using one. Many standardized achievement tests use separate answer sheets with little or no difficulty at the third grade level. The use of a separate answer sheet represents a test taking skill that should be taught to students, and practice in the skill should be provided early in the school program. Part of a homemade answer sheet that is adaptable to both true-false and multiple-choice items is shown in Fig. 7.2.

3. *Group items of the same format (true-false, multiple-choice, or matching) together.* Each different kind of objective item requires a different set of directions. Grouping items of the same format together makes it possible to write a concise and clear set of directions that will apply throughout that part of the test. The different kinds of item also require different response sets or approaches to the item on the part of the examinee. The examinee is better able to maintain an appropriate response set or approach if the items of the same type are grouped together.

Course _____ Name _____

Exam _____ Date _____

Instructions: Read the directions on the test sheet carefully, and follow
them exactly. For each test item, mark your choice for the
correct answer by blocking out the letter which corresponds to
the best answer for the test item.

Item	Answer	Item	Answer	Item	Answer
1	A B C D E	26	A B C D E	51	A B C D E
2	A B C D E	27	A B C D E	52	A B C D E
3	A B C D E	28	A B C D E	53	A B C D E
4	A B C D E	29	A B C D E	54	A B C D E

Figure 7.2
Part of a homemade answer sheet.

4. *Within item type, group items dealing with the same content together.* This practice will help reduce the feeling that the test lacks unity or coherence and will encourage a more integrated approach to the items on the part of the student. It will also help both the student and the teacher to see strong and weak points of the student in dealing with the content.

5. *Arrange items so that difficulty progresses from easy to hard.* This is most important when testing time is limited so that some items on the test will not be attempted by all students. Those unattempted items should be the more difficult ones that the examinee would have been less likely to answer correctly even if he had reached them. On power tests this kind of arrangement is supposed to have some psychological advantages in encouraging students, particularly young children and less able students to continue to attempt the items on the test rather than giving up. However, the practice is supported by professional judgment rather than by empirical evidence.

6. *Write a set of specific directions for each item type.* A good set of directions will provide information about how the examinee is to record his answers, the basis on which he is to select his answers, and the scoring procedures that will be used.

For a test made up of multiple-choice items that will not be corrected for guessing and for which separate answer sheets are used, one might use the following set of directions.

Directions: Read each item and decide which choice *best* completes the statement or answers the question.

Mark your answers on the separate answer sheet. Do *not* mark them on the test booklet. Indicate your answer by blacking out on the answer sheet the letter corresponding to your choice. That is, if you think that choice B is the best answer to item 1, black out the B in the row after No. 1 on your answer sheet.

Your score will be the number of right answers, so it will be to your advantage to answer every question, even if you are not sure of the right answer.

Be sure your name is on your answer sheet.

For a test made up of true-false questions in which answers are to be recorded on the test paper and the total score will be corrected for guessing, the following set of directions could be used.

Directions: Read each of the following statements carefully.

If all or any part of the statement is false, circle the F in front of the statement.

If the statement is completely true, circle the T in front of the statement.

Your score will be the number of right answers minus the number of wrong answers, so *do not guess blindly.* If you are not reasonably sure of an answer, omit the question.

Be sure your name is on your test.

7. *Be sure that one item does not provide clues to the answer of another item or items.* Unless one is very careful in assembling items for a test, the answer to an item may be given away by a previous item. All of the items that are finally selected should be carefully checked because it is possible for a true-false or completion item to give clues to the answer of a multiple-choice item or vice-versa. Thus in this example the true-false item provides a cue to the answer to the objective item.

EXAMPLE

1. T F   The spores of the bacteria causing botulism are present in soil and air.

2. Which of the following bacteria form spores?

A. Staphylococcus causing "food poisoning"
B. Bacillus causing botulism
C. Bacillus causing typhoid fever
D. Pneumococcus causing pneumonia

8. *Be sure that the correct responses form essentially a random pattern.* Some classroom teachers attempt to make their job of scoring easier by establishing a regular pattern of correct answers. For example, on a true-false test they will use a repetitive pattern such as T, T, F, F, F or on a multiple-choice test a pattern such as A, C, B, D. When this is done, some test-wise students may discover the pattern and use it as a means of answering items that they really do not know. On 4-option multiple-choice tests, there is a tendency for the correct answers to appear more frequently in the second and third positions than in the first and last positions. It is desirable on a multiple-choice test to have the correct answer in each of the possible response positions about the same percentage of the time. For example, on a 4-option multiple-choice test of 50 items, one might check to see that each response position contains the keyed answer in not less than 10 nor more than 15 items.

SCORING THE OBJECTIVE TEST

A basic decision that needs to be made before the test is given is whether a correction for guessing will be used. Students should be told whether the correction will be used because it may influence their strategy in taking the test. Test experts are not in complete agreement about the usefulness of the correction for guessing.

It is well known that there are marked differences among examinees in their tendency to guess on an objective test when they are not sure of the answer. These differences in willingness to guess introduce some variation in scores that is not related to real differences in achievement among students. One intended purpose of instructing examinees not to guess and of imposing a penalty for wrong answers is to try to make the guessing behavior more alike for all examinees.

Waters (1967) studied the effects of different scoring formulas on the number of items omitted on a test. The scoring formulas used were: rights only; rights $-$ $\frac{1}{4}$ wrongs; rights $-$ wrongs; rights $-$ $2 \times$ wrongs; and rights $-$ $4 \times$ wrongs. He found that the number of omits did increase as the penalty for wrong answers increased, but that the examinees receiving the more severe scoring penalties did not omit as many items as they should have if they were to achieve the highest score. He also found that the average number of items right was about the same for all scoring patterns. It appears that neither the instruction not to guess, with a threat of penalty for wrong answers, nor the instruction to answer every question, whether you are sure of the answer or not, persuades all people to behave the same way on an objective test. The probability of taking a risk appears to depend as much on the person's personality as on the test directions.

The formula for correction for guessing that is generally used is

$$\text{Corrected score} = R - \frac{W}{n - 1}$$

where R is the number of questions answered correctly,
  W is the number of questions answered incorrectly,
  n is the number of answer choices for an item.

Note that questions for which examinees do not give an answer, that is, omit, do not count in this formula for guessing. On a true-false test where there are only 2 possible answers, $n - 1$ in the formula becomes $2 - 1$, or 1, and the correction for guessing is the number of right answers minus the number of wrong answers.

The two examples below, one based on a true-false test and one on a multiple-choice test, illustrate how the formula works.

EXAMPLE 1

Type of Test	n	Student Performance		
		R	W	Omits
True-false	2	48	20	7

$$\text{Corrected score} = 48 - \frac{20}{2 - 1} = 48 - \frac{20}{1} = 28$$

EXAMPLE 2

Type of Test	n	Student Performance		
		R	W	Omits
Multiple choice	5	48	20	7

$$\text{Corrected score} = 48 - \frac{20}{5 - 1} = 48 - \frac{20}{4} = 43$$

The formula assumes (1) that a person either knows the right answer or else guesses—that is, that he never responds on the basis of misinformation—and (2) that all choices are equally attractive to a person who does not know the answer. These assumptions are rarely justified. On the one hand, a good item writer formulates misleads so as to capitalize on the misconceptions of the poorly informed. On the other hand, the person with partial information or with some shrewdness about objective items can often eliminate one or two options from consideration. The correction formula is, therefore, at best a rough and approximate adjustment that can compensate for gross differences in readiness to mark items.

Guessing on tests presents the most serious problem in tests that are highly speeded or that have items with only 2 answer choices. The scores obtained from such tests will probably be more dependable if they are corrected for guessing. In multiple-choice tests that have 4 or 5 answer choices and liberal enough time limits to permit all or most examinees to attempt every item, a score that is simply the number of right answers is quite satisfactory and there is little or no gain from correcting for guessing.

There have been a number of suggestions made for more complex scoring patterns for objective tests, particularly multiple-choice items. Most of these increase scoring time and to some extent test taking time. Some of these appear to produce small gains in precison of measurement per item, but it is not clear that they provide a gain per minute of testing time. Readers who are interested in these variations are referred to special treatments of the problem (Ebel, 1965; Davis, 1959; Combs et al., 1955).

ANALYZING AND USING THE RESULTS OF OBJECTIVE TESTS

An analysis of the responses pupils make to the items on a test can serve two important purposes. In the first place, the item responses provide diagnostic information for studying the learning of the class and the failures to learn and for guiding further teaching and study. In the second place, the responses to the separate items and a review of the items in the light of these responses provide a basis for preparing better tests another year.

The basic analysis that is needed is a tabulation of the responses that have been made to each item on the test. We need to know how many pupils got each item right, how many chose each of the possible wrong answers, and how many omitted the item. It helps our understanding of the item if we have this information for the upper and lower fractions of the group, and perhaps also for those in the middle. From this type of tabulation we can answer such questions as the following for each item:

1. How hard is the item?
2. Does it distinguish between the better and poorer students?

3. Do all the options attract responses, or are there some that are so unattractive that they might as well not be included?

A simple form can be prepared for recording the responses to each item, like that shown in Fig. 7.3. This can be put on a separate card for each item, and then the information can be accumulated in a permanent item file. This form is planned for a multiple-choice item with as many as five choices, but can be used for true-false items by using only the A and B columns.

		A	B	C	D	E	Omit
Item: Which one of the following states was formed from the Northwest Territory?							
		A. Indiana					
		B. Iowa					
		C. Montana					
		D. Oregon					
Option							
		A	B	C	D	E	Omit
Upper	25%	10					
Middle	50%	17		1	2		
Lower	25%	5	1	1	3		

Figure 7.3
Form for recording item analysis data.

To illustrate the type of information that is provided by an item analysis, we present below certain items from a social studies test, together with the analysis of responses for each item. This test was given to 100 high school seniors who had had a course in current American problems. There were 95 items on the test. The highest score on the test was 85 and the lowest score was 14. The test papers were arranged in order of total score, starting with the score of 85 and ending with the score of 14. The top 25 papers were selected to represent the upper group (score range 59 to 85) and the last 25 papers were selected to represent the lower group (score range 14 to 34). The count of responses is based on the 25 cases from the top and the 25 cases from the bottom of the group. The responses made to each item by each individual in the upper and lower groups were tallied to give the frequency of choosing each option. These frequencies are shown on the right. The correct option is underlined. Each item is followed by a brief discussion of the item data.

EXAMPLE

253
writing test
items

Item 1: "Everyone's switching to Breath of Spring Cigarettes!" is an example of the propaganda technique called

		Upper	*Lower*
A.	glittering generality.	0	2
B.	bandwagon.	25	20
C.	testimonial.	0	2
D.	plain folk.	0	1
	(Omit)	0	0

This is an easy item, since all 25 in the upper group and 20 in the lower group get it right. However, it does differentiate in the desired direction, since what errors there are fall in the lower group. The item is also good in that all of the wrong answer choices are functioning; that is, each wrong answer has been chosen by one or more persons in the lower group. Two or three easy items like this would be good ice-breakers with which to start a test.

EXAMPLE

Item 2: There were no federal income taxes before 1913 because prior to 1913

		Upper	*Lower*
A.	the federal budget was balanced.	3	5
B.	regular property taxes provided enough revenue to run the government.	9	15
C.	a tax on income was unconstitutional.	13	0
D.	the income of the average worker in the U.S. was too low to be taxed.	0	5
	(Omit)	0	0

This is a difficult item but a very effective one. That it is difficult is shown by the fact that only 13 out of 50 got it right. That it is effective is shown by the fact that all 13 getting the item right were in the upper group. All of the wrong options attracted some choices in the lower group and all of the wrong options attracted more of the lower group than the higher group. Incidentally, an item such as this shows how faulty the idea of "blind guessing" often is when an item is effectively written. In this item the majority of the lower group concentrated upon one particular wrong option that was particularly plausible and appealing.

EXAMPLE

Item 3: Under the "corrupt practices act" the national committee of a political party would be permitted to accept a contribution of

		Upper	Lower
A.	$10,000 from Mr. Jones.	15	6
B.	$1,000 from the ABC Hat Corporation.	4	6
C.	$5,000 from the National Association of Manufacturers.	2	6
D.	$500 from union funds of a local labor union.	4	7
	(Omit)	0	0

This item turned out poorly. First, the item is very difficult; only 8 out of the 50 or 16 percent of the students got it right. Second, the item is negatively discriminating, that is, correct answers were more frequent in the lower group than in the upper group. There are two possible explanations for the item analysis data: (1) the item was ambiguous especially for students who knew the most or (2) the students have not learned the provisions of the "corrrupt practices act." There are two things that point to the second as the more probable explanation; the concentration of responses of the upper group at option A and the apparently random responses of the lower group that indicate random guessing. In order to arrive at the correct answer to the item the student would have to know (1) the limit placed on contributions to the national committee of a political party, (2) who is forbidden to make contributions, and (3) what kind of organization the National Association of Manufacturers is. The teacher would have to discuss the item with the class to determine where the difficulty lies but one might guess that it is points 1 and 3 that are causing difficulty in the upper group.

EXAMPLE

255
restricted-
response tests

Item 4: The term "easy money" as used in
economics means

		Upper	Lower
A.	the ability to borrow money at low interest rates.	21	17
B.	dividends that are paid on common stocks.	0	0
C.	money that is won in contests.	0	0
D.	money paid for unemployment compensation.	4	8
	(Omit)	0	0

This item shows some discrimination in the desired direction
(21 versus 17), but the differentiation is not very sharp. The
response pattern is one that is quite common. Only two of the
four choices are functioning at all. Nobody selects either the B
or C choices. If we wished to use this item again, we might try
substituting "wages paid for easy work" for option B and
"money given to people on welfare" for option C. The repeat
of the vowel "easy" in option B and the idea of getting money
for not working in option C might make the item more difficult
and more discriminating.

Item statistics such as these can be used not only for evaluating the items but to guide review and restudy of the material
with a class. The items that prove difficult for the class as a
whole provide leads for further exploration. Discussion of these
items with the class should throw light on the nature of the
misunderstanding. The misunderstanding may in some cases
be cleared up by brief further discussion, although in some
cases a fuller review of the topic may be indicated. It is desirable, if local policies permit, to let pupils have their answer
sheets and a copy of the test and to make the answer key
available to them, so that they can themselves use the test as a
guide to review and clarification of the points they missed. An
examination should teach as well as test.

RESTRICTED-RESPONSE TESTS

So far we have directed our attention solely to tests made up of
structured-response objective items. There may also be occasions when a test for a local situation can with advantage consist of free-response items. The distinguishing feature of all free-
response test exercises is that the answer is *produced* by the ex-

aminee in response to the question or problem that is presented. The response may be very brief—a single word or a number—in which case the item approaches the objectivity of a structured-response item. Or, at the other extreme, the response may be an extended essay.

There are certain educational objectives that without question can be more successfully appraised by extended essay responses. These are objectives that focus on selecting, arranging, organizing, and expressing ideas, and those that focus on producing original or ingenious solutions to problems. However, we may question whether in practice these are the objectives for which essay questions have typically been used or the qualities that typically determine what rating a reader will assign to an essay response. Knowledge of facts, correctness and effectiveness of English usage, and legibility of handwriting all can be demonstrated to influence the score on essay tests. Furthermore, reading a pile of essay exams is a laborious and a subjective undertaking. An essay examination provides an assessment of relatively low reliability, in part because of variations within and among readers, in part because of the "lumpy" sampling that results from a small number of questions to cover a domain of knowledge. Without further elaboration, we present in Table 7.3 a table summarizing our perception of the advantages and shortcomings of essay, short-answer and objective test items.

We conclude by giving some suggestions relating to the preparation of short-answer and completion types of item, and finally some suggestions on the writing and the reading of essay questions.

The restricted-response exercise can be in the form of a question (short-answer) or of a statement with blanks to fill in (completion). Generally these two forms are interchangeable, that is, the same problem could be presented either as a question or as a statement to be completed. To be classified as a restricted-response item, the question or statement must be answerable with a word, a date, a number or a phrase, a list of several words, or at most with no more than two or three sentences. The restricted-response question is not very flexible and should be used sparingly on locally made tests. Items of this type are best suited for testing knowledge of vocabulary, names or dates, simple comprehension of concepts, and ability to solve quantitative problems. Quantitative problems that yield a specific numerical solution are "short-answer" by their very nature.

Factor	Essay	Short Answer, Completion	Objective
Can measure ability to solve novel problems	+ +	+	+ +
Can measure ability to organize, integrate, or synthesize	+ +	+	− −
Can measure originality or innovative approaches to problems	+ +	+	− −
Can isolate specific abilities in subject area from general skills of writing, spelling, and language usage	− −	−	+ +
Has potential value for diagnosis	− −	+	+ +
Can sample adequately the objectives of instruction	− −	−	+ +
Can sample adequately the content of instruction	− −	−	+ +
Is free from opportunities for guessing answer	+ +	+ +	− −
Gives consistent scores from scorer to scorer	− −	−	+ +
Is accurate in differentiating levels of competency among examinees	− −	−	+ +
Can be scored by unskilled clerk or machine	− −	−	+ +
Can be scored quickly	− −	−	+ +
Takes little time for writing items	+	+	−

Though short-answer questions have a simple, straightforward structure, there are still many bad exercises of this type written by inexperienced test makers. The most common faults found in locally made items are ambiguity of meaning, lack of precision in stating the question, and triviality of the content being measured. When constructing completion items, teachers too frequently lift a sentence from a textbook and remove one or two words. This practice is undesirable for two reasons: (1) a sentence out of context loses much of its meaning and (2) too great a premium is placed on rote memorizing of textbook material. The section that follows offers some guidelines for improving the construction of short-answer and completion items.

WRITING RESTRICTED-RESPONSE QUESTIC

1. *Be sure that each item deals with important content; do not measure trivia.* The information that a student is required to recall on a test should be important in the area. Avoid the type of item that could quite justifiably be answered, "Who cares?" Ask yourself in each case whether knowing or not knowing the answer would make a significant difference in the individual's competence in the area being appraised. Both the examples of poor questions given below measure trivial information, but both appeared in a teacher-made test on health in the eighth grade. No revision is suggested for the items since the information called for could be of no significance in an eighth grader's understanding of health or health practices.

EXAMPLE

Poor: Short answer: How many cases of smallpox occurred in the United States in 1950? (*Answer:* 39)

Poor: Completion: In 1965, only 1 out of (10) Americans provided for adequate dental care.

2. *Be sure the question or statement poses a specific problem to the examinee.* A short-answer question or completion item should be written in such a way that a student who knows the material will know what the one desired answer is. Look at the examples of short-answer and completion items labeled *Poor.* For both of the questions, the answer desired was nicotine. However, as the questions are written many words or phrases other than nicotine would be factually correct and reasonably sensible: chlorophyll, pigments, veins, moisture, starch, cells, leaf tissue, poison. The problem needs to be more specifically defined as is done in the revised statements.

EXAMPLE

Poor: Short answer: What does the tobacco leaf contain? (Nicotine)
    Completion: The tobacco leaf contains (nicotine).

Better: Short answer: What is the name of the poisonous substance found in tobacco leaves? (Nicotine)
    Completion: The poisonous substance found in tobacco leaves is named (nicotine).

3. *Be sure that the answer that the student is required to produce is factually correct.* Look at the poor examples given below. The answer the test maker wanted was cirrhosis of the liver, but alcohol per se does *not cause* cirrhosis of the liver; it is the nutritional deficiency that is frequently associated with excessive drinking of alcohol that leads to cirrhosis of the liver.

EXAMPLE

Poor: Short answer: What organic disease of the liver is caused by alcohol? (Cirrhosis of the liver)

Completion: Alcohol causes an organic disease called (cirrhosis) of the liver.

Better: Short Answer: What organic disease of the liver is common among people who drink large amounts of alcohol and have inadequate diets? (Cirrhosis of the liver)

Completion: People who drink large amounts of alcohol and have inadequate diets frequently suffer from an organic disease called (cirrhosis) of the liver.

4. *Be sure the language used in the question is precise and accurate in relation to the subject matter area being tested.* The sample completion item appeared on an eighth grade health test. From a biological standpoint, the statement is imprecise in calling genes "particles" and inaccurate in using the adjectives "strong" and "weak" instead of "dominant" and "recessive." The revision of the question shows how it could have been stated in a more precise way without giving the answer away.

EXAMPLE

Poor: Some of the small particles inside chromosomes are stronger than others. These stronger ones are said to be (dominant) while the weaker ones are said to be (recessive).

Better: A mother has type A blood and a father has type O blood. Four children are born in the family, all of whom have type A blood. From this one would conclude that the genes for type A blood are (dominant) to those of type O.

5. *If the problem requires a numerical answer, indicate the units in which it is to be expressed.* This will simplify the problem of scoring and will remove one source of ambiguity in the examinee's answer. In the poor example below, the answer can be given as 4 cups, 2 pints, or 1 quart, and if the student does not designate the units in which he is expressing his answer, the teacher may have difficulty in determining whether the student really knows the answer.

EXAMPLE

Poor: What is the recommended daily minimum requirement of milk for a 14-year-old boy?

Better: The recommended daily requirement of milk for a 14-year-old boy is (4) cups.

6. *In a completion item, omit only key words.* The blank in a completion item should require the student to supply a fact or term that is important in the area being appraised. Do not leave the verb out of a completion statement unless the purpose of the item is to measure knowledge of verb forms. In the sample item the teacher should decide whether he wants to test for knowledge of the word "glycogen," of the place where excess glucose is stored in the body, or of a function of the liver, and write the item accordingly.

EXAMPLE

Poor: The liver (stores) excess glucose as glycogen.

Better: In normal body metabolism, excess glucose in the blood is stored in the liver in the form of (glycogen).

7. *In an achievement test, do not leave too many blanks in a completion statement.* Overmutilation of a statement reduces the task of the examinee to a guessing game. Overly mutilated statements may be appropriate when one is trying to appraise creativity or originality with words, but not when one is trying to appraise factual knowlege.

EXAMPLE

Poor: The ___(1)___ whose primary ___(2)___ is ___(3)___ are the ___(4)___ .
    (*Answer:* 1, teeth; 2, function; 3, cutting; 4, incisors.)

Better: The teeth whose primary function is cutting are called the (incisors).

8. *In a completion item, put blanks near the end of the statement rather than at the beginning.* The student should know what question he is being asked before he encounters the blank.

EXAMPLE

261
restricted-
response tests

Poor: The _____ gland is an example of an endocrine gland.

Better: An example of an endocrine gland is the _____ gland.

PREPARING THE TEST FOR USE

The main objectives to be sought in preparing a restricted-answer test for administration are that the test format be easy for examinees to understand and follow and that the responses be convenient for the test maker to score. Some suggestions that will help to achieve these ends are given below.

1. *If both completion and short-answer questions are used on the same test, put items of the same type together.* Each type of question requires a different set of directions and a somewhat different mental set on the part of the students.

2. *Have students write their answers on a separate answer sheet.* Students should have ample space for recording their answers. Since the size of handwriting varies with different students, it is very difficult to judge how much space each will need. The teacher will also find it easier to score papers if the answers are recorded in a uniform manner. For short-answer questions blue books or blank sheets of paper can be used and the students can be instructed to number their answers to correspond to the question. For completion items, an answer sheet can be dittoed or mimeographed containing the number of each question, with a line extending from the number on which the student can record his answer.

3. *Write a set of directions for each item type that is used on the test.* The directions should be simple but complete. They should include such things as how and where the student is to record his answers, the score value of each question, and whether spelling will be considered in judging the adequacy of the answer. For quantitative problems the student should be instructed whether he is to show all of his work or merely record the answer. For short-answer questions the student should be instructed whether his answers must be writtten in complete sentences.

4. *So far as possible, group items dealing with the same content or skill together,* If this is done, it may help to reduce the feeling that the test is made up of unrelated bits and pieces. The examinee will also be able to concentrate on a single area of content at a time rather than having to shift back and forth among areas of content. Furthermore, the teacher will have an easier job of analyzing the test results for the group or for the individual since she will be able to see at a glance whether the errors are more frequent in one content area than another.

SCORING THE TEST

1. *Check the answer key against a sample of papers before scoring any paper.* Checking the prepared key against a few papers, preferably of those who are known to be good students, may disclose one or more items to which students have consistently given a response different from that in the key. This may arise either from a clerical error in preparing the key or from an interpretation of the question by students that differs from the one the instructor had intended. When this occurs, and if the alternative interpretation is defensible, the key should be corrected or extended to include the variant. In an item such as, "Give an example of a communicable disease," a number of answers could be correct. Sometimes in making the original key the teacher does not think of some possible answers, and the key may need to be extended as scoring proceeds.

2. *If spelling and sentence structure, as well as accuracy of content, are to be scored, provide a separate score for each.*

3. *Correct errors and make comments on each question as it is scored or provide a complete set of answers for each student when the papers are returned.* This practice provides better direction to students' learning from a test and has also been shown to increase motivation for student learning.

4. *Generally speaking, score each question either right or wrong and assign equal weight to each question.* A well-written restricted-response question will pose a very specific problem to the student and should be scored either 0 for wrong or 1 for correct. Awarding partial credits creates difficulties in scoring. The issue of partial credit generally arises in those questions presenting a quantitative problem or in completion questions that include more than 1 blank. Although awarding partial credit for correct method of work in a quantitative problem or for correctly filling some of the blanks in a completion item may make for happier relations with the students, it contributes little or nothing to the measurement effectiveness of a test.

The practice of having some questions count more in the total than others on a purely arbitrary basis contributes nothing to the test and increases scoring difficulties. If the teacher believes that some content or some skills are more important than others, he should have more questions based on that content or requiring that skill.

Although students at all levels of education need practice to develop writing skills, it is very doubtful that an examination is the appropriate place to provide this practice. Rather, the major advantage of the essay type of question lies in its potential for measuring the student's abilities to organize, integrate, and synthesize his knowledge; to use his information to solve novel problems; and to be original or innovative in his approaches to problem situations. To realize this potential requires that each question be carefully phrased so that it will require the student to reveal these kinds of abilities. Merely casting a question in essay form does not automatically insure that these abilities will be assessed.

Look at the following two essay questions.

EXAMPLE

Question 1

What methods have been used in the United States to prevent and control communicable diseases?

Question 2

Table 1

CAUSES OF DEATH AND RATE FOR EACH IN 1900 AND 1967

	Death Rate per 100,000 People	
Cause of Death	**1900**	**1967**
1. Pneumonia	175.4	21.8
2. Diarrhea and enteritis	139.9	2.0
3. Diseases of the heart	137.4	399.9
4. Cancer	64.0	160.9
5. Diphtheria	40.3	0.02

Examine the data provided in the table shown above.

Explain how changes in knowledge, in medical practice, and in the conditions of life in the United States between 1900 and 1967 account for the changes in death rate shown in the table.

To answer question 1 the student needs only to recall information and write it down in much the same form in which it was presented in the textbook or in class. On the other hand, question 2 requires that the student recall something about the characteristics of each of the diseases and disease conditions, and about methods of transmission or conditions that affect incidence of disease. He must then relate these to such things as immunization, chemotherapy, improvements in sanitation, and the increasing proportion of older people in the population. Question 2 seems more clearly appropriate for an essay question.

To realize the value of the essay question for appraising the ability to use information, to organize materials, or to use language effectively depends not only upon writing questions appropriate to elicit these abilities but also upon being able to structure the situation so that other factors do not obscure the desired appraisal. In the typical essay examination differences in knowledge of basic factual material hide differences in ability to use and organize those facts and time pressures often militate against the student's producing his best writing.

The "open-book" examination has been suggested as one means of partially evening out differences in factual knowledge. In this form of examination the students have access to any data in their texts or their notes. Realistically, we cannot expect to wash out all differences in knowledge by an open-book examination. The able student knows what to look for in the book and where to find it; the poor one can spend a whole period aimlessly leafing through the pages. However, there seem to be other advantages to the open-book examination. Feldhusen (1961) reported that college students who were given open-book examinations felt that this type of examination was more effective in promoting learning, reducing worry and tenseness about the examination, and reducing cheating. He also reported that, although students spent less time memorizing factual material in preparing for an open-book than for a closed-book examination, they spent as much or more time on general review of the material.

The time pressures of the typical essay testing situation can be eased by assigning essay questions as an out-of-class examination or by having very liberal time limits. If the former is done, we not only minimize time pressures but also gain the advantages of the open-book examination. Under these conditions, the student has time not only to write carefully but also to edit his writing, and the teacher can get samples of his best writing under optimal conditions. An out-of-class examination does introduce other problems, such as the possibility of help from parents or others. We can never be sure how much the final product is a result of the student's own efforts and how much should be attributed to others. Because of this, some essay testing must continue to be done under supervised conditions, but the out-of-class essay examination can be a valuable teaching device.

WRITING THE ESSAY QUESTIONS

The following suggestions are presented as guides to writing more effective essay questions.

1. *Have clearly in mind what mental processes you want the student to use in answering before starting to write the question.* The teacher or test constructor must understand as fully as possible the kinds of student response that represent the ability or abilities to be measured before determining the kinds of stimulus material needed to elicit those responses. For example, a teacher who wants to use the essay question to evaluate eighth graders' ability to think critically about health information may identify as evidence of critical thinking the abilities to evaluate the adequacy of an authority, to recognize bias or emotional factors in the presentation, to distinguish between verifiable and unverifiable data, to recognize the adequacy of data, to check statements against other known data, and to determine whether data support the conclusion. Once he has decided that these competencies should be appraised, he can then select, adapt, or create stimulus materials that will require students to display these abilities.

2. *Use novel material or organization of material in phrasing essay questions.* Generally speaking, we want the essay question to appraise students' ability to use information. To determine whether students can do this, we must put them in a situation where they must do more than merely reproduce the material as it has appeared in the text or in the classroom lecture and discussion. Questions 1 and 2 on page 263 are good illustrations of this point. Question 1 does not require students to use information but merely to reproduce it, whereas question 2 does require them to use it.

3. *Start essay questions with such words or phrases as "Compare," "Contrast," "Give the reasons for," "Give original examples of," "Explain how," "Predict what would happen if," "Criticize," "Differentiate," "Illustrate."* The use of words or phrases such as these, combined with novel material, will help to present tasks requiring students to select, organize, and use their knowledge. Don't start essay questions with such words as "what," "who," "when," and "list," since these words tend to lead to tasks requiring only the reproduction of information.

4. *Write the essay question in such a way that the task is clearly and unambiguously defined for each examinee.* We want the score that a student gets to be a reflection of how well he or she can do a specified task, not of how well he or she can figure out what the task is supposed to be. And, too, in large-scale testing programs we want the task to be perceived in the same way by all paper graders, so that a student's score will be affected as little as possible by who scores the paper. Luck in guessing what is wanted for an answer and disagreements in the quality of answers produced can be reduced by writing essay questions that set a clearly defined task for the examinee.

Thus a question such as "Discuss the organizations that contribute to the health of the community," is global, vague, and ambiguous. First, what is meant by the word "discuss"? Does it imply listing organizations and their activities? Criticism and evaluation of what they do? Identification of gaps in the organizational structure? Second, does the teacher expect students to consider only government organizations or does she expect students to consider the whole gamut of public and private organizations that contribute to the health of a community? Third, what does the teacher mean by "contribute to the health of the community"? Does she want the student to confine the answer to the kinds of contribution that involve enforcement of health regulations, direct treatment of illness, and preventive medicine, or does she want the student to include contributions through education and research? The question as written requires that the student guess what the teacher wanted for an answer, and the score is likely to depend on how lucky the student is in guessing.

A better way to phrase the question so that each examinee will interpret it the same way would be:

Using tuberculosis as an example, indicate how each of the following organizations could be expected to contribute to the prevention of the disease or the cure or care of persons with the disease.

     (a) Local and state health departments
     (b) United States Public Health Service
     (c) Department of Agriculture
     (d) The National Lung Association
     (e) The American Public Health Association

The question as it has been rephrased provides for a more common basis for response without sacrificing the freedom of the student in answering the question. (The revised question also clearly indicates that the task will be difficult for the typical eighth grade student in terms of whom the blueprint on pp. 208–209 was conceived.)

5. *A question dealing with a controversial issue should ask for and be evaluated in terms of the presentation of evidence for a position, rather than the position taken.* On many issues that individuals and society face there are no generally agreed-upon answers. Yet these controversial issues constitute much of what is genuinely vital in education. In these areas it is not defensible to demand that a student accept a specific conclusion or solution. However, it is reasonable to appraise him on how well he knows, can marshall, and can utilize the evidence upon which a specific conclusion is based. Thus the question "What laws should Congress pass to improve the medical care of àll citizens in the United States?" has no generally accepted answer. But we could reasonably ask a student to respond to such a question as the following: "It has been suggested that the cost of all medical care provided by physicians and the cost of all medications be borne by funds provided by the federal government. Do you agree or disagree? Support your position with logical arguments." In this type of question the teacher should *not* grade the student on the position he takes but only on the basis of how well he defends or supports his position.

6. *Be sure the essay question asks for the behavior that you really want the student to display.* Teacher-made essay tests quite frequently have questions such as "Give your best definition of good health"; "What do you think is the difference between active and passive immunity?"; "In your opinion what factors have contributed to the decreasing number of cases of diphtheria between 1900 and 1967 in the United States?" Usually, in these questions the teacher is not interested in what the student's opinion is but in whether the student knows the factual material. The questions should be rewritten to read, "Define good health"; "Explain the differences between active and passive immunity"; "What factors have contributed to the decreasing number of cases of diphtheria in the United States between 1900 and 1967?" (When this is done, it becomes clear that the questions are too factual in nature to be good essay questions.)

7. *Adapt the length and complexity of the answer to the maturity level of the students.* Though at all levels the distinctive value of the essay question lies in its ability to require the respondent to select and organize his own ideas in his own way, the organization and expresssion that we can reasonably expect an elementary school or junior high school pupil to produce is quite restricted in amount and conceptual level. A question such as

that on p. 263 may be too elaborate, too conceptually sophisticated, and too long for such a group.

PREPARING THE ESSAY TEST FOR USE

To make the most of essay questions as indicators of student
achievement certain precautions should be taken. In addition
to the suggestions on p. 217 that are general to all types of test,
the following merit consideration.

1. *Be sure that the students do not have too many or too lengthy
questions to answer in the time available.*
2. *If several essay questions are to be given, try to have a range of
complexity and difficulty in the questions.*
3. *In most classroom tests, require all students to answer the same
questions.*
4. *Write a set of general directons for the test.*
5. *Specify the point value for each question on the test.*

Adequate appraisal of student achievement with an essay
test requires not only well formulated questions but also sound
and consistent judgment of the quality of the answers.

Formal research provides little systematic guidance for improving the scoring of essay tests, but the following suggestions
are offered, stemming from accumulated professional experience. These suggestions should help the teacher to maintain a
more consistent standard for judging the answers across all students and make him more consciously aware of the basis for his
ratings, thereby enabling him to feed back more specific comments to the student on his performance and help him to reduce irrelevant factors that might influence his judgment of the
quality of the answers.

1. *Decide in advance what qualities are to be considered in judging the
adequacy of the answer. If more than one distinct quality is to be appraised, make separate evaluations of each.*
2. *Prepare an answer guide or model answer in advance showing
what points should be covered.*
3. *Read all answers to one question before going on to the next.*
4. *After scoring the answer to one question for all papers, shuffle or
rearrange the papers before starting to score the next question.*
5. *Grade an answer without knowing who wrote it, so far as possible.*
6. *If papers are to be returned, write comments and correct errors on
answers.*

1. Prepare a statement of the objectives for a course or a unit of a course that you are teaching or hope to teach.

2. Which of the objectives in (1) could be measured effectively by a written test? Which only partially or not at all? Why is a written test inadequate for these? How might these objectives best be appraised?

3. Based on the objectives identified in the first part of (2) and a course outline, prepare a blueprint for a test to evaluate the unit or course.

4. In a junior high school one teacher takes complete responsibility for preparing the common final examination for all the classes in general science. This teacher makes the examination up without consulting the other teachers. What advantages and disadvantages do you see in this procedure? How could it be improved?

5. One objective that is often proposed for the social studies program in the secondary school is to increase the pupil's "critical reaction to the news in different news media." How could the formulation of this objective be improved so that progress toward it could be measured?

6. The following were included in a school system's formulation of the objectives of a unit on health. Criticize each of these, revising it if there are ways in which it could be improved.

(*a*) Makes posters illustrating good health habits.

(*b*) Demonstrates health consciousness.

(*c*) Points out relationships between improvements in sanitation and drop in occurrence of disease.

(*d*) Appreciates the critical role of bacteria for sickness and health.

(*e*) Shows knowledge of and a lasting improvement in health habits.

7. Look at the blueprint for the examination on a unit on health that appears on pp. 208–209. For which of the cells in this blueprint would it be appropriate to use (*a*) extended-response exercises, (*b*) restricted-response exercises, and (*c*) structured-response items? What factors influenced your decisons?

8. For which of the following tests would it be important to correct scores for guessing? Give the reason or reasons for your decision.

(*a*) A 100-item true-false test. All students answered all questions.

(*b*) A 70-item multiple-choice test of spatial relations. Each item has 5 answer choices. For each item 1 or more than 1 answer choice may be correct. All students answered all questions.

(*c*) A 50-item multiple-choice test with 4 answer choices, one of which is the keyed answer. Only 40 percent of the examinees completed all items.

(*d*) A 60-item multiple-choice test with 4 answer choices, 1 of which is the keyed answer. Ninety percent of the students answered all items.

9. A college teacher has given an objective test to a large class, scored the papers, and entered the scores in the class record book. What further steps might the teacher take before returning the papers to the students? Why?

10. Collect some examples of poor items you have seen on tests. Indicate what is wrong with each item.

11. Construct 4 multiple-choice items designed to measure understanding or application in some subject area in which you are interested.

12. Prepare a short objective test for a small unit that you are teaching or plan to teach. Indicate the objectives that you are trying to evaluate with each item.

13. Criticize the following features of an essay test planned for a ninth grade social studies class:

(*a*) There will be 10 questions on the test.
(*b*) Each student will answer any 5.
(*c*) Each question will have a value of 20 points.
(*d*) One point will be taken off for each misspelled word and each grammatical error.
(*e*) A 5-point bonus will be given for neatness.
(*f*) Time for the test will be 40 minutes.

14. Criticize each of the following essay questions:

(*a*) Instead of talking just abut France's industry and agriculture alone, we talked about them as part of the Common Market. What are the advantages to France as a member of the Common Market? What products, raw materials, and agricultural products does France contribute to the Common Market? (ninth grade social studies)

(*b*) What should scientists do to make sure that scientific discoveries are used for the benefit of mankind rather than for the destruction of mankind? (eighth grade science)

(*c*) Select a character from a novel or short story that you have read this year. Give the name of the character and the title and author of the work in which he appeared. In a well-written paragraph, explain how this character has influenced your life. (twelth grade English literature)

(*d*) Discuss essay-type tests. (college undergraduate class in tests and measurements)

SUGGESTED
ADDITIONAL READING

271
suggested
additional
reading

Adkins, Dorothy C. *Test construction.* *(2nd Ed.)* Columbus, Ohio: Charles E. Merrill, 1974.

Coffman, William E. Essay examinations. In R. L. Thorndike (Ed.), *Educatonal measurement.* (2nd Ed.) Washington, D.C.: American Council on Education, 1971.

Colwell, R. *The evaluation of music teaching and learning.* Englewood Cliffs, N.J.: Prentice-Hall, 1970.

Ebel, Robert L. How to write true-false test items. *Educational and Psychological Measurement,* 1971, 31, 417–426.

Ebel, Robert L. Evaluation and educational objectives. *Journal of Educational Measurement,* 1973, 10, 273–279.

Ebel, Robert L. Can teachers write good true-false items? *Journal of Educational Measurement,* 1975, 12, 31–35.

Eduational Testing Service. *Multiple-choice questions: A close look.* Princeton, N.J.: Educational Testing Service, 1973.

Frisbie, David A. Multiple-choice versus true-false: A comparison of reliabilities and concurrent validities. *Journal of Educational Measurement,* 1973, 10, 297–304.

Frisbie, David A. The effect of item format on reliability and validity: A study of multiple-choice and true-false achievement tests. *Educational and Psychological Measurement,* 1974, 34, 885-892.

Gronlund, Norman E. *Stating behavioral objectives for classroom instruction.* Toronto: Macmillan, 1970.

Gronlund, Norman E. *Preparing criterion-referenced tests for classroom instruction.* New York: Macmillan, 1973.

Hakstian, A. Ralph and Wanlop Kansup. A comparison of several methods of assessing partial knowledge in multiple-choice tests: II. Testing procedures. *Journal of Educational Measurement,* 1975, 12, 231–239.

Hales, Loyde W. and Edward Tokar. The effect of the quality of preceding responses on the grades assigned to subsequent responses to an essay question. *Journal of Educatonal Measurement,* 1975, 12, 115–117.

Harrow, Anita J. *A taxonomy of the psychomotor domain: A guide for developing behavioral objectives.* New York: David McKay Co., 1972.

Henryssen, Sten. Gathering, analyzing, and using data on test items. In R. L. Thorndike (Ed.), *Educational measurement.* (2nd Ed.) Washington, D.C.: American Council on Education, 1971.

Huck, Schuyler and William Bounds. Essay grades: And interaction between graders' handwriting clarity and the neatness of examination papers. *American Educational Research Journal,* 1972, Ix, 279–283.

Kansup, Wanlop and A. Ralph Hakstian. A comparison of several methods of assessing partial knowledge in multiple-choice tests: I. Scoring procedures. *Journal of Educational Measurement,* 1975, 12, 219-230.

Kibler, Robert J., Donald J. Cegala, Larry L. Barker, and David T. Miles. *Objectives for instruction and evaluation.* (Rev. ed.) Boston: Allyn and Bacon, 1974.

Krathwohl, David R. *Taxonomy of educational objectives, Handbook II:*

Affective domain. New York: McKay, 1964.

Krathwohl, David R. and David A. Payne. Defining and assessing educational objectives. In R. L. Thorndike (Ed.), *Educational measurement* (2nd Ed.) Washington, D.C.: American Council on Education, 1971.

Krypsin, William J. and John F. Feldhusen. *Developing classroom tests: A guide for writing and evaluating test items.* Minneapolis, Minn.: Burgess Publishing Company, 1974.

Mager, Robert F. *Preparing instructional objectives.* (2nd Ed.) Belmont, Calif.: Fearon, 1975.

Metfessel, Newton S., William B. Michael, and Donald Kirsner. Instrumentation of the Taxonomy of Educational Objectives in behavioral terms. In David A. Payne and Robert F. McMorris (Eds.), *Educational and psychological measurement.* (2nd Ed.) Morristown, N.J.: General Learning Press, 1975.

Morse, H. T. and G. H. McCune. *Selected items for the testing of study skills and critical thinking.* Washington, D.C.: National Council for the Social Studies, 1971.

Mueller, Daniel J. An assessment of the effectiveness of complex alternatives in multiple choice achievement test items. *Educational and Psychological Measurement,* 1975, 35, 135–141.

Mueller, Daniel J. and Allan Shwedel. Some correlates of net gain resultant from answer changing on objective achievement test items. *Journal of Educational Measurement,* 1975, 12, 251–254.

Pascale, Pietro J. Changing initial answers on multiple-choice achievement tests. *Measurement and Evaluation in Guidance,* 1974, 6, 236–238.

Payne, D. A. *The assessment of learning: Cognitive and affective.* Lexington, Mass.: D. C. Heath and Co., 1974. Chapter 8.

Peterson, Candida C. and James L. Peterson, Linguistic determinants of the difficulty of true-false test items. *Educational and Psychological Measurement,* 1976, 36, 161–164.

Schwarz, Paul A. Prediction instruments for educational outcomes. In R. L. Thorndike (Ed.), *Educational measurement.* (2nd Ed.) Washington, D.C.: American Council on Education, 1971.

Slakter, Malcolm J. and Kevin D. Crehan. Longitudinal studies of risk taking on objective examinations. *Educational and Psychological Measurement,* 1975, 35, 97–105.

Synd, R. B. and A. J. Picard. *Behavioral objectives and evaluation measures: Science and mathematics.* Columbus, Ohio: Charles E. Merrill, 1972.

Tinkleman, Sherman N. Planning the objective test. In R. L. Thorndike (Ed.), *Educational measurement* (2nd Ed.) Washington, D.C.: American Council on Education, 1971.

Wesman, Alexander G. Writing the test item. In R. L. Thorndike (Ed.), *Educational measurement.* (2nd Ed.) Washington, D.C.: American Council on Education, 1971.

CHAPTER EIGHT
STANDARDIZED ACHIEVEMENT TESTS

The last chapter dealt with locally produced tests prepared by a teacher or group of teachers for their own use in their own classes. This chapter deals with centrally produced tests brought out by a test publisher or state or national testing agency for widespread use in a large number of schools and school districts. Though the forms of test exercises in the two categories of instrument may often be quite similar, the two have certain fundamental differences in design and function. Let us consider those differences.

DISTINCTIVE FEATURES OF CENTRALLY PRODUCED TESTS

Centrally produced tests differ from those developed locally by a teacher or group of teachers in three main respects, one a matter of degree and two a matter of kind.

In the first place, much more time and professional skill can usually be invested in a centrally produced test or test battery. Since the publisher hopes that the product will achieve widespread acceptance and use over a period of several years, he is willing to invest substantial amounts of time and money in the steps of reviewing current curricula, preparing blueprints of content and skill, writing test exercises, carrying out editorial review of items to clear up ambiguities and guarantee that there is a clearly best answer, completing item analyses to provide a statistical check upon how items actually behave, and assembling a balanced set of pretested items. In the second place, since the test is designed to be used in many, often widely dispersed, localities, the design of the centrally produced test is built around the common objectives of education that are widely shared by many school systems. It eschews the local and idiosyncratic in favor of the widespread and universal. The third and most distinctive feature of most centrally-produced tests is the availability of norms. The term "standardized test" implies the availability of normative data, and publishers of these tests provide a range of normative information to help give meaning to test scores.

Normative data provide for a particular type of meaning, in that they emphasize comparison with others. They permit statements about how Hilary is doing in relation to others of her age, or others of her grade, or others from the same type of school system in which she is enrolled. They permit statements about how Hilary is doing in math relative to her performance in reading or in relation to her performance on a test of scholastic aptitude. They permit statements about how Hilary's school is doing in comparison with schools the country over, or schools of a particular type, or schools in a particular type of community. The primary role of standardized tests is comparison—of an individual or group with others, of different aspects of performance within an individual or group.

If we take account of these characteristics, and relate them to the discussion in Chapter 6 of the types of decision in which achievement test results may be helpful, we come to the following conclusions as to the ones for which standardized tests are likely to be helpful:

1. Day-by-day instructional decisions must depend primarily on locally constructed tests, rather than standardized surveys, though some mini-tests are now being prepared for nation-wide distribution.

2. Student appraisal decisions should be based primarily on locally constructed tests covering what has been taught specifically in a given unit or course.

3. Diagnostic and remedial decisions can with advantage use information both from published diagnostic tests and from focused tests developed locally. These tests are discussed on pp. 167–169 and in Chapter 6.

4. Placement decisions call for a broad appraisal in an area and can often use standardized tests to identify entry level of performance on a uniform score scale. This usage is described on pp. 177–182.

5. Counseling and guidance decisions usually call for the

normative comparisons that standardized tests make possible; this issue is considered on pp. 182–189.

6. Selection decisions tend to imply comparison with others, and for these comparisons adequate norms are often important. See pp. 189–191.

7. Curricular decisions between alternative programs imply a broadly based comparison in which standardized measures can play a role, often supplemented by measures developed locally for distinctive special objectives. Tests for these purposes are considered in Chapter 6.

8. Public and policy decisions, as with curricular decisions, call for a comprehensive and comparative view of how well a school is doing, and for this the broad survey and comparison that a standardized test permits has significant value. We shall return to this issue in Chapter 14.

TYPES OF STANDARDIZED TESTS

Many of the early objective achievement tests that were developed were tests within a single subject, unrelated in their conception and in their standardization to tests in any other subject. Later these separate, uncoordinated tests were supplemented by coordinated batteries prepared for a single publisher by a team of authors. These coordinated batteries have several important advantages. Planning is comprehensive, and the components are designed so that they appear to the authors to provide an integrated coverage of the major academic skills or the major curricular areas. Each part is planned with an awareness of the other parts, so that duplication should be minimized and joint coverage of important material is guaranteed. Recognizing that human judgment is fallible and human vigilance is imperfect, we may expect that the result may fall short of this ideal, but it does constitute a target that at least may be approximated.

More important is the fact that all of the subtests of such a battery have been standardized on the same sample of students. In discussing the appropriate uses of standardized tests we have made repeated reference to comparisons—comparisons within and between individuals, comparisons within and between groups. These comparisons are relatively direct and straightforward when norms for all parts of the battery are based upon the same group of students; they become much more "iffy" when the reference group changes from test to test. Of course there are possible drawbacks in the "package deal"

Table 8.1
Content Coverage by Widely Used Achievement Batteries

	California Achievement Tests	Comprehensive Tests of Basic Skills	Iowa Tests of Basic Skills	Metropolitan Achievement Tests	SRA Achievement Tests	Stanford Achievement Series
Reading:						
Decoding skills	1.5– 4.0	a	1.6–3.5	K7–4.9	1.5–2.5	1.5–6.9
Vocabulary	1.5–12	2.5–10	1.6–9.5	1.5–9.5	1.5–9.5	1.5–9.5
Comprehension	1.5–12	2.5–10	1.6–9.5	K7–9.5	1.5–9.5	1.5–9.5
Language:						
Punctuation	1.5–12	2.5–10	1.6–9.5	3.5–9.5	2.5–9.5	3.5–9.5
Capitalization	1.5–12	2.5–10	1.6–9.5	3.5–9.5	2.5–9.5	3.5–9.5
Usage	2.0–12	2.5–10	1.6–9.5	3.5–9.5	2.5–9.5	3.5–9.5
Spelling:		2.5–10	1.6–9.5	2.5–9.5	2.5–9.5	1.5–9.5
Math (Arithmetic):						
Computation	1.5–12	2.5–10	1.6–9.5	K7–9.5	1.5–9.5	1.5–9.5
Concepts	1.5–12	2.5–10	1.6–9.5	2.5–9.5	1.5–9.5	1.5–9.5
Problems	1.5–12	2.5–10	1.6–9.5	2.5–9.5	1.5–9.5	1.5–9.5
Study Skills:						
Maps		2.5–10	1.6–9.5	b	4.5–9.5	
Graphs and Tables		2.5–10	1.6–9.5	b	4.5–9.5	
Library and Reference	c	2.5–10	1.6–9.5		4.5–9.5	d
Science:				5.0–9.5		2.5–9.5
Social Studies:				5.0–9.5		2.5–9.5
Listening:	1.5–2.0		1.6–3.5			1.5–6.9

a A few items at lowest level.
b Some included in *Social Studies*.
c A few items in *Reading* test 2.0–12.
d Few items in *Language* test.

of a complete battery. Comparing different batteries, we may prefer an arithmetic test from one, a language test from another, and a reading test from still a third, on the basis of their correspondence to our local curriculum and objectives. But all told, for the types of comparison for which standardized tests are appropriately used, the gains from unified norms (and test design) seem to outweigh any loss from having to accept a package one or two elements of which are judged to be less than ideal.

Table 8.1 shows in summary form the structure and content and the grade range of six of the most widely used survey achievement batteries. All of these cover the grade range 3 through 9 where the bulk of achievement testing takes place. All cover the basic skills of reading, arithmetic, spelling, and language usage. These skill areas tend to be the ones in which objectives are most uniform and most universal from school system to school system. The *Metropolitan Achievement Tests* and the *Stanford Achievement Tests* provide tests designated *Science* and *Social Studies,* but the batteries are also provided as "basic" batteries without these content subtests. There is relatively less agreement as to what is taught in these content areas, and consequently a nationally uniform test is less likely to be appropriate for use in a local situation.

Some of the batteries provide test levels for use in the first and second grades, and the *Metropolitan* even offers a test for use toward the end of kindergarten. Naturally these early tests tend to be quite different from tests at the elementary grades and above, both in emphasis and in manner of presentation. Presentation is largely oral, pacing of the presentation being in the hands of the test administrator. Since basic reading skills have not been established, much of the material in the test booklet is pictorial. At the earliest levels, the tests tend to be limited to simple reading and number skills.

To give some idea of how the form and content of a test changes from the most elementary to the more advanced levels, we show in the following example items similar to those in, but not actually used in, the parts of the *Metropolitan* related to reading.

EXAMPLE

Primer Level (Grade K to 1.4)

Listening for sounds

Picture sounds (22 items): Look at the pictures of the ball, the kite, and the tree. Which one starts with a sound like *cat?* Put a mark under it.

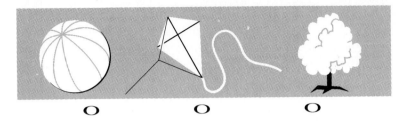

O   O   O

Letter sounds (8 items): Mark under the letter that stands for the beginning sound in *top*.

g   n   t   s
O   O   O   O

Word sounds (9 items): Mark under the word *tall*. He is a *tall* boy.

fall   tell   tall   talk
O   O   O   O

Reading

Letter recognition (11 items): Mark under the letter R.

R   P   B   W
O   O   O   O

Word-picture matching (17 items): Which word tells what the picture is about?

O   mouse

O   house

O   hat

O   howl

Sentence-picture matching (5 items): Mark in the space beside the sentence that tells about the picture.

O   The birds are flying.

O   The bird is sitting.

O   The boys are jumping.

Primary I (Grade 1.5–2.4)
Word Knowledge
   Word-picture matching (see Primer) (35 items)
Word Discrimination
   Word sounds (see Primer) (35 items)

Reading

Sentence-picture matching (see Primer) (13 items)

Stories (33 items):

John and Mary like to play ball.
John throws the ball.
Mary catches the ball.

What does Mary like to play?

- O **ball**
- O **dolls**
- O **jacks**

Primary II (Grade 2.5–3.4)

Word Knowledge

Word-picture matching (see Primer) (17 items)

Synonyms (23 items):

To *strike* is to O **hit** O **cry** O **fall** O **jump**

Word Analysis

Word sounds (see Primer) (35 items)

Reading

Sentence-picture matching (see Primer) (13 items)

Stories (see Primary I) (31 items)

Elementary (Grade 3.5–4.9)

Synonyms (see Primary II) (50 items)

Word discrimination–sentence Completion (36 items):

Please _____ and lock the door.

clothes   close   cause   class

Reading

Stories (see Primary I) (44 items)

Intermediate (Grade 5.0–6.9)

Advanced (Grade 7.0–9.5)

Synonyms (50 items)

Stories (45 items)

We can see from a comparison of the successive levels that the presentation shifts from teacher-paced oral-aural format to a pupil-paced entirely written format. Pictures are used a good deal at the lower levels, where basic decoding skills are still being established. And at the earlier levels a fair amount of emphasis is given to word analysis and decoding skills, whereas at the higher levels emphasis is purely on knowledge of word meanings and reading of continuous text. The few brief examples cannot, of course, give a picture of the gradually increasing length and complexity of the "stories" that are to be read, or of the expanding variety of comprehension questions that are based upon them.

Two things stand out in this analysis. One is that there is a progressive shift in the nature of what is tested in standardized achievement tests to match the capabilities of the maturing students. The other is that, especially at the higher levels, the test provides a broad survey of complex skills rather than a specific analysis of sharply defined competencies. These statements would, in general, hold true of other test batteries and of other subject areas.

The survey achievement tests are basically designed to yield a fairly reliable score for each individual for each of the skill areas. (Reliability coefficients in the high 80s or low 90s would be fairly typical.) They can also be expected to provide a highly reliable composite assessment of average achievement pooled over the skill areas. The composite score for battery total provides a gross undifferentiated indication of whether a child has been making superior, average, or below par progress in basic educational skills—an indication that can be compared with earlier measures, with that of classmates, and with evidence of academic potential. The decisions to which such a global assessment can make a useful contribution are somewhat limited. It may help in identifying some children who should be encouraged to start thinking about post-secondary education. It can serve to identify initially children who present the most serious learning problems. It can help in the placement of a transfer student who has moved from one school to another.

For most decisions for which a survey battery is used, interest tends to center on the subtest scores and the profile of strengths and weaknesses. If Peter's achievement level is below par, where do his most serious shortcomings lie? How is he progressing in reading, taken by itself? How is Ms. Albertson's class progressing in mastery of arithmetic concepts, as compared to computational skills? In what respects do the schools of the Peterboro district appear better than average? In what respects do they show deficiencies? Do the differences reflect intended differences in curricular emphasis, or do they indicate a situation that should be a cause for concern and of efforts at remediation?

When it comes to classroom instructional decisions, even the subtest scores on a survey achievement battery provide only limited help. So Peter is a full grade below his current grade placement in capitalization skills—what is to do about it? So Ms. Albertson's class shows an average grade equivalent a half-grade lower in arithmetic concepts than in arithmetic computation. What steps should Ms. Albertson take? What should she teach or re-teach? One way to seek the answer is to look at the specific questions on the capitalization test that Peter failed, or the specific arithmetic concepts that many of the children in Ms. Albertson's class did not know. Through their computerized test scoring services, test publishers have been moving in the direction of reporting back more and more detailed information about the responses of single children and of class groups. Thus there are report forms that will indicate just which items Peter got wrong on the capitalization subtest, for example, perhaps grouping them by the capitalization rule that they exemplified. From this the teacher can see whether Peter made errors in capitalizing at the beginning of a sentence, at the beginning of a quotation, for names of persons, for names of places, and so forth. Ms. Albertson can see the frequency of error in each of these situations for all the students in her class. This type of microanalysis of the test results has the potential for providing specific identification of difficulties and specific cues for instruction. Through these reports the publisher tries to assist in what test makers have always urged that teachers should do, that is, dig beneath the normative test score to identify the specific test exercises with which individuals and the class as a whole are encountering difficulty.

This type of detailed analysis of success and failures on specific items can be quite suggestive for guiding teaching. However, the limitations of a survey test for this purpose are very real. In the first place, there are in many cases only 1 or 2 items dealing with a specific skill. Any individual child may get the item right by a lucky guess, or fail it because of distraction by some element of the problem not really relevant to the basic skill it is designed to test. And 1 or 2 items are hardly enough to permit a reliable "mastery" or "nonmastery" decision for a single child. What failure on an item *can* do is to alert the teacher to the need to test that skill more fully with a mini-test focused specifically on the skill called for by the failed item. Similarly, failure on an item by a substantial fraction of students in a class suggests the need to test that skill more thoroughly in order to have evidence to judge reliably what fraction of the class lacks mastery of the skill.

A further issue, in relation to the class rate of success or failure on an item is whether the class could have been expected to know the answer to that question: On the one hand, has the skill been taught either recently or at some time in the more remote past? On the other, what success rate is typical of students at this grade level? The first question can only be answered on the basis of local knowledge of what has been taught in the present class and in previous grades. Some help on the second question may be provided by the publisher, who may provide tables showing success percentage by item and by grade level.

If the microanalysis of test results is to be helpful to a teacher, the analysis should be in the teacher's hands as soon as possible after the testing. When test results are centrally processed, as tends to be the case for a large part of present-day standardized testing, there is inevitably a lag of several weeks between testing and receipt by the teacher of the report of the test results. Each added week of delay makes the results less timely for instructional decisions concerning specific children or the class group. New learning has taken place—and, alas, previously learned material may have been forgotten—and the details of the descriptive picture have become less accurate. Thus it is important that all possible steps be taken to expedite completion of a testing program, assembly of answer sheets from the participating schools, and shipment of the materials to the processing agency. From that point on one is at the mercy of the U. S. Mail and the agency carrying out the scoring and report preparation. The problem of turnaround time is likely to be particularly serious in statewide testing programs, if there is a requirement that returns from all school systems be received before test analysis can be carried through. There have been instances in which processing delays due to technical and to political issues have delayed reporting beyond the year in which the test results were obtained. By the time these results were in the hands of the teachers, it was too late for any use to be made of the results for instructional planning for specific pupils.

DIAGNOSTIC ACHIEVEMENT TESTS

Diagnosis relates primarily to the single individual. Sarah gets a low score on a survey test of reading comprehension. Why? Peter gets a low score on the arithmetic section of the achievement battery. What are the sources of the difficulty? Much, probably most, diagnostic testing is carried out with single pupils after it has been determined from a survey test or from the observations of the teacher that the pupil is not making satisfactory progress in reading, arithmetic, or some other segment of the school program. The tests of one diagnostic reading test were listed and briefly described in Chapter 6 (pp. 174–175). However, some tests are available that are intended to serve a diagnostic function and that are designed for group administration. We shall describe one of these, indicating what it undertakes to do and what problems arise in its use and interpretation.

The *Stanford Diagnostic Arithmetic Test, Level III,* is designed for use from the middle of the fourth to the middle of the eighth grade. To give a picture of the test, we list below the subtests, giving in each instance an item that is similar to (but not identical with) one of the early and one of the late items in that subtest. Shown also are the number of items in the subtest and the allocation of testing time.

Test 1: Concepts of Numbers and Numerals
    Part A: Number Systems and Operations (30 items, 20 minutes)
$$\square \times 5 = 5$$
$$(3 \times 4) \times 5 = 3 \times (4 \times \square)$$
    Part B: Decimal Place Value (26 items, 20 minutes)
$$2000 + 500 + 70 + 3 = ?$$
$$7200 \div 100 = ?$$
        (*a*) 7.2   (*b*) 72   (*c*) 720   (*d*) 720,000

Test 2: Computation with Whole Numbers
    Part A: Addition and Subtraction (20 items, 12 minutes)

436	1235
759	$-$ 756
285	?
?	

    Part B: Multiplication (18 items, 20 minutes)

340	247
$\times$ 24	$\times$ 358
?	?

    Part C: Division (18 items, 30 minutes)

$$9 \overline{)\ 162} \qquad\qquad 38 \overline{)\ 1746}$$

Test 3: Common Fractions
    Part A: Understanding (22 items, 20 minutes)

$$\frac{2}{3} = \frac{?}{6} \qquad \text{Reduce to simplest terms } \frac{24}{36}$$

    Part B: Computation (28 items, 28 minutes)

$$\frac{3}{5} + \frac{1}{3} = ? \qquad\qquad 3 \div \frac{3}{4} = ?$$

Test 4: Decimal Fractions and Percentages (48 items, 35 minutes)
        $$1.4 \times 200 = ? \qquad\qquad 3\% \text{ of } \$60.00 = ?$$

Test 5: Number Facts (Presented Orally)
 Part A: Addition (26 items, 5 minutes)
   $4 + 5 = ?$ $7 + 8 = ?$
 Part B: Subtraction (26 items, 5 minutes)
   $8 - 5 = ?$ $12 - 7 = ?$
 Part C: Multiplication (26 items, 5 minutes)
   $4 \times 6 = ?$ $8 \times 7 = ?$
 Part D: Division (26 items, 5 minutes)
   $36 \div 4 = ?$ $48 \div 6 = ?$
 Part E: Carrying (26 items, 5 minutes)
   $36 + 6 = ?$ $6 \times 6 + 5 = ?$

From an examination of the test outline as shown above, supplemented by study of the test manual, a number of points become clear.

In the first place, the 13 diagnostic scores, 8 based on printed test materials and 5 on orally presented number fact exercises, correspond approximately to the areas of arithmetic concepts and arithmetic computation as these are presented in survey achievement batteries. There is no attempt to test application of computational skills to verbally stated problems. That is, knowing *what* to do is not tested; the test is limited to fluency in carrying out a clearly stated arithmetical exercise. If we wish to probe specific weaknesses in analyzing problems and determining what sequence of operations to carry out, an entirely different sort of test would be required. Any diagnostic test explores only some, not all of the sources of difficulty in a curricular area.

A second observation would be that administration of the battery requires a substantial commitment of time. Including time for distributing and collecting booklets and giving directions, the authors estimate a time requirement of 4 hours and 10 minutes. They recommend spreading the testing over seven sittings—which presumably would be spread out over a week or more. The time may be well spent if at the beginning of the year a teacher wishes to take stock of where the class and the individuals in it stand with respect to their arithmetic skills. And the time is necessary if one is to get an adequately reliable assessment of each of a number of distinct skills. (Reliabilities of the separate subtests range from about .80 to .90.) However, the time requirements do bring home the fact that diagnostic testing is a time-consuming enterprise, whether for an individual or a group. The investment of time can be justified only if the test results are going to be analyzed carefully and used to guide further instruction.

A further observation is that the scores, especially on the eight printed tests, provide only an inital step in diagnosis. If Peter's scores are compared with the norms for his grade group and it is found that he falls farthest behind the norms in multiplication of whole numbers, we still do not know what it is about multiplication that is giving him trouble. We have some guidance on where we should focus our further scrutiny, but we still need to make a microanalysis of Peter's errors in multiplication problems to see if there are a few identifiable errors in conception or procedure that are the source of repeated errors, or whether the errors seem to arise from weaknesses in underlying number facts. That is, having tentatively identified an area of weakness, we need to observe the process of Peter's functioning in that area to determine exactly what he does wrong, and to generate hypotheses as to why he is doing it. A thorough diagnostic study typically calls for observation of *process* as well as *product* of pupil performance.

If weakness on a particular subtest is peculiar to one person in a class, we look for the shortcomings in that person's learning. If the class as a whole falls especially low in some subtest we ask whether teaching of those skills or understandings has been done poorly, or whether the introduction of certain topics has been delayed in the local curriculum. That is, a discrepancy between local performance and national norms signifies a problem only if the local curriculum parallels the national pattern in the time at which topics are introduced. If a topic (such as fractions) has not yet been taught to a particular class, obviously there is no reason to be concerned if the topic has not been mastered. Interpretation of class average profiles on such a diagnostic battery must be made in the light of the group's past instructional history and instructional emphasis.

Because the subtests in a battery provide meaningful diagnostic cues only when the material covered by a subtest has been taught to the pupils, we may question whether the material on fractions and decimals provides useful diagnostic information for fourth and fifth grade groups. One cannot identify deficient performance on a subtest if the average performance is very close to a zero score. Raw scores corresponding to the 50th and 25th percentiles are shown for each subtest for each grade range in the norm tables in Table 8.2, along with the number of items in the subtest. From this table it is clear that the subtests on division of whole numbers, on fractions, and on decimals would be of no diagnostic value in the fourth and fifth grades. The *average* pupil gets only a few of these items right, and there is little room to differentiate between the average

Table 8.2

Raw Scores on Subtests of *Stanford Diagnostic Arithmetic Test* *(Form W)* Corresponding to 50th and to 25th Percentiles

Subtest	Number of Items	50th Percentile				25th Percentile			
		4.5–5.5	5.5–6.5	6.5–7.5	7.5–8.5	4.5–5.5	5.5–6.5	6.5–7.5	7.5–8.5
Number System and Operations	30	15	19	22	23	10	14	15	17
Decimal Place Value	26	14	17	19	21	9	14	15	17
Addition and Subtraction	20	17	19	19.5	19.5	14	17	17.5	18
Multiplication	18	10	14	15	16	6	12	13	14
Division	18	4	13	15	16	2	9	13	13
Fractions: Understanding	22	4	10	13	17	2	6	9	12
Computation	28	3	10	18	22	1	5	9	16
Decimal Fractions and Percentages	48	9	16	21	28	4	11	16	20

and the *deficient* pupil. Table 8.2 also brings out one further feature of diagnostic tests. This is that in general the better adapted a test is to display serious deficiency, the poorer it will be for identifying levels of excellence. Thus the test of addition and subtraction of whole numbers makes essentially no distinctions among the top half of the grade group even at the fifth grade level. There is an essential incompatibility between the functions of diagnosing deficiency and assessing all degrees of excellence. The test that is good for the one purpose is unlikely to be good for the other. Usually a diagnostic test should be designed more like a criterion-referenced or mastery test, so that the expected score is close to a perfect score and so that there is a wide range of below-par scores to express degrees of deficiency.

SECONDARY SCHOOL AND COLLEGE LEVEL ACHIEVEMENT TESTS

At the elementary school level, standardized tests tend to focus on the basic skills of operating with words and numbers. At the secondary school and college levels, the emphasis shifts to the substance of particular curricular areas, and even to particular courses. Since the curriculum becomes more and more differentiated, with the core that is common to all students representing a smaller fraction of the total, there is less of a function for a uniform comprehensive assessment.

Survey test batteries do continue in use at the high school level. We will comment briefly on two rather different patterns for a high school battery, and then discuss some of the tests and test series that are available for separate subjects and courses.

A test battery that grew out of the need, at the end of World War II, to evaluate and give credit for educational experiences obtained in the armed forces, is the *Iowa Tests of Educational Development.* Since the battery was originally designed to evaluate experiences that might have been quite varied in type and content, the tests tended to emphasize general knowledge and ability to read with understanding material from different fields of knowledge, and subsequent editions have maintained that same format. In its present version the battery is composed of the following tests:

1. *Understanding of Basic Social Concepts.*
2. *General Background in the Natural Sciences.*
3. *Correctness and Appropriateness of Expression.*
4. *Ability to do Quantitative Thinking.*
5. *Ability to Interpret Reading Materials—Social Studies.*
6. *Ability to Interpret Reading Materials—Natural Sciences.*
7. *Ability to Interpret Reading Materials—Literary.*
8. *General Vocabulary.*
9. *Sources of Information.*

The emphasis on getting, using and interpreting material of various types and from various sources is apparent in the test titles. Almost all of the subtests make a substantial demand upon reading skills, and most of the subtests are highly correlated with one another. As a result, while the test provides a good prediction of later academic performance,* the subtests are not very effective as diagnostic tools, and do not correspond closely enough to what is taught in any specific course to have value as measures of course outcomes. The battery might have value in indicating how effective a total school program has been in developing informed literacy.

More conventional, and more representative of other high school batteries would be the *Tests of Academic Progress,* designed for use in grades 9 to 12. There are six tests in the battery, as follows:

---

* The college admissions tests of the American College Testing Program test battery correspond closely to four of the ITED tests.

287
secondary
school and
college level
achievement
tests

1. *Social Studies.*
2. *Composition.*
3. *Science.*
4. *Reading.*
5. *Mathematics.*
6. *Literature.*

As can be seen from the titles, the battery is a mixture of skills (reading, writing, and perhaps mathematics) and of content (social studies, science, literature). However, even in the content areas there is a fair amount of emphasis on functional knowledge, for example, interpretation of data and of experimental designs in science. Such adaptations bring the tests closer to the common core of secondary education, make them more generally usable and perhaps more useful for comparing different schools and curricula and for guidance decision relating to a particular student. However, it makes them less useful as measures of what has been taught in any specific course.

In addition to batteries such as those just described, there are series of tests the titles of which correspond rather closely to those of specific courses. One extensive series was developed by the Cooperative Test Division of the Educational Testing Service. The nature of the tests is suggested by the titles of the tests in the field of mathematics: *Structure of the Number System, Arithmetic, Algebra I, II, and III, Geometry, Trigonometry, Analytic Geometry, Calculus.* Another series is represented in the *Evaluation and Adjustment Series* published by Harcourt, Brace, Jovanovich. This series includes tests in *Chemistry, Physics, Biology, American History, Algebra, Geometry, and Listening Comprehension* among others. Typically the tests in these series are designed for students who have completed some specific course—beginning algebra, biology, world history, and the like. Norms are usually based on samples of students who have completed such a course, with whatever selective factors may have entered into that choice. There is little attempt to maintain comparability of the score scale from one field to another, so comparisons across fields are rather questionable. Test content may in some cases match course content well enough so that the test can play a role in the end-of-year evaluation of each student, but such a step should be reviewed with care before it is entered upon.

One role that has been suggested for tests that are designed to match specific courses is that of exemption from the specific course requirement. In part because many young people have received various kinds of training in the armed forces, in part in recognition of the fact that some individuals may have been educated through other media than formal schooling—through reading, through radio and television, through work experiences—it has seemed desirable to some educators to provide through examinations a channel for accrediting such experience. The *College Level Examination Program* of the Educational Testing Service is such a channel.

The *CLEP* was set up to provide a uniform nationwide procedure for evaluating experience claimed as the equivalent of a specific college course. Examinations have been prepared for 35 areas ranging from Accounting and Afro-American History to Tests and Measurements, Trigonometry, and Western Civilization. Normative data have been obtained from college students who have completed the designed course, as well as from the samples who have taken the equivalency test. Scores are presented as standard scores that range from 200 to 800, with 500 representing the average score for the basic reference population. The manner in which the results from such a test will be used is determined by the college to which the student is applying and from which he wishes equivalency credit. As with any accrediting or licensing examination, the decision as to what constitutes a minimum acceptable level is quite arbitrary. Though general normative data may be available for those who have taken the course for which the examination is a substitute, it is likely that no data will be available specifically for the college to which an individual is applying. It is then necessary to determine intuitively at what score level the balance shifts in favor of the gain in time saved and away from the risk of sending ahead an inadequately prepared person. The use of examinations for licensure and certification is widespread in our society, and the logical or empirical bases upon which qualifying scores are set are often largely unexamined.

STATEWIDE ACHIEVEMENT TESTING PROGRAMS

There has been some tendency in recent years for an expansion of mandated statewide testing programs. Typically, in these programs, all the public schools of a state are required to give a specified test or battery of tests at specific grade levels. In some instances, forms of already published tests have been used, but more often tests have been produced by or for the state Department of Education. These have frequently been based on a systematic formulation of relatively specific objectives by committees of educators within that state, in an attempt to fit the testing more closely to the objectives and sequence of instruction within the state. Involvement of teachers in the design of the test blueprint is intended to overcome the objection that the test exercises do not match what the schools have been teaching.

In most instances the focus of statewide programs has been upon evaluation at the level of school or school system, and test forms have been designed with that end in view. A testing program can be formulated that will be highly effective at the level of school or school system but be inappropriate for evaluating single pupils.

ITEM SAMPLING

It is usually true that testing time is sharply limited, and it is certainly true that an externally mandated program will be more acceptable to a local school system if it calls for no more than an hour or so of each pupil's time. On the other hand, the number of different specific objectives that a blueprint committee can identify in only a single curricular area is very large indeed. Given this conflict between desire for a manageably brief test and for comprehensive curricular coverage, what reconciliation is possible? One that has been undertaken is to produce a number of forms of the test—perhaps as many as 10 or 12—each one of which *samples* from the total domain of the curriculum. Each child then takes some one form of the test, but the forms are rotated so that within a given class, school, or school system all forms are equally represented. Since each child has taken a test form, all the children in a class or school are equally weighted in the average, and since the test forms have been rotated all the test items are equally represented in the average. The pooled results then provide appraisal of a broadly representative sample of the curriculum, and even subtest scores corresponding to fairly narrow curricular segments can be represented by enough test items to provide a reasonably complete and varied coverage of that segment. The term *item sampling* has been applied to this procedure, since each form of the test is one sample from the total pool of items. Such an item sampling procedure permits a fairly complete diagnostic profile of strengths and weaknesses for a particular school or school system, expressing results for a defined skill area either in terms of absolute mastery or in relation to other schools or systems within the state.

At the national level the item sampling technique has been used in the National Assessment of Educational Progress, in which each examinee is tested with only a fraction of the total pool of items. In the Assessment analyses are carried out initially at the level of the single item, and data are aggregated by region, by type of community, by sex, by ethnic group, and in other ways. Comparisons are then made between different strata (subgroups) and for the same stratum at different points in time. For example, the percentage of paragraphs judged to be coherent in short essays written by students, with testing carried out in 1969 and again in 1974, were as follows.

	17-Year-Olds		13-Year-Olds		9-Year-Olds	
	1969	1974	1969	1974	1969	1974
Male	87	75	76	76	54	41
Female	84	78	73	79	60	45

The data provide a picture, in this case somewhat discouraging, of trends in one facet of educational performance by age and sex groupings in our schools.

The item sampling technique especially, and in general any procedure that tries to sample very broadly over the elements of the curriculum, is of limited value in appraising the performance of single pupils. With item sampling, different pupils will have taken different tests. In any mandated program that must fit into a limited block of time the sampling of items on a specific educational objective will usually be so limited that a conclusion regarding mastery by Susie Stein will be so unreliable as to provide a most meager basis for any teaching decision.

TESTING FOR MINIMUM COMPETENCY

A type of mandated program that appears to be emerging in a number of states is one that is designed to appraise "minimal competency" in certain core curriculum areas. As a reaction against policies of automatic promotion and of awarding a diploma without regard to demonstrated competence, states are establishing or considering various test procedures designed to guarantee a certain level of competence in all graduates and to deny a diploma to those who do not demonstrate that level. As is too often the case, legislators who direct by law that something *shall* be done often provide little guidance as to *how* it will be done. Development of an examination to assess minimum competency presents a number of serious problems.

The first problem would seem to be: Competence in what? In what broad segments of the curriculum is competence to be demanded? Only in certain very basic reading, language, or mathematical skill, or more broadly in the domains of human knowledge? Suppose that this question has been answered, and that one of the agreed upon areas is mathematics. The next problem is to agree upon what constitutes minimum competence in mathematics. Is it to be represented by mastery (at some specified level) of a catalogue of specific skills such as "addition of three 2-digit whole numbers" or "conversion of such fractions as halves, thirds, quarters, and fifths to decimals"? Should it be defined normatively as "performance on a representative arithmetic test at a level equal to the average sixth grade student"? Or should it be defined in still some other way? What if the definition turns out to be unrealistically high, and a large fraction of high school students fail to reach it? What will be the political impact of this, and how feasible will it be to make appropriate adjustments?

Preparation of minimal proficiency tests presents no special problems, once a definition of the domain and level has been reached. However, such a test should be rather different from the usual ability test. Since one is interested only in a decision at one specific ability level, the test should be designed to be maximally sensitive *at that level.* There will be no need to have in the test those difficult items that differentiate between average and superior competence. Nor will there be any point in including very easy items that can be answered successfully even by those of low competence in the skill in question. The items can appropriately be targeted at a narrow band of difficulty, and should be items that differentiate as sharply as possible between those falling just below and those falling just above the magic dividing line. It will not be possible to do this with precision, and inevitably the test will differentiate over a fairly wide range of competence, but the better the test is at differentiating the minimally competent from the hopelessly inept, the poorer it will be at expressing degrees of excellence.

SUMMARY STATEMENT

Most standardized tests are broad survey measures of areas of achievement, though some tests aspiring to be diagnostic are also on the market. The survey tests are useful primarily in connection with selection, placement, guidance, curricular, and public policy decisions. Adequate diagnostic testing is a time-consuming enterprise, and typically has been reserved for those pupils who show serious deficiencies in some broad area of achievement.

At the secondary and college levels centrally produced achievement tests are being called upon to provide evidence both of outstanding competence—to serve as a basis for advanced placement—and of minimal competence as a basic outcome of schooling. Statewide programs of testing are in a state of flux as educators vacillate between attempts to make objective referenced interpretations of achievement in local schools and attempts to make global appraisals of the effectiveness of different schools and school systems.

QUESTIONS AND EXERCISES

1. For which of the following purposes would a standardized test be useful? For which should a teacher expect to make his own test? Why?

(*a*) To determine which pupils have mastered the addition and subtraction of fractions.

(*b*) To determine which pupils in a class are below expectation in arithmetic computation.

(*c*) To determine the subjects in which each pupil in a class is strongest and weakest.

(*d*) To determine for a class which punctuation and capitalization skills need further teaching.

(*e*) To form subgroups in a class for the teaching of reading.

2. Get a curriculum guide covering the content and objectives of a subject that you are teaching or plan to teach. Examine a standardized achievement test for that subject. Which of the objectives in the curriculum guide are adequately measured by the test? Which ones are not? How adequately is the content covered by the test?

3. Make a critical comparison of two achievement test batteries for the same grade. How do they differ? What are the advantages of each from your point of view?

4. The manual of test W states that it can be used for diagnostic purposes. What should you look for to determine whether it has any real value as a diagnostic aid?

5. Why should we be specially concerned about the reliability of the scores resulting from a set of diagnostic tests? What implications does this have for using and interpreting such tests?

6. A senior high school, which draws from three feeder junior highs, has a special accelerated program in mathematics. What are the advantages and disadvantages of selecting students for this program on the basis of a standardized achievement test in mathematics given at the end of the 9th grade?

7. You have given a standardized achievement battery in October to your 4th grade class. How might you, as a teacher, use the results?

8. Using a centralized scoring service, a school buys item analysis data that show the percent of pupils answering each item correctly for each grade and each classroom in the school. How could the school as a whole use these results? How could individual teachers use them?

9. In high school H, where pupils are assigned to English sections on a presumably random basis, the principal finds that there are marked discrepancies in the distribution of grades awarded by different teachers. How could results from a standardized test help the principal in dealing with this problem?

10. Miss Carson, a 6th grade teacher, says: "I am not as much interested in a pupil's level of performance as I am in the growth that he shows while he is in my class." From a measurement point of view, what problems does this point of view raise?

11. The school system of Centreville is proposing to introduce a revised mathematics curriculum on an experimental basis in selected elementary schools. They wish to evaluate the effectiveness of the program before introducing it throughout the system. How adequate would a standardized achievement test in elementary school mathematics be for this evaluation? What problems would arise? How might these be dealt with?

12. A state legislature has passed a law requiring all students to show adequate competency in skills needed for everyday living before they are awarded a high school diploma. In order to implement the legislation what is the *first* problem that needs to be solved? What would be the advantages and disadvantages of using (a) a centrally constructed test by the State Education Department, (b) locally constructed tests by each school, and (c) a national published achievement test to determine adequate competency?

13. Give an example of a situation where it would be appropriate to use item-sampling techniques in a testing program. Give an example of a situation where it would be inappropriate to use item-sampling techniques.

Ebel, Robert L. Standardized achievement tests: Uses and limitations. In L.R. Aiken, Jr. (Ed.), *Readings in Psychological and Educational Testing*. Boston: Allyn and Bacon, 1973.

Jorgenson, Gerald W. An analysis of teacher judgments of reading level. *American Educational Research Journal*, 1975, 12, 67–75.

Sax, Gilbert The use of standardized tests in evaluation. In W. James Popham (Ed.), *Evaluation in Educaton*. Berkeley, Calif.: McCutchan, 1974.

Shoemaker, David M. Toward a framework for achievement testing. *Review of Educational Research*, 1975, 45, 127–147.

The scoring of children: Standardized testing in America. *The National Elementary Principal*, 54, July/August, 1975.

CHAPTER NINE
STANDARDIZED TESTS OF INTELLIGENCE OR SCHOLASTIC APTITUDE

WHAT IS AN APTITUDE?

In previous chapters we have been interested in tests as measures of the end results of school instruction. In this chapter and the next we shall be interested in tests as predictors of some future performance by the individual. However, whether our interest centers on outcomes of past learning or on potential for the future, all we can test is *present performance.*

Present performances are tied with varying degrees of closeness to organized school instruction. Thus the American student who can decipher the meaning of *Arma virumque cano,* or of

$$6 \, r \, (\,) \, c \, \frown \, — \, \frown \, r \, 6 \, \frown \, 6.$$

almost certainly learned these in school, in Latin class in the one case and in shorthand class in the other, and mastery of these tasks serves only as an indicator of progress resulting from systematic instruction. Other performances depend jointly on school and out-of-school experiences—understanding words, working out quantitative problems, following the train of thought in a complex prose passage. These are taught in school, but perfected also in the day-by-day experiences of life. Still others relate to what is taught in school only very remotely—such as tasks involving problem solving with spatial, pictorial, and other nonverbal materials, and, of course, all the performances that are mastered before the child gets to school.

It should be emphasized that *any* performance depends to some degree upon life experiences—if not upon school experiences. Any verbal test requires that a person must have learned to speak the language; any pictorial test calls for an acquaintance with the objects that are portrayed; any test of whatever sort requires that the person must have learned to put forth effort and do his best in test situations. By the same token, *any* performance depends to some extent on the genetic potential of the person—his genetic potential as a human being and his specific genes as an individual. Thus the aptitude tests that we discuss in this chapter and the next differ from achievement tests discussed in Chapter 8 only in being *less* dependent upon specific segments of school instruction and in being used to make inferences about the future, rather than to draw conclusions referring to the past. They cannot claim to be pure measures of innate potential for learning.

297
general
intellectual
ability as a
psychological
construct

GENERAL INTELLECTUAL ABILITY AS A PSYCHOLOGICAL CONSTRUCT

Very early in the history of psychological measurement, psychologists became interested in assessing general ability to deal with and manipulate the domain of ideas and relationships among ideas. Though the interest was motivated in part by a scientific concern to understand and describe intellectual functioning, it was motivated in part by very practical needs to identify children with intellectual deficits that would make it difficult for them to progress normally in school, or, at a more severe level, individuals who would have difficulty in meeting the basic intellectual demands of life—in an extreme case, people who wouldn't have "sense enough to come in when it rains."

Tests designed to assess the level of general cognitive functioning have been called *intelligence tests* in the psychological literature, or *IQ tests* in popular discussion. However, psychologists have never been able to agree very precisely on a definition of "intelligence" or on exactly what it does and doesn't include. In recent years there has been a tendency to play down the term "intelligence," since the term has come to carry a surplus of both meaning and feeling, and instead to speak of "general cognitive ability" or "scholastic aptitude." The last term brings out specifically the function of these tests as predictors of school performance.

Whatever the designation, abundant evidence indicates that a wide variety of tasks that depend upon one's stock of ideas

298

standardized
tests of
intelligence or
scholastic
aptitude

and facility in working with relationships among ideas cluster together to form a generalized skill in cognitive functioning. This ability influences performance on a wide range of test tasks and has implications for functioning in school and in the broader tasks of life. In this chapter we consider the form that these tests have taken, evidence of their generality over a range of tasks and their stability over time, issues concerning their validity for school and nonschool criteria, and problems in their interpretation and use.

GROUP TESTS OF COGNITIVE FUNCTION

Most ability testing carried on in this country is done with group tests that can be given to a whole class at one time. We shall describe one series of group tests to illustrate some of the characteristics of instruments of this type. A listing of other widely used series, with their key characteristics, will be found in Appendix Four.

The *Cognitive Ability Tests* (Thorndike, Hagen, and Lorge, 1968, 1972) are made up of four distinct parts. For use in the primary grades there is a nonreading test in which all directions are given orally. For grades 4 through 13 there are a verbal test, a quantitative test, and a nonverbal test. Each test is made up of several subtests within which the items have the same form and progress from easy to difficult. Each is available in several levels, so as to provide tests of appropriate difficulty for persons of different levels of intellectual maturity.

The primary test has 4 subtests: oral vocabulary, relational concepts, multimental, and quantitative concepts. The material in the test booklet is entirely pictorial, and sample items are shown in Fig. 9.1. The tasks are presented to the pupil orally. For the 4 items in the illustration, the oral directions are substantially as follows:

Oral Vocabulary: "Fill in the oval under the picture that shows the rat . . . the rat."
Relational Concepts: "Fill in the oval that shows the ball is on the chair . . . the ball is on the chair."
Multimental: "Look at the row of pictures. One does not belong with the others, One is different. Fill in the oval under the one that does not belong with the others.
Quantitative Concepts: "Find the box that has two sets of two sticks in it . . . two sets of two sticks. Fill the oval under that box.

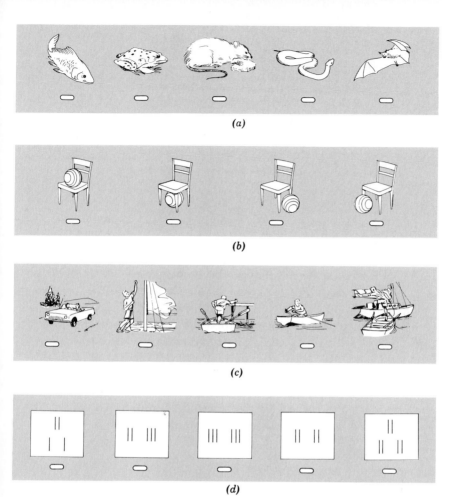

Figure 9.1
Sample *Cognitive Ability Test* items. (a) Oral Vocabulary; (b) Relational
Concepts; (c) Multi-Mental; (d) Quantitative Concepts (Reproduced by
permission of Houghton Mifflin Co.)

The verbal test includes four subtests designated respectively
vocabulary, sentence completion, verbal classification, and verbal analogies. An example of each type of item is shown in Fig.
9.2. The correct answer has been underlined for each item. In
order to provide tasks that are suitable for children as low as
the fourth grade and as high as the beginning of college (which
means difficult enough for most adults), this test has been produced in a "multilevel" format. The items in each subtest
range from easy fourth grade to difficult thirteenth grade.
However, pupils of a given age or grade take only part of the
tasks, starting and stopping at different places. There are eight

300
standardized
tests of
intelligence or
scholastic
aptitude

overlapping levels of the test. Thus for the vocabulary test the normal testing pattern would be as follows:

Grade	Level Taken	Begins at Item	Ends at Item
4	A	1	25
5	B	6	30
6	C	11	35
7	D	16	40
8	E	21	45
9	F	26	50
10–11	G	31	55
12–13	H	36	60

Each pupil is tested with 25 vocabulary items, and these can be picked to be the most appropriate for his group's ability level. The total test is made up of 100 items, 25 of each of the four types shown in Fig. 9.2.

Because the ability to handle ideas and relationships of a quantitative nature seems somewhat different from the ability to work with verbal ideas and relationships, a separate quantitative test has been prepared. The types of item used in this test are shown in Fig. 9.3. In the first subtest the examinee must determine which of 2 quantities is greater. In the second he must find the choice that logically continues the series. In the third he must arrange numbers and operation signs to produce one of the answer choices.

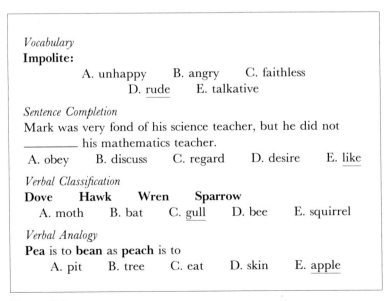

Vocabulary
Impolite:
    A. unhappy   B. angry   C. faithless
          D. rude   E. talkative

Sentence Completion
Mark was very fond of his science teacher, but he did not
_____ his mathematics teacher.
  A. obey   B. discuss   C. regard   D. desire   E. like

Verbal Classification
Dove   Hawk   Wren   Sparrow
  A. moth   B. bat   C. gull   D. bee   E. squirrel

Verbal Analogy
Pea is to **bean** as **peach** is to
    A. pit   B. tree   C. eat   D. skin   E. apple

Figure 9.2
Sample verbal test items like those used in the *Cognitive Abilities Test.*

Quantitative Comparison
    Column I   Mark A if I is more than II   Column II
               Mark B if I is less than II
     5 × 0   Mark $\overline{\text{C}}$ if I is equal to II   5

Number Series
 18   16   14   12   10
          A. 7 $\underline{\text{B. 8}}$ C. 9   D. 10   E. 12

Equation Building
 1   8   9   +   −
       $\underline{\text{A. 0}}$ B. 3   C. 8   D. 9   E. 18

Figure 9.3
Sample quantitative test items like those in the *Cognitive Abilities Test.*

In order to have a measure of reasoning that does not require verbal ability, and especially one that makes no demands
upon reading skills, a nonverbal series is also provided. Samples of the 3 item types—figure analogies, figure classification,
and figure synthesis—are shown in Fig. 9.4. In the first 2, the
one correct answer must be chosen. In the figure synthesis test
the examinee must determine whether each "complete shape"
can be made by placing the "given pieces" beside each other.
The nonverbal test is also prepared in the multilevel format,
permitting the examiner to select the range of difficulty most
appropriate for the group.

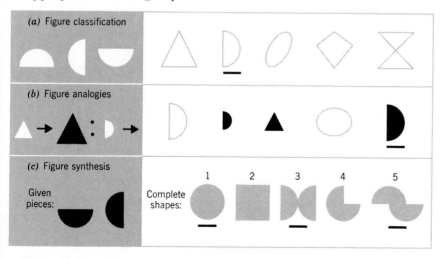

Figure 9.4
Sample nonverbal items like those in the *Cognitive Abilities Test.*

302
standardized
tests of
intelligence or
scholastic
aptitude

Evidence for the existence of a general cognitive ability running through this rather wide range of test tasks is found in the substantial correlations among the four batteries within a grade group. These were found to be approximately as follows.

	Verbal	Quantitative	Nonverbal
Primary*	.60	.58	.66
Verbal		.75	.66
Quantitative			.72

* A time interval of two years elapsed between testing with the primary and the other tests. The other three were given at the same time.

Thus it is evident that all of the tests tap to a considerable extent some common skills of cognitive functioning. However, as we shall see presently, the reliabilities of the separate tests are around about .90, so that it is also true that each measures functions somewhat different from those measured by the others. The uniqueness of each test is enough to permit it to have some distinctive meaning apart from the others. All of the tests show fairly good correlations with measures of school achievement, but for most subjects the verbal test is a somewhat better predictor. However, the verbal test calls for reading and for facility with English. Thus the nonverbal test could be expected to give a more adequate picture of the ability level of a child from a Spanish-speaking environment or of a child who had experienced particular difficulty in learning to read. The quantitative test has advantages in predicting performance in mathematics and related areas of academic performance.

The *Cognitive Ability Tests,* and a number of others, follow a pattern of several separately timed subtests. We have also already mentioned the graduated multilevel format. A few tests mix all types of item together in what is called an omnibus arrangement (*Henmon-Nelson, Otis-Lennon*). Many tests are published in three or four distinct levels, each of which is designed to be used in a range of several grades, and must, therefore, contain some items easy enough for the slower pupils in the lowest grade and some hard enough for the brighter pupils in the highest grade.

Tests for children in the primary grades usually call for the responses to be marked in the test booklet itself. In the upper elementary grades separate answer sheets are often used, though consumable test booklets in which the answers are marked are also used to some extent. Most tests for older groups use separate answer sheets. Electronic optical scanning devices have now been developed to the point that it is possible to score by machine even the primary level tests where the pupil has marked his response in the test booklet.

A number of group tests of intelligence are listed and briefly characterized in Appendix Four, Section A. We will next turn our attention to two widely used individual tests—tests that must be given to one examinee at a time in a face-to-face interview type of setting.

THE REVISED
STANFORD-BINET TESTS
OF INTELLIGENCE

The individual test that over the years has had the widest use with young children is the *Stanford-Binet,* brought out by Lewis M. Terman in 1916 as an adaptation of the earlier work of Binet and Simon in France. A revised version of the test was published by Terman and Merrill; this was somewhat further revised in 1960 and restandardized in 1972 (Terman and Merrill, 1973). The current revision, which uses the best items from the two forms of the test brought out in 1937, is known as *Form L-M.* It provides a set of subtests for each of 20 levels of ability, starting with tests suitable for the average 2-year-old and going up to four levels suitable for differentiating the abilities of average and superior adults. To illustrate the content of the test, we have picked four levels at different points on the scale and listed the subtests of each level with brief descriptions.

2½-Year Level

1. *Identifying Objects by Use* (card with 6 small objects attached).
   "Show me the one that we drink out of," etc.
   Three out of 6 for credit at this level.

2. *Identifying Parts of Body* (large paper doll).
   "Show me the dolly's hair," etc.
   Six out of 6 parts for credit at this level.*

3. *Naming Objects* (5 small objects).
   "What is this?" (Chair, automobile, etc.)
   Five out of 5 for credit.

4. *Picture Vocabulary* (18 small cards with pictures of common objects).
   "What's this? What do you call it?"
   Eight out of 18 for credit at this level.*

5. *Repeating Two Digits.*
   "Listen; say 2." "Now, say 4, 7," etc.
   One out of 3 for credit.

* Scored also at one or more other levels.

304

standardized
tests of
intelligence or
scholastic
aptitude

6. *Obeying Simple Commands* (4 common objects on table).
"Give me the dog."
"Put the button in the box."
Two out of 3 correct for credit.

6-Year Level

1. *Vocabulary* (graded list of 45 words).
"When I say a word, you tell me what it means. What is an orange?" etc.
Six words to receive credit at this level. Words like tap, gown.*

2. *Differences.*
"What is the difference between a bird and a dog?"
"Wood and glass?"
Two out of 3 correct for credit.

3. *Mutilated Pictures* (5 cards of objects with part missing).
"What is gone in this picture?" or "What part is gone?"
Four out of 5 for credit.

4. *Number Concepts* (twelve 1-inch cubes).
"Give me 3 blocks. Put them here."
Four out of 5 different numbers correct.

5. *Opposite Analogies.*
"A table is made of wood; a window of _____."
Three out of 4 correct for credit.

6. *Maze Tracing* (mazes, with start and finish points marked).
"The little boy wants to go to school the shortest way without getting off the sidewalk. Show me the shortest way."
Two right out of 3 for credit.

12-Year Level

1. *Vocabulary* (same as 6-year level).
Fifteen words correct for credit at this level. Words like juggler and brunette.

2. *Verbal Absurdities* (5 statements).
"Bill Jones' feet are so big that he has to pull his trousers on over his head. What is foolish about that?"
Four out of 5 right for credit at this level.

3. *Picture Absurdities.*
Picture showing person's shadow going wrong way. "What is foolish about that picture?"

4. *Repeating 5 Digits Reversed.*
"I am going to say some numbers, and I want you to say them backwards."
One out of 3 correct for credit.

* Scored also at one or more other levels.

5. *Abstract Words.*
     "What do we mean by pity?"
     Three out of 4 for credit at this level.

6. *Sentence Completion* (4 sentences with missing words).
     "Write the missing word in each blank. Put just one word in each."
     Three out of 4 required for credit at this level.

Superior Adult-Level II

1. *Vocabulary* (same as 6-year level).
     Twenty-six words for credit at this level. Words like mosaic, flaunt.

2. *Finding Reasons* (2 parts).
     "Give three reasons why a man who commits a serious crime should be punished."
     Both parts right for credit.

3. *Proverbs* (pearls before swine, etc.).
     "Here is a proverb and you are supposed to tell what it means."
     One out of 2 correct for credit.

4. *Ingenuity.*
     A 5-pint can and a 3-pint can to get exactly 2 pints of water.
     Three out of 3 problems correct for credit.

5. *Essential Differences.*
     "What is the principal difference between work and play?"
     Three out of 3 correct for credit.

6. *Repeating Thought of Passage.*
     Short paragraph on the value of life.
     Four out of 7 essential ideas must be reproduced for credit.

The above examples illustrate the variety of material included in the test. Note that the specific tests vary from one level to another. Many of the tests at the lower age levels are quite concrete, dealing with little objects and pictures. At the upper levels the tests tend to be more abstract and quite heavily verbal. The various tests include tasks calling for display of past learnings, perception of relations, judgment, interpretation, sustained attention, immediate memory, and other cognitive processes. However, interest is focused on the common core of cognitive ability running through the varied tasks, and these are combined to provide a single overall index of mental ability.

The tasks were selected so as to be of appropriate difficulty for the average child of the age level to which they were as-

306

standardized
tests of
intelligence or
scholastic
aptitude

signed. In testing a child the examiner begins at a level where the child is likely to succeed, but only with some effort. If the child fails these and appears discouraged, the examiner will drop back to an easier level. Otherwise he will move ahead level by level until he reaches a level at which the child fails all tests. When the uppper limit has been established, the examiner will be sure to go back and establish the level at which the child can do all the tests. Often a few quite easy tests will be given at the end to build up the child's morale.

The child is credited with the basal age at which he passes all tests plus a credit for tests passed at more advanced levels. Each test passed at a given level credits the child with the same number of months of mental age. Thus where there are six tests at each year age level, passing a single test gives a credit of 2 months of mental age. For example, child A

Passed all tests at 6-year level	= 6 yrs. basal age
Passed 3 of 6 tests at 7-year level	= 6 mos. credit
Passed 1 of 6 tests at 8-year level	= 2 mos. credit
Failed all tests at 9-year level	= 0 credit
Resulting in a mental age of	6 yrs., 8 mos.

Level of achievement is expressed as a mental age, arrived at as indicated above. The mental age describes the level at which the child is performing. But this takes no account of the child's life age. Performance in relation to a group of children of his own age is expressed as an IQ. The IQs for the current revision of the Stanford-Binet are deviation IQs, that is, they are essentially standard scores for which the mean is 100 and the standard deviation 16 at each age level. Insofar as the normative groups are adequate and comparable from one age to another, an IQ has the same meaning at one age as at any other. Tables for converting MAs to IQs are provided from age 2-0 (2 years, 0 months) up to age 18-0. For individuals over 18 years of age the table is entered with a chronological age of 18-0.

THE WECHSLER
INTELLIGENCE SCALES

The second major series of individual ability tests is the *Wechsler Intelligence Scales*. Wechsler worked initially on a scale to measure cognitive abilities in adults, whereas the Binet scales had been designed for and were appropriate primarily for children. Content of the *Wechsler Adult Intelligence Scale* (*WAIS*)

(Wechsler, 1955) was selected with an eye especially to its appropriateness for use with adults. At the same time, the test was organized in the format of a series of distinct subtests, each starting with easy items and progressing to more and more difficult items of the same sort. The titles of the subtests are given below. In each case the subtest is illustrated by an item of roughly average difficulty. (The illustrative items are similar to those in the test, but are not actually included in it.)

Verbal Subscale

1. *General Information.*
   What day of the year is Independence Day?
2. *Similarities.*
   In what way are *wool* and *cotton* alike?
3. *Arithmetic Reasoning.*
   If eggs cost 60 cents a dozen, what does 1 egg cost?
4. *Vocabulary.*
   Tell me the meaning of corrupt.
5. *Comprehension.*
   Why do people buy fire insurance?
6. *Digit Span.*
   Listen carefully, and when I am through, say the numbers right after me.

        7   3   4   1   8   6

   Now I am going to say some more numbers, but I want you to say them backward.

        3   8   4   1   6

Performance Subscale

7. *Picture Completion.*
   I am going to show you a picture with an important part missing. Tell me what is missing.

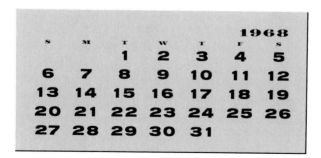

8. *Picture Arrangement.*
   The pictures below tell a story. Put them in the right order to tell the story.

308
standardized
tests of
intelligence or
scholastic
aptitude

9. *Block Design.*

Using the four blocks, make one just like this.

10. *Object Assembly.*

If these peices are put together correctly, they will make something. Go ahead and put them together as quickly as you can.

11. *Digit-Symbol Substitution.*

Code

△	○	◻	✕	8
1	2	3	4	5

Test

△	8	✕	○	△	◻	8	✕	△	8	etc.

Each subtest of the *WAIS* yields a separate score, which is then converted into a standard score for that subtest. The subtest standard scores are combined in three different groupings to yield total scores, and from these total scores three different types of IQ may be read from norm tables. The three IQs are (1) a verbal IQ from subtests 1 through 6; (2) a performance IQ from subtests 7 through 11; and (3) a total IQ from all the subtests put together. The separate verbal and performance IQs may have diagnostic significance in the case of certain individuals with verbal, academic, or cultural handicaps. The IQ on the *WAIS* is also a standard score, but set to make the mean of the normative sample 100 and the standard deviation 15.

As we have indicated, the original *Wechsler Intelligence Scale* was designed for adults. It was suitable for use with adolescents and with adults of all ages. Subsequently, however, the material has been extended downward to make tests for children. The same general pattern of subtests has been used, although the tasks change their character somewhat as one gets down to the younger age levels. In fact, one may question whether the parallelism between the nature of the subtests for 4-year-olds and for adults is real or only superficial. Two lower levels of the test are now available. *The Wechsler Intelligence Scale for Children* (*WISC*) was originally published in 1949, and has been published in a revised form in 1974 (Wechsler, 1974). It is recommended by its publisher for use with children 6 to 16 years of age. The *Wechsler Preschool and Primary Scale* (*WPPSI*) (Wechsler, 1967) is offered for use with children from 4 to 6½.

The features that distinguish the *WAIS* from the *Stanford-Binet* are:

1. Original test items specifically designed for adults.
2. Organization by subtests rather than by age levels.
3. Provision for separate verbal and nonverbal IQs.

310

standardized
tests of
intelligence or
scholastic
aptitude

All these features seem like sound adaptations in a test for adults. Most psychometricians would probably agree now in preferring the *WAIS* as a measure for adolescents and adults, though its relation to academic success is perhaps not as clearly established as is that of the *Stanford-Binet*. (As a matter of fact, at these ages a printed group test would usually seem more appropriate for academic prediction.)

With the addition of the *WISC* and the *WPPSI*, the Wechsler series can now be used with children as young as 4 years of age. The *WPPSI* is fairly new and evidence on its validity is rather limited. Therefore, for children up to the age of 6 or 7, the *Stanford-Binet* must still be considered the standard instrument. For children from 7 to 15, a decision between the two tests is not an easy one. The *Binet* is reported to be somewhat more difficult and time consuming to give. The usual *Binet* procedure of carrying the examinee through to the point where he encounters a long series of failures is judged to be a seriously upsetting matter for some emotionally tense children. The separate verbal and performance IQs of the *WISC* should be quite useful in some cases in understanding children whose verbal development is either very accelerated or retarded, and may have diagnostic value for some children with special educational disabilities. However, the *Binet* is probably a somewhat more reliable measure. (No directly comparable data are available.) The ultimate basis for choice will be the validity of the inferences that can be made from each in the situations in which they are actually used. Prediction of academic success can apparently be made about equally well from either test. It seems likely that the two tests are about equally useful for children with mental ages of 7 or above.

ABBREVIATED INDIVIDUAL TESTS

A major problem in using individual intelligence tests is that they are distressingly costly in time of trained examiners. This has led to various attempts to provide abbreviated adaptations of the *Binet* or *Wechsler*, as well as to produce other shorter and simpler individual tests. Abbreviations of the *Binet* or *Wechsler* that omit either certain subtests (Doppelt, 1950) or a fraction of the test items (Mogul and Satz, 1963; Slosson, 1963) correlate quite well with the complete test but are less reliable, as would be expected with a shortened test.

Of all the subtests in the *Binet* and *Wechsler,* the one that has consistently shown the highest correlation with total score has been the vocabulary test. This has led several test makers to produce picture-vocabulary tests as abbreviated test devices. The *Full-Range Vocabulary Test* (Ammons and Ammons, 1948) uses a set of 16 plates, each with 4 pictures on it. A word is spoken, and the examinee indicates which of the 4 pictures it refers to. The plates are reused with words of increasing difficulty, so that a total of 80 words can be tested. The same general procedure is used with the *Peabody Picture Vocabulary Test* (Dunn, 1959) except that a different set of pictures is used for each of the words tested. Thus the materials required are kept very simple, and a quick estimate of ability is obtained. The score is, of course, highly dependent upon a limited verbal type of ability, but the procedure functions fairly efficiently within that limitation.

TESTS NOT DEPENDING ON LANGUAGE OR CULTURE

Most of the widely used general cognitive ability tests depend to some degree on language and include tasks presented in verbal terms. They also assume some familiarity with the objects and activities of a particular culture. It is probably efficient to assess the cognitive functioning of most persons within a common culture in this way because, to a considerable degree, our mental functioning is carried out through the medium of language and involves the world with which we are familiar. However, for some groups or situations this is not so. The most obvious example is that of groups who do not speak the common language, or speak it only slightly. When an individual has little command of English, results from a verbal test in English are in large measure meaningless. A less obvious case, but one that may be equally important, is the individual whose cultural background is different from that represented in the test (for example, a person who has never owned anything on which he would have fire insurance—see item 5 on p. 307). For use with such groups or individuals, test makers have attempted to produce tests that tap important cognitive functions but do not depend upon language or, it is hoped, upon a specific cultural background.

Reference has already been made to the Nonverbal Scale of the *Cognitive Ability Tests* and to the Performance IQ of the Wechsler series. These are nonverbal in the sense that lan-

312

standardized
tests of
intelligence or
scholastic
aptitude

guage is used only to give the directions, and these directions can be translated into the language of the examinee. Two other tests may be mentioned that have been used widely in crosscultural studies as measures of cognitive maturity—the *Progressive Matrices Test* (Raven, 1956) and the *Draw-a-Man Test* (Harris, 1963). The *Matrices Test* presents tasks of the form illustrated in Fig. 9.5. A two-dimensional set of stimulus figures is presented with one cell (here the lower right-hand one) blank. The examinee must choose from among the options given the

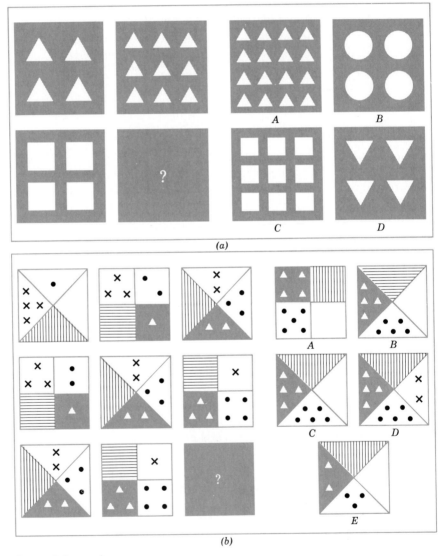

Figure 9.5
Matrices items.

option that fits the empty cell. He must perceive the relationship of successive figures in each dimension and identify the choice that fits the dual (or multiple) relationships. The simplest items involve color and pattern and are relatively easy tasks of perceptual matching. The difficult items involve abstract relationships of shape, direction, and number changing in complex ways.

The *Progressive Matrices* was originated and developed in England, and much of the research with it has been carried out in European, African, or Asiatic countries. Thus there is limited evidence on how it correlates with the tests used in the United States or what its validity is for predicting school success, job performance, or other life criteria in the American setting. Its freedom from language and apparently limited dependence on cultural variables has made it a popular instrument for use in developing countries or with culturally diverse groups.

The *Draw-a-Man Test* is perhaps the simplest there is so far as procedure is concerned. A child is asked to draw first a man and then a woman, being instructed "Make a picture of a man. Make the very best picture that you can; take your time and work very carefully . . . Be sure to make the whole man, not just his head and shoulders." A scoring scheme has been provided that allocates points for completeness and maturity of representation. Thus, 5 points can be earned for eyes: (1) eyes present; (2) brow or lashes; (3) detail of pupil; (4) vertical-horizontal proportion; and (5) direction of glance.

As used in a large-scale survey of children and adolescents in the United States (Harris, 1974), the test yielded average correlations of .84 between two drawings, one of "a person" and the other of the "self," and this value might be considered an estimate of alternate-forms reliability of the procedure. Average correlation for children in an age group with an abbreviated version of the *WISC* was about .45. We estimate that the correlation with a full-length *WISC* would be .50 or a little higher. It is of interest that for this test the difference between black and white children in the United States was only about one-third as great as the difference found for the abbreviated *WISC*. To the extent that the drawing is an expression of intellectual maturity it presents a much more favorable picture of the ability of black children than do the more conventional tests using verbal and abstract tasks.

The validity of nonverbal tests and tests designed to depend as little as possible on a specific culture has not been very thoroughly or comprehensively explored. For predicting school

314

standardized
tests of
intelligence or
scholastic
aptitude

success for the usual American school child, they are pretty clearly less effective than the more widely used verbal tests. Their validity for other than school criteria mostly remains to be determined. Their value seems to lie primarily in use with atypical individuals and groups. A child who is a poor reader often performs poorly on verbal tests of aptitude, and a score from a nonverbal test provides a cue as to whether his disability is specifically in the language area or whether the cognitive deficit is more general. For groups with a different language, and perhaps also a different culture, the nonverbal measure overcomes the language barrier and perhaps in part the cultural difference.

INFANT AND PRESCHOOL TESTS

The first intelligence tests were made for school-age children. However, it was not long before the theoretical interests of child psychologists and the practical needs of child-care and placement agencies stimulated the attempt to develop procedures for appraising cognitive abilities of preschool children and even of infants. Any appraisal procedures with young children obviously had to be individually administered. Also, they had to be based upon behavior that was spontaneously exhibited by or could be elicited from children of the age being studied. Infant tests, therefore, had to take on a very different character from later appraisals. Arnold Gesell (1940) pioneered in designing tests based on observation of the child's postural, perceptual, manipulative, and social responses. Does he sit up? Stand up? Walk? Will he turn to look at a light? Notice a face? Can he pick up a block? A spoon? A little pellet? By what type of a grasping motion? How does he react to strange adults? To another infant?

Observations of large numbers of infants showed a typical developmental sequence in the different aspects of the child's development. Performance B followed A, and was followed by C. Norms have been established representing the average age at which a particular behavior manifests itself. The child may be assigned a developmental age based upon the behavior he shows. Retests after a short interval show the child to be fairly consistent in his level of performance. If he is advanced at one testing, he will tend to be advanced at another within a few days or weeks. The developmental schedules provide a moderately reliable picture of the individual *at a particular point in time.*

Developmental scales to cover the age range from 2 to 30 months have been assembled subsequently by Cattell (1960) and Bayley (1969).

What significance does acceleration or retardation in development during the first year or so of life have for predicting later intelligence? The answer for normal children in normal home environments is shown in Table 9.1, which gives, for one rather typical study, the correlation of infant tests, given at the ages of 1 to 12 months, with intelligence tests at various later ages. The picture seems quite clear. For these normal infants, without any particular pathology, the infant tests give a fairly good prediction of developmental status a few months later, but their value as predictors drops rapidly as the time interval increases. The infant tests provide essentially *no* prediction of intellectual status at school age.

When there is some sort of neuropathology, however, the situation may be rather different. In one longitudinal study of infants seen in a hospital, usually because some pathology of the central nervous system was suspected (Knoblock and Passamanick, 1967), the correlation between *Gesell Developmental Quotient* at an age of 16 to 52 weeks and *Stanford-Binet* IQ at 6 to 10 years of age was .70. However, the sample of 135 included 40 cases that were judged to have some type of pathological condition, and these had an average IQ on retesting of 55. Thus schedules for the systematic observation of infants seem to

Table 9.1

CORRELATION OF INTELLIGENCE TESTS DURING FIRST YEAR OF LIFE WITH LATER MEASURES*
(Correlations based on pooling of successive tests)

Age at Later Test	Age at Initial Test			
	1, 2, 3 Mos.	4, 5, 6 Mos.	7, 8, 9 Mos.	10, 11, 12 Mos.
4, 5, 6 mos.	.57			
7, 8, 9 mos.	.42	.72		
10, 11, 12 mos.	.28	.52	.81	
13, 14, 15 mos.	.10	.50	.67	.81
18, 21, 24 mos.	− .04	.23	.39	.60
27, 30, 36 mos.	− .09	.10	.22	.45
42, 48, 54 mos.	− .21	− .16	.02	.27
5, 6, 7 yrs.	− .13	− .07	.02	.20
8, 9, 10 yrs.	− .03	− .06	.07	.19
11, 12, 13 yrs.	.02	− .08	.16	.30
14, 15, 16 yrs.	− .01	− .04	.01	.23
17, 18 yrs.	.05	− .01	.20	.41

* Tests used were: 1–15 months, *California First-Year Mental Scale;* 18 months–5 years, *California Preschool Scale;* 6 years and older, *Stanford-Binet* (Bayley, 1949).

316
standardized
tests of
intelligence or
scholastic
aptitude

have some value in identifying children who will later be classified as mentally defective, but no value on the positive end for forecasting degrees of intellectual talent.

There have been a number of different tests prepared primarily for use with preschool children, that is, in the age range from about 18 months to 5 years. As a matter of fact, as we have seen, the *Stanford-Binet Intelligence Scale* has tests going down to the 2-year level and may be considered a preschool test. It would compare very favorably with the other tests available for this age level, though it is somewhat more verbal than many of the others. A good many of the preschool tests have tended to get away from the verbal material that appears so heavily in group tests for older children and also in the *Stanford-Binet.*

One test for preschool children that has received wide use is the *Merrill-Palmer Scale* (Stutsman, 1931). This is most suitable for children from 2 to 4, though it can be used with children slightly older and slightly younger. The test is made up of 38 little subtests, of which only four call for verbal response by the child. A number of the tasks call for gross motor coordination (standing on one foot) or finer eye-hand coordination (building block tower, cutting with scissors). Form and object perception and motor control combine in a number of formboards in which cutouts must be fitted into the appropriate hole. The tasks make use of a variety of materials interesting to the child, blocks, pictures, scissors, balls, etc., so that cooperation can usually be obtained, a real problem with children at these ages.

The *Merrill-Palmer Scale* has fairly satisfactory reliability, especially above about 30 months. Correlations with retests 6 months later have been reported (Ebert and Simmons, 1943) as follows for different age groups:

24 months	.63
30 months	.76
36 months	.78
42 months	.80

The correlation with school-age *Binet* is about .40 for a *Merrill-Palmer* test at age 2; about .45 to .50 for one at age 4.

The *Minnesota Preschool Scale* (Goodenough et al., 1940) is another example of a test designed for preschool groups. The 26 tests in this scale tend to be more like those of the *Binet*. Six tests taken at random from one form of the *Scale* are described briefly.

Test 2: Pointing Out Objects in Pictures. Card with man, chair, apple, house, and flower on it. Child is asked to point to each in turn.

Test 5: Imitative Drawing. Experimenter makes vertical stroke; then a cross. Child is asked to imitate each in turn.

Test 8: Imitation. A set of 4 cubes, on which experimenter taps in specified sequence. Child instructed to imitate the sequence of taps.

Test 14: Colors. Cards red, blue, pink, white, and brown. Child is asked to name the color.

Test 20: Paper Folding. Examiner folds paper with three consecutive folds. Child is asked to copy exactly.

Test 24: Giving Word Opposites. Child is asked to give words meaning opposite of cold, bad, thick, dry, dark, and sick.

Test materials are quite simple. Copying, imitating, and re-sponding to simple verbal relations enter into a number of the tests.

This test appears to be somewhat more reliable than the *Merrill-Palmer.* Correlation between two forms of the test given within a few days of each other was found to be .89. Below 3 years, this test did not correlate very well with later *Binets,* but the *Minnesota* given between 3 and 4 gave a correlation with *Binets* at school age of about .60. However, IQs on the *Minnesota Preschool Scale* have quite a different spread from those for the *Binet,* so a preschool IQ on this test is not readily equated to later *Binet* performance (Goodenough and Maurer, 1942).

A recently developed test for preschoolers that has some in-teresting possibilities is the *McCarthy Scales of Children's Abilities* (McCarthy, 1972). This test yields not only an overall General Cognitive Index but also separate scores for verbal, perceptual, quantitative, memory and motor development. The scores rep-resenting these several aspects of development are overlapping and show positive correlations with one another, but do also have some distinctiveness, so that they may measure usefully distinguishable aspects of maturity. Thus in one study (Kauf-man, 1973) of a small group in first grade, correlations with later reading and math achievement scores were as follows.

		Reading	Math
773	Verbal	.20	.27
774	Perceptual	.49	.48
775	Quantitative	.42	.57
776	Memory	.33	.55
777	Motor	.05	−.07

The small size of the group (N = 31) indicates that these re-sults need not be taken too seriously, but they do suggest that

318
standardized
tests of
intelligence or
scholastic
aptitude

the parts of the test may differ rather substantially in their validity as predictors of academic achievement. The test is too new and published results from its use too limited to permit any dependable conclusion on the value of its several scores. They will appeal to the clinically oriented test user who considers patterns of strength and weakness important clues for understanding a child.

GROUP VERSUS INDIVIDUAL TESTS AS MEASURES OF INTELLIGENCE

We have seen that intelligence tests fall into two main patterns, group tests and individual tests. The types of task presented to the examinee are a good deal alike in both patterns. However, the two procedures have certain significant differences. These may be summarized as follows.

Group Tests	*Individual Tests*
Problems presented in printed booklet, read by examinee. Personal contact with examiner a minimum.	Problems presented orally by examiner in face-to-face situation.
Tasks usually presented and test timed as a unit, or separate time limits for each subtest.	Problems presented one at a time, usually without indication of time limits.
Individual usually responds by selecting one of a limited set of response options printed in the test booklet.	Individual usually responds freely, giving whatever response seems appropriate to him.

These differences in procedure have several important implications for the conduct of testing and for the results that may be obtained from such testing. In the first place, when test tasks are presented orally to the subject and he does not have to read them for himself, his performance is much less dependent upon his reading skills. The child who has lagged behind in acquiring these skills is not penalized for this specific failure.

The effect of reading disability upon intelligence test performance is shown clearly in a study (Neville, 1965) comparing individual *WISC* scores and *Lorge-Thorndike Verbal* test scores for good, mediocre, and poor readers in a fifth grade class. Reading groups were defined by scores on the reading section of the *Metropolitan Achievement Test* at the end of the fourth grade. Intelligence tests were given during the fifth grade to 18 pupils in each reading group. IQs on the tests were as follows.

	Lorge-Thorndike Verbal	WISC Verbal	WISC Performance	WISC Total
Good readers	113	110	106	109
Mediocre readers	95	96	96	96
Poor readers	82	89	94	90

The verbal group test shows a good deal more relationship to the reading test than does either part score or the total score on the individual test. The difference between good and poor readers is 31 IQ points for the group test and from 12 to 21 for the individual test.

The results reported above are probably somewhat extreme, because reading ability was defined by a test involving a test of word knowledge as well as of connected reading, and word knowledge is also directly measured in the *Lorge-Thorndike* test. Furthermore, the study was carried out with elementary school children, for whom the actual mechanics of reading still present some problems. One may anticipate that less difference would be found for high school or college students. Moreover, some current group tests are either partly or wholly nonlanguage in their content and would be relatively independent of reading skills. However, this study points out very clearly the caution with which group test performance must be interpreted for a person who departs markedly from the average in his reading skills. A low group test score for a poor reader cannot be taken at face value. It should always be checked by giving a test that does not involve reading.

The presentation of problems one at a time by an examiner is also a factor of some significance in determining what the test is likely to yield. Especially with younger children, maintaining continuity of attention and effort on a group test may be a problem, and variations in this respect are certainly a significant factor in test score. When each problem is separately presented by the examiner, this serves to reestablish the child's orientation to the task and can help to maintain his effort. What is equally important, the examiner is in a position to observe lapses of interest and effort and to take some account of them in interpreting the results.

The individual intelligence test is essentially a well-standardized interview situation. The tasks to be presented to the examinee are precisely formulated, and detailed standards are provided for evaluating his responses. However, the face-to-face relationship of an interview prevails. This offers the alert examiner a wealth of opportunities for observing the examinee

320

standardized
tests of
intelligence or
scholastic
aptitude

and noting poor motivation, distractibility, signs of anxiety and upset, and other cues that will help in interpreting the actual test performance. At the same time, the demands upon the examiner are considerably heavier. If valid testing is to result, the tasks must be presented in a standard way, interest and cooperative effort must be maintained, and a uniform standard must be applied in evaluating responses.

It is also possible that some examinees may be more comfortable and relaxed in the anonymity of a group test. An individual test session is a period of quite intense social interaction, and the child or adult who has some difficulty in relating to other persons may "clam up" in the highly personal context of the test session.

The free-response item in the individual test fits into the interview setting of the individual test and reinforces both its strengths and its limitations. Potentially, the free response of the examinee can tell us more about him than the mere record of which option he has chosen from a set of 5. There is more of the quality of his own behavior available to us. We can see just how he goes about defining a word, whether by class and differentia (that is, an orange is a round, orange colored, citrus fruit) or by use (an orange is to eat). We can note the speed and sureness of his attack on a problem task. But we must also depend on the examiner to interpret and evaluate the responses, and at this point subjectivity is likely to creep into the examining. Careful attention must be paid to the standard samples provided in the test manual, and experience under supervision is indicated before an examiner can expect to give and score an individual intelligence test in a way that will yield results comparable to those of other examiners.

In general, the limitations of group tests are most acute and the advantages of individual tests most pronounced with young children. Printed group tests cannot be used successfully with children below school age. Children at this age cannot read and have difficulty in manipulating a pencil, following instructions, or maintaining sustained attention for the period that is required for taking a test. These same factors continue to present fairly serious problems for testing in the primary grades. However, the factor of cost makes individual testing impractical for most large-scale users of tests, so that with older individuals the overwhelming majority of the ability tests used are paper-and-pencil group tests.

RELIABILITY AND STABILITY OF MEASURES OF COGNITIVE ABILITY

321

reliability and
stability of
measures of
cognitive ability

To give some impression of the reliability of measures of general cognitive ability at different ages we have assembled the data shown in Table 9.2. The results are in each case excerpted from the authors' manual for the test and are generally based on representative samples of cases. The procedure for estimating reliability is indicated, and in some instances estimates produced by different procedures appear together so they can be compared.

Even with tests of very young children, the internal consistency of individually administered measures of cognitive functioning is reported to be quite high. The manual of the *Bayley Scales of Infant Development* (Bayley, 1969) reports split-half correlations of about .90 for children only 3 or 4 months old. For preschool age children, split-half correlations for the General Cognitive Scale of *McCarthy's Scales of Children's Abilities* (McCarthy, 1972) are reported as about .94. The manual for the recent revision of the *Wechsler Intelligence Scale for Children* indicates reliabilities for school age children averaging about .96.

Unfortunately, none of the above tests provide alternate forms, so it is not possible to determine how consistently a child would perform on a different form given on a different day— say a week or a month later. Such data were available for Forms L and M of the *Stanford-Binet* (Terman and Merrill, 1973), and correlations ranged from .85 to .95 for different age groups. For ages from 2 to 6 the median correlation was .88, whereas for ages above 6 the median was .93.

Group tests can first be administered at the kindergarten level, and then only with some difficulty. However, they show reasonably high internal consistency even at that level. Thus the manual for the *Cognitive Ability Test, Primary* (Thorndike, Hagen, and Lorge, 1968) reports Kuder-Richardson reliabilities of .90 for kindergarteners. At higher levels, the reliabilities of group tests approach, but apparently do not quite reach, those for individual tests. Thus Kuder-Richardson reliability estimates for the *Cognitive Ability Tests* (Thorndike, Hagen, and Lorge, 1972) in grade 3 and above are about .94 for the verbal test, .92 for the quantitative tests and .93 for the nonverbal test.

Alternate-form reliabilities for group tests are appreciably lower than estimates from a single testing. Thus, for the Lorge-

322

standardized
tests of
intelligence or
scholastic
aptitude

Thorndike Multilevel (Lorge, Thorndike, and Hagen, 1966), the median values are as follows:

	Verbal	Nonverbal
Odd–Even	.93	.93
Alternate Form	.90	.84

The lower values to be expected with alternate forms must be kept in mind whenever a publisher provides only evidence from testing with a single form.

Table 9.2

REPRESENTATIVE GENERAL ABILITY TEST RELIABILITIES

Test	Procedure	Age	Correlation
Werner and Bayley Mental Scale			
1933–35 edition	Split-half	1–15 mo.	.83*
	Retest, 1 mo.	1–15 mo.	.82*
1958–61 edition	KR #20	1–15 mo.	.90*
McCarthy— General Cognitive	Split-half	3 yrs.	.94
		5 yrs.	.94
		7½ yrs.	.94
	Retest, 1 mo.	3–3½ yrs.	.91
		5–5½ yrs.	.89
		7½–8½ yrs.	.90
WPPSI	Split-half	4 yrs.	.92
		5 yrs.	.93
		6 yrs.	.94
	Retest, 11 wks.	5½ yrs.	.92
WISC–R	Split-half	7½ yrs.	.95
		11½ yrs.	.96
		15½ yrs.	.95
	Retest, 1 mo.	6½–15½	.95
CAT Primary	KR #20	K	.90
	Retest, 13 mo.	Gr. 2	.90
		K–Gr. 1	.72
		Gr. 1–2	.80
		Gr. 2–3	.82
CAT Multilevel Verbal	KR #20	Gr. 3	.96
		6	.94
		9	.94
Quantitative		3	.93
		6	.92
		9	.92
Nonverbal		3	.95
		6	.93
		9	.93

* Median of correlations for single age groups.

Generally speaking, the reliability of measures of general cognitive ability is quite satisfactory, and these are among the most dependable psychological measuring instruments. However, the chance errors in a score such as an IQ are still enough to require that we be quite tentative in our interpretation. Thus Table 9.3 shows the spread of IQs that could have been expected on Form M of the *Binet* if that form had been given to a group of pupils all of whom had received exactly the same IQ on Form L. Note that the IQs spread over a range of more than 25 points, and that less than a third of the cases fall in the center 5-point interval. And it must be remembered that these figures are for the *Stanford-Binet,* one of our most reliable tests. Thus an IQ of 100 must not be thought of as meaning "exactly 100," but rather "probably between 95 and 105, *very* probably between 90 and 110, almost certainly between 85 and 115.

Table 9.3
EXPECTED DISTRIBUTION OF *STANFORD-BINET* FORM M IQs FOR CASES ALL WITH FORM L IQs OF 100

IQ	f
113+	3
108–112	9
103–107	23
98–102	30
93–97	23
88–92	9
87 and below	3

In addition to knowing the precision with which an intelligence test appraises an individual's abilities at a particular time, we would like to know how consistently the individual maintains his position in his group from one year to the next or over a considerable span of years. How confidently can we predict what scholastic aptitude an individual will show when he is of college age from his performance on a test at age 2? Age 6? Age 10? Evidence on this point is presented in Figs. 9.6 and 9.7.

Fig. 9.6 shows the findings from one extensive study using individual tests. The final test is the *Stanford-Binet* in every case. The initial test is the *California Preschool Scale* up through 5 years and the *Stanford-Binet* after that age. Note that for the early tests the prediction is rather poor and drops as the interval is increased. A test at age 2 correlates only .37 with one at age 6 and .21 with one at age 14 or 15. A correlation as low as this

324
standardized
tests of
intelligence or
scholastic
aptitude

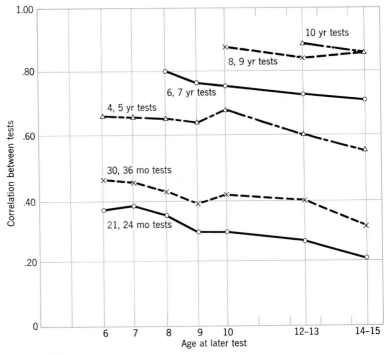

Figure 9.6
Effect of age at initial testing and test-retest interval on prediction of
later *Stanford-Binet* IQ from earlier Test. (Adapted from Honzik,
McFarlane and Allen, 1948.

indicates that a test at the age of 2 is essentially useless as an
indicator of where the individual will stand during his school
years. As we go up the age range, however, the correlations are
progressively higher and the drop is less. A test given at age 8
or 9 correlates .88 with one at age 10 and still correlates .86
with one at age 14 or 15. For normal children in a typical
environment, a *Stanford-Binet* at age 8 or 9 appears to provide
almost as accurate a forecast of ability near the end of high
school as would the same test given several years later.

   Two sets of data on stability of group test performance over
time are presented in Fig. 9.7. The two follow the same general
pattern, though they differ a good deal in detail. As the time
interval increases the correlation coefficient tends to drop more
or less steadily. The earlier tests at around grade 3 or 4 correlate perhaps .50 to .60 with the end-of-high-school test, but for
a test in grade 9 or 10 the correlation is .70 to .80. In these
studies of group tests, different tests were used at the different
ages. For this reason, it is not clear how much the lower correlation over the longer intervals is due to growth changes in the
children over a span of years and how much it is due to

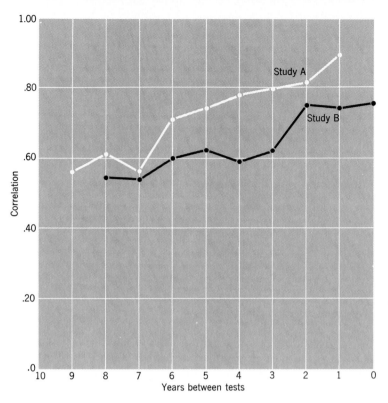

Figure 9.7
Effect of test-retest interval on prediction of group intelligence at end of
high school from earlier group tests. (Study A adapted from J. E.
Anderson, 1939; Study B adapted from R. L. Thorndike, 1947.)

changes in the material included in the tests. From the practical point of view, Fig. 9.7 suggests that a group intelligence test
needs to be supplemented by new testing every 3 or 4 years if
pupil records are to provide an accurate indication of current
ability level.

During the years of maturity, stability of intelligence test
performance is marked even over long intervals. Owens (1954),
retesting Iowa State University students some 30 years later
when they were about 50 years old, found a correlation of .77
with their scores as college freshmen. In another 25-year longitudinal study (Bradway and Thompson, 1962), correlations
were obtained as shown below.

	1941 *Binet*	1956 *Binet*	1956 *WAIS*
Preschool *Binet* (1931)	.65	.59	.64
Adolescent *Binet* (1941)		.85	.80
Adult *Binet* (1956)			.83

326
standardized
tests of
intelligence or
scholastic
aptitude

Several factors probably combine to produce the lack of stability over time observed in early intelligence tests. First, individual differences in maintenance of attention and effort are much more important in the young child than they are at a later date. Second, the types of performance that serve as marks of intelligence change in nature from infancy through childhood, becoming more and more verbal, abstract, and symbolic. Finally, in a young child a major part of intellectual growth is still to take place, while in an older child much or most of the growth has already occurred. Thus the correlation between an intelligence test given to 15-year-olds and one given to the same group 10 or 20 years later is high because by age 15 intellectual growth is nearly complete (Bloom, 1964).

PRACTICAL IMPORTANCE OF ABILITY AS MEASURED BY COGNITIVE ABILITY TESTS

To what extent are the individual differences that are brought out by tests of general cognitive ability important in the practical affairs of life? Do they enable us to predict to a useful degree how an individual will perform in school, on a job, or in other life adjustments?

APTITUDE TESTS AND SCHOOL SUCCESS

First let us consider academic success. From the many hundreds of investigations of scholastic aptitude test scores in relation to academic success, a number of conclusions can safely be drawn. These may be summarized as follows.

1. *The correlation of aptitude test scores with school marks is substantial.* Viewing all the hundreds of correlation coefficients that have been reported, a figure of .50 to .60 might be taken as fairly representative. Though this constitutes a very definite relationship, it is only necessary to turn back to Fig. 2.7 and the discussion of correlation on p. 49 to realize that there are still many marked discrepancies between aptitude test score and what a particular youngster does in school.

2. *Higher correlations have been found in elementary schools than in high schools and in high schools than in colleges.* Past studies have indicated a drop in correlation from perhaps .70 in elementary school to .60 in high school and .50 in college. The drop in correlation is probably to be explained by the decreased range of intellectual ability in the college groups. A relatively small percentage from the lower half of a school population have gone on to college, and specific colleges draw from an even more restricted ability range. Although more and more young people are going to college, the clientele of specific colleges continues to be fairly homogeneous in ability, and this results in lower correlations.

3. *Previous school achievement has given correlations with later school success as high as or higher than aptitude test scores.* In predicting college marks, for example, high school record has usually shown correlations at least as high as those resulting from a scholastic aptitude test at entrance.

4. *Aptitude test and achievement combined give still better prediction.* By pooling information on previous school achievement and aptitude test score, the correlation with later school achievement can be raised above that yielded by either factor alone. The two types of information supplement one another. School marks provide evidence on motivation and on study skills and habits of work, as well as on basic ability; the uniform, objective aptitude test compensates for the variability in standards of achievement from school to school.

5. *Aptitude tests correlate higher with standardized measures of achievement than with school marks.* Correlations between a scholastic aptitude test score and total score on an achievement battery in the .70s or even .80s are not unusual. Thus, for representative samples of 500 in each grade, the *Cognitive Ability Tests* gave correlations with the *Iowa Tests of Basic Skills*, averaged over grades, as follows:

Iowa	C.A.T. Verbal	C.A.T. Quantitative	C.A.T. Nonverbal
Vocabulary	.81	.66	.55
Reading	.80	.66	.56
Language	.78	.69	.57
Study Skills	.77	.74	.65
Arithmetic	.73	.77	.62
Composite	.85	.77	.68

6. *The degree to which scholastic aptitude tests are related to academic success depends upon the subject matter.* As one would expect, the more academic subjects, which depend more completely upon the same kinds of verbal and numerical symbol as those that bulk so large in scholastic aptitude tests, show the higher correlations. Thus one early summary of studies in secondary and higher education (St. John, 1930) reported an average correlation of .46 with natural science grades and .38 with English

328
standardized
tests of
intelligence or
scholastic
aptitude

grades and foreign language grades, but only .28 with shop work and .22 with grades in domestic science.

The fact that tests designed to assess intelligence correlate with academic achievement and school progress is unquestioned. From the very way in which the tests were assembled it could hardly be otherwise. How these facts should be capitalized upon in educational planning and individual guidance is a more troublesome matter. We will return to it later in the chapter.

GENERAL COGNITIVE ABILITY IN RELATION TO OCCUPATIONAL LEVEL

We turn our attention now to out-of-school accomplishments and consider how scores on general cognitive ability measures relate to achievement in the world of work. There are two types of questions that we may raise: (1) How do workers in different kinds of job compare in measured ability? (2) Within a given kind of job, to what extent is aptitude related to job success?

In relation to the first question, we may look at selected data from Project Talent appearing in the *Career Data Book* (Flanagan et al., 1973). Project Talent is a project in which a 5 percent sample of U. S. high school students were tested in 1960 and have been followed up since that time. The *Career Data Book* reports results from a 5-year follow-up of the students who were in grades 11 and 12 at the time of the original testing. Although only about one-third of the students completed the follow-up questionnaire, this still remains by all odds the largest-scale longitudinal study that has been carried out, and substantial numbers were identified who were employed in or training for a wide range of occupations.

The talent battery of tests included no one test that was specifically designed as a measure of general intellectual ability. However, a composite of several of the tests would provide a score that is a reasonable approximation to such a general ability measure. We have pooled measures of reading comprehension, abstract reasoning, and arithmetic reasoning to produce such a composite.

Table 9.4 shows medians and quartiles for each of 24 occupations selected as representing the major types of occupation in the U. S. The data are reported on a standard score scale for which the mean is 100 and the standard deviation is 20. The table shows that occupational differences are real, and fairly substantial in a number of cases. Furthermore, the differences probably should be considered minimum estimates since (1) all the groups had at least reached grade 11 and the school dropouts in some occupations would not be included in these data, and (2) for the higher levels of occupation these were persons still in training for the occupation with the possibility of further screening out before the candidates reached their occupational goal. However, while noting a range of median values from 119 for high school math teachers to 91 for laborers, one should also note the substantial overlap for different occupational groups. A quarter of the laborers got as high scores on this intellectual composite as the average electronic technician, and a quarter of these, in turn, got scores as high as the average electrical engineer. Though differences between groups are real, variability within each group is substantial.

329
practical
importance of
ability as
measured by
cognitive ability
tests

Table 9.4

ESTIMATE OF GENERAL INTELLECTUAL ABILITY IN DIFFERENT OCCUPATIONS*

	Sex	No.	Q_1	Med.	Q_3
Electrical engineer	m	713	105	114	124
H. S. math teacher	f	421	110	119	128
Registered nurse	f	2260	101	109	120
Physician	m	591	109	118	128
Certified public accountant	m	728	99	109	120
Manufacturing manager	m	235	98	109	119
Clergyman	m	508	99	110	120
Social worker	f	758	99	110	121
Lawyer	m	1110	106	115	125
Librarian	f	293	103	113	125
Artist, sculptor	f	156	101	112	122
Music teacher	f	223	101	112	121
Electronics technician	m	720	93	104	114
Laboratory technician	f	441	90	103	115
Business proprietor	m	811	88	100	113
Salesman (misc.)	m	961	88	101	113
Machinist	m	680	87	98	111
Auto mechanic	m	270	82	95	109
Carpenter	m	180	83	95	106
Plumber	m	224	82	94	106
Secretary	f	2830	91	103	114
Bookkeeper	f	399	90	102	114
Hairdresser	f	719	85	97	109
Laborer	m	927	80	91	104

* Scale: Mean = 100, standard deviation = 20

330
standardized
tests of
intelligence or
scholastic
aptitude

COGNITIVE ABILITY TEST SCORES
AND JOB SUCCESS

What can we say about the relationship of cognitive ability test scores to success within particular jobs? A summary of the findings reported in a number of different studies is presented in Table 9.5.

When the criterion being predicted is success in a training program, the average correlations tend to run from .40 to .50 (with the one exception of the .18 for vehicle operators), and these values are not greatly different from the values obtained for success in school. When the criterion is one of job proficiency, the correlations are uniformly lower, ranging from $-.10$ for sales clerks to .33 for salesmen, and averaging about .20 over all occupations. In part, the lower correlations may be due to limitations in the *criterion* of job success. Whether success is measured by supervisors' ratings, as is usually the case, or by some index of production on the job, the indicator is likely to be unreliable and biased by a number of considerations that have nothing to do with the real efficiency of the worker. Insofar as this is true, no test given to the individual can be expected to predict the criterion.

However, deficiencies in the criterion are only part of the story. A wide range of factors other than ability to handle abstract ideas enter into practically any job performance. And in the many jobs that are of a routine and repetitive nature, fluency in working with ideas, beyond a basic minimum level, may be a doubtful asset or even, in some work settings, a liability.

Table 9.5
VALIDITY OF INTELLIGENCE TESTS AS PREDICTORS OF TRAINING AND PROFICIENCY CRITERIA[*]

	Training	Proficiency
Executives and administrators		.30
Foremen		.25
Clerks	.48	.30
Sales clerks		$-.10$
Salesmen		.33
Protective service	.53	.25
Personal service	.50	.07
Vehicle operators	.18	.14
Trades and crafts	.41	.18
Industrial workers	.38	.19

[*] Adapted from E. E. Ghiselli, 1966.

All in all, we may conclude that (1) measures of general cognitive ability are related to occupational group membership, and (2) though the relationship of test score to job success is usually positive, it is likely to be quite low. Prediction of on-the-job achievement appears a good deal less accurate than prediction of school achievement.

TESTING THE CULTURALLY DIFFERENT

There is a good deal of debate as to how (or whether) tests of general cognitive abilities should be used with groups that differ from the white, middle class, English speaking group from which most test makers have come and that has constituted the reference point for most test development. It has been contended that the tests are unfair, irrelevant, or other wise inappropriate for minority group persons, persons for whom standard English is not the first language, or persons who have been deprived in some way in terms of their early environment.

There is abundant evidence that aptitude test performance is influenced by general cultural background. Recruits in the United States Army showed a gain equivalent to almost one full standard deviation between World Wars I and II (Tuddenham, 1948). Tennessee mountain children showed IQs in 1940 averaging 10 points higher than found for children in the same area in 1930 (Wheeler, 1942). Even for a while after World War II, restandardizations of ability tests found a rising trend in general population norms.* These changes are associated with a complex of social changes, including longer years of schooling for children and for their parents, greater accessibility and mobility of people—especially those in the rural areas—, the development and almost universal availability first of radio and then of television, and perhaps improvement in the materials and procedures of education.

The shifts that have just been described are upward shifts, reflecting extended and enriched experiences, especially in the preschool years. They document the positive effects of an environment that provides experiences related to the abilities called for by tests of cognitive skills. However, there are other

---

* There has been some evidence of a reversal of this trend in the past decade.

332
standardized
tests of
intelligence or
scholastic
aptitude

environments that provide a less adequate background for coping with the tasks that cognitive ability tests present. The environments may be characterized by some or all of the following:

1. A home language other than standard English—either a foreign language or a nonstandard dialect.

2. Home values that place little emphasis on book learning and getting ahead in school.

3. Home social and economic pressures that make it difficult for parents to provide a stable and supportive environment for the child.

4. Parents who have not learned how to function as teachers of their young children.

5. A shortage of the material possessions and lack of the economic stability that provides toys, books, and games as well as relaxed and comfortable living conditions.

6. A sense of separation and alienation from the dominant culture.

To the extent that some definable group, such as blacks or Spanish-speaking persons, is generally characterized by some of these factors, one can expect that ability test scores will be affected. A long series of studies (Loehlin et al., 1975) has documented the lower test scores of black children in the United States. There seems little question that a substantial part of this deficit is to be accounted for by environmental deficits of the types we have mentioned. Whether all of the difference is to be attributed to conditions of life is probably unanswerable in any definitive way. The deficiency is not peculiarly or even primarily in verbal measures. Thus Lesser, Fifer, and Clark (Lesser et al., 1965) studied test performance on several types of ability measure for middle class and lower class children from Jewish, Negro, Puerto Rican, and Chinese families. The results are shown in Fig. 9.8. It can be seen that the Negro child performed relatively *better* on verbal tests than on any other type. It should also be noted that the differences in level between middle class and lower class children appeared within each ethnic group and seemed large compared to the differences between ethnic groups.

Whatever the original patterns of causation, by the time a child comes to school, and even more completely by the time he is a candidate for admission to a program of higher education or a job, the differences are there. The issue then becomes: What do any test results signify, in the case of persons from a deprived group, so far as potential for future achievement is

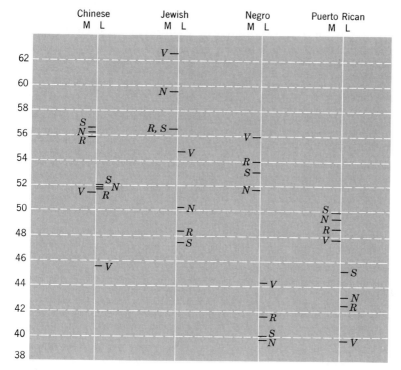

Figure 9.8
Relative Achievement of Middle class (M) and lower class (L) children of
different ethnic groups. Key N-number; R, reasoning; S, spatial; and V,
verbal. (Adapted from Lesser, Fifer and Clark, 1965.)

concerned? Are the relationships between measures of present
ability and future outcomes as high for pupils from limited
backgrounds as for the generality of pupils? For a given score,
how should the prognosis be modified, if at all, by knowledge
that the score was earned by a pupil from a meager environment? Since his score may have been held down by his environmental limitations, should we predict a higher school or job
performance for him than for his more favored classmate who
matches him in initial score? Should we predict essentially the
same outcome for both? Or does experience indicate that the
child from the more limited background will lapse back to a
lower final level?

These questions are easier to ask than they are to answer.
This is so in part because the answer may vary a good deal
depending upon the age at which the initial measure is obtained. The answer will also depend very markedly upon what
happens to the person in the interval between initial testing
and the final assessment of outcomes. Because for a considerable period public policy discouraged keeping separate records

334
standardized
tests of
intelligence or
scholastic
aptitude

by race and socioeconomic level, there is less information than we might like on the predictive accuracy of aptitude test measures for black pupils and for general groups of pupils from low socioeconomic families. Studies of the prediction of academic achievement in predominantly black colleges (Stanley and Porter, 1967) yield correlations of much the same size as those found in other institutions. Again, when studied in integrated college settings, a given level of aptitude test score seems to predict about the same level of achievement for black and for white students (Cleary, 1968). Readiness tests given to entering first grade children have been found to predict end-of-year achievement about equally well for Negroes, Mexicans, and Orientals as for Caucasian children (Mitchell, 1967). When no intervention is made to ameliorate conditions under which ghetto children grow up, the prognosis seems to be less favorable for a ghetto child than it is for a middle class child starting at the same test level. There is some tendency (Coleman, 1967) for the lower socioeconomic black child to drop further down in the distribution of his agemates the older he gets. Programs to break into the cycle of impoverishment and low ability have been numerous in recent years. These tend, in almost all cases, to emphasize *early* intervention, accepting the proposition that effective intervention must take place early in the life history of the individual, while initial language and thought patterns are being established. Under these circumstances it appears to have been possible to produce appreciable positive shifts in the mental growth curves, though it is still not clear how permanent the gains have been.

EXPECTED ACHIEVEMENT

One of the problems faced by any teacher or guidance worker is to know what level of achievement can reasonably be expected of any given child, and as a corollary of this, whether the child is doing as well as could reasonably be expected. The literature on underachievement would fill a good-sized library, and much of it is nonsense. At the very crudest level, we could set the same standard of expectancy for all children of a given age—and in a sense this is what the schools do when they admit all children to school at age 6 and expect all pupils to learn to read in the first grade. No tempering of expectation is introduced based upon other facts that are known about the child—his home background or his performance on a test of academic aptitude. Any child who falls below the average of all children is thought of as an underachiever, and educational effort and public concern are focused on bringing all children up to average—"up to the norm." This conception of what is to be expected is illustrated in diagram (*a*) of Fig. 9.9.

But we now know that all 6-year-olds or all 10-year-olds are *not* the same—with respect to either native endowment or life experiences. The differences show up on our measures of academic aptitude as well as on any other measures that we can apply to children. How shall we take these differences into account in setting expectations and in conceiving of underachievement? One possibility is to expect each child to achieve in school at a level exactly matching his performance on measures of scholastic aptitude. The child who falls at the 99th percentile in aptitude is then expected to fall at the 99th percentile on achievement, the one at the 75th to be also at the 75th, and the one at the very bottom in aptitude to be at the very bottom in achievement. Any discrepancy through which

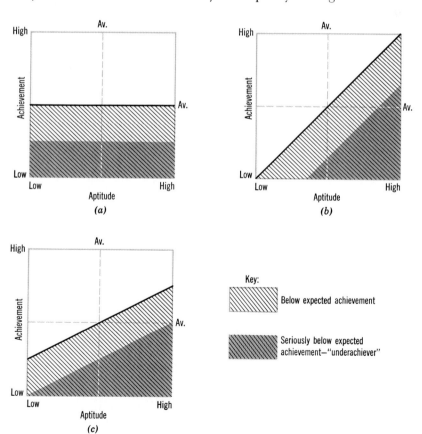

Figure 9.9
Three Conceptions of expected Achievement.

336

standardized
tests of
intelligence or
scholastic
aptitude

achievement falls below aptitude is conceived as underachievement. This conception is shown in diagram (*b*) of Fig. 9.9.

But this conception is just as faulty as the conception that the same standard should be set for all. This second conception implies a +1.00 correlation between measures of aptitude and of achievement, and we simply do not find such a correlation. Nor should we. Putting aside for the moment errors of measurement, which are very real in both aptitude and achievement appraisals, the two involve somewhat different things. Especially as we consider marks by teachers, these reflect interest, effort, ability to understand what the teacher wants, and skill at pleasing him, as well as capability in some special segment of academic content. So the correlation of aptitude with achievement is positive but far from perfect, and the pupils at the very top in measured aptitude will be above average, but usually not at the very top in achievement. The realistic situation is displayed in diagram (*c*) of Fig. 9.9. A child at a given aptitude score level must be viewed in relation to the *average achievement of all pupils at his aptitude level.* He should be considered an underachiever if he falls seriously below that average performance.

A number of test publishers who offer both a measure of scholastic aptitude and a measure of academic achievement provide some type of joint norms table indicating the level of achievement to be expected for a person who has performed at a particular level on the aptitude test. The tables often are provided separately by school grade or by chronological age. These tables are designed to help the teacher or guidance counselor judge whether the pupil is "doing as well as should be expected" in the light of his performance on the aptitude test.

The basic data from which tables of expected achievement are prepared are two-dimensional scatter-plots of achievement versus aptitude of the sort that we first encountered in Chapter 2. Taking a slice from such a plot, we can find the *average* achievement for a given level on the aptitude test, and this average value is certainly our best estimate of the expected value. However, very few children will fall exactly at the average value, and the question that we then have to face is whether the person falls far enough above or below the average of pupils at his or her aptitude test level for it to be a matter of concern to us. A few publishers have produced actual percentile tables of achievement-for-aptitude-level. A fraction of such a table, based on the *Cognitive Abilities Test, Nonverbal* and the *Iowa Tests of Basic Skills*, is shown in Fig. 9.10 on pages 338–341.

The presentation of the information in Fig. 9.10 is a little difficult to follow at first exposure. Let us try to make clear how the table is to be read. There are four sections of the table shown. Each section applies to fifth graders in a given Standard Age Score range on the Cognitive Abilities Test, Nonverbal—the first to those with SASs below 70, the second to those in the range 70–79, the third 80–89, and the fourth 90–99. The complete table included additional sections for 100–109, 110–119, 120–129, and 130 and over, and, of course, for other grades.

Within a given section the column on the extreme left shows the grade equivalent (GE), but without a decimal point. That is, the entry 45 should be read 4.5, or fifth month of the fourth grade. Each of the other columns refers to one of the subtests of the ITBS, that is, Vocabulary, Reading, and so forth. The entries in each of these columns are percentiles.

Knowing a child's SAS, we select the section of the table that corresponds to that SAS. Within the section, we select the column corresponding to the subtest in which we are interested, and the row corresponding to the pupil's grade equivalent (GE) on that subtest. Thus, if fifth grader Louise had obtained an SAS of 95 and a reading grade equivalent of 4.5, the table shows that her achievement is at the 42nd percentile within her SAS group.

We would interpret this as meaning that she falls just a bit below the average performance for girls of her SAS level. A grade equivalent of 3.4 would fall at the 14th percentile, given Louise's SAS, and would lead us to believe that she was a rather serious underachiever. However, if Sally, with an SAS on the aptitude measure of 68, had a reading grade equivalent of 34, this would be at the 45 percentile for her ability group, and the performance would be quite consistent with expectation for a person of her ability.

A full table like Fig. 9.10 is certainly the best way of making data on expected achievement available to test users. One sees directly not only whether a pupil is above or below what would have been predicted from knowledge of his aptitude test score but also how extreme his deviation is from the group average.

However, these discrepancy scores are somewhat tricky creatures at best, and are to be approached with a good deal of circumspection.

First, no "aptitude" tests are pure measures of native potential. They are measures of what have sometimes been called "developed abilities." And those abilities are influenced by many of the same factors that influence academic achievement. A stimulating and supportive home environment, good language skills, interest in reading, application to school learn-

338
standardized
tests of
intelligence or
scholastic
aptitude

Figure 9.10

PERCENTILE DISTRIBUTION OF *ITBS* GRADE EQUIVALENTS BY *COGNITIVE ABILITIES TEST STANDARD AGE SCORE*: GRADE 5, NONVERBAL

SAS LEVEL: Below 70

	Voc.	Rdg.	Test L: Language					Test W: Work-Study				Test M: Math.			Comp.
GE	V	R	L-1	L-2	L-3	L-4	L-T	W-1	W-2	W-3	W-T	M-1	M-2	M-T	C.
60			99												
59			98						99						
58			98	99	99	99			98						
57			97	98	98	98			98				99		
56			96	98	98	98		99	97			99	98		
55			95	97	97	97		98	96			98	98		
54		99	94	97	96	96		98	95	99		97	97		
53		98	93	96	95	95	99	97	93	98		96	96	99	
52	99	98	92	94	94	94	98	96	92	97	99	95	94	98	
51	98	97	91	93	92	93	98	95	90	96	98	93	93	97	
50	97	96	89	92	90	92	97	94	88	94	97	92	91	96	99
49	96	95	88	91	89	91	96	92	86	92	96	90	88	94	98
48	94	93	86	89	87	89	95	90	84	90	94	87	85	92	97
47	93	92	84	88	84	88	93	88	82	88	92	84	82	90	96
46	91	90	82	86	82	86	92	85	79	85	89	81	80	87	95
45	89	88	80	84	79	84	90	82	75	81	86	78	77	84	94
44	87	85	78	81	77	81	88	79	72	77	82	74	73	80	92
43	85	82	75	78	74	79	86	75	69	72	77	70	69	76	90
42	82	79	72	75	70	76	83	71	65	67	72	65	65	71	87
41	78	76	69	71	67	73	80	67	61	62	67	60	61	65	84
40	74	72	66	68	64	70	77	63	58	57	61	56	58	60	79
39	70	69	63	64	60	66	73	59	54	53	56	51	54	55	73
38	66	65	60	60	56	63	69	55	50	49	50	47	50	50	65
37	62	60	56	57	52	60	64	51	45	46	45	42	47	46	57
36	58	55	52	53	48	56	58	47	41	42	40	38	43	41	50
35	54	50	48	49	44	53	51	44	38	38	35	35	40	37	44
34	50	45	45	46	41	50	45	40	35	34	30	31	37	32	38
33	46	40	42	42	37	46	40	36	32	31	25	27	34	27	31
32	42	36	39	38	33	42	34	32	29	27	21	24	30	23	25
31	39	31	36	35	30	39	28	28	27	24	17	21	26	19	20
30	35	27	33	31	27	35	23	25	24	21	13	18	23	16	16
29	32	24	30	28	24	31	18	22	21	18	10	15	20	13	12
28	29	20	28	25	21	28	15	19	19	15	8	13	18	11	9
27	26	17	25	23	19	24	12	16	17	13	6	11	15	9	7
26	23	15	23	20	17	21	10	14	15	11	4	9	13	7	5
25	20	13	20	17	15	18	8	12	13	9	3	7	11	5	4
24	17	11	18	15	13	16	6	10	11	7	2	5	10	4	3
23	15	10	16	12	11	13	5	8	10	6	1	3	8	3	2
22	12	8	14	10	10	11	4	6	8	5		2	7	2	1
21	10	6	12	9	8	10	3	5	7	4		1	5	1	
20	8	5	10	7	7	8	2	4	6	3			4		
19	6	4	8	6	6	6	1	3	5	2			3		
18	4	3	6	5	5	5		2	4	1			2		
17	3	2	5	4	4	4		2	3				1		
16	2	2	4	3	3	3		1	2						
15	1	1	3	2	3	2			1						
14			2	1	2	1									
13			2		1										
12			1												

Figure 9.10 (*Continued*)

339
expected
achievement

PERCENTILE DISTRIBUTION OF *ITBS* GRADE EQUIVALENTS BY *COGNITIVE ABILITIES TEST STANDARD AGE SCORE:* GRADE 5, NONVERBAL

SAS LEVEL: 70–79

GE	Voc. V	Rdg. R	Test L: Language L-1	L-2	L-3	L-4	L-T	Test W: Work-Study W-1	W-2	W-3	W-T	Test M: Math. M-1	M-2	M-T	Comp. C.
65			99												
64			98			99									
63			98	99		98									
62			97	98	99	98			99						
61			96	98	98	98			98						
60			95	97	98	97			98						
59	99		94	97	97	97	99	99	97	99		99	99		
58	98	99	93	96	97	96	98	98	96	98		98	98		
57	98	98	92	95	96	96	98	98	95	98		98	97	99	
56	97	98	91	94	95	95	97	97	94	97		97	96	98	
55	96	97	90	93	94	94	97	96	93	96	99	96	95	98	
54	94	96	89	92	92	93	96	95	91	95	98	94	94	97	99
53	93	94	88	91	91	92	95	94	89	94	97	93	92	96	98
52	91	93	86	89	90	90	94	92	87	92	96	91	90	95	98
51	90	92	84	88	88	89	93	90	84	90	94	89	87	94	97
50	88	90	82	86	86	88	92	88	81	87	92	87	84	92	96
49	86	88	80	84	83	86	90	86	78	84	90	85	81	90	94
48	83	86	78	81	81	84	88	84	75	81	87	82	77	87	93
47	81	83	76	79	78	82	86	81	72	77	83	79	73	83	92
46	79	80	74	77	76	80	84	78	68	73	79	75	70	79	90
45	76	77	71	74	73	77	81	74	64	69	75	71	66	75	87
44	73	74	68	72	70	75	79	70	60	65	70	67	62	70	83
43	70	70	65	69	67	72	76	66	56	61	65	62	58	65	79
42	67	66	62	66	63	69	73	62	53	56	60	57	55	59	74
41	63	61	59	63	59	66	69	58	49	52	54	53	51	53	68
40	60	57	56	60	56	63	64	54	45	49	48	48	48	48	61
39	56	53	52	57	52	60	59	50	42	45	43	43	44	42	54
38	52	49	49	53	48	56	54	46	39	41	37	39	41	37	47
37	49	45	45	49	44	53	49	42	36	37	31	35	37	32	41
36	46	41	42	46	40	50	44	38	33	33	26	31	33	27	35
35	43	37	40	42	36	46	38	35	30	29	22	28	30	23	29
34	40	34	37	38	33	43	32	31	28	26	18	24	27	19	24
33	36	30	34	35	29	40	27	28	25	23	15	21	24	16	20
32	33	27	31	31	26	36	22	25	23	20	12	18	21	13	16
31	30	24	28	28	23	33	18	22	20	17	9	16	19	11	13
30	28	21	25	25	20	30	14	19	18	15	7	13	16	9	10
29	25	18	23	22	18	27	11	17	16	12	5	11	14	7	7
28	22	16	20	19	16	24	9	15	14	10	4	9	12	6	5
27	19	14	18	16	14	21	7	12	12	8	3	7	10	4	3
26	17	12	16	14	12	18	5	10	10	7	2	5	9	3	2
25	14	10	14	12	11	15	4	8	8	6	1	3	7	2	1
24	12	8	12	10	10	13	3	7	7	4		2	6	1	
23	10	6	10	8	8	11	2	5	6	3		1	4		
22	8	5	9	7	7	9	1	4	5	2			3		
21	6	4	8	6	6	8		3	4	2			2		
20	4	3	6	5	5	6		2	3	1			1		
19	3	2	5	4	4	4		1	2						
18	2	2	4	3	3	3			1						
17	1	1	3	2	3	2									
16			2	1	2	1									
15			2		1										
14			1												

340
standardized
tests of
intelligence or
scholastic
aptitude

Figure 9.10 *(Continued)*

PERCENTILE DISTRIBUTION OF *ITBS* GRADE EQUIVALENTS BY *COGNITIVE ABILITIES TEST STANDARD AGE SCORE:* GRADE 5, NONVERBAL

SAS LEVEL: 80–89

GE	Voc. V	Rdg. R	Test L: Language L-1	L-2	L-3	L-4	L-T	Test W: Work-Study W-1	W-2	W-3	W-T	Test M: Math. M-1	M-2	M-T	Comp. C.
74			99												
72			98			99									
70			97	99	99	98									
68			96	98	98	98									
67			95	98	98	97	99								
66	99		94	97	97	97	98								
65	98		94	97	97	96	98		99	99					
64	98	99	93	96	96	96	98	99	98	98					
63	97	98	92	95	96	95	97	98	98	98		99	99		
62	97	98	91	95	95	95	97	98	97	97		98	98		
61	96	97	90	94	94	94	96	97	96	97		98	97	99	99
60	95	96	89	93	93	93	96	97	95	96	99	97	96	98	98
59	94	95	88	92	92	92	95	96	94	96	98	96	95	98	98
58	93	94	87	91	91	91	94	95	93	95	98	95	94	97	97
57	92	93	86	90	90	90	93	94	91	94	97	94	93	96	96
56	91	92	84	88	89	88	92	93	90	92	96	93	92	95	95
55	89	90	82	87	88	87	91	92	88	90	95	91	90	94	94
54	87	88	81	85	86	86	90	90	85	88	94	89	88	92	92
53	85	86	79	83	84	84	89	88	83	85	92	87	85	91	91
52	82	84	76	81	82	82	87	85	80	83	90	85	82	89	89
51	80	81	74	79	80	80	85	82	76	80	88	82	79	86	87
50	77	79	72	76	78	78	82	79	73	76	85	79	75	82	85
49	75	76	69	74	75	76	80	75	70	73	82	76	71	78	83
48	72	73	66	71	72	74	78	71	67	70	78	72	67	74	80
47	69	70	63	68	69	72	75	67	64	66	73	68	63	69	77
46	66	67	60	65	66	69	72	63	61	62	68	64	59	64	73
45	63	64	57	62	63	67	69	59	58	58	63	59	55	59	69
44	60	60	54	59	59	64	65	56	54	53	58	55	51	55	65
43	57	57	51	55	55	61	61	52	50	49	52	50	47	50	60
42	54	53	48	52	51	58	57	48	47	45	45	46	44	45	54
41	50	49	45	48	47	55	53	45	44	41	39	42	40	40	48
40	47	44	42	44	43	52	48	41	40	37	34	38	36	36	42
39	44	40	39	41	39	48	43	38	36	33	29	34	33	31	37
38	40	36	36	37	36	45	38	35	33	30	24	30	30	26	32
37	37	32	34	34	33	42	34	31	30	26	19	26	26	21	27
36	34	29	31	30	30	40	30	28	28	23	15	22	23	17	21
35	31	26	28	27	27	37	25	25	25	20	12	18	21	14	16
34	29	23	26	25	24	34	21	22	22	17	9	15	18	11	12
33	26	20	23	22	22	32	17	20	20	15	7	13	16	9	9
32	23	17	21	19	19	29	13	17	17	12	6	10	14	7	6
31	21	15	19	17	16	26	10	14	15	10	5	8	12	5	4
30	19	13	17	15	14	24	7	12	13	8	4	6	10	4	3
29	16	11	15	13	12	21	5	10	11	7	3	5	8	3	2
28	14	10	13	11	10	18	4	8	10	5	2	4	7	2	1
27	12	8	12	9	9	16	3	6	8	4	1	3	6	1	
26	10	7	10	8	8	14	2	5	7	3		2	5		
25	8	6	9	7	7	12	2	4	6	2		1	4		
24	6	4	7	6	6	10	1	3	5	2			3		
23	4	3	6	5	5	8		2	4	1			2		
22	3	2	5	4	4	6		2	3				2		
21	2	2	4	3	3	5		1	2				1		
20	1	1	3	2	2	4			1						
19			2	1	2	3									
18			1			2									
17						1									

Figure 9.10 (*Continued*)

341
expected
achievement

PERCENTILE DISTRIBUTION OF *ITBS* GRADE EQUIVALENTS BY *COGNITIVE ABILITIES TEST STANDARD AGE SCORE:* GRADE 5, NONVERBAL

SAS LEVEL: 90–99

GE	Voc. V	Rdg. R	Test L: Language					Test W: Work-Study				Test M: Math			Comp. C.
			L-1	L-2	L-3	L-4	L-T	W-1	W-2	W-3	W-T	M-1	M-2	M-T	
80				99		99									
78			99	98	99	98									
76			98	97	98	97									
74			97	96	97	96	99								
73			96	96	97	96	98								
72	99	99	96	95	96	95	98		99						
71	98	98	95	94	96	94	97	99	98						
70	98	98	94	94	95	93	97	98	98	99					
69	97	97	93	93	95	92	96	98	97	98		99	99		
68	97	97	92	92	94	91	96	97	97	98		98	98		
67	96	96	90	91	93	90	95	97	96	97	99	98	98		99
66	95	95	89	90	92	89	94	96	95	96	98	97	97	99	98
65	94	94	88	88	91	88	92	95	94	95	98	96	96	98	98
64	93	93	86	87	90	86	91	94	93	94	97	95	95	98	97
63	92	92	85	86	88	85	90	93	92	93	96	94	94	97	96
62	91	91	83	84	87	83	89	92	90	91	95	93	92	96	95
61	89	89	81	82	86	82	87	90	89	90	94	91	91	94	94
60	88	87	79	80	84	80	85	89	87	88	93	90	90	93	92
59	86	85	77	78	82	78	83	87	85	86	91	88	88	92	91
58	84	83	75	76	80	76	81	85	83	84	89	86	86	90	89
57	81	80	73	74	78	74	79	83	80	81	87	83	84	87	87
56	79	78	71	71	76	72	77	80	78	78	84	80	81	85	85
55	76	75	68	69	73	70	74	77	75	76	82	77	78	82	82
54	72	72	66	67	71	67	72	74	72	73	79	74	74	79	78
53	69	69	64	64	68	65	69	70	69	70	75	70	71	75	75
52	66	66	61	61	65	62	67	66	66	67	71	66	67	71	71
51	62	62	58	58	62	60	64	62	63	63	67	62	63	66	67
50	59	58	55	55	59	57	60	58	60	59	63	58	58	61	62
49	56	55	52	52	56	54	57	55	57	56	58	54	54	56	58
48	52	52	50	49	53	52	54	51	54	52	53	50	50	51	54
47	49	49	47	47	50	50	50	48	50	48	48	47	47	46	49
46	46	45	45	44	46	47	46	44	46	44	44	43	44	42	45
45	43	42	42	41	43	44	43	40	43	40	40	40	41	39	41
44	40	39	40	38	40	42	40	37	40	36	36	37	38	35	37
43	37	37	37	35	37	40	36	33	37	33	31	33	35	31	32
42	35	34	35	32	34	38	32	30	34	30	27	30	32	27	28
41	32	31	33	29	31	36	29	27	31	27	23	27	29	23	25
40	30	28	30	27	28	33	26	24	28	24	19	24	26	19	21
39	27	26	28	24	25	31	23	21	26	21	16	21	23	16	17
38	25	23	26	22	23	29	20	18	23	19	13	18	20	14	14
37	22	21	23	20	20	27	17	16	21	16	10	16	18	11	11
36	20	18	21	17	18	25	14	14	19	14	8	13	16	9	8
35	18	16	19	15	16	23	12	12	17	12	6	11	14	8	6
34	16	14	16	13	14	21	10	10	15	11	4	8	12	6	4
33	14	12	14	12	12	19	8	8	13	9	3	6	10	4	3
32	12	10	12	10	10	17	6	7	11	7	2	4	8	3	2
31	11	9	11	9	9	15	4	6	10	6	2	3	7	2	1
30	10	7	10	8	7	13	3	5	8	5	1	2	6	1	
29	8	6	8	7	6	12	2	4	7	4		1	5		
28	6	5	6	6	5	10	1	3	6	3			4		
27	5	3	5	5	4	8		2	4	2			3		
26	4	2	4	4	3	7		1	3	1			2		
24	2	1	2	2	2	5			2				1		
22	1		1	1	1	3			1						
20						1									

342

standardized
tests of
intelligence or
scholastic
aptitude

ing will all have some effect on aptitude measures, just as they will on academic achievement. Thus, when we set a low expectancy for achievement on the basis of low "aptitude" we may be saying in part "because this child has not achieved, he cannot be expected to achieve," and we may be perpetuating in our expectations the child's past failure to learn.

Second, just because of the substantial correlation between measures of scholastic aptitude and of academic achievement, the discrepancies between them are appraised at a pretty low level of reliability. Thus the percentile values reported in Fig. 9.10 are much less dependable than percentiles that would be reported for a complete grade group or age group. The reliability of these difference scores range from about .50 to .70 for different sections of the achievement test, wheareas the reliabilities of the aptitude and achievement tests taken separately are around .90. So it is only as the individual shows a rather extreme deviation, in percentile terms, from the average value of his SAS group that we can say with confidence that his achievement falls above or below expectation.

COGNITIVE ABILITY TESTS AND SCHOOL DECISIONS

There is a wide range of decisions about or by students for which tests of cognitive abilities have been or might be used. We shall review some of these and consider gains that may result and problems that may arise from such use.

ADMISSIONS DECISIONS

At all levels of the educational system, some schools are selective. At the elementary level these tend to be private schools of good reputation where there are more applicants for admission than can be accommodated. At the secondary level such private schools are joined by a limited number of specialized public high schools that focus on intensive academic preparation in the sciences or arts and that have a large pool of eager candidates for admission. At the college and university level, most institutions are selective to a degree—some very selective—though the concept of admission open to all secondary school graduates is accepted in some community colleges and public universities.

When admission is selective, some type of academic aptitude test is frequently required as *one* item of information to be considered by the school or college in arriving at the decision to admit. At the primary level some private schools rely upon the *Stanford-Binet*. Use may also be made of one of the academic readiness tests discussed on pp. 381–383. Group tests are generally used at the higher levels, sometimes commercially available tests but often "secure" tests, revised each year and prepared specifically for such a testing program. At the secondary level the Educational Testing Service produces the *Secondary School Admissions Test*, and for college admissions the *College Entrance Examination Board Scholastic Aptitude Test*. (The other major college admissions testing program is the somewhat more achievement oriented *American College Testing Program Assessment*.)

When a test such as any of the above is used, often being combined with a review of previous school achievement when secondary or college admission is being considered, much greater homogeneity of the resulting a student population is usually achieved. Transforming *College Board SAT* scores to the same scale that is used for the *Stanford-Binet*, one estimates, for example, that 90 percent of Radcliffe College students have scores that are the equivalent of deviation IQs of 130 or over. This is an extreme case, but in a number of the more selective colleges 90 percent fall above a DIQ equivalent of 120.

Clearly, the rate at which instruction can proceed, the type of reading material that can be used, and the abstractness with which verbal and quantitative ideas can be presented is vastly different in such institutions from those in a southern state college in which the *average* score is equivalent to a DIQ of 93. One does not find much *specific* documentation of the ways in which instruction in highly selective schools, from the primary grades through the university, differs from that in nonselective full-range-of-ability institutions. One senses that it will certainly be *easier* to teach in a highly selective school, and that the student whose capabilities match the demands of such a setting will learn more in that setting. He will read more, write more, work more independently, range more widely through the accumulated culture. It depends upon one's conception of the good society whether one views the accelerated progress of a relatively small fraction of the population as a social as well as an individual good.

Admission decisions are typically handled at the administrative level, the duty being assigned to a person or persons who specialize in that function. This makes possible a degree of stability in criteria and standards that is less likely in some of the more informal and decentralized uses of test results.

PLACEMENT DECISIONS

Within a school there may be a number of placement decisions. These are called for when there are alternatives on

344

standardized
tests of
intelligence or
scholastic
aptitude

courses to be taken (e.g., algebra vs. business arithmetic), or rate of movement through the course (e.g., algebra in 1 academic year, or spread over 2). Though placement is likely to be based on prior achievement in the specific subject or upon a specific prognostic test, there are instances when neither of these is available. Then a general measure of cognitive functioning may be of some help in deciding which program or treatment is most suitable for each candidate. Or the ability measure may receive some weight as a supplement to previous achievement.

There are two rather distinct forms of placement. In one the goals of both programs are the same, and only the means to reach them differs. This would be true, at least approximately, in the choice between a 1-year and a 2-year presentation of beginning algebra. Previous arithmetic achievement, possibly supplemented by an algebra prognosis test , might well be the best basis for decisions in this case. In the other form both the goals and the routes to attainment of those goals differ, as, for example, in the choice between algebra and business arithmetic. A general ability measure may be of some value in determining what general educational goals seem realistic for an individual—for example, whether college education is an appropriate objective—and this may influence in turn the specific courses that the individual will find it appropriate to take.

Placement decisions, which are internal to a school, are likely to be the responsibility of guidance personnel or of a designated person or persons in the department concerned, with greater or less participation by the student himself.

GROUPING DECISIONS

In most larger schools there are enough children of a given age so that several classroom groups are needed in order to provide for them. Groups may be assembled pretty much at random, or some systematic procedure for grouping may be introduced. One approach that has been widely used over the years is to try to achieve some sort of "homogeneous grouping." When homogeneous grouping has been attempted, general cognitive ability measures have sometimes been used as the basis, or one of the bases, of such grouping. The rationale underlying grouping has been that the teacher will then be able to adapt the tempo and content of instruction to the characteristics of the class that is being taught.

Over the last 50 years there has been a host of studies attempting to appraise the effectiveness of various patterns of homogeneous or ability grouping. The work has been reviewed recently by Findley and Bryan (1971). In general, the gains from attempting to apply homogeneous grouping to the great majority of students, the middle 95 percent, seem to be slight and inconsistent. Of course grouping per se accomplishes nothing. It is what goes on in the classroom that may make a difference. And the general trend of the research results suggests that the adaptations that teachers make in response to grouping are not substantial enough or crucial enough to make a noticeable improvement in student achievement.

Special classes for the extreme deviates in cognitive functioning represent a somewhat different problem. At the lower end of the range of ability there comes a point where the child appears to be unable to profit from regular classroom instruction and to require a different learning environment. Placing a child in a special class is a drastic step, and the decision to do so should not be made lightly. Evidence of cognitive functioning is quite relevant, and that evidence may be gotten by test as well as by observation of the child in the school setting. Since test performance is influenced by language, by social background, and by adaptation to the examiner, it seems clear that no absolute level of test score should be set by law or policy as the basis for special class placement, but rather that the test results should be one datum that enters, with others, into the decision to put a child into a special class for mentally retarded children.

WITHIN-CLASSROOM DECISIONS

Decisions concerning admissions, placement, and grouping occur largely at the administrative level in a school. Decisions that involve primarily the classroom teacher for which general ability tests may be of value are decisions relating to diagnosis, to remediation, and to referral. At the crudest level a diagnostic judgment asks whether the child is achieving at the level that can appropriately be expected. This is a somewhat tricky judgment, and we have discussed it at some length in a previous section (pp. 334–342). Diagnosis is carried a step further by the comparison of semantic (verbal) and figural (nonverbal) measures of ability, providing evidence on whether a child has nonverbal abilities that may suggest other channels for learning. Appraisal of verbal and nonverbal abilities represents, of course, only a first step in the diagnostic study to determine whether a child shows some mental retardation, or a specific learning disability.

If the decision is toward a specific learning disability, the

346
standardized
tests of
intelligence or
scholastic
aptitude

pattern of ability test scores may provide cues for remedial work. If the problem seems more acute, the pattern of ability test results, in combination with measures of achievement and observations of classroom behavior, may suggest to the teacher the need for specialized help and the desirability of referral of the child for remedial instruction or for more intensive diagnostic study.

On the positive side, measures of general scholastic aptitude may be used by a teacher to consider with a student his future educational and vocational plans. Especially at the secondary school level, results from one or more scholastic aptitude tests can help to identify those students who should give serious thought to going on to college, and perhaps continuing in one of those postgraduate forms of professional training that make heavy cognitive demands.

GUIDANCE DECISIONS

Tests of general cognitive ability have an obvious function in the educational program as sources of information important to persons responsible for counseling and helping the child with problems of personal and social adjustment, making provisions for special educational activities for him, helping him to decide on appropriate educational objectives, and working with him to formulate vocational plans. In plans and decisions of all these types it is important to have a clear picture of the pupil's intellectual abilities as one aspect of the total picture of the pupil as an individual.

In educational guidance, information about scholastic aptitude is especially important. This information should receive very serious consideration in deciding what is an appropriate educational objective for the pupil; that is, whether to plan for college and if so the kind of college to plan for, or what type of high school curriculum to select. In vocational counseling, more specialized ability measures, of the kinds we shall consider in the next chapter, are desirable as a supplement to the general intelligence test, but these specialized tests are not so important for educational planning. For understanding a child who is having problems in school, whether with his school work or with his personal adjustments, an estimate of his intellectual level is essential. As we have indicated elsewhere, individual tests and nonlanguage tests are highly desirable supplements to the usual group test when any reading or language handicap is suspected.

Though aptitude tests usually depend less directly upon specific teaching than do achievement tests, it must be recognized that any test performance is in some degree a function of the individual's background of experience. Aptitude tests are distinguished at least in part by their function—to predict future accomplishments.

Among the most thoroughly explored and widely used aptitude tests are tests of cognitive abilities to which the designation "intelligence test" or "IQ test" has typically been attached. As these have been developed, they have tended to emphasize abstract cognitive abilities, abilities to deal with ideas and symbols, and they may even be thought of as primarily scholastic aptitude tests.

The two main patterns of tests have been group tests and individual tests. Group tests, resembling the short-answer achievement test in format, are much more economical to use and are satisfactory for many purposes when the examinees are normal groups of school age or older. However, the individual tests have a number of advantages and are useful particularly with (1) young children, (2) emotionally disturbed cases, and (3) cases with special educational disabilities.

Special tests have been developed for infant and preschool groups, for groups with educational and language handicaps, and for groups from varied cultures and social classes. These may be of practical value in special cases, though they serve more often as research tools.

Results for these tests with school-age children are about as reliable as any of our psychological measurement tools. The widely used individual tests such as the *Stanford-Binet Intelligence Scale* and the *Wechsler Intelligence Scales* are probably somewhat more reliable than the typical group test, though the differences are not large. In spite of the high reliability, appreciable differences may be expected between one testing and another.

When general ability test scores are studied in relation to achievement in the world, the most clear-cut relationships are with academic achievement. However, it is also true that there are substantial differences in test performance between persons in different types of job. Furthermore, success in at least some types of job has been found to be related to the abstract cognitive abilities measured by such tests.

Group differences in intelligence test scores (that is, sex, race, age differences) must be interpreted quite tentatively, in view

348

standardized
tests of
intelligence or
scholastic
aptitude

of the differences in background for these different groups. However, *individual* differences in the tests are important facts, which we need to use wisely in helping individuals in their adjustment to the world of the school and of work.

QUESTIONS AND EXERCISES

1. It has been proposed that all intelligence tests should really be called scholastic aptitude tests. What are the merits and the limitations of this proposal?

2. In what respects is it preferable to rely upon a good aptitude test for an estimate of a pupil's intelligence than upon ratings by teachers?

3. In each of the following situations would you elect to use a group intelligence test or an individual intelligence test? Why?

(*a*) You are studying a boy with a serious speech impediment.

(*b*) You are selecting students for a school of nursing.

(*c*) You are preparing to counsel a high school senior on educational and vocational plans.

(*d*) You are making a study of the Mexican children in a school system in Arizona.

(*e*) You are working with a group of delinquents in a state institution.

(*f*) You are trying to identify the sources of the difficulty for a child who is a nonreader.

4. If you were routinely giving an aptitude test, in which of the following situations would you use the *Raven's Matrices* rather than the *Stanford-Binet?* Why did you decide as you did?

(*a*) For testing Puerto Rican children entering school in New York City.

(*b*) For selecting children for a special class of gifted children.

(*c*) For evaluating intelligence in a school for the deaf.

(*d*) For studying children who have reading problems.

5. What are the implications for child placement agencies of the data on infant tests presented on p. 315?

6. Are the usual group intelligence tests more useful for those students who are considering professional occupations or those considering occupations in the skilled trades? Why?

7. What are the main conclusions that you would draw from Table 9.4 p. 329? What are the limitations of the data presented in this table?

8. A news article reported that a young woman who had been committed to a mental hospital with an IQ of 62 had been able to raise her IQ to 118 during the 3 years she had spent there. What is misleading about this news statement? What factors could account for the difference between the two IQs?

9. In what respects are intelligence tests better than high school grades as predictors of college success? In what respects are they less good?

10. Why do intelligence tests show higher correlations with standardized achievement tests than they do with school grades?

11. Comment on the statement: "College admissions officers should discount scholastic aptitude test scores of applicants who come from low socioeconomic groups."

12. You are a fourth grade teacher and have just received back the results for your class from the citywide administration of the *Cognitive Abilities Tests* in the fourth grade. What use might you make of the results? What additional information would you need?

13. An eighth grade student had received the following Standard Age Scores on the *Cognitive Abilities Test, Verbal*: Grade 4—98, Grade 6—116, Grade 8—104. What would be the best figure to represent the child's "true" scholastic aptitude level?

14. A school in a prosperous community gave *Stanford-Binet* intelligence tests to all entering kindergartners and all first graders who had not been tested in kindergarten within the first week or two of school. How desirable and useful a procedure is this? Why?

15. A school system wanted to set up procedures to identify pupils to receive remedial instruction in reading. These were to be those pupils whose reading was falling seriously behind their potential for learning to read. What would be a sound procedure for accomplishing this?

SUGGESTED ADDITIONAL READING

Anastasi, A. Common fallacies about heredity, environment, and human behavior. *ACT Research Report No. 58.* American College Testing Program, 1973.

Asbury, Charles A. Selected factors influencing over- and underachievement in young school-age children. *Review of Educational Research,* 1974, 44, 409–428.

Bradley, Robert H. and B.M. Caldwell, Early home environment and changes in mental test performance in children from 6 to 36 months. *Developmental Psychology,* 1976, 12, 93–97.

Butcher, H.J. Intelligence and creativity. In P. Kline (Ed.), *New Approaches in Psychological Measurement.* New York: John Wiley & Sons, 1973.

Casler, Lawrence. Maternal intelligence and institutionalized children's developmental quotients: A correlational study. *Developmental Psychology,* 1976, 12, 64–67.

350
standardized
tests of
intelligence or
scholastic
aptitude

Churchill, William D. and Stuart E. Smith. Relationships between the 1960 Stanford-Binet Scale and group measures of intelligence and achievement. *Measurement and Evaluation in Guidance*, 1974, 7, 40-44.

Cunningham, Walter R. and J.E. Birren. Age changes in human abilities: A 28-year longitudinal study. *Developmental Psychology*, 1976, 12, 81-82.

Hopkins, Kenneth D. and Glenn H. Bracht. Ten-year stability of verbal and nonverbal IQ scores. *American Educational Research Journal*, 1975, 12, 469-477.

Loehlin, John C., Gardner Lindzey, and J.N. Spuhler. *Race differences in Intelligence.* San Francisco: W.H. Freeman and Company, 1975.

The myth of measurability. *The National Elementary Principal*, 54, March/April 1975.

National Center for Health Statistics. *Intellectual development of chil-dren by demographic and socioeconomic factors.* DHEW Publication No. (HSM) 72-1012. Public Health Service. Washington, D.C. Government Printing Office, December 1971.

Samuel, William, David Soto, Michael Parks, Peter Ngissah, and Benjamin Jones. Motivation, race, social class, and IQ. *Journal of Educational Psychology*, 1976, 68, 273-285.

Sattler, Jerome M. *Assessment of intelligence.* Philadelphia: W. B. Saunders Co., 1974.

Solmon, L.C. *Schooling and subsequent success: Influence of ability, background, and formal education.* ACT Research Report No. 57. Iowa City, Iowa: The American College Testing Program, April 1973.

Thorndike, R.L. *The concepts of over- and under-achievement.* New York: Bureau of Publications, Teachers College, Columbia University, 1963.

CHAPTER TEN
THE MEASUREMENT OF SPECIAL APTITUDES

The tests reviewed in Chapter 9 are tests of general cognitive ability. In many cases they result in a single score that represents an overall appraisal of the individual's ability to deal with abstract ideas and relationships. However, a number of them produce two or more scores of a more specialized nature that are designed to provide more specific and analytical information about the individual, for example, the verbal and performance IQs of the *Wechsler* scales. Concern for specific information on more restricted segments of the ability domain has led to the development of test batteries and single tests to measure specialized aptitudes. It is these tests that we shall consider in the present chapter. We will direct our attention first to batteries and tests designed for vocational guidance and vocational selection. Then we will consider specialized tests for prognosis and prediction in single school subjects and in special types of school. Finally, we will take a brief look at tests in the specialized fields of art and music, and at efforts to appraise "creativity."

VOCATIONAL APTITUDE BATTERIES AND TESTS

One of the practical matters with which psychologists first became concerned was guiding young people into types of work in which they would be happy and successful and selecting for an employer those persons who would be efficient and satisfied in the jobs he was trying to fill. As psychologists began to study jobs, it seemed apparent that different ones required different special abilities as well as different levels of general cognitive ability. The automotive mechanic required a good deal of mechanical knowledge but little verbal fluency, while the lawyer needed verbal comprehension but not mechanical skill. The bookkeeper needed good ability with numbers, while the watchmaker needed fine coordination of finger movements. The ability requirements of jobs appeared to differ along a number of specialized dimensions.

At the same time, research demonstrated that human abilities are to some degree specialized. This has been shown in studies of the correlations between different tests. Consider the correlations shown in Table 10.1 among six tests of a battery used for classification of men in the U.S. Air Force (DuBois, 1947). Note that the correlation between the first two tests is relatively high, much higher than the correlations of these two with the remaining four tests. These two are both tests that are quite verbal in nature and they appear to define a factor of ability to deal with verbal relationships. Tests 3 and 4 are both numerical tests and are substantially correlated. Tests 5 and 6, which correlate substantially with each other, both involve speed of visual perception.

There has been a large volume of research on the organization and structure of human abilities during the last 50 years. Much of it has employed a technique known as *factor analysis* to try to tease out the underlying ability factors. Factor analysis starts with a table of correlations such as we have shown in Table 10.1, but ordinarily with a much larger table including a much larger number of test variables. By computational procedures that we shall not go into in any detail here (for an introduction to factor analysis, see Cronbach, 1970), the factor analyst attempts to identify a small number of underlying factors that can account for the complete set of relationships among the test variables. Each test has a *loading* on each of the factors,

Table 10.1
INTERCORRELATIONS OF SELECTED AIR FORCE APTITUDE TESTS

	1	2	3	4	5	6
1. Reading Comprehension	.....	**.50**	.05	.23	.13	.11
2. Navigator Information	**.50**	.....	.16	.25	.17	.15
3. Numerical Operations	.05	.16	.....	**.44**	.27	.11
4. Dial and Table Reading	.23	.25	**.44**	.....	.39	.23
5. Speed of Identification	.13	.17	.27	.39	.....	**.43**
6. Spatial Orientation	.11	.15	.11	.23	**.43**	.....

corresponding to the correlation of the test with the factor, and the analyst tries to arrive at a pattern of factor loadings that is simple and psychologically meaningful. The correlations in Table 10.1 can be quite well represented by the set of loadings on three factors shown below.

	Factor		
	1	2	3
Reading Comprehension	.72	.04	.04
Navigator Information	.70	.14	.08
Numerical Operations	.08	.71	.00
Dial and Table Reading	.28	.57	.30
Speed of Identification	.13	.37	.58
Spatial Orientation	.13	.02	.63

Note that *Reading Comprehension* and *Navigator Information* have substantial loadings on the first factor, which can perhaps be identified as a verbal factor. *Numerical Operations* has an appreciable loading only on factor 2, which we can call a number factor. *Dial and Table Reading* has its largest loading on factor 2 (number), but this is a complex test calling, in some measure, for all three of the factors. The last two tests, which are primarily speeded perceptual tests, have their largest loadings on factor 3, and this we will therefore call a perceptual factor. However, *Speed of Identification* also has an appreciable loading on factor 2, and since this test has nothing to do with numbers, this loading suggests that our interpretation of factor 2 as a number factor may need to be modified to include the aspect of speed. The interpretation of factors is something that must be contributed by the investigator, from his understanding of the nature of the tests that do and do not show loadings on a given factor.

Research has indicated that one can distinguish quite a number of special ability factors, such as verbal comprehension, word fluency, numerical fluency, perceptual speed, mechanical knowledge, spatial visualizing, and inductive and deductive reasoning. It is also true that most of these abilities are to some degree related to each other. The tests of general cognitive ability discussed in the last chapter reflect a pooling of several of these separate factors, together with accentuation of their common core.

The data on essentially cognitive or intellectual abilities lend themselves to several alternate interpretations, portrayed visually in Fig. 10.1, depending upon how we choose to think of the core of overlap among different tests.

One interpretation that has been put forth most vigorously by English psychologists (Vernon, 1960) pictures individual differences in cognitive abilities as resembling, essentially, a branching tree, with the main trunk being a general intellectual ability, two main branches representing school related as opposed to "practical" ability, and the smaller branches corre-

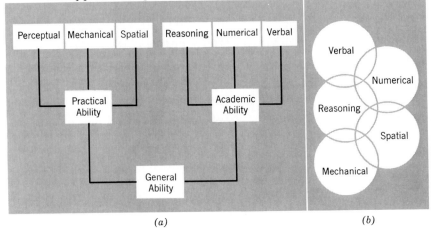

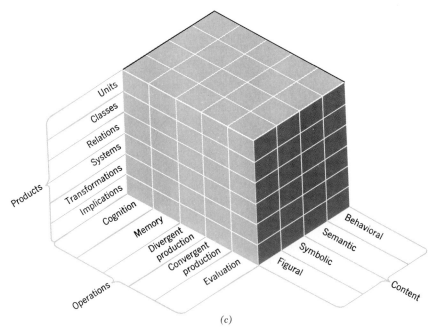

Figure 10.1
Ways of conceiving cognitive abilities
(a) Hierarchical structure,
(b) Multiple factor structure;
(c) Guilford's three-way structure.

sponding to more specialized verbal, numerical, spatial, mechanical, and other abilities. A second interpretation, set forth initially by Thurstone (1938) in this country and followed by many of his disciples, pictures a limited number of separate factors, each appearing in some types of test and life performance, with each measure dependent on only two or three of the set of factors. No one of Thurstone's factors was considered to be really general in nature, or to rank above any of the others. Thurstone had originally identified seven factors, but the number had been gradually increased as other investigators worked with other kinds of test. A review of ability test research in 1951 (French, 1951) tentatively identified 59 different factors of all sorts as having been found by investigators up to that date.

In a systematic analysis that carried the notion of specialized factors still further, Guilford (1967) proposed that intellect could be analyzed in terms of a three-dimensional structure on the basis of (1) what kind of material was acted on, (2) what actions were carried out with it, and (3) what products were produced. Guilford proposed a $4 \times 5 \times 6$ structure that resulted in 120 cells, and he has carried on a monumental research program of test development and analysis to see whether tests can be generated that correspond to each of the logically identifiable cells.

Through theoretical research on the nature of abilities on the one hand and applied research on the validity of specific tests for specific jobs on the other, psychologists have been guided in the design of aptitude test batteries for use in educational and vocational guidance and in personnel selection and classification. Since about 1940 these batteries have come to occupy quite central positions in the testing scene, so we will need to study them in some detail. First, we will examine two of the most widely used batteries, one oriented primarily toward school use and the other toward industrial use. Then we will review some of the evidence on validity and consider the advantages and limitations of a battery of this sort.

THE DIFFERENTIAL APTITUDE TEST BATTERY

This battery was originally brought out by The Psychological Corporation in 1947 as a guidance battery for use at the secondary school level, and revised and streamlined forms were produced in 1963 and 1972. In the design of the battery some attention was paid to having separate tests with low intercorrelations, but the main focus was on getting measures that would be meaningful to high school counselors. As a result, with the exception of the test of clerical speed and accuracy, intercorrelations are about .50. However, since the reliabilities of the parts are about .90, it is clear that more than one single ability is being measured. The eight subtests are briefly described and illustrated below.*

1. *Verbal Reasoning.* Items are of the double analogy type, that is, ? is to A as B is to ? Five pairs of words are provided to complete the analogy.

_____ is to night as breakfast is to _____.

A. supper—corner
B. gentle—morning
C. door—corner
D. flow—enjoy
E. supper—morning

2. *Numerical Ability.* Consists of numerical problems emphasizing comprehension rather than simple computational facility.

3 = ? % of 15

A. 5
B. 10
C. 20
D. 30
E. none of these

3. *Abstract Reasoning.* A series of problem figures establishes a relationship or sequence, and the examinee must pick the choice that continues the series.

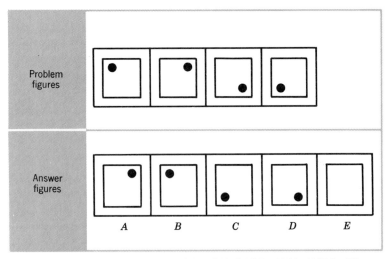

4. *Space Relations.* A diagram of a flat figure is shown. The examinee must visualize and indicate which solid figure could be produced by folding the flat figure, as shown in the example below.

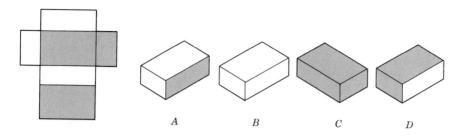

A   B   C   D

5. *Mechanical Reasoning.* A diagram of a mechanical device or situation is shown, and the examinee must indicate which choice is true of the situation.

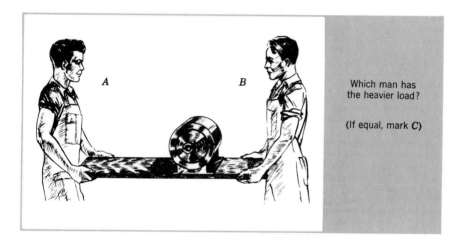

Which man has the heavier load?

(If equal, mark *C*)

6. *Clerical Speed and Accuracy.* Each item is made up of a number of combinations of symbols, one of which is underlined. The examinee must mark the same combination on his answer sheet.

Test Items						Sample of Answer Sheet				
V. <u>AB</u>	AC	AD	AE	AF		AC AE AF **AB** AD (V)				
W. aA	aB	BA	Ba	<u>Bb</u>		BA Ba **Bb** aA aB (W)				
X. A7	7A	B7	<u>7B</u>	AB		**7B** B7 AB 7A A7 (X)				
Y. Aa	Ba	<u>bA</u>	BA	bB		Aa **bA** bB Ba BA (Y)				
Z. 3A	3B	<u>33</u>	B3	BB		BB 3B B3 3A **33** (Z)				

7. *Language Usage: Spelling.* A list of words is given, some of which are misspelled. The examinee must indicate for each word whether it is correctly or incorrectly spelled.

EXAMPLE

	Right	Wrong
gurl	::	::

8. *Language Usage: Sentences.* A sentence is given, divided by marks into four subsections. The examinee must indicate which section—A, B, C, or D—contains an error; if there is no error, he marks E.

EXAMPLE

1. Ain't we / going to / the office / next week?   :: :: :: :: ::
      A   B   C   D   A B C D E

The tests of the *DAT* are essentially power tests, with the exception of the *Clerical Speed and Accuracy Test,* and time limits are in most cases 30 minutes. Total testing time for the battery is about 5 to 5½ hours, and it requires at least two separate testing sessions. Percentile norms are available for each grade from the eighth through the twelfth. Norms are provided for each of the subtests, and also for the combination of *VR* and *NA*, which may be used as a general appraisal of scholastic aptitude. An illustration of the profile form on which results may be plotted is shown on p. 142.

THE GENERAL APTITUDE TEST BATTERY (GATB)

The *General Aptitude Test Battery* was produced by the Bureau of Employment Security, U. S. Department of Labor, in the early 1940s. It was based upon previous work in which experimental test batteries had been prepared for each of a number of different jobs. Analysis of the more than 50 different tests that had been prepared for specific jobs indicated that there was a great deal of overlapping among certain ones of them, and that only about 10 different ability factors were measured by the complete set of tests. The *GATB* was developed to provide measures of these different factors. In its most recent form it includes 12 tests and gives scores for 9 different factors. One is a factor of general mental ability (*G*), resulting from scores on three tests (*Vocabulary, Arithmetic Reasoning,* and *Three-Dimensional Space*) that are also scored for more specialized factors. The other factors, and the tests that contribute to each, are described below.

1. *Verbal Aptitude.* Score is based on one test, *Number 4, Vocabulary.* This test requires the subject to identify the pair of words in a set of four that are *either* synonyms or antonyms.

EXAMPLES

| a. cautious | b. friendly | c. hostile | d. remote |
| a. hasten | b. deprive | c. expedite | d. disprove |

2. *Numerical Ability.* The appraisal of this aptitude is based upon two tests. The first of these, *Number 2, Computation,* involves speed and accuracy in simple computations with whole numbers.

EXAMPLES

Subtract (−)   256   Multiply (×)   37
                83   8

The second test entering into the *Numerical Ability* score, *Number 6, Arithmetic Reasoning,* involves verbally stated quantitative problems.

EXAMPLE

John works for $1.20 an hour. How much is his pay for a 35-hour week?

3. *Spatial Aptitude.* One test, *Number 3, Three-Dimensional Space,* enters into appraisal of this aptitude. The examinee must indicate which of four 3-dimensional figures can be produced by folding a flat sheet of specified shape, with creases at indicated points.

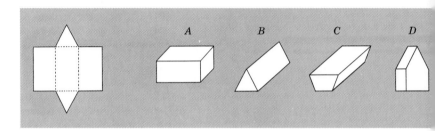

EXAMPLE

4. *Form perception.* This aptitude involves rapid and accurate perception of visual forms and patterns. It is appraised in the *GATB* by two tests, *Number 5, Tool Matching,* and *Number 7, Form Matching,* which differ in the type of visual stimulus provided. Each requires the examinee to find from among a set of answer choices the one that is identical with the stimulus form.

EXAMPLE: TOOL MATCHING

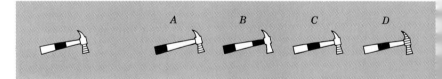

EXAMPLE: FORM MATCHING

361
vocational
aptitude
batteries and
tests

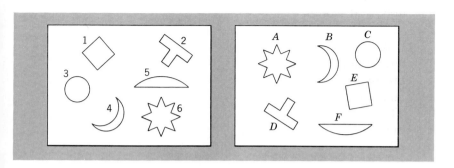

5. *Clerical Perception.* This aptitude also involves rapid and accurate perception, but in this case the stimulus material is linguistic instead of purely spatial. The test, *Number 1, Name Comparison*, presents pairs of names and requires the examinee to indicate whether the two members of the pair are identical, or whether they differ in some detail.

EXAMPLES

> John Goldstein & Co—John Goldston & Co.
> Pewee Mfg. Co.—Pewee Mfg. Co.

6. *Motor Coordination.* This factor has to do with speed of simple but fairly precise motor response. It is evaluated by one test, *Number 8, Mark Making.* The task of the examinee is to make three pencil marks within each of a series of boxes on the answer sheet to yield a simple design. The result appears approximately as follows:

etc.

Score is the number of boxes correctly filled in a 60-second test period.

7. *Manual Dexterity.* This factor involves speed and accuracy of fairly gross hand movements. It is evaluated by two peg-board tests, *Number 9, Place,* and Number 10, *Turn.* In the first of these the examinee uses both hands to move a series of pegs from one set of holes in a pegboard to another. In the second test the examinee uses his preferred hand to pick a peg up from the board, rotate it through 180°, and reinsert the other end of the peg in the hole. Three trials are given for each of these tests, and score is the total number of pegs moved or turned.

8. *Finger Dexterity.* This factor represents a finer type of dexterity than that covered by the previous factor, calling for more precise finger manipulations. Two tests, Number 11, *Assemble*, and Number 12, *Disassemble*, use the same piece of equipment. This is a board with 50 holes in each of two sections. Each hole in one section is occupied by a small rivet. A stack of washers is piled on a spindle. During *Assemble*, the examinee picks up a rivet with one hand, a washer with the other, puts the washer on the rivet, and places the assembly in the corresponding hole in the unoccupied part of the board. He assembles as many rivets and washers as he can in 90 seconds. During *Disassemble*, he removes the assembly, returns the washer to its stack, and returns the rivet to its original place. Score is the number of items assembled or disassembled as the case may be. The apparatus tests are all arranged so that at the completion of testing the equipment has been returned to its original condition, and is ready for the testing of another person.

A comparison of the *GATB* and the *DAT* brings out that the *DAT* has tests of mechanical comprehension and language that the *GATB* lacks, while the *GATB* includes form perception and several types of motor test that are missing in the *DAT*. Thus the *GATB* is more work oriented and less school oriented in its total coverage. Inclusion of the several types of motor test results in somewhat lower correlations, on the average, for the *GATB*, though the "intellectual" tests correlate about as highly as those of the *DAT*. The correlations among the different aptitude scores of the *GATB* are shown in Table 10.2 for a group

Table 10.2

INTERCORRELATIONS OF *GATB* APTITUDE SCORES FOR 100 HIGH SCHOOL SENIORS

	G	V	N	S	P	Q	K	F	M
G—Intelligence	.....	.73	.74	.70	.43	.35	−.04	−.05	−.06
V—Verbal	.73	.....	.42	.40	.34	.29	.13	−.03	.06
N—Numerical	.74	.42	.....	.34	.42	.42	.06	−.03	.01
S—Spatial	.70	.40	.34	.....	.48	.26	−.03	.01	−.03
P—Form Perception	.43	.34	.42	.48	.....	.66	.29	.27	.23
Q—Clerical Perception	.35	.29	.42	.26	.66	.....	.29	.20	.16
K—Motor Coordination	−.04	.13	.06	−.03	.29	.29	.....	.37	.49
F—Finger Dexterity	−.05	−.03	−.03	.01	.27	.20	.37	.....	.46
M—Manual Dexterity	−.06	.06	.01	−.03	.23	.16	.49	.46	.....

of 100 high school seniors. Excluding the correlations with *G*, which involves the same tests appearing in *V*, *N*, and *S*, the correlations range from −.06 to .66. The three motor factors show fairly marked correlations, but they are practically unrelated to the remaining tests. The perceptual and intellectual factors also show quite a bit of relationship to one another, and this is most marked between the two types of perceptual factor.

There are quite substantial correlations between the corresponding factors of the *DAT* and the *GATB*. Representative values from one study (U. S. Employment Service, 1967) are as follows.

Verbal	.74
Numerical	.61
Space	.65
Clerical	.57

However, the correlations are low enough so that it is clear that the tests cannot be considered identical. One important difference is the fact that the *DAT* tests are in most cases purely power tests, while the *GATB* tests are quite highly speeded.

OTHER APTITUDE BATTERIES

Since use of the *GATB* is limited to state employment services, it is worth mentioning one generally available battery that was intended primarily for industrial use. This is the *Employee Aptitude Survey* developed by Psychological Services, Inc. (1963). The battery was developed with an eye to the practical realities of testing in industry, and most of the tests are only 5 minutes in length. The battery includes tests designated as follows.

1. *Verbal Comprehension.*
2. *Numerical Ability.*
3. *Visual Pursuit.*
4. *Visual Speed and Accuracy.*
5. *Space Visualization.*
6. *Numerical Reasoning.*
7. *Verbal Reasoning.*
8. *Word Fluency.*
9. *Manual Speed and Accuracy.*
10. *Symbolic Reasoning.*

In the technical manual, occupational group norms are provided for persons working in some 52 different occupations, and validity data for samples in over 30 occupations. This is a battery that is likely to be useful to personnel officers in various sorts of business and industrial settings.

A number of other batteries have been developed in the past 30 years, and several are briefly described in Appendix Four, Section B.

VALIDITY OF APTITUDE BATTERIES

Now we must inquire into the usefulness of aptitude batteries such as the *DAT* and the *GATB,* asking to what extent such a battery can provide us information that permits us to make better, more varied, and more differentiated predictions than those that are possible from a test of general cognitive ability or scholastic aptitude. The types of prediction with which we are most likely to be concerned are predictions of success in specific school subjects or major fields, predictions of success in specific jobs for which the individual is an applicant, and predictions of success in general fields of the world of work.

Differential prediction of academic success. We have seen that scholastic aptitude tests have fairly good overall validity for predicting academic success. One thing that we might hope is that an aptitude battery would tell us in *which* subject areas a student is *most* likely to be successful. Will Wilma do better in English or in mathematics, in science or in French, in mechanical drawing or in history? A battery can do this to the extent that different tests in the battery are valid for different subjects. To what extent is this the case?

The manual for the *DAT* provides extensive data on the correlations of each of the subtests with achievement in a number of school subjects. Some of these results are summarized in Table 10.3. This table shows the median value of the correlations, and also ranks the eight subtests, and the combination of verbal and numerical, with respect to their correlations with each subject.

The first thing to notice is that certain subtests are among the highest for almost all subjects. Thus *Verbal Reasoning* and *Numerical Ability* are each among the better predictors for all subjects. Recognizing this, the authors of the *DAT* provided a single score combining these two subtests. We can see from the table that VR + NA is as good a predictor or better than *any* of the subtests for *all* subjects, including typing and industrial arts. To a considerable extent the abilities that underlie academic ability are general abilities, and a common scholastic

Table 10.3

MEDIAN CORRELATION OF *DIFFERENTIAL APTITUDE TEST* SCORES WITH SCHOOL GRADES IN DIFFERENT SUBJECTS

Test	English	Mathe-matics	Science	Social Studies, History	Lan-guages	Typing	Indus-trial Arts
Verbal Reasoning (VR)	.52(2.5)*	.40(4)	.50(2)	.49(3)	.46(4)	.38(4)	.32(4)
Numerical Ability (NA)	.50(4)	.52(1.5)	.48(3)	.49(3)	.41(5)	.43(2)	.32(4)
VR + NA	.57(1)	.52(1.5)	.56(1)	.55(1)	.54(1)	.44(1)	.36(1)
Abstract Reasoning (AR)	.42(6)	.41(3)	.40(5)	.37(6)	.25(6)	.34(6)	.35(2)
Clerical Speed and Accuracy (CSA)	.28(8)	.20(9)	.24(9)	.26(8)	.16(9)	.30(7)	.24(8)
Mechanical Reasoning (MR)	.22(9)	.24(8)	.28(8)	.22(9)	.17(8)	.26(8)	.27(7)
Space Relations (SR)	.30(7)	.30(6.5)	.34(7)	.30(7)	.20(7)	.24(9)	.32(4)
Spelling (Spell.)	.46(5)	.30(6.5)	.38(6)	.42(5)	.48(3)	.36(5)	.19(9)
Grammar (Gram.)	.52(2.5)	.39(5)	.46(4)	.49(3)	.50(2)	.40(3)	.30(6)

* Number in parentheses shows rank of that test for that subject.

aptitude test will give about as good a prediction of any of them as we can get.

At the same time, Table 10.3 does show a little indication of differential validity. *Spelling* and *Grammar* are somewhat more useful as predictors of English grades than of grades in industrial arts, and conversely *Abstract Reasoning* and *Space Relations* are somewhat more useful for industrial arts than they are for English. But this is the sharpest distinction that appears in the table. Even in this case, the validity of the test battery as a predictor of *difference* in achievement between English and industrial arts appears to be no more than .20 or .25. Thus we are able, primarily, to predict general level of educational achievement; differential prediction of performance in one area rather than another must be made only very tentatively at best.

Prediction of specific job success.   We may next ask how successful a battery of aptitude tests will be in predicting the success of workers in a specific job. Will tests have validity high enough to make them useful either to a State Employment Service or to an employer in selecting workers for employment? Will different tests predict success in different jobs? The manual for the *GATB* provides an impressive array of data on the differences between workers in different jobs and on correlations of the tests with success either in training programs or on the job. The data often fall short of being ideal because the validation is concurrent (rather than predictive); because the data are for workers already employed rather than job applicants; because the samples are small; because the sample may be limited to workers in a single plant or company; and because there is no independent cross-validation.* However, the accumulation of data is quite impressive, and provides the best available pool of data in which a common battery was validated against criteria of success in a wide range of different jobs.

We have selected from the total array of jobs 23 in which the number of cases was at least 100 and in which correlations of test scores with a job criterion were available. The evidence is presented in Tables 10.4 and 10.5 and, for four of the jobs, in Fig. 10.2 (p. 362). Table 10.4 shows average standard scores (using a norm system in which the mean is 100 and the standard deviation is 20) for each occupational group. Group differences are clearly quite marked, both in level and in pattern. Thus computer programmers are highest in the factor scores representing G (general intelligence) and N (numerical) and on these two scales they fall more than 1.5 standard deviations above the population mean. By contrast, electronics assemblers fall well below the population average in N, and are highest in motor coordination and manual dexterity, where they fall half a standard deviation above the general population average. To bring out the patterning, the highest mean score for each occupation has been shown in the table in boldface type.

Table 10.5 on p. 368 shows validity coefficients for each factor against a job-success criterion for each occupation. The criterion was, in most cases, some type of rating by a supervisor. The first nine columns of the table show validity coefficients for single factor scores, including all coefficients that differed significantly from zero. Thus it is possible to see which tests gave a prediction for which jobs and how good the predictions were. In every instance at least one of the nine factors correlated with job success at a level significantly different from zero, though many of the correlations are small. Most are in the 20s, though a few go up to the 40s and 50s. There is clearly a fair amount of differential patterning of the validity coefficients. Thus the spatial factor has correlations of .50 with success as a dental assistant and as a tool-and-die maker, but is

---

*Especially in exploratory studies in which a battery of tests is being tried out, it is important to verify validities discovered in an initial study by checking the same tests with a new independent sample, a process to which the term *cross-validation* has been applied.

Table 10.4

MEAN *GATB* FACTOR SCORES* FOR SPECIFIC OCCUPATIONS

Occu-pation Code	Title	General Intelligence	Verbal	Numerical	Space	Form Perception	Clerical Perception	Motor Coordination	Finger Dexterity	Manual Dexterity
020	Computer programmer	**132**	125	131	122	120	128	117	109	113
078	Medical technologist	126	127	122	117	126	**130**	122	114	117
079	Dental assistant	104	105	102	107	116	**117**	114	112	114
	Surgical technician	97	102	93	97	107	**108**	**108**	106	107
193	Air traffic control specialist	**118**	114	115	113	109	111	112	101	106
195	Case worker	116	**120**	112	105	102	119	115	99	98
202	Stenographer, typist	106	104	106	108	**119**	113	114	105	103
208	Typesetter, perforator operator	110	113	106	104	107	120	114	102	101
212	Teller, bank	111	111	110	107	115	**120**	114	107	101
213	Tabulating machine operator	111	109	112	106	110	**120**	112	106	107
219	Clerk, general office	108	109	111	101	114	**123**	117	106	107
241	Claim adjuster	**116**	109	**116**	114	114	111	107	......	......
276	Salesman, construction machinery	**113**	109	107	111	100	104	102	97	107
317	Food service worker	82	85	80	91	100	91	91	96	98
319	Fountain girl	95	98	95	95	85	104	104	87	97
355	Nurse aide	89	95	85	91	101	**104**	**104**	99	102
	Psychiatric aide	95	97	90	95	91	**100**	**100**	86	94
375	Patrolman	112	110	106	112	88	106	96	91	91
529	Asparagus sorter	96	99	91	96	108	99	101	101	**117**
601	Tool-and-die maker	109	100	105	**119**	97	101	104	97	**108**
690	Fancy stitcher (shoes)	93	93	91	94	111	99	101	106	115
712	Dental-laboratory technician	96	96	91	102	98	99	**101**	95	**101**
726	Electronics assembler	95	100	89	100	104	105	111	**108**	**113**

Factor

* Score scale with mean of 100 and standard deviation of 20.

Table 10.5
VALIDITY OF *GATB* FACTOR SCORES AND OCCUPATIONAL APTITUDE PATTERNS FOR SPECIFIC OCCUPATIONS

Occu-pational Code	Title	Factor									Occupational Aptitude Pattern
		General Intel-ligence	Verbal	Numer-ical	Space	Form Per-ception	Clerical Per-ception	Motor Coordi-nation	Finger Dexterity	Manual Dexterity	
020	Computer programmer	.36		.40	.24					.28	#1 .28
078	Medical technologist	.57	.22	.40	.51	.28	.22		.21		
079	Dental assistant	.34	.32	.24	.32	.20	.22				#3 .23
	Surgical technician		.28	.27		.19	.22			.19	#3 .27
193	Air traffic control specialist		.21	.22						.18	#36 .18
195	Case worker	.39	.37	.41							
202	Stenographer, typist					.20	.42	.30	.18		
208	Typesetter, perforator operator	.30	.21	.31			.25	.17	.45		#36 .25
212	Teller, bank										
213	Tabulating machine operator	.34	.22	.36	.20		.15				#9 .21
219	Clerk, general office	.26	.22	.23			.15				#13 .16
241	Claim adjuster	.20	.20	.32			.26	.31			#6 .24
276	Salesman, construction machinery	.32	.19	.29	.23			.22	.26		
317	Food service worker					.18		.22	.21	.35	#32 .19
319	Fountain girl	.23	.15	.25		.23				.28	
355	Nurse aide	.31	.25	.29			.24	.21	.19	.22	
	Psychiatric aide					.20		.19			
375	Patrolman				.23	.19		.23	.17	.18	
529	Asparagus sorter	.60	.30	.48	.50	.40	.36			.16	#34 .20
601	Tool-and-die maker	.28	.19	.30	.29	.50	.45	.53	.49	.46	#31 .47
690	Fancy stitcher (shoes)										
712	Dental-laboratory technician	.32	.21	.20	.32			.22	.21	.24	#28 .43
726	Electronics assembler	.23		.19	.22	.20			.28	.29	#16 .17

not significantly related to success in 13 of the 23 jobs. Manual dexterity is a significant factor for fancy stitchers and food service workers, but not for 12 of the jobs. There are 8 of the jobs in which the general intelligence factor fails to show a significant correlation, and so on down the line.

The last column in Table 10.5 shows the validity of occupational aptitude patterns for the 13 of the 23 occupations for which this information is reported. In their original use of the *GATB* for screening individuals for a specific job, the U. S. Employment Service staff established minimum qualifying scores on the two, three, or four aptitude factors that appeared to be most effective in differentiating successful workers in the job from those who either were unsuccessful in it or did not enter it. Thus, for the specific occupational specialty *computer programmer, business,* the qualifying scores were: G,115; V,105; N,110; and S,105. In order to develop a more manageable counseling and screening procedure the Employment Service undertook to group occupations into families in which, either on the basis of validity data or of an analysis of the job, the aptitude requirements were judged to be similar. A total of 36 families were set up, each with its unique pattern of cutting scores. Thus occupational pattern #1, which includes engineers of all types, physicians, and urban planners, as well as computer programmers, has cutting scores set at: G, 125; N, 115; and S, 115. Pattern #36, which includes a wide range of stenographers, stenotypists, and typists, has cutting scores set at: G, 105; Q (clerical perception), 100; and K (motor coordination), 90.

The relationships between qualifying on the aptitude pattern and being judged successful on the job, shown in this last column, are positive and statistically significant in each case, but none of them is large. The whole array of 196 validity coefficients for jobs for which the validity of the classification into "accepted" and "rejected" is made on the basis of the proposed occupational aptitude pattern is as follows.

Validity	Number of Coefficients
.60+	9
.50–.59	23
.40–.49	42
.30–.39	62
.20–.29	51
.10–.19	9

The median of these 196 coefficients is .36. To show what this level of validity would mean in the case of a job in which $\frac{1}{3}$ of those tested were rated as unacceptable on the basis of the tests and $\frac{1}{3}$ of the employees were rated as unsatisfactory by their supervisor, the following example is provided.

| | Rated on Job | |
Rated on Tests	Unacceptable	Acceptable
Acceptable	15	52
Unacceptable	18	15

Thus, with the definitions of acceptable and unacceptable provided in the example, 78 percent of those passed by the tests turned out to be acceptable on the job as compared with 45 percent of those failed on the test. This appears to be a representative picture of the effectiveness of a test battery for prediction of job performance.

In Fig. 10.2 we have taken four jobs and assembled all the evidence relative to the effectiveness of the test battery for differentiating degree of success in each job. Each of the four charts shows the evidence relating to one job. The nine rows in the chart show the data for the nine factor scores of the *GATB* battery. For each row there are two bars, the upper one representing scores of workers judged successful and the lower bar the scores of workers judged unsuccessful. The bar includes a range from $+1$ standard deviation to -1 standard deviation, and the long mark in the middle represents the mean of the group. Thus, looking at the group of computer programmers, we see that they are superior on all the measures, but that the superiority is greatest, on the average, in general intelligence and in numerical ability. On these tests, not only is the average high, but the groups are relatively homogeneous (that is, the bars are short). Furthermore, on these two factors there is a relatively large difference between the workers judged successful and those judged unsuccessful. Stenographers differ less from the general average and in their case the various lines of evidence point to the perceptual measures as especially important. Patrolmen are most outstanding in manual dexterity but most homogeneous in general intelligence. Electronics assemblers show a peak on manual dexterity, and this differentiates the better from the poorer workers, but the long bars indicate that the group is quite heterogeneous.

A comparison of the four charts will provide a reasonable

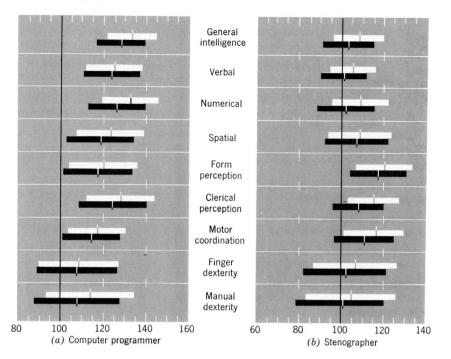

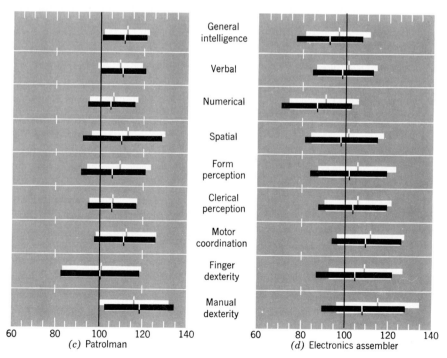

Figure 10.2

Ability profiles for four occupations.

picture of the degree to which different abilities describe different occupations and predict success in them.

A large number of separate studies of aptitude tests in relation to job success have been summarized by Ghiselli (1973). Where a number of different sources provided correlations between scores on some type of test and success in a general category of job, he combined all the available data to produce a kind of pooled composite validity index. Selections from his report are shown in Table 10.6. Each entry is an average, often of a number of correlations.

The pooled correlations reported by Ghiselli do not go above .30. Correlations in the teens and 20s are fairly typical. For a given category of job, the variation in validity from one type of test to another is rather modest. Thus these results present a rather less optimistic picture of the value of tests of special aptitudes than that portrayed in the *GATB* results in Table 10.5.

The less promising picture may stem in part from the blurring resulting from combining quite a span both of jobs and of tests within a single coefficient. It may be, however, that the large numbers of cases represented in Ghiselli's composite correlations are more stable, less subject to chance fluctuations, and consequently less likely to yield large correlations than are the rather small U. S. Employment Service samples. The true picture of validity of tests as predictors of success at a given job in a given company, and of the distinctiveness of different abilities as predictors for different types of jobs probably lies somewhere between the pictures presented in these two tables.

Table 10.6

AVERAGE VALIDITY OF DIFFERENT SORTS OF TEST FOR JOB PERFORMANCE IN BROAD CATEGORIES OF JOBS (ADAPTED FROM GHISELLI, 1973)

	Intellectual Abilities	Spatial, Mechanical Abilities	Perceptual Accuracy	Motor Abilities
Executives, administrators	.30	-.23	.24	.13
Foremen	.26	.22	.27	.15
Clerical occupations	.28	.17	.29	.16
Sales clerks	-.03	.14	-.02	.09
Salesmen	.19	.18	.04	.12
Protective service	.22	.18	.21	.14
Personal service	.27	.13	.10	.15
Vehicle operators	.16	.20	.17	.25
Trades and crafts	.25	.23	.14	.19
Industrial occupations	.20	.20	.20	.22

There are two somewhat different and complementary ways of thinking about test results (or any other data) in relation to jobs and job choice. We may call these, in order to have convenient labels, the *taxonomic* and the *predictive* models. Let us illustrate them, for the sake of simplicity, using two groups: engineering school students and law school students.

TAXONOMIC APPROACH

In the taxonomic approach we would ask: In what ways are these two groups different? What facts that we may know about them will serve to distinguish them most clearly and sharply? With relation to a single counselee, the corresponding question would be: Is he or she more like engineering students or more like law students? A special branch of statistical analysis called *discriminant analysis*, has grown up to answer such questions.

Given a body of data on the two groups in our illustration, we can seek out the items on which the groups are most different, and try to combine the data in such a way as to increase still further the separation of the groups. The data shown in Table 10.7 were drawn from *The Career Data Book* of *Project Talent (Flanagan et al., 1973)*, and represent average percentile values for the two groups (as well as a third group of auto mechanics) on a number of interest and ability measures. The testing was done while the students were still in high school, so the data indicate the extent to which high school data are capable of predicting group membership some 5 years later.

There are several differences of moderate size between law and engineering students on the ability tests, most noteworthy the superiority of the engineers on tests of mechanical comprehension and spatial visualizing. However, the really large differences between the groups are in their expressed interests. The engineering students were dramatically higher on mechanical-technical interests (38 percentile points), and substantially higher in interest in physical science and math. The law students were substantially higher in interest in public service (politics), literary-linguistic activity, business, and sales.

How well can the two groups be separated by a composite of these measures? In another *Project Talent* report Cooley and Lohnes (1968) develop a composite score based on both ability and interest tests that they label "Technical versus Sociocultural." This is the most important single dimension spreading

Table 10.7

MEDIAN PERCENTILES OF LAW STUDENTS, ENGINEERING STUDENTS, AND AUTO MECHANICS ON ABILITY AND INTEREST MEASURES, AND BETWEEN-GROUP DIFFERENCES

	Median Percentiles			Group Differences	
	Law Students	Engineering Students	Automotive Mechanics	Engineering —Law	Engineering —Mechanic
Ability Test					
English	85	77	31	−8	46
Reading Comprehension	83	74	35	−9	39
Creativity	75	77	50	2	27
Mechanical Comprehension	62	79	50	17	29
Visualizing (3-dimensional)	62	76	50	14	26
Abstract Reasoning	70	77	43	7	34
Arithmetic Reasoning	79	79	45	0	34
Introductory Math	84	87	38	3	49
Arithmetic Computation	73	69	31	−4	38
Interest Scores					
Physical Science, Math	63	84	37	21	47
Biological Science, Medicine	66	61	33	−5	28
Public Service (Politics)	76	47	34	−29	13
Literary-Linguistic	76	50	28	−26	22
Social Service	59	43	34	−16	9
Artistic	55	53	36	−2	17
Musical	59	54	50	−5	4
Sports	48	37	32	−11	5
Hunting-Fishing	36	36	46	0	−10
Business	63	38	30	−25	8
Sales	57	37	40	−20	−3
Computational	56	58	42	2	16
Office	46	48	47	2	1
Mechanical-Technical	24	62	74	38	−12
Skilled Trade	23	37	65	14	−28
Farming	32	38	57	6	−19
Labor	26	35	65	9	−30

out some 24 college major field groups. On this composite score the typical engineering student fell at the 84th percentile, the typical student heading for law at the 31st. Only about 7 percent of law school students score as high as the average engineering student. Thus, from the taxonomic point of view, future law and engineering students are two groups that can be separated quite effectively in high school by a combination of ability and interest, with primary emphasis on the interest measures.

Table 10.7 also shows the median scores for a group of automotive mechanics. These also may be compared with the engineering students, and again the groups are clearly very different. In this case, however, more of the large differences are on the ability tests. Not surprisingly, the engineering students score higher on all of these, but especially on the measures of basic mathematics and of English language skills. Many of the interest differentials are quite small, the biggest being the contrast of physical science interest with trade and laboring interests. A composite score that would most effectively separate these two groups would combine information on language and mathematics achievement with that on professional-scientific versus trade-laboring interests, and there seems little question that the separation would again be very effective.

When we try to use test data in a taxonomic approach, we face two related problems: (1) How many categories is it fruitful to try to separate at a given stage in a client's vocational development? (2) What way of combining the test evidence will permit the most effective separation of those categories? Cooley and Lohnes (1968) suggest that during secondary education the 12 categories shown in Table 10.8 may be as many

Table 10.8
TWELVE MAJOR CAREER FIELDS

1. Biological and medical sciences, Ph.D. or M.D.	Biomedical researchers Medical doctors
2. Biological and medical sciences, D.D.S., M.S., or B.S.	Dentists Pharmacists Biologists
3. Physical sciences and mathematics, Ph.D.	Research scientists Mathematicians
4. Physical sciences and engineering, M.S. or B.S.	Applied scientists Engineers
5. Skilled and technical, with post-high school Training	Skilled and technical workers
6. Laborers, no post-high school training	Miscellaneous Laborers
7. Clerks and office workers, no post-high school training	Clerks Office and service workers
8. Noncollege, nontechnical, with post-high school training	Accountants Office equipment operators Salesmen
9. Business, B.S. or B.A.	Businessmen Auditors
10. Business, graduate school	Managers Executives
11. Sociocultural, B.S. or B.A.	Welfare workers Artists Musicians Counselors Teachers
12. Sociocultural, graduate school	Lawyers Social scientists

as will be useful in guiding secondary school students. They conclude that no more than three composite scores from the full battery of *Project Talent* data are useful in differentiating these groups. The dimensions may be labeled as follows.

1. *Science-Oriented Scholasticism.* This dimension identifies those with academic interests and abilities, especially those with a quantitative and scientific slant.

2. *Technical versus Sociocultural.* This dimension separates those with abilities and interests primarily in things and amounts from those with interests and abilities relating to people and language.

3. *Business versus Cultural.* This serves primarily to separate those whose primary interests are practical and material from those primarily interested in culture for its own sake.

PREDICTIVE APPROACH

By contrast with the taxonomic model, the predictive model focuses on some measure of success within a *specific occupation*. A set of data for engineering students and students of automotive mechanics is shown in Table 10.9. The criterion measure is in each case school grades, and the predictors are the factor scores of the *GATB* (described on pp. 359–362). In the predictive model little or no attention is paid to differences *between* groups. Rather, attention is focused on success *within* the group that is taking some particular program of training or working in some particular job. The data on engineering students in Table 10.9

Table 10.9
VALIDITY COEFFICIENTS OF *GATB* TESTS FOR PREDICTING GRADES IN ENGINEERING AND AUTO MECHANIC SCHOOL

	Engineering	Automotive Mechanic
V (Verbal)	.40	.18
N (Numerical)	.38	.18
S (Spatial)	.11	.48
P (Form Perception)	.11	.14
Q (Clerical Perception)	.30	.12
K (Motor Coordination)	.25	−.11
F (Finger Dexterity)	.08	.27
M (Manual Dexterity)	.01	−.04
N	164	50

suggest that the best prediction of engineering school grades would be produced by some combination of *Verbal, Numerical* and *Clerical Perception* scores.

We can determine, for this sample of cases, the best combination of tests and the manner in which they should be combined to give the most accurate prediction of the criterion score.* Table 10.10 shows the best sets of 2, 3, 4, or more tests to be used for predicting grades, how the tests should be combined, and what the correlation of the composite score with grades would have been. For example, the set of two tests that would be best to use would be V and N. They should be combined with almost equal weight, but giving a little more weight to the V score (.29 to .26). The indicated combination yields a correlation of .46 with grades. From the table it is possible to see how the correlation improves as additional tests are added. The first one or two additions make a noticeable increase in the accuracy of prediction, but after that the increments become progressively smaller since the most promising tests have already been included and the remaining tests tend also to overlap the ones that have been included.

It may seem odd that the measures of P and M are incorporated in the prediction with minus signs, even though the original validity coefficients for these tests were positive. This sometimes happens when a test with quite low validity overlaps markedly with other more valid tests. In this instance one suspects that P gets at some aspect of sheer speed of perception and response that also affects a number of the other tests. It is known that all the tests of the *GATB* are quite speeded. This

Table 10.10

COMBINATIONS OF FACTOR STANDARD SCORES TO PREDICT ENGINEERING SCHOOL GRADES

Number of Factors	Combination of Tests	Multiple Correlation
2	$.29\,V + .26\,N$	.46
3	$.27\,V + .25\,N + .21\,Q$	.51
4	$.30\,V + .32\,N - .20\,P + .26\,Q$	.54
5	$.30\,V + .28\,N - .35\,P + .26\,Q + .22\,K$	.56
6	$.29\,V + .28\,N - .33\,P + .26\,Q + .26\,K - .10\,M$	.57
8	$.30\,V + .28\,N + .00\,S - .34\,P + .25\,Q + .25\,K + .12\,F - .16\,M$	.58

* The statistical techniques of multiple regression are more technical and specialized than can appropriately be presented in this book. The interested reader will find them presented in many standard statistics texts, such as Kerlinger and Pedhazur 1973.

speed factor may blur the measures of verbal and numerical ability and we may be improving their effectiveness as predictors by eliminating the effects of speed statistically through the subtraction procedure.

Unfortunately the voluminous data from Project Talent provide, at this time, no analyses organized within the predictive model, so it is not possible to compare directly the tests that differentiate engineers from other groups with those that predict success in engineering school. However, it can be noted that for the *GATB* data the best single predictor of engineering school grades is the *V* (*Verbal*) score, and the data from Table 10.7 indicate that a high verbal score would certainly *not* identify a high school student as more like engineers than like lawyers. What difference there is runs in the opposite direction. Thus those tests that are the best predictors *within* an occupation may have very limited effectiveness in differentiating *between* occupations.

When tests are administered by an employer primarily to serve his needs, the predictive model seems to be the appropriate one. The employer is interested largely in how successful the applicant is likely to be in the specific job for which he is an applicant, and wants to identify the test or tests that give the best prediction of probable success within practical limits of testing time. Sometimes the applicant may be a candidate for, or available for assignment to, a number of different jobs. Then the employer is interested in knowing how well each applicant is likely to do in each job, so that available manpower may be allocated most efficiently. This type of concern with the classification and assignment of personnel is most characteristic of a military organization in which a great variety of functions must be discharged with a relatively undifferentiated pool of manpower. In all of these settings the predictive model appears to fit the demands of the situation.

When tests are used for counseling individuals about their futures the situation is rather different. The counselee is interested not only, and perhaps not primarily, in his probable degree of success in a specific occupation. He is interested in how well satisfied he will be with a field of work. Furthermore, he is usually prepared to consider a wide range of possible occupations. He needs help in appraising the large set of possible alternatives. He needs help in answering the question, "What am I like?" so far as the world or work is concerned. In this context, the taxonomic model has a good deal of appeal. It tries to locate the individual in the total job space and to help him to see how congruent his abilities, interests, and temperament are with the several options that he faces at any particular point in his vocational development.

The last three columns of Table 10.11 show the mean scores of each of the 12 career groups defined in Table 10.8 on each of the three discriminant dimensions defined on p. 376. The scale on which these means are reported is one in which the overall mean is 50 and the standard deviation is 10. The results for the first two dimensions are charted in Figure 10.3. To provide an idea of the spread within each occupational group, and the overlapping of the different groups, an ellipse is lightly sketched in, showing the region around the centroid within which 50 percent of the group could be expected to fall. Each shaded area defines the 50 percent of cases in the group that are clustered around the average person. The extent of overlap of the shaded areas gives some idea of the similarity of the groups. Thus a person with a 40 on Dimension I and a 48 on Dimension II is in the "inner 50 percent " for the group of laborers, the group of clerks and office workers, and the group of skilled and technical, and clearly "belongs" to any of those groups. The person is not far outside the boundary of the inner group of noncollege, nontechnical, but is remote from all of the college and graduate school groups. It can be noted that much of the area in the diagram "belongs" to at least two, and often three or four of the 12 groups.

Inspection of Figure 10.3 shows that the first discriminant dimension does a pretty good job of separating out groups that differ substantially in educational level. Relatively few persons

Table 10.11

DISCRIMINANT FUNCTION CENTROIDS FOR 1965 5-YEAR FOLLOW-UP CAREER PLAN GROUPS.

Plan-Group		Dimension I	Dimension II	Dimension III
1	MED*	64	48	54
2	BIO	55	47	50
3	RES	62	41	52
4	ENG	54	44	48
5	TEC	43	46	51
6	LBR	38	48	53
7	CLK	41	52	50
8	ACT	45	53	49
9	BUS	52	52	46
10	MGT	59	51	45
11	WEL	53	54	52
12	PRF	59	54	53

* The abbreviations refer to the categories given in Table 10.8.

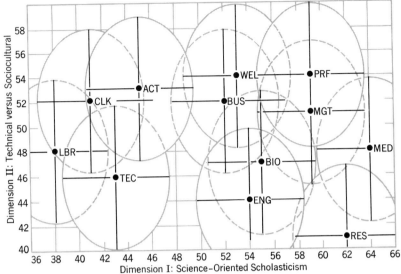

Figure 10.3
Centroids of five year follow-up career plan groups in discriminant plane.

with no post-high school education surpass the average college graduate on this dimension. The dimension appears to identify fairly well those with the inclination and ability to complete a college education. On the second dimension there is a good deal of overlapping, but the physical scientists and engineers are fairly well separated from the nontechnical groups. If we had plotted the third dimension, we would have noted even more overlapping for that dimension.

It is not easy to express the amount of overlapping in educational or occupational groupings. We have attempted to do so in Fig. 10.3 using an arbitrary 50 percent boundary, but persons from each group do lie outside that boundary. It is still more difficult to judge how the facts that we observe should be used in career decision making. The taxonomic approach that data such as these represent describes the existing situation, existing at a particular point in time. Building counseling on such data assumes that the way things have been in the past is the way that they should be and will be in the future. This may be a generally reasonable assumption, in that the structure of education and of work is not likely to undergo sudden or drastic changes. But it *is* an assumption, and may well prove inaccurate in many details, or even in some main features.

We must also question the degree to which general trends should be prescriptive for the individual case. A point on a

Table 10.12
PROFILE FOR BILLIE WILLIAMS

Occupational Group	Centour*
1. Medical sciences and practice, M.D., Ph.D.	12
2. Biological and medical sciences, D.D.S., M.S., B.S.	80
3. Physical sciences, mathematics, Ph.D.	18
4. Physical sciences, engineering, M.S., B.S.	78
5. Skilled and technical, post-high school training	14
6. Laborers, no post-high school training	5
7. Clerks, office workers, no post-high school training	8
8. Noncollege, nontechnical, post-high school training	12
9. Business, B.S., B.A.	40
10. Business, graduate school	40
11. Sociocultural, B.S., B.A.	30
12. Sociocultural, graduate school	25

* The *centour* is the boundary marking the percentage of cases as far from the group average or centroid as Billie Williams is. That is, Billie is more like Group 2 than 80 percent of those who were actually members of Group 2, but is more like Group 6 than only 5 percent of those who were actually in Group 6.

chart describes only the average of a group, and any selected region encompasses only some specified fraction of the group. Individual members of the group deviate from the average in varying degrees and in many directions. What a counselor might appropriately do, given that the data have been organized to permit him or her to do so, is to report to the counselee what percentage of each group is farther from the centroid than the counselee. Thus, if Billie Williams has scores on the two main discriminant dimensions of 54 and 46, the report might read like that in Table 10.12.

Such a report indicates that a person like Billie *could* be found in any one of the occupations (as is true for most combinations of scores), but is most similar to college graduates in fields 2 and 4 that involve biological and physical sciences and their application. Such a report provides a reasonable and realistic basis for further discussion and meditation. If the point corresponding to Billie's two scores were marked on a chart like Fig. 10.3, it is easy to see in what direction Billie deviates from each group; while the profile indicates the degree of deviation.

PROGNOSTIC TESTS

One group of aptitude tests is made up of tests designed to predict readiness to learn or probable degree of success in some specific subject or segment of education. These are called prognostic tests. A group of tests in this category that have been widely heralded and have received considerable use are the "reading readiness" tests. These tests are designed to be used with children, usually shortly after their entry into the first grade, to give the school as accurate an indication as possible of the child's ability to progress in reading. They provide information the teacher can use in assembling working groups within the class, in deciding upon the amount and type of prereading activities to provide, and in judging how soon to start a formal reading program. In some communities where kindergarten attendance is quite general, tests at the end of kindergarten are looked to as one basis for organizing first grade groups for the following year. The sorts of task that appear in these tests may be seen from Table 10.13.

If you compare the tasks in Table 10.13 with the sample test items for general ability tests shown on pp. 299–301, you will be aware of a substantial degree of similarity. In both, knowledge of word meanings appears. Both deal with recognition of sameness and differences, with analysis and classification. However, the reading readiness tests tend to emphasize more exclusively the materials of reading, letters and words. They include the components or early stages of the reading task. The basic question now becomes: Does the special slant of the reading readiness test result in increased validity? Is the special test an improvement over a measure of general academic aptitude? This is the question that must be raised for any type of prognostic test or special academic aptitude test.

Table 10.13
TYPES OF TASK INCLUDED IN REPRESENTATIVE READING READINESS TESTS

Type of Test Task	Gates-MacGinitie	Harrison-Stroud	Lee-Clark	Metropolitan	Murphy-Durrell
Recognition of words	✻	✻			
Recognition of letters	✻			✻	✻
Discrimination of sounds	✻	✻			✻
Blending of sounds	✻				
Comprehension of verbal material—words, sentences, directions	✻	✻	✻	✻	
Visual form discrimination or matching	✻	✻	✻	✻	
Copying symbols	✻			✻	
Number concepts				✻	
Learning words in standard lesson					✻

The general trend of the evidence does seem to support the higher validity of the readiness tests specifically designed to forecast progress in learning to read, though incisive comparative studies are hard to find. The correlations of reading readiness tests with reading measures at the end of the first grade are typically about .60 to .65, and the subtests that have the highest validity have fairly consistently been those quite directly involving component reading skills, that is, recognizing or discriminating the visual form of letters or words. These correlations are probably somewhat higher than a generalized aptitude test would give for this specific criterion—reading performance at the end of grade 1.

Prognostic tests have been developed for various other subjects and levels, and the last few years have witnessed some renewal of interest in these tests. Carroll and Sapon (1958) and Pimsleur (1966) have each brought out a battery of foreign language prognosis tests, and the *Symonds Foreign Language Prognosis Test* has been restandardized. The older *Orleans Algebra Prognosis Test,* and *Geometry Prognosis Test* have been revised (Orleans and Hanna 1968, 1969). The authors of all these tests offer evidence to show that the specialized tests provide a better prediction of achievement in the special subject area than is possible from a general measure of scholastic aptitude. However, we may still question whether, within the areas of academic achievement, special prognostic tests can improve the predictions based upon a combination of measures of general intelligence and previous academic achievement in related areas enough to justify their use. The demonstration that they can has not been sufficiently impressive to result in widespread adoption of the tests.

Special prognostic tests seem likely to be more useful as predictors of success in rather special types of academic task that have had no counterparts at earlier levels of school experience. Thus the *Turse Shorthand Aptitude Test,* for which a correlation of .67 with later achievement in shorthand has been reported, may be useful as a supplement to other information about a pupil in evaluating probable success in shorthand training, to the extent that such training continues to be offered. The *ERC Stenographic Aptitude Test* and the *Bennett Stenographic Aptitude Tests* have given comparable results. These tests include such tasks as spelling, transcribing symbols, dictation under speed pressure, and word discrimination.

PROFESSIONAL SCHOOL APTITUDE BATTERIES

One other group of aptitude tests, so-called, are the tests that have been developed to select individuals for particular types of professional training. Many types of professional school, sometimes individually but more often operating through their professional organizations, have instituted testing programs for the selection of their students. Testing programs have been in operation for selecting students for engineering, law, medicine, dentistry, veterinary medicine, nursing, and accounting, to mention a few.

The tests used in these professional school batteries tend to be tests of reading, quantitative reasoning, and apprehending abstract relationships, with the balance and emphasis shifted somewhat to conform to the academic emphasis of the particular training program. They are largely minor variations upon the same theme—a relatively high-level measure of scholastic aptitude and achievement. The different professional aptitude tests would correlate very substantially with one another or with a measure of general academic aptitude, and indeed it should be expected that they would, because the abilities required to succeed in training for the different professions have much in common. The similarities outweigh the differences. The common core is adapted to a particular professional field, for example, by giving more emphasis to quantitative materials for engineering and more to verbal materials for law. It is supplemented in some cases by rather highly specialized tests, for example, a test of chalk carving for dentistry. These variations are superimposed upon the basic theme of scholastic aptitude and achievement.

MEASUREMENT OF MUSICAL APTITUDE

When we come to such fields as music and art, the inadequacy of general scholastic aptitude measures becomes quite apparent. Grades in these subjects are usually among those least well predicted by general measures of scholastic aptitude. Furthermore, the specialized nature of outstanding talent in these fields has long been recognized. Our problem is to determine what the components of this talent are and devise ways of appraising them.

In musical ability one large component is executive or motor, the ability to master the patterns of action required for playing an instrument. Aptitude measures have largely avoided this domain, perhaps because of its specificity to a particular instrument. Most measurement has been directed toward the perceptive and interpretive aspects of music.

Hearing music involves in the first place various types of sensory discrimination—discrimination of pitch, of loudness, of temporal relations. It involves in the second place perceiving the more complex musical relations in the material, interval relationships, the pattern of a melody, the composition of a chord, the relationship of a harmony to a melody. Third, it involves esthetic judgments about the suitability and pleasingness of a melody or harmony, a rhythmic pattern, or a pattern of dynamics.

The most thoroughly investigated musical aptitude test battery, the *Seashore Measures of Musical Talents,* is directed primarily toward measuring simple sensory discriminations, though with some attention to perceiving slightly more musical material. The subtests, listed below, analyze music down so far that very little music remains.

1. *Discrimination of Pitch:* judging which of two tones is higher.

2. *Discrimination of Loudness:* judging which of two sounds is louder.

3. *Discrimination of Time Interval:* judging which of two intervals is longer.

4. *Judgment of Rhythm:* judging whether two rhythms are the same or different.

5. *Judgment of Timbre:* judging which of two tone qualities is more pleasing.

6. *Tonal Memory:* judging whether two melodies are the same or different.

The items are on phonograph records, with a series of items of each type. Within each type the judgments become progressively more difficult.

The analytic approach to musical aptitude is evident in the above list of subtests. Critics have contended that the analysis has removed the tests a great way from any genuinely musical material and that fine discriminations of pitch, time, and intensity are really not called for in the activities of the musician. Validity studies of the *Seashore* tests have been somewhat conflicting, yielding appreciable correlations with measures of musical success in some instances and very low correlations in others. The value of the analytic tests is still a matter of doubt and controversy.

A more recently developed test that is based on more complex and more genuinely musical material is the *Gordon Musical Aptitude Profile* (Gordon, 1965). This test, recorded on tape, consists of tests of musical perception in which the examinee must judge whether an "answer" phrase is the same as or different from the "question" phrase. There are four such subtests in which the comparison is to be based, respectively, on (1) melody, (2) harmony, (3) tempo, and (4) meter. These are followed by three subtests in which the examinee must judge which of two musical selections is better. In the first, or phrasing test, two renditions differ in musical expression; in the second, or balance test, the two renditions have different endings; in the third test, designated style, the two renditions differ in tempo.

The test appears to have been developed with a good deal of psychometric sophistication and thoroughness. Reliability is quite acceptable—in the .70s for the seven separate subscores, the .80s for the three main sections, and .90 to .95 for the composite score based on all of the parts. The test is relatively new (published in 1965) so that available validity data are largely those supplied by the author in the test manual, but these seem generally promising and, in certain instances, quite dramatic. Thus seven correlations with music teachers' estimates of the musical talent of members of their choral or instrumental group were reported as ranging from .64 to .97!

In an exemplary longitudinal study, Gordon (1967) followed up groups of students over a three-year period. Tests were given in the fourth or fifth grade, and were put away and not made available to either music teachers or evaluators of the pupil's performance. Complete classes were tested, composed of pupils who had had no previous formal musical training. For the 3 years of the follow-up, they received 1 period a week of instrumental instruction. Each pupil was tested with a standard set of performance tests for his instrument—"etudes" that were tape recorded and judged without knowledge of who was performing. In addition, teacher ratings were obtained, and an achievement test on music reading and notation was given.

Correlations of total test score with the three criterion measures at the end of one, two and three years were as follows.

	1 Year	2 Year	3 Year
Performance test	.53	.69	.68
Achievement test	.61	.61	.71
Teacher rating	.37	.39	.35

The test clearly provides a good prediction of later musical performance, one that appeared to get better the longer the period of musical training that is covered. It is worth noting that objective and unbiased performance measures were more predictable than were the ratings by teachers.

TESTS OF ARTISTIC APTITUDE

Several types of test have been available relating to aptitude for art, but the field has been rather dormant in recent years. In the first place,there have been tests of esthetic judgment. That field is now fairly well dominated by the *Meier Art Judgment Test*. Each item consists of a pair of pictures of art objects. One is an acknowledged masterpiece. The other is that same masterpiece, systematically distorted in some respect (balance, proportion, shading, etc.). The test booklet indicates the aspect in which the two pictures differ, and the examinee must select the better picture of the pair.

A test of the judgmental aspect of art ability is the *Graves Design Judgment Test*. This differs from the *Meier Test* in that all the items consist of abstract and nonrepresentational material. The members of a pair differ in some single aspect of design, that is, balance, symmetry, variety. Judgment of design is presumably divorced from any particular object or content.

In an attempt to get at the productive, as distinct from the purely judgmental, aspect of art, certain tests (*Horn, Knauber*) require the subject to produce drawings based on certain limiting "givens." In the *Horn Art Aptitude Inventory* a pattern of lines and dots is provided, and from this material the examinee must produce a sketch. The type of item is indicated in Fig. 10.4. The products must be evaluated by subjective rating, according to standards given by the authors, but they present some evidence that this can be done rather reliably even by nonartists. The *Knauber Art Ability Tests* use various assigned drawing tasks, including also problems in shading, perspective, and composition.

Art tests have generally been fairly successful in differentiating art students or art teachers from other groups. However, it has been argued that they accomplish this because they are in large measure achievement tests rather than aptitude measures. There has been relatively little study of these tests as aptitude measures with untrained individuals. Studies of art students have indicated that test performance is reasonably

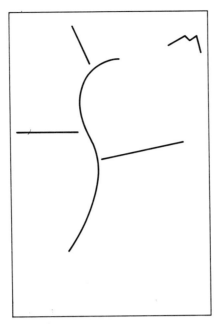

Figure 10.4
Example of type of items used in *Horn Art Aptitude Inventory*

predictive of later art school success. Thus Horn and Smith (1945) found a correlation of .66 between score on the *Horn* test at the beginning of the year and average faculty rating of success in a special high school art class at the end of the year. Barrett (1949) correlated four art tests with grades in a ninth grade art course and with ratings of pupils' art products, with the following results.

	Course Grade	Ratings of Product
McAdory Art Test	.10	.13
Meier Art Judgment Test	.37	.35
Knauber Art Ability Test	.33	.71
Lewerenz Fundamental Art Abilities Test	.40	.76

The last two tests, requiring production of drawings by the examinee, had about the same correlation with grades as did the *Meier Art Judgment Test* but much higher correlations with appraisals of student products.

We can see from the above that the test tasks that require art students to do the sorts of task they will be taught to do in art class predict their later achievement. How far down to untrained pupils this can be pushed remains to be determined.

Since the keying of art tests of all types depends upon a pooling of judgments, obtaining a high score requires conformity to accepted esthetic standards. There is real question as to the applicability of these tests (or the tests of musical aptitude) in a distinctly different culture. There is also the possibility, though it is a fairly unlikely one, that a highly talented but unconventional person will be penalized on the tests.

APPRAISING CREATIVITY

Consideration of tests in the field of music and art leads us rather naturally to the topic of creativity. One criticism that has been directed at ability tests of the usual type is that they focus on what may be called *convergent thinking.* In convergent thinking the examinee is called upon to zero in on *the* right answer to a problem for which an answer has already been determined. He is asked to define a word, solve an arithmetic problem, find the next number to continue a series, or identify the one thing that doesn't belong in a set. Often he chooses the right answer from among 4 or 5 choices that are supplied to him. The critics point out, however, that much of life's activity involves *divergent thinking,* the generating of novel responses to situations, responses that are original, unusual, varied, and hopefully effective in handling the largely unstructured problem that the person is called upon to solve.

In recent years a number of investigators have attempted to develop tests of divergent thinking and perhaps of creativity. Guilford included divergent thinking as one of the five operations upon intellectual materials in his *Structure of Intellect* (see p. 354), and he and his students have undertaken to produce a number of tests that exemplify this function. Typically, the tests call upon the examinee to generate multiple responses to a problem, for example, different uses for a wire coat hanger. The responses are scored in terms of fluency (number of responses), flexibility (number of different categories of responses), and originality (number of rare responses given by few other respondents). Torrance (1966) has produced tests oriented more toward young children and toward graphic or pictorial as well as verbal response. Thus in one test the subject is presented with a page of plain circles, and his task is to make each circle into a picture, producing as many pictures and as varied a set as he can.

If "divergent thinking" or "creativity" are to be useful constructs for educational and psychological measurement, tests for these qualities must (1) be relatively uncorrelated with the tests of convergent thinking that make up conventional aptitude batteries; (2) show some coherence in the sense that different tests of "creativity" correlate with each other; and (3) have some significant correlates in the world of practical events. The tests have had only modest success on any of these counts. Correlations with conventional tests of convergent thinking are not high, but they are generally positive and appreciable. Correlations of different "creativity" measures have been modest at best and the notion of a generalized trait of creativity receives only limited support. The extent to which the creativity tests are predictive of achievement either in or out of school is still a matter of controversy, some investigators reporting substantial relationships and others failing to find any. Thus the tests must still be thought of as research tools rather than as instruments that are of proved value for use either in schools or in industry.

SUMMARY STATEMENT

Though tests of general cognitive ability bear some relationship to success in many fields, efficient vocational guidance or personnel classification calls for tests more specifically directed at the abilities called for by each kind of job. Analytical studies of human abilities support the genuineness and importance of these special abilities. Numerous tests of special abilities have appeared, and more recently tests of this sort have been organized into comprehensive aptitude batteries for use in vocational guidance or personnel classification.

Data from tests of separate aptitudes may be organized in either a predictive or a taxonomic model. From the point of view of the employer concerned with selection or classification, the predictive model is probably the more appropriate. However, for guidance of individual vocational choices the taxonomic model may well be more suitable. Aptitude tests show modest validity within the context of either model, but neither prediction nor differentiation is precise enough to give comfort to the testing enthusiast.

Special tests to evaluate readiness to undertake particular educational tasks have also been developed. The most widely used of these are reading readiness tests. Other types of prognostic test have been less widely used, perhaps because their function is reasonably well served by measures of scholastic aptitude and academic achievement. Professional school aptitude batteries appear to be variations upon the basic theme of scholastic aptitude tests.

The fields of music and art have produced a number of ability tests. However, highly analytic tests have not been very clearly successful. More complex tests involve an unknown admixture of previous training. These show reasonably good validity and may provide an improved and at least relatively objective way of appraising status, and hence promise, in the field.

Tests of "divergent thinking" and "creativity" are currently attracting a good deal of attention, but their usefulness as psychometric tools is still uncertain.

QUESTIONS AND EXERCISES

1. A number of aptitude test batteries have been developed for use at the secondary school level and with adults, but almost none for the elementary school. Why is this? Is it a reasonable state of affairs?

2. What are the advantages in using a battery such as the *Differential Aptitude Tests* instead of tests selected from a number of different sources? What are the limitations?

3. Step by step, what would need to be done to set up a program for selecting students for a dental school?

4. Mugwump University has professional schools in law, medicine, and engineering. Taking a taxonomic approach, what properties would a counselor want in a test battery to be used to help students choose among these three professional schools.

5. If the counselor emphasized a predictive approach, what properties would he desire in the test battery?

6. A vocational high school offers programs to train bookkeepers, cosmetologists, dental assistants, and stenographers. Studies with the GATB have yielded the data on means, standard deviations, and correlations with supervisory ratings shown below for these four occupations. As a counselor in the school, how would you use this information in helping students to choose among the four programs?

	Verbal			Numerical			Spatial			Manual Dexterity		
	Mean	S.D.	r	Mean	S.D.	r	Mean	S.D.	r	Mean	S.D.	r
Bookkeeper	106	16	.51	112	15	.37	103	20	.38	105	21	.36
Cosmetologist	96	15	.24	92	13	.31	100	16	.25	98	17	.07
Dental assistant	106	13	.26	102	14	.34	107	16	.30	115	19	.36
Stenographer	105	12	.21	105	14	.24	106	16	.06	103	21	.09

7. At the beginning of the 12th grade Mary Jones took the battery of tests used in Project Talent, and her scores gave values for the three discriminant dimensions of 62, 58, and 55 respectively. Which of the 12 broad career planning groups of Table 10.8 (p. 375) does she most resemble? What should a counselor's immediate objective be for Mary?

8. How sound is the statement: "The best measure of aptitude in any field is a measure of achievement in that field to date."? What are its limitations?

9. What are the differences between a reading readiness test and an intelligence test? What are the advantages of using the readiness test rather than an intelligence test for first grade pupils?

10. To what extent are tests like the *Horn Art Aptitude Inventory* measures of aptitude? To what extent are they measures of achievement?

11. In what ways could a follow-up study of graduates of a high school help in improving the school guidance program?

12. Why have aptitude test batteries shown up better in discriminating *between* jobs than in predicting success *within* a single job category?

13. What special problems arise in attempting to measure an attribute such as "creativity"? What procedures seem to have promise for overcoming these problems?

14. Have the students in a class write down all the uses they can think of for *old newspapers*. Try to set up a scoring system for the results to appraise (1) fluency, (2) flexibility, and (3) creativity. What problems did you encounter in the data gathering and analysis?

15. What do psychologists hope to accomplish by *factor analysis?* What problems do they encounter when they use these procedures?

SUGGEST
ADDITIONAL READI

Bennett, G.K., H.G. Seashore, and A.G. Wesman. *Fifth edition manual for the Differential Aptitude Tests, Form S and T.* New York: The Psychological Corporation, 1974.

Fleishman, E.A. On the relation between abilities, learning, and human performance. *American Psychologist,* 1972, 27, 1017–1032.

Ghiselli, E. *The validity of occupational aptitude tests.* New York: Wiley, 1966.

Hunt, J. McV. and G.E. Kirk. Criterion-referenced tests of school readiness: A paradigm with illustrations. *Genetic Psychology Monographs,* 1974, 90, 143–182.

Kogan, Nathan and Ethel Pankove. Long-term predictive validity of divergent-thinking tests: Some negative evidence. *Journal of Educational Psychology,* 1974, *66,* 802-810.

Steckler, V. A review of the Nonreading Aptitude Test Battery, *Journal of Employment Counseling,* 1973, *10,* 17-20.

United States Department of Labor: Manpower Administration. *Manual for the U.S.E.S. General Aptitude Test Battery.* Washington, D.C.: U.S. Employment Service, 1970.

United States Department of Labor: Manpower Administration. *Manual for the U.S.E.S. Nonreading Aptitude Test Battery.* Washington, D.C.: U.S. Employment Service, 1970.

CHAPTER ELEVEN
QUESTIONNAIRES AND INVENTORIES FOR SELF-APPRAISAL

The last chapters have been devoted to measures of ability: what the individual *can* do under test conditions and motivation to do his best. We shall move on now to measurement of other aspects of personality—to the appraisal of what one *will* do under the natural circumstances of life. Both in discussions of personality and in efforts to develop instruments of appraisal, we must recognize that the person is a unified whole. Any aspects or traits that we may separate out are separated out for our convenience. They do not exist as separate entities, but are only aspects of or ways of looking at the unitary person. However, it is inevitable that we do pick the person to pieces to study and understand him. We cannot look at everything at once.

Personality itself has many different aspects, of which the following may be distinguished.

Temperament refers to an individual's characteristic mood, activity level, excitability, and focus of concern. It includes such dimensions as cheerful-gloomy, energetic-lethargic, excited-calm, introverted-extroverted, and dominant-submissive.

Character relates to those traits to which definite social value is attached. They are the "Boy Scout" traits of honesty, kindliness, cooperation, industry, and such.

Adjustment is a term that we shall use to indicate how well the individual has been able to make peace internally and with the surrounding world. Insofar as the individual can comfortably accept himself and his world, insofar as his ways of life do not get him into trouble in his social group, he will be considered well adjusted.

Interests refer to tendencies to seek out and participate in certain activities.

Attitudes relate to tendencies to favor or reject particular groups of individuals, sets of ideas, or social institutions.

METHODS OF STUDYING PERSONALITY

Most of the evaluation techniques to be considered in this and the following chapters have to do with one or more of the aspects of personality identified above. To what sources may we go for evidence on these aspects when we wish to study an individual? First, we can see what the individual has to say about himself or herself. Second, we can find out what others say about him or her. Third, we can see what he or she actually does, how he or she behaves in the real world of things or people.

SELF-REPORTS

One obvious source for information about a person is that person. No one else has as intimate and continuous a view of Johnny as Johnny has of himself. He is aware of hopes and aspirations, worries and concerns that may be well hidden from the outsider. To get at the individual's view from the inside, we may use interviews, probing those areas that seem sensitive or significant. Another approach is to incorporate the questions that might be asked in a face-to-face interview into a uniform questionnaire or *personality inventory*. The choices the individual makes in responding to the set of questions are scored in various ways to provide self-description. These procedures will be elaborated in this chapter, and their strengths and weaknesses pointed out.

APPRAISAL THROUGH THE OPINION OF OTHERS

For some purposes, we may be interested in how a person is perceived by his or her fellow beings. Is Ellen seen as a friendly fellow worker? A fair teacher? An industrious pupil? A convincing salesperson? A generally desirable employee? The opinion of others may be the significant fact in certain settings. It is also a very convenient way of getting a summary appraisal of someone. For these reasons rating procedures have been widely used. We shall consider their values and limitations in Chapter 12.

It can be argued that for practical purposes an individual's personality is what that person does, rather than what he or she says or what is said about him or her. The problem is to develop procedures for appraising genuine behavior not distorted for the purpose of making a good impression. Some attempts have been made to do this by putting individuals in test situations of various types. The test situations may appear to be ability tests, but in fact be scored for factors other than the ability that the examinee believes is being measured. The test situations may involve fantasy and imaginative production. The situations may involve various forms of group interaction. In some instances behavior is scored objectively, in others it is rated by an observer or assessor, while in still others it leads to a rather elaborate and intuitive clinical interpretation.

Behavior may also be studied in natural settings—the play group, the classroom, the office. When this is done the investigator typically functions as an observer, recording and possibly also evaluating the actions that occur. Different ways of obtaining and analyzing behavior samples will be considered in Chapter 13.

INTERVIEW

If we wish to find out about a person, one way to do so is to ask that person questions and to evaluate the answers. This inquiry may be to some degree, structured, controlled, and standardized with respect only to the questions asked, with respect to both the questions and the possible answers, or with respect to neither questions nor answers. If we think of questions and answers as representing two dimensions that may extend from very fluid to very structured and controlled, we can represent several forms of questioning as shown in Fig. 11.1. Falling at the structured, controlled end of the continuum with respect to *both* question and response are the many self-report inventories of which we shall speak later in the chapter. These present each person with a uniform set of questions in predetermined order, and provide a limited set of categories or options from among which a choice must be made.

The typical application blank is equally structured so far as the questions are concerned, but provides more flexibility on the response side. The responses are often (though not always) constructed by the respondent, providing opportunity for a response that is uniquely descriptive of him.

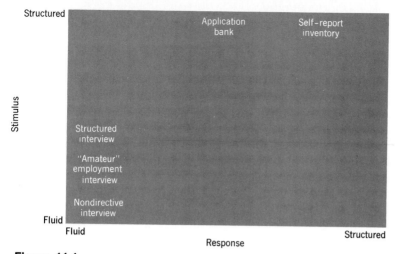

Figure 11.1
Relationships among self-descriptive technique.

At the other extreme—that is, the open, and unstructured end for both question and response—is the nondirective, therapeutic interview and, often, the untrained employment interview. It is impossible to tell in advance, or from one case to the next, either what questions will be asked or what form the responses will take. This is, for the interview, both a strength and a weakness. It is a strength in that it makes it possible to adapt the questioning to the individual case, following up in depth those lines of inquiry that seem most relevant and productive. It is a weakness in that it makes it very unlikely that the same evidence will be obtained for all interviewees. In the extreme case there may be large gaps in the interview coverage, and highly relevant material may be missed because the appropriate questions were not asked. This variation in what is covered certainly accounts, in part, for the discouragingly low consistency that emerges in the impressions that different interviewers get when they interview the same person.

The problem for the interview is to maintain the virtues of flexibility while at the same time achieving a reasonable degree of uniformity. One approach to this has been to develop various patterns of structured interview, in which a specified set of topics is systematically covered, but not always in the same order or in the same detail. This approach is intermediate in degree of structure and control in the stimulus (question) dimension, and pretty open and fluid in the response dimension. Through training and through an interview record form, interviewers are led to cover systematically a set of topics that have been identified as relevant and to record the relevant

INTERVIEWING

INTERVIEW GUIDE

LISTEN	COMMENT	INQUIRE
Be Receptive and Responsive	Make Conversation	Probe: What? How? Why?

Keep Questions Open-Ended.

INTRODUCTION

Cover:
Greeting
Small talk
Opening question
Lead question

Look for:
Appearance
Manner
Self-expression
Responsiveness

WORK EXPERIENCE

Cover:
Earliest jobs,
    part-time, temporary
Military assignments
Full-time positions

Ask:
Things done best? Done less well?
Things liked best? Liked less well?
Major accomplishments? How achieved?
Most difficult problems faced? How handled?
Ways most effective with people? Ways
    less effective?
Level of earnings?
Reasons for changing jobs?
What learned from work experience?
What looking for in job? In career?

Look for:
Relevance of work
Sufficiency of work
Skill and competence
Adaptability
Productivity
Motivation
Interpersonal relations
Leadership
Growth and development

EDUCATION

Cover:
Elementary school
High school
College
Specialized training
Recent courses

Ask:
Best subjects? Subjects done less well?
Subjects liked most? Liked least?
Reactions to teachers?
Level of grades? Effort required?
Reasons for choosing school? Major field?
Special achievements? Toughest problems?
Role in extracurricular activities?
How financed education?
Relation of education to career?
Consider further schooling?

Look for:
Relevance of schooling
Sufficiency of schooling
Intellectual abilities
Versatility
Breadth and depth of knowledge
Level of accomplishment
Motivation, interests
Reaction to authority
Leadership
Team work

Figure 11.2
Guide for employment and assessment interviewers. (Copyright © 1972, 1973 by The
Psychological Corporation, New York, N. Y. Reproduced by permission.

EARLY YEARS (OPTIONAL)

Cover:
Family and home
Guidance and discipline
Individual and group
    activities
Neighborhood and
    community

Ask:
What did father do for a living?
Describe parents' interests? personalities?
How about brothers and sisters? Contrast
    with self?
Parents' expectations? How strictly raised?
How spend time? play? chores? organizations?
How describe neigbhorhood? community?
Effect of early influences?

Look for:
Socio-economic status
Parental examples
Attitudes toward achievement,
    work, and people
Emotional and social
    adjustment
Basic values and goals
Self-image

PRESENT ACTIVITIES AND INTERESTS

Cover:
Special interests and hobbies
Civic and community affairs
Living arrangements
Marriage and family
Finances
Health and energy
Geographical preferences

Ask:
Things like to do in spare time?
What social activities?
Extent involved in community?
Describe home? and family?
Opportunities to build financial reserve?
What kind of health problems? physical check-up?
Reaction to relocation?

Look for:
Vitality
Management of time,
    energy, and money
Maturity and judgment
Intellectual growth
Cultural breadth
Diversity of interests
Social interests
Social skills
Leadership
Basic values and goals
Situational factors

SUMMARY

Cover:
Strengths
Weaknesses

Ask:
What bring to job? What are assets?
What are best talents?
What qualities seen by self or others?
What makes you good investment for employer?

What are shortcomings?
What areas need improvement?
What qualities wish to develop further?
What constructive criticism from others?
How might you be risk for employer?
What further training, or experience, might
    you need?

Look for:
PLUS (+) AND MINUS (−)
Talents, skills
Knowledge
Energy
Motivation
Interests
Personal qualities
Social effectiveness
Character
Situational factors

CLOSING REMARKS

Cover:
Comments regarding interview and applicant
Further contacts to be made
Course of action to be taken
Cordial parting

information provided on each. In this way the lapses and biases of the single interviewer are minimized. A record form that is used by one group of personnel psychologists in training interviewers and for guidance of novice interviewers is shown in Fig. 11.2 on pages 398–399.

The popularity of the interview is *not* based primarily upon its demonstrated validity as a device for appraising people. In fact, evidence for the validity of the impressions or conclusions derived from interviews is spotty and rather contradictory. Interview procedures are basically subjective, variable, and heavily dependent upon the skill of the interviewer. It has been demonstrated repeatedly that different interviewers interviewing the same person come up with quite varied impressions of that person. The variability arises in part from variation in the questions asked and the lines of inquiry intensively pursued. It arises in part from differences in interpretation and evaluation of the responses the interviewee makes. The typical interview is not a precise or efficient psychometric technique. Furthermore, individual interviews place very heavy demands upon the time of interviewing personnel, demands that may be prohibitive in a number of situations. To economize on interviewer time, then, and to provide an inquiry that is uniform in presentation and procedure for evaluation, the printed questionnaire has been developed. The self-report questionnaire or inventory is essentially this: a standard set of questions about some aspect or aspects of the individual's life history, feelings, preferences, or actions, presented in a standard way and scored with a standard scoring key.

The alternative approaches to interrogating an individual have opposite advantages. One trades off the objectivity, reliability, comparability from person to person, and economy provided by the multiple-choice inventory for the flexibility and adaptability to the individual case provided by the interview. A potential user must decide in each situation what compromise of these values is most suited to his needs.

THE BIOGRAPHICAL DATA BLANK

An obvious and important use of the questionnaire is as a means of eliciting factual information about the individual's past history. Place and date of birth, amount and type of education and degree of success with it, nature and duration of previous jobs, hobbies, special skills, and a host of other biographical facts can be determined most economically through a blank filled out by the individual. It is the economy and efficiency of this approach that makes it particularly appealing. Though the reports may be inaccurate in some respects, each individual is probably the richest single repository for such factual personal information.

The problems in using questionnaires to elicit facts are primarily problems of communication. When questions are preformulated and appear in printed form and answers are written down, misunderstanding may occur either in the respondent's interpretation of the question or in the using agency's interpretation of the response. If there is no personal interaction, these misunderstandings cannot be cleared up with an oral question or a further probing into the area of uncertainty. It is important, therefore, that a fact-finding questionnaire be very carefully worded and that it be tried out in preliminary form with small groups to make sure that the ambiguities have been cleared out of it.

An interview to supplement the questionnaire may be desirable in order to permit clarification of any of the responses to questionnaire items that are puzzling to the user or to get fuller information on some points. As a matter of fact, one appropriate use of self-report inventories of all types is to provide a jumping-off place for an interview, the questionnaire providing leads that may be followed up in the interview.

Sometimes the factual information on an application blank has been used to determine whether the applicant meets certain specified minimum requirements for a job; that is, is 21 years of age, has a valid driver's license, and so on. Sometimes it is used as part of the raw material available to a personnel officer, director of admissions, or scholarship committee, on the basis of which a clinical decision is made as to the individual's desirability as an employee or a student. Increasingly in recent years biographical data blanks have been analyzed item by item and empirical keys have been developed to predict some criterion of job or life performance.

Thus a study (McGrath, 1960) of the application blanks and purchase contracts of samples of new car buyers identified 24 items that discriminated between those who completed payments for their cars and those who had the cars repossessed. When the scoring key developed on one sample of cases was applied to a new second sample, score correlated approximately 0.50 with completion of payments in the new sample. Loughmiller and others (1973) reported cross-validated validities of approximately .40 for a biographical data key as a predictor of a composite criterion of success as a medical practitioner. Other situations to which empirical weighting of the items in an application blank or a biographical inventory have recently been applied with promising results are in the prediction of creativity in adolescents (Schaefer and Anastasi, 1968) and in scientists (Buel et al., 1966), of job turnover in unskilled (Scott and Johnson, 1967) and clerical (Buel, 1964) employees, and of sales, research, and general engineering interest (Chaney and Owens, 1964). Thus, the procedure appears to have promise in quite a range of practical situations. Determination of the proper scoring weights is a fairly major research undertaking (England, 1961), but once a scoring system has been developed the scoring of individual blanks proceeds rapidly. If the number of applicants justifies doing so, it is even possible to prepare biographical data blanks in multiple-choice form with separate answer sheets and to score these by machine as one would any standard test.

INTEREST INVENTORIES

Questions that almost every person has asked at some time or other are, What kind of a job shall I plan for? What kind of a work career will be most suitable for me? To answer that question we need to know not only what kind of work a person will be *able* to do well, but also what kind of work that person will find interesting and personally satisfying. Will it be the work of a TV repairman or that of a bank teller? That of a department store salesperson or that of a service station attendant? That of a lawyer, or that of a physician? This information may be of concern to an employer, who wants an employee who will be stable and satisfied in the job. It is certainly of importance to the person entering the world of work, for whom a career in which he or she can find satisfaction and pleasure is one of life's major concerns.

It is for this reason that the development of inventories to assess interests and values has been a major preoccupation of a number of testing and personnel psychologists. You might ask, Well, if you want to know what job Susie or Peter would find interesting, why don't you just ask them? And of course a certain amount of information can be obtained by this head-on attack. But there are many occupations that Susie or Peter may never have thought about, so that they have never formulated an expression of interest in them. And there are many jobs, perhaps most jobs, concerning which they have only the sketchiest of impressions of what the job entails—what tasks are done and under what circumstances. It is for these reasons that a more indirect approach seems attractive.

In the inventory approach, quite a series of statements is presented the examinee, naming jobs, activities, and situations, and the examinee indicates preferences between or liking for one or more of the choices. Response typically takes one of two contrasting forms—a categorical response of liking, indifference, or dislike, or a choice between alternative situations or activities. Items illustrating the format of five of the better known and more widely distributed inventory series (but not drawn from the actual content) are shown below.

EXAMPLES

Strong Vocational Interest Blank (399 items) and *Strong-Campbell Interest Inventory* (325 items)

Occupations:

	L (Like)	I (Indifferent)	D (Dislike)
Electrician			
School subjects:			
Astronomy	L	I	D
Amusements:			
Bowling	L	I	D
Activities:			
Watching sports telecasts	L	I	D

Ohio Vocational Interest Survey (280 items)*

Prepare food in a restaurant	D	d	n	l	L
Drive a large truck	D	d	n	l	L
Answer letters in an office	D	d	n	l	L
Teach young children	D	d	n	l	L

Holland Vocational Preference Inventory (160 items)

Athletic coach	Yes	No
Forester	Yes	No
Physician	Yes	No
Janitor	Yes	No

*D = Dislike very much   d = dislike   n = neutral   l = like
L = like very much

Minnesota Vocational Interest Inventory (158 sets)*

	L	D
Put up kitchen shelves	0	0
Spade up a garden	0	0
Hang wallpaper	0	0
Drive a big truck	0	0
Drive a taxi	0	0
Drive a garden tractor	0	0

*L = like most   D = like least

Kuder Occupational Interest Survey (100 sets) and *Kuder Preference Record (Vocational)* (168 sets)*

	Most	Least
Repair a car's engine	M	L
Calculate batting averages	M	L
Sell magazines door-to-door	M	L
Sing in a choral group	M	L
Do volunteer work in a hospital	M	L
Camp out in the woods	M	L

*M = like most   L = like least

In the first three patterns of responding illustrated, the examinee responds to each item individually, recording a positive, negative, or (in the first two) neutral response to that item. In the last two patterns he ranks the three options in a set, marking the most and least liked and thus indicating that the other alternative falls in the middle. The *forced choice* pattern of the last two patterns has appealed to some test makers because it evens out any "yes-saying" tendency—that is, an orientation that might lead some test takers to set a very low standard for indicating liking for an activity and others to set a considerably more severe personal standard. Such a tendency has been called a *response set;* an *acquiescence set* is one of a number of stylistic patterns that may distort the meaning of inventory responses.

However, the forced-choice type of item has its own limitations. Since every person *must* make the same number of choices and rejections, the procedure washes out any *real* differences between persons in range and degree of interests, so that each person must have as many lows as highs and any genuine differences in general level of enthusiasm are lost. The relationships among the several scores tend also to be distorted, since the forced pattern of choosing means that for every interest area chosen some other area must be rejected. The result is that the average correlation among scores for such a forced-choice instrument must be negative (approximately $-1/(n-1)$, where n is the number of different scales on the instrument).

STRONG-CAMPBELL INTEREST INVENTORY

We shall now describe in some detail the *Strong-Campbell Interest Inventory,* since it is the most recent member of a family of inventories that goes back to the 1920s and has been the subject of almost 50 years of research. We shall indicate how the *Strong-Campbell* differs from Strong's earlier version of the interest inventory, and later we shall compare other current inventories with the *Strong-Campbell.*

As indicated on p. 403, the *Strong-Campbell* is composed of 325 items referring to occupations, school subjects, activities, amusements, types of people, and so forth, for which the examinee expresses liking, indifference, or dislike. The type of score that is most characteristic of the Strong series of inventories is one that indicates the degree to which a person is similar, in his interests, to persons in a particular occupation.

In order to establish the scoring key for an occupation, Strong (and subsequently Campbell) compared the responses of persons within an occupation to those of a reference group of persons-in-general. Since the responses of men and women show substantial differences on a number of interest items, the comparisons have been carried out separately for men and for women. That is, male psychologists, for example, have been compared with a group of men-in-general and female psychologists, with a group of women-in-general. The in-general samples were each designed to represent in equal numbers persons from some 50 different occupations.

To illustrate the results, consider the percentages of persons responding "Like" to the two occupations Artist and Farmer. The results were approximately as follows.

	Artist	**Farmer**
Female psychologists	76%	24%
Women in general	59	24
Male psychologists	55	23
Men in general	41	30

For the occupation Artist there is a considerably greater percentage of psychologists than of persons-in-general marking "Like," and this is true for both women and men. Thus this response would be scored $+1$ for the psychologist key in both sexes. The item Farmer does not show much differentiation for either sex, and would probably be scored 0 in both cases. If it were to be given a weight for men, the weight would be -1, since fewer male psychologists chose this response. Each response (L, I, D) to each item is examined in this way, and a weight assigned ($+1$, 0, or -1). The total score on the Psychologist key is the sum of the item responses. A raw score is obtained in this way for each of the occupations for which a key has been developed, with separate keys prepared for women and for men. To produce directly comparable scores for the different occupations, a standard score conversion has been set up, based on the sample of persons in the specific occupation, such that the mean for that sample is 50 and the standard deviation is 10.

Interpretation is based on the standard scores. In general, a score of 45 or over is considered "similar" to those in the occupation, since it falls well within the score distribution of members of the occupation. A score of 25 or less is considered "dissimilar," since a score this low would be very rare for a person in the defining group of occupation members. Scores from 26 to 44 are viewed as rather uninformative, since they are neither clearly similar to nor distinctly different from those received by the group in the occupation.

Scores are provided for 57 female groups and 67 male groups, but not always for the same occupation. (It is still hardly possible to assemble an adequate female sample of merchant marine officers or an adequate male sample of home economics teachers.) Members of each sex are scored for all 124 scoring keys, but primary attention is paid to the like-sexed keys in interpreting the score profile. Illustrated in Table 11.1 is the profile of high and of very low scores for Susan Snow, a registered nurse who was training to become a rehabilitation counselor.

It is, of course, possible to look at the scores for single scales and to note, for example, that Susan's greatest similarity is to female social workers and that a counselor scale is in the high group. We also note that registered nurse is not one of the high group for Susan. It is perhaps at least as informative to look at the complete set of high and low scores, especially for the own-sex group. Thus most of the high-scoring scales for Susan are for occupations that involve working with words or people, of-

Table 11.1
STRONG-CAMPBELL OCCUPATIONAL PROFILE FOR SUSAN SNOW

Female Scales			Male Scales		
Occupation	Occupational Theme*	Score	Occupation	Occupational Theme*	Score
Similar to:					
Social worker	(S)	63	Speech pathologist	(IS)	57
Social science teacher	(SEC)	55	Lawyer	(E)	55
YMCA staff worker	(SE)	53	Social worker	(S)	53
Speech pathologist	(IS)	51	Librarian	(A)	50
Librarian	(A)	49	Elementary teacher	(SEA)	49
Secondary guidance counselor	(SCE)	49	English teacher	(AS)	49
English teacher	(AS)	47	Musician	(A)	49
Language teacher	(A)	47	Priest	(S)	48
			Advertising executive	(A)	46
			Chamber of Commerce executive	(ES)	45
			Social science teacher	(SEC)	45
Very Dissimilar to:					
Veterinarian	(I)	14	Navy officer	(RI)	14
Art teacher	(A)	13	Police officer	(RES)	12
Medical technician	(IR)	12	Veterinarian	(RI)	10
Engineer	(IR)	11	Architect	(ARI)	9
Instrument assembler	(RC)	10	Forester	(RI)	8
Mathematician	(I)	10	Math-Science teacher	(IRS)	8
Chemist	(IR)	4	Farmer	(RC)	6
Physicist	(I)	− 2	Agribusiness manager	(ERC)	5
			Highway patrol officer	(RE)	0
			Skilled craftsman	(R)	0
			Vocational agriculture teacher	(RCE)	− 3

* The letters in parentheses represent the vertices of Campbell's *General Occupational Theme* scales shown in the diagram on p. 408.

ten both. Low-scoring scales tend in many cases to involve science or the outdoors, or both. We can speculate that a basis for initiating steps to move out of nursing into counseling is Susan's orientation toward verbal-social rather than toward scientific-concrete occupations.

The *Strong-Campbell Inventory* has added two types of scale that were not included in the original *Strong Vocational Interest Blank*. The first of these are called *General Occupational Theme Scales*. They stem basically from a conception of interests and personality developed by Holland (1966). The 6 scales are thought to be representable in the form of a hexagon, as shown below.

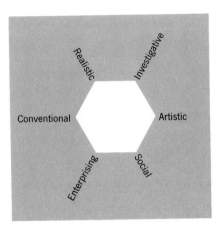

Vertices that are adjacent are thought to express compatible or related interests, and opposite vertices to represent incompatible interests. Each theme is described not only by the occupations that appear to relate to it, but also by a set of adjectives that are thought to be typical of a person in whom that theme is predominant. Thus a person high on the Realistic theme is described as "robust, rugged, practical, and physically strong . . . stable, natural and persistent . . ." The person is said to have conventional political and economic goals; rarely to perform creatively in the arts or sciences; and to like to build things with tools.

Susan Snow's standard scores on the general themes are reported and interpreted as follows.

Theme	Standard Score	Interpretation
Realistic	38	Moderately low
Investigative	46	Average
Artistic	57	Average
Social	55	Moderately high
Enterprising	51	Average
Conventional	41	Moderately low

Campbell has classified the specific occupational scales under one or more of the general occupational themes, and the theme or themes are indicated in the profile by the capital letters in parentheses. The 4 female occupational scales on which Susan scored highest are all classified as having a social theme (sometimes in combination with others), while 5 of her 6 lowest involve the investigative and 4 of 6 the realistic theme. Thus the general themes do tend to bear out the impression gained earlier from an inspection of the specific scales on which high and low scores were obtained. They provide a general framework within which the more specific information of the occupational scales can be organized.

Finally, the *Strong-Campbell Inventory* provides what are called *Basic Interest Scales*. These are scores based on small clusters of items in which the items correlate fairly substantially with each other and appear to share common manifest content. The nature of the scales can be made clearer by listing them, showing Susan Snow's standard scores on each scale, and the interpretive statement that would accompany that score. The results were as shown in Table 11.2.

For Susan, these scores add little that is new. They do perhaps give a somewhat better sense of the content that contributes to her high and low scores for specific occupations. Thus

Table 11.2
STANDARD SCORES FOR INDIVIDUAL SCALES FOR SUSAN SNOW

Scale	Standard Score	Interpretation
Agriculture	39	Rather low
Nature	40	Rather low
Adventure	48	Average
Military	45	Average
Mechanical	37	Rather low
Science	40	Rather low
Mathematics	39	Rather low
Medical Science	44	Average
Medical Service	52	Average
Music/Dramatics	59	Average
Art	50	Average
Writing	56	Average
Teaching	60	Rather high
Social Service	63	Rather high
Athletics	45	Average
Domestic Arts	61	Average
Religious	54	Average
Public Speaking	53	Average
Law/Politics	58	Rather high
Merchandising	51	Average
Sales	50	Average
Business Management	52	Average
Office Practices	40	Rather low

her high social worker standard score certainly stems in part from her rather high standing on social service activities and perhaps from her rather high interest in teaching. It is probably reinforced by her below average interest in agriculture and mechanics, since these are not activities that are likely to appeal to social workers as a group. Some examinees will show more dramatic peaks and hollows in their response to specific content areas. We will see more systematic development of homogeneous area scales when we turn presently to the *Kuder Preference Record.*

A few collateral scores are also reported in the *Strong-Campbell* that permit a check upon accuracy and style of responding or that give supplemental information about the examinee.

KUDER PREFERENCE RECORD, VOCATIONAL

An interest inventory that contrasts rather sharply with Strong's series of instruments is the *Kuder Preference Record, Vocational.* The difference in type of item has already been noted on pp. 404–405. At this point we must consider the difference in type of score derived from the items.

Whereas in the original *Strong* item weights were determined solely on the basis of the item's ability to differentiate a particular occupational group from men-in-general, Kuder selected items that defined a particular area of interest, such as mechanical, clerical, or persuasive. An item was selected in part on the basis of its content and in part from the statistical evidence that it did correlate with an appropriate cluster of related items. In this way 10 content-related and statistically cohesive scales were developed. Table 11.3 gives the designation of the scales, and shows the profiles of group averages for four occupational groups. Thus male psychologists were notably high on the *Scientific* and *Literary* scales, and low on the *Persuasive* scale. Their lowest scale was the highest for insurance salesmen. Female physicians were high on *Scientific* and *Outdoor* interests and very low in *Clerical* interest. Not all groups showed clearly differentiated patterns; thus female bookkeepers and cashiers had no really low interest areas, and only a mild elevation for *Computational* interests.

The 10 area scores of the *Kuder* seem somewhat more directly descriptive of a person than do scores on specific occupational scales. To describe a person as high in scientific and outdoor interests and low in clerical and persuasive interests probably communicates a clearer picture of a person than to say the person is high in physician, chemist and forester inter-

Table 11.3
MEAN *KUDER OCCUPATIONAL INTEREST* PERCENTILE RANKS OF PERSONS IN SELECTED OCCUPATIONS

	Men		Women	
Scale	Psychologists	Insurance Salesmen	Physicians	Bookkeepers and Cashiers
Outdoor	*	33	84	*
Mechanical	28	26	77	34
Computational	67	35	47	77
Scientific	84	31	86	45
Persuasive	13	84	22	62
Artistic	56	41	60	55
Literary	84	54	58	61
Musical	52	61	45	65
Social Service	60	52	63	42
Clerical	30	58	11	59

* Data not reported

ests and low in interests for banker, accountant, and life insurance salesman. However, to interpret a *Kuder* profile in specific occupational terms requires a further step that may not be too easy or satisfactory: matching an individual's profile with the typical profile for the occupation in question. Thus in the past the *Kuder Preference Record, Vocational* has often been considered an appropriate exploratory instrument to map out an individual's interests in general terms, and the *Strong* a more focused instrument to examine specific vocational possibilities. With developments in both camps, the distinction in function between the two has become blurred. We see this more clearly as we consider the *Kuder Occupational Interest Survey (KOIS)*.

KUDER OCCUPATIONAL INTEREST SURVEY

With the *KOIS*, Kuder moved into the camp of empirically keyed inventories. The item type was the same triad pattern used for the *Kuder Preference Record* (see p. 404). However, the scores reported could be thought of as the correlation between the individual's choices and the choices that were typical of the criterion group. That is, to the extent that the responses by an examinee were those made frequently by psychologists, that person got a high coefficient for *Psychologist;* and to the extent that he chose responses made rarely by psychologists, the person's coefficient would be low or even negative. In this comparison no reference is made to persons-in-general. For each score, reference is made only to the specific criterion group.

The report form for the *KOIS* shows coefficients for 37 female occupational groups and 75 male occupational groups, 19 female college majors, and 29 male college majors. Counselors are encouraged to pay attention primarily to the high scores, especially those within .06 of the highest for a given counselee. The 10 highest scores in each category are listed by the scoring machine to bring them to the user's attention. The record for a young woman working for an advanced degree in psychological measurement is shown in Table 11.4.

The 10 highest scores show quite a diversity, so perhaps attention should be focused on those above the dotted lines— within .06 of the highest value. It is encouraging that a number of psychological and of quantitative occupations appear among these, providing confirmation of the appropriateness of a quantitative branch of psychology for this young woman. However, the college major scales indicate a breadth of interest extending into languages and social science that suggest a humanist as well as a scientist orientation toward the career field.

Table 11.4
KOIS HIGH SCORES FOR FEMALE MEASUREMENT MAJOR

Occupational Scales, Female Norms		College Major Scales, Female Norms	
Psychologist	.66	Psychology	.61
Psychologist, Clinical	.63	Biological Science	.60
Computer Programmer	.61	English	.59
Social Worker, Psychiatric	.59	Foreign Language	.58
Social Case Worker	.57	History	.55
Bookstore Manager	.55	Health Professions	.52
Physical Therapist	.54	Mathematics	.52
Social Worker, Medical	.54	General Social Science	.51
Science Teacher, HS	.53	Elementary Education	.50
Social Worker, School	.53	Political Science	.50

Occupational Scales, Male Norms		College Major Scales, Male Norms	
Psychology Professor	.60	English	.58
Psychiatrist	.59	Foreign Language	.58
Psychologist, Clinical	.59	Biological Science	.54
Mathematician	.58	Physical Science	.51
Pediatrician	.58	Psychology	.51
Chemist	.54	Art and Art Education	.49
Computer Programmer	.54	Music and Music Education	.49
Librarian	.54	Sociology	.49
Statistician	.54	Elementary Education	.47
Psychologist, Counseling	.53	History	.47

To some users the *KOIS* has seemed less discriminating than the *Strong Inventory*. This is because the *Strong* focuses on what is *different* in the interests of a particular occupational group, what distinguishes them from other groups and from persons in general. By contrast, the *KOIS* deals only with similarities, and since people in a wide range of jobs have a good deal in common, the scores received for quite different occupations are often quite similar.

One other empirically keyed inventory is the *Minnesota Vocational Interest Inventory*. Since tests of the *Strong* series had been developed primarily for counseling with college students, and had focused on business and professional occupations, a need was felt for an inventory directed specifically at the skilled trades; the distinctive feature of the *MVII* is that it is focused on blue-collar jobs. Keys have been developed to differentiate specific trades from tradesmen in general, following in general the technique used by Strong. However, items are of the forced-choice format (see p. 404). The test is reasonably effective in differentiating groups already in different trades, but data on the predictive effectiveness of the *MVII* are rather limited.

Finally, mention may be made of the *Ohio Vocational Interest Survey* (see items on p. 403). This is an instrument designed for use in high school, and is based on the rationale that occupations can be classified in terms of the level (high, moderate, low) at which they require activities involving data, persons, and things.* Items have been developed to exemplify each of the possible combinations of these categories. For example, teaching, counseling, and social work are thought to represent the top level of demand for working with data and people, but the lowest level for working with things. Each of 24 occupational clusters is represented in the inventory by a set of 11 items, and the student receives a percentile score based on responses to the set. A consistency-of-response index for the set is also reported.

RELIABILITY AND VALIDITY OF INVENTORIED INTERESTS

Scores on most interest inventories are quite stable over short periods of time, such as 2 weeks or a month. Correlations of about .90 are typical of those reported in the manuals for both the *Strong* and the *Kuder* series.

---

* Three levels of each category produce 27 possible combinations $(3 \times 3 \times 3)$, but only some of these were considered to be represented in the world of work.

For the *SVIB* there is evidence (Mallinson and Crumrine, 1952; Strong, 1943, 1951, 1952) that interests show a good deal of stability over time, at least in adolescents and adults. Data on the average correlation at different ages and over different periods may be summarized as follows.

	Upper Elementary School	High School	College Freshmen	College Seniors
1 or 2 years	.55	.65	.80	.....
3 to 5 years	.30	.....	.75	.75
6 to 10 years	.....	.50	.55	.70

The stability is low in the elementary school, but for persons of college age stability compares favorably with that for tests of general cognitive ability.

In appraising the validity of an interest inventory as a *description* of how the individual feels about activities and events in the world about him, the main issue is the truthfulness of his responses. There isn't really any higher court of appeal for determining a person's likes and preferences than the individual's own statement.

A number of studies have indicated that inventories such as the *Strong can* be faked (Garry, 1953; Longstaff, 1948). If a group of examinees is told to try to respond the way that life insurance salesmen would, they are generally rather successful in making themselves appear like life insurance salesmen. However, this is not an indication that the blank *will* be faked, even when used as an employment device.

When the inventory is used for counseling and to help the respondent, as is most often the case, there is probably little reason to anticipate intentional faking. The individual may be expected to report his likes and dislikes as he knows them. Self-knowledge is often imperfect, so reports may be inaccurate in some respects. Thus, we may say that we would like to attend symphony concerts because of a feeling that that is the thing to say, but our actions may belie this statement; we may in fact listen only to country and western music. This lack of self-insight is a real problem. But it is probably mitigated somewhat in the inventory approach to interests, where isolated points of poor insight will have only minor effects upon a final score.

The validity of interest inventories as predictors of later behavior is another matter. Scoring keys for the *Strong* were established by comparing persons who were already in an occupation with persons-in-general. Occupational interest profiles for the *Kuder Preference Record* have also been prepared by determining the average level in each of the interest areas for individuals already working in the occupation. But the common interest patterns of individuals in a field of work may have grown out of their work. The workers may have come to exhibit certain common patterns from the very nature of their work experience. The crucial evidence on predictive validity would come from testing a group *before* it entered the world of work and determining whether those who later entered and continued in a particular occupation had shown distinctive interest patterns *before* they entered the occupation. This is an expensive operation, expensive in the time that must elapse before persons can become settled in their occupation and expensive in the dissipation of cases among literally hundreds of occupations.

Strong (1951) was able to follow some groups who were tested as college undergraduates and obtained some evidence on the extent to which students with interests characteristic of a particular occupation tended to enter that occupation and to persist in it. The occupation in which the typical individual was actually working 10 years later ranked second or third for that person among all the scales of the *Strong*. Considering group averages, those who remained in an occupation had received higher interest scores for that occupation than for any other occupation, and higher scores than those who switched to some other occupation.

Berdie (1965) located the twelfth grade *SVIB* records of students who had completed specialized professional programs at the University of Minnesota. Percentages showing high interest (standard scores of 40 or above) on each of four scales are shown below in relation to the professional training completed.

High Interest on Scale for	Completed Training in			
	Medicine	Law	Accounting	Mechanical Engineering
Physician	49	2	6	21
Lawyer	18	50	18	2
Accountant	5	19	43	6
Engineer	33	0	15	73

Although the relationship falls well short of perfection, it is clear and striking and the discrimination among the groups is quite sharp.

McCully (1954) followed up a group of men who had been given the *Kuder Preference Record* as a part of Veterans' Administration counseling at the end of World War II. They were located several years later, and their occupation determined. Table 11.5 shows the average standard scores on each of the 10 *Kuder* interest areas for those occupational groups that were large enough to justify study. The results show clear-cut and fairly substantial differences in pattern of interest for different occupations. Thus evidence with respect to both the *Strong* and the *Kuder* indicates that they have a certain amount of validity as predictors of occupational choice.

INTEREST AND ABIL

It is important not to confuse measures of interest and ability. Interest measures tell us nothing directly about ability and, generally speaking, the relationships between interests and abilities are quite low. A representative set of correlations is shown in Table 11.6. Correlations of .20 or more are shown in boldface type; there are only six correlations as great as .20 and only one over .30. Highest correlation is between verbal ability and literary interest, next is between spatial ability and artistic interest, and third is between numerical ability and computational interest. The correlations all make sense, but they are also all quite modest in size. Interest measures and ability measures deal with two distinct aspects of fitness for a field of study or work. Each provides information that supplements the other. Interest is not a substitute for ability, and, conversely, ability to learn the skills of a job is no guarantee of survival or satisfaction in the job.

Standardized interest inventories have been developed primarily for their contribution to vocational counseling and job placement. With this purpose in mind, they are directed at groups of high school age or older. The *Kuder*, with its relatively general interest areas, has been used satisfactorily at about the ninth grade and above. The *Strong*, focusing on specific occupations and with a particular emphasis upon occupations at the professional level, is suitable primarily for senior high school pupils with definite plans to go to college, and for college groups. As in almost all inventories, these instruments involve a good deal of reading. Their use with individuals who fall below eighth or ninth grade reading level would probably present serious problems.

Table 11.5

MEAN *KUDER* STANDARD SCORES OF DIFFERENT OCCUPATIONAL GROUPS*

	Mechani-cal	Computa-tional	Scientific	Per-suasive	Artistic	Literary	Musical	Social Service	Clerical
Accounting and related	**−78**	**152**	−32	37	**−82**	19	2	−14	**118**
Engineering and related	**56**	45	**82**	−16	7	1	−21	−46	−41
Managerial work	−28	44	−18	**56**	−27	19	−15	−2	42
Clerical—computing and recording	−27	**67**	−9	9	−50	4	3	−14	**68**
General clerical work	−19	−3	−31	−9	−14	22	3	17	30
Sales—higher	−65	−14	−40	**111**	**−54**	38	17	18	30
Sales—lower	−19	−12	−25	**79**	−32	10	6	15	16
General farming	22	−25	−16	−37	−4	−49	−42	12	−10
Mechanical repairing	**81**	−21	3	−40	28	−28	−30	−40	−29
Electrical repairing	**66**	−3	27	−35	5	−41	−13	−19	−29
Bench crafts (fine)	**63**	−5	12	−24	38	−23	−20	−33	−2

* Based on a mean of 0 and a standard deviation of 100 for the reference group of 2,797 employed veterans. Means greater than ½ standard deviation are shown in bold type.

Table 11.6
CORRELATION OF APTITUDE AND INTEREST FACTORS*

Kuder Interest Scale	General Aptitude Test Battery Factor								
	General Intel-ligence	Verbal	Numer-ical	Spatial	Form Per-ception	Clerical Per-ception	Motor Coordi-nation	Finger Dexterity	Manual Dexterity
Outdoor	.01	−.07	−.04	.11	−.04	**−.20**	−.19	−.04	−.04
Mechanical	−.02	−.06	−.04	.19	−.02	−.12	−.11	.08	.06
Computational	.14	.06	**.25**	.12	.10	.15	.07	.03	.12
Scientific	.16	.10	.10	.12	.04	−.02	−.03	.10	.04
Persuasive	−.12	−.07	.01	−.16	−.11	.06	.07	−.08	.02
Artistic	.10	.07	−.10	**.26**	.07	−.04	.04	.12	.04
Literary	.14	**.32**	.04	.00	.02	.06	.05	−.07	.00
Musical	−.02	.06	−.08	.04	−.05	.04	.07	.00	−.11
Social Service	−.10	−.09	.04	**−.20**	.06	.04	−.01	−.04	−.04
Clerical	**−.24**	−.14	.06	−.18	−.02	.08	.00	−.02	.00

* Adapted from the *Manual* of the *General Aptitude Test Battery.*

Self-report inventories have been extensively developed in the areas of temperament and personal adjustment. In these areas we again encounter instruments developed to yield scores for internally consistent clusters of behaviors, as in the *Kuder Preference Record,* and instruments built with keys based on reference to some external criterion, as in the *Strong Vocational Interest Blank.*

The basic material of all temperament questionnaires is much the same. They draw from an extensive catalogue of statements about actions and feelings. To these the individual responds by indicating whether each is or is not characteristic of him. In many cases, a "?" or "uncertain" category is provided for a person who does not wish to endorse an unequivocal "Yes" or "No" answer. In the case of adjustment questionnaires, questions are culled from case studies, writings on various types of adjustment problem, suggestions of psychiatrists, and similar sources. For the normal dimensions of temperament, a review of psychological and literary treatments of personality differences and a systematic scrutiny of previous questionnaires, together with the personal insights of the investigator, provide the raw material for assembling items.

There are a large number of temperament and adjustment inventories. We shall describe three in some detail, illustrating distinctively different patterns. These are the *Guilford-Zimmerman Temperament Survey,* the *Minnesota Multiphasic Personality Inventory (MMPI),* and the *Thorndike Dimensions of Temperament (TDOT).* Then we shall undertake a more general evaluation of the validity of inventories in this area and of the conditions under which one may expect them to be of value.

THE GUILFORD-ZIMMERMAN TEMPERAMENT SURVEY

The *Guilford-Zimmerman Temperament Survey* was the final development in a series of instruments on which Guilford worked, each of which has attempted to identify and measure a number of internally coherent dimensions of personality that are clearly distinct from one another. Guilford started with a pool of items and studied the intercorrelations among them, using the methods of factor analysis referred to on p. 352. He identified distinct personality factors, or *foci,* and tried to build up clusters of items to measure each. The objective was to get separate scales that were internally coherent and relatively independent of other scales. Thus, if a factor of "sociability" were identified, the attempt would be to get a cluster of items focusing on "sociability" that correlated substantially with each other, so that the person who subscribed to one item also would be likely to subscribe to others. This cluster should be quite distinct from other clusters relating to "dominance," "impulsiveness," and so forth, so that the correlations between the different clusters would be quite low. This is the same basic approach as the one used for the *Kuder Preference Record.*

The *Guilford-Zimmerman* inventory provides scores appraising the clusters named and characterized below. Each cluster is characterized both by descriptive phrases and by two illustrative items.*

General Activity. A high score indicates rapid pace of activities; energy, vitality; keeping in motion; production, efficiency, liking for speed; hurrying; quickness of action; enthusiasm, liveliness.

EXAMPLES

You start to work on a new project with a great deal of enthusiasm. (+)
You are the kind of person who is "on the go" all of the time. (+)

Restraint. A high score indicates serious mindedness; deliberateness; persistent effort; self-control; *not* being happy-go-lucky or carefree; *not* seeking excitement.

EXAMPLES

You like to play practical jokes upon others. (−)
You sometimes find yourself "crossing bridges before you come to them." (+)

Ascendance. A high score indicates habits of leadership; a tendency to take the initiative in speaking with others; liking for speaking in public; liking for persuading others; liking for being conspicuous; tendency to bluff; tendency to be self-defensive.

EXAMPLES

You can think of a good excuse when you need one. (+)
You avoid arguing over a price with a clerk or salesman. (−)

* Reproduced by permission of the Sheridan Psychological Services, Inc.

Sociability. A high score indicates one who has many friends and acquaintances; who seeks social contacts; who likes social activities; who likes the limelight; who enters into conversations; who is *not* shy.

EXAMPLES

You would dislike very much to work alone in some isolated place. (+)

Shyness keeps you from being as popular as you should be. (−)

Emotional Stability. A person with a high score shows evenness of moods, interests, etc.; optimism, cheerfulness; composure; feelings of being in good health; *freedom from* feelings of guilt, worry, or loneliness; *freedom from* day dreaming; *freedom from* perseveration of ideas and moods.

EXAMPLES

You sometimes feel "just miserable" for no good reason at all. (−)

You seldom give your past mistakes a second thought. (+)

Objectivity. The high scorer is defined as *free from* the following: egoism, self-centeredness; suspiciousness, fancying hostility; ideas of reference; a tendency to get into trouble; a tendency to be thin-sknned.

EXAMPLES

You nearly always receive all the credit that is coming to you for things you do. (+)

There are times when it seems everyone is against you. (−)

Friendliness. High scores signify respect for others; acceptance of domination; toleration of hostile action; *freedom from* hostility, resentment, or desire to dominate.

EXAMPLES

When you resent the actions of anyone, you promptly tell him so. (−)

You would like to tell certain people a thing or two. (−)

Thoughtfulness. The high-scoring person is characterized as reflective, meditative; observing of his own behavior and that of others; interested in thinking; philosophically inclined; mentally poised.

EXAMPLES

You are frequently "lost in thought." (+)

You find it very interesting to watch people to see what they will do. (+)

Personal relations..   High scores signify tolerance of people; faith in social institutions; *freedom from* self-pity or suspicion of others.

EXAMPLES

There are far too many useless laws that hamper an individual's personal freedom. (−)

Nearly all people try to do the right thing when given a chance. (+)

Masculinity.   The high-scoring person is interested in masculine activities; not easily disgusted; hardboiled; inhibited in emotional expression; resistant to fear; unconcerned about vermin; little interested in clothes, style, or romance.

EXAMPLES

You can look at snakes without shuddering. (+)

The sight of ragged or soiled fingernails is repulsive to you. (−)

Since each of these clusters can be thought of as a dimension having two ends; just as we have north and south, east and west, there is an opposite end of each dimension that can be characterized as just the reverse of the description given above. Items marked (−) characterize this opposite end. Of course, most people do not score at either extreme on these dimensions. Here, as elsewhere, a continuous range of variation, with most people occupying an intermediate position, is the characteristic pattern. Most people are neither outstandingly active nor conspicuously lethargic, neither clearly ascendant nor clearly submissive. People can rarely be well described by clear-cut personality *types*. They are better described as showing different *traits* in varying *degrees*.

Choosing the names for the clusters presented above was a bit of a problem, because the clusters do not correspond exactly to the language labels we bring with us. Each cluster is defined by the items that went into it and that were grouped together because they actually went together in the responses of people taking the inventory. The titles are approximate. Each cluster can be understood more exactly only by a close study of the items of which it is composed.

Table 11.7 shows the reliabilities of the separate scores and the intercorrelations of the scores. The reliabilities cluster about .80 and are adequate, though not strikingly high. The attempt, in developing this inventory, was to identify a number of relatively independent aspects of personality. This means that the correlations of the different scores *should* be low. They tend to be. However, certain of the scores show rather substantial correlations. Attention may be directed to *Ascendance* and *Sociability, Emotional Stability* and *Objectivity, Friendliness* and *Personal Relations,* and *Restraint* and *Thoughtfulness.* These pairs of scores are far from independent, and the information provided by the scores is overlapping. In a sense the inventory is only partially efficient because of the duplication in the different scores. It is as if we were in part saying the same thing over again. In most cases, however, each score provides information about a new and distinctive aspect of the individual.

The *Guilford-Zimmerman Inventory* has several characteristics that it may be well to summarize at this time.

1. It is based upon the responses of normal everyday people, not of the overtly maladjusted or the institutionalized.

2. Its scales are set up by internal analysis, by study of the "going together" of groups of items.

3. Responses are taken at face value. Their significance is assumed to be given by their obvious content.

4. The respondent may endorse as many or as few of the items as he wishes; his choices are not forced or constrained.

Table 11.7

INTERCORRELATIONS AND RELIABILITIES OF THE 10 SCALES OF THE *GUILFORD-ZIMMERMAN TEMPERAMENT SURVEY**

| Scale | Intercorrelations | | | | | | | | | Relia- |
	2	3	4	5	6	7	8	9	10	bility†
1. *General Activity*	−.16	.34	.35	.34	.14	−.17	.24	−.03	.30	.79
2. *Restraint*		−.08	−.21	.08	.05	.25	.42	.14	−.01	.80
3. *Ascendance*			.61	.35	.41	−.25	−.19	−.04	.29	.82
4. *Sociability*				.23	.36	−.06	.04	.18	.21	.87
5. *Emotional Stability*					.69	.37	−.13	.34	.37	.84
6. *Objectivity*						.34	−.04	.43	.32	.75
7. *Friendliness*							−.03	.50	.26	.75
8. *Thoughtfulness*								.22	−12	.80
9. *Personal Relations*									.35	.80
10. *Masculinity*										.85

* Reproduced by permission of the Sheridan Supply Company.
† Kuder-Richardson formula, based on 912 college students.

424
questionnaires
and inventories
for self-
appraisal

THE MINNESOTA MULTIPHASIC
PERSONALITY INVENTORY

By contrast, let us consider the *Minnesota Multiphasic Personality Inventory,* which differs radically with respect to the first three characteristics from the *Guilford-Zimmerman Temperament Survey.* The *Minnesota Multiphasic Personality Inventory* was originally developed as a tool for studying individuals suspected of exhibiting some degree of psychopathology. With this objective, a pool of items was assembled from statements appearing in books on psychiatry and abnormal psychology and from case-study records. The attempt was to make the array of statements about symptoms, actions, and attitudes comprehensive, including all that seemed at all promising as indicators of personality malfunctioning. The items were tried out on a group of "normals" and on a number of hospitalized groups selected as representing specific patterns of maladjustment. The process of developing scoring keys was basically the same as that for the *Strong Vocational Interest Blank;* that is, the items in a given key were those that differentiated a particular pathological group from the group of "normal" people-in-general. Nine clinical scales were developed in this way, and, supplemented by a *Social Introversion* scale, these nine provide the basic score profile for the test.

The scale labels, and the types of group upon which they were originally based, are presented briefly below.

1. *Hypochondriasis (Hs).* Individuals showing excessive worry about health, often accompanied by reports of obscure pains and disorders.

2. *Depression (D).* Individuals suffering from chronic depression, feelings of uselessness and inability to face the future.

3. *Hysteria (Hy).* Individuals who have reacted to personal problems by developing physical symptoms such as paralysis, cramps, gastric complaints, or cardiac symptoms.

4. *Psychopathic Deviate (Pd).* Persons showing lack of deep emotional response, irresponsibility, and disregard of social pressures and the regard of others.

5. *Paranoia (Pa).* Persons tending to be excessively suspicious and sensitive, with feelings of being picked on or persecuted.

6. *Psychasthenia (Pt).* Patients troubled with excessive fears (phobias) and compulsive tendencies to dwell on certain ideas or perform certain acts.

7. *Schizophrenia (Sc).* Patients characterized by bizarre and unusual thought or behavior, and a subjective life tending to be divorced from the world of reality.

8. *Hypomania (Ma).* Persons tending to be physically and mentally overactive, with rapid shift in ideas or actions.

9. *Masculinity-Femininity (Mf).* Persons tending to identify with the opposite sex, rather than their own.

The flavor of the items in the *MMPI* is best conveyed by quoting a sample; the first 5 items in the full set of 555 are quoted below. After each item are listed the code designations of the scales for which the item is keyed. The symbols (+) and (−) tell whether it is the "Yes" or the "No" response that adds into that key.

EXAMPLES*

1. I like mechanics magazines.   *Mf*(−)
2. I have a good appetite.   *Hs*(−), *D*(−), *Hy*(−)
3. I wake up fresh and rested most mornings.   *Hs*(−), *Hy*(−), *Pt*(−)
4. I think I would like the work of a librarian.   *Mf*(+)
5. I am easily awakened by noise.   *D*(+)

Raw scores on the *MMPI* are converted to standard scores with a mean of 50 and a standard deviation of 10. Though all points on an individual's profile are examined, attention tends to be focused particularly on any scores of 70 or over. The profile of a psychiatric patient is shown in Table 11.8 together with the type of interpretive statement that might be elicited† by such a profile. Obviously this is a person with fairly severe adjustment problems.

The *MMPI* was originally developed in the psychiatric hospital, but use of the instrument has spread far beyond those limits. It has been used widely as a screening device for personality problems in colleges, military and governmental groups, and as a research tool in literally hundreds of studies in all sorts of settings.‡ This widespread use of an instrument and a set of

---

† The statements follow those programmed into the computer at the Mayo Clinic and used for computerized interpretation of *MMPI* results.
‡ This is one of the half-dozen most widely studied psychometric devices, and up to 1971, no less than 3,840 theses, articles, and books had appeared using or studying it.

Table 11.8
**MMPI PROFILE AND INTERPRETIVE COMMENTS FOR
PSYCHIATRIC PATIENT**

Scale	Standard Score	Comment
F*	74	Interpret profile with caution. Respondent admits a large number of unusual experiences, feelings, or symptoms. May have significant psychiatric problems. Consider psychiatric evaluation.
K*	50	Neither defensive nor self-derogating.
Hs	82	Great number of chronic physical complaints and preoccupation with bodily functions. Much functional pain, fatigue and weakness likely.
D	89	Severely depressed, worrying, indecisive, and pessimistic.
Hy	79	Probably immature, egocentric, and demanding. Prone to develop circumscribed functional complaints such as headaches or backaches.
Pd	64	Independent or mildly nonconformist.
Mf	71	Probably sensitive and idealistic with high esthetic, cultural, and artistic interests.
Pa	53	Respects opinions of others without undue sensitivity.
Pt	82	Respondent is aware of and concerned about asocial attitudes and emotional impulses but unable to control them.
Sc	87	Probable feelings of unreality, bizarre or confused thinking and conduct. May have strange attitudes and false beliefs.
Ma	43	Low energy and activity level. Difficult to motivate. Apathetic.
Si	83	Introverted, shy, and socially inept.

* See p. 428 for a discussion of these scores.

scales with a basically psychopathological orientation raises serious questions of both a methodological and an ethical nature. We will consider first a number of problems of measurement methodology, and then the ethical issues that arise in the use of an instrument of this type.

Heterogeneity of scoring keys. The empirical procedure, in which items were placed in a particular scoring key if they were responded to differentially by the modest-sized hospitalized clinical group, led to a rather mixed array of items in a number of the scoring keys. Some refer to fairly obvious clinical symptoms, while others, which have been labeled "subtle" items, appear to have nothing to do with the particular pattern of pathology. These two subgroups of items are not only different in apparent nature, but also unrelated (even slightly negatively related) statistically. Thus the items making up a score lack coherence. It seems likely that much of the variation in score among a group such as college students is produced by variations in responding to the "subtle" items, since few of them are likely to ascribe to themselves the more obvious symptoms of pathology. So the scores may represent some quite different aspect of personality in normal groups than is suggested by the pathological criterion groups on which the keys were originally established.

Overlapping of scales. The instrument exhibits a characteristic (which tends to be true of the *Strong Vocational Interest Blank* and other empirically keyed instruments, as well) of extensive overlapping among certain of the scales. Different scales show positive correlations that run as high as .80 (*Sc* with *Pt*). The correlations arise in part because some of the same items are keyed for several scales, in part because items of similar flavor are keyed in different scales; and in part from certain response sets that we shall examine presently. As a result it appears that a large part of what is being measured by the nine regular scales could be accounted for by two or at most three underlying common factors. The complete score profile appears to be a redundant and, perhaps, inefficient way of describing the personality differences that the scales do, in fact, assess.

Response sets. Associated with their obvious pathological reference, many of the items of the *MMPI* have a very low level of desirability as a form of behavior to attribute to oneself. Judges assessing the items are reasonably consistent in rating the different items for social desirability, and these social desirability ratings have a number of interesting correlates. First, social desirability has a very substantial correlation, .86 in one study, with the probability of endorsing the item. The "better" something is generally perceived to be, the more likely people are to say it is true of them. Second, the tendency to mark socially desirable items is itself a reliable individual characteristic. A group of items selected and keyed to yield a social desirability score provides a score that is as stable and dependable as any of the other scores produced by the instrument. Third, this social desirability score shows very substantial correlations (mostly negative) with many of the other scores on the *MMPI*. In part the instrument is measuring the individual's tendency to be self-defensive vs. self-derogatory.

The authors of the test have recognized this problem, and have devised several scales to try to identify either conscious or unconscious distortion of results. There are four such *verification* or *correction* scales.

1. ? The number of items on which the individual refuses to mark either "Yes" or "No," seen as an indication of defensiveness and withdrawal from the test task.

2. L The number of obviously "good" but extremely improbable behaviors that the examinee claims, seen as an indication of rather naïve defensiveness and overclaiming.

3. F The number of very rare and unusual responses that the individual makes, seen as a sign that the respondent may not have understood and followed the directions.

4. K The tendency to choose responses given by clinically identified abnormals who had shown normal profiles on the test, seen as an indicator of subtle defensiveness and tendency to describe oneself in a good, a "socially desirable" light.

However, the problem of dealing with response sets is far from completely solved. It remains a problem in part because it is hard to tell how much of "social desirability" responding represents a relatively superficial response set on the part of the individual, how much represents a more deep-seated defensiveness, and how much represents a completely genuine high level of self-regard.

A corollary response set that has been of some concern on the *MMPI* is one of acquiescence or "yes-saying." The structure of the instrument is such that most of the items are phrased so that a "Yes" answer means endorsing some symptom or behavior as characteristic of oneself. Thus any element of suggestibility, of readiness to agree, would lead to endorsing many symptoms. And, to the extent that the symptoms are preponderantly unfavorable ones, acquiescence would lead to elevated scores on a number of the clinical scales.

In contrast with the *Guilford-Zimmerman*, we note that the *MMPI:*

1. Is based upon the distinctive responses of selected groups of persons—in this case, groups each presenting a particular psychopathology.

2. Has scales that are defined by these abnormal groups.

3. Is not concerned with the apparent meaning of an item, but only with whether it functions—whether it serves to differentiate between the abnormal and the control group.

It thus follows the general pattern of the *Strong Vocational Interest Blank.* In common with the *Guilford-Zimmerman,*

4. It permits any number of items to be endorsed, leaving the respondent free of constraint in this regard.

Let us look now at an inventory that makes use of the forced-choice pattern of response.

This inventory was designed to assess 10 bipolar normal dimensions of temperament that have a good deal in common with those included in the *Guilford-Zimmerman Temperament Survey*. The polarities have been labeled as follows.

1. *Social versus Solitary.*
2. *Ascendant versus Withdrawing.*
3. *Cheerful versus Gloomy.*
4. *Placid versus Irritable.*
5. *Accepting versus Critical.*
6. *Tough-Minded versus Tender-Minded.*
7. *Reflective versus Practical.*
8. *Impulsive versus Planful.*
9. *Active versus Lethargic.*
10. *Responsible versus Casual.*

However, the form of presenting the items is somewhat distinctive.

The basic format consists of 20 sets of 10 items each. In a given set there is one item relating to each of the above 10 polarities. Items were selected in terms of their intercorrelations—high with their own scale and as low as possible with the other nine scales. The items put together in a set have been rather closely matched on popularity, that is, the frequency with which they are chosen by people as being descriptive of them, and consequently may be presumed to be fairly well matched on social desirability. The examinee is instructed to select the 3 items in each set that are *most* descriptive of him and the three that are *least* descriptive. The remaining four may be presumed to be intermediate. The examinee gets a high "sociable" score if he chooses the items expressed in the sociable direction ("I like noisy parties") as most characteristic of him and items stated in the solitary direction ("Sometimes I just have to get away from people") as least characteristic.

Note that the instrument uses a forced-choice format and that the choices are among items matched for popularity. This is intended to minimize the role of any response sets of social desirability or acquiescence.* The sets of 10 items require the

---

* However, individuals instructed to "fake good" *do* still show consistent tendencies to raise or lower specific points in their profile. A "verification" key has been developed (Thorndike, 1968) that will identify 83 percent of "fakers" at a cost of 6 percent of presumably honest responses.

examinee to balance each dimension against all other nine each time he makes a choice, so that each set of choices provides the maximum amount of information. The instrument is not fully ipsative (that is, the 10 scores do not have to add up to the same total for every one), because half the items are stated in terms of one end and half in terms of the other end of the polarity, but the combination of forced-choice form of the item sets and of initially selecting items with low relationships to scales other than their own produces a set of scores with relatively low intercorrelations (of the 45 scale intercorrelations, only 2 for men and 4 for women are as high as .30). Scores show good correlations with self-ratings and modest correlations with ratings by associates. Some groups, such as salesmen, show very distinctive profiles. Other aspects of validity remain, for the most part, still to be investigated.

EVALUATION OF TEMPERAMENT
AND ADJUSTMENT INVENTORIES

How well can one hope to describe termperamental characteristics and personal adjustment through the individual's responses to a series of questions? Perhaps we can clarify the issue by asking what a person must do to fill out an inventory adequately. Completing one of these inventories usually requires that the respondent be (1) able to read and understand the item, (2) able to stand back and view his own behavior and decide whether the statement is or is not true of him, and (3) willing to give frank and honest answers. Each of these points raises certain issues about the validity of self-report instruments.

One problem in inventories of all types is that of *reading load.* This problem is partly one of sheer amount of reading. Especially in inventories that try to appraise a number of different traits, it is usually necessary to have several hundred items to provide enough scope and reliability. The slow reader may have trouble getting through so much verbiage, or may give up and start responding without really reading through the item. In part the problem is one of level of reading, that is, of the complexity of structure and abstractness of ideas involved. If the vocabulary or concepts are beyond the respondent's comprehension, he may again give up the attempt really to understand and may respond in a superficial or random fashion. (The *F* scale of the *MMPI* was designed to protect against this hazard.) Thus inventories are of questionable value for those of low literacy, be they adults or children.

Related to, but somewhat different from the problem of *reading* the items in an inventory is the problem of *interpreting* them. Suppose the question is phrased, "Do you often like to do things by yourself?" The reader may be able to decode this statement perfectly competently, but still have trouble deciding (1) how frequently this type of event has to occur to be "often"; (2) what kinds of "things" are referred to—that is, studying, going walking, going out to dinner; and (3) whether liking implies an active seeking out or a passive acceptance of solitary activity. Variation in interpretation could produce quite a variation of response, and interpretation problems of this sort can arise for highly literate persons as well as for poor readers.

A second problem is that of *self-insight*. Inventories require the individual to conceptualize and classify his own behavior—to decide whether certain descriptions or classifications of behavior are true of him. This implies a certain ability to stand back from himself and view himself objectively that may be difficult to achieve. In fact, the person whose adjustment is most unsatisfactory may be the one who is least able to achieve this objectivity and to face his own deficiencies. Studies have shown repeatedly that those who are rated low by their associates on some desirable trait tend to overrate themselves grossly. Thus an ill-tempered girl is likely not to recognize her own irascibility; an overbearing boy may be unaware of his boorishness.

When inventories are built according to the pattern of the *Strong VIB* or the *MMPI,* such a lack of self-insight may not be of crucial importance. For these inventories the keying of an item is based not on its obvious content but on the empirical fact that it does distinguish between criterion groups. If Rachel has marked that she would like to repair a clock, she has behaved in the way that engineers typically behave. The question of whether engineers on the one hand or Rachel on the other, *really* want to repair a clock is not central to our interpretation. The point is that they have both reacted to the question in the same way, so we give Rachel a credit on the engineer key of the *Strong.* On the other hand, when items and scores are interpreted on the basis of their manifest content and taken at face value, as is true of the *Guilford-Zimmerman* inventory or the *Kuder Preference Record,* noninsightful responses will lead to an untrue picture of the person who makes them.

A third problem is the willingness of the respondent to *reveal* the way he perceives or feels about himself. For personality inventories, frank and honest response by the examinee is es-

sential for a valid picture. In most cases the general significance of the items is reasonably apparent to the reader.
Moderately sophisticated examinees (that is, college upper-
classmen) usually find it possible to "fake good" or "fake bad"
on self-descriptive inventories (Yonge and Heist, 1965), though
they seem to be less able to simulate a particular pattern of
strength or weakness. Even when the subject cannot fake successfully, a person who *tries* to do so will certainly give a distorted picture of himself. Inventory scores will be useful only
when most respondents are answering in the way that they
consider to represent themselves. The importance of providing
protection against distortion is sufficently great so that control
scores to detect it have been introduced into the *MMPI* and
certain other inventories.

The possibility of consciously distorting one's score means
that personality or adjustment inventories cannot be used, or
can be used only with caution, when the examinee feels threat-
ened by the test or feels that it may be used against him.
Inventories have not generally proved useful in an employ-
ement situation, perhaps for this reason. If an inventory is given
to elementary school pupils (and perhaps in high school and
college) in the typical school setting, in which a test is something to do your best on and the teacher is often someone to get
the best of, one is inclined to doubt whether many of the pupils
will be willing to reveal personal shortcomings that they may
be aware of. Generally speaking, in any practical situation we
should consider an adjustment inventory to be no more than a
preliminary screening device that will locate a certain number
of individuals who *may* be having problems of adjustment or
may be in conflict with their environment. Final evaluation
should always await a more personal and intensive study of the
individual. Furthermore, a good score on an adjustment inventory is not a guarantee of good adjustment; it may characterize
a person who is protective, defensive, or unable to face and to
acknowledge very real problems.

Personality inventories are a product of the middle-class
American culture. The extent to which items have equivalent
meaning for other national cultures, or even for the lower socioeconomic level in America, has not been fully explored. Some
additional caution is necessary in interpreting results for members of other cultural groups.

The issue of invasion of privacy.   Whenever an individual is
called upon to provide personal information, the issues of invasion of privacy and even of self-incrimination are potential

problems. The problem becomes important in proportion as the information sought is private and possibly derogatory in nature, as is true of a psychopathology-oriented inventory such as the *MMPI*.

If the self-reported information is being used only in the individual's behalf and is freely and willingly given, as would be typical of information provided in the context of counseling or therapy, then the problem of invasion of privacy is minimal. Ethical behavior on the part of the person gathering the information, whether by interview or by questionnaire, requires only that the confidentiality of the information be maintained, and that it be used only for the purpose for which it was obtained. When information is gathered for research purposes, a similar guarantee of confidentiality is ethically required, but in addition "informed consent" seems a reasonable requirement. That is, the individual should voluntarily agree to provide the information, knowing what kind of information he is being called upon to supply and, in general terms, how it will be used.

The most serious questions of invasion of privacy arise when the individual is asked to supply information that may, in fact, be used against him, as in a selection or an employment situation. How much right does a school or college, an industrial employer, or an agency of local or federal government have to require the individual to provide information about himself that may be used to screen him out of training, employment, or a role in national affairs? Of course the rights of the individual are not absolute; the claims of society and its institutions must also receive consideration. Under some circumstances, as with highly sensitive positions central to the national security, the concerns of society may be paramount. Again, a university has some responsibility to invest its resources in students who are likely to provide to society a return (though not necessarily an economic return) on the investment. Even an industrial concern has responsibilities to its stockholders, its other employees, and its customers to function efficiently and produce products or services of good quality. Thus we are faced with a weighing of competing values: how serious is the intrusion upon the individual on the one hand, and how crucial is the information to a genuine and important social gain on the other? These questions have been raised more thoughtfully and insistently in recent years.

Evidences of validity. Those inventories that have been developed as measures of adjustment usually show a moderate level of *concurrent* validity. That is, they differentiate between groups established on other grounds as differing in adjustment. Thus the *MMPI* was set up to distinguish between diagnosed pathological groups and normals, and continues to do so in new groups. Other inventories have been tested by their ability to differentiate less extreme groups and have stood up fairly well under the test.

When it comes to *predictive* validity, the results are less encouraging. In civilian studies (Ellis, 1946, 1953; Ghiselli and Barthol, 1953; Super, 1942) temperament or adjustment inventory scores have generally failed to predict anything much about the future success of the individual either in school, on the job, or in his personal living. Military experience with these instruments (Ellis and Conrad, 1948) has been somewhat more promising. There have been a number of studies showing substantial relationship between scores based on inventories and the susequent judgment resulting from a psychiatric interview. Relationships to subsequent discharge from the service have also been sufficiently good to indicate that an inventory could serve a useful function as a device to screen for careful interview those who appeared to be potential misfits.

The practical use of temperament and adjustment inventories. We must now ask what use *should* be made of temperament and adjustment inventories in and out of school. In the light of the factors that can distort scores, and the limited validity these instruments have shown as predictors, we must conclude that they should be used very sparingly. Our feeling is that an adjustment inventory should be used only as an adjunct to more intensive psychological services. If facilities are available to permit intensive study of some of the group by psychologically trained personnel, an inventory may serve as a means of identifying persons likely to profit from working with a counselor. However, there is little that a classroom teacher can do to dig behind and test the meaning of an inventory score. Accepted uncritically, the score may prove very misleading. We believe that little useful purpose is served by giving an adjustment inventory and making the results available to the teacher, especially the teacher of an elementary school child.

Multidimensional temperament inventories have shown some fairly substantial differences, based on concurrent testing, between persons in different occupations (Cattell, Eber, and Tatsuoka, 1970). However, there have been almost no genuinely predictive studies. Though the concurrent studies suggest that there are fairly substantial temperamental differences between persons in different occupations, the evidence is a good deal more limited than is the case for interest measures. It *may* be that persons having certain patterns of temperamental characteristics should be guided toward or away from certain types of job. This seems plausible to many people. However, our information about the personality patterns in specific occupations is too limited and the range of variation within occupations is probably too wide to make practical use of such personality appraisals at the present time.

ATTITUDE QUESTIONNAIRES

One further type of self-report instrument that has received a good deal of use in psychological research and in educational program evaluation is the questionnaire designed to assess attitudes with respect to some group, social institution, social concept, or proposed action. We differentiate between attitude mapping and attitude measurement. In *mapping* one sinks many separate shafts into an attitude domain to see what the range and scope of attitudes is in some group or groups, whereas in *measurement* one tries to get a relatively precise appraisal of the intensity of some specific attitude in each individual. We shall illustrate each as we describe the procedures for developing an attitude measure for the domain of women's liberation.

ATTITUDE MAPPING

Attitude mapping is seen in the various public opinion surveys by such organizations as the Gallup Poll or the Michigan Survey Research Center. The surveyor attempts to identify some current issues within an attitude domain and to get a response with respect to each. For example, in the area of women's liberation or women's rights we might include such questions and response alternatives as those shown below.

1. If a husband and wife both have jobs and the woman is offered a job in a distant city that is better than her husband's she should

(*a*) accept it, and expect her husband to move.

(*b*) accept it, and leave it to her husband to decide what he wants to do.

(*c*) accept it only if her husband also finds a job in the new location.

(*d*) turn it down and keep her present job.

2. If a married woman who has been working has a child she should

(*a*) stay home and care for the child until it is of school age.

(*b*) return to work and expect her husband to share equally in the care of the child.

3. In the matter of sexual expression a woman should
   (*a*) have complete freedom, in or out of marriage.
   (*b*) exercise complete restraint until married.
   (*c*) have complete freedom only until marriage.

Analysis of the results would typically take the form of percentages of respondents choosing each alternative. Data might be broken down for subgroups by age, region, religion, marital status, and other factors of interest. Thus it might plausibly be expected that women would endorse more frequently the statements affirming equality and independence for women, that these would be endorsed more often by younger persons, and that religious affiliation would be related at least to response on the third question.

ATTITUDE MEASUREMENT

In attitude measurement we are interested primarily in getting a score having adequate reliability that can represent the intensity of each person's sentiments toward or against the attitude object—in this case liberation and equality for women. We start by assembling—from reading, from associates, from the recesses of our own consciousness—a catalogue of statements covering possible views on the target concept. These should range from the most positive and favorable to the most negative and unfavorable, and will usually cover various subfacets of the attitude domain. In the case of women's liberation they would cover equal employment opportunities, child care, sexual freedom, personal independence, degree of role differentiation, and so forth. Each statement should be clear and brief, present a single idea, and be focused on feeling rather than fact, attitude rather than information.

The total pool of items is usually much too long to use as a measuring instrument, so it is necessary to select a subset of items. This is often done by having the items reviewed and rated by a corps of judges. The judges' function is not to indicate agreement or disagreement with the item, but rather to assess where the statement falls on a pro-anti scale in relation to the target concept. Usually a 7- or 9-point scale is used. The scale points might range from 9, very strongly favorable toward womens' freedom and status, through 5, neutral, to 1, very strongly hostile toward womens' freedom and status. The purpose of the rating is to find (1) where on the pro–anti dimension a given statement falls, and (2) how well a group of judges can agree as to the statement's meaning. We wish eventually to select a set of statements that represent all degrees of favorableness and unfavorableness, and statements that convey nearly the same meaning to everyone. The position of an item on the scale of favorableness–unfavorableness is indicated by the median rating that it receives from the judges; its ambiguity by the spread of ratings as given by the semi-interquartile range. Consider the following two statements.

	Median	Q
A wife's job and career are just as important as her husband's.	8.1	1.0
Feminine fashions are a device to hold women in an inferior role.	7.0	3.1

The first statement seems promising for inclusion in the final attitude instrument. It is a strongly "pro" statement, and judges are in good agreement as to just where it falls on the attitude dimension. The second is a poor statement. Though on average it is rated as implying a moderately favorable position towards women's liberation, there is great disagreement among raters as to just what the statement does signify. It was assigned by different judges to all positions from scale step 1 to scale step 9. Furthermore, about 10 percent of the judges marked it as irrelevant to the attitude dimension under study. Because of its high ambiguity, it was dropped from further consideration for the scale.

Given the judge's ratings, we can now select a reasonably brief set of statements that have clear meaning, that represent all degrees of intensity of pro and anti views, and that cover the main facets of the domain being studied. The statements can usually best be presented to subjects in the format shown in Fig. 11.3 on page 438, in which the respondent indicates degree of acceptance of each statement. Responses can be scored 4, 3, 2, 1, 0, the direction of the scoring depending upon whether the statement is pro or anti. That is, on statements 1, 2, 4, 6, 7, 10, 11, 12, 13, 15, and 20, in which agreement indicates attitudes favorable to women's rights, a value of 4 would be assigned to the AA (strongly agree) response while on the remaining staements the value of 4 would be assigned to the DD (strongly disagree) response. The possible score would thus range from 80 (most strongly favoring women's liberation) to 0 (most hostile). A score of 40 could be considered neutral.

A sample of the results obtained from administering the scale to 133 students in measurement classes is shown in Table

ATTITUDE TOWARD WOMEN'S LIBERATION

Read each statement. Then circle the symbol that best represents your reaction to the statement, according to the following scale:

AA — strongly agree with the statement.
a — tend to agree with the statement.
? — undecided. Neither agree nor disagree.
d — tend to disagree with the statement.
DD — strongly disagree with the statement.

(AA) a ? d   DD   1. Men and women should receive the same pay for the same work.

(AA) a ? d   DD   2. No woman should have to bear a child unless she chooses to.

AA   a ? d **(DD)**   3. Most women are unsuited by temperament for supervisory or administrative jobs.

(AA) a ? d   DD   4. There should be no clubs or public places that are restricted to a single sex.

AA   a ? d **(DD)**   5. Woman's place is in the home.

(AA) a ? d   DD   6. Standards for promotion should be the same for men and for women.

(AA) a ? d   DD   7. A wife's job and career are just as important as her husband's.

AA   a ? d **(DD)**   8. Men and women are basically different in their make-up, and suited to fill different roles.

AA   a ? d **(DD)**   9. A woman who follows a career can seldom expect to have a satisfactory home life.

(AA) a ? d   DD   10. There are no inborn psychological differences between men and women.

(AA) a ? d   DD   11. Men should share equally in housework—getting meals, cleaning, etc.

(AA) a ? d   DD   12. Every woman should have an independent career if she wants one.

(AA) a ? d   DD   13. In matters of sex, there should be a single standard for men and for women.

AA   a ? d **(DD)**   14. The workers for Women's Liberation are frustrated female failures.

(AA) a ? d   DD   15. Except for physical strength, anything a man can do women can do equally well.

AA   a ? d **(DD)**   16. Women's Liberation is of interest only to a few women on the lunatic fringe.

AA   a ? d **(DD)**   17. It doesn't make sense to make a large investment in a woman's education, because she is likely to marry and not use her advanced training.

AA   a ? d **(DD)**   18. By nature, women are submissive and men dominant.

AA   a ? d **(DD)**   19. The natural role for a woman is a secondary supporting one.

(AA) a ? d   DD   20. In all respects, men and women should receive just the same treatment.

Figure 11.3
Sample attitude scale.

Table 11.9

439
attitude
questionnaires

SELECTED RESULTS FOR ATTITUDE SCALE ON WOMEN'S LIBERATION*

Score	Percentile	Group Percentage	Falling above Median
75	90th	Women	61%
68	75th	Men	29
61	50th	Over 30	41
		Under 30	57
51	25th	Single	55
40	10th	Other	46
		Catholic	39
		Other	57

* Reliability (split-half): .89.

11.9. The scale shows quite satisfactory reliability. In general these students tended to endorse statements favorable to women's rights, and the more strongly favorable positions (above the median) appeared more often among women, students under 30, the unmarried, and the non-Catholic.

Alternative formats. Attitude measures sometimes take other formats. One simple change would be to present a set of statements such as those shown, being careful also to include some neutral statements, and to direct the respondent to mark either (1) *all* statements agreed with or (2) the statements—possibly a specified number—that *best* represent that respondent's view. With this format it is important to have accurately determined scale values for each statement, since the score that an individual receives is the average of the scale values of the statements that the person endorses.

A slightly different approach is to select a somewhat shorter set of statements that are very homogeneous in content, differing only in degree of some specific attitude. An example, relating to the acceptability of abortion might take the form shown below.

1. Abortion should be legal whenever a woman wishes one.
2. Abortion should be legal if the doctor recommends it.
3. Abortion should be legal when pregnancy is the result of rape or incest.
4. Abortion should be legal when the health or well-being of the mother is endangered.
5. Abortion should be legal when the life of the mother is endangered.
6. Abortion should not be legal under any circumstances.

These six statements presumably represent a gradient of permissiveness. A person who agrees to statement (1) would presumably agree to (2)–(5), and one who agrees to (2) but not (1) could be expected to agree to (3)–(5) (if the statements are in correct order). Thus a person's position on this continuum could be defined by the highest statement accepted. A scale of this type has some logical advantages, in that the same scale value always means the same statements accepted, but this type of scale (called a Guttman scale, after the psychologist who promoted it) is limited to quite specific and homogeneous attitude domains.

Semantic differential. One other approach to attitude assessment is worthy of mention. This is the so-called semantic differential. The procedure grew out of studies by Osgood and others of the structure of the domain of meaning represented by adjectives. Osgood, Suci, and Tannebaum (1957) reported, on the basis of factor analytic studies, that most of the variations in meaning that are expressed by different adjectives can be represented by three main dimensions. These have been designated *evaluative, potency,* and *activity.* Adjective pairs that represent each of these main dimensions are shown below.

Evaluative

good	—	—	—	—	—	—	—	bad
nice	—	—	—	—	—	—	—	nasty
fair	—	—	—	—	—	—	—	unfair

Potency

strong	—	—	—	—	—	—	—	weak
capable	—	—	—	—	—	—	—	helpless
dominant	—	—	—	—	—	—	—	submissive

Activity

energetic	—	—	—	—	—	—	—	lazy
busy	—	—	—	—	—	—	—	idle
active	—	—	—	—	—	—	—	passive

A set of adjectives such as these can be used to get at a person's perception of any target object. The target can be a general concept such as women's liberation, or abortion, or it can be a specific person such as one's teacher or oneself. Usually the order of the adjectives is scrambled, and the "positive" and "negative" poles of some pairs are reversed on the page, so as to reduce thoughtless, stereotyped responding. A scale with 7 steps is presented, as in the illustration above, and the respondent is asked to indicate how the target concept or person appeared to him by making a mark on the appropriate point between the two adjectives. That is, if the respondent reacts to women's liberation as very good, a check is made on the step nearest to "good"; if women's liberation is perceived as neither especially good nor especially bad, a check is made midway between "good" and "bad"; and so forth.

The semantic differential provides a quick and easy way to collect impressions on one or several target objects. However, the sets of adjective pairs often seem of questionable appropriateness for a target object, and it may stretch a person's imagination to respond. One suspects that often the responses may be at a rather superficial and purely verbal level.

'One limitation of *all* the attitude assessment procedures that we have described is that they involve solely a verbal response. They communicate what the person is willing to say he believes or feels. The respondent may not be prepared to be entirely open and forthright with us. More importantly, a person's actions may not correspond to the verbally endorsed beliefs and feelings. A child who subscribes verbally to statements of good will toward members of one or another ethnic group may still avoid that group when picking playmates or persons to attend a birthday party—or may not. The verbal statements of attitude must be recognized as just that. Though it may be of interest in its own right to determine that after a particular college course or a particular television program students have changed in the verbally stated attitudes that they will endorse, it must not automatically be assumed that other aspects of their behavior toward the target object will have changed. In research studies a number of more directly behavioral, and usually unobtrusive indicators of attitude have been studied (Webb et al., 1966). For example, attitudes toward drinking have been surveyed by examining the variety of bottles in garbage cans; a functional measure of attitudes toward ecology might be a count of the cans and bottles scattered along the roadside.

SUMMARY AND EVALUATION

In this chapter we have considered self-report inventories as instruments for studying personality. An inventory of this sort is essentially a standard set of interview questions presented in written form.

The individual's report about himself has one outstanding advantage. It provides an "inside" view, based on all the individual's experience with and knowledge about himself. However, self-reports are limited by the individual's

1. Ability to read the questions with understanding.
2. Self-insight and self-understanding.
3. Willingness to reveal himself frankly.

One type of questionnaire that has proved valuable in selection and placement is the biographical data blank, in which a person provides factual information about his past history. A scoring key developed for the particular job has been found to have useful validity in several different instances.

Interest inventories provide satisfactorily reliable descriptions of interest patterns. These patterns persist with a good deal of stability, at least after late adolescence, and appear to be significant factors for vocational planning.

The validity of adjustment and temperament inventories is more open to question. Inventories of all types can be distorted to some extent if the individual is motivated to distort his responses. Thus the integrity of the responses depends upon the motivation of the person examined. This depends, in turn, upon the setting in which and purposes for which the inventory is used. In school, industrial, or military use of adjustment inventories, one suspects that the motivations may often favor distorted responses. In any event, inventories of this type have not generally shown high validity. They should be used only with a good deal of circumspection.

Attitude questionnaires have been developed to score the intensity of favorable or unfavorable reaction to some group, institution, or issue. Though these represent only verbal expressions of attitude, they are useful research tools.

QUESTIONS AND EXERCISES

1. How much should an interview be structured in advance by the interviewer? What may be gained from such structuring? What may be lost?

2. Write 2 or 3 questions to be used as part of a biographical data blank for selecting door-to-door cosmetics salespersons. Indicate the rationale for each question. How would you decide which questions to keep in the final form of the blank?

3. Consider the following four interest inventories: (1) *Strong-Campbell Interest Inventory;* (2) *Kuder Preference Record, Vocational;* (3) *Kuder Occupational Interest Survey;* (4) *Minnesota Vocational Interest Inventory.* Which one (or ones) would you recommend for each of the following uses? Give the reasons for your choices.

(*a*) A college sophomore wants counseling on choice of major field and on vocational plans.

(*b*) A counseling program is being set up for students entering a vocational high school that has a number of different trade programs.

(*c*) An inventory is desired for use in a tenth grade course exploring careers and the process of occupational choice.

(*d*) A counseling service for adults wants an inventory to use with college graduates.

4. It has been found that the scales for the same or very similar occupations on the *Strong Vocational Interest Inventory* and the *Kuder Occupational Interest Survey* often show quite low correlations with one another. Why does this happen? What is its theoretical significance? What is its practical significance?

5. Table 11.6 on p. 418 shows correlations between ability scores on the *GATB* and interest scores on the *Kuder Preference Record.* What do you conclude from this table? What significance does your conclusion have for vocational counseling and vocational choice.

6. Most civilian studies have failed to find interest or adjustment inventories very useful in personnel selection. What are the reasons for this?

7. Compare the advantages and disadvantages, for personnel selection or academic admissions, of the information obtained from

(*a*) An interview.

(*b*) A personal history form.

(*c*) A self-descriptive inventory.

8. What is meant by the term "response set"? What are some potentially important response sets? How might they influence the interpretation of results on personality inventories?

9. How serious a problem is invasion of privacy with personality measures? What uses of such measures are acceptable? What controls on their use should be introduced? How and by whom?

10. What conditions must be met if a self-report inventory is to be filled out accurately and give meaningful results?

11. How much trust can we place in adjustment inventories given in school to elementary school children? What factors limit their value?

12. What important differences do you notice between the *Guilford-Zimmerman Temperament Survey* and the *Minnesota Multiphasic Personality Inventory?* For what purposes would each be more suitable?

13. What types of distortion of the image of a person are the control scales (*L, K, F, ?*) in the *MMPI* intended to identify or correct for? What would be the analogous issues in ratings of one person by another person? How might one adapt the ideas of control scales to ratings by other persons?

14. What factors limit the usefulness of paper-and-pencil attitude scales? What other methods might a teacher use to evaluate attitudes?

15. Prepare the rough draft for a brief attitude scale to measure teachers' attitudes towards objective tests.

SUGGESTED ADDITIONAL READING

Borgen, Fred H. and Gregory T. Harper. Predictive validity of measured vocational interests with black and white college men. *Measurement and Evaluation in Guidance*, 1973, 6, 19–27.

Campbell, D. P. *Handbook for the Strong-Campbell Vocational Interest Blank.* Stanford, Calif.: Stanford University Press, 1971.

Cascio, Wayne F. Accuracy of verifiable biographical information blank responses. *Journal of Applied Psychology*, 1975, 60, 767–769.

Cegelka, Patricia Thomas, Clayton Omvig, and David L. Larimne. Effects of aptitude and sex on vocational interests. *Measurement and Evaluation in Guidance*, 1974, 7, 106–111.

Goldberg, L. R. A historical survey of personality scales and inventories. In P. McReynolds (Ed.), *Advances in Psychological Assessment.* Vol. 2, Palo Alto, Calif.: Science and Behavior Books, 1971, 293–336.

Harmon, Lenore W. Sexual bias in interest measurement. *Measurement and Evaluation in Guidance*, 1973, 5, 469–501.

Heneman, Herbert G. III, and Donald P. Schwab. Interviewer validity as a function of interview structure, biographical data, and interviewee order. *Jounal of Applied Psychology*, 1975, 60, 748–753.

Payne, David A., Frank E. Papley, and Robert A. Wells. Application of a biographical data inventory to estimate college academic achievement. *Measurement and Evaluation in Guidance*, 1973, 6, 152–156.

Prediger, D. J. and N. S. Cole. *Sex-role socialization and employment realities: Implications for vocational interest measures.* ACT Research Report No. 68. Iowa City, Iowa: The American College Testing Program, January 1975.

Prediger, Dale J. and Gary R. Hanson. The distinction between sex restrictiveness and sex bias in interest inventories. *Measurement and Evaluation in Guidance*, 1974, 7, 96–104.

Schmitt, Neal. Social and situational determinants of interview decisions: Implications for the employment interview. *Personnel Psychology*, 1976, 29, 79–101.

Ulrich, L. and D. Trumbo. The selection interview since 1949. *Psychological Bulletin,* 1965, 63, 100-116.

Whetstone, Robert D. and V. Robert Hayles. The SVIB and black college men. *Measurement and Evaluation in Guidance,* 1975, 8, 105-109.

Wiggins, Jerry S. *Personality and prediction: Principles of personality assess-* *ment.* Reading, Mass.: Addison-Wesley, 1973, 656pp.

Zytowski, Donald G. Predictive validity of the Kuder Preference Record, Form B, over a 25-year span. *Measurement and Evaluation in Guidance,* 1974, 7, 122-129.

Zytowski, Donald G. (Ed.) *Contemporary approaches to interest measurement.* Minneapolis, Minn: University of Minnesota Press, 1973.

CHAPTER TWELVE
THE INDIVIDUAL AS VIEWED BY OTHERS

In the last chapter we considered the information about personality that could be gotten from inventories in which the individual describes himself. A second main way in which an individual's personality shows itself is through the impression made upon others. The second person serves as a reagent reacting to the first personality. How well does A like B? Does A consider B a pleasing person to have around? An effective worker? A good job risk? Does A consider B to be conscientious? Trustworthy? Emotionally stable? Questions of this sort are continually being asked of every teacher, supervisor, former employer, minister, or even friend. We must now inquire how fruitful it is to raise such questions and what precautions must be observed if the questions are to receive useful answers.

LETTERS OF RECOMMENDATION

The most fluid form for getting an impression of person A through the eyes of a person B is to invite B to talk or write to you about A. Such a communication could be obtained in any setting, but occurs most commonly when person A is a candidate for something: admission to a school, a scholarship or fellowship, a job, membership in a club, or a security clearance. Person A then furnishes the institution, placement agency, or employer the names of people who know him well or know him in a particular capacity, and that agency obtains statements about A from B and C, who know him.

How useful and how informative is the material that is included in free, unstructured communications describing another person? Actually, in spite of the vast numbers of recommendations written every year, very little of a solid and factual nature is known about their adequacy or the effectiveness with which they discharge their function. Opinion as to their value varies widely. Some critics maintain that recommendations tend to perpetuate and even promote the introduction of irrelevant considerations into appraisal of applicants. Thus Lewis (1972) writes, speaking of applicants for faculty positions in chemistry, "Non-academic factors such as an individual's skill in interpersonal relations are as much a part of academic assessment as is diligence. Those who are amiable, docile, and of sound mind receive special approbation." However, factual studies of the reliability and validity of the information obtained from a letter of recommendation or of the extent to which recommendations influence the action taken with respect to an applicant are fragmentary in the extreme.

One analysis (Siskind, 1966) of 67 letters written for 33 psychology internship applicants found 958 statements to be distributed as follows:

1. Positive statements	838	(87%)
2. "Don't know" statements about a characteristic	17	(2%)
3. Statements referring to natural shortcomings, the result of inexperience or youth	44	(5%)
4. Other statements indicative of shortcomings	59	(6%)

Siskind suggests that the letter writers "want to see angels" among their students or that they "only want to write about angels." In any event, it is easy to see that the vast preponderance of positive statements makes the discriminating use of such reference letters difficult.

Readers *do* use such letters, and there is evidence (Harrington, 1943) that they are able to agree fairly well in judging how positive a letter is, and that there is a moderate degree of consistency ($r = .40$) between letters written about a given person. One clue as to how this occurs comes from a study (Peres and Garcia, 1962) of adjectives used in a series of letters written in support of applicants for engineering jobs. Of 170 different adjectives extracted from the letters, almost all were positive in tone, but when these were applied as ratings to "best" and "worst" present employees, the adjectives differed enormously in the degree to which they differentiated these groups. Thus the applicant could be called "congenial," "helpful," and "open" or he could be called "ingenious," "informed" and "productive." The first three were applied about equally often to the best and poorest workers, while the last three were highly differentiating between these two groups. Apparently, the validity of the inferences drawn from a letter of reference depends to a considerable extent upon the degree to which the recipient has learned to "read between the lines," weighting the nice things that are said by an appropriate "discrimination factor" that identifies whether it is the job-relevant or the tangential virtues that are mentioned.

The extent to which a letter of recommendation provides a *valid* appraisal of an individual and the extent to which it is accurately diagnostic of outstanding points, strengths, or weaknesses, is almost completely unknown. However, one cannot be very sanguine. Most of the limitations that we shall presently discuss in connection with more structured rating scales apply with at least equal force to uncontrolled letters. In addition, in the latter each respondent is free to go off in whatever direction fancy dictates, so that there is no core of content common to the different letters about a single person or to the letters dealing with different persons. One letter may deal with A's social charm; a second with B's integrity; and a third with C's originality.

Although, as we have just seen, a user of recommendations does develop an internal weighting schema for comments of different kinds, such a schema is probably neither very precise, very stable, nor very uniform from reader to reader. Add to this the facts that (1) the applicant usually is more or less free to select the persons who will write about him and may be expected to pick those who will support him and that (2) recommenders differ profoundly in their propensity for using superlatives, and the prospect is not a very rosy one.

Further research studies of the validity of free descriptions of one person by his fellows are urgently needed. In the meantime, recommendations will continue to be written—and perhaps to be used. We must turn our attention to more structured evaluation procedures.

RATING SCALES

Undoubtedly, it was, in part, the extreme subjectivity of the unstructured statement, the lack of a common core of content or standard of reference from person to person, and the extraordinary difficulty of quantifying the materials that gave impetus to the development of rating scales. Rating procedures attempt to overcome just these deficiencies. They attempt to get appraisals on a common set of attributes for all raters and ratees and to have these expressed on a common quantitative scale.

We all have had experience with ratings, either in making them or in having them made about us or, more probably, in both capacities. Rating scales appear in a large proportion of school report cards, more clearly in the nonacademic part. Thus we often find a section phrased somewhat as follows:

	1st Period	2nd Period	3rd Period	4th Period
Effort	_____	_____	_____	_____
Conduct	_____	_____	_____	_____
Citizenship	_____	_____	_____	_____
Cooperation	_____	_____	_____	_____
Adjustment	_____	_____	_____	_____
	H = superior S = satisfactory U = unsatisfactory			

Many civil service agencies and industrial firms send rating forms out to persons listed as references by job applicants, asking for evaluations of the individual's "initiative," "originality," "enthusiasm," or "ability to get along with people." These same companies or agencies often require supervisors to give merit ratings of their employees, rating them as "superior," "excellent," "very good," "good," "satisfactory" or "unsatisfactory" on a variety of traits or in overall usefulness. Colleges, medical schools, fellowship programs, and still other agencies call for ratings as a part of their selection procedure. Beyond these practical operating uses, ratings have been involved in a great many research projects. All in all, vast numbers of ratings are called for and given, often reluctantly, in our country week by week and month by month. Rating other people is a large-scale operation.

Often ratings are retrospective, summarizing the impressions developed by the rater over an extended period of contact with the ratee. Sometimes they are concurrent, arising out of an interview or a period of observation. Almost universally, a rating involves an evaluative summary of past or present experiences in which the "internal computer" of the rater processes the input data in complex and unspecified ways to arrive at the final judgment. By contrast, in systematic observational procedures (to be considered in the next chapter) the observer tries to function only as an accurate recorder, leaving the synthesis and interpretation of the observations as a separate process.

The most common pattern of rating procedure presents the rater with a set of trait names, perhaps somewhat further defined, and a range of numbers, adjectives, or descriptions that are to represent levels or degrees of possession of the traits. He is called upon to rate one or more persons on the trait or traits by assigning him or them the number, letter, adjective, or description that is judged to fit best. Two illustrations are given of rating scales, drawn from a program for evaluation of management personnel.* The first is one of a series of trait ratings. This part of the evaluation instrument calls for ratings of the following traits: job know-how, judgment, leadership, ability to plan and organize, communication ability, initiative, dependability, and human relations. For the trait of leadership, the rater is instructed as shown below. The actual rating scale follows these instructions.

LEADERSHIP

Consider his ability to inspire confidence. How much respect does he command as an individual, not merely because of his position? Do people look to him for decisions? Is he afraid to "stick his neck out" for what he believes? Does he have teamwork?

| Completely lacking. Definitely a follower with equals. Does not try to convince others that his way is best. | Tries to lead with some success, but has never achieved a strong position. Is passive in directing his subordinates. | Good leader. People wait to hear what he has to say. Respected by colleagues. People call for his opinion. | Exceptional leader. Able to take over and pull things into shape. People seem to enjoy going along on his side. Is respected by subordinates and colleagues. |

An overall summary rating is also called for, and this takes the form shown on p. 451.

* These were made available through the courtesy of the Personnel Department of Mack Trucks, Inc.

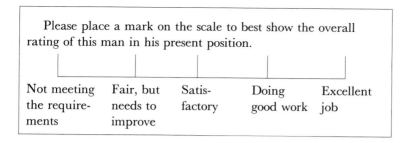

These are only illustrations of a wide range of rating instruments. We shall turn presently to some of the major variations in rating patterns. Right now, however, let us consider some of the problems that arise when one tries to get a group of judges to make these appraisals.

PROBLEMS IN OBTAINING SOUND RATINGS

The problems in obtaining accurate and valid appraisals of an individual through ratings are of two main sorts. First, there are the factors that limit the rater's *willingness* to rate honestly and conscientiously, in accordance with the instructions given to him. Second, there are the factors that limit his *ability* to rate consistently and correctly, even with the best of intentions. We shall need to consider each of these in turn.

FACTORS AFFECTING THE RATER'S WILLINGNESS TO RATE CONSCIENTIOUSLY

When ratings are collected it is commonly assumed that each rater is trying his best to follow the instructions that have been given, and that any shortcomings in the ratings are due entirely to human fallibility and ineptitude. However, this is not necessarily true. There are at least two sets of circumstances that may impair the integrity of a set of ratings: (1) The rater may be unwilling to take the trouble that is called for by the appraisal procedure; and (2) the rater may identify with the person rated to such an extent that he or she is unwilling to make a rating that will hurt that person. Each of these merits some elaboration.

Unwillingness to take the necessary pains. At best, ratings are a bother. Careful and thoughtful ratings are even more of a bother. In some rating procedures the attempt is made to get away from subjective impressions and superficial reaction by introducing elaborate procedures and precautions into the rating enterprise. Thus in one attempt to improve efficiency rating procedures for Air Force officers (Preston, 1948) an elaborate form was introduced that was to serve as a combined observational record and rating form. Fifty-four specific critical behaviors were described relating to officer efficiency. Scales were prepared describing degrees of excellence in each type of behavior. The accompanying instructions called upon raters to observe their ratees for a period before the official ratings were to be given and to tally on the rating form instances that had been observed of desirable and undesirable acts within each of the behavior categories described on the scale.

In theory this was admirable, because it tied the final ratings closely to systematic observations of the subordinates' actions. However, after a year or two of use this form was discarded, in part at least because of its complexity and because raters were not willing to devote the time and the thought that would have been required to maintain the rather elaborate preliminary observational records on which the ratings were to be based.

One suspects that to some degree perfunctoriness in carrying out the operation of rating is a factor contributing to lowered effectiveness in many rating programs. Particularly if the number of pupils or employees to be rated is large, the task of preparing periodic ratings can become a decidedly onerous one. Unless raters are really "sold" on the importance of the ratings, the judgments are likely to be hurried and superficial ones, given more with an eye on finishing the task than with a concern for making accurate analytical judgments.

Identification with the persons being rated. Ratings are often called for by some rather remote and impersonal agency. The Civil Service Commission, the Military Personnel Division of a remote headquarters, the personnel director of a large company, or the central administrative staff of a school system are all pretty far away from the first line supervisor, the squadron commander, or the classroom teacher. The rater is often closer to the persons being rated, the workers in his office, the junior officers in his outfit, the pupils in his class, than to the agency that requires the ratings to be made. One of the first principles of supervision or leadership is that "the good officer looks out for his men." Morale in an organization depends upon the conviction that the leader of the organization will take care of the members. When ratings come along, "taking care of" becomes a matter of seeing to it that one's own people fare as well as—or a little better than—those in competing groups.

All this boils down to the fact that in some situations the rater is more interested in providing a "break" for the people whom he is rating and in seeing that they get at least as good treatment as other groups being rated than he is in providing accurate information for the using agency. This situation is aggravated in many governmental official agencies by a policy of having the ratings public and requiring that the rater discuss with the person being rated any unfavorable material in the ratings. A further aggravation is produced by setting up administrative rulings in which a minimum rating is specified as required for promotion or pay increase. No wonder, then, that ratings tend to climb or to pile up at a single scale point. There is a tendency for the typical rating, accounting for a very large proportion of the ratings given, to be "excellent." "Very good" almost becomes an expression of dissatisfaction, while a rating of "satisfactory" is reserved for someone you would get rid of at the very first opportunity.

It is important to realize that a rater cannot always be depended upon to work wholeheartedly at giving valid ratings for the benefit of the using agency, that making ratings is usually a nuisance to him, and that he is often more committed to his own subordinates than to an outside agency. A rating program must be continuously "sold" and policed if it is to remain effective. And there are limits to the extent to which even an active campaign can overcome a rater's natural inertia and his interest in his own little group.

FACTORS AFFECTING THE RATER'S ABILITY TO RATE ACCURATELY

Even when raters are presumably well motivated and doing their best to provide valid judgments, there are still a number of factors that operate to limit the validity of those judgments. These center around the lack of opportunity to observe, the covertness of the attribute, ambiguity of the quality to be observed, lack of a uniform standard of reference, and specific rater biases and idiosyncrasies.

Opportunity to observe the person rated. One factor that must always be borne in mind as a consideration limiting the accuracy of rating procedures is limited opportunity on the part of the rater to observe the person being rated. Thus a teacher teaching four or five different class groups of 30 pupils each and seeing many pupils only in a class setting may be called upon to make judgments as to the "initiative" or "flexibility" of these pupils. A college instructor who has taught a class of 100 students will receive rating forms from an employment agency or from the college administration asking for similar judgments. The truth of the matter is that effective contact with the person to be rated has probably been too limited to provide any adequate basis for the judgment that is being requested. True, the ratee has been physically in the presence of the rater for a good many hours, possibly several hundred, but these have been very busy hours, concerned primarily with other things than observing and forming judgments about pupil A. Pupil A has had to compete with pupils B, C, D, and on to Z and also with the primary concern with teaching rather than judging.

In a civil service or industrial setting much the same thing is true. The primary concern is with getting the job done, and although in theory the supervisor has had a good deal of time to observe each worker, in practice he has been busy with other things. We may be able to "sell" supervisors on the idea of devoting more of their energy to observing and evaluating the persons working for them, but there are very real limits to the amount of effort that can be withdrawn from a supervisor's other functions to be applied to this one.

We face not only the issue of general opportunity to observe, but also that of specific opportunity to observe a particular aspect of the individual's personality. Any person sees another only in certain limited contexts, in which only certain aspects of behavior are displayed. The teacher sees a child primarily in the classroom, the foreman sees a workman primarily on the production line, and so forth. We might question whether a teacher in a thoroughly conventional classroom has seen a child under circumstances that might be expected to bring out much "initiative" or "originality." The college instructor who has taught largely through lectures is hardly well situated to rate a student's "presence" or "ability to work with individuals." The supervisor of a clerk doing routine work is poorly situated to appraise "judgment." Whenever ratings are proposed, either for research purposes or as a basis for administrative actions, we should ask with respect to each trait being rated: Has the rater had a chance to observe these people in enough situations of the sort in which they could be expected to show variations in this trait so that his ratings can be expected to be meaningful? If the answer is "No," we would be well advised to abandon the rating of the trait in question.

In this connection it is worthwhile to point out that persons in different roles may see quite different aspects of the person to be rated. Pupils see a teacher from quite a different vantage point than does the principal. Classmates in Officer Candidate School have a different view of the other potential officers than does the drill instructor. In getting ratings of some aspect of an individual, it is always appropriate to ask who has had the best chance to see the relevant behavior displayed. It would normally be to this source that we should go for ratings.

Covertness of trait being rated.   If a trait is to be appraised by an outsider, someone other than the person being rated, the trait must show on the outside. It must be something that has its impact on the outside world. Such characteristics as appearing at ease at social gatherings, having a pleasant speaking voice, and participating actively in group projects are characteristics that are essentially social. They appear in interaction with other persons and are directly observable. They are *overt* aspects of the person being appraised. By contrast, attributes such as "feeling of insecurity," "self-sufficiency," "tension," or "loneliness" are inner personal qualities. They are private aspects of personality and can only be inferred crudely from what the person does. They are *covert* aspects of the individual.

An attribute that is largely covert can be judged by an outsider only with great difficulty. Little of inner conflict or tension shows on the surface, and when it does show it is often in masquerade. Thus deep insecurity may express itself as aggression against other pupils in one child, or as withdrawal into an inner world in another. The insecurity is not a simple dimension of overt behavior. It is an underlying dynamic factor that may break out in different ways in different persons or even in the same person at different times. Only a thorough knowledge of the individual, combined with a good deal of psychological insight, makes it possible to infer from the overt behavior the nature of his underlying covert dynamics.

One can see, then, that rating procedures will be relatively unsatisfactory for the inner, covert aspects of an individual. Qualities that depend upon very thorough understanding of a person plus wise inferences from his behavior will be rated with low reliability and little validity. Ratings have most chance of being accurate for those qualities that show outwardly as a person interacts with other people, the overt aspects. Experience has shown that these can be rated more reliably, and one feels confident that they are rated more validly. The validity lies in part in the fact that these social aspects of behavior have their meaning and definition primarily in the effects of one person on another.

Ambiguity of meaning of dimension to be rated. Many rating forms call for ratings of quite broad and abstract traits. Thus in the illustration on p. 449 we included, among other attributes "citizenship" and "adjustment." These are neither more nor less vague and general than ones included in other rating schedules. But what do we mean by "citizenship" in an elementary school pupil? By what actions is "good citizenship" shown? Does it mean not marking up the walls? Or not spitting on the floor? Or not pulling little girls' hair? Or bringing newspaper clippings to class? Or joining the Junior Red Cross? Or staying after school to help the teacher clean up the room? What *does* it mean? Probably no two raters would have exactly the same things in mind when they rated a group of pupils on "citizenship."

Or consider "initiative," "personality," "supervisory ability," "mental flexibility," "executive influence," or "adaptability." These are all examples from rating scales in actual use. Though there is certainly some core of uniformity in the meaning that each of these terms will have for different raters, there is with equal certainty a good deal of variability in meaning from one rater to another. In proportion as a term becomes abstract, its meaning becomes variable from person to person, and such qualities as those listed above are conspicuously abstract.

The rating that a given child will receive for "citizenship" will, then, depend upon what "citizenship" means to the rater. If it means to rater A conforming to school regulations, A will rate certain children high. If to rater B it means taking an active role in school projects, the high ratings may go to quite different children. A first problem in getting consistent ratings is to achieve consistency from rater to rater in the meanings of the qualities being rated.

Uniform standard of reference. A great many rating schedules call for judgments of the persons being rated in some set of categories such as

Outstanding, above average, average, below average, unsatisfactory.
Superior, good, fair, poor,
Best, good, average, fair, poor.

Outstanding, superior, better than satisfactory, satisfactory, unsatisfactory.

Superior, excellent, very good, good, satisfactory, unsatisfactory.*

But how good is "good"? Is a person who is "good" in "judgment" in the top tenth of the group with whom he is being compared? The top quarter? The top half? Or is he just *not* one of the bottom tenth? And what *is* the group with whom he is supposed to be compared? Is it all persons of his age? All employees of the company? All persons in a particular job? All persons in the same job with the same length of experience? If the last, how is the rater supposed to know the level of judgment that is typical for persons in a particular job with a particular level of experience?

The problem that all these questions are pointing up is that of forming a standard against which to appraise a given ratee. Variations in interpretation of terms and labels, variations in definition of the reference population, and variations in experience with the members of that background population all contribute to variability from rater to rater in their standards of rating. The phenomenon is a familiar one in academic grading practices. Practically every school that has studied the problem has found enormous variations among faculty members in the percentages of A's, B's, and C's that they give in comparable courses. The same situation holds for any set of categories, numbers, letters, or adjectives, that may be used. Standards of interpretation are highly subjective and vary widely from one rater to another. One person's "outstanding" is another person's "satisfactory."

Raters differ not only in the level of ratings that they assign, but also in how much they spread out their ratings. Some raters are conservative, and rarely rate anyone very high or very low; others tend to go to extremes. This difference in variability of ratings serves also to reduce the comparability of ratings from one rater to another. These differences among raters appear not to be a chance matter but to be a reflection of the personal characteristics and value structure of the rater. Thus in one study (Klores, 1966) it was found that supervisors who placed importance on a supervisor's personal relationships with subordinates gave higher and less variable ratings than supervisors who placed importance on providing structure in the work situation.

* One marking system from Indonesia is reported to have categories translated as: Excellent, Very Good, Good, Sufficient, Average, Below Average, Less, Very Less, Ugly, Very Bad.

Specific rater idiosyncrasies. Not only do raters differ in general "toughness" or "softness." They also differ in a host of specific idiosyncrasies. The experiences of life have built up in each of us an assortment of likes and dislikes and an assortment of individualized interpretations of the characteristics of people. You may distrust anyone who does not look at you while he is talking to you. Your neighbor may consider any man a sissy who has a voice pitched higher than usual. Your boss may consider that a firm handshake is the guarantee of a strong character. Your tennis partner may be convinced that blonds are flighty. These are rather definite reactions that may be explicit and clearly verbalized by the person in question. But there are myriad other more vague and less tangible biases that we carry with us and that influence our ratings. These biases help to form our impression of a person and color all aspects of our reaction to him. They enter into our ratings too. In some cases, our rating of one or two traits may be affected. But often the bias is one of general liking for or aversion to the person, and this generalized reaction colors all our specific ratings. Thus the ratings reflect not only the general subjective rating standard of the rater, but also his specific biases with respect to the person being rated.

A different type of idiosyncrasy that is likely to influence overall judgments of effectiveness on a job (or in an educational program) is idiosyncrasy as to what types of behavior are desirable. Thus Barrett (1966) found wide differences among supervisors of employees in closely similar jobs in the attributes that were considered important. Some raters considered "solving problems on one's own initiative" among the most important things a subordinate could do and some considered it among the least important. To the extent that such differences in values prevail, it is inevitable that supervisors will fail to agree on who are their more effective subordinates.

THE OUTCOME OF FACTORS
LIMITING RATING EFFECTIVENESS

What is the net result of these factors affecting the raters' willingness to rate conscientiously and ability to rate accurately? The effects show up in certain pervasive distortions of the ratings, in relatively low reliabilities, and in doubt as to the basic validity of rating procedures.

The generosity error. We have pointed out that the rater is often as much committed to the people he is rating as he is to the agency for which ratings are being prepared. Over and above this, there seems to be a widespread unwillingness on the part of raters, at least in the United States, to damn a fellow human with a low rating. The net result is that ratings tend quite generally to pile up at the high end of any scale. The unspoken philosophy of the rater seems to be "one person is as good as the next, if not a little better," so that "average" becomes in practice not the midpoint of a set of ratings but near the lower end of the group. It is a little like the commercial classification of olives, where the tiniest ones are called "medium," and they go from there through "large" and "extra large" to "jumbo" and "colossal."

If the generosity error operated uniformly for all raters, it would not be particularly disturbing. We would merely have to remember that ratings cannot be interpreted in terms of their verbal labels and that "average" means "low" and "very good" means "average." Makers of rating scales have countered this humane tendency with some success by having several steps on their scale on the plus side of average, so that there is room for differentiation without having to get disagreeable and call a person "average."

It is differences between raters in the degree of their "generosity error" that are more troublesome. To correct for such differences is a good deal more of a problem. We shall consider presently some special techniques that have been developed for that purpose.

The halo error.   Limitations in experience with the person being rated, lack of opportunity to observe the specific qualities that are called for in the rating instrument, and the influence of personal biases that affect general liking for the person all conspire to produce another type of error in ratings. This is a tendency to rate in terms of overall general impression without differentiating specific aspects, to allow the total reaction to the person to color judgment of each specific trait. This effect is called *halo*.

We can illustrate halo by the table on p. 460, involving ratings of World War II student airplane commanders by their instructors (Army Air Force 1947). The table shows the intercorrelations of four rather distinct characteristics of the students when ratings were given by the same instructor, in comparison with reliability, as estimated by correlations for rating of the same trait made by two different instructors.

	Intercorrelations			Between Rater Reliability
	2	3	4	
1. Eagerness	.77	.77	.59	.39
2. Foresight		.86	.62	.61
3. Leadership			.66	.56
4. Instrument flying				.32

Whereas the between-rater reliability of the judgments averaged out to be .47, the correlation among different traits by the same rater averaged .71. Thus when the same person looked he tended to see the same thing even for rather different traits, while different raters tended to see different things even for the same trait.

Of course, some relationship among desirable traits is to be expected. We find correlation among different abilities when these are tested by objective tests and do not speak of the halo effect that produces a correlation between verbal and mechanical ability. Just how much of the relationship between the different qualities on which we get ratings is genuine and how much of it is spurious halo is very hard to determine. That some of the relationship is due to inability to free oneself from general biases seems clear, however, from examples such as the one just given.

Reliability of ratings. Studies have shown repeatedly that the between-raters reliability of conventional rating procedures is low. Symonds (1931) summarized a number of studies and concluded that the correlation beween the ratings given by two independent raters for the conventional type of rating scale is about .55. There seems to be no good reason to change this conclusion after the lapse of years. When the two ratings are uncontaminated—that is, the raters have not talked over the persons to be rated—and when the usual type of numerical or graphic rating is used, the resulting appraisal shows only this very limited consistency from rater to rater.

If it is possible to pool the ratings of a number of independent raters who know the persons being rated about equally well, reliability of the appraisal can be substantially increased. Studies have shown (Remmers, et al., 1927) that pooling ratings functions in the same way as lengthening a test, and that the Spearman-Brown formula (p. 90) can legitimately be applied in estimating the reliability of pooled independent ratings. Thus, if the reliability of one rater is represented by a correlation of .55, we have the following estimates for the reliability of pooled ratings:

    2 raters .71
    3 raters .79
    5 raters .86
    10 raters .92

Unfortunately, in many important practical situations it is impossible to get additional equally qualified raters. An elementary school pupil has only one regular classroom teacher; a worker has only one immediate supervisor. Adding on other raters who have more limited acquaintance with the ratee may weaken rather than strengthen the ratings.

Reliability data on some of the newer types of rating devices to be discussed presently appear somewhat more promising. These data will be presented as the methods are discussed. One of the gains from basing ratings on specific tangible behaviors will be, it is hoped, that the objectivity, and hence the reliability, of the judgments will be increased.

Validity of ratings. All the limiting and distorting factors that we have been considering make us doubtful about the validity of ratings. Rater biases and rater unreliability operate to lower validity. However, it is usually very difficult to make any statistical test of the validity of ratings. The very fact that we have fallen back on ratings usually means that no better measure of the quality in question is available to us. There is usually nothing else against which we can test the ratings.

In one context the validity of ratings is axiomatic. If we are interested in appraising how a person is reacted to by other people, that is, whether a child is well liked by his classmates or a foreman by his work crew, ratings *are* the reactions of these other persons and are directly relevant to the point at issue.

When ratings are being studied as predictors, statistical data can be obtained as to the accuracy with which they do in fact predict. This is something that must be determined in each setting and for each type of criterion that is being predicted. That ratings are in some cases the most valid available predictors is shown in studies of the ratings of aptitude for military service that have been given at the U.S. Military Academy (Personnel Research Section, 1953). These ratings by tactical officers and by fellow cadets correlated more highly with later ratings of performance as an officer than did any other aspect of the man's record at West Point. Correlations with ratings of effectiveness in combat in the war in Korea were about .50. This criterion is again a rating, but it is probably as close to the real "payoff" as we are likely to get in this situation. In other situations, of course, ratings may turn out to have no validity at all. Each type of situation must be studied for its own sake.

IMPROVING THE EFFECTIVENESS OF RATINGS

So far we have painted a rather gloomy picture of rating techniques as devices for appraising personality. It is certainly true that the hazards and pitfalls in rating procedures are many. But for all their limitations, there are and will continue to be a host of situations in which we will have to rely on the judgments of other people as a means of appraising our fellow men. The sincerity and integrity of a potential medical student, the social acceptability of a would-be salesman, the conscientiousness of a private secretary can probably only be evaluated through the judgment that someone makes of these qualities in the individuals in question. What can be done, then, to mitigate the defects of rating procedures? We shall consider first the design of the rating instrument and then the planning and conduct of the ratings.

REFINEMENTS IN THE RATING INSTRUMENT

The usual rating instrument has two main components: (1) a set of *stimulus variables* (the qualities to be rated) and (2) a pattern of *response options* (the ratings that can be given). In the simplest and most conventional forms, the stimulus variables consist of trait names and the response options consist of numerical or adjectival categories. Such a form was illustrated on p. 449. This type of format appears to encourage most of the shortcomings discussed in the preceding section. Consequently, many variations and refinements of format have been tried out in an attempt to overcome or at least minimize these shortcomings. The variations have manipulated the stimulus variables, the response options, or both. Some of the main variations are described below.

REFINEMENTS IN PRESENTING THE STIMULUS VARIABLES

Bare trait names represent unsatisfactory stimuli for two reasons. In the first place, as we pointed out on p. 456, the words mean different things to different people. The child who shows "initiative" to teacher A may show "insubordination" to teacher B, whereas teacher B's "good citizen" may seem to teacher A a "docile conformist." In the second place, the terms are quite abstract and far removed in many cases from the realm of observable behavior. Consider "adjustment," for example. We do not observe a child's adjustment. We observe a host of reactions to situations and people. Some of these reactions are perhaps symptomatic of poor adjustment. But the judgment about the child's adjustment is several steps removed from what we have a chance to observe.

Users of ratings have striven to get greater uniformity of meaning in the traits to be rated, and they have attempted to base the ratings more closely upon observable behavior. These attempts have modified the stimulus aspect of rating instruments in three ways.

1. *Trait names have been defined.* "Social adjustment" is a rather nebulous label. It can be given somewhat more substance by elaborating on what the label is supposed to refer to, as in the following example.

Social Adjustment. Interest in and skills of interacting with both children and adults in work and play situations. Willingness both to give and to take in interpersonal situations. Conformity to basic social norms of behavior.

The elaboration attaches somewhat more substance to a very intangible concept, and should provide for somewhat greater uniformity of meaning among a group of raters.

There is no question that an expanded definition of each attribute to be appraised is a desirable first step in improving rating procedures. However, we may doubt that a brief verbal definition will go very far toward overcoming the individual differences in meaning that different raters attach to the term and, consequently, to the rating task.

2. *Trait names have been replaced by several more limited and concrete descriptive phrases.* The abstract and inclusive term "social adjustment" might be broken down into several components each relating to a more limited aspect of behavior. Thus we might have:

Working with other children.
Playing with other children.
Interacting with teacher and other adults.
Conforming to basic social norms and standards.

A judgment would now be called for with respect to each of the more restricted, and, hopefully, more tangible aspects of pupil behavior.

3. *Each trait name has been replaced with a substantial number of descriptions of specific behaviors.* This carries the move toward concreteness and specificity one step farther. Thus the rubric "working with other children" might be replaced with something like:

Working in groups with other children:
  Takes an active part in group enterprises.
  Makes and defends suggestions.
  Accepts majority decisions.
  Does his share of the work.
  Helps others with their work.

A similar subdivision would be carried out for each of the three other major headings. These items are still more tangible and specific. There should be much less ambiguity as to what it is that is to be observed and reported on, though there is still an element of interpretation in deciding, for example, what level of involvement constitutes "taking an active part."

The replacement of one general term with many specific behaviors gives promise of achieving more uniformity of meaning from one rater to another. It may also bring the ratings in closer touch with actual observations that have been made of the behavior of the individual who is being appraised. If it is the case that the trait to be rated is one that the rater has really had no opportunity to observe, the attempt to replace the trait name with specific observable behaviors will often make this fact painfully apparent and will force the designer of the instrument to rethink the problem of relating his instrument to the observations that the rater has really had an opportunity to make.

The gains that a list of specific behaviors achieves in uniformity of meaning and concreteness of behavior judged are not without cost. The cost lies in the greatly increased length and complexity of the rating instrument. There are limits to the number of different judgments that can be asked of a rater. Furthermore, the lengthy, analytical report of behavior may be confusing to the person who tries to use and interpret it. The lengthy list of specific behaviors will probably prove most effective when (1) judgments are in very simple terms, such as simply present-absent, and (2) there are provisions for organizing and summarizing the specific judgments into one or more *scores* for broad areas.

REFINEMENTS IN FORM
OF RESPONSE CATEGORIES

465

improving the
effectiveness of
ratings

Expressing judgments about a ratee by selecting some one of a set of numbers, letters, or adjectives is still common on school report cards or in civil service and industrial merit rating systems. However, these procedures have little other than simplicity to commend them. As we saw on p. 457, the categories are arbitrary and undefined. No two raters interpret them in exactly the same way. A rating of "superior" may be given to 5 percent of employees by one supervisor and to 25 percent by another. One man's A is another man's B. Subjective standards reign supreme.

.Various attempts have been made to manipulate the response options to try to achieve a more meaningful scale or greater uniformity from rater to rater.

Percentage of groups. To try to produce greater uniformity from rater to rater and to produce greater discrimination among the ratings given by a particular rater, judgments are sometimes called for in terms of percentage of a particular defined group. Thus a professor rating an applicant for a fellowship is instructed to rate each candidate according to the following scale:

> Falls in the top 2 percent of students at his level of training.
> In top 10 percent, but not in top 2 percent.
> In top 25 percent, but not in top 10 percent.
> In top half, but not in top 25 percent.
> In lower half of students at his level of training.

Presumably the specified percentages of a defined group provide a uniform standard of quality for different raters. However, the stratagem is usually only partially successful. Individual differences in generosity are not that easily suppressed.

Graphic scale. A second variation is more a matter of form than clarity of definition. Rating scales are often prepared so that judgments may be recorded as a check at some appropriate point on a line, instead of by choosing a number, letter, or adjective, as in the scale below.

Responsibility for Completing Work

Very
high   Average   Very
                                                                       low

The pattern often makes a fairly attractive page layout, is compact and economical of space, and seems somewhat less forbidding than a form that is all print. However, this particular variation does not seem to have much advantage other than attractiveness and convenience. One study (Blumberg et al., 1966) that compared various numerical and graphic formats for presenting the rating task found format to be quite insignificant as a determinant of the ratings that were given.

Behavioral statement. We have seen that the stimuli may be in the form of relatively specific behavioral statements. Statements of this sort may also be used to present the choice alternatives. Thus we may have an item of the following type.

Participation in School Projects

Volunteers to bring in materials. Suggests ideas. Often works overtime.	Works or brings materials as requested. Participates, but takes no initiative.	Does as little as possible. Resists attempts to get him to help.

Here three statements describing behavior are combined with a graphic scale, and are used to define three points on the scale. The descriptions may be expected to lend more concreteness and uniformity of meaning to the scale steps. However, these editorial provisions do not completely overcome rater idiosyncrasies, which continue to plague us.

A whimsical development of a rating form that provides a fairly clear illustration of behavioral statements is shown in Figure 12.1.

Man-to-man scales. An early attempt to get more uniformity of meaning into the response scale, developed as far back as World War I, used men instead of numbers, adjectives, or descriptions to represent the scale points. The rater is asked to think of someone he has known well who was very high on the quality being rated. That person's name is then entered on the rating form to define the "very high" point on the scale. In the same way, the names of other persons known well by the rater are entered in spaces to define "high," "average," "low," and "very low." The five names then define levels for the trait. When a person is to be rated the rater is instructed to compare

Figure 12.1

EMPLOYEE PERFORMANCE APPRAISAL

Area of Performance	Degree of Performance				
	Far exceeds job requirements	Exceeds job requirements	Meets job requirements	Needs Improvement	Does not meet minimum requirements
Quality of work	Leaps tall buildings in a single bound	Leaps tall buildings with a running start	Can leap short buildings with prodding	Bumps into buildings	Fails to recognize buildings
Promptness	Is faster than a speeding bullet	Is as fast as a speeding bullet	Would you believe a slow bullet?	Misfires frequently	Wounds self when handling guns
Adaptability	Walks on water	Readily keeps head above water	Washes with water	Drinks water	Chronically waterlogged
Communication	Talks with God	Talks with the angels	Talks to himself	Argues with himself	Loses arguments with himself

him with the five persons defining the levels on the trait. The rater is to judge which person the new ratee most closely resembles on the trait in question. The value assigned corresponds to the step on the scale that person occupies.

It was thought that the man-to-man feature would lend concreteness to the comparisons and overcome the tendency of some raters to be consistently generous. In cases in which all raters have a wide range of acquaintance, so that their scale persons may be expected to be fairly comparable, the procedure may make for more uniformity from rater to rater. But such scope of acquaintance and thoroughness of familiarity with suitable scale persons is likely to be somewhat unusual in the practical situations in which ratings must be made. Implicit comparison with other persons is involved in any rating enterprise, but explicit use of particular persons to define the steps on a rating scale has not been widely adopted.

Present–absent. When a large number of specific behavioral statements are used as the stimuli, the response that is called for is often a mere checking of those that apply to the individual in question. The person is then characterized by the statements that are checked as representing him. The rating scale becomes a behavior checklist. The set of items on p. 464 might constitute part of such a checklist.

If this type of appraisal procedure is to yield a score, the statements must be scaled or assigned score values in some way. The simplest way is merely to score them $+1$, -1 or 0, depending upon whether they are favorable, unfavorable, or neutral with respect to a particular attribute (that is, perseverance, integrity, reliability, etc.) or a particular criterion (that is, success in academic work, success on a job, responsiveness to therapy, etc.) An individual's score can then be the sum of the scores for the items checked for him.

If the additional elegance seems justified, more refined scaling procedures can be applied to the statements. A statement's scale value can be based on its judged significance or the degree to which it has actually discriminated between successful and unsuccessful individuals. The score an individual receives is then based on an averaging of the scale values of the items that were checked as describing him. The reliability of such a checklist of scaled items has been found to be quite satisfactory in some instances. An early study (Richardson and Kuder, 1933) reported a correlation of .83 between total score given by two independent raters when rating salesmen. More recently (Ross et al., 1965) split-half reliabilities from .72 to .95 and retest reliabilities from .77 to .93 were reported for scores on the four scales (aggressive, withdrawn, prosocial, and passive-aggressive) of the *Pittsburgh Adjustment Survey Scales* applied to elementary school boys.

Only limited use has been made of checklists as devices to yield scores on each individual, but they seem to present a promising pattern. They come the closest of any of the rating procedures to self-report inventories on the one hand and to ability tests on the other. A behavior checklist is in a sense a personality inventory that has been filled out by someone other than the person being described. The items can be selected and scored in much the same way.

One well-known behavior checklist that is more like an ability test is the *Vineland Social Maturity Scale* (Doll, 1953, 1965). This checklist is made up of items relating to self-help, self-direction, communication, socialization, and the like. Selected items from different levels of the scale are shown in Table 12.1. Norms were established for each item of the scale, representing the age at which the behavior appears on the average. The checklist is filled out by a rater who knows the child being appraised. Items the child does or can do are checked. A basal

Table 12.1
ITEMS SELECTED FROM THE *VINELAND SOCIAL MATURITY SCALE*

Item No.	Age Level (in years)	Item
1	0–1	"Crows," laughs
6	0–1	Reaches for nearby objects
11	0–1	Drinks from cup assisted
15	0–1	Stands alone
19	1–2	Marks with pencil or crayon
28	1–2	Eats with spoon
34	1–2	Talks in short sentences
37	2–3	Removes coat or dress
40	2–3	Dries own hands
44	2–3	Relates experiences
51	4–5	Cares for self at toilet
53	4–5	Goes about neighborhood unattended
68	7–8	Disavows literal Santa Claus
70	7–8	Combs or brushes hair
78	10–11	Writes occasional short letters
80	10–11	Does small remunerative work

age is established for which all items are positive, and the person being rated is automatically given credit for all earlier items. Points are given for additional items passed. The table of norms gives developmental age equivalents for the point scores, and a developmental quotient may be computed that indicates the individual's rate of progress toward self-sufficiency and independence.

The checklist pattern has been used as a simple descriptive instrument, as in school reports to the home. The procedure is attractive in this setting because it can give information on specific aspects of pupil development. However, forms tend to become complicated and to confuse many parents, so this type of reporting has not been widely adopted.

Frequency of occurrence, or typicality. Instead of reacting in an all-or-none fashion to an item, as in the checklist, the rater can be given the choices that the behavior is "always," "usually, "sometimes," "seldom," or "never" characteristic of the ratee.* Or the ratee may be characterized as "very much like," "a good deal like," "somewhat like," "slightly like," or "not at all like" the behavior described in the statement. The terms indicating frequency or resemblance may vary; the ones given are only suggestive. An individual's score could now take account both of the significance of the statement and the frequency or typicality that is checked. That is, an important attribute could receive heavier credit than a minor one, and a check at the "always" step more credit than a check at "usually."

Indefinite designations of frequency or degree of the sort that are being suggested here will be differently interpreted by different raters, so the old problem of differences in rater standards reappears. Moreover, when the number of specific behaviors being checked is substantial, a simple present-absent checking correlates quite highly with the more elaborate form.

Ranking. In those cases in which each rater knows a substantial number of ratees, he may be asked to place them in rank order with respect to each attribute being studied. Thus a teacher may be asked to indicate the child who is most outstanding for contributing to the class projects and activities

---

* In formulating items to be responded to with the categories "always," "usually," etc., one must take care that no term expressing frequency is included in the statement of the item. Otherwise, one is faced with the syntactic atrocity of judging that Johnny "always" "usually accepts majority decisions."

"over and beyond the call of duty," the one who is second, and so on. Usually, the ranker will be instructed to start at both ends and work in toward the middle, since the extreme cases are usually easier to discriminate than the large group of average ones in the middle. This is sometimes formalized as *alternation ranking*, that is, picking the highest and then the lowest, the next highest and then the next lowest, and so on. In order to ease the task of the ranker, tie ranks may be permitted. If no tie ranks are permitted, the ranker may feel that the task is an unreasonable one, especially in a group of some size.

Ranking is an arduous task for the ranker, but it does achieve two important objectives. First, it forces the person doing the evaluation to make discriminations among those being evaluated. The ranker cannot place all or most of the persons being judged in a single category, as may happen with other reporting systems. Second, it washes out individual differences among raters in generosity or leniency. No matter how kindly the ranker may feel, he must put somebody last, and no matter how hardboiled he is, someone must come first. Individual differences in standards of judgment are eliminated from the final score.

If scores based on rankings by different judges are to be combined, there is one assumption that is introduced in rankings that may be about as troublesome as the individual differences in judging standards that have been eliminated. If we are to treat rankings by different judges as comparable scores, we must assume that the quality of the group ranked by each is the same. That is, we assume that being second in a group of 20 represents the same level on the trait being appraised, whichever group of 20 it happens to be. Usually there is no direct way of comparing the different subgroups, so about all we can do is assume that they are comparable. If the groups are fairly sizable and chosen more or less at random from the same sort of population, this may be a reasonable assumption. But with small groups or groups selected in different ways, the assumption of comparability may introduce substantial amounts of error into any scores based on ranks.

Ranks as such do not represent a very useful score scale. The meaning depends upon the size of the group: being third in a group of 3 is very different from being third in a group of 30. Furthermore, steps of rank do not represent equal units of a trait. As we saw in our discussion of percentile norms (Chapter 4), in the usual bell-shaped distribution, 1 or 2 ranks at the extremes of a group represent much more of a difference than the same number of ranks near the middle of the group. For

that reason, it is common practice to convert ranks into normalized standard scores in order to get a type of score that has
uniform meaning without regard to the size of the group and
uniform units throughout the score range. Special tables have
been prepared to facilitate this conversion, and tables for
groups of all sizes up to 25 may be found on pp. 90–92 of
Symonds (1931).

Behaviorally anchored rating scales.   A method that has recently been popular for developing performance evaluation instruments is one that calls upon the supervisors who will later
be the ones to use the rating scales to participate in their development. Work proceeds in three stages.

1. A group of future raters, through a period of discussion,
agrees upon the dimensions that can be distinguished as aspects of performance of a job. In one early application of the
method (Smith and Kendall, 1963) head nurses agreed upon
the following dimensions as applicable to medical-surgical
nurses:

Knowledge and judgment

Conscientiousness

Skill in human relations

Organizational ability

Objectivity

Observational ability

2. The potential users generate a pool of "critical incidents"
of actually observed behavior to illustrate superior, average,
and inferior performance in each of the dimensions. Raters in a
new group are then called upon to assign each incident to the
dimension to which it applies. For further analysis, only those
incidents are retained for which there is a high degree of agreement in assignment to a given dimension.
3. Each person in a new group of judges indicate where on
a scale of excellence each statement falls. The average level
and the consistency of these judgments are scrutinized, and a
subset of items is retained in which each shows good agreement
among judges and for which the complete set shows a wide
range of average scale values. By way of illustration, the following 3 items are drawn from the scale entitled *Interpersonal Relations with Students* on an instrument for college faculty (Harari

and Zedeck, 1973). The scale has a possible range from 1 (low) to 7 (high).

473
improving the
effectiveness of
ratings

Scale Value	Statement
6.8	When a class doesn't understand a certain concept or feels "lost," this professor could be expected to sense it and act to correct the situation.
3.9	During lectures, this professor could often be expected to tell students with questions to see him during his office hours.
1.3	This professor could be expected to embarrass or humiliate students who disagreed with him.

In application, the set of statements for each dimension is provided, and the rater indicates which statement comes closest to describing the person being rated. Users have reported (Campbell et al., 1973) that this procedure "yielded less method variance, less halo error, and less leniency error" than more conventional rating procedures.

The procedures for scale development are quite time consuming, and the resulting instrument tends to be a little cumbersome. More experience is needed before one can judge whether gains from the procedure are maintained in further use, and are sufficiently large to justify the additional work.

THE FORCED-CHOICE PATTERN

All the variations considered so far operate on the same basic pattern. The rater considers one attribute at a time and assigns the ratee to one of a set of categories or places him relative to others on that particular attribute. We shall now consider a major departure from that pattern. The essence of the procedure we consider now is that the rater considers a *set* of attributes at one time and decides which one (or ones) most accurately represents the person being rated. Thus an instrument developed for evaluating Air Force technical-school instructors (Highland and Berkshire, 1951) included sets of items such as the following

(a) Patient with slow learners.

(b) Lectures with confidence.

(c) Keeps interest and attention of class.

(d) Acquaints classes with objective for each lesson.

The rater's assignment was to pick out the 2 items from the set that were *most descriptive* of the person being rated.

Note that all the statements in the above set are nice things to say about an instructor. As a matter of fact, they were carefully matched, on the basis of information from a preliminary investigation, to be just about equally nice to say about an instructor. But they differ a good deal, again based on preliminary investigations, in the extent to which they actually distinguish between persons who have been identified on other evidence as being good and poor instructors. The most discriminating statement is (*a*) and the least discriminating is (*b*). Thus we could assign a score value of 2 to statement (*a*), 1 to (*c*) and (*d*), and 0 to (*b*). A person's score for the set would be the sum of the credits for the 2 items marked as most descriptive of him. His score for the whole instrument would be the sum of his scores for 25 or 30 such blocks of 4 statements. Such a score was found to have good split-half reliability (.85 to .90), so that this instrument provided a reliable score for the individual's desirability as an instructor in the eyes of a single rater. This does not, of course, tell anything about the agreement that would be found between different raters.

By casting the evaluation instrument into a forced-choiced format, the maker hopes to accomplish three things.

1. *To eliminate variation in rater standards of generosity or kindliness.* Since the items in a set are all equally favorable things to say about a person, the kindly soul should have no particular tendency to choose one rather than another, and the true nature of the ratee should be the controlling factor.

2. *To minimize the possibility of a rater intentionally biasing the score.* In the ordinary rating scale the rater is in pretty complete control of the situation. He can rate a person up or down as he pleases. In the forced-choice type of instrument, it is hoped that the rater will be unable to identify which are the significant choices and therefore will be unable to throw the score one way or the other at will. However, though there are some indications that a forced-choice instrument is less fakeable than an ordinary rating scale, it is still far from tamper-proof in the hands of a determined rater.

3. *To produce a better spread of scores and a more nearly normal distribution of ratings.* By making all options equally attractive, one minimizes the effect of the generosity error, it is hoped, and gets a more symmetrical spread of scores. Again, there is indication that this result is achieved at least in part.

Forced-choice formats generated a good deal of interest, some research, and a certain amount of practical use during the period from 1945 to 1965, but the burden of preparing them and negative reactions to them on the part of raters have resulted in a gradual decline in interest in recent years.

REFINEMENTS IN THE RATING PROCEDURES

The best-designed instrument cannot give good results if used under unsatisfactory rating conditions. Raters cannot give information they do not have and cannot be made to give information they are unwilling to give. We must, therefore, try to pick raters who have had close contacts with the ratees and ask them for judgments on attributes they have had an opportunity to observe. We should give them some guidance and training in the type of judgment we expect them to make, and if possible they should have opportunity to observe the ratees *after* they have been educated in the use of the rating instrument. When there are several people who know the ratees equally well, ratings should be gathered from all of them and pooled. Every effort should be made to motivate the raters to do an honest and conscientious job. Let us consider these points further.

Selection of Raters.   For most purposes the ideal rater is the person who has had a great deal of opportunity to observe the person being rated in those situations in which he would be likely to show the qualities on which ratings are desired. (Occasionally it may be desirable to get a rating of the impression that a person makes on brief contact or in a limited experimental situation.) It is also desirable that the rater take an impartial attitude toward the ratee. The desirability of these two qualities, thorough acquaintance and impartiality, is generally recognized in the abstract. However, the goals may be only partially realized in practice.

Administrative considerations usually dictate that the rating and evaluation function be assigned to the teacher in the school setting and to the supervisor in a work setting. The relationship here is in each case one of direct supervision. There is generally a continuing and fairly close personal relationship. But the relationship is a one-directional and partial one. The teacher or supervisor sees only one side of the pupil or worker, the side that is turned toward the "boss."

Those qualities that a boss has a good chance to see, primarily qualities of work performance, can probably be rated adequately by the teacher or supervisor. Thus in one study (Judy, 1952) of airplane mechanics it was found that the ratings by a pair of supervisors on "job know-how" were as reliable as the pooled ratings by eight coworkers in a plane maintenance crew and that the supervisors' pooled rating correlated .53 with a written proficiency test, whereas the pooled rating for the co-workers correlated only .43. However, those qualities that show themselves primarily in relationships with peers or subordinates will probably be evaluated more soundly by those same peers and subordinates. The validity of the U. S. Military Academy peer ratings described on p. 461 is a case in point.

The lack of agreement between supervisor and pupil ratings of teachers is suggested in some of the following correlations from different studies

Pupil's rating of excellence versus principal's rating (Cook and Leeds, 1947)	.39
Pupil's rating of excellence versus composite of 5 judges (Lins, 1946)	.28
Mean pupil rating of effectiveness versus administrator's rating (Brookover, 1940)	.08
Student versus administrator rating on general teacher effectiveness (Reed, 1953) School I	.40
School II	.50

A certain amount of overlap does exist, but the ratings appear also to have a good deal of uniqueness. The bird's eye and worm's eye views are not the same.

Who should choose the raters?   The selection of persons to rate applicants for jobs or fellowships requires consideration from another point of view. In this setting the applicant is usually asked to supply a certain number of references or to submit evaluation forms filled out by a certain number of individuals. The choice of the evaluators is usually left up to him, and we may anticipate that he will select persons he believes will rate him favorably. It might be more satisfactory if the applicant were asked to supply the names and addresses of persons who stood in particular relationships to him and who should therefore be able to supply relevant information, rather than leaving the applicant free to pick his own endorsers. A job applicant might be asked to give the names of his immediate supervisors in his most recent jobs, a fellowship applicant to list the name of his major advisor and of any instructors with whom he had taken two or more courses. Thus we are shifting the responsibility of determining who shall provide the ratings from the applicant to the using agency. Such a shift should reduce the amount of special pleading for the applicant.

Selection of qualities to be rated.   Two principles appear to apply in determining the types of information to be sought by rating procedures. First, it seems generally undesirable to use rating procedures to get information that can be provided satisfactorily by some more objective and reliable indicator. A score on a well-constructed aptitude test is a better indicator of cognitive ability than a supervisor's rating of intellect. When accurate production records exist, they are to be preferred to a supervisor's rating for productivity. Ratings are something to which we resort when we do not have any better indicator available.

Second, we should limit ratings to relatively overt qualities, ones that can be expressed in terms of actual observable behavior. We cannot expect the rater to look inside the ratee and tell us what goes on within. Furthermore, we must bear in mind the extent and nature of the contact between rater and person rated. For example, a set of ratings to be used after a single interview should be limited to the qualities that can be observed in an interview. The interviewee's neatness, composure, manner of speech, and fluency in answering questions are qualities that should be observable in a single interview. His industry, integrity, initiative, and ingenuity are not, though these qualities might be appraised with some accuracy by a person who has worked with him for a time. Ratings should be of observable behavior—observable in the setting in which the ratee has been observed.

Educational program for raters.   Good ratings do not just happen, even with the proper raters and the proper instrument for recording the ratings. Raters must be "sold" on the importance of making good ratings and taught how to use the rating instrument. Pointing out the importance of "selling" a rating program is easier than telling how to do it. As indicated earlier, inertia on the one hand and identification with the ratee on the other are powerful competing motives. We cannot provide a course in direct selling at this point, but a job of selling needs to be done in almost any program for gathering ratings. Furthermore, the selling must continue if thoughtfulness and integrity of the appraisals are to be maintained.

It is desirable that raters have practice with the specific rating instrument. A training session, in which the instrument is used under supervision, is often desirable. The meanings of the attributes can be discussed, sample rating sheets can be prepared, and the resulting ratings reviewed. The prevailing generosity error can be noted, and raters cautioned to avoid it. Further practice can be given, in an attempt to generate a more symmetrical distribution of ratings. Training sessions will not eliminate all the shortcomings of ratings, but they should reduce somewhat the more common distortions considered earlier.

Observations made as a basis for ratings.   One objection to ratings is that they are usually made after the fact and are based on general unanalyzed impressions about the person rated. An attempt to get away from this dependence on general memory is sometimes made by introducing the rating program well in advance of the time at which the final ratings are to be called for. It is hoped that the raters will then be on the alert for and take specific note of behavior relating to the qualities to be rated. A record form can be developed in which critical areas of performance are identified, and space is provided for recording instances of desirable, as well as undesirable actions on the part of the ratee. A section from such a form, designed for use in evaluating student nurses (Fivars and Gosnell, 1966) is shown in Fig. 12.2, pp. 480–481. A final rating for each section would be based upon a review of the incidents, both positive and negative, that had been observed and recorded by the supervisor. However, recording of this type does call for a high level of commitment to, and cooperation in, the rating program. When that level of involvement is achieved, advance notice and systematic recording may be expected to improve the rating process. Situations of this sort are probably rare, however.

Pooling of ratings by several raters.   One of the limitations of ratings is low reliability. If several people have had a reasonably good chance to observe the ratee, reliability can be improved by pooling their independent ratings (see pp. 460–461). Unfortunately, the number of persons well placed to observe a person in some particular setting—school, job, camp, and so on—is usually limited. Often only one person has been in close contact with the ratee in a particular relationship. He has had only one homeroom teacher, only one foreman, only one tent counselor. Others have had some contact with him, but it may be so much less that their judgments add little to the judgment of the rater most intimately involved.

Note that we specified the pooling of *independent* ratings. If the ratings are independently made, the "error" components will be independent and will tend to cancel out. If, however, the judgments are combined through some sort of conference procedure, we cannot tell just what will happen. Errors may cancel out, wisdom may win, or the prejudices of the most dogmatic may prevail. Pooling independent judgments is the only sure way of balancing out individual errors and has been found in several studies (Personnel Research Section, 1952) to be more satisfactory than the conference type of procedure.

NOMINATING TECHNIQUES

If a teacher is to understand pupils, he must have some awareness of the values and standards that the group sets for its members—the peer culture—and of the role that each child plays in the group of his contemporaries—the peer group. The standards and values of his peers provide the sanctions and the rewards that are very influential in determining how a person will act and how content he will be in the group setting. The peer group can be quite a cohesive unit. In such a group any action by a teacher with respect to an individual child is often viewed not only as an action for or against him but also as an action for or against the group to which he belongs and which identifies with him. Thus, in order both to understand the individual and to understand how acts with respect to individuals affect the group climate, it is important to appraise the role of the individual in the group.

Studies have shown (Gronlund, 1959) that teachers do, in general, have a fairly good sense of which children are and which are not accepted by their peers. A correlation of about .60 between teacher ranking and the pooling of choices by members of the peer group appears to be fairly typical. But even a correlation of this size leaves room for marked discrepancies in perception of some individuals within a class. It is often difficult for a teacher to attribute to an active and, perhaps, troublesome child his true level of influence with his peers. So, to improve understanding of the social interplay in a classroom, of the reputation of each pupil among his peers, and the patterns of attraction and repulsion, peer ratings are often helpful.

A rating procedure that is very simple and quite effective for obtaining appraisals by peers is the *nominating technique.* We will consider this technique first as applied to social choices and rejections and then as applied more generally to trait ratings.

To improve their understanding of the social structure in a classroom, the patterns of friendship and leadership, teachers

Student's Name

_____

Behaviors Needing Improvement
1. *Planning, organizing, and adapting nursing care*
   a. Failed to organize nursing care for maximum patient benefit.
   b. Failed to collect all equipment necessary for patient care.
   c. Took unwise shortcuts in giving nursing care.
   d. Failed to adapt procedure to situation.
   e. Used inadequate or improper substitute equipment.

Date	Item	What Happened

2. *Checking*
   a. Failed to check Kardex in administering medication, treatment.
   b. Did not check cards, labels, or names in medication procedure.
   c. Failed to see that laboratory orders were carried out.
   d. Did not question inconsistent medication, treatment, diet order.
   e. Failed to check requisition, equipment, or supplies.
   f. Neglected to check patient's condition.

Date	Item	What Happened

3. *Meeting the patient's adjustment and emotional needs*
   a. Refused request, was unkind, tactless, or indifferent.
   b. Did not provide recreational or diversional activity.
   c. Failed to recognize social service, spiritual, other needs.
   d. Did not explain or reassure patient about test, treatment, or policy; or misinformed patient.

Date	Item	What Happened

Figure 12.2
Observational Record form to serve as a basis for rating. (After Fivars and Gosnell, 1966.) (Reproduced by permission of John C. Flanagan and of the Macmillan Company.)

may use the simple expedient of asking pupils to name their choices of best friends or of work partners. For example, a teacher might say to a class: "For our unit on Mexico, we are going to need some committees of children who will work together on some part of the project. I would like to know which children you would like to have on a committee with you. Put

Behaviors to Be Encouraged

1. *Planning, organizing, and adapting nursing care*
   A. Organized nursing care plan or equipment efficiently.
   B. Anticipated needs of others.
   C. Adapted nursing care plan to overcome difficulties.
   D. Adapted nursing care procedures to patient's needs
   E. Used adequate substitute equipment when necessary.
   F. Devised or suggested new technique for welfare of patient or for ward efficiency.

Date	Item	What Happened

2. *Checking*
   A. Checked Kardex frequently for new orders.
   B. Made special checks in medication procedure.
   C. Checked to see that laboratory orders were carried out.
   D. Noted inconsistency in medication, treatment, diet order.
   E. Checked equipment and supplies for shortage or defects.
   F. Made special checks on signs and condition of patient.

Date	Item	What Happened

3. *Meeting the patient's adjustment and emotional needs*
   A. Was reassuring, kind, and considerate to patient.
   B. Made arrangements for recreational or diversional therapy.
   C. Noted social service, home nursing, spiritual, other needs.
   D. Adapted explanation of teaching to patient's understanding.
   E. Effectively taught patient health principles or home care.

Date	Item	What Happened

your name on the top of the piece of paper I gave you. Then under it put the names of the children you would especially like to have on your committee."

Such a procedure produces a set of nominations or choices for work partners. It is possible to show these choices pictorially by a diagram such as that shown in Fig. 12.3. This is called a *sociogram,* and the procedure of constructing a sociogram is called *sociometry.*

From the sociogram shown in Fig. 12.3 we can see that A and B are the most sought after members of the group: these are the "stars." Pupils J and O did not choose anyone and were not chosen by any other pupils; they are isolates. Pupils H and I chose each other, but were not chosen by any other pupils. Except for the mutual friendship between them, they too are isolates. Pupils P, Q, M, and N are fringers; they do not really belong to any of the groups but do make choices within the group.

Figure 12.3 shows the pattern of choices and attractions within the group. It would also be possible to have children indicate those class members whom they would definitely *not*

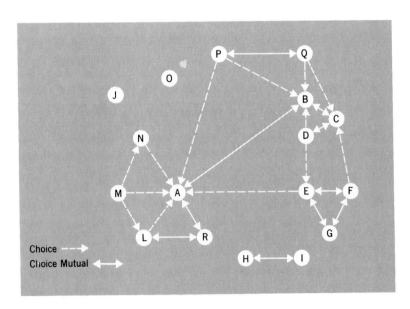

Figure 12.3
Sociogram of fourth grade class.

want to associate with. Calling for rejections presents some slight risks to individual and class morale but does permit a more complete picture of group structure.

The sociogram in Fig. 12.3 indicates that this is not a closely knit group. The rather large number of isolates and fringers and the linkages across from one "clique" to the other suggest an unstable pattern that is in the process of changing and reforming. Thus the sociogram might represent a class at the beginning of the school year, in which a residue of last year's friendships is mixed with new currents and in which pupils from other class groups and other schools are not yet integrated into the group. It is in such a setting as this that the teacher can be most effective in bringing isolates into the group or promoting new friendships.

After the teacher has determined which children are without friends or are relatively isolated in the group, he or she should try to find out why this is the case. Sometimes the explanation may be very simple. The child may be new to the group and have not yet had time to find his place in it. The normal opportunities to get acquainted, furthered by the teacher's efforts to bring out the new child's assets, may be all that is required. The child may be older or younger than the rest of the group, having friends in other classes or outside of school. The child may not live near any of the other children in the class. At other times the reasons may be more subtle, and it may take a good deal of discreet sleuthing for the teacher to find out why Willie and Alice are not chosen by their classmates.

When the reasons are understood the teacher can often help to remove them. Sometimes the simple process of coaching the child so that he develops competence in athletics may turn the trick. The teacher can arrange seats so that a child is placed near one for whom he expressed preference. Sometimes helping a child to develop everyday social graces or to improve personal appearance is all that is needed to make him acceptable. If an isolate or fringer has special mechanical or artistic skills, giving him an opportunity to use these in class group activities may be effective.

In general, the teacher can help a child become integrated with and accepted by the peer group by (1) providing opportunity for developing friendly relations, (2) improving social skills, and (3) building up a sense of accomplishment or competence.

Sociometric choices describe the present flow of interaction among children rather than indicating any strong and permanent emotional structuring. However, the structuring of a class group affects the general emotional climate of the classroom. In a class where there are many isolates or children who are "fringers," that is, not completely accepted by a clique, the morale of the group tends to be low and group planning and coordinated group action is made more difficult. It is also true that a teacher dealing with one child is quite frequently dealing with the clique to which the child belongs.

Sociograms frequently point up mistakes that a teacher makes in characterizing a child. Thus, when the teacher has judged a child and his position in his peer group by adult standards, sociometric devices point out these mistakes and give the teacher a framework for understanding behavior that taken by itself may seem unexplainable.

Sociograms have been used in various nonschool situations. In industry they have been used to form work groups and have been found to stimulate production. They have been used in institutions, especially those for juvenile offenders, to select house groups.

The sociogram by itself tells the teacher only what children are selected or rejected, not the reasons for selection and rejection. It is most useful when used in conjunction with good anecdotal records. For successful use, especially when rejections are asked for, there needs to be a friendly feeling between the teacher and the class. Furthermore, the teacher should actually use the nominations as far as possible in the way in which he has told the class he would use them.

The teacher should also remember that group structure is not static, especially in younger age groups. One sociogram made at the beginning of a school year will rarely provide an adequate picture of group structure through the year. Furthermore, neither choices nor rejections can be taken entirely at face value. When, as is sometimes the procedure, the number of choices is limited to "three best friends," failure to choose a particular pupil need not mean lack of friendly feeling for him. Choices may reflect the prestige of the person chosen and a desire to be associated with that prestige, rather than a link of friendship. The culture pattern in certain age groups dictates that rejections follow sex lines. Class and caste distinctions also introduce cultural factors influencing choice and rejection. A sociogram is at best a rough and tentative picture of the social currents and climate of the group.

A final word of caution should be sounded about attempting to use sociometric data to reconstruct a group or modify a child's role in it. We have offered some suggestions as to ways in which a teacher may try to help the relatively isolated child. However, any such manipulations call for a good deal of subtlety. Heavy-handed attempts by the teacher to manipulate the pupils in the group may only aggravate the ills he is trying to cure.

Other patterns for obtaining peer evaluations have been developed, and they have been used for other purposes beside the preparing of sociograms and the studying of social currents within the group. A slightly more complex form is the *Ohio Social Acceptance Scale,* in which each pupil reacts to each other pupil in the group, checking him under one of the following six categories: (1) My very, very best friends, (2) My other friends, (3) Not friends, but okay, (4) Don't know them, (5) Don't care for them, (6) Dislike them. From the pooled pupil responses, a score may be obtained for each child indicating the extent of his acceptance within the group. This or some other similar format provides a simple procedure for obtaining ratings by a group of peers, and their simplicity makes them usable even with elementary school children.

The *Syracuse Scales of Social Relations* (Gardner and Thompson, 1958) provide for an even more elaborate rating system, in which each pupil sets up his own person-to-person scale in relation to a person to "talk over your troubles with" and of a person to help you "make or do something," Each pupil in the class is then located by the pupil at some point on this scale. Results can be summarized in terms of average ratings given or received by a single pupil, or the class as a whole, and particular constellations of mutual attraction can be sought out.

Nominations may be used at any age level, and may be made with respect to any type of characteristic. For example, they have frequently been used in the armed services in Officer Candidate School, where each member of a unit may be asked to nominate a specified number of individuals in his unit who have shown the greatest evidence of "leadership" during the training course. He may also be asked to nominate those who have shown the *least* indication of leadership.

Taking all the nominations for the group as a whole, it is possible to arrive at a score for each individual, giving a plus for each favorable nomination and a minus for each unfavorable nomination.

A variation of the nominating procedure that has been used with school children has usually been referred to as the "Guess Who" technique or as "Casting Characters." In this procedure, the children are instructed somewhat as follows.

Suppose we were going to put on a class play. The characters in the play are described below. For each character, you are to put down the names of one or more children in the class who would be good for that part because he or she is just like that anyway.

"This person is always cheerful and happy—never grouchy or cross.

"This person is always butting in and telling other people how to do things. He cannot mind his own business.

"This person is very quiet and doesn't get into games or do things with other children."

The number of characters can be extended as desired. Each "character" is a description in fairly concrete terms of a quality of behavior in which the investigator is interested. Descriptions of opposite ends of a scale can be included—that is, friendly versus unfriendly, dominating versus submissive, and so on—and can be treated as positive and negative nominations on a single scale. Each child receives a score for each "character," based on the number of nominations he receives.

The attractive feature of the nominating pattern is its simplicity, which makes it rather painless to administer and usable with young groups or groups with little sophistication or experience in rating. It is feasible because the large number of raters make it possible to use a simple count of nominations instead of a rating of the usual type. However, nominating procedures do sometimes generate resistance. Students in military training programs have been known to "rig" the choices so as not to injure the chances of fellow students, and parent groups have reacted sometimes violently when children were asked to make negative responses of rejection or separation from their classmates. It is important to be aware of these sensibilities in students and in a community.

SUMMARY AND EVALUATION

In spite of all their limitations, evaluations of persons through ratings will undoubtedly continue to be widely used for administrative evaluations in schools, civil service, and industry, as well as in educational and psychological research. We must recognize this fact and learn to live with it. Granting that we shall continue to use ratings of different aspects of personality, we should do so with full awareness of the limitations of our instruments, and we should do so in such a way that these limitations are minimized.

The limitations of rating procedures arise out of the following.

1. A humane unwillingness to make unfavorable judgments of our fellows, which is particularly pronounced when we identify to some extent with the person being rated (generosity error).

2. Wide individual differences among raters in "humaneness" or, in any event, in leniency or severity of rating (differences in rater standards).

3. A tendency to respond to other persons as a whole in terms of our general liking or aversion and difficulty in differentiating out specific aspects of the individual personality (halo error).

4. Limited contact between the rater and person being rated—limited both in amount and in type of situation in which seen.

5. Ambiguity in meaning of the attributes to be appraised.

6. The covert and unobservable nature of many of the inner aspects of personality dynamics.

7. Instability and unreliability of human judgment.

In view of these limitations it is suggested that ratings will provide a most accurate portrayal of the person being rated when the following criteria are met.

1. Appraisal is limited to those qualities that appear overtly in interpersonal relations.

2. The qualities to be appraised are analyzed into concrete and relatively specific aspects of behavior, and judgments are made of these behaviors.

3. A rating form is developed that forces the rater to discriminate and/or that has controls for rater differences in judging standards.

4. Raters are used who have had the most opportunity to observe the individual in situations in which he would display the qualities to be rated.

5. Raters are "sold" on the value of the ratings and trained in the use of the rating instrument.

6. Independent ratings of several raters are pooled when there are several persons qualified to carry out ratings.

Evaluation procedures in which the significance of the ratings is somewhat concealed from the rater present an interesting possibility for civil service and industrial use. This is true particularly when controls on rater bias are introduced through forced-choice techniques or a correction score.

Peer-nominating techniques have interesting possibilities for use in schools and other group settings. They permit sociometric analyses of the interpersonal relations of pupils in a classroom or the workers in a shop. "Guess Who" nominations permit a simple type of rating in the early grades.

QUESTIONS AND EXERCISES

1. If you were writing to someone who had been given as a reference by an applicant for a job in your company or for admission to your school, what should you do in order to obtain the most useful evaluation of the applicant?

2. Make as complete a list as you can of the different ratings used in the school that you are attending or the school in which you teach. What type of a rating scale or form is used in each case?

3. In the light of such evidence or opinion as you can obtain, how effective are the ratings that you identified in the previous question? How adequate a spread of ratings is obtained? How consistently is the scale used by different users? What is your impression of the reliability of the ratings? Of their freedom from halo and other errors?

4. What factors influence a rater's willingness to rate conscientiously? How serious is this issue? What can be done about it?

5. Why would three *independent* ratings from separate raters ordinarily be preferable to a rating prepared by the three persons working together as a committee?

6. In the personnel office of a large company, employment interviewers are called upon to rate job applicants at the end of the interview. Which of the following characteristics would you expect to be rated reasonably reliably? Why?

   (*a*) Initiative.
   (*b*) Appearance.
   (*c*) Work background.
   (*d*) Dependability.
   (*e*) Emotional balance.

7. In a small survey of the report cards used in a number of communities the following 4 traits were most frequently mentioned as found on the report cards: (1) courteous, (2) cooperative, (3) health habits, (4) works with others. How might these be broken down or revised so that the classroom teacher could evaluate them better?

8. Which of the following would influence your judgment of a person in an interview? In what way?

(*a*) A very firm grip in shaking hands.

(*b*) Wearing a "loud" necktie.

(*c*) Generally pausing for a moment before replying to a question.

(*d*) Playing with keys on a key ring.

(*e*) Having a spot on his or her coat.

(*f*) Looking at the floor all during the interview.

9. Compare the reactions of several class members or of several acquaintances on the items of question 8. How general are the reactions? What basis in fact is there for them?

10. What advantages do ratings by peers have over ratings by superiors? What disadvantages?

11. What are the advantages of ranking over rating on a rating scale? What are the disadvantages?

12. Suppose that a forced-choice rating scale had been developed for use in rating the teachers in a city school system in order to get an evaluation of their effectiveness. What advantages would this rating procedure have over other types of rating? What problems would be likely to arise in using it?

13. Make up a "Guess Who" form that might be useful to a teacher in finding out about the pupils in a class. If a class group is available to you, try the form out and analyze the results. What precautions should be taken in using the results?

14. Using a class group taught by some class member or made available by the instructor, get each child's choices for other children to work on a committee. Plot the results in a sociogram. What do the results tell you about the class and the pupils in it? What limitations would this sociogram have for judging the status of an individual child among his classmates?

15. Suppose you have been placed in charge of a merit rating plan which is being introduced in some company. What steps would you take to try to get as good ratings as possible?

SUGGESTED
ADDITIONAL READING

Bernardin, H. John, Mary B. La-Shells, Patricia C. Smith, and Kenneth M. Alvares. Behavioral expectation scales: Effects of developmental procedures and formats. *Journal of Applied Psychology,* 1976, 61, 75–79.

Burnaska, R.F. and T.D. Hollman. An empirical comparison of the relative effects of rater response biases on three rating scale formats. *Journal of Applied Psychology,* 1974, 59, 307-312.

Campbell, J.P., M.D. Dunnette, R.D. Arvey, and L.W. Hellervik. The development and evaluation of behaviorally based rating scales. *Journal of Applied Psychology,* 1973, 57, 15-22.

Centra, John A. Self-ratings of college teachers: A comparison with student ratings. *Journal of Educational Measurement,* 1973, 10, 287-295.

Elmore, Patricia B. and Donald L. Beggs. Consistency of teacher ratings of pupil personality traits in a classroom setting. *Measurement and Evaluation in Guidance,* 1975, 8, 70-74.

Hakel, Milton D. Normative personality factors recovered from ratings of personality descriptors: The beholder's eye. *Personnel Psychology,* 1974, 27, 409-421.

Jaeger, Richard M. and Tom D. Freijo. Race and sex concomitants of composite halo in teachers' evaluative rating of pupils. *Journal of Educational Psychology,* 1975, 67, 226-237.

Keaveny, Timothy J. and Anthony F. McGann. A comparison of behavioral expectation scales and graphic rating scales. *Journal of Applied Psychology,* 1975, 60, 695-703.

Laosa, Luis M., J.D. Swartz, and D.B. Witzke. Cognitive and personality characteristics of high school students as predictors of the way they are rated by their teachers: A longitudinal study. *Journal of Educational Psychology,* 1975, 67, 866-872.

Rich, Jordan. Effects of children's physical attractiveness on teachers' evaluations. *Journal of Educational Psychology,* 1975, 67, 599-609.

CHAPTER
THIRTEEN
BEHAVIOR
TESTS
AND
OBSERVATIONS

In the last two chapters we have considered the possibilities of getting information on personality from the individual's self description and from the impression that he has made upon others who have interacted with him. Both of these have been retrospective approaches, based on the accumulation of past experiences—experiences of oneself in the first case, experiences of another person in the second. We turn now to the possibilities of getting information about a personality from observing a current sample of the individual's behavior.

There are two main types of setting in which we may observe a sample of a person's behavior. On the one hand, we may devise some sort of testing situation, one that is perceived by the person being appraised as a test, and observe his performance within the boundaries of that defined test situation. Or on the other hand, we may observe his behavior in a naturalistic setting, for example, in the classroom, the playground, or the office, where we hope that the person under observation will be largely or completely unaware that any attention is being paid to what he does. The first section of this chapter will deal with testing approaches; the second with observation in naturalistic settings.

When we give a test to let us sample a person's behavior, so that we may draw some conclusion about that person's personality, we want it to be a representative sample of the way in which that person will typically behave. We are not interested in "best" behavior. However, many of the forms of behavior in which we are interested are ones that a person can manipulate, at least to a degree, if he or she chooses to do so. The person can attempt to put on a facade of honesty, vigor, assertiveness, or sweet reasonableness if this is what the test situation seems to call for. For this reason it is often necessary that the purpose of the testing be somewhat camouflaged, that the procedures be indirect, and that the relevant behavior that is actually observed and scored be quite different from that which is the apparent focus of the test as seen by the examinee.

INDIRECT MEASURES OF HONESTY

The need for indirectness is well illustrated by a battery of honesty tests developed almost 50 years ago by Hartshorne and May (1928). The battery, which constituted an early classic study of "character" testing and education, still represents a landmark in testing in this field and illustrates both the essentials of a testing approach and the range of problems encountered in this type of testing.

May and Hartshorne developed a comprehensive series of tests of honesty. These included situations in which the individual had a chance to cheat, situations in which he had an opportunity to lie, and situations in which it was possible for him to steal. Some of the situations are described below.

1. *Cheating on a test by copying.* A test is given dealing with some topic related to school work, word knowledge, for example. The papers are collected. The next day the papers are passed out, and each pupil is allowed to score his own paper when the answers are read aloud. As a matter of fact, however, the papers have been accurately scored before they are returned without any marks being made on the paper. The amount that the pupil copies in and scores his own paper above the correct score is used as an indication of cheating.

2. *Cheating on a test by adding on.* A speeded arithmetic test is given, and at the end of 3 minutes pupils are told to stop work. However, for several minutes papers are left on their desks while the teacher or test administrator is busy doing something else. Later a second test is given after which the papers are immediately collected. When performance on the first testing surpasses performance on the second test by a specified amount, this is taken as evidence that the examinee added onto his work after the time limit was up and before the papers were collected.

3. *Cheating in a game—peeking.* The game is illustrated in Fig. 13.1. The instruction is to shut one's eyes and then put a dot in

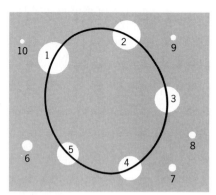

Figure 13.1
Aiming test. (After Hartshorne and May, 1928.)

each circle in turn. Norms are prepared, based upon children tested with their view blocked so that they could not peek. A child who performs unduly well, as determined by the "peekproof" norms, is assumed to have peeked and helped himself.

4. *Cheating in an athletic contest.* As a part of a "field day," each child is given a hand dynamometer to squeeze as a test of strength of hand. Three "practice" squeezes are given, and the adult observer unobtrusively notes and later records the best performance on these. Then the pupil is told to make additional squeezes "for the record." While the child makes the squeezes, the adult is obviously busy with another child, and not watching. The child records this performance on a record blank. Since fatigue tends to set in on successive squeezes, it is unlikely that a child will show improvement. If the performance reported surpasses the practice squeezes by a specified amount, it is assumed that the child has been unduly optimistic in recording his performance.

5. *Lying—self-glorification.* In this test the child is asked a series of questions. Each question has to do with standards of behavior that are universally applauded but seldom achieved. Thus one question reads "Do you always obey your parents cheerfully and promptly?" and another, "Do you always smile when things go wrong?" It is hard to know how many of a set of statements like this a child might truthfully endorse, but an attempt was made to determine this by having groups of graduate students think back to their childhood and respond as would have been true of them then. The child who marks an excessive number of items is deemed to be not angelic but untruthful.

6. *Stealing.* A game is devised that uses a number of coins.

These are in a box, and one box is passed out to each child. After the game is over, each child is told to put the coins back in the box and fasten it up. The boxes are collected. They have been unobtrusively coded, so it is possible to tell which child had which box. A check of the coins in the boxes makes it possible to determine which children have helped themselves to one or more of the coins.

As can be seen from the brief descriptions, the tests are rather involved and require extensive stage managing. The details of the testing situation seem fairly critical, that is, how sure the child feels that he is free from observation, the manner in which the children are occupied when they are stopped in their work, and so forth. And it is crucial that the "security" of the test be maintained, for if the true purpose of the test were suspected, examinees could immediately conform to the approved social standard.

EVALUATION OF BEHAVIOR TESTS OF HONESTY

How reliable and how valid are these situational tests of honesty? Reliability estimates are shown in Table 13.1 We can see that the reliabilities of single tests are rather modest, averaging about .50. In comparison with the aptitude and achievement tests discussed in earlier chapters, these reliabilities are disappointing. The score of a pupil on any single test of the set used by May and Hartshorne would provide only the roughest indication of the typical behavior of that child. A single test would need to be extended by adding on several additional tests of the same sort if a satisfactorily stable and dependable measure were to be obtained. The single tests would appear to be useful primarily for the comparison of different groups of pupils.

Table 13.1
RELIABILITIES OF TESTS USED FOR MEASURING DECEPTION (FROM HARTSHORNE AND MAY, 1928)

Type of Test	Reliability Coefficient
1. Copying from a key or answer sheet	.70
2. Adding onto one's score on a speeded test	.44
3. Peeping when one's eyes should be shut	.46
4. Faking a solution to a puzzle	.50
5. Faking a score in a physical ability test	.46
6. Lying to win approval	.84
7. Getting illicit help at home	.24

When it comes to validity, we are put to it to find any satisfactory outside standard against which to evaluate the tests. Teachers' ratings of pupils may be taken as one limited and imperfect criterion, and the classroom cheating tests showed a modest correlation with this criterion (average about .35). But before we look for outside criterion measures, we should perhaps ask how the different kinds of honesty tests correlate with each other.

Considering four different types of cheating test carried out in the classroom situation, the authors found that on the average a test of one type correlated with a test of one of the other types only to the extent of .26. When some type of classroom cheating test was correlated with cheating in an athletic contest, the average correlation was found to be only .16, and with the stealing test the average correlation was .17. The lying test, also given in the classroom, averaged .23 with the other classroom tests and .06 with the two out-of-classroom tests.

The reliabilities of the single tests are low; the correlations between the different sorts of tests are a good deal lower. When the correlations involve different settings (that is, classroom versus gymnasium) or different types of behavior (that is, cheating versus stealing), the correlations drop still further. Many of them are not far from zero. Score on any one test depends only slightly upon a common factor running through all of the tests, and depends, to a considerable extent, on factors unique to that specific test situation.

What does this outcome signify?

From the practical point of view, it indicates that no one honesty test, and probably no battery of honesty tests, is going to permit us to make accurate predictions of behavior on some other test or in a life situation. Our ability to identify the store clerk who will pilfer from the store or the citizen who will "chisel" on an income tax return will be very meager, unless we can test these individuals in closely similar situations. The specifics of the test situation on the one hand and the life situation on the other will water down any relationship.

From a theoretical point of view, it gives us a picture of behavior as dependent only to a modest degree upon generalized personality traits. The concept of trait is a useful one for organizing our description of a person. And there *is* an underlying coherence and continuity that gives meaning to his actions. But those actions are also situation bound, and the specific habits of responding to specific situations are as important determiners as are broad underlying traits. This phenomenon is not peculiar to objective behavior tests; it also characterizes the items of self-report inventories. In fact, a single behavior test is in many ways like a single item on an inventory. Thus in a sense the test that provides the pupil an opportunity to revise his answer sheet as he scores it really asks a specific question in behavorial terms, to wit: Would you change the wrong answers if you scored your own paper? The series of tests collectively provide a multi-item behavior inventory. Collectively they describe the underlying trend of the individual's behavior, but it is still true that his response to any one specific situation will be predictable only to a limited extent from his standing on the general trait and will depend, to a substantial degree, on factors unique to the specific situation.

OTHER TYPES OF PERFORMANCE TEST

The May and Hartshorne measures were devious and indirect only from the point of view of the examinee. To the person reading about them the relationship between the behavior being observed and the trait being inferred from the behavior is clear and apparent. The trait indicators have a good deal of face validity, and are readily identified as corresponding to the trait that is being inferred from them.

This has not always been the case. Some trait indicators may be qualitatively quite removed from the trait that they are found to indicate. For example, Eysenck (1952) developed a battery of performance measures to identify neuroticism. Some of the measures that he found to discriminate between normal and neurotic groups were (1) the amount of body sway in response to a direct suggestion of falling, (2) the number of unusual responses on a multiple-choice free association test, (3) the speed of dark adaptation, (4) the number of food aversions, and (5) the length of time breath could be held. The battery score from a battery of 8 to 10 such specific tests appeared to have quite high reliability and to discriminate fairly sharply between a normal and a neurotic group. Thus the tests did not *seem* to have validity, but validity in this case was based entirely on relationship to an outside criterion. The tests didn't "look like" measures of neurotic tendency, but rested upon their empirical validation. Such empirical validation stands in need of repeated confirmation when the content of the test responses bears little apparent relationship to the inferences made from them.

Another illustration of an indirect set of performance tests is found in the tests developed by Witkin and others (1962) of an attribute that they call *field dependence.* Field dependence is a way of perceiving in which the person is unduly influenced by and dependent upon the totality of the surrounding (typically visual) field. Three tests that correlate fairly substantially and that are used collectively to assess field dependence are the following.

1. *Tilting chair in a tilting room.* The subject is required to adjust the chair in which he sits to a vertical position when the tilted "room" gives visual cues that conflict with the postural cues from his own body.

2. *Rod and frame.* The subject is required to adjust a rod to a vertical orientation when the only visual reference is a frame that has been tilted at an angle to the normal vertical-horizontal orientation.

3. *Embedded figures.* The subject must find a simple figure that has been "hidden" in a more complex diagram.

This set of tests, primarily perceptual in nature, tends to bridge the gap between measures of ability and measures of personality. A number of tests of this sort have sometimes been spoken of as tests of "cognitive style." The tasks are cognitive in nature, but they are used for the insight that they give into personality characteristics. Thus a person who is *independent* of the surrounding field on the three perceptual tests is reported to be more self-sufficient in his social relationships, to have more elaborated defenses and controls to channel his impulses and direct his actions, to show problems of overcontrol, over-intellectualization, and isolation when he presents a personality disturbance.

The availability of measures of field dependence has led to a welter of studies of the attribute and its correlates, with somewhat inconsistent findings. Clearly, the perceptual tests that are used as indicators of the attribute do depend in large part on factors of general cognitive ability and of spatial visualizing ability (Vernon, 1972). Whether they assess important traits beyond these two intellectual dimensions seems still an open question.

The most extensive effort to develop objective personality tests is represented by a catalogue of such measures developed by R. B. Cattell and his associates (1967) to appraise many of the personality factors that he had identified in factor analytic studies of self-descriptive inventories and of ratings. The array of possible measures is imposing, but their validity and practical utility remain largely untested. At the present time the book is more a catalogue of possibilities for the research worker than a set of tested practical tools.

One feature that is common to many of the objective behavior tests is that they are indirect and "unobtrusive" measures. They are designed to make the examinee "task-oriented" rather than self-oriented. That is, the focus of his attention and effort is in getting an individual or group task completed quickly or effectively. By recording or observing some aspect of his performance that is only indirectly related to the assigned task, we hope to get information on his typical mode of functioning. The presumed advantage of this oblique approach is that we are able to bypass the defenses that an individual sets up against direct inspection of his personality. However, this advantage is gained only at considerable cost. The cost lies sometimes in the more involved, elaborate, and costly procedures for data collection. It lies sometimes in the lack of any obvious rationale for the test score, as when a measure of body sway is used as an indicator of neuroticism or when some category of response to an inkblot is interpreted as implying emotionality. When the significance of an item of behavior is not clearly implied by the nature of the act itself, as it is when hitting another child is counted as an aggressive act, it becomes crucial to validate and revalidate each indicator beyond the shadow of a doubt. It is the shakiness of this independent validation that leaves so many indirect assessment procedures so much in question at the present time.

These approaches are appealing, in that they presumably cannot be distorted by the subject to give a desired impression. However, the procedures are complex and time consuming, and the predictive validity of the tests for socially important criteria is still largely undetermined. A large amount of research is needed before we will know whether objective testing to appraise personality can be useful.

PROJECTIVE TECHNIQUES

The behavior samples that have been described so far in this chapter have in each case been focused on a specific attribute or construct: honesty, neuroticism, field dependence. There is however, a group of techniques for obtaining behavior samples that are viewed as providing at one time evidence on a host of diverse aspects of personality structure and personality dynamics. These have most generally been called *projective techniques*. Their common feature has been that they present the examinee with a somewhat ambiguous and unstructured set of stimulus materials, and call upon him to impose his own structure upon these materials. The product is a complex protocol that is then analyzed following a set of guidelines that are themselves often more elaborate than the original response materials; the protocol is interpreted in relation to many facets of personality.

The two most widely known and most exhaustively investigated projective techniques are the *Rorschach Psychodiagnostic* (over 4,580 published references as of 1971) and the *Thematic Apperception Test* (over 1,760 references). The *Rorschach* consists of 10 plates containing ink blots similar to the ones illustrated in Fig. 13.2. These are presented to the subject with very general instructions—approximately, "People see all sorts of differ-

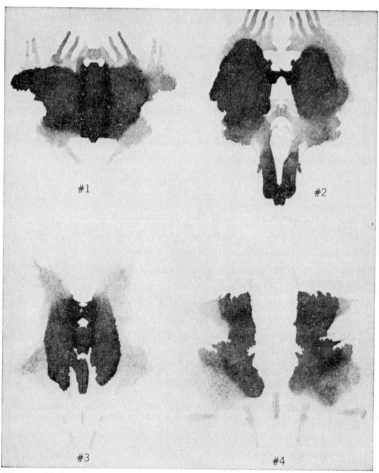

Figure 13.2
Rorschach-type inkblots.

ent things in these cards. I'd like you to tell me what you see." The several responses to each card are recorded, and a further inquiry is carried out to determine where in the blot the subject saw each percept and what aspects of the blot (shape, color, shading, etc.) determined the response.

Possible responses to card #2 might include, for example, "two witches playing pattycake," "head of George Washington," "atomic explosion," "a white eagle," and "two hands with thumbs pointing toward each other."

In the *Thematic Apperception Test (TAT; see* Murray et al., 1938) the examinee is shown a picture such as the one illustrated in Fig. 13.3 and asked to write a story about it. In this story the respondent is to tell what is happening, what led up to it, and what the outcome will be. Several pictures are used and the record consists of the set of stories produced in response to them. A sample story, illustrating what might be produced in response to the picture in Fig. 13.3 is the following.

This young girl wants to go out on her own and lead a good life, but this old woman wants to control her and make her do things as the old woman wants them done. Some of the things the old woman has told the girl were bad, but the girl had to do them anyway. She hates the old hag and gets tired of the control that the old woman has over her and kills the old hag. No one ever found out that the girl killed the woman so she is free to do what she wants.

Figure 13.3
Sample picture from *Murray Thematic Apperception Test.*

Both the *Rorschach* and the *TAT* generate an extended record of responses that serves as the raw material to be analyzed, and clearly there could be many different procedures for coding, scoring, and/or interpreting the material in that record. Procedures for handling a *Rorschach* record have been elaborated in great detail, and several competing systems exist (Exner, 1969). Procedures for handling *TAT* story material are more informal, and vary a good deal depending upon the purpose for which the results are to be used. For example, one group of investigators has been interested in using the stories to assess achievement motivation, while another group has used them to get evidence on the time span in the individual's perception of his world. In these, and in all other projective materials, the interpretive systems have become quite elaborate, and an extensive training and apprenticeship is called for before the user is viewed as competent to draw inferences from the complex record.

Projective techniques are used in so many different ways, and different users and investigators have tried to draw such a wide range of inferences from them, that it is almost impossible to make any general statement about the validity of the procedures. In general, the accumulated evidence on validity does not inspire the hard-nosed psychometrician with confidence in their utility. At the same time, many clinicians have strong convictions that the response protocol provides a rich source for insights and hypotheses about the examinee's personality structure and dynamics. And it is also possible that the responses may provide useful material for research studies of perceptual and cognitive styles, motivational factors, and cultural effects. Even if the procedures turn out to have very limited practical validity, they may still be useful as research tools. One point on which all would agree, enthusiast or critic, is that these are procedures to be interpreted only by the specialist who has had extensive training in psychological theory and in the instrument in question. The teacher, counselor, or personnel officer will at most be a good second-hand user of the interpreted results from such instruments.

SITUATIONAL TESTS AND ASSESSMENT PROGRAMS

One approach to assessing an individual's personality is to place the person in a fairly complex and demanding task situation and to then observe how he or she goes about dealing with it. The task situation is kept the same for all persons being evaluated, and in this sense it is a standard test. However, the appraisal is often made by one or more observers, and in this sense it partakes of the subjectivity and some of the problems of the rating procedures that were discussed in the last chapter. Probably the first large-scale use in this country of the combination of situational tests and observer ratings for human assessment was the program by the Office of Strategic Services (Assessment Staff, OSS, 1948) to screen personnel for special undercover and counterinsurgency tasks in World War II. However, current application of these procedures occurs largely in the recruitment and appraisal of managers in business and industry. It is reported that more than 100,000 persons have been assessed in the Bell System, and lesser numbers in other major corporations.

The basic research study in the Bell System has been described by Bray, Campbell, and Grant (1974). Evidence on the validity of assessment procedures is summarized by Huck (1973). Since the Bell System program is fairly typical, the procedures will be described in some detail, and evidence will be presented on validity of the appraisals for predicting advancement in the management hierarchy.

The total manager assessment process is typically a 2-day enterprise that includes in its span conventional general ability tests (of the sort described in Chapter 9) on the one hand and an interview focused on work history and work attitudes (as considered in Chapter 11) on the other. However, for the present we will focus on those situational tests included in the assessment that represent a pattern that we have not considered before. These might be characterized in general as *simulations* of some aspect of the work of a manager, and are designed to give the candidates a chance to display through their actions in a semistandardized test situation some of the qualities of leadership, decisiveness, planfulness, and sensitivity to others that might influence a person's effectiveness in a managerial role. Let us examine three types of task that appear in the Bell System assessment.

LEADERLESS GROUP DISCUSSION

A group of about six persons to be assessed is brought together to discuss and reach a common decision on a problem of the type that a manager might face. One scenario often used involves picking a foreman to be promoted to the next level of management. Each assessee is provided with a brief sketch of the strengths and weaknesses of "his subordinate," and organizes an initial oral presentation to the group. After all the presentations have been completed, there is a period of discussion leading to selection of one candidate to receive the promotion, and perhaps a rank ordering of the other candidates. The assessee is instructed: "Because you will be judged on your skill in arguing for your candidate you should try to convince the group that your candidate is well qualified for promotion. As a group, however, you will want to select the person who will make the greatest contribution to your company." The discussion is monitored by observers who prepare a report on each assessee's performance, both in initial presentation and in the discussion. The reports are later read to the assessment staff, together with reports from the other procedures, and are expected to contribute to rating of such qualities as oral communication skill, human relations skill, perception of social cues, behavior flexibility, need for approval of peers, resistance to stress, energy, and organizing and planning.

THE IN-BASKET

This test is responded to individually and independently by each person being assessed. The scenario is that the assessee has suddenly had to take over the job of a district manager. The assessee has arrived on a Sunday and finds a pile of memos and correspondence on the desk. As background, the assessee is provided with some information about the district and the staff. Given a limited amount of time (3 hours) to work on the material, the person being assessed must assimilate it, establish some order of priority for action, and leave instructions for subordinates as to what action is to be taken during the following week while he or she is away. The person then prepares notes and memos dealing with these actions as a record of his or her decisions.

After the work period is over, the candidate is interviewed by a member of the assessment staff in order to get a picture of his or her method of attacking the task and the rationale for the chosen priorities and actions. The assessor prepares a report on the candidate, covering such aspects as written communication skills, human relations skills, creativity, need for approval of superiors, inner work standards, tolerance of uncertainty, resistance to stress, energy, organizing and planning, and decision making.

In this simulation a group works together as the managers of a small manufacturing company or as traders on a security exchange. Decisions must be made to buy and sell in response to the changing prices and conditions that are presented to the group. Decisions are required to be group decisions, so that for effective performance the group has to work together with some decisiveness and judgment. Again the performance of the group is monitored, and a descriptive report is prepared on each participant. The reports contribute to the eventual ratings on such factors as behavior flexibility, need for approval of peers, tolerance of uncertainty, resistance to stress, energy, organization and planning, and decision making.

It is clear that these situational exercises are rather different from "tests" as these have been presented in previous chapters. In the first place, a number of them are group situations, involving the interaction between each candidate and the other members of the group. The interactive situation has potential for bringing out aspects of a person's behavior in relation to others that could hardly appear in the conventional test setting. In the second place, the performance of a candidate is often described—initially, at least—rather than scored, and of course, this description is dependent upon the perceptiveness and retentiveness of the observer. The description permits a completeness and vitality in the record that a score might well lose, but does so at the risk of a good deal of subjectivity. In the third place, each situation to which an individual is exposed provides only a part of the input that is synthesized in a final set of trait ratings of the individual, and these ratings lead to a summary judgment of how well he is likely to succeed in the occupational career for which he is being assessed—typically that of a business manager. How well do the procedures work? Let us look at some representative results.

First, the matter of reliability. There is a good deal of evidence on between-rater reliability. Compared with the typical rating procedures that we considered in the last chapter, the consistency of trained assessors rating the records of the same observed behavior sample is comforting. Adequate reliability is achieved, it appears, because the assessors *do* receive practice and training, and because they are reacting to a *specific* current sample of behavior, rather than to impressions drawn from a varied and haphazard past experience with the ratee. The more critical question is whether a candidate's performance at one testing session with one set of tasks corresponds to the same individual's performance at some subsequent occasion when assessed by a different team of assessors on a new set of tasks.

The clearest evidence on this point comes from a report by Moses (1973) of an investigation in which a group of telephone company employees who had previously gone through a 1-day Early Identification Assessment were processed some months later through the regular 2-day Personnel Assessment Center. The second assessment was entirely independent of the first, and neither candidates nor assessment staff knew anything about the results from the first assessment. Some of the correlations between ratings on the first and the second assessment are shown in Table 13.2. Final overall appraisal of effectiveness is the most stable of the judgments, followed closely by scholastic aptitude. However, all of the more specific ratings show a moderate consistency from one assessment session to another. In view of the fact that the specific tasks were different, the team of assessors was different, and a period of some months had elapsed between assessments, the results seem rather encouraging.

What validity does the final rating have as a predictor of managerial progress? The most crucial study is the Bray, Campbell, and Grant study previously referred to, because all the assessment data and predictions have been kept secure and no information has ever been provided to the men or to their supervisors. Thus there has been no possibility of contamination in which the assessment results and predictions might have influenced what happened to the man in his career. The percentage of personnel reaching "middle management" after 8 years with the company is shown in Table 13.3, as a function of assessment center prediction and of job conditions during the period of work. Clearly, both the qualities of the candidate, as perceived by the assessment team, and the type of job situation

Table 13.2
CORRELATIONS OF RATINGS OBTAINED ON TWO INDEPENDENT ASSESSMENTS

Overall rating for probable progress in management	.73
Leadership	.56
Energy	.52
Decision making	.53
Forcefulness	.62
Oral communication skills	.49
Written communication skills	.57
Scholastic aptitude	.72
Need for peer approval	.50

Table 13.3

**PERCENTAGE OF ASSESSEES REACHING MIDDLE
MANAGEMENT AS A FUNCTION OF ASSESSMENT
PREDICTION AND WORK CONDITIONS**

	Assessment Prediction		
Level of Job Challenge	Will Reach Middle Management	Will Not Reach Middle Management	Total
High	76	61	71
Moderate	55	33	43
Low	33	5	11
All cases	64	32	50

in which the person landed were related to that person's probability of progressing in the management hierarchy. The man
predicted to advance was twice as likely to progress to middle
management as the man predicted not to, while the person
who was placed in a setting of high job challenge was almost
twice as likely to have progressed as the one in a moderate-
challenge job, and six times as likely as one in a low-challenge
job. The two factors in combination give an even better forecast. The relationships displayed in Table 13.3 correspond to
correlations* of .48 for assessment prediction, .57 for job challenge, and .64 for the two in combination.

It is of some interest to see which trait ratings were especially related to the overall assessment rating, and also which trait
ratings were especially related to management level at the
time of reassessment 8 years later. Some results are shown in
Table 13.4. Of special interest is the close correspondence in
order of magnitude for the two sets of correlations. The correspondence is represented by a correlation of .94 between the
two sets. Apparently the assessors were doing something right!

SYSTEMATIC OBSERVATION

So far we have been considering relatively uniform and standardized test situations as settings in which behavior may be
observed and evaluated. The comparability from person to
person of such situations has a strong appeal. However, there
are also important advantages in observing behavior in the
naturally occuring settings of daily life.

* These are tetrachoric correlations.

Table 13.4

507
systematic
observation

CORRELATION OF TRAIT RATINGS WITH OVERALL ASSESSMENT AND WITH LEVEL OF MANAGEMENT REACHED

	Overall Rating	Level Reached
Human relations skills	.66	.32
Organizing and planning	.61	.28
Decision making	.59	.18
Oral communication skills	.53	.33
Energy	.51	.28
Scholastic aptitude	.46	.19
Range of interests	.45	.23
Tolerance of uncertainty	.39	.30
Need for approval of peers	−.16	−.17
Social objectivity	.04	.13
Number of cases	207	123

The situations of everyday life are probably less uniform from person to person than the test situations that we stage. Also, they are not loaded to bring forth the behaviors in which we are specially interested. However, the very naturalness of real life events and the fact that we do not have to stage special events just for testing purposes make observation of natural situations appealing to us.

Of course we observe the people with whom we associate every day of our lives, noticing what they do and reacting to the ways in which they behave. Our impressions of people are continuously being formed and modified by our observations of them. But these observations are casual, unsystematic, and undirected. If we are asked to document with specific instances our judgment that Helen is a leader in the group or that Henry is undependable, we are usually put to it to provide more than one or two concrete observations of actual behavior to document our general impression. Observations must be organized, directed, and systematic if they are to yield dependable information about an individual.

We should perhaps pause to draw a distinction between the observational procedures that we discuss now and the rating procedures that we considered in Chapter 12. The basic distinction is this: When we are collecting observations, we want the observer to function as nearly as possible as an objective and mechanical recording instrument, whereas when we gather ratings we want the rater to synthesize and integrate the evidence that he has. The one function is purely that of providing an accurate record of the number of social contacts, suggestions, aggressive acts, or whatever the category of behavior may be in which we are interested. The *observer* serves merely as a somewhat more flexible and versatile camera or recording machine. In *rating*, by contrast, the human instrument must judge, weight, and interpret.

Systematic observational procedures have been most fully developed in connection with studies of young children. They seem particularly appropriate in this setting. On the one hand, the young child has not developed the covers and camouflages to conceal himself from public view as completely as has his older brother or sister, so there is more to be found out by watching him. On the other hand, he is less able to tell us about himself in words. So it has been in the study of infants and nursery school children that observational procedures have had their fullest development.

Extracting a meaningful, dependable, and relatively objective appraisal of some aspect of an individual's personality from observing a sample of his behavior is far from easy. In the first place, behavior flows as a complex and continuous stream with no sharp breaks or clear units. The preschooler is at the sand table making a "cake" at one moment, moves on to listen to the teacher talking to a group, and then on to build a house with the giant blocks. On the way he picks at his nose, takes a playful poke at some other child, and shouts to the teacher (or the world in general) "See me! See what I've made." But this is only a partial report. No verbal description can capture the full detail of even 5 minutes of the life of an active child. What should be observed? When and for how long? What can be done to make the observations accurate and reliable? How should the observations be organized and summarized? What do the observations *mean* so far as the personality of the child is concerned? Let us consider some of the issues and some of the efforts to resolve them.

WHAT TO OBSERVE

If anything meaningful is to emerge from observation of the complex flow of behavior, the observations must have some focus. We must be looking at something or for something—for indications of leadership, or of insecurity, or of sociability, or of emotional strain, or of energy level, or of aggressiveness, or of dependency, or often for indicators of several such personal attributes at the same time. The research or practical problem with which we start specifies what aspect or aspects of behavior it is important to observe, and our plan for observing follows from definition of the behavior aspects that will be relevant to the problem.

BEHAVIORS THAT REPRESENT A PERSONALITY ATTRIBUTE

Even when we have decided what *attribute* we are interested in, we still have the problem of deciding what *behaviors* shall be accepted as indicators of that attribute. Consider the following behaviors.

Crying.
Hitting another child.
Holding on to a teacher's hand or apparel.
Calling attention to what he has done.
Tattling on another child.
Volunteering information in a discussion.

Which of these should be tallied as indicators of "dependency" in a kindergartener? What other behaviors should be added? This is the type of decision that must be made as wisely as possible, in the light of broad familiarity with children's behavior and the dynamics underlying it, if the observational data are to have real meaning.

WHEN AND HOW LONG TO OBSERVE

Observational data are of two major sorts—systematic and incidental. For the present we concentrate on programs of systematic observation. Anecdotal procedures for recording incidental observations will be considered in a later section of the chapter. When we embark on a program of systematic observations, we must decide where, when, and for how long each person is to be observed. The decision represents a compromise between the cost of extended observations on the one hand and the need for a representative and reliable picture of the person on the other. Since both persons and situations vary from day to day, it is generally preferable to have a number of relatively brief periods of observation on different days than to have one or two longer periods. The sample of the person's behavior will be more representative and the score we obtain will be more reliable. However, the practical reality factors of travel time and administrative convenience limit the number of occasions upon which it is feasible to observe a particular child or group. Furthermore, in too brief a sample of behavior it may be difficult to judge what a particular action signifies. So the final decision is a practical compromise between cost and comprehensiveness, between completeness of context and multiplication of occasions.

An expedient that has appeared to work well in a number of cases has been to break each single period of observation up into quite short segments. These may be no more than a minute or even ½ minute in length. Then the observation that is made is merely the occurrence or nonoccurrence of the particular category of behavior during each small segment of time. Thus we might observe each child for ten 5-minute periods, each on a different day. The 5-minute periods might each be subdivided into ten ½-minute periods. For each of the ½-minute periods we would observe whether the particular child did or did not exhibit any of a set of defined aggressive behaviors. Each child would then receive a score, with a possible range from 0 to 100, indicating the number of periods in which he produced aggressive acts. Such scores, based on an adequate number of short samples of observed behavior, have been found to show quite satisfactory reliability. Thus, for example, Olson (1929) found the reliability for twenty 5-minute observations of children's nervous habits to be .87 in one case and .82 in another.

Naturally it will be desirable to plan to make observations in settings where the behavior that we are interested in is likely to appear. Observations of aggressive acts for example, could be made more profitably during a period of free play than during a period devoted to listening to stories or to watching television.

TRAINING OBSERVERS

Even with a carefully defined set of behaviors to be observed, disagreements arise between observers. Some of these are unavoidable because of fluctuations of attention or variation of scoring on close judgments. Others can, however, be eliminated by training. Practice sessions in which two or more observers make records of the same sample of behavior, compare notes, discuss discrepancies, and reconcile differences provide one means of increasing uniformity. Practice sessions watched and later criticized by an already trained observer represent another. Such procedures make for uniformity of interpretation and standard application of the observation categories.

THE MECHANICS OF RECORDING OBSERVATIONS

An essential for accurate observational data is some procedure for immediate recording of what was observed. The errors and selectivity of memory enter in to bias the reporting of even outstanding and unusual events. In the case of the rather ordinary and highly repetitive events that are observed in watching a child in preschool, for example, an adequate account of what was observed is only possible if the observations are recorded immediately. There is so much to see and one event is so much like others that to rely upon memory to provide an accurate after-the-fact account of a child's behavior is fatal. This is certainly the case in any attempt at complete and systematic recording, though we shall find a place for selective observation and anecdotal recording of significant incidents of behavior some time after they have taken place.

Any program of systematic observation must, therefore, provide some technique for immediate and efficient recording of the events that are observed. There are many possibilities for facilitating recording of behavior observations. One that has been widely used has been to develop a systematic code for the categories of behavior that are of interest. Thus preliminary observations will have served to define the range of aggressive acts that can be expected from 3- and 4-year-olds. Part of the code might be set up as follows: h = "hits," p = "pushes," g = "grabs materials away from," n = "calls a nasty name," and so forth. A record blank can be prepared, divided up to represent the time segments of the observations, and code entries can be made quickly while the child is observed almost without interruption.

If the observer is skilled in standard shorthand, of course, fuller notes of the observation can be taken. These can be transcribed and coded or scored later. In some cases, when a research project has liberal financial backing, more complete photographic or videotape recordings of the observations may make possible a permanent record of the behaviors in a relatively complete form. These records can then be analyzed at a later date. Such resources are likely to be the exception, however, and in many cases it will be necessary to plan a simple and efficient code to provide an immediate and permanent record of what was observed. The important objectives here are to do away with dependence on memory, to get a record that will preserve as much as possible of the significant detail in the original behavior, and to develop a recording procedure that will interfere as little as possible with the process of observing the child.

ILLUSTRATIVE STUDIES USING DIRECT OBSERVATION

The ways in which direct observation has been used in studying aspects of the child's behavior and the impact of educational experiences upon him can best be indicated by selected illustrations. We have chosen several examples of quite different types of observational procedures and quite different problems to illustrate the applications of direct observation.

PERSONALITY DIFFERENCES IN NEWBORN CHILDREN

The study that we shall describe first (Birns, 1965) asked the rather simple question (but not necessarily one that is simple to answer): Are there consistent differences in children at or near the time of birth? We are limited in what we can observe in neonates, but responsiveness to stimulation seemed to be one observable trait. Arrangements were made, therefore, to stimulate babies with a soft tone, a loud tone, a cold disk, and a pacifier several times during the first 4 or 5 days of life. Each stimulus was presented three times at each of four different sessions, and two or three trained observers scored the intensity of the infant's response. The observers of the infant could report his responses as (1) inhibition or diminution of activity then underway, (2) no response, or (3) response rated on a 5-point scale from (1) "small eye, toe, or finger flicker; refers to movement of only one body part" to (5) "hard crying and any activity; major intense overall activation."

Two types of evidence were offered to support the proposition that there are consistent individual differences in responsiveness. First, responsiveness to the four different stimuli was compared, with the finding that the typical correlation of intensity from one to another stimulus was about .50. Second, responsiveness was compared across the four separate test sessions, and it was found that the typical correlation between separate sessions was about .40. These two findings were interpreted as supporting the position that consistent individual differences in an aspect of personality are already in existence within the first few days of life.

PERSONALITY VARIABLES AND "IDENTIFICATION"

The study we have just reported used observation in connection with the application of specific stimuli. A different pattern is illustrated in the next study (Sears et al., 1965) in which observation was carried on of children engaged in the normal activities of a preschool program. The observations provided one kind of data within a more extensive study of children's identification with their parents. Observations were focused on dependency, aggression, and adult role taking.

The observation period for a given child was 10 minutes, and this period was divided into segments, each 30 seconds long. For each 30-second segment, the observer recorded the dominant behavior category from among a list of 29. The designations of some of these are as follows.

Giving facts and demonstrating knowledge	(Adult role)
Using real adult manerisms	(Adult role)
Touching and holding others	(Dependency)
Positive attention seeking	(Dependency)
Direct physical aggression	(Antisocial aggression)
Tattling	(Prosocial aggression)

The schedule of observations was planned so that a child was observed at various times of day, on various days of the week, and by different members of the team of observers. The average number of 10-minute observation periods for any one child was 38. That is, the child was observed for a little more than 6 hours in total.

The score for a given child on a given behavior category was the proportion of time periods during which that behavior was coded as the dominant one. Categories were combined in various ways to give more comprehensive and stable scores. The reliability of certain of these combined scores for the total observation series is shown below, estimated in the one case from the correlation between observers and in the other from different segments of the series of observations.

	Between Observers	Between Time Periods
Total score—adult role	.77	.73
Total score—dependency	.74	.63
Total score—antisocial aggression	.85	.79
Total score—prosocial aggression	.74	.73

It can be seen that 6 hours of observation is none too much to provide dependable appraisals of these behaviors.

The sample studied consisted of only 40 children,* 20 boys and 20 girls, so that relationships reported must be considered quite tentative. From the extensive array of relationships reported among observational variables and of these with other types of measure, we shall pick out only a few illustrative items. In general, the aggressive behaviors were more coherently structured in the group as a whole than either dependency or adult role behaviors. That is, as a general trend, the child who was high on one type of aggressive behavior tended to be high on others. However, for boys, "tattling" did not seem to belong in the aggressive cluster, while for girls, "injury to objects" was unrelated to other aggressive actions. Only for girls did different types of adult role behavior group together, and dependency behaviors appeared to have very little unity and cohesiveness for either sex. It appeared that active attention getting, based on the individual's performance or product, was a very different type of behavior with very different significance in the life economy of the individual from the dependency exhibited in touching, holding, being near, or seeking reassurance from an adult. Generally speaking, hypothesized relationships between dependency and identification with adults were not confirmed by the results of the study.

TEACHER BEHAVIORS INFLUENCING PUPIL ATTITUDES AND ACHIEVEMENT

A somewhat different application of techniques of direct observation is in the study of teacher inputs, of what goes on in a classroom, and its relationship to pupil outputs of knowledge or of attitude. Flanders (1965) studied verbal interaction in the classroom. Observers in the classroom recorded 6 hours of events in each class. A record was made about every 3 seconds, using the set of categories shown in Table 13.5.

Flanders' interest centered primarily on the impact of the "indirect influence" forms of teacher talk as compared with the "direct influence" forms. Sixteen social studies and 16 mathematics classes were observed, and the classes with the most "indirect" teachers were compared with those with the most "direct" teachers with respect to attitudes toward the teacher and achievement in a standard unit that was taught during the time that the observations were being made. The essential results are summarized in Fig. 13.4 on p. 516, which shows the

---

* One of the practical problems of studies using observational procedures is that the time investment needed per child tends to be so great that samples studied are small, and results correspondingly undependable.

average achievement and attitude scores of each group, as well as the range extending 1 standard deviation on either side of the mean. In this study, the classes of the more "indirect" teachers consistently showed up better on both the attitude and the achievement measures. Of course, it is not entirely clear whether using "indirect" measures is a cause or merely a

Table 13.5
CATEGORIES FOR INTERACTION ANALYSIS, 1959

Teacher Talk	Indirect Influence	1.* *Accepts Feeling.* Accepts and clarifies the tone of feeling of the students in an unthreatening manner. Feelings may be positive or negative. Predicting or recalling feelings are included. 2.* *Praises or Encourages.* Praises or encourages student action or behavior. Jokes that release tension, but not at the expense of another individual, nodding head or saying "um hm?" or "go on" are included. 3.* *Accepts or Uses Ideas of Student.* Clarifying, building, or developing ideas suggested by a student. As teacher brings more of his own ideas into play, shift to category 5. 4.* *Asks Questions.* Asking a question about content or procedure with the intent that a student answer.
	Direct Influence	5.* *Lecturing.* Giving facts or opinions about content or procedure; expressing his own ideas, asking rhetorical questions. 6.* *Giving Directions.* Directions, commands, or orders which students are expected to comply with. 7.* *Criticizing or Justifying Authority.* Statements intended to change student behavior from unacceptable to acceptable pattern; bawling someone out; stating why the teacher is doing what he is doing; extreme self-reference.
Student Talk		8.* *Student Talk—Response.* Talk by students in response to teacher. Teacher initiates the contact or solicits student statement. 9.* *Student Talk—Initiation.* Talk initiated by students. If "calling on" student is only to indicate who may talk next, observer must decide whether student wanted to talk.
Silence		10.* *Silence or Confusion.* Pauses, short periods of silence, and periods of confusion in which communication cannot be understood by the observer.

* There is NO scale implied by these numbers. Each number is classificatory, designating a particular kind of communication event. To write these numbers down during observation is merely to identify and enumerate communication events, not to judge them.

symptom of good teaching, but there is at least a chance that the work of teachers can be improved by training them to make more use of the "indirect" categories of verbal interaction.

Another illustration of the use of systematic observation as a technique for studying elementary school pupils and their teachers, appears in a study of the use of behavior management techniques in the classroom (Rollins et al., 1974). Teachers in an urban low socioeconomic school had been instructed in the use of positive reinforcement procedures to encourage desirable conduct and academic activities in their classrooms. Systematic observation was used before and after the training both to determine whether the teachers in the experimental classes did increase their use of positive reinforcements and decrease their use of punitive responses and to see whether any related changes appeared in the behavior of pupils.

Observation was set up in 5-minute cycles. During the first cycle, positive and negative reinforcing behaviors of the teacher were tallied; during the second cycle disruptive behaviors by pupils were tallied; during the third cycle attentive versus off-task behaviors were observed. Illustrative of disruptive behaviors were unauthorized leaving of one's seat, making loud noises, disturbing other pupils by talking to them, poking them,

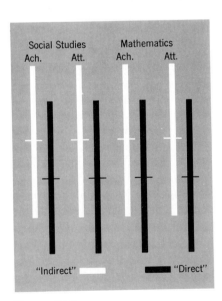

Figure 13.4
Attitude and achievement of classes taught by "direct" and "indirect" teachers. (Adapted from Flanders, 1965.)

or messing with their possessions. Check observers were used periodically and good interrater reliability was reported.

The training program appeared to have been remarkably effective in changing teacher behavior, since teachers in the experimental classes displayed something like four times as many positive reinforcements per student as teachers in control classes, and used many less punishments. Observations of the pupils indicated perhaps a third as many disruptive activities and a substantial increase in the percentage of attentive behavior. Finally, the gain in reading test grade equivalent over an 8 month period averaged (over all grades) about 7 months in the experimental groups as compared with about 4 months in the control groups. Thus in this study the systematic observations served to document the changes in classroom events that accompanied, and may have been responsible for, noteworthy differences in classroom achievement.

The illustrations we have just sketched in have shown methods of direct observation used in rather different ways and applied to quite different problems. These examples are representative of many specific studies from among which the selection was made. They suggest the range of usefulness of this way of studying the individual person or groups of persons.

VALUES AND LIMITATIONS OF SYSTEMATIC OBSERVATION

We have described the nature of systematic observation, outlined some of the precautions necessary if the procedure is to be satisfactorily reliable and objective, and illustrated the application of the method to different sorts of research study. Now let us undertake an appraisal of the method, indicating some of its strengths and some of its limitations as a way of studying personality.

ADVANTAGES OF DIRECT OBSERVATION

Procedures based on direct observation of the behavior of others have a number of features that make them attractive as personality evaluation devices. Some of the more significant points are considered below.

A record of actual behavior. When we observe an individual, we get a record of what he actually *does*. We are not dealing with his rationalizations and protestations. If our observational procedures have been well planned and our observers carefully trained, our score is in large measure free from the biases and idiosyncrasies of the particular observer. Our record of the individual is not a reflection of what he thinks he is, or of what someone else thinks he is. His actions speak to us directly. If, as will be true in many cases, our concern is in what the person does or the way in which his behavior has been changed, then observation of his behavior is the most direct, and in many ways the most satisfying, way of getting the relevant information.

Applicable in a natural situation. One great advantage of observational techniques is that they can be applied to the naturally occurring situations of life. Observation is not restricted to a test situation, though we saw when we were describing situational tests that observation is often an important adjunct to a test situation. Observation can be carried out in the nursery school, in the classroom, in the cafeteria, on the playground, at camp, in the squadron day room, or anywhere individuals work or play in a public setting. There are, as we shall point out presently, practical difficulties and limitations that arise in stage managing the observations. But, in spite of these, direct observation is a widely applicable approach to studying individual personalities operating in a normal nontest setting.

Usable with young children and others for whom verbal communication is difficult. Observation is possible with small children, no matter how young. As a matter of fact, the younger the child, the easier it is to observe him. The infant is completely unself-conscious, and we can sit and watch what he does with no special procedures or precautions. With older children it becomes necessary either to screen the observer from the subjects being observed or adapt them to him. The observer may be separated by a one-way vision screen so that he can see the child or children but they cannot see him. However, the requirement to provide such a physical setting seriously restricts the situations in which observation may be done. More often, and more simply, the observer may be present long enough and function sufficiently unobtrusively so that the subjects come to pay no attention to him, accepting him as a natural part of the surroundings.

The value of direct observation is greatest where its application is most feasible—with young children. Young children are quite limited in their ability to communicate through language. They do not have much experience or facility in analyzing or reporting their feelings or the reasons for their actions. They are often shy and resistant with strangers. For these groups especially, direct observation provides an important avenue of approach.

LIMITATIONS OF DIRECT OBSERVATION

The factors we have just described contribute to the attractiveness of direct observation as a technique for studying individuals. However, this approach is by no means the answer to all our measurement problems. A number of factors seriously limit the usefulness of observational techniques. These range from very practical and down-to-earth considerations, which we shall consider first, to more fundamental theoretical issues.

Cost of making the observations. Observation is costly primarily in the demands that it makes on the time of trained observers. In the illustrations we gave, each child or class was observed for a number of observation periods extending in some instances to several hours. When observations are to be made of a substantial number of individuals or class groups, the hours rapidly mount up. Systematic direct observation and recording of behavior is for this reason alone limited in its use to research projects, in which the necessary time commitments can be made. In routine school operations it is not practical to find the manpower required to make direct observations routinely of each pupil.

The cost of direct observation lies not merely in the observer time required in making the recordings. Any form of special setting or any form of mechanical recording represents an additional cost. Furthermore, when the original record is a running diary account, a motion picture, or a video tape of an individual's or a group's actions, analysis of the records is also likely to be time consuming.

Fitting the observer into the setting. There is always a question of whether having an observer in any setting, watching and making notes of what goes on, will actually change what happens. In many of the situations we wish to observe, it is not practical to have the observer invisible. We hope, often with justification, that after an initial period of getting used to the observer all persons being observed will take the observer completely for granted and ignore him or her. However, this is easier in some situations than others. When the group is small, when it is necessary for the observer to follow its activities very closely, or when the group meets for too short a time to get used to being observed, the members may not be too successful in coming to think of the observer as a piece of the furniture.

Eliminating subjectivity and bias. When observational procedures are used, it is found necessary to use all possible precautions to keep the observer's interpretations and biases out of the observation. It is especially desirable that the observer not know too much about the study that is being done, not know what experimental treatment a specific child is receiving, and not know test scores or other facts about a person who is being observed. The objective is to have the observer function purely as a recording instrument that is sensitive to, and makes a record of, certain categories of behavior. Most of the precautions described on pp. 510-511 are directed toward that end. But at best we are only partially successful. The observer is always human. We may minimize the subjective influence, but we cannot eliminate it. Especially when the phenomena being studied are complex or involve an element of interpretation, we must beware of the role of the observer in the final result.

Determining a meaningful and productive set of behavior categories to observe. Any observation is selective. Only certain limited aspects of the individual's behavior can be observed and recorded. Furthermore, if observations are to be treated quantitatively they must be classified, grouped, and counted. Any system of classification is a somewhat arbitrary framework that we impose upon the infinitely varied events of life. It is not always easy to set up a framework that serves our purposes well. Thus you may very well feel that the categories of behavior described on p. 515 do not cover well the range of teacher actions, or that the types of activity included under a given heading are inappropriate to that heading. Or we may have classified aggressive acts in terms of the overt behavior, hitting, pushing, or grabbing, whereas for our purposes it might have been better to classify by the precipitating event (if we could observe it): aggression in response to conflict over property, or as a reaction to verbal disparagement, or after thwarting of some activity in progress. In any event, scores based upon observations of behavior can be no more significant and meaningful than the categories devised for analyzing that behavior.

Determining the significance of an isolated item of behavior. Because of the need to achieve reliability and objectivity, the tendency has been to focus observation upon rather small and discrete acts, or at least to break the analysis of observational material up into small and discrete acts. There is a real danger that when this is done the meaning of the behavior, the true significance of the action, will be lost. We observe that 3-year-old A hugs 3-year-old B. Is this an act of affection? Or is it, as seems frequently the case at this age, an act of aggression? If the observation stands alone, we have no way of telling. Or suppose that A hits B. This is fairly clearly an aggressive act, but what does it signify in the life economy of A? Is it a healthful and adjustive reaction to earlier domination by B, a bursting of bonds that have shackled A? Or is it a displaced aggression built up by domination at home by a parent or older sibling? Or does it signify any one of a number of other things?

The external character of observation.   What the illustration just given brings out is that observation is external. The "outsideness" is exaggerated when little bits of behavior are analyzed out of context. But the "outsideness" is a fundamental feature of any observational approach to studying behavior. We always face the problem of determining the meaning of the behavior and must recognize that what we have before us is only what the person does, not what it signifies.

INFORMAL OBSERVATION—
THE ANECDOTAL RECORD

The systematic and continuous observations of pupil behavior considered in the previous section are essentially research tools. They are too time consuming to be practical and usually too specialized to be useful to classroom teachers trying to build up a better understanding of their pupils. However, every teacher is observing his pupils from day to day, and there is no reason why those observations should not be informally recorded as a guide to his own increased understanding or to that of others who will later deal with the pupils. Such reports of informal teacher observations of pupils have been called *anecdotal records.*

But why should the observations be *recorded?* Who should be observed? What should be recorded? How should the records be kept? What steps should be taken to organize and summarize them? What problems are commonly encountered in making and using anecdotal records? These are some of the points we shall need to consider.

Of course teachers learn from observing pupils, but why record the separate observations? Why not trust to the teacher's memory to summarize in his own mind the observations he makes from day to day and allow him to report his evaluation of a pupil in a term-end descriptive statement or set of ratings?

The answer lies partly in the fallibility of human memory and the inadequacy of human beings as assemblers and combiners of facts about another person. We make many observations of other people, but we make *so* many that they all melt together in our memory, and only a rare few of the most striking experiences continue to retain their individuality. Even these become warped and distorted with the lapse of time. And the way the sharper memories are distorted, together with the flavor of the stew that is made of our blurred recollections of ordinary day-to-day experiences, depends as much on the rememberer as on the event. Our general reaction to a child, flavored by all our ingrained prejudices and warped by what we have heard about him or by our initial experiences with him, provides the framework into which our observations are fitted. All of the sources of difficulty with personality ratings discussed in the previous chapter bear witness to the fallibility of general impression and unguided memory. By contrast, a record of an event is one dependable datum that will remain unchanged from the time we made it until the time we want to refer to it. A set of such records provides stable evidence on which later appraisals can be based.

A further reason for not relying upon summary impressions of a child, as reported by the teacher at intervals, is that such reports have generally not proved too informative or useful. They are likely to be couched in general terms, often moralistic in tone, evaluating rather than describing, and telling more about the teacher's reactions to the child than about the child.

Wilhelmina does not work nearly as hard as she should. She seems to be a bright child, and does well when she really tries. She can be very annoying at times.

What do we now really know about Wilhelmina? What chance do we have of understanding her or of working with her more effectively? We have a fairly good picture of a teacher's dissatisfaction, but know very little of a factual nature about the child.

Making a record of an observation of child behavior, a prompt record while the behavior is still fresh in the mind, can be a corrective for the limitations and distortions of memory. Such a record can come, with practice, to provide a relatively direct and objective report of actions, with the reactions of the observer kept down to a minimum.

> During art class Wilhelmina was very slow in starting work. She stopped her own work several times during the period to wander around the room and look at what other pupils were doing and tell them what was wrong with their pictures. May and Jane each told her to mind her own business and leave them alone.

This notation provides an item of factual information that can help us to know and understand Wilhelmina. It is a specific excerpt of behavior. Put together with a number of others, it may yield a factual and meaningful picture of the child.

Finally, a set of observational records provides a type of documentation for a report about a person, whether to school authorities, to parents or to a potential employer, that lends weight and substance to the report. Just as a statement about academic performance carries more conviction when it is based upon the evidence of objective test performance, so statements about interpersonal relationships seem more factual and dispassionate if they are documented with a set of actual instances of the behavior being reported.

WHO SHOULD BE OBSERVED?

Anecdotal records may serve two rather different sorts of purpose. A first purpose may be to give teachers practice in studying children, with a view to deepening their understandings and increasing their sympathetic insights. If the records are serving as part of an in-service educational program in child study, it may be well to concentrate observations on two, or at most three or four, pupils. This will permit a completeness of observation and a fullness of reporting that would not otherwise be possible. The children will ordinarily be selected for observation in terms of the teacher's special interest in them. However, it would probably be unfortunate to focus exclusively or even primarily upon "problem" cases. There is much to be learned and much light to be cast on the child with special problems by studying the "normal" child, with his or her normal problems, quirks, and idiosyncrasies.

In schools in which anecdotal records have become a part of the basic cumulative record system, anecdotes should be reported for each child in the class group. In this case, it will naturally be necessary to be content with a much more limited sample of observations for any single child.

WHAT SHOULD BE RECORDED?

This question divides into two. Which incidents should be made a matter of record? What should be included in the record of each?

Items worthy of recording. Anecdotal records provide an informal and largely qualitative picture of certain aspects of an individual's behavior. There is no point in using them for aspects of his behavior that can be appraised by more objective and accurate methods. Intellectual ability, academic achievement, and creative skills are better shown by standardized tests on the one hand or by pupil products on the other. It is primarily aspects of social functioning or adjustment to personal problems that one hopes to illuminate by records of incidents of school behavior. The interactions of a child with the other children in the room, evidences of acceptance or rejection, aggression or withdrawal, events that throw light on the child's role in the group and his reaction to it are fit material for our pen. Indications of personal tensions and adaptations to them, habitual mood and temper, or special crises and adjustments are worth recording. We may ask in each case: What can this incident tell a reader who does not know the child—a guidance worker, a subsequent teacher—that he could not find out in some simpler, more objective way?

Material to be included in an anecdote. An anecdotal record should be an accurate factual report of an event in a child's life, reported with enough of the setting and enough detail so that it is a meaningful item of behavior. Such a report is far from easy to prepare. Experience with teachers who are starting to try to write anecdotes about their pupils indicates that there are three common deviations from this prescription.

   1. *The anecdote evaluates, instead of reporting.* It tells the teacher's reaction to the child. "John was a very difficult child today" is a report of how the teacher felt about John, not of what he did.

   2. *The anecdote interprets, instead of reporting.* It gives the teacher's conclusions as to the reasons for behavior, instead of or as well as a report of what actually occurred. For example, we may see an item that reads: "Oscar simply cannot keep still in class now. He is growing so fast that he is restless all the time." The second sentence is pure interpretation, based upon extremely meager evidence, as far as we can tell. It tells us nothing about what happened. Explanations and interpretations are all very well in their place, if they are kept tentative and thought of only as hypotheses for further testing. But they should be clearly distinguished from description. The primary function of an anecdotal record is to describe a child's behavior.

3. *The anecdote describes in general terms, rather than being specific.* A report of this type would be the following: "Mary is not well accepted by the other children in the class. She usually stands on the sidelines at recess and does not take part in the games." This summarizing statement may be of some value in providing a picture of the child. However, it lacks the objectivity and concreteness that characterize the description of a single specific event. It incorporates more of selection and evaluation than we would like in our basic raw material.

A good anecdotal record has the following features.

1. It provides an accurate description of a specific event.
2. It describes the setting sufficiently to give the event meaning.
3. If it includes interpretation or evaluation by the recorder, this interpretation is separated from the description and its different status is clearly identified.
4. The event it describes is one that relates to the child's personal development or social interactions.
5. The event it describes is either representative of the typical behavior of the child or significant because it is strikingly different from his usual form of behavior. If it is unusual behavior for the child, that fact is noted.

The following three anecdotes are presented as conforming fairly well to the above specifications. Note that no attempt is made to phrase the anecdotes in full sentences. The emphasis is on ease of recording rather than on grammatical elegance. You may find it worthwhile to check them off point by point and see how you would like each changed to make it a more useful and meaningful piece of data about a child.

Class: 5A   *Pupil:* Henry K.   *Date:* 3/15/76

Class working as a group, Richard serving as chairman, discussing plans for class exhibit for local "Visit Your School Week." Henry's hand up and trying to talk almost continuously. Interrupted other children 4 or 5 times. Interruptions largely caustic or facetious com-

ment. When Richard told him he was "out of order" because someone else was talking, he said, "Aw, nuts to you," and paid no more
attention to the discussion.

(Typical of Henry's behavior a number of times lately. Aggres-
sively seeking attention, then withdraws if rebuffed.)

Class: 8D   *Pupil:* Peter Y.   *Date:* 4/25/75

Peter drowsed off in social studies discussion period after lunch
today. Faraway look; then eyes closed. Came to with a start when
spoken to. Seemed attentive for few minutes, then dropped off again.
Sleepy throughout the period.

(Same sort of thing several times in past 2 weeks. Is something
preventing him from getting enough sleep? What is it?)

Class: 6B   *Pupil:* Betsy R.   *Date:* 10/6/75

Coming into class after morning recess Betsy slapped Sue, reason
unknown. While getting seated, had a row with Jane about owner-
ship of a pencil. Later in morning, pinched Ellen. 2 or 3 other squab-
bles before lunch. Standing by herself after lunch, not playing with
other girls.

(Very unusual for Betsy. Usually even tempered, well liked, and
the center of the group.)

HOW SHOULD ANECDOTAL RECORDS BE KEPT?

The exact mechanical format of anecdotal records is of secondary importance compared with the considerations of content.
However, the usefulness of records will depend upon the ease
with which the records for a particular pupil may be assembled, studied, and summarized. It is also important that the
sheer mechanical burdens of keeping the records be kept to a
minimum. One of the main practical problems in the use of
anecdotal records has been the clerical burdens they impose.

If an anecdote is to be a faithful record of an event, it should
be recorded as immediately as possible while memory of the
event is still fresh. Unfortunately, immediate recording is
rarely feasible. At best, some time elapses before the observer
has a free moment in which to note down a record of the
behavior. This interval should be kept as short as possible, and
in every instance the record should be made on the same day
that the behavior is observed.

The appropriate form for keeping records will depend upon
the primary purpose for which they are being kept. If the records are serving to guide the teacher's study of two or three
particular pupils, they may well be kept in the form of two or
three separate logs or diaries. Successive entries should then be
dated and entered in sequence in a notebook, on sheets of

typewriter paper, or on file cards. When records are being made from time to time on all the pupils in a school, as a part of the regular cumulative record system of the school, a uniform method of recording that facilitates filing the records of each child in his individual file folder will be needed. The record form should be evaluated in terms of the total record system. If an individual file folder is used, an 8½ × 11 sheet of paper will often prove suitable. The record form should provide space for identifying information (class, pupil, date, person making the record), the anecdote itself, and possibly for an evaluating comment.

WHAT SHOULD BE DONE
TO ORGANIZE OR SUMMARIZE RECORDS?

Each original anecdotal record is an item of information about an individual. A series of records provides a whole set of such items. But for data to be useful they must be organized, summarized, and interpreted. The data in such an intelligence test as the *Binet* consist of a series of responses to specific items that are summarized in a mental age or IQ. Although the significant elements in a set of anecdotal records cannot be summarized as simply, some attempt at bringing the items together into an organized picture of the individual will usually be desirable.

At intervals, perhaps once a semester or possibly oftener if a child is being studied intensively, the anecdotes on an individual should be reviewed carefully. Recurring patterns should be noted. Any progressive changes should be brought out. A thumbnail sketch of the individual, as shown by the anecdotes, should be prepared. The attempt should be made to relate the anecdotal material to other facts that are known about the child: his health, intellectual ability, academic achievement, home surroundings, and family pattern. A tentative interpretation of the patterns may be attempted, if it is recognized that any interpretation is to be thought of as a set of very tentative hypotheses. In the summary, as in the records themselves, the descriptive summary and the interpretation of it should be kept clearly differentiated.

WHAT USE SHOULD BE MADE
OF ANECDOTAL RECORDS?

Like any other evaluation procedure, anecdotal records have value only if they are used. Several appropriate uses may be identified.

By the person making the records.   As noted earlier, the process of accumulating records and studying and organizing the results should help the maker to understand better the specific person being studied. A series of such studies may, it is hoped, provide more general insights into students' social and motivational responses to the classroom or work situation.

By later teachers.   Anecdotal observations about a child can give a later teacher a head start in understanding the child's assets and difficulties. There is a legitimate concern lest the early teacher's biases and negative responses handicap the child in his later endeavors. But this concern is much less relevant when the earlier record is a report of samples of behavior. If the report is primarily descriptive rather than evaluative, it can provide a valuable background for interpreting his actions in his new social group.

With parents.   Teachers face an important responsibility for reporting to parents, and it is desirable that those reports have as much credibility as can be provided for them. To be able to cite specific instances in support of statements about interpersonal behaviors or social interactions is to bolster the credibility of what might otherwise seem a very subjective judgment.

With other school personnel.   In those cases in which a counselor, special teacher, or school psychologist is called in to work with a child in relation to his educational or personal problems, it helps to have the problems defined in part by observations of samples of his behavior. Again, when periodic narrative statements are to be entered on report forms or in school records, these records can be made more specific and related more directly to the child's behavior if samples of that behavior are available to refer to.

With potential employers.   At a higher level, as for example, in professional school, there may be occasion to prepare a letter of recommendation, or some form of evaluation for a student. The evidence available in a set of anecdotal reports of class or clinical performance can provide the evidence to guide and support such an evaluation.

WHAT PROBLEMS ARISE IN MAKING AND INTERPRETING ANECDOTAL RECORDS?

We have already indicated a number of the problems in making and using anecdotal records in the previous sections. These and some other issues will be considered in this section.

Problems arising out of the selection of items. The number of anecdotes that could be written about any individual is almost limitless. The written record must consist of a relatively small fraction of these, chosen by the observer as being significant or as typical of the child. The quality of the accumulated data depends upon the shrewdness and impartiality of this selection. Both the significance and the truthfulness of the picture will depend upon the ability of the observer to select items to record that are illuminating and truly representative. Bias by the observer can easily creep into both the selection and the recording of the items. For a child whom the teacher dislikes, it is easy to pick out and record only situations in which he appears in a bad light. If the teacher is unduly preoccupied with academic achievement or an orderly classroom, incidents relating to nonachievement or disorder may take a dominant role in the record. It is hard to know how much bias is introduced in a set of anecdotes by selectivity of this sort, but the problem is certainly a very real one.

Problems relating to the phrasing of the anecdote. Difficulties here center around the tendencies, which we have already considered, to include evaluation, interpretation, and generalities and to leave out the specific factual description. Problems of literary style are also occasionally a matter of concern. In this regard, the thing to remember is that anecdotes are valued not as literary gems but for the information they convey. Brevity and clarity, not literary elegance, are the objectives even to the point of writing in phrases rather than sentences.

Problems relating to the clerical burden. One of the most serious practical problems in any school program of anecdotal records is the sheer clerical burden of preparing, filing, and summarizing the records. These problems have tended to limit the systematic use of anecdotal records to preschools, where classes are small and where personal-social development is quite central to the school's concern, and to private schools and a few public schools in which the resources are far above the national average. Bearing in mind the burdens that a program of anecdotal records places upon the staff, any school system should move into anecdotal recording cautiously. Recording should be tried first for a few pupils in each class and gradually expanded only if it seems to be yielding useful information. Recording procedures should be kept as simple as possible. Literary style and elegance of format should be minimized.

Problems relating to use. Like any other evaluation procedure, anecdotal records are useful only if they are used. One must take care that the records do not become an end in themselves. The records must be accessible. They must be summarized periodically, so that the user can refer to a concise summary. School personnel should be encouraged and trained to use them.

One specific problem is a feeling on the part of some teachers that they do not wish to be biased by what a previous teacher has said about a child. When what the previous teacher has said is primarily an expression of his reactions to the child, with a strong admixture of personal prejudice, this unwillingness is understandable. When the anecdotes and the summary become factual and descriptive, there is no longer any reason to object to having the information. It is as important for the teacher to start the year with information about the status of a child's personal and social development as it is to be informed about his reading and number skills.

PSEUDOANECDOTAL RECORDS

There appear in the student files of many school systems what we might refer to as "pseudoanecdotal records." These consist of narrative and evaluative statements by teachers, in which they characterize the social relationships, work habits, or personal appearance of a child. These are not in any real sense anecdotal *records,* because they are not in any direct way based on *observations* of the child. They are summarizing, subjective appraisals of the child, including whatever aspect of his or her impression a teacher saw fit to record. Though they may have some value, they should be recognized for what they are, and not confused with the type of record we have been discussing earlier.

SUMMARY EVALUATION
OF ANECDOTAL RECORDS

An anecdotal record provides a medium for recording the observation of a significant item of pupil behavior. When teachers have developed skill in selecting incidents and in describing them objectively, when the mechanics of record-keeping and summarizing are kept within reasonable bounds, and when the records are available for use by those whose concern it is to understand the individual pupil, such records can be a significant aid to working with children.

One approach to personality appraisal is the direct measurement or the observation of some aspect of behavior. We may attempt to elicit typical behavior by actual test situations, such as those represented by the honesty tests of May and Hartshorne. These have the advantage that they can be scored as directly and objectively as an ability test. However, the tests are complex to develop and stage, have rather modest reliability, yield results that seem to be rather specific to the particular test situation, and are not readily adaptable to many of the aspects of personality in which we are interested.

One group of techniques for obtaining and evaluating behavior that has received a great deal of attention over the past 40 years comprises the projective techniques. These yield a sample of responses to relatively unstructured stimulus materials, and the responses are analyzed and interpreted to yield a wide range of inferences about the person who produced them. Evidence on the reliability and validity of the resulting inferences is very mixed, and we can hardly recommend the techniques with confidence. In any case the use of these techniques should be limited to specialists who have had extended training in their scoring and interpretation.

The situational test represents a compromise between a standard test and an observational procedure. A lifelike test situation is developed, into which the examinee is placed. Typically, it is a social situation involving some type of interaction with other individuals and structured to emphasize the facets of the personality in which the investigator is particularly interested. Group discussion or group problem solving represents one promising type of situation. For evaluation of the examinee's behavior, however, reliance is placed on observation and ratings. This permits a good deal more freedom in planning the test situations, and many sorts of interpersonal behavior may be observed.

Behavior in naturally occurring situations also has been studied by techniques of direct observation. Steps that have been taken to refine the everyday observations we make of people include (1) limitation of observations to a single aspect of behavior, (2) careful definition of the behaviors falling within this category, (3) training of observers, (4) quantification of observations, as by a procedure of taking many short samples, and (5) development of procedures for coding and recording the observations.

Direct observation has the advantages of (1) representing actual behavior, (2) being applicable to natural life situations, and (3) being usable with young children and others with whom verbal communication is difficult. However, observational procedures present a number of problems, including (1) cost, (2) difficulty of fitting the observer into the situation, (3) difficulty of eliminating observer bias, (4) difficulty of setting up meaningful and productive categories to observe, (5) difficulty in determining the meaning of isolated bits of behavior, and (6) the fact that an observer inevitably has an outside view of the person whom he observes.

Systematically scheduled observation is rarely practical for teachers, job supervisors, or other persons for whom personality appraisal is secondary to other aspects of their job. Such a person may use informal anecdotal records to accumulate information about a pupil or employee. Informal observations should be factual reports of significant items of behavior; they should avoid evaluation, interpretation, and vague generalities. Recording of observations should be kept as simple as possible and the record should be reviewed and interpreted periodically to give an organized picture of the person who has been observed.

QUESTIONS AND EXERCISES

1. In their studies of honesty, Hartshorne and May report quite low correlations between different behavior tests of honesty. If this is true for other qualities as well, what does it mean for our understanding of people?

2. Try to design several behavior tests for some trait other than honesty.

3. What basis is there for expecting a projective test to work? Why should we be able to tell anything about a person from the types of responses that he gives to projective test materials?

4. Why has there been such a divergence of opinion between clinical psychologists and specialists in measurement as to the value of projective tests?

5. What are the distinctive advantages of procedures such as leaderless group discussions, in-baskets, and business games, in comparison with paper-and-pencil ability tests? What special problems do they present?

6. Plan a situational test for use in a school or industrial situation. What would you hope to get from this test that you could not get in other ways? What would be the difficulties of using such a test as you have proposed?

7. How could the class discussion that takes place in most classes serve as the basis for systematic observation? Make a plan for recording these observations.

8. In a research study, you propose to use systematic observations of school children as a method of studying their social adjustment. What problems would you encounter? What precautions would you need to take in interpreting the results?

9. What advantages do systematic observations or short sample observations have over the observations of everyday life? What limitations do these more specialized procedures have?

10. If you are working in a classroom, make anecdotal records on some one child over a 1-week period. Observe as well as you can the guides for making anecdotal records given on pp. 524–525. What difficulties did you encounter in making the records?

11. Criticize the following anecdotal records:

(*a*) "Mary continues to be a nuisance in class. She is noisy and not only fails to do her own work but keeps other children from doing theirs. I don't know what I am going to do about it."

(*b*) "John had a good deal of trouble with his arithmetic today. He didn't seem to be able to get the idea of reducing fractions to a common denominator. Out of several problems he was able to identify the lowest common denominator only once."

12. In some educational situations, such as the clinical part of the education of nurses, evaluation depends entirely on observations made by a supervisor. For such a situation, compare the advantages and disadvantages of (1) systematic, regularly scheduled observations and (2) a program of anecdotal records.

13. As a class group, assemble the experiences of a number of schools or school systems in using anecdotal records. How many use them currently? With what sorts of group? What sorts of problem are they encountering? How many have tried them and abandoned them? For what reasons?

SUGGESTED ADDITIONAL READING

Asher, James J. and James A. Sciarrino. Realistic work sample tests: A review. *Personnel Psychology,* 1974, 27, 519–533.

Banister, D., and M. Bott. *Evaluating the person.* In P. Kline (Ed.), *New Approaches in Psychological Measurement.* New York: John Wiley & Sons, 1973.

Bigoness, William J. Effect of applicant's sex, race, and performance on employers performance ratings: Some additional findings. *Journal of Applied Psychology,* 1976, 61, 80–84.

Brandt, R. M. *Studying behavior in natural settings.* New York: Holt, Rinehart and Winston, Inc. 1972.

Brown, Bob Burton and Jeaninne N. Webb. *The use of classroom observation techniques in the evaluation of educational programs.* TM Report 49. ERIC Clearinghouse on Tests, Measurement and Evaluation, Educational Testing Service, December 1975.

Fitzpatrick, Robert and Edward J. Morrison. Performance and product evaluation. In R. L. Thorndike (Ed.), *Educational Measurement.* (2nd Ed.) Washington,

D. C.: American Council on Education, 1971.

Herbert, John and Carol Attridge. A guide for developers and users of observation systems and manuals. *American Educational Research Journal,* 1975, 12, 1–20.

Hinrichs, John R. and S. Haanperä. Reliability of measurement in situational exercises: An assessment of the assessment center method. *Personnel Psychology,* 1976, 29, 31–40.

Hundleby, John D. The measurement of personality by objective tests. In P. Kline (Ed.) *New Approaches in Psychological Measurement.* New York: John Wiley & Sons, 1973.

Mayer, Steven E. and Anita I. Bell. Sexism in ratings of personality traits. *Personnel Psychology,* 1975, 28, 239–249.

Semeonoff, Boris. New developments in projective testing. In P. Kline (Ed.), *New Approaches in Psychological Measurement.* New York: John Wiley & Sons, 1973.

Simon, Anita and E. Gil Boyer. *Mirrors for behavior III: An anthology of observation instruments.* Wyncote, Pa.: Communications Materials Center, 1974.

CHAPTER FOURTEEN
PLANNING A SCHOOL TESTING PROGRAM

We want to give some standardized test in our school. What would you recommend?

I am on a committee to revise the testing program for our schools. These are the tests we plan to use, and the grades in which we plan to use them. Will you criticize this plan?

Probably every teacher or tests and measurements faces requests like these each semester. What standardized tests should be used? When should they be used? What constitutes a sound testing program?

THE CART AND THE HORSE

The trouble is that there is really no answer to such questions. Or, rather, the only answer is another series of questions. Before asking "What tests should we give," we must ask, "What decisions are we going to need to make for which test results might provide useful input? When are we likely to need to make them? Will they arise for all or most students, or only for a few? Who will be responsible for the decision? Administrator? Teacher? Parent? Student?" Unless there are some decisions in relation to which the test results will be useful, giving tests can be a rather futile enterprise. What profit is there in a reading readiness test if all members of a class study reading together from the same primer at the same rate and time? Why give a reading test in the tenth grade if there are no provisions for differentiated individual work or remedial instruction? A functioning testing program should grow out of explicitly stated needs for specific kinds of information and plans for the ways that the test results will be used in decision making. A testing program can be planned only in terms of the purposes it is to serve. Tests given with no particular use in mind *may* find a use, *may* create their own market but it hardly seems likely.

The starting place is the school, its curriculum, its students, its staff, and the decisions that need to be made for, with, and by students. It cannot be expected that each single teacher will have seen in advance how test data can be used in forwarding his activities with his class. Learning to use test information represents one aspect of in-service growth. But a testing program unrelated to local needs, local resources, and local levels of sophistication is unlikely to function effectively. Planning that does not center around constructive use of the test results and provide for increasing the total staff's understanding of the tests that are used in the program is likely to be sterile. For tests are given to be used, not to be filed. More important than planning *what* tests are to be *given* is planning *how* the tests are to be *used*.

This is why planning a testing program in the abstract or in a vacuum is so unsatisfactory. Defining functions and purposes is the horse. Let us put him out in front, and the cart carrying a program of tests will follow after.

FUNCTIONS OF A TESTING PROGRAM

The phrase *testing program* as used in this chapter refers to an organized schoolwide or systemwide program for administering a uniform battery of tests. We are restricting the use of the term to those programs in which the local school authorities have full control over which tests will be given, when they will be given and to whom they will be given. The term, as we are using it, does not include the wide variety of teacher-made tests that are prepared for use within a single class or school, the specialized testing procedures that may be carried on to study individual students, nor the testing programs that are controlled by agencies other than local school authorities—agencies such as the College Entrance Examination Board (CEEB) or state education departments.

Although, in our use of the term *testing program*, we stress local control and local needs, many of the needs for the information that tests can supply and many of the functions to be served by a testing program are common from one school system to another. We have discussed ways of using the results of various kinds of standardized tests in previous chapters. See Chapter 6 for a full discussion of the types of decision for which achievement tests may prove useful, Chapter 9, for uses of intelligence and prognostic tests, and Chapter 11, for uses of temperament and adjustment inventories.

In Table 14.1 we present a summary of the most justifiable uses of test results. This summary may serve as a checklist to guide a review of local needs and uses. However, the applicability of these functions must always be checked in the local setting. One must ask, "Can we, or do we wish to, use tests for this purpose in our schools?"

Table 14.1
FUNCTIONS OF A TESTING PROGRAM

Classroom Functions	Guidance Functions	Administrative Functions
Diagnosing learning difficulties	Preparing evidence to guide discussions with parents about their children	Assigning students to classroom groups
Evaluating discrepancies between potential and achievement	Helping the student make immediate choices	Placing new students
Appraising gains or growth in achievement	Helping the student to set educational and vocational goals	Helping to determine eligibility for special groups
Grouping students for instruction within a class	Improving counselor, teacher, and parent understanding of problem cases	Evaluating curricula, curricular emphasis, and curricular experiments
Planning instructional activities for an individual		Improving public relations
Identifying students who need special diagnostic study and remedial instruction		Providing information for outside agencies
Determining reasonable achievement levels for each student		

QUALITIES DESIRED
IN A TESTING PROGRAM

What are the general characteristics of a good school testing program? We shall consider three briefly: relationship to use, integration, and continuity.

RELATION TO USE

We have indicated in Table 14.1 a number of functions for which standardized tests are used in some school systems. The first step in planning a testing program for your schools is to review these and possibly other functions and determine how tests will be used in your schools. The testing should then be planned in relation to these uses. Tests should be selected and the times at which they are given should be chosen so that the needed information will be available and as up to date as possible at whatever time it will be used to assist in some decision.

Thus suppose teachers in the first grade wish to use test results to help them form subgroups that will move into reading at different rates. Their need is then for a reading readiness test. If almost all pupils go to kindergarten, the test might be scheduled for the end of the kindergarten year, say, in May. But more likely one will want to give the test in the first grade, early in the fall, as soon as the pupils have settled down in their new class.

Or suppose that a differentiated high school program is available for the 3 years of senior high school, and that counselors and pupils work out plans for the high school program during the spring of the ninth grade in the light of available information on pupil aptitudes and achievement. In this setting a program of aptitude and achievement testing during the first semester of the ninth grade will provide relevant and current information. Here, as everywhere, the important thing is to provide *what* will be used *when* it will be used.

INTEGRATION

The testing program should be seen as a whole. Information that is needed in the sixth grade is not unrelated to the information that was obtained in the fifth grade or to information that will be useful in the seventh grade. Each item of information gathered should be obtained at such a time and in such a way that it will make the maximum contribution to the total. Several aspects of integration merit consideration.

In an integrated program it will usually be desirable to use the same series of tests over the grade range for which the series is appropriate. For example, if the *Metropolitan Achievement Tests* are being used to measure progress in basic skills, it will probably be desirable to use them in any grade from first up to sixth, and possibly to eighth or ninth, in which an achievement battery is being used. The advantages are that norms are based upon the same sampling of communities from grade to grade, and the tests conform to a common outline of content and format. Thus scores from one grade to the next are more nearly comparable, so that a truer picture may be obtained of pupil growth.

Integration implies particularly integration among the several divisions of the school program. Tests in junior high school should be planned in relation to those already given in the elementary school, and those in senior high school take account of junior high testing. A cognitive ability test given in the sixth grade need not be followed by a similar test at the beginning of the seventh grade. If aptitude tests are given in the ninth grade, there is limited gain from a similar battery in the tenth.

Integration among divisions of the school implies continuity of school records. The records accumulated about a pupil in the elementary school should follow him, in whole or in part, when he goes on to the secondary school. It may be that the complete record, especially if it is a very full one, should not stay in the active record file. However, key information should carry over into the record system of the higher school, and the full record should be available for reference if need be. At the same time, however, information should be updated with the most recent test results (and other student information), so that decisions can be based upon the most current information about a student.

Integration means, finally, timing testing so that insofar as possible multiple purposes can be served. An attempt to serve two masters is always a compromise. However, it sometimes represents a sound use of limited resources. Thus a test of cognitive abilities given fairly early in the sixth grade can serve adequately for sectioning and guidance in the seventh grade and still be available as a resource for studying problem cases in grade 6. A scholastic aptitude test in grade 10 or 11 gives as good a prediction of college success as one taken in May of the senior year and is also available for counseling purposes during 2 or 3 years of high school.

CONTINUITY

The potential values of a testing program increase as it is continued over a period of years. Advantages of continuity in the program are twofold. On the one hand, data accumulate in the records of the individual pupil. There are available to contribute to an understanding of the youngster not merely the results of tests given during the present year but also the data from earlier testings one or more years ago in lower grades. Present status can be seen in perspective in relation to earlier records. We can see whether Jerry's academic problems in the sixth grade have developed recently or whether they represent merely the continuation of an early trend; we can determine whether the difficulty Mary is having with long division is new or whether it has its roots in early difficulties with arithmetic fundamentals.

Continuity also is of importance in permitting a school system to get to know the particular tests it is using. We have emphasized at various points that a good deal of caution must be exercised in applying national norms to a local setting. Local use of a test or test series over a period of time permits the development of local standards of expectancy. This may take the form of an informal and implicit tempering of national norms in interpreting local performance. It may take the form of an actual set of local norms. Thus a suburban community with a very high percentage of pupils going on to college may find that percentiles based on its own school population provide a more appropriate framework for judging the academic status of its pupils than do national age or grade norms.

Getting to know tests implies getting to know what they measure, as well as establishing local standards of expectancy. If teachers work with the tests and results, they will come to know what the test covers, what cues for diagnosing group strengths and weaknesses can be drawn from it, and what its limitations are. Both types of familiarity are desirable when teachers are using test results to help them with their work. For this reason a school system will ordinarily wish to continue to use the same tests over a period of years, changing them only when they become out of date or when a study of other available tests indicates that there are ones available that represent a definite improvement over those that have been used in past years.

SUGGESTED PRIORITIES IN A TESTING PROGRAM

At the beginning of the chapter we indicated an unwillingness to prescribe a particular pattern for a testing program. This unwillingness stems in part from the differnt functions the program may serve in different schools. It stems also from the wide variation in financial and professional resources available in different school systems. However, there is a general core of uniformity, in spite of diversity, and the same types of test are available to all schools. That being so, we shall offer some suggestions on the tests we consider likely to prove most generally useful in a program at the different levels.

A PROGRAM FOR THE ELEMENTARY SCHOOL

In the elementary school concern centers on helping the individual to master the tools of learning and communicating while he or she is learning to live and work in a group of peers. At the same time, the individual is building up a background of experience, knowledge, and understanding. It is in this setting that tests must function. Though it is difficult to arrange choices in an ordered sequence, since tests relate to each other and function in teams, we have attempted to do so roughly.

In all subsequent discussion it is assumed that children have been adequately examined for vision and hearing and general health status. We have thought of these measures as part of the physical examination rather than as part of the school testing program. They are, of course, of fundamental importance in guaranteeing a profitable educational experience for each child. There is nothing more tragic than the so-called "stupid" child in the back row, who gets nothing out of school because he cannot hear what the teacher is saying or cannot see what is written on the blackboard.

Reading tests. We are disposed to give first place in our program of elementary school testing to tests of reading ability. Reading has always been the key avenue for acquiring all types of organized knowledge. Though in the present-day world its supremacy is challenged somewhat by movies, radio, and television, learning from books will continue to be at the heart of education, especially at the higher levels. For this reason, aiding the school in making early identification of poor progress in reading and in keeping track of reading progress through the school years seems to be among the most useful services a testing program can perform.

If very meager resources permit only a single reading test, we suspect that we would give it at the end of the second or beginning of the third grade, to identify individuals for special help for a year or so before they reach the greater variety of content and the more extensive demands upon independent reading during the later elementary grades. However, we would like to be able to give a reading test every year or two from the beginning of the second grade throughout the elementary school.

Group academic aptitude test.   To aid in interpreting reading test results and other aspects of academic achievement, to help in setting expectations for pupils, and to aid in understanding problem cases, we would like to have results from a test of general cognitive ability. When we are thinking in terms of a minimum program and are considering the practical realities of time and cost, we must settle for a group test. If it is to be used in conjunction with our early third grade reading test, it should be a nonreading ability test. But group tests given as early as the beginning of the third grade do not have too satisfactory reliability or stability over time. If we can afford only a single group test, we would probably do well to delay it until the fourth or fifth grade, when the results are more dependable. If a test is to be given in the second or third grade, we would want to be able to include at least one more group ability test during the upper elementary grades, fourth, fifth, or sixth, the choice of grade depending upon plans for testing in junior high school. We would not object to additional tests, given fairly adequate resources. These would serve primarily to increase the reliability of our appraisal. We would be glad to have both verbal and nonverbal measures of cognitive ability.

Basic skills battery.   Competing with the academic aptitude test for second place in our program would be a battery covering the basic skill subjects. This would, of course, include reading and could replace the separate reading test. If the battery could be given only once, we would probably choose to give it in grade 3 or 4 where the results could be used by the school for planning individual programs of instruction for pupils or for fitting pupils into special programs of remedial instruction. However, we would like to be able to test children with such a battery every year, starting in the third grade or possibly the second. We have a certain bias in favor of carrying out this testing in the fall, so that the fresh results may be available for use by the teacher who has worked with the testing.

Reading readiness test.   On the assumption that the teachers in our school have an individualized program of instruction in reading for the first grade, we would place a reading readiness test next upon our list. We might possibly move it higher. We would view this test as a partial guide to the first grade teacher in organizing subgroups for reading instruction and as a basis for helping to evaluate the progress of individual pupils.

The four types of test listed so far are the ones commonly found in school testing programs. Other types of test will be found much less frequently. Some are not used because of cost, some because what they have to offer seems less important.

Individual intelligence tests. For most students in the elementary school, adequate appraisal of general intellectual abilities can be obtained from group tests. There are situations, though, in which an individual intelligence test could be very useful. Most of these situations are those in which one is working intensively with an individual who has severe learning disabilities or emotional problems. We tend to view the individual intelligence tests as being supplementary to the regular school testing program.

Achievement tests in content subjects. Some of the achievement batteries for the upper elementary grades include tests dealing with content areas of science and social studies. Although each school must decide for itself whether these tests offer valid appraisals of its curriculum, we feel that the nature of their content is such that they have limited usefulness either for helping teachers in instructional decisions relating to students or for helping to evaluate the curriculum in the school. We do not recommend them as important features of an elementary school program.

Other types of measure. Other types of test may be required for studying individual children. These include the diagnostic tests used in the special study of children with disability in a particular subject. They also include the techniques of clinical testing used by school psychologist in studying a problem case. However, these represent supplements of the testing program rather than a basic part of it.

We have not recommended paper-and-pencil personality inventories because of (1) serious doubts as to the validity of the information they provide for an elementary school child and the soundness of the interpretations and constructive use that school personnel can make of the results; and (2) the objections of parents to the kinds of question that are asked in these inventories. This does not mean that personality development of the elementary school child is of no concern to the school.

Rather, it means that understanding the child as a person must depend upon observations of each pupil by the teacher and other school personnel.

A PROGRAM FOR THE SECONDARY SCHOOL

In the secondary school the student faces a number of educational choices and decisions. He has to make choices of particular subjects or between different curricula. At the same time, he must start thinking about future educational or vocational plans. The curriculum has, to a considerable extent, moved beyond the basic skills toward increased emphasis on specialized subject matter. These shifts in emphasis appear to call for a corresponding shift in the pattern of the school testing program.

In planning a testing program for the secondary school we want to be sure that the diverse needs of both the college-bound and noncollege-bound student are met. The secondary school testing program should take into consideration college entrance tests such as the *CEEB Preliminary Scholastic Aptitude Test* and *Scholastic Aptitude Test,* and the tests of the American College Testing Program that are taken by the college-bound students. However, one of the most common faults of secondary school testing programs is the failure to provide for adequate appraisal of the noncollege-bound student. These students need counseling as much as, if not more than, the college-bound students. The planning of instructional activities and curricula for them requires an understanding of their general and specific abilities as well as of their status and progress in basic skills. There is a real need for schools to gather data on the effectiveness of their programs for the noncollege-bound student. The order of priority that we propose is outlined below.

Scholastic aptitude test.   When several distinct high school curricula are available, a student must decide upon the kind of curriculum that he will pursue in high school. A related decision is how many academic courses he will take at one time and the level of the courses that is most suitable for him. During his high school program, he must decide how far up the educational ladder he will seek to go. A scholastic aptitude test is of value as a supplement to school grades in arriving at these decisions. It is also of value in interpreting the student's progress in school and in setting reasonable levels of expected achievement for him.

By high school age, the abilities measured by a scholastic aptitude test have become fairly well stabilized. There is little systematic shift from one year to the next. Thus a tenth-grade test will serve to estimate scholastic aptitude at the end of the twelfth grade as well as one given later. For this reason, if only a single test is to be given, it may be given early, so that it can be used throughout the school program. Tests of both verbal and nonverbal abilities can be used to obtain a more complete description of the student's abilities.

Reading test.   Skill in reading is important for both college-bound and noncollege-bound students. However, there is relatively little to be gained by giving a reading test unless the school provides either a developmental or remedial reading program. When such resources *are* available, results of reading tests can be used to place individuals in the appropriate program. Since the constructive use of a reading test implies appropriate action, it is desirable that the testing be done early in the program of the school, preferably in the eighth or ninth grade.

Tests of special aptitudes.   For counseling students it is desirable to have appraisals of specialized aptitudes as well as general scholastic aptitude. Tests of specialized aptitudes are usually not well adapted for use below the eighth grade. The particular time at which they are used will depend upon the guidance program of the school. Testing should be timed so that results will be available when the counselor and the student must work together to decide on the student's program in secondary school. Usually these kinds of decision must be made either in the eighth or ninth grade.

At this level, an educationally oriented battery such as the *Differential Aptitude Test Battery* is especially appropriate. If such a battery is used, it can take the place of the general scholastic aptitude test since certain subtests can be combined to give a suitable estimate of scholastic aptitude. For the noncollege-bound student, a vocationally oriented aptitude battery such as the *General Aptitude Test Battery* could be given in the eleventh or twelfth grade.

Achievement tests in content areas.   Standardized achievement tests in the content areas for secondary schools have some value in helping students make decisions about their future educational plans and also in helping the school to evaluate various aspects of its curriculum. Such tests are particularly of value in the ninth or tenth grades. They have little value for individual guidance if they are given in the twelfth grade.

Interests.   Although interests of a student are of value in helping him to make vocational and educational decisions, we have placed interest inventories relatively low in priority in a secondary school testing program. One reason for doing so is that interests of students of secondary school age are relatively unstable. Especially for college-bound students, the types of decision that build upon vocational interests can usually be deferred until after the end of secondary school by which point interest patterns have become somewhat more stabilized. Another reason is that the type of interest inventory that is appropriate at the secondary school level usually provides somewhat scanty data on the validity of the scores. If an interest inventory is given at the time that pupils first begin to think about and discuss the world of work, as is done in the ninth grade of some schools, it should be one, such as the *Kuder Preference Record*, that evaluates in terms of general interest areas rather than providing ratings for specific jobs. Early testing with such an inventory could appropriately be supplemented by a second testing with a more job oriented inventory, such as the *Strong-Campbell Vocational Interest Blank* or the *Minnesota Vocational Interest Inventory* in the eleventh or twelfth grades, especially for students who are not planning to go to college and who will be entering the world of work.

Prognostic tests.   We place prognostic tests very low in priority in our secondary school testing program. By the time that the student enters secondary school, there are usually extensive data on his abilities and achievement that can be used to estimate his probability of success in such fields as algebra and foreign languages. We doubt that the use of a special prognostic test for a subject will increase the accuracy of prediction of success in the subject enough to justify the additional testing. We also think it is undesirable to base decisions on admitting students to courses on the results of a single test.

Personality and adjustment inventories.   We have serious reservations about the practical value of paper-and-pencil techniques for assessing personality at this level also. We do not recommend giving these kinds of inventory routinely to all students. However, this does not exclude their use by well-trained counselors or school psychologists for studying individual students.

A TESTING PROGRAM FOR THE COLLEGE

At the college level the diversity in programs, characteristics of students, and goals of students becomes even greater than at the high school level. This diversity is reflected in the functions that standardized tests are expected to serve at the college level. The primary functions served by standardized tests at the college level are (1) admissions, (2) academic placement, and (3) guidance and counseling of the individual student. Except for testing for admissions and placement, the college testing program is likely to be highly individualized to serve the needs of the student who has requested counseling.

Much of the admissions testing for both 2-year and 4-year colleges is done by external testing agencies, either the College Entrance Examination Board (CEEB) or the American College Testing Program (ACT). These tests will be discussed in the section on external testing programs.

The problem of placing students in appropriate courses or sections of courses after admission to college arises in four general situations: (1) placement in freshman courses; (2) advanced placement for those students who have taken college-level courses in secondary schools; (3) credit for and exemption from courses that a student has studied outside of the formal classroom structure; and (4) placement of students transferring from another college. For placement in freshman courses, colleges have used either the relevant achievement test of the CEEB or the college freshmen level of the standardized achievement tests discussed in Chapter 8. If the CEEB achievement tests are used, they are usually taken by the student while in high school. If other standardized tests are used, they are usually given to all freshman as a part of the freshman testing program, often during a freshman orientation week.

Advanced placement for those students who have taken college level courses in secondary schools is usually accomplished through the use of *CEEB Advanced Placement Examinations.* These examinations are administered once each year, in May, and the results are available for use before the student enters college. The *College Level Examination Program* of the CEEB was established to enable those who have reached the college level of education outside the classroom through correspondence study, television courses, on-the-job training, independent reading, or any other means to demonstrate their level of achievement and to use the test results for college credit or placement. The same test series has been used for admission, placement, and guidance of students who wish to transfer from one institution to another. There are two types of examination in the program: (1) the *General Examinations* that appraise achievement in five basic areas of the liberal arts: *English Composition, Humanities, Mathematics, Natural Sciences,* and *Social Sci-*

ences-History: and (2) the 16 *Subject Examinations* designed to appraise achievement in specific college courses.

The major function of standardized testing in colleges is for guidance of individual students. This guidance may be educational, vocational, or personal. At the college level, problems in these areas tend to be individual rather than general.

Furthermore, these services are likely to be offered only when the student requests them, although the request may come as a result of outside pressure. This suggests that the tests used should be selected in light of the problem being presented by each student; therefore the emphasis is on a highly individualized rather than on a uniform testing program.

There are some colleges, particularly 2-year colleges, that require no uniform examinations of all students for admission to the college. In these colleges, a uniform freshman testing program could provide data that would be useful in placing students and in counseling students, In many colleges the number of students who have difficulty in maintaining satisfactory scholastic standing is great enough to justify gathering common data on all students so that they are available for counseling. The priorities that we suggest are oriented toward these common guidance needs.

Scholastic aptitude. Since a substantial number of college students have difficulty in maintaining satisfactory scholastic standing, evidence on scholastic aptitude is often needed as a basis for counseling with respect to academic difficulties. Separate appraisal of verbal and quantitative abilities may be of value in permitting a more diagnostic appraisal. The test should be given at the time of admission so that the results may be available for use throughout the college program.

A battery of special aptitude tests could be used in place of the scholastic aptitude test. However, there appears to be somewhat less need for special aptitude tests in a college population than at the secondary level. The decision to go on to college has already somewhat narrowed down the range of occupations for which the group is preparing; the tests of mechanical, spatial, and clerical abilities are of rather less significance for college students than for a high school group.

Reading. A measure of reading ability contributes some further basis for understanding problems of academic failure. It has a special function if the college provides a reading clinic in which remedial instruction may be obtained. A reading test given at the time of college entrance and interpreted in conjunction with the scholastic aptitude test provides one basis for locating students who might advantageously receive such special help.

Interests.   With final vocational choices drawing close, early in college appears to be a time at which a vocational interest test might be given advantageously to all students. Thus, if a test of interest in specific vocations, such as the *Strong-Campbell Vocational Interest Blank*, is given during the sophomore year, the results can be available for consideration at the time that choices of major field are made. Since interest patterns at that age remain quite stable, the scores will be suitable for special counseling throughout the remainder of the college course.

Adjustment.   The typical adjustment inventory is better suited to college students than it is to less mature and less educated groups. When extensive counseling services exist, such an inventory might be administered routinely in order to identify individuals for further study. However, we have serious reservations as to the value of such a procedure. Ordinarily, at the college level counseling is initiated at the request of the client. We question how effective or useful collegewide screening and bringing in students for conferences is likely to be. Use of the scores by departmental advisers and others without special training is hardly to be recommended.

SUMMARY OF SUGGESTED PROGRAMS

Let us emphasize again that any testing program needs to be formulated by personnel in the local situation who are aware of local conditions, local purposes, and local resources. The proposals that have been outlined in this section are, at most, rough general guides. The highlights of this discussion have been organized in tabular form in Table 14.2. The most highly recommended tests are marked with a double asterisk. Tests considered useful supplements in an extensive testing program or of value for certain special purposes receive a single asterisk. Procedures deemed of doubtful value are indicated by a question mark. When there is no mark, it indicates that the type of test is considered inappropriate, impractical, or of little value at that level for a classwide or schoolwide testing program.

Table 14.2
SUGGESTED TESTS FOR SCHOOL TESTING PROGRAM

Type of Testing	Educational Level		
	Elementary	Secondary	College
Group academic or scholastic aptitude	**	**	**
Reading	**	**	**
Basic academic skills	**	?	
Reading readiness	**		
Individual intelligence	*	?	?
Achievement in content subjects	?	**	*
Personality inventory		?	?
Interest inventory		*	**
Special aptitude tests or battery		**	*
Prognostic tests for special subjects		?	

PLANNING A TESTING PROGRAM

We have been discussing the possible functions, the qualities desired, and some suggested priorities in a school testing program. In the last analysis, though, each school system must assume the responsibility of planning and carrying out its own program. An outsider who knows nothing about the particular school system cannot design a good program for use there nor can a school system obtain an effective program just by taking over a program from a neighboring school system.

Each school system must decide on who will have responsibility for planning and directing the school program. The first responsibility of the group or person responsible for the testing program is to determine how the test results are to be used in the local situation. Then they must decide what tests will be given, in what grades, and at what time of the school year. Last, they must set the broad policies for scoring the tests and reporting the results. In the following sections we will discuss considerations related to planning a testing program.

PARTICIPATION IN PLANNING

The potential users of test results are classroom teachers, guidance personnel, specialists such as school psychologists and remedial reading teachers, supervisors, and administrative personnel. All of these people are faced with making decisions.

The time that the decision needs to be made and the information needed to make it will vary. Since the results of the testing program should serve all potential users, the program must, of necessity, represent compromises in the selection of tests and in the time of the school year in which they will be administered. To achieve continuity and integration of the program, representation from all levels of the school, kindergarten through grade 12, should participate in the planning as a group, although some of the work may be done in subgroups.

In selecting achievement tests one must know the nature of the curricula and the objectives and emphasis on objectives at each level of education in the local system. In a school the people who are or should be most familiar with the objectives and nature of the curriculum in each area are the classroom teachers, subject-matter specialists, and supervisors of instruction; therefore representatives from these categories should have a major role in selecting achievement tests.

Counselors, school psychologists, remedial reading specialists, and other specialists have a relationship with students and parents that is somewhat different from the relationships that classroom teachers have. The types of problem and issue that they face are also somewhat different. In addition they tend to have more background in testing than do classroom teachers and should be expected to have more psychometric sophistication. These people should also be represented on the planning committee both for the contribution they can make in the selection of tests and to make sure that they have the information they need at the time it is needed.

Prinicipals of schools, superintendents, and assistant superintendents face quite different problems from the other two groups. The administrative personnel are more likely to be involved in reporting to parent and community groups on the effectiveness of programs and the school as a whole. They must initiate or support requests for revision of programs and for budgets to add new programs or more or new kinds of personnel. They also need to be represented in the planning of the testing program.

In the climate that exists in many communities in 1976 it might be advisable to involve representatives of parent or other community groups in the planning of a school testing program. Although the involvement of such groups does not have to be continuous, there should be some systematic procedure for bringing into the deliberation of the committee on the testing program the opinions and concerns of this group.

Although the planning of a testing program should involve many people, one person needs to be designated in a school system as having major and ultimate responsibility for coordinating and carrying out the program. The title that this person carries varies from one school system to another but, just for convenience, we shall use the title of director of testing.

The duties of the director of testing may include (1) coordinating the activities of the planning committee; (2) maintaining an up-to-date file of specimen tests; (3) providing for periodic review of the testing program and the use being made of test results; (4) planning the budget for the testing program; (5) carrying out such administrative details as ordering, storing, and distributing tests, making out detailed schedules for testing, and collecting tests or answer sheets for scoring; (6) providing for the scoring of the tests either by a test-scoring agency or locally; (7) planning and supervising analysis and tabulations of test results; (8) reporting test results to school personnel, parent groups, and the board of education; and (9) providing for in-service education of school personnel in administering, interpeting, and using tests.

Reviewing the list of possible duties of the director of testing, two things are quite clear. One is that directing a school testing program effectively requires a lot of time. Therefore the person filling the position should be assigned the duty as a recognized part of the job and have enough time allocated to discharge the functions. Responsibility for the school testing program should not be added on to a full load of other duties. The second thing that should be clear is that the person filling such a role should have an educational and experience background in testing and in statistics as well as having some administrative and leadership qualities.

SELECTING TESTS FOR THE PROGRAM

It has been indicated in previous sections that the kinds of tests to be given in a school depend upon the kind of information that the school needs in order to make decisions. For some kinds of decision, one will need the information given by an achievement test; for others, one will need academic aptitude tests; and for still others, one will need specialized aptitude batteries. The initial decision, then, involves the kinds of test that are needed; but a further choice must be made of one test out of the many that are available in each category.

In the selection of an achievement test one should be concerned, first, that the test match well the objectives and curricular emphasis of the school, and, second, that the test have psychometric characteristics adequate to guide the kinds of decision that the school wishes to make in using the results. The selection of other types of test such as academic aptitude tests and specialized aptitude tests should be made primarily on the basis of their psychometric qualitites. Although members of the test selection committee might quite appropriately react to the format and attractiveness of a particular test of this kind, the most crucial questions are: What evidence do the test authors provide for the validity of the test for the kinds of decision and interpretation that we want to base on the test results? How good is this evidence? Is the reliability adequate for the kinds of interpretations and uses that we want to make? How adequate are the norms for our purposes? Judgments of the adequacy of the technical data presented require some sophistication in statistics and test theory. A well-qualified director of testing could provide this service.

After a tentative selection has been made of all the tests to be used in the program, the totality should be examined critically to determine how much new and different information is obtained from each of the tests. One of the most common faults of school testing programs is redundancy. That is, time and money are invested in two or more tests that get very nearly the same information from the same students at the same point in time. For example, a plan for testing ninth grade students in February using both the *Differential Aptitude Test* (*DAT*) and a general aptitude test is inefficient and redundant. The combined scores from the *Verbal Reasoning Test* and the *Numerical Ability Test* of the *DAT* yield about the same information as that obtained from the general aptitude test. Since much more information can be obtained from the *DAT* than from the general aptitude test, if time and funds permit giving the longer and more complete aptitude battery, the general aptitude test should be dropped. It is probable that some other kind of test, or a general ability test at some other point in the student's school career would add a greater amount of new and useful information. Thus one should look for gaps as well as duplication.

FREQUENCY AND TIME OF TESTING

Among the decisions that need to be made in planning a testing program are how frequently the selected tests are to be given, in what grades, and at what time of the year. To some extent the time of year that a particular kind of test can be given is limited by the nature of the test. For example, if an achievement test in algebra is to be given to ninth grade students, it only makes sense to give it after the students have completed the course of study. On the other hand, an achievement test covering the basic skills of learning can be administered at almost any time. In the previous section on priorities in a testing program we have indicated our preferences for both grade placement of various kinds of test and the time of the year for giving those tests. However, the decision should be made in terms of local uses to be made of the test results and the time that the information is needed.

When considering the grades in which the tests are to be given, the committee should also decide on the level of the test to be used and whether adjustments in level are to be made within a particular grade. For example, if an achievement test battery is planned for the beginning of the fifth grade, are all students in the fifth grade to be given the level of the test designed for that grade? If so, we can expect that students who are poor readers will answer very few questions and thus will be appraised inadequately. We would obtain a more accurate appraisal of what such a student *can* do if we gave him a lower level test. If the testing situation permitted, we might gain by grouping pupils for testing in accordance with their expected level of achievement and then testing each such group with the level most appropriate for it, without regard for official grade labels. The problem becomes more acute when there is an ungraded organization in the school. In this kind of organization, we would want to determine the placement of the tests according to the instructional level of the student, not by the number of years he has been in school.

When planning for frequency of testing, overtesting should be avoided. Redundancy in testing is one form of overtesting. A second type of overtesting can be illustrated by elementary school testing programs that provide for administering an achievement battery in October and again in May in each of grades 2 through 6. It is difficult to justify such a heavy testing program. Certainly, the differences in scores obtained from tests given in May in one grade to those given the following October are likely to be meaningless, and the results from the May testing are obtained too late in the year to have much use for any instructional or guidance decisions. A third type of overtesting is the administration of a general intelligence test in every year of the school program. In general, if the results of any test administered in the program are not used, then one is overtesting.

TEST SCORING AND TEST ANALYSIS

One aspect of the planning of a testing program is deciding how the tests are to be scored and what kinds of analysis are to be made. Several factors have combined to move test scoring and analysis out of the hands of the classroom teacher and into the domain of specialized service agencies. On the one hand, there are provisions in a number of union contracts limiting the nonteaching duties that teachers may be called upon to carry out. On the other, there has been a steady improvement in the technology for optical scanning of record forms that makes possible very rapid and accurate test scoring by optical scanners. Some scanners (e.g., Digitek) are available at a price that makes it economical for a large school system to operate its own centralized scoring service. However, more versatile scanners, and ones that can read answers marked directly on a test booklet, are available in specialized test-scoring service agencies (e.g., Measurement Research Center, Iowa City, Iowa). Especially for smaller school systems, the testing service agencies make possible an accuracy of scoring and a completeness of analysis of test results that is not possible relying solely on local resources.

Scoring and reporting services offered by the major test publishers have become more varied and more elaborate with each passing year. In many cases it is possible to get, for a price, some or all of the following.

1. Printed class lists showing part and total scores, both raw scores and percentiles, stanines, or some other type of converted score, for each pupil in the class.

2. A pressure-sensitive label for each pupil that can be affixed to the permanent record form, showing all of the above information.

3. A printout for each pupil, showing which items were right and perhaps which wrong answers were chosen for each item gotten wrong.

4. A summary printout for each class, showing the number of pupils getting each item right, the items being coded to show the objective that each is presumed to measure.

5. Distributions of raw or converted scores, together with means and standard deviations, for separate classes, grade groups in a school building, and grade groups in a school system.

6. Identification of students scoring at or near a chance level, who might with profit be tested with a lower level of the test.

7. Achievement scores expressed in relation to aptitude test performance, reported either as a percentile rank in a specific aptitude group or as an expected achievement level that can then be compared with obtained achievement test score.

Though they have in some instances become so complex as to be self-defeating, these reports are potentially very helpful, on the one hand in relation to recording and interpreting the test results for specific pupils and on the other in communicating to administrators, the school board, and the broader public the evidences of strength and weakness in a local program. You will need to examine the publishers' catalogues to determine exactly what is available.

At the present time, many tests for the primary grades are produced in machine-scorable booklets, in which the answer choices are marked directly on the booklet, and the whole booklet is fed through the optical scanner. For grades 4 and above most published tests use a separate answer sheet.

Many classroom teachers feel that children are penalized when they have to use answer sheets, particularly the densely packed answer sheets such as MRC and Digitek. Studies (Dizney et al., 1966; Hayward, 1967; Miller, 1965; Slater, 1964) reveal no consistent differences in scores on unspeeded tests for students in grades 4 through 9, using different kinds of answer sheets. One study (Clark, 1968) showed slight but statistically significant differences between marking on the test booklet and using a separate answer sheet for slow-learning students, age 11 through 16. It is important to determine whether separate answer sheets were used in normative testing for a test, because norms will be strictly applicable only if local procedures conform to those used in the normative testing.

SETTING POLICY ON REPORTING RESULTS

Anticipating the date when test results become available, one needs to establish policies on who will receive reports of the results and how these results will be reported. In elementary and secondary schools, no disagreements are likely to arise on making the results of standardized achievement tests available to all professional personnel in the school, but some disagreement does exist on whether classroom teachers should have free access to aptitude test results. Since the results of aptitude tests are useful in planning learning activities for students and for helping to diagnose student difficulties in learning, it seems illogical to withhold such information from the classroom teacher who has major responsibilities for these functions. The reason given in a number of schools that withhold aptitude test results from teachers is that they misuse the results. If this is indeed the case, then the constructive action would be to plan in-service activities to improve the teacher's competence in interpreting and using the results, rather than to withhold the information.

A more important issue is what information on test results should be communicated to parents or to students. To some extent, the decision has been taken out of the hands of school personnel by the Buckley-Pell Amendment,* which gives parents and students the legal right to examine any records maintained by the school on a given student. When left to their own devices, schools have tended (Goslin, 1967) to be reluctant to report actual test scores, tending rather to concentrate on reporting to parents the school's interpretation of the test results. In a good many school systems results from testing have been reported only when the parent or (at the secondary level) the student has requested information. The importance of adequate interpretation can hardly be questioned. Raw scores are readily misinterpreted by a person unfamiliar with the nature of the test or with test norms, measurement error, and the like. It is important, therefore, that the school system plan when and in what way test results will be made available to students and/or their parents, and plan also for procedures and persons who will give the information in a way in which it can be understood and used constructively.

Our opinion is that everyone concerned with or about the student should routinely receive some type of information about his performance on all kinds of standardized test. To us the question is not whether everyone should receive information, but how to give the information in such a way that it can be understood and used constructively by all concerned. We shall consider ways of doing this in a later section. The planning committee should decide on the policy and make plans to see that the policy is implemented.

A third aspect of policy to be considered is whether the results of the testing program for the system as a whole are to be reported routinely to lay groups. There are various groups

* To *Public Law 93–380, Elementary and Secondary School Act of 1974.*

in any community who may be potential audiences; for example, parent-teacher associations, the board of eduation, the general community that supports the schools by paying taxes, and groups with special interests. Decisions about reporting to such groups are usually made at a high administrative level, but since all school personnel have a vested interest in the picture of school accomplishments being presented to these groups and since they are also frequently called on to interpret or explain the reasons for the results, the making of policy regarding how and to whom such reports shall be made should be the responsibility of a group with widely based representation.

LOGISTICS OF A SCHOOL TESTING PROGRAM

Carrying out a program of testing throughout a school system is a fairly complex undertaking. If the testing is to proceed smoothly, and if standard testing conditions are to be maintained, a certain amount of advance planning is needed. The necessary tests and accessory materials need to be ordered and distributed to separate schools and classes. Supplementary local instructions need to be prepared and distributed. Detailed schedules for testing need to be prepared and distributed. Testers and proctors must be trained. Detailed arrangements for scoring the tests or collecting the tests for scoring must be made. In-service education activities must be planned for teachers who need help in the interpretation and use of the results. Reports of the results need to be prepared and submitted to various groups. Some of the more important issues in carrying out a testing program are discussed in the sections that follow.

SCHEDULING OF TESTS

After the original decision has been reached as to what tests are to be given, in which grades they are to be given, and at what time of the year they are to be given, an exact testing schedule must be worked out. The schedule for testing should be made available at the beginning of the year to all classroom teachers and other school personnel so that other school activities will not be planned for the same time. Tests should probably not be scheduled immediately before or after a major school holiday such as Christmas. If testing is to be done in the fall, it probably should not be scheduled before the third or fourth week of the session, especially in elementary school.

The schedule should permit regrouping of children for testing. We have mentioned previously that it is desirable to administer a level of a test that is at an appropriate difficulty level for the student. For example, in the fifth grade classes in a school system, there may be students for whom a third grade level of a test would be most appropriate, or others for whom a sixth grade level would be most appropriate. Out-of-grade testing is highly desirable in these situations and the schedule should provide for it. If the program requires testing of kindergarten or beginning first grade students, the schedule should provide for dividing the total class into small groups of not more than 10 to 15 students in order to provide the best testing conditions.

The most fundamental concerns in scheduling are that tests be given under standard conditions and that these conditions permit each examinee to perform at his best level. Thus any unit of time scheduled for testing should be long enough to permit administration of a complete test, including a realistic allowance for distributing and collecting papers and for giving instructions. The novice is likely not to realize how much time is required beyond the basic testing time. Testing schedules should not be made too tight.

Moreover, when more than a single test is to be given, as in the case of standardized aptitude or achievement test batteries, it is undesirable to give too many of the tests in one day or at a single sitting. For younger children especially, a break should be provided between parts of the test, and the program of testing should be divided into several segments and spread over several days. A number of the manuals for test batteries suggest ways in which the total testing time can be divided advantageously for children at different age levels. The purpose of the spread-out schedule is, of course, to minimize loss of interest and effort especially on the part of young children and of children who find the tests somewhat difficult and frustrating.

Secondary to the above considerations are those of economy and administrative convenience. Economy is achieved by reusing the same test booklets several times. When tests with separate answer sheets are to be used in several classes, a fairly complex testing schedule may be necessary in order to permit this re-use. (This schedule should provide some time for screening out booklets that have been marked up by examinees.) Greater flexibility of scheduling will be possible if the tests are purchased as separates, rather than bound together in a single booklet, because one class can use one part of the battery while some other class is using another part.

In departmentalized schools with class periods of a fixed length, it is administratively convenient if a unit of testing fits into a single class period. Many test publishers have taken account of this in designing their tests. However, this type of convenience should not be permitted to distort or interrupt the administration of any test. Enought time should be provided to permit the completion of a test at a single sitting. If the program of testing is worth doing, it is worth the upsetting of administrative routines.

PLANNING FOR TESTING OF ABSENTEES

Whenever tests are scheduled over several days, one runs into the problem of students who are absent from one or more of the testing sessions. Some provision should be made for testing these absentees at other times, so that the data on students will be as complete as possible.

PREPARATION OF STUDENTS FOR TESTING

Advance preparation of students for testing has as its objectives (1) establishing optimum motivation and cooperation during testing and (2) assuring that students are familar with the procedures for the test, so that they will not be handicapped by novel and unfamiliar procedures.

Optimum motivation is that which results in serious and sustained effort without undue anxiety and tension. Because of wide pupil differences, it is not possible to achieve this ideal with every examinee. However, some advance explanation of and discussion about the tests may help to achieve it. The attitude should be conveyed that the tests are genuinely important, but not a desperate "life-or-death" matter. Constructive uses of the test results for individual guidance and educational adaptation can well be stressed. The older the students, the more complete the advance briefing that can profitably be given to them.

Since tests are designed to measure aptitudes and achievements rather than the tricks and skills of test-taking, it is desirable that all examinees have an opportunity to get acquainted with the general character of the test items and the mechanics of testing in advance. Some of the large-scale testing agencies, such as the Educational Testing Service and the Educational Records Bureau, prepare for distribution to examinees leaflets that describe the tests and give sample items. A school system might find it profitable to prepare similar practice materials for its own testing program.

When separate answer sheets are to be used by students for the first time, it may help to give advance practice with the mechanics of the answer sheet. The teacher might provide a similar answer sheet to be used with one of his or her own tests, or with sample items prepared to resemble those of the test itself.*

ENVIRONMENT FOR TESTING

The desirable environment for testing is one in which examinees are (1) physically comfortable and emotionally relaxed, (2) free from interruptions and distractions, (3) conveniently able to manipulate their test materials, and (4) sufficiently separate to minimize tendencies to copy from one another.

The conditions of lighting and ventilation for testing should be at least as good as those maintained for teaching in a normal classroom. Especially for young children, the familiar surroundings of their own classrooms are to be preferred to those of cafeterias or auditoriums, where crowding and lack of good conditions for writing and for handling test materials may also be problems.

Casual interruptions in the classroom can be minimized by a "Test in progress—Do not disturb" sign on the door. Arrangements should be made with the school administration to suspend fire drills, public address announcements and, insofar as possible, bells and other unrelated signals during a period when testing is being carried out in one or more classes. Other steps to minimize delays and distractions include (1) seeing either that each examinee has an extra pencil, or that spare pencils are readily available, (2) making sure that children (especially young ones) have had a chance to visit the toilet before testing starts, and (3) providing clear instructions as to what to do for those examinees who finish their work completely before the time limit is up.

To be able to manipulate test materials conveniently, the examinee should have a desk or table on which to write, and enough room so that he can spread both the test and the answer sheet out before him. Working in chairs, perhaps with a lap board, in an auditorium or gymnasium is far from ideal,

* Special practice materials are available from some publishers of standardized tests.

especially if tests are speeded so that delays in paper handling can lower the score of the examinee.

The problem of proctoring an examination (and sometimes of maintaining order) is made a good deal easier if desks or seats are well separated.

SELECTION AND PREPARATION
OF TEST ADMINISTRATORS

The administration of most group tests is simple enough so that any teacher should be able to handle it satisfactorily after a little special preparation and practice. However, some schools may find it more convenient administratively to have this function discharged by special personnel from the guidance staff or from the school psychologist's office. No matter who administers the test, all prospective administrators should have some in-service training with the specific tests that are to be used. The training has the objectives of (1) making the examiners thoroughly familiar with the tests and test manual and (2) standardizing procedures with respect to certain recurring problems and questions that frequently arise.

One worthwhile familiarization experience for examiners is "giving the test" to each other, that is, by reading the directions aloud exactly as they are given in the manual, and raising questions with one another. Taking the tests, at least in part, is another way of anticipating problems that are likely to arise in giving them. A few of the issues that are likely to arise in assuring standard and opimum testing conditions are the following:

Verbatim directions. The examiner must understand that the directions in the manual for giving the test must be read verbatim. The examiner should not paraphrase the directions, add anything to them, or leave anything out. Studies on the effects of altering directions of a test (Lamb, 1967; Yamamoto and Dizney, 1965) have shown that changes in directions have differential effects on student performance. Changes from the published directions violate the standard conditions of the test and may invalidate the norms.

Answering questions. The principle to guide the examiner in answering student questions is that the student should have a clear understanding of what he is supposed to do. He should not be confused by the mechanics of testing or at a loss as to what the nature of the test is. Therefore, before testing starts, the examiner should use his best efforts to make the procedures and the task clear. He can repeat or paraphrase instruction, go over the practice examples, and, possibly, even supplement them. He should encourage questions at this point, and make every effort to clear up any misunderstandings.

Once a specific test starts, questions should be discouraged. Obviously, no help may be given on specific items, and no cues should be provided as to whether a pupil's answer is right or wrong. Questions on general procedure can be dealt with by repeating or paraphrasing the directions, but when a child expresses perplexity on a specific item he must be stalled off with "I'm sorry. I can't answer that. Do the best you can. If you get stuck go on to the next item."

Timing. If the test has sections with very short time limits, that is, 1 or 2 minutes, each examiner should be provided with a stopwatch. For other tests a watch with a second hand will suffice. When using an ordinary watch, a written record should be made of the exact time that a subtest was started and of the time that it is to stop, so that timing will not be thrown off by memory lapses. A simple homemade form will facilitate such recording.

Proctoring. The examiner should circulate around the room, especially when a new subtest is being started, to check on the work of the examinees. He should check to make sure that each student is working on the correct pages, and that he is marking his responses in the proper place if a separate answer sheet is being used. Individual children may need to be encouraged to keep working or to go back and check their work.

CENTRALIZED ADMINISTRATION

Some schools attempt to obtain uniformity in administration of tests through the use of closed circuit television or the school intercommunication system. Hopkins et al. (1967) described an experiment in the use of closed circuit television for testing fifth and sixth grade classes. They found that for large classes (55-90 pupils) the televison administration resulted in higher mean scores, but for the regular size classes (20-35 pupils) teacher administered tests yielded higher scores. The differences between the two modes of administration were only about 0.2 of a grade equivalent.

Although one does gain uniformity in administration through highly centralized procedures, the gain is obtained through loss of flexibility in dealing with emergency or special situations in the classroom. No opportunity is provided to give extra instruction to slow groups on the procedures for handling test materials. If highly centralized administration of tests is done in a school system, it becomes very important to give adequate preparation to the students before testing.

SCORING

Most schools buy test-scoring services, but sometimes tests are scored by classroom teachers. If the scoring is done by classroom teachers, adequate controls should be set up to insure that it is done accurately. Errors are particularly likely to creep into such operations as subtracting a correction for errors, adding part scores to make a total score, and going from raw to converted scores. It is especially important to check these steps. Surveys have repeatedly indicated the inaccuracy of teachers in scoring tests. If at all possible, the school system will find it advantageous to buy scoring services, since these will produce more accurate results and be less expensive in the long run.

RECORDING RESULTS OF TESTS

Since test results are likely to be most meaningful if one has a cumulative picture of the student's development as he progresses through school, all test results for a student should be recorded on a permanent record card. The simplest and easiest way to keep a record of a student's performance on tests is to buy the test-scoring service that provides a pressure sensitive label reporting his scores; it is then necessary only to provide space on the cumulative record card for pressing on the labels. The space should provide for keeping the results of tests of the same type together; that is, all achievement test labels in one section, all general aptitude test results in another section, and all specialized aptitude tests in another section.

If the school does not purchase such a scoring service, then all of the information shown on the label should be entered by hand on the permanent record card.

CHECKING ON DISCREPANT RESULTS

There are a number of ways that systematic errors can occur in test results. When administering a test, the examiner can make a mistake in timing and give either less or more time than the instructions allow. When using tests in the multilevel format, students can be given wrong answer sheets or started in the wrong place. If tests are scored locally, gross errors can be made in counting the number right or in using a correction formula for arriving at the score. The wrong table can be used for transforming raw scores to converted scores or the table can be read incorrectly. For these reasons, all test results should be examined carefully for consistency and reasonableness before they are used.

A test may be inconsistent with others given at the same time, as when a student who has consistently scored 2 or more years above his grade placement on all parts of an achievement battery obtains an IQ of 80 on a group aptitude test. Instead of blithely labeling him an "overachiever," one should make sure that there have been no gross errors in administering, scoring, or recording the aptitude test. A test may be inconsistent with results from an earlier test of the same type, as when a student who fell at the 98th percentile on a test in the fifth grade falls at the 25th percentile on a similar test in the seventh grade. Results of a test can be inconsistent for a whole class, as when one fifth grade class shows a marked drop in reading test scores both in terms of their fourth grade scores and in terms of other similar fifth grades in the system. Such a result for a whole class usually indicates some serious error in the adminstration of the test.

A list should be made of all cases showing seriously discrepant results, and these should be carefully checked. The papers should be rescored to make sure that the scoring is accurate. Computations and reading of norm tables involved in obtaining converted scores should be verified. Transcription of these scores should be checked. If no error is found in any of these steps, it may be desirable to refer the student for retesting with another form of the suspect test before a permanent record is made of the result.

PRESENTING THE RESULTS OF TESTING TO THE PUBLIC

We believe that a school or school system will get the maximum return from its investment in a program of standardized tests if the results of testing are reported to all persons or groups of persons who need the information. In any community we find a number of groups to whom test results could be reported. First, there are the individual students and their parents. Second, there is the staff in the schools which has responsibility for instruction, curriculum, administration, and pupil personnel services. Third, there are official lay bodies, such as the board of education, that have responsibility for setting overall policy both in educational and budgetary matters. Fourth, there are special interest groups such as parent-teacher associations, whose support the school system wants. Fifth, there is the general public whose taxes and votes support the schools. Test results are reported to these various groups in order to achieve different goals; the groups differ in sophistication with reference both to education and to educational testing; and they differ from each other in the kinds of information that they need. However, in spite of these differences and whatever the audience, the general purpose of the report should be to summarize, organize, and interpret the test results so that a meaningful picture of the school's or the individual's accomplishments will emerge.

REPORTING THE RESULTS OF A PROGRAM OF TESTING

Before one can plan effective procedures for reporting the results of a program to any group, one must be very clear just what it is that one wants to communicate. What are the specific questions that one is attempting to answer through the use of test data? An explicit statement of these questions can help to make clear the ways in which the test data need to be analyzed and reported.

The general question "How well do students in each grade of our schools perform in relation to the national normative sample?" requires only a tabulation of all scores within a grade on each test and the computation of some kind of average score. This average score can then be compared to the national norms for building or system averages. On the other hand, if one asks "How effective have our curricular efforts been for students of different aptitude levels and different socioeconomic levels?" one must first group the students in each grade by socioeconomic level and within socioeconomic levels by the level of performance on a test of scholastic aptitude. Within each subgroup, achievement scores will be tabulated, and average scores computed. Finally, one will have to search out some normative data for similar subgroups of pupils, and display the data for one's own school in comparison with this reference group.

Most of the questions that are likely to be asked involve various types of comparison. Some of the kinds of comparison that may be of significance are the following.

1. Comparisons of local group performance with national norms or more specialized norms.

2. Comparisons of local group performance on achievement tests with the level of performance on scholastic aptitude tests.

3. Comparison of achievement in different subject matter areas.

4. Comparison of the effectiveness of the school program with students of different racial, socioeconomic, or ability characteristics.

5. Comparison of different schools in the system or of different class groups within a school.

6. Comparison of groups that were taught in different ways or that had different curricula.

7. Comparison of the same group of individuals at different grade levels.

8. Comparison of groups at different grade levels within a school or school system.

The kinds of analysis that can be done of test results are limited by the types of comparison data that are available for the test and by the number of students in the grade or system who have certain characteristics. For example, a director of testing might want to compare the average score of each grade in his school system to other schools of similar ability and socioeconomic level in the nation. To accomplish this he would need national norms of building averages by average intelligence and socioeconomic level of the building. In 1976, there were no such norms for any achievement test. Or suppose that a particular school wants to look at its achievement test results for each grade separately by ability level, but has in each grade only 5 to 10 students who fall below an IQ of 100 on the aptitude test that it uses. A separate analysis based on a sample size of 5 to 10 is likely to be so unstable as to be meaningless, so the ability range over which this analysis would be possible in this school would be quite limited.

The results of a program of testing may be presented either as written reports or orally. Most school systems will find it advantageous to use both methods, preparing a written report for permanent reference and using oral reports for effective communication with most groups. Important results should be presented in both tabular and graphic form. For each class and school or subgroup of interest, scores will need to be tallied separately for each significant subtest. The scores useful in answering most questions will ordinarily be converted scores; that is, grade scores, standard scores, or percentiles for a particular grade group. If scores are to be compared across subtests, percentiles or standard scores that have comparable meanings across tests should be used instead of grade scores. Average scores (mean or median) will need to be obtained for each group. Howevever, the simple average provides limited information, so for a more complete picture of the results, some measure of variability such as the standard deviation or the semi-interquartile range should also be computed. When reporting to school personnel, one might compute the 10th, 25th, 75th, and 90th percentiles in addition to the median, so as to provide a more complete picture of the performance of the group. All of these will have to be organized in both tabular and graphic form.

Good graphic representation can facilitate understanding of the test results but one must guard against distorting the data in graphs in such a way that they lead to incorrect interpretation. The most common form of distortion comes from showing only part of the vertical scale. By doing this it is sometimes possible to expand a part of the scale so that quite small differences appear to be quite large. One should also try to keep graphs as simple as possible; putting too many different things on one graph only confuses the audience. Illustrations of graphs representing kinds of test data are shown in Figs. 14.1 through 14.5.

Figure 14.1 shows the median level of achievement for

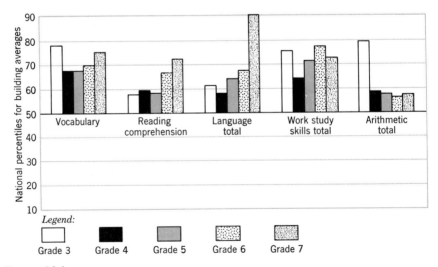

Figure 14.1
Centreville median achievement by subject area and grade level in comparison to national norms by system averages.

grades 3 through 7 for the Centreville school system. This graph makes it particularly easy to compare different grades within each subject area, but it also permits comparisons across subject areas for a single grade group. Such a graph would be suitable for showing any type of audience how the average performance in each grade of this school compares to national norms for system averages. It is particularly suitable for lay audiences. To construct a graph of this type that presents an accurate picture, we need to have norms for building averages. We are displaying averages for our school, and they should be compared with averages from other schools. Fig. 14.2 shows the median performance of the same seventh grade compared to general national norms for individuals and to national norms for individuals who scored at the same IQ level as the average for this seventh grade. Comparison of Figs. 14.1 and 14.2 with respect to the height of the bars on each of the tests brings out

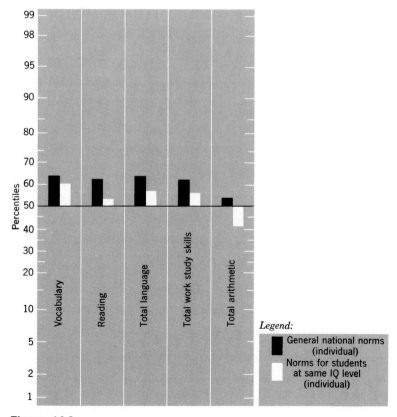

Figure 14.2
Achievement of median seventh grade Centreville student in relation to general national norms and in relation to norms for students of same IQ level. (*Iowa Tests of Basic Skills.*)

the effect of using norms for individuals rather than for system averages. Although both graphs show that this seventh grade performs above average on all tests, only Fig. 14.1 accurately shows how far the typical performance of this seventh grade surpasses the national norm for average scores of seventh grade classes. Yet, since there are no norms for building averages by intelligence levels for the test used in this system, Fig. 14.2 has some value despite its limitations. First, it focuses attention on the fact that this seventh grade should be expected to perform above the average. Second, it draws attention to the relatively poor performance of the group on arithmetic in relation to other seventh grade students with similar aptitude test scores.

Fig. 14.3 on p. 571 shows another way of comparing level of achievement and level of intelligence. In this school system the *Stanford Achievement Tests* (1964 edition) and the *Otis Intelligence Test, Beta* were given to all seventh grade classes. The graph shows the performance in reading comprehension by the middle half of those seventh graders who obtained scores at each stanine level on the intelligence test. This type of graph is particularly valuable for presentation to school personnel because it shows quite clearly that the reading program in the school was less effective for students who fell at or below the sixth stanine on the intelligence test.

Figures 14.4 and 14.5 on pp. 572 and 573 illustrate one way of presenting a picture of both typical performance and range of performance of a group. In these graphs, the bars representing achievement extend from the 10th percentile to the 90th percentile. The performance of the middle 50 percent is shown by the broad portion of the bar and the median is indicated by a horizontal line across the broad bar. The amount of detail in the graph makes it more suitable for school personnel than for most lay groups. Figure 14.4 permits comparisons among subtests for the seventh grade and Fig. 14.5 shows the performance of the same group of students in spelling from the fourth through the seventh grades.

It is perhaps worth emphasizing here that the test results displayed in any set of graphs and tables constitute only raw facts, not meaningful interpretations or conclusions. These interpretations must be supplied by the educator who is acquainted with the circumstances surrounding the test scores. Thus, if little emphasis has been given to arithmetical computation in the school system for which seventh grade results are presented in Fig. 14.4, one would not expect high performance.

If a school gives little emphasis to a particular skill in an early grade but increases its emphasis on that skill in later grades, low achievement at an early grade should be expected; the school should present the analysis of the test data across grades, as in Fig. 14.5, to show whether the expected improvement in achievement does occur in the later grades. On the other hand,

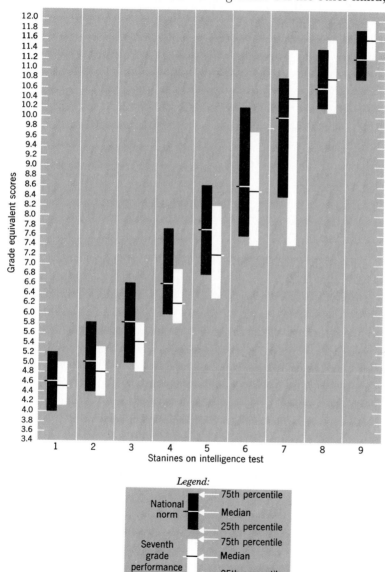

Figure 14.3
Comparison of performance on *Reading Achievement Test* by level of performance on intelligence test for Easton Seventh grade. (*Advanced Battery, Stanford Achievement Tests* 1964 Edition.)

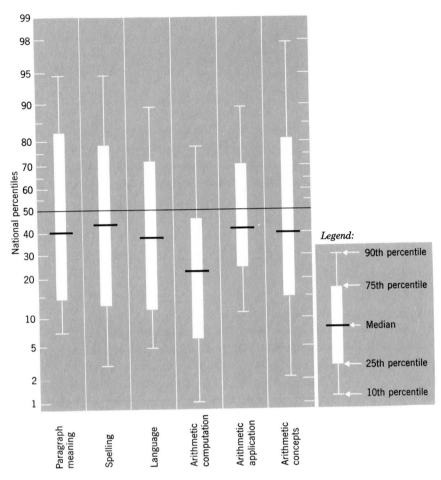

Figure 14.4
Median achievement and range of achievement in Easton seventh grade
in comparison with national norms. (*Stanford Achievement Tests,* 1964
Edition.)

school teachers and administrators need to face frankly those
situations where they have been less successful than they expected to be or wished they were.

Many schools find it particularly difficult to make known
results such as those shown in Fig. 14.4. The school from which
these results were taken had a median stanine of 4 on the *Otis
Intelligence Test.* Such a school may try to explain away the
results on the basis that the average ability level of its seventh
grade students is below that of the national normative sample.
However, Fig. 14.3 shows that even when the level of ability is
taken into account, the test results in reading are still poor on

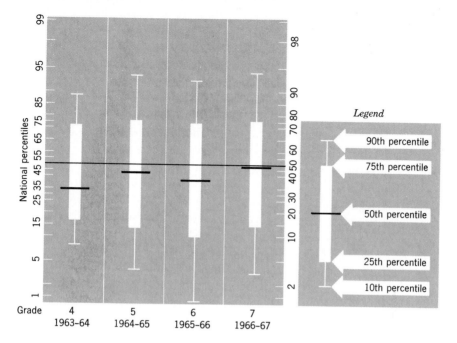

Figure 14.5
Achievement of same students in grade 4 (1963-64) through grade 7
(1966-67) in spelling.

the whole, and a similar analysis for arithmetic would probably show a similar picture. Faced with such test results, personnel in some schools are inclined, like the proverbial ostrich,
to bury the reports deep in a file where they will never be seen,
or even to discontinue the standardized testing program. But
refusal to face a problem will not make it go away; ignorance
of how well (or poorly) children are reading will not help to
make them better readers. Instead, analysis of test results
should serve as a stimulus to determine why such results were
obtained. The personnel in the school could seek answers to
such questions as: Do we have a highly mobile student body?
Are the quantity and quality of instructional materials for
reading adequate for the kinds of student we have? Do the
classroom teachers get enough help from supervisors and reading specialists? How much instructional time in reading does
each child in each grade receive? Are class sizes too large for
the teacher to provide for individual differences?

Item analysis data can be particularly helpful to a school
system in understanding the strengths and weaknesses of its
program. These could be used to help the educator interpret
the test results.

574
planning a
school testing
program

REPORTING TEST RESULTS
FOR THE INDIVIDUAL

As noted earlier, parents now have a legal right to examine any records that the school maintains on their children, including test scores. But this implies positive action by the parent. What should a school do about routinely reporting test results to *all* parents? When and by whom should test results be reported? In what form should they be presented?

A printed report is at best a rather cold and impersonal form of communication, and it is subject to misinterpretation by the layman who has little experience with tests and testing concepts. For this reason it often seems best that interpretations of test results be given in face-to-face conferences with student or parent. Most schools have some provision for parents to visit the school periodically and to have some type of contact with their child's teacher and/or a member of the guidance staff. Such visits could be scheduled advantageously some time after the results from a test administration become available.

At the time of such a conference, it would be desirable to have on hand a record of performance that can be given to the student or parent to keep. Many test publishers provide a record form designed to be given to students or sent home to parents. These record forms vary considerably. The best ones provide a simple description of the nature and purposes of the tests, an explanation of how to interpret the reported scores, and some kind of profile for recording the student's scores. Almost all of them provide for reporting exact scores, usually percentiles or stanines. The personnel in a school should examine the published reporting form for the test they use to decide whether they want to report test results in that way.

A school could design a report form for its own students. Such a form should provide for reporting the student's standing on all important subtests of the test battery used and should provide information on the nature and purpose of the tests. Since scores are not perfectly exact and parents and pupils may tend to overinterpret exact scores, it seems better to have a form that displays scores in rather broad categories. Fig. 14.6 on p. 575 shows a type of report form that a school system could construct for its own use. In this form scores are grouped into 5 categories: High—95th percentile or higher; Above average—76th percentile to 94th percentile; Average—25th percentile to 75th percentile; Below Average—6th to 24th percentile; and Low—5th percentile or lower. Any test that has percentile norms can be entered on such a form. The student's

Name: _____ Dawkins, Roy _____

School: Centreville Elementary

Grade: ___4___

Date Tested: April 1968

Score Category	Vocab-ulary	Read-ing	Spell-ing	Capital-ization	Punc-tuation	Usage	Maps	Graphs	Refer-ences	Arith. Con-cepts	Arith. Prob-lems	L-T Intelli-gence Test
High (95th percentile or higher)												
Above Average (76th percentile to 94th percentile)		N	N L I	N				N				N
Average (25th percentile to 75th percentile)	N				N L I	N L I	N		N	N	N	L
Below Average (6th percentile to 24th percentile)	L I	L I		L I			L I	L I	L I	L I	L I	
Low (5th percentile or below)												

Figure 14.6

Report of performance on *Iowa Tests of Basic Skills* and *Lorge-Thorndike Intelligence Tests*.

Key: N, standing in relation to national norms for 4th grade students

L, standing in relation to 4th grade students in Centreville school system

I, standing in relation to 4th grade students in national sample with similar intelligence test scores.

standing on each test can be shown in relation to general national percentile norms, local percentile norms, or percentile norms by intelligence test score. The use of the report form can be illustrated by taking the record of Roy Dawkins, a fourth grade student in the Centreville Elementary School who was given the *Iowa Tests of Basic Skills* and the *Lorge-Thorndike Intelligence Test* in April 1968. His performance on the tests is shown in Table 14.3 in terms of grade equivalent scores, general national percentiles, local percentiles, and national percentiles by intelligence level.

Roy's scores have been entered on the record form by using N to indicate national percentile norms, L to indicate local percentile norms, and I to indicate ability level percentile norms. Of course, only one type of norm could be used, or a separate form could be used for entering each type of norm. The use of all three on the same form is advantageous if one wants to emphasize the differences in Roy's standing in relation to the three reference groups. Before holding a conference with Roy or his parents, the teacher or counselor should assemble available data on Roy's performance in the classroom and, if possible, examine his answer sheet on the achievement tests in order to have more specific information on Roy's strengths and weaknesses.

The oral report should include a short explanation of the tests. The student or parent should be permitted to look at the

Table 14.3
TEST RESULTS FOR ROY DAWKINS

Test	Grade Equivalent	General National Percentile	Local Percentile	National Percentile by Intelligence Level
Vocabulary	4.4	41	19	21
Reading	4.4	42	22	16
Spelling	6.4	82	76	84
Capitalization	5.8	71	49	65
Punctuation	5.0	56	33	38
Usage	5.0	55	52	34
Maps	4.0	28	08	16
Graphs	4.4	40	20	23
References	4.1	31	17	17
Arithmetic Concepts	4.1	31	19	14
Arithmetic Problems	4.2	34	20	20
Lorge-Thorndike Intelligence Test (IQ = 112)	5.2	78	55	

record as the teacher or counselor gives the interpretation. The interpretation might be something like the following.

Roy's aptitude for school work is somewhat better than average among fourth graders in the country as a whole but it is just about average among the fourth grade students in the Centreville schools. We would predict that he would most probably be somewhat above average in achievement when compared to a national sample of fourth graders but only about average in achievement among Centreville fourth graders. Let's see how Roy's achievement meets our expectation.

In vocabulary and reading, Roy is just about average according to national norms but is somewhat below average in the Centreville fourth grade. His achievement on these tests indicate that he is likely to have some difficulty in keeping up with his school work for the rest of this school year and in the fifth grade. Roy is a slow reader and has difficulty in getting the main idea of a passage and answering questions that are not specifically answered in the reading material. We plan to work intensively with Roy on these skills for the rest of the year. You can help at home by using opportunities to encourage him to learn and use new words and to read during his free time.

In spelling, Roy is somewhat above average in relation to the national norm group, Centreville fourth graders, and his ability level. His spelling is one of his strong points. His scores on the capitalization, punctuation, and usage tests are about average for his ability level and among Centreville fourth graders.

Although Roy's scores on map reading and use of references are average according to national norms and his score on graphs is above average in terms of national norms, he is somewhat below average on all of these tests among our fourth graders and lower than we would expect him to be according to his ability level. Mastery of the skills measured by these tests is important in our mathematics, science, social studies, and language programs. If Roy is to achieve satisfactorily in these programs, he must gain better mastery of these skills. We plan to form some small groups of students like Roy and give them special work on these skills. From time to time, we will be giving Roy some special exercises on these skills to be done at home. You can help by seeing that Roy does these.

On the two arithmetic tests, Roy's scores were about average on national norms but below average for our fourth grade students and for his ability level. Roy is having difficulty with fundamental operations and needs more practice on number facts. We will work with Roy on these skills. You might try to encourage Roy to practice arithmetic skills at home by using natural situations that involve money or measurement.

In the sample interpretation we have tried to illustrate three qualities that an interpretation should have:

1. It should be set in the frame of reference of the particular student. Test scores should be interpreted in terms of what is known about the student's aptitude and about his educational or vocational goals.

2. It should be directed toward positive and constructive action. It should emphasize the assets in a test profile or it should be oriented toward remedial action when achievement falls below what aptitude would lead one to expect.

3. It should be factual and dispassionate, rather than appearing to pass judgment on the individual. Test results should be reported truthfully and accurately.

The flavor should be one of working with the student and his parents to realize common goals rather than one of passing judgment on him.

EXTERNAL TESTING PROGRAMS

Up to this point the discussion of testing programs has been limited to those over which the local school system has full control. In planning its own testing program, a school should take into consideration the external testing programs that are under the control of agencies outside the local system. There are three types of external testing program that involve large numbers of students in the elementary and secondary schools: (1) college admissions and placement programs, (2) national scholarship testing programs, and (3) state-mandated testing programs. Each of these will be discussed briefly in the sections that follow.

COLLEGE ADMISSIONS AND PLACEMENT PROGRAMS

The oldest of the college admissions testing programs is the one conducted by the College Entrance Examination Board (CEEB). The Board began in 1900 to administer entrance tests for a limited number of "Ivy League" colleges. Early tests were essay in character, but an objective *Scholastic Aptitude Test* was introduced in 1926, and subsequently the achievement tests were gradually converted to objective format. The volume of College Board testing increased slowly at first, but then more and more rapidly as the number of schools requiring the tests increased and the percentage of young people aspiring to go to college mounted.

The College Entrance Examination Board administers its tests at testing centers all over the world. Papers are centrally scored, and the results are reported to the colleges the individual has designated, to his school, and to the individual himself. Generally, these tests are taken by the student during his senior year in high school. However, there were always some who took the tests as juniors and in 1959–1960 the College Board formalized the *Preliminary Scholastic Aptitude Test* for administration to college-bound juniors in secondary schools for use in guidance and for early admission to college. Further information about the tests in the series can be obtained from the publications of the College Board.

A second and newer program for college admissions, designed for smaller and less selective colleges than those for which the College Board program was tailored, is the American College Testing Program. The battery for this program consists of four tests of general skills in *English, Mathematics, Social Studies* and *Science,* respectively. Tests are administered at centers spread over the United States. Further information about the program can be obtained from the American College Testing Program, Iowa City, Iowa.

Certain states also run programs for admission to state-operated colleges. These vary considerably from state to state. Information about them can usually be obtained either from the major state university or the state Department of Education.

Finally, there are various programs for admission to graduate schools or professional schools. The most widely used admission tests for graduate schools are the *Graduate Record Examination* administered by the Educational Testing Service and the *Miller Analogies Test* administered by the Psychological Corporation. Special tests are used by professional schools in such fields as law, medicine, dentistry, and accountancy. Information about the relevant tests can usually be obtained from the national association of the profession, from the admissions office of a professional school, or from one of the agencies mentioned above.

The Advanced Placement Program of the CEEB has been described in the section on college testing programs. Descriptions of the Advanced Placement Program and the tests can be obtained from the publications of the Board.

580
planning a
school testing
program

TESTING PROGRAMS
FOR SCHOLARSHIP AWARDS

Testing programs used in connection with scholarship awards represent one special development of some interest. The need for these programs arises from the fact that substantial scholarship funds come from sources outside of any particular university—from foundations, industry, and federal and state governments—so that some general appraisal of applicants is needed that is not related to the programs or policies of any single institution. The most ambitious testing program of this type is the one administered by the National Merit Scholarship Corporation. Identification of "semifinalists" has been based on the *Preliminary Scholastic Aptitude Test*. Since it has been the policy of the Corporation that awards be prorated by states, in proportion to the number of high-school seniors, the standard to qualify as a semifinalist has varied fairly widely from one state to another. (It has also been the policy that the cash value of the award vary depending upon the financial status of the family.)

Final award of scholarships has been based upon performance on College Entrance Examination Board tests, and upon such other factors as the evaluating panels choose to consider.

Other less extensive scholarship testing services have been developed and offered to the public by the College Board, the Educational Testing Service, and certain state testing agencies.

STATE-MANDATED TESTING PROGRAMS

A number of states have mandated that certain tests be given in particular grades throughout the state. Some of the states use published standardized tests for the mandated program, but other states, such as New York, use tests that are constructed by the state Education Department. The statewide programs have usually been instituted to serve two purposes: (1) quality control; that is, to help determine the effectiveness of the educational programs in local communities; and (2) to provide information that would help the state to allocate to the local school systems either special state funds or federal funds under state control.

The typical pattern found in state-mandated programs is to require testing in certain specified grades. Generally, the tests used focus on the basic skills, although some, like the *New York State Regents Examinations*, have been designed to appraise achievement in college preparatory type courses in grades 9 through 12.

CONCERNS ABOUT EXTERNAL
TESTING PROGRAMS

581

concerns about
external testing
programs

External testing programs of all kinds have caused educators considerable concern. Although each of the external programs has been designed to serve a valid educational purpose, one may ask whether these purposes at times conflict with other purposes of the schools where the tests are administered. Concern of the educators about external testing programs focuses on the effect that the tests have on the student who has to take them and on the educational program of the school.

Some educators feel that students in the secondary school are required to take too many external tests and that the time spent on these tests could be better spent on regular school work. However, most of the external tests for college admission and placement or for scholarship awards are administered outside of the regular school time, usually on Saturdays. Students are likely to take, at most, two or three during a year. Although scheduling the tests may be a nuisance for school administrators—and testing agencies must give some consideration to this—the burden on the time of the student can scarcely be considered serious.

Since college admissions tests loom as an important obstacle to secondary school students seeking admission to college, teachers, counselors, and others have expressed concern over the effects of anxiety on the test scores. A number of studies (S. B. Sarason et al., 1960; I. G. Sarason, 1961) have found statistically significant negative correlations between measures of test anxiety and scores on other tests. The negative correlations found in such studies do not, of course, indicate a direct causal relationship. One does not know just from the correlation whether high levels of anxiety caused the low test scores or whether previous low test scores caused the present high level of anxiety. French (1962) compared the performance of high school students on the CEEB *Scholastic Attitude Test* under anxiety-arousing and relaxed conditions. He found that performance was essentially the same under the two conditions and that the concurrent validity of the test, as shown by correlation with high school grades, was just about the same under the two conditions.

A third concern, again related to college admissions testing, arises from pressure from students and parents for the school to set up programs for coaching students for the tests. The College Entrance Examination Board (1968) has sponsored or conducted a number of studies on the effects of coaching. The conclusion from the studies is that coaching is unlikely to produce appreciable gains on the test. This, however, will probably not prevent some schools and pupils from continuing to spend time trying to "beat the test."

A fourth concern stems from the feeling that college admissions testing programs are unfair or biased against minority groups. The studies that have considered this issue (Cleary, 1968; Munday, 1965; Stanley and Porter, 1967) have shown the accuracy of prediction of college success, using either the CEEB test or ACT, to be about the same or higher for black as for white students.

The fifth concern is that the external tests may pervert the educational program of the school, because the tests come to control the curriculum and the teachers focus on preparing for the tests. This problem is most likely to arise when the external tests are concerned with specific segments of the school curriculum, as is the case with the *New York State Regents Examinations.* Since the performance of student, teacher, and school are all judged to some extent by performance on the tests, they may assume a disproportionate importance. Anyone acquainted with secondary schools in New York State knows of classes that spend weeks, even months, in review of past Regents Examinations. One can certainly question whether this is the most rewarding investment of time for student and teacher.

Even when the test is less closely tied to the curriculum, the test may affect it through what the test does and does not emphasize. Thus it has been argued that the relatively small role for actual writing in recent English tests of the College Board has reinforced a tendency to reduce the number and variety of compositions called for in high school English courses, and has strengthened an undesirable trend. Certainly, it is important that external testing programs present desirable models, emphasizing the important goals of education and not distorting the pattern of the school program. When the testing programs deal with achievements of a nature sufficiently broad and basic that they go beyond specific courses and course objectives, the danger of an unfavorable impact seems reduced.

In spite of the concerns that educators may have about the external testing programs, these programs are likely to be around for a long time. Persons responsible for developing the internal program for their own school system should become familiar with state-mandated programs of testing, as well as other external programs, asking themselves what local needs these programs can serve. They can then plan their own program of testing so that it supplements rather than duplicates the information provided by the mandated programs.

SUMMARY

Our central theme in this chapter has been that tests are given to be used and that uses are determined by local needs. An effective school testing program is related to local needs and helps build a continuous picture of the students' development from kindergarten through grade 12.

Table 14.1 summarizes the variety of functions that tests are often called upon to serve. Discussion of these functions may guide a local group in defining their purposes in testing. Planning for a school testing program and setting up policies related to it should be done by a committee that has representation from all levels of school personnel, but one person, the director of testing, should be assigned overall supervision for the program. Suggested priorities for a testing program for elementary and secondary schools and for colleges were given. These were summarized in Table 14.2.

Suggestions were given for carrying out the testing program so that standardized conditions are maintained. The importance of good cumulative records of test scores was stressed. The need to check scores for reasonableness was pointed out.

Effective use of test results requires setting up procedures for analyzing and interpreting the results to various interested publics. Group results need to be organized effectively in graphs and charts that reveal significant comparisons. Oral and written reports need to be given to school personnel and lay audiences. The need to report the results of testing for an individual student to the student and his or her parent was stressed. Methods of reporting test results for an individual were discussed. Emphasis was placed on giving a sound interpretation of the score in terms of educational or vocational goals of the student rather than on reporting exact scores that are likely to be misused or misinterpreted.

Finally, external testing programs that impinge upon the school's own program were reviewed. The major external programs discussed were the CEEB and ACT examinations for college entrance, the National Merit Scholarship tests, and state-mandated programs. The concerns of educators over the external tests were discussed.

QUESTIONS AND EXERCISES

1. Suppose you have just started to work in a particular school system and you have been told that one of your major assignments during the first year will be to revise the testing program now in use in the school system. What would be the first steps that you would take? Why would you take these steps?

2. "In school systems where programs are truly individualized for each child, a program of standardized achievement testing has no place." What is your reaction to this statement? On what do you base your response?

3. It has been suggested that if an elementary school uses a general achievement battery such as the *Stanford Achievement Test* or the *Iowa Tests of Basic Skills* each year, then any intelligence test it uses should be a nonverbal test. What are the arguments for this position? What are the arguments against it?

4. A school system wants to take parts of several achievement batteries to form an achievement battery that the teachers feel will be more suitable for the local curriculum. The system proposes to develope local norms and use only these for interpretation. What are the advantages and disadvantages of the proposal?

5. A secondary school, grades 9-12, in which approximately 70 percent of the graduates take no further education, has a strong vocational program, jointly supported by the school and local industries. In grades 11 and 12 there is a work-study program in which the students spend half the time in apprentice training and half in academic work. How should the testing program for this school differ from that in a suburban high school in which 80 percent of students go to college?

6. A special liberal arts college is being set up to take students not eligible for regular college admission who have promise for completing a liberal arts program. The college will accept any student with promise over 18 years of age whether he has completed high school or not. Programs are to be set up to remedy deficiencies that students might have. Plan a testing program that would help the new college admit students and place them.

7. A school system gives a battery of achievement tests consisting of vocabulary, reading comprehension, spelling, English usage, and mathematical concepts and reasoning in October of each year in grades 2 through 6. It also gives a general intelligence test in grades 2, 4, and 6. How can the results of the testing be used in each of the following situations? How must the data from the testing be analyzed to respond to each problem? What would the limitations of test results be?

(a) The students in the system are to be reassigned. Parents of children in school A object to sending their children to school B because they feel that the achievement level of their children will decrease.

(b) The school system has appointed a committee to revise the elementary mathematics program.

(c) One school in the system has had an ungraded organization for 5 years. School personnel want to keep it but the Board of Education wants to put the school under the graded organization because of costs.

8. A state Department of Education wants to start a statewide testing program in grades 2, 4, 6, 8, 10, and 12. The Department needs data on reading, language, mathematics and general scholastic ability. The data are to be used to judge the effectiveness of educational efforts throughout the state and to allocate special funds. The following proposals have been made. What are the advantages and disadvantages of each of the proposals?

(a) The state will construct tests of its own and norm them on the school population in the state.

(b) A committee selected from various school districts in the state will select five published tests in each area. Local schools can then choose one of the five to use. Schools may test at any time between October 1 and December 31.

(c) A committee selected from various districts will select the best available published standardized test in each of the areas. All schools in the state must give the same test at the same time of the year.

9. Below are given data on *Stanford Achievement Test, Arithmetic Problem Solving* scores obtained by sixth grade students in the Paradise School System between 1970 and 1974. All tests were given during the first week in October.

Year	N	P_{10}	P_{25}	P_{50}	P_{75}	P_{90}
1970	273	4.2	5.4	6.4	8.0	11.3
1971	268	4.1	5.1	6.1	7.9	11.1
1972	277	3.1	4.4	5.9	7.4	9.5
1973	273	3.1	4.0	5.7	7.0	9.0
1974	275	3.0	3.8	5.2	7.0	9.0

Suggest several hypotheses to account for these results. What further information would you need to evaluate the reasonableness of the different hypotheses?

10. In the table below are shown the scores of Roger Tuthill, tested at the end of the fourth grade. Prepare a report to be used in conference with Roger's parents.

GRADE 4—TESTED MAY 1974

	National Norms			Local Norms	
	Grade Equivalent	Percentile Rank	Stanine	Percentile Rank	Stanin
Word knowledge	4.0	30	4	9	2
Word discrimination	4.9	55	5	25	3
Reading	4.2	35	4	28	3
Spelling	5.0	55	5	19	3
Language	5.5	67	6	18	3
Arithmetic computation	6.7	98	9	96	8
Arithmetic problem solving and concepts	7.8	98	9	99	9

11. In the previous question data were provided in terms of both local and national norms. What do the differences between the two tell about the nature of the local 4th grade group?

12. A school system gave the *Stanford Achievement Tests* to all pupils in the fifth grade in May. The *Otis-Lennon Mental Ability Test* had been given at about the same time. Grade equivalents for the 10th, 25th, 50, 75th, and 90th percentiles for each test are shown below. Prepare a report to interpret these results to the Board of Education or a group of interested parents.

STANFORD ACHIEVEMENT TESTS
GRADE 5—TESTED MARCH 1974

	P_{10}	P_{25}	P_{50}	P_{75}	P_{90}
Word meaning	3.3	4.2	5.0	5.7	6.8
Paragraph meaning	3.7	4.8	5.5	6.5	7.8
Spelling	3.6	4.4	5.4	6.8	7.9
Language	3.2	4.1	5.5	6.5	7.6
Arithmetic computation	3.9	5.0	5.7	6.5	7.3
Arithmetic concepts	4.0	4.7	5.5	6.4	7.5
Arithmetic application	3.7	4.5	5.5	6.6	7.6
Otis-Lennon Mental Ability Test IQ	81	91	98	112	120

13. A statewide testing program has been planned in which each pupil takes some one of 10 forms of a 30-minute achievement test. In total, the 10 forms give a wide sampling of the statewide objectives of instruction. Results are averaged over forms and pupils for each school and school system. How desirable is this pattern of testing (1) for enabling state and local administration to monitor achievement in each school, and (2) for helping teachers in their instructional plans for individual children?

14. What are the advantages of the Buckley-Pell Amendent requiring parent and/or student access to school testing records? What problems does this legal requirement raise?

SUGGESTED ADDITIONAL READING

Ayrer, James E. and Thomas C. McNamara. Survey testing on an out-of-level basis. *Journal of Educational Measurement,* 1973, 10, 79–84.

Borgen, Fred H. Differential expectations? Predicting grades for black students in five types of colleges. *Measurement and Evaluation in Guidance,* 1972, 4, 206–212.

Ferguson, R.L. and E.J. Maxey. *Trends in the academic performance of high school and college students.* ACT Research Report No. 70. Iowa City, Iowa: The American College Testing Program, January 1976.

Hoepfner, Ralph. Published tests and the needs of educational accountability. *Educational and Psychological Measurement,* 1974, 34, 103–109.

Lenning, O.T. *Predictive validity of the ACT tests at selective colleges.* ACT Research Report No. 69. Iowa City, Iowa: The American College Testing Program, August 1975.

Mauger, Paul A., and C.A. Kolmodin, Long-term predictive validity of the Scholastic Aptitude Test. *Journal of Educational Psychology,* 1975, 67, 847–851.

Munday, L.A. *Declining admissions test scores.* ACT Research Report No. 71. Iowa City, Iowa: The American College Testing Program, February 1976.

Pfeifer, C. Michael Jr. Relationship between scholastic aptitude, perception of university climate, and college success for black and white students. *Journal of Applied Psychology,* 1976, 61, 341–347.

Towle, Nelson J. and Paul F. Merrill. Effects of anxiety type and item-difficulty sequencing on mathematics test performance. *Journal of Educational Measurement,* 1975, 12, 241–249.

Tyler, Ralph W. National assessment—Some valuable by-products for school. In L.R. Aikin, Jr. (Ed.), *Readings in Psychological and Educational Testing.* Boston: Allyn and Bacon, 1973.

Womer, Frank B. National assessment of educational progress. In G.H. Bracht, K.D. Hopkins, J.C. Stanley (Eds.) *Perspectives in Educational and Psychological Measurement.* Englewood Cliffs, N.J.: Prentice-Hall, 1972.

CHAPTER FIFTEEN
MARKS AND MARKING

One educational activity closely related to the problems of measurement is that of evaluating student performance in some segment of schooling and recording and reporting that evaluation. Typically, the evaluation is summarized in some condensed and highly abstract symbol. A survey (NEA, 1967) of over 600 school systems indicated that a system of numerical or letter grades was used in about 80 percent of the systems, except in the first grade, where the percentage was 73, and in the kindergarten, where it was 17. More recent evidence (Pinchak and Breland, 1974) indicates that, at the secondary level at least, the situation has not changed.

Use of these highly condensed symbols to convey the teacher's evaluation has frequently been criticized, for reasons that we shall consider presently, but the alternatives that have been offered to replace the conventional A, B, C, D, F and percentage systems have introduced problems of their own, and no fully satisfactory replacement for the course grade seems to be at hand. Especially in secondary school and college, it seems likely that marks will be with us for some time to come. Thus it is important that we understand marks and marking both as cultural and as psychometric phenomena.

Marks and marking have been very deeply imbedded in the educational culture. They have become the basis, in whole or in part, for a wide range of actions and decisions within a given educational institution, between levels in the educational structure, and in the relations of the educational system to the outside world. Eligibility for admission to certain programs or departments, for scholarship aid, for membership on athletic teams, even for continuing in school at the higher levels has been determined in some measure by academic standing. Admission to college or graduate school has been based, in part, on grades received at the previous academic level. Thus there are many points within the school at which marks interact with the administrative and instructional process. It is for this reason, in part at least, that marking systems have been so durable and so resistant to change.

Like any other deeply ingrained aspect of a culture, marks and marking procedures are often taken for granted, with a minimum of rational analysis of their nature and their functions. As we examine them, our approach should be, in part, that of the cultural anthropologist, who looks at a set of odd but presumably meaningful behavior patterns and tries to understand the functions they serve and the manner in which they relate to the total culture of which they are a part. We should put aside our personal involvement, look at the phenomenon with the cold eye of the social scientist, try to identify the forces that shape and sustain present grading practices, and the pressures within the educational culture that make the practices at one and the same time both somewhat irrational and highly resistant to change.

FUNCTIONS SERVED BY MARKS

Marking and reporting practices are sustained partly by tradition, but partly by the real functions that they serve with a greater or lesser degree of adequacy. These functions relate to the needs of students themselves, to the needs of parents (or parent substitutes) in charge of the pupils and responsible for their upbringing, to the needs of the school in which the pupils are enrolled, to the needs of schools to which they later may be candidates for admission, and to those of employers or others in adult society to whom the students may someday relate. Let us examine each of these categories of need to see how well marking and reporting practices serve them.

Students need information about themselves to guide present learning and plans for the future. They need immediate feedback to tell them what they know and where their errors and deficiencies lie. Daily exercises, recitations, and quizzes provide this type of feedback. It is provided most completely and effectively in programmed instructional materials, in which students receive immediate confirmation or correction of their responses. Periodic marks and report cards are too remote from learning activities to provide this type of specific direction of day-by-day learning.

Students need information defining what it is appropriate and important for them to learn. Again, what the teacher assigns as learning tasks, and especially what he or she *corrects, grades, and returns to the pupils* defines for them what is considered important in school. Thus White and Boehm (1967) found that pupils in the elementary school tended to agree that spelling and arithmetic were the things that it was important to learn, because these were the papers that their teachers graded. But here again, it is testing and immediate feedback that are central, rather than a mark on a report card once in 6 or 8 weeks.

Students need information as to the sort of persons they are. Is he the sort of person who is good with words? With numbers? In science? In art? Is she the sort of person who should plan to go on to college? To major in chemistry? Course marks can and should play a part in building up this self-picture, though the variability of marking standards from school to school, department to department and teacher to teacher presents many barriers to achieving a clear and accurate image. However, with all their technical limitations, marks remain one of the best predictors of later marks, and so are important in conveying information about likelihood of success in college generally, or in specific institutions or programs. Results for somewhat over 100,000 students followed up in a major American College Testing Program study (Hoyt and Munday, 1966) showed the correlation with college freshman grades to be .58 for a composite of high school marks, .55 for a composite of standardized test scores, and .65 for the optimum combination of both types of information. So marks have a significant role to play in informing the individual (as well as the institution to which he may later apply) of his prospects for academic success.

Clearly, the pupil or the parent who looks at a report from the school and asks the question: What kind of learner am I? (is Johnny?) needs help in interpreting the marks. With the enormous variation that exists among teachers and among schools and colleges, even a skilled counselor has his talents stretched to make a sound judgment as to what any given record signifies in terms of any specific educational decision. But the marks shown on a report card consitute one important type of evidence of educational potential to be interpreted to pupil or parent. One of the standards for any marking and reporting system is that it be as interpretable as possible.

Parents have need for information about their child. They need information, at the simplest level, to reassure them that their child's school experience is proceeding satisfactorily or to alert them if problems are developing. The usual report card serves this need, at least at a minimal level, but the amount of information that can be conveyed by a single symbol is so limited that many schools have felt a need to supplement the conventional report form in various ways. The 1966 NEA survey showed that about half the school systems scheduled conferences with parents of elementary school children—but the percentage dropped to about 25 in junior high and 20 in senior high. In the primary grades a third of the schools included narrative comments on the pupil in their reporting, a practice that occurred for about one-fifth at grade 4 and only about a tenth in junior and senior high school.

Especially when a child is encountering educational difficulty, the conventional report card becomes a most inadequate communication medium. It can do little more than register the teacher's dissatisfaction with a pupil. It does not convey a diagnosis of the source of the difficulty or provide to either pupil or parent any suggestions for remedial action. Thus, at best but without any certainty that it will do so, it can cause the parent to seek out the teacher to find out more about the problem and what school and family can jointly do about it. This global and purely negative character of a low mark is its greatest weakness.

Parents need information to help them plan for their child's future. Their need here is one shared with the pupil, and the values and limitations of marks are those considered earlier. Again, parents need help in interpreting marks, together with standardized test data, in terms of the realistic expectancies that they present for future choices and actions. Most parents are poorly qualified to use either marks or standardized test scores for decision making, except as the implications of these data are interpreted to them, so persons who provide the interpretation play a very key role.

Teacher evaluations, typically recorded as marks but sometimes amplified with narrative comments or anecdotal reports, serve a variety of functions within the economy of the educational system itself. Many of these functions are primarily administrative, though these may be quite central to the students' educational future. The most obvious of these is the decision to admit—to college on the basis of secondary school grades, to graduate school on the basis of grades in college.

At the college level, probation and dismissal at one end and honors and distinction at the other stem from the pervasive grade-point average. In between, eligibility for admission to more advanced courses or for major study in a field may be based in considerable extent upon having "passed" or achieved a specified level in previous courses. In the culture of an educational system that is selective in its parts, if not in its entirety, these are administrative decisions that must be made, and if they are not made on the basis of teacher evaluations as recorded in course marks, they will be made in terms of special examinations or other procedures. There are also, of course, a host of nonacademic decisions in which marks play a role, such as eligibility to be a member of athletic teams—aspects of the college culture that have a sometimes disturbing reality and importance.

It is these actions, so crucial to the individual student and so central to the functioning of the educational institution, that account for much of the irrationality of marking practices and of their resistance to rational change. An assortment of vested interests and personal convictions get bound up in grading systems and standards, and these can be as highly resistant to change as dietary habits that had their origins and rationale in an ancient prerefrigeration era. Thus a science department that wishes to hold majoring in its field down to a limited number of the most promising students finds it convenient to grade severely in the introductory course so that most freshmen are discouraged from taking, and few can qualify for, advanced work in the department. An individual professor who fortifies his ego with the conviction that "standards must be maintained" can take satisfaction in the high rate of failure and the infrequency of As in his classes—a trend that one of his colleagues might take to be evidence of poor teaching. Marking practices are expressions of individual and group value systems as much as they are dispassionate reports of student behavior. Should students in an "honors" section receive grades that reflect their achievement in relation to their total class, or in relation only to each other? And what about a "slow" or "minimum fundamentals" section? Should a student be penalized for handing in papers late, or get extra credit for doing optional work? Should students with the same level of scholastic aptitude get, on the average, the same grades irrespective of the subject or department involved? These are all questions of value that rarely are examined in detail and upon which members of a faculty seldom come to genuine agreement. As long as disagreement exists within the local educational culture on questions of value such as these, the technical efforts of the psychometrician to introduce a consistent rationale into grading practices will be futile.

TECHNICAL QUESTIONS IN SOUND MARKING PROCEDURES

Now that we have explored, in general terms, the role of marks in the educational culture, let us turn to some of the more specific and technical problems relating to the assignment of marks to pupils. We will organize the discussion around six main questions:

1. On what should a mark be based?

2. How should component data be weighted in arriving at a mark?

3. In how many categories or subdivisions should marks be reported?

4. What fraction of students should receive each mark?

5. In relation to what frame of reference should marks be formulated and how can they be related to that frame?

6. How can standards be equated from section to section, course to course, and department to department?

Note that many of these questions are phrased in terms of a "should," and that issues of value as well as fact arise in connection with each one of them. As we consider these questions in turn, we shall have to address ourselves first to the underlying issues of value and then to the problems of technique and implementation.

ON WHAT SHOULD A MARK BE BASED?

This question really breaks down into two parts: (1) What characteristics of a student should be represented in a mark, and (2) What types of evidence should be gathered to provide evidence on the designated characteristic or characteristics? The first question can be rephrased by asking: Should a mark represent as pure and accurate an appraisal of competence in a segment of the curriculum as can be devised, or should it be modified by factors other than that competence? Some of the potential modifiers are:

(*a*) Amount of work completed, as well as final level of competence reached. It is not unusual for teachers to permit students to raise their marks by doing additional amounts of work, giving only limited attention to the quality of the work and almost entirely without regard to whether the additional work results in any higher level of competence on the part of the student. The mark then comes to signify conscientiousness and industry as well as, or perhaps even instead of, competence.

(*b*) Mechanical aspects of work completed—neatness, legibility, correctness in the mechanics of written or oral expression. These are factors that the school welcomes and strives for in the work of its pupils, but one is impelled to ask how many of these factors should influence and how much they should influence a mark that reports competence in, say, history or biology.

(*c*) Aptitude, as this is indicated to the teacher by the results of scholastic aptitude tests or by the section to which the pupil is assigned. Should all pupils be judged in relation to a common standard, or should each be judged in relation to some indicator of potential to achieve?

Aside from personal convictions and a personal value system, it would seem that the only criterion that can be brought to bear on these questions is the criterion of use. For what purposes will a mark be used? In the light of these uses—such uses as we have discussed earlier in the chapter—what is the best foundation for a marking system? It seems to us that most purposes are best served by a mark that is as pure and unadulterated a measure of competence as can be devised, but others may see values in modulating competence by one or more other types of consideration. We would hope that the introduction of other factors is done as a result of a thoughtful examination of the issues, rather than as a casual and unanalyzed decision.

When the foundations for allocation of marks have been thought through by the instructor or by the teaching group, it is then essential to decide what types of test, exercise, written report, or other behavior will provide evidence of the achievements that the mark is to represent. The choice of types of evidence can best be based upon the same type of analysis of the objectives of a course that was proposed in Chapter 7 as the basis for designing a well-balanced test. If the objectives have been clearly identified in behavioral terms, this statement will point to the types of evidence that will provide an indication of the extent to which those objectives have been achieved.

HOW SHOULD COMPONENT DATA
BE WEIGHTED?

595

technical
questions in
sound marking
procedures

A scrutiny of the list of objectives will usually suggest that certain class activities, certain assignments and exercises, certain reports and papers, and certain examinations are appropriate media for gathering evidence of the extent to which a student has achieved the course objectives. These separate indicators must be combined in some way if a single symbol is to be used to report a student's performance. How shall the weight for each component be determined?

In the last analysis, two factors determine the desirable effective weight for a given datum, that is, a test, a paper, a recitation, and so on. The first of these is the validity of the information that it provides. Validity in this context signifies the importance of the knowledge or skill that is reflected in the datum and the faithfulness with which it is reflected, uncontaminated by other irrelevant factors (such as verbal fluency or penmanship). Usually, the validity of a type of datum can only be assessed through judgment, possibly a pooled judgment of several instructors in an area. A second, but relatively minor consideration is reliability. The less reliable datum that incorporates a relatively large component of measurement error deserves a smaller weight, other things being equal, than the more reliable one. We may generally anticipate that reliability will be highest by a considerable margin for a carefully prepared objective test, intermediate for essay tests and for papers and essays, and lowest for the on-the-wing appraisal of oral contributions and participation in class. These trends should temper somewhat the weights that would otherwise be assigned on the basis of the judged validity of the datum.

Once an instructor has decided what weight to allocate to each kind of datum, it is necessary to be sure that each does, in fact, receive that weight. Suppose that an instructor has given a 90-item objective exam for which the score is the number of items right, and a term paper that has been evaluated on a 5-point scale ranging from 5 = excellent to 1 = unsatisfactory, and that he has decided that in the final assessment of his students the exam should carry twice as much weight as the term paper. Suppose, further, that the two sets of scores have the following characteristics:

	Exam	Paper
Mean	63	3.2
Standard deviation	11	0.55

What must be done to these scores to produce the desired result?

Note the standard deviations. That for the exam is 20 times as great as that for the paper. If we were simply to add the two scores for each individual, the exam would have 20 times as much effect as the paper in determining the individual's standing on the combined score. But this instructor wants its effect to be twice as great—so he must multiply the scores on the term paper by a factor of 10, making the mean 32 and the standard deviation 5.5 (see p. 131). The 2 standard deviations are then in the ratio of 2 to 1, and the effective weights are what the instructor set out to produce. In summary, the effective weight of each component is determined by its standard deviation. To give variables the desired effective weights, one must multiply each variable by a factor that will adjust the standard deviations to the desired ratio. The desired multiplying constant C, can be found from the formula:

$$C_B = \frac{Wt_B \cdot SD_A}{Wt_A \cdot SD_B}$$

where Wt_A and Wt_B are the desired weights for two components;

SD_A and SD_B are the standard deviations of the components;

A is the component that is being used as an "anchor" variable; and

B is one of the variables whose weight is being adjusted to bring it into line with variable A.

HOW MANY CATEGORIES SHOULD BE USED?

Evaluations may be reported very crudely in only two categories such as "Pass" and "Fail," in three or four categories, in the widely used 5-letter A, B, C, D, F set of categories, in a 15-category system that attaches plusses and minuses to the above letters, or in a percentage system that nominally can take any one of 100 values. How can we decide which is to be preferred? As usual, the issues are partly those of value and partly those of fact.

Arguments concerning the values involved tend to center around deemphasizing the competitive pressures and the presumably irrelevant goals represented by marks. It is maintained that this can best be accomplished by a very coarse grading system which, in effect, makes only a few gross discriminations. This gain is bought, of course, at the expense of most of the information that the marking system might possibly supply about the individual. In a pass-fail system we know only that a student has been judged passable in a course, except for the often extremely small fraction who are judged to have failed. Or, in a 3-point system, we know for the great bulk of students that they have been judged neither inadequate nor outstanding. Marks recede into the background except for the small group who fail, and perhaps for another small group who aspire to honors.

As the number of discriminations increases beyond a 2- or 3-category system, distinctions begin to be of importance for all students. If the number of categories is small, there are relatively few students who fall close to dividing lines between categories, and for these a very major gain or loss occurs depending on which way the decision goes. As the number of categories increases, the number of borderline decisions increases correspondingly, but each decision becomes less crucial in the total academic record of the student. There is a trade-off of increased frequency of potential error or unfairness in grading for decreased size and importance of that error.

The issue of fact that is relevant to the number of grading categories is the reliability of the evidence on which the decision is being made. Each component that enters into a final grade, as well as the grade itself, has an appreciable (if often unknown) standard error of measurement. If this error is large relative to the unit in which grades are reported, many of the discriminations that are reported will be without substance or meaning. Consider the following situation, which is artificial but is believed to be fairly realistic.

A school reports grades in a percentage system. For a particular course, the grades have a mean of 85, a standard deviation of 7, a range from 53 to 98, and a reliability of .80.

Given the above data, we can determine that the standard error of measurement of this final grade is $7\sqrt{1 - .80} = 3.1$ percentage points. Harking back to our discussion of reliability in Chapter 3, we can recall that this means that about one-third of our grades will differ from the person's hypothetical "true grade" by as much as 3 points and in 87 percent of cases the score assigned to a person will differ by at least 1 point from the one we would have assigned if we have known his true score! How useful is it to carry discriminations to this level of fineness if it means that 87 percent of the reported values are "wrong"? Even if the reliability of the final grade were .95, a value that is probably never reached in practice, there would still be 75 percent of "wrong" grades.

Suppose we grouped our data, and divided the score range into a smaller number of categories. How often would the reported grade be the "right" grade? Percentage of correct assignments at four levels of reliability and three degrees of coarseness of grading are estimated below.

Categories	Reliability			
	.60	.70	.80	.90
15 (A+ to F−)	27%	31%	37%	50%
5 (A to F)	70	77	85	96
3 (Honors, Pass, Fail)	91	95	98	99.9

The assumptions upon which the above table is based are complex, somewhat arbitrary, but still probably reasonably realistic. They seem to suggest that trying to make discriminations into *more* than 15 categories is a fairly futile exercise, and that even this degree of fineness strains the precision of our judgments. Of course, being "wrong" by 1 or 2 categories on a finely divided scale is not a crucial matter, but trying to make discriminations that are far beyond the limits of our evidence seems a fairly fruitless enterprise.

HOW MANY SHOULD GET WHAT MARK?

Over a period of 50 years a great deal has been written, much of it nonsense, about the appropriate frequency distribution of the symbols that represent marks. Two primary principles need to be emphasized in this regard. First, the symbols that represent marks are basically an ordinal, not a cardinal system. No one would question that, in our conventional 5-letter system, A is better than B, B better than C, and so on down to F. But there is no such universal consensus that the 5 or 6 steps do or should represent *equal* steps of quality, so that an A is just as much better than a B as a D is better than an F. Second, the symbols are embedded in an educational culture in which the cultural role of the symbols is at least as important as their psychometric properties. The specification that a student must repeat a course if he is to receive credit for it is a sociocultural decision, not a psychometric one. The decision that a student shall be eligible to take further advanced courses in a department is a sociocultural one, not a psychometric one. It is these practical consequences that flow from a grade that determine its real meaning, and the custodians of the culture, not the statisticians, must decide to what proportion of a student group these consequences should accrue.

In most educational institutions, an uneasy equilibrium is reached between the grading symbol system and the social consequences of particular grades. Percentage of academic failure remains fairly stable from year to year; average grades within a department maintain themselves at a fairly stable level, though varying from department to department; new faculty members are informally initiated into the culture and maintain its general character, though superimposing their individual idiosyncrasies upon it. But the equilibrium is an intuitive, unexamined sort of thing.

Grade-point average has been found to be unresponsive to real changes in the characteristics of the student population (e.g., see Baird and Feister, 1972), but seems to be subject to the same sort of inflationary pressures that have been plaguing the economy.* The rationale for instructor, course, and department differences in distribution of grades is, to say the least, obscure. The cultural norms as to how grading symbols are used throughout a school or college deserve conscious scrutiny to make sure that the categories are, in fact, being used in ways that serve the purposes of the institution itself and the larger educational system of which it is a part.

One possible decision, after such a scrutiny, is that successive symbols should represent equal steps along an interval scale. How is one to achieve equal units for a composite of various types of information expressed in various units, which may or may not be equal? There may well be question as to whether this can be done in a way that will give much confidence in the outcome. However, one technique that has a certain reasonableness for courses that are taken by large and relatively unselected groups of students is to assume that competence is distributed in accordance with the normal curve. The range of the normal curve can then be divided into equal segments, and the percentage of cases falling in each segment determined from a table such as the table in Appendix One. One solution to this problem is shown below.

Symbol	Standard Score Range on Normal Curve	Percentage of Cases
A	$+1.5$ to $+2.5$ or higher	7
B	$+0.5$ to $+1.5$	24
C	-0.5 to $+0.5$	38
D	-1.5 to -0.5	24
F	-2.5 or below to -1.5	7

* It is a commonly reported experience that average grades have tended upward over a time span during which objective measures of achievement were standing still or tending downward.

Thus, if this system were applied to a freshman survey math course, 7 percent would be awarded As, 24 percent Bs, and so on.

Of course, the fact that it is possible to assign marks by such a system does not mean that it is sensible to do so. This can only be judged in terms of the impact that such a procedure will have upon the practical actions that flow from the allocation of marks. Is it socially desirable, in the context of the institution in question, that 7 percent fail freshman math? Would the purposes of the institution be better served if the percentage were larger? Smaller? *Should* the percentage failing equal the percentage getting an A? Only a wise examination of the purposes of the institution and the impact of the failure percentage upon those purposes can provide an answer.

IN RELATION TO WHAT FRAME OF REFERENCE SHOULD MARKS BE ASSIGNED?

There are three quite different reference frames within which marks may be assigned. We may label these

1. Performance in relation to perfection.
2. Performance in relation to potential.
3. Performance in relation to peers.

Performance in relation to perfection has been discussed in some detail in Chapter 6 in relation to criterion-referenced tests. There may be some limited segments of curricular material for which it is possible to make a complete catalogue of that which exists to be learned. Common examples would be (1) the 100 multiplication "facts," (2) the symbols representing the chemical elements, (3) the names of the bones in the body. When the number of items is finite and definable, it is possible to test the examinee with all or a representative sample of them, and report his performance as a percent of perfect performance.

However, as indicated earlier, the learning to which the concept of complete mastery applies represents only a fairly small fraction of school learning. Even for these the notion of mastery may be somewhat illusory, because we may have to specify the task so completely that it becomes trivial. Thus a child who can answer the question "What does 4×5 equal?" may fail on the question "What will four 5-cent candy bars cost?" Does the child "know" the multiplication combinations if he cannot apply them in a problem context? Thus complete mastery as a frame of reference for the use of marking symbols is of quite limited utility.

One frame that has had a fair amount of support is that of using symbols to report performance in relation to some estimate of potential to perform. It is argued that the type of information that is useful—in part, to a school, but especially to a parent—is whether achievement measures up to what the individual's underlying talents make possible. We are dealing here with the issue of under-and overachievement discussed in Chapter 9. And we face many of the same technical problems that we faced at that time. How do we get a measure of "potential" that is independent of and uncontaminated by present achievement? Can teachers make the required judgment of achievement-in-relation-to-potential, divorcing it from simple achievement? One study addressed specifically to this point (Halliwell, 1960) indicates pretty clearly that they cannot, and that those who received high ratings were the bright youngsters—not the "overachievers." In addition to a serious question of whether teachers *can* make the required judgments in a sufficiently reliable and valid manner, there is also the question, in relation to a number of the contexts in which marks are used, of whether this really is the desired information to be conveyed by a marking symbol. When decisions relate to more advanced courses to be taken or recommendation for further education or for a job, what one may wish to know is not whether Sarah does the best she can, but what she can, in fact, do.

The third reference frame, performance in relation to peers, undertakes to express individual performance in relation to some reference group. This is the type of referent that is used in standardized test norms, as described in Chapter 4, where the peer group is some very farflung national sample. Such a reference group has been used, at least to a limited extent, to calibrate grading practices nationwide in Swedish schools, but usually the reference group for school marks is conceived in much more limited terms. It may be the total student body of the institution or some unit of it, the total group taking some course, the total group in a particular instructor's section, or the shadowy and ill-defined total group of previous students that shape an instructor's impressions of what is good, or average, or poor performance. Problems in the use of a peer group as a reference frame involve first the value judgment of what peer group provides the most appropriate reference frame and then the technical problems of anchoring the marks that are awarded to that frame.

Arguments for using a very inclusive reference frame, for example, the total freshman class in a college or all the sixth graders in a school system, center on matters of fairness and equity. An individual of a given level of ability, it is argued, should have an equal chance of getting a particular mark no matter what teacher, class group, or subject area is involved. However, this conception of equity to the individual comes into conflict with other values in the educational system. For the student, an issue is that of providing for each individual an opportunity for success at his or her own level. This would imply evaluating the individual in terms of progress from a previous level of competence, and is closely related to the idea of achievement in relation to potential. For the institution and for society, it can be argued that needed levels of particular talents (specifically, cognitive and intellectual talents) vary as between different fields and occupations, and that the reference group should be persons in a specific field, such as physics or vocational agriculture, rather than the total body of students.

The simplest reference frame is one that does not go beyond the single instructor. Marks could then be assigned either in relation to a specific class group or in relation to the more general but more vague inner standard held by the instructor. If the specific class is used to provide the reference frame, there is always the possibility that the students in one class may be in some way unrepresentative, so that each student may receive either an unfair penalty or an unwarranted bonus because of the nature of that reference group. If the "inner standard" is used, one is troubled by its subjectivity and its variability from instructor to instructor and possibly from time to time for a given instructor.

Which evil is the lesser depends primarily on the size and randomness of the group in a class. If the class is very small, that is, 10 or 15, there would seem to be little question that the "inner standard" needs to be called on to check the representativeness of that class. As the group gets larger, and especially as it is known that no special selective factors have been operating to send a particular type of student into it, one gradually gets more and more faith in the equivalence of successive samples from a common population, and one is prepared to assign marks on a predetermined basis treating the total group as a uniform reference frame. The shift from "inner standard" to "class reference group" is a matter of degree. With intermediate-size classes of 25 to 40 pupils, one might be inclined to temper any standard allocation of grades somewhat to take account of one's impression of the caliber of the group in relation to others taught previously or concurrently, while in large lecture courses of 100 or more, one might reasonably feel that the uniformity of successive groups was much more to be trusted than the stability of one's own subjective judgment.

EQUATING STANDARDS

Whenever a general group is selected to provide the reference frame, some technique is needed to anchor any specific group to that frame. There must be some item or items of information available for the complete reference group (or a fair and representative sample of it). When the reference group is all the students in all the sections of a course, and the course has been so taught that it includes a core of common content and objectives, an examination on that common core provides a reasonable anchoring device. For more diverse groups one might use grade-point averages in previous courses or scores on a common scholastic aptitude test as a rough anchor.

Let us work through an illustration to show how an anchoring test might be used. Suppose that a college has three sections of a general psychology course, taught at different hours by different instructors, but using a common text and syllabus. The instructors, working together, have assembled a common final examination that they agree is equally suitable for each of their sections. A few items may be more appropriate for one section, but these are balanced by a few more appropriate for each of the others. The exam is given to all sections and the results are as shown in Table 15.1

Table 15.1
SCORES IN THREE SECTIONS OF COURSE

Score	Section 1	Section II	Section III	Total Group
85–9	1	2	1	4
80–4	2	4	1	7
75–9	3	7	1	11
70–4	5	9	6	20
65–9	6	6	6	18
60–4	6	7	19	32
55–9	4	5	19	28
50–4	5	4	3	12
45–9	2	2	2	6
40–4	4	0	0	4
35–9	0	3	2	5
30–4	2	1	0	3
N	40	50	60	150

It is the college grading policy that in unselective introductory courses, the allocation of grades will ordinarily be approximately 15 percent As, 25 percent Bs, 40 percent Cs, 15 percent Ds and 5 percent Fs, and the instructors agree that they know of nothing peculiar about this year's introductory psychology course that would require a change in this policy. Working from the distribution of total scores for the total class, we have 15 percent of 150 = 22, so the top 22 students, approximately, should represent As. These are students with scores of 75 or over.* The next 25 percent × 150 = 38 students, representing Bs are those with scores of 65—74. Continuing on down, we get the complete picture shown in Table 15.2.

This table specifies the *number* of each grade to be awarded within each section, but does not specify *which individuals* are to receive which grade. This would presumably be based on each student's complete record, giving only the desired weight in the total to the common anchor test. Thus a pupil in section I who earned only a B on the common test might be one of those eventually awarded an A because of the excellence of the rest of his record. In practice, it might be agreed that each instructor would be permitted to make minor deviations from his allocated frequencies when near ties occurred, or when other evidence suggested a somewhat different shape of the distribution of performance in his group.

As set forth, the example illustrated a strict equipercentile conversion from the anchoring test to the final mark. That is, the percentage of each grade awarded corresponds, step by step, with the percentage in that category on the common test. This is not unreasonable when the anchor test clearly and directly represents the common elements in the objectives of the specific course. When anchoring is based on some more indirect indicator of competence, such as general gradepoint av-

---

* The frequency distribution was designed so the letter breaks come out at even class-intervals, which would not ordinarily be the case with real data.

Table 15.2
GRADE DISTRIBUTION IN THREE SECTIONS

			Section I		Section II		Section III	
Grade	Score	Total	No.	%	No.	%	No.	%
A	75–89	22	6	15	13	26	3	5
B	65–74	38	11	28	15	30	12	20
C	55–64	60	10	25	12	24	38	63
D	40–54	22	11	28	6	12	5	8
F	Below 40	8	2	5	4	8	2	3

erage or a measure of scholastic aptitude, it may seem reasonable to temper the variation among groups based on this indirect indicator, letting each group regress somewhat closer to the general average. Thus, in our illustration, section II would be allocated more than 15 percent of As but less than 26 percent; section III less than 15 percent, but more than 5 percent. The less directly relevant the anchor measure, the more tempering that would be appropriate—so that general grade-point average might be given essentially no weight in determining what would be an appropriate number of As, Bs, and Cs in, for example, a course in piano playing.

Statistical methods of controlling standards within sections of a course, or even between courses, work reasonably well for large courses with a common curriculum, and for fairly general student groups. They run into difficulties when groups are small or specialized. Under these circumstances, any rigid adherence to certain percentages of particular grades seems unwarranted. Sampling variations in the character of the group from one semester to another will be too large, and variations in the nature of students enrolling for different courses too marked. Under these circumstances, the reference group tends to become the somewhat ill-defined one that a single instructor carries around imbedded somewhere in his cortex of "the typical English 212 student," against which he rates his present class. Clearly, this is a highly subjective, unstable, and individualistic reference frame. However, it is the one that *does* control grading standards in a very large part of contemporary education, and it will certainly continue to do so. When a course is quite specialized or when the student group is one that has quite distinctive characteristics, it may be inevitable that this be so.

SUMMARY STATEMENT

Marks and marking systems are deeply embedded in the educational culture and serve, though limpingly, a number of legitimate educational ends. For this reason, they are likely to survive for some time to come. Among the purposes served with at least a minimal level of success are (1) informing parents about how their child is perceived by the school, (2) helping to form the individual's picture of himself as a learner and to set his goals for further levels of learning, (3) regulating the flow into specific programs and activities within an educational institution, and (4) monitoring admission to later educational institutions and the world of work.

Like any deeply ingrained aspect of a culture, grading and marking practices involve motivations that are only partly accessible to inspection at the conscious level, and are correspondingly resistant to change. Before practices can be made psychometrically more sound, their bases must be brought out and subjected to conscious, even self-conscious scrutiny. Since many, perhaps most, of the issues relating to the assignment of marks are issues of value, an examination of marking practices must address itself first and foremost to a clarification of these values. A few suggestions are offered of psychometric procedures for attaining specific values of equivalence and comparability, if it is decided that these are values worth seeking.

QUESTIONS AND EXERCISES

1. It has been proposed that while the A, B, C, D, F system of grading is relative, a percentage system represents an absolute appraisal. What are the arguments for and against this point of view? Are there any systems of appraisal that are based on an absolute standard? Identify one, and give the evidence to support your position.

2. In what ways is the marking system in a school similar to a rating procedure? In what ways does it differ? What factors that limit the effectiveness of ratings also limit the effectiveness of a marking system? How could the suggestions for improving ratings given in Chapter 12 be used to improve marking procedures in a school?

3. How is the general level of ability of the class that a student is in likely to affect the marks that student will get? How ought it to affect them?

4. What should be the role of student self-appraisal in evaluating educational progress? What are the limits of such appraisal?

5. Try to get copies of the report cards used in one or more school systems. Examine them, and compare them with the cards obtained by other class members. What similarities and differences do you note? What shortcomings do you feel they have?

6. Talk to a school principal or superintendent and find out what changes have been made in reporting practices while he or she has been in the school system. Why were they made? How satisfied is he with the result? What provisions are made for parent-teacher conferences? How satisfactorily have these worked out? What problems have arisen? How well does the present system of marking and reporting serve the functions listed on pp. 589–593?

7. What problems arise when one tries to have marks on a report card take account of aptitude and effort?

8. Comment on the proposition: "A course grade is most useful when it measures as accurately as possible the pupil's mastery of the direct objectives of the course and is not messed up with any other factors."

9. For a course that you teach or plan to teach, list the types of evidence you would plan to consider in arriving at a course grade. Indicate the weight to be given to each. Why have you allocated the weights in this way?

10. You have decided to give equal weight, in a biology course, to (1) a series of quizzes, (2) a final exam, and (3) laboratory grades. A study of the score distributions shows that the quiz SD equals 10, the exam SD equals 15, and the laboratory SD equals 5. How must you weight the raw scores in order to give the desired weight to the three components of the final grade?

11. When is it appropriate to "mark on a curve"? When not? When it is, how should the fraction to get each grade be determined?

12. What steps would you propose to take to reduce differences between instructors in grading standards?

13. In college Y there are 10 sections of freshmen English. What steps could be taken to assure uniform grading standards, so that a student is not penalized by being in a particular section?

14. It has been proposed that "schools should abandon marks and report only 'Pass' and 'Fail' for students." What would be the gains from such a procedure? What would be the losses? How would the functions now served (admittedly imperfectly) by marks be discharged? How adequate would these alternative procedures be?

15. A school principal remarked to his board of education: "We have higher standards than Mason High. Our passing mark is 70, and theirs is only 65." What assumptions is he making in this statement? How defensible are they?

16. It has been suggested that marks must be approached as a cultural rather than a psychometric phenomenon. What merit is there in this point of view? What are some of its implications?

SUGGESTED ADDITIONAL READING

Adkins, Dorothy C. *Test construction* (2nd Ed.) Columbus, Ohio: Charles E. Merrill, 1974, Ch. 9.

Austin, D. B. Grading systems. In L. C. Deighton (Ed.), *The Encyclopedia of Education*, Vol. 4. New York: Macmillan and Free Press, 1971, 181–185.

Baurenfeind, Robert H. Goal cards and the measurement of educational progress. In David A. Payne and Robert F. McMorris

(Eds.), *Educational and Psychological Measurement.* (2nd Ed.) Morristown, N. J.: General Learning Press, 1975.

Baurenfeind, Robert H. Grading on the bulb. *Measurement and Evaluation in Guidance,* 1973, 5, 483–487.

Cureton, Louise W. The history of grading practices. *Measurement in Education.* East Lansing, Mich.: National Council on Measurement in Education, 1971.

Gilman, David Alan. The economics and psychology of the report card. *Measurement and Evaluation in Guidance,* 1974, 7, 157–162.

Goldman, R. D., D. E. Schmidt, B. N. Hewitt, and R. Fisher. Grading practices in different major fields. *American Educational Research Journal,* 1974, 11, 343–357.

Goldman, Roy D. and Barbara Newlin Hewitt. Adaptation-level as an explanation for differential standards in college grading. *Journal of Educational Measurement,* 1975, 12, 149–161.

Gronlund, Norman E. *Improving marking and reporting in classroom instruction.* New York: Macmillan, 1974.

Hiner, N. R. An American ritual: Grading as a cultural function. *The Clearing House,* 1973, 47, 356–361.

Hoyt, D. P. The relationship between college grades and adult achievement. *ACT Research Reports,* No. 7, Iowa City, Iowa: The American College Testing Program, 1965.

Hunt, Richard A. Student grades as a feedback system: The case for a confidential multiple grade. *Measurement and Evaluation in Guidance,* 1972, 5, 345–359.

Kindsvatter, R. Guidelines for better grading. *The Clearing House,* 1969, 43, 331–334.

Millman, J. Reporting student progress: A case for a criterion-referenced marking system. *Phi Delta Kappan,* 1970, 52, 226–230.

Milton, Ohmer and John W. Edgerly. *The testing and grading of students.* New Rochelle, N. Y.: Change Magazine, 1976.

Pinchak, B. M. and H. M. Breland. Grading practices in American high schools. *The Education Digest,* 1974, 39, 21–23.

Scully, M. G. Grade inflation. *The Chronicle of Higher Education,* October 7, 1974, 9(3), 2.

Soderberg, L. O. Grading: An old problem revisited. *Improving College and University Teaching,* 1974, 22, 244–246.

Terwilliger, J. D. *Assigning grades to students.* Glenview, Ill.: Scott, Foresman and Company, 1971.

Thomas, R. M. Records and reports. *Encyclopedia of Educational Research.* (4th Ed.) New York: Macmillan, 1969, pp. 1104–1111.

Thorndike, R. L. Marks and marking systems. *Encyclopedia of Educational Research.* (4th Ed.) New York: Macmillan, 1969, 759–766.

Warren, J. R. *College grading practices: An overview.* Report 9. Washington, D. C.: ERIC Clearinghouse on Higher Education, 1971.

Warren, Jonathan R. *The continuing controversy over grades.* TM Report 51. ERIC Clearinghouse on Tests, Measurement and Evaluation, Educational Testing Service, November 1975.

Williams, R.G. and H. G. Miller. Grading students: A failure to communicate. *The Clearing House,* 1973, 47, 332–337.

Williams, Reed G., Martin J. Pollack, and Nancy A. Ferguson. Differential effects of two grading systems on student performance. *Journal of Educational Psychology,* 1975, 67, 253–258.

CHAPTER SIXTEEN
SOCIAL AND POLITICAL ISSUES IN TESTING

During the last 60 years standardized testing has expanded in scope and variety to such an extent that at some point it touches the life of almost every person in the country. The school child receives a standardized test battery to appraise his academic progress. If he does very poorly he may be tested with an individual test to help determine whether he needs placement in a special class, and if he does extremely well he may (less often) be tested individually to help appraise whether a program of special acceleration or enrichment is called for. If he aspires to college, he probably takes one or more nationwide college admissions test, and if he goes on to professional school, he may be required to take a specialized aptitude-achievement battery for admission. He may encounter one or more tests as he applies for a job, and will meet a classification test battery if he enters the Armed Forces. If he seeks help in the process of educational or vocational choice, tests may be specified to provide some of the information needed in the process of decision making, and if he comes to a counselor for help with a personal problem tests may still face him.

In view of the wide prevalence of tests in education, in industry and in government, it is hardly surprising that testing, meaning primarily standardized testing on an institutionwide basis, has become a matter of social and political concern. This concern is one manifestation of a more general concern with the rights of the individual citizen and of groups of citizens in our society. That more general concern has manifested itself in many ways in the last generation—in concern for women's rights, in concern for the rights of ethnic and racial minorities, in concern for rights of privacy and the separation of one's private life from one's public or working life. To the extent that results from testing appear to constitute a potential threat to rights of individuals or groups, testing has come under scrutiny and sometimes under attack.

It is our purpose in this chapter to examine some of the dangers and inequities that have been ascribed to testing, to inquire into the merits of the criticisms and see what precautions are called for to meet them, and to try to see how testing can be handled so as to maximize the social and individual values while minimizing social and individual hazards.

TESTING AS A THREAT TO INDIVIDUAL RIGHTS

In what respects should we be concerned with testing as a threat to the rights of the individual, whether a child or an adult? We shall consider the threat under three headings: invasion of privacy, self-incrimination, and physical or psychological damage.

INVASION OF PRIVACY

Recent years have seen an increasing legal and political concern about all types of inroads into individual privacy. The widespread and sometimes apparently irresponsible use of credit bureaus, the advent of computers and data banks in which information about persons can be mechanically and impersonally stored, and a temper that says a person's life is his own business have all sensitized society to any procedure that may probe into an individual's personal being and reveal it to others. Personality inventories have been the most frequent targets of this concern, because the questions that they ask are in their very nature highly personal and potentially revealing. Consider questions such as the following.

Do you have trouble making new friends?
Did you ever want to run away from home?
Do you sometimes have thoughts that are too bad to talk about?

These certainly ask the individual to make public—to whomever will have access to the answer sheet—some quite covert and personal aspects of the respondent's inner life. We may well ask under what circumstances and to whom such revelations appropriately may be called for.

Though the personal inroads are less obvious, a mathematics test that causes a person, in effect, to say "I don't do arithmetic very well" can also be conceived as calling for a personal revelation that the individual might prefer not to make. When is it reasonable to demand such information? Under what circumstances may a social need to know override an individual's right to keep his own secrets? We offer a number of criteria that may be applied, but hardly by any mechanical formula, to judge when it is reasonable to require an individual to demonstrate what he can do or to report what he believes and feels.

1. *For whose benefit will the information be used?* When the information is being assembled in order to provide specific help to the individual who provides it, objection to collecting it will be minimized. Such a situation arises when classroom tests are given and used to identify specific skills on which specific pupils need further practice, or when diagnostic tests are given as guides to planning remedial work as in reading. Such a situation arises when a student comes to a counseling center to seek help in career planning or with a personal problem, and questionnaires or inventories are given to provide the counselor *and* the client with information to help the counseling process. When some general social good is anticipated from the information, as when achievement test data serve to guide a state or city in the allocation of financial resources for education, one is also not inclined to be critical, so long as the demands on the time and effort of the examinees are reasonable. Another type of social good is found in licensing examinations that protect the public from incompetent practitioners of important functions—from driving a truck to removing an appendix.

The most severe restriction of such tests seems to be indicated when the information sought will be used solely for the selfish benefit of some person or group other than the one supplying the information (and perhaps to the detriment of the latter). The most obvious illustration is the use of selection tests and self-report inventories by employers. However, even here it can be argued that it benefits society if individuals in each job are those who will be most effective and most satisfied in that job.

2. *How relevant is the information to the decisions that must be made?* What is its degree of validity? Even when the goal is praiseworthy, there is no point in gathering evidence whose relevance is so limited that it provides almost no help on the decisions that are to be made. And, conversely, the more directly relevant the information is, the more one is justified in calling upon the individual to provide it—always assuming that the uses to be made of it are themselves defensible. Ideally, degree of relevance should have been established by previous research. However, especially in research studies themselves, it may in a number of cases have to be presumptive relevance estimated on rational grounds.

3. *If the information is to be gathered for a social good, how crucial is that good?* A group of students was asked whether it would be acceptable to gather data on job candidates' emotional stability. The percentages saying "yes" for each of several jobs were as follows.

Clerical employee	34%
Airline pilot	75
Astronaut	83

The above difference may reflect in part a judgment of the relevance of emotional adjustment to functioning in the three jobs. But it also almost certainly reflects a perception of the amount of social damage or loss that might result from having a person "blow his stack" in each of the three settings. Society will be well advised to be more uncompromising in the standards that it sets for its surgeons than those it applies to its sausage salesmen. The rights of the individual may have to yield more when the rights of others are crucially involved.

4. *How "personal" is the information that is sought?* Some questions are perceived as much more "nosey" than others. Thus, in a questionnaire study in the context of personnel selection, Rosenbaum (1971) found inquiry about the items below was most often considered to be an invasion of privacy.

Sexual habits	81%
Amount of savings	66
Political beliefs	64
How income is budgeted	63
Frequency of church attendance	60
Description of spouse's personality	59

Topics that were rarely viewed as an invasion of privacy included a wide range of biographical and historical facts about schooling and prior work history, but also evidence on vocational aptitudes (2.5 percent), physical handicaps or disabilities (3.5 percent), work goals (9.5 percent), IQ (9 percent), interests (11 percent), and hobbies (12 percent). Five broad factors were identified in the set of 66 items, and most items could be grouped in these five clusters. The designation of the clusters, and the average percentages considering those items an invasion of privacy were as follows.

I.	Family background and influences	(17 items)	49%
II.	Personal history data	(19 items)	3
III.	Interests and values	(11 items)	12
IV.	Financial management data	(7 items)	52
V.	Social adjustment	(7 items)	16

If these results are accepted, it appears that tests of ability and assessments of interest will be relatively acceptable in this context, while probing personality inventories dealing with matters of politics, religion, finances, and sex are potentially explosive. Possibly in a different context the order might be different, but the results provide a tentative guide as to where invasion of privacy is likely to arise as a serious issue.

5. *Has there been provision for "informed consent"?* One procedure for minimizing the offensiveness of any invasion of privacy is to give a test, questionnaire, or other procedure only after obtaining the "informed consent" of the person, or of a parent or guardian in the case of a minor child. Informed consent implies that the person has been told what information will be collected, why it is to be collected, and how it will be used, and that he or she has then agreed to proceed with the test or other procedure. It implies that the consenter is competent to understand what information is being provided and to decide on the appropriateness of participation. This may be questionable when the consenter is of limited ability or from a limited or different background from that of the investigator. Increasingly, informed consent has been introduced as a federal requirement in psychological (as well as medical) research and service.

Informed consent raises problems both for the tester and the person being tested. For the person being tested, there must exist a genuine freedom to refuse if consent is to mean very much. Thus an applicant who very much wants a job, or a prisoner who feels his privileges will depend upon his cooperation, is under considerable pressure to accept whatever testing (or other) demands are made. Under such circumstances it is especially important that the demands be reasonable in their own right, and that the tester not rely upon consent to justify unreasonable demands.

From the point of view of the tester, one type of problem arises from the word "informed," and one from the very fact of inviting refusal by making consent an explicit positive act. The first problem arises when it is essential that the examinee remain somewhat naive about the nature and purpose of a test procedure. Consider the honesty tests described briefly on pp. 492-494. What would happen to the results on those devices if the tester came in the day before and announced: "Boys and girls, tomorrow we will have some tests to see whether you will cheat, lie and steal." The children are now informed—in a rough sort of way. But the process of informing them will have made their scores meaningless. Their behavior on the tests will have been radically altered. This is an extreme case, but somewhat the same problem arises whenever the purpose of a test— or of a psychological experiment—is to some degree covert and devious. In some situations informing the respondent may destroy his usefulness for the investigation.

The other problem in requiring explicit consent is that it invites refusal, a refusal that might never have arisen if acquiescence in the procedure had been taken for granted. It is particularly in such projects as norming tests or carrying out surveys of abilities or attitudes, in which results for a representative sample are critically important, that refusals and drop-outs are a serious problem. If, as one suspects is often the case, the refusers differ significantly from the consenters, then the resulting sample is biased, and the nature and amount of that bias is usually unknown. The consequent distortion of results may seriously reduce or even destroy their meaning and usefulness.

6. *To what extent may consent be assumed?* We have long operated as though the presence of an individual in a certain role in a certain setting implied permission to gather certain types of information on him. Perhaps the most obvious instance is the largely automatic acceptance of the appropriateness of testing of students by their teacher, both to provide formative evaluations of progress to guide further instruction and to provide summative evaluations in terms of which the teacher judges the adequacy and quality of each student's performance. We have generally considered that the applicant for a job, through the very act of applying, implies consent for the employer to gather certain types of information as these relate to his or her potential value as an employee. The question is: What types of information? Similarly, a person coming voluntarily for counseling implies by that act some willingness to have the counselor probe into his or her inner life. This implied consent is still probably accepted as real, but its appropriate limits are being scrutinized a good deal more critically than they have been in the past.

7. *Is the individual's anonymity protected?* One final factor that mitigates the intrusion into an individual's affairs is a guarantee of anonymity. In most research studies there is no interest in specific persons, and after the data are collected names are no longer needed.* Sometimes no identification is needed even when the data are originally gathered. When this is so, any threat to personal privacy is, of course, very much reduced.

SELF-INCRIMINATION AND RIGHT TO REBUTTAL

A concern related to invasion of privacy, but still distinguishable from it, is that of self-incrimination. In the words of the Fifth Amendment to the Constitution of the United States, no person shall "be compelled in any criminal case to be a witness against himself," and our culture tends to extend this notion to noncriminal contexts. We view with concern procedures that *force* an individual, either because of the pressures brought to bear on him or because of the concealed and indirect inferences that are made from his responses, to give information that will be used to his own disadvantage. Yet we recognize that the individual who seeks some special personal gain—entry to a training program, a job, even bank credit—has some responsibility to justify receipt of that special consideration, and that the attempt at justification may involve some risk. Perhaps a reasonable view might be that the potential gains for the individual should at least balance the demands made upon him for information that may prove derogatory.

When an individual stands accused in a court of law, he has the right to face his accuser, hear the evidence against him, and offer evidence to refute the accusation. One concern with some uses of test data is that this situation does not prevail. The examinee doesn't see his test results, doesn't know how they are being interpreted, and isn't aware of what decisions are being based upon them.† In view of the less than perfect reliability of test scores, the occurrence of occasions when the individual is for some reason "off his feed" and performs poorly, and the reality of occasional scoring, converting, or copying errors in handling scores, the possibility that an individual may be condemned by an erroneous score is sufficiently real for one to

---

* Some longitudinal studies *do* require the continuing identification of persons, and in these studies the protection of anonymity is a special problem.

† Of course, this concern is not specific to test results, but applies to any secret dossier that is maintained on an individual.

wish to give the examinee (or a parent, if the examinee is a young child) an opportunity to see the score and react to it. The reaction might take the form of a description of mitigating circumstances. It might take the form of a request for a retest. It might take the form of presentation of other compensating information. In any event, if the results are made available to, and perhaps discussed with, the concerned individual, it avoids the impression of star chamber proceedings in which the individual is forced to provide information that is then kept secret and used in secret ways. This concern about the secrecy of academic records, including test results, has been crystallized in the Buckley-Pell Amendment, which specifies that school records must be made available to parents and/or students. Implementing this requirement generates some substantial practical problems for schools—and may perhaps encourage them to do less testing and to keep less complete records—but it does also provide a safeguard against the types of faulty test results referred to above.

PHYSICAL OR PSYCHOLOGICAL RISK

A third concern that has been expressed is that testing may perhaps invade the rights of the individual by subjecting the person tested to "physical or psychological risk." It is hard to see how any of the standard psychological or educational tests of the types that we have considered in this book can subject the examinee to *physical* risk that is greater than the normal hazards of living. However, there may be some possibility of increased psychological risk. Tests can be somewhat anxiety provoking. Personality inventories may raise issues and set the individual to thinking about aspects of his or her feelings and actions that provoke worry. Poor performance on an ability test may be damaging to a person's self-esteem. If some extra anxiety, worry, or self-derogation are considered to represent psychological hazards, it must be acknowledged that test taking and test results may at times contribute to them. The problem is to judge the severity of the hazard and to balance it against the countervailing benefits either to the person tested or to the larger society in which that person will function.

A somewhat different type of risk is that which may be attendant upon classifying or categorizing the individual (Hobbs, 1975). All of us have a natural, but sometimes regrettable, tendency to try to simplify the infinite complexity of the world by placing events—and persons—in categories to which labels can be attached, and then dealing with the event or person as a representative of the class rather than as an individual. This labeling carries with it a cluster of implications as to what the person is like, can do, and can be expected to become. A host of such implications attach to such a label as "mentally retarded," "specific learning disability," "emotionally disturbed," or "delinquent," and the label carries with it prospects for the future treatment of that person in the educational and the social system.

Labeling is at best an oversimplified description, even when the label is appropriately applied. Furthermore, many labels are likely to be thought of as explanations, rather than simply as descriptive classifications. Instances of mislabeling are a particular matter of concern, and the prospect that test results may frequently play a role in mislabeling persons from economically depressed or culturally different backgrounds is one basis for concern about hazard to the individual as a result of testing.

Those of us who make tests, and those of us who use them, must be continuously on guard against the tendency to label and to categorize glibly. We must continuously insist that a test score is *one descriptive* fact about a person, and that this fact can only be fully understood in terms of the total past and present context of the person. It is an exacting challenge to all who work in the helping professions—teachers, counselors, social workers—to know each pupil or client thoroughly enough, and to put all the information together wisely enough so that the person is understood and helped, and not merely labeled.

POSSIBLE HAZARDS TO RIGHTS OF GROUPS

A concern is sometimes expressed that tests may be used to deprive certain groups of a fair chance to receive certain social goods, especially educational and job opportunities. To the extent that tests are used mechanically as selection and placement devices, and to the extent that certain groups in our society—ethnic and racial minorities or poor people more generally—do less well on those tests, tests *do* become the instruments through which access to education and jobs is disproportionately barred to members of these groups. The question that must be faced is whether they are unjustly barred, and, more generally, what constitutes fair and equitable use of tests in personnel selection, placement, and classification.

The question of fair use has its psychometric side when one inquires into the relationship between test scores and job performance, both within groups and between different ethnic or socioeconomic groups. But it also has a philosophical and political side when one asks what values society accepts as desirable goals for a system of personnel allocation and utilization. How much weight should the U. S. society give to maximizing productivity of its educational or industrial establishment (in whatever terms "productivity" is defined)? How much weight should it give to balancing opportunity between different segments of the society, or to extinguishing any existing educational and occupational differentials? Psychometric research may be able to provide some, admittedly crude, estimates of the cost in productivity of forcing numerical equality among groups in selection and placement decisions, but purely psychometric research cannot say whether the cost in relation to one type of value is justified by the gain in quite a different value.

POSITIVE VALUES THAT TESTING IS DESIGNED TO ACHIEVE

So far we have considered primarily the hazards and problems that may arise from the use of tests so far as the individual is concerned and so far as groups in our society are concerned. However, there is another side of the coin. Testing is carried out to a considerable extent to achieve positive outcomes both for the individual and for the larger society. We should now turn our attention to a consideration of those positive outcomes. Then, finally, we may try to reconcile the hazards and the gains and see what kind of approach to the use of test results will accomplish the most in terms of positive values and the least in terms of hazards.

INDIVIDUAL GOODS THAT TESTING MAY ACHIEVE

At various points in this book we have spoken of testing in relation to decisions—to the decisions that are inevitably going to be made for a person or by a person in the course of education and life. The credo of those of us who make tests or teach about tests is that the use of tests will permit (but certainly not guarantee) better, wiser decisions.

Decisions about a person, concerning primarily the most effective content and method for educating that person. For the last 70 years educators and psychologists have recognized that persons show substantial differences in learning capabilities and learning styles. Educators have tried in various ways to adapt to these differences and to individualize instruction. Any attempt to adapt instruction to the characteristics of a specific person means a whole series of decisions as to what pattern of instruction is best suited to that person at a given moment in time. How rapidly and in what way should a child be introduced to reading? Should a child be taught arithmetic primarily by a "discovery" approach or by practice and habituation? Should a child be taught algebra, and if so when and at what tempo? These are decisions that have to be made if instruction is to be anything but a lock-step carrying of everyone through the same sequence at the same rate and in the same way.

Of course these decisions can be based wholly on the subjective judgments of a teacher, aided by such informal tests as that teacher chooses to construct and employ. But there have seemed to be advantages in supplementing those judgments with objective appraisals based on a uniform set of exercises that are systematically related to critical skills or aptitudes and permit comparison with the performance of groups of learners with defined characteristics (of age, grade, sex, etc.). It has become increasingly clear that relationships between human characteristics on the one hand and optimal patterns of instruction on the other are more complex than our formulations have sometimes indicated. It is apparent that we still have much to learn about how and how much to modify instructional materials, methods, or goals to optimize the learning experiences of a particular individual or group. But the problems and decisions exist. Tests comprise one source of relevant information that a wise person can use in making better decisions, and these better decisions constitute one of the important values that we try to achieve through testing.

We have much to learn about the ways in which human characteristics interact with instructional modes to make for effective learning. We have a good deal to learn about techniques of instructional management that will permit different instructional modes to flourish side by side in the same classroom. We have room for improvement of our techniques of diagnosis and prescription for children who have shown specific learning difficulties. But we have made progress, and in this progress testing has played an honorable role.

Decisions about the treatment that a person is to receive are, of course, not limited to educational institutions. To the extent that the staffs of mental hospitals, prisons, and other custodial institutions accomplish more than a purely custodial function, they must determine what each person in their care is like and the focus of each person's problems in order to plan a program of treatment or care that is best for that person. Testing serves as one tool to help complete these pictures.

Decisions by a person, concerning choices and future plans. It is obvious that every person has many choices to make in life that depend upon knowing what sort of a person he or she is. And there is no question that many people feel a need for help in those choices. Help may take the form of information as to what the world is like—what careers there are and what each implies, what types of educational programs exist and what demands each will make. But help may also take the form of telling the individual more about himself—how his abilities, interests, or temperament match the demands of different training or career options. This help to the individual in achieving better self-knowledge represents one of the important values that testing hopes to achieve.

SOCIAL GOODS THAT TESTING TRIES TO ACHIEVE

Testing functions not only in the interests of a specific individual for whom the test results may provide useful information and guidance in that person's educational and vocational career, but also for the social group of which the person is a part. We can identify a number of social problems in which testing can and should play a constructive role.

Protection from incompetence and ineptitude. In a wide range of occupations it is important that all of us be protected from those who cannot perform competently. We see this perhaps most clearly in such a field as medicine. We would all agree that it is socially desirable that medical practitioners be competent and that some guarantees be set up to protect the public from practitioners lacking adequate knowledge and skill. Of the various bases for assuring competence in a practitioner in some field, tests to assess knowledge and the application of that knowledge represent one important component. The field of medicine has seen some most interesting developments in licensing examinations that have involved assessing not only the individual's mastery of the content of the field but also the ability to apply it in diagnosis of individual cases and in prescription of proper treatment. Obviously no test can provide a perfect assessment of performance in a professional or work specialty, but it can provide one important safeguard from the individual who is uninformed or inept.

Efficient use of social resources.   Related to the protection of persons from the incompetent practitioner is the protection of society from the waste of its resources in training individuals who are unlikely to progress in the specialized skill that is involved. Again we can take medicine as an illustration. Medical training is a scarce and heavily subsidized resource, and the provision of the necessary faculty and laboratories for training medical students is an expensive demand upon society. With places for training practitioners at a premium, it becomes important to society that those who are given the opportunity to receive this training be persons who are likely to profit from it and to succeed in the specialty for which they are being trained. The problem is less acute in areas in which the training is less costly and in which shortages are less severe, but in principle the issue of efficient utilization of social resources becomes a good that one hopes to achieve by appropriately valid selection procedures.

Efficient utilization of social resources can be thought to apply not only to training programs but also to resources for production If a worker is ineffective in using expensive equipment for industrial production this represents a social cost, though one that is perhaps less recognized as a general concern of society. However, over the years the improved efficiency of the operation of our whole productive establishment has been one of the goals of personnel testing.

Efficient educational procedures.   Education is an expensive enterprise, and its costs have been mounting. "Productivity" in education is not easy to assess—though performance on well-designed achievement measures provides one indication of the yield from the educational enterprise. However, one has an uncomfortable feeling that there is nothing in education to match the gains in industrial productivity over the last 50 years. Thus it becomes increasingly important to monitor and guide the educational enterprise in order that it may be as effective as possible.

Testing has a role in appraising the outcomes of education, and especially in the evaluation of curricular innovations and instructional changes. It has a role in the routine monitoring of a school's or school system's overall effectiveness. It has a further role in adjusting the program of instruction to the individual learner. For example, during the last 15 or 20 years there has been a good deal of research directed toward the notion of "cognitive style" and particular patterns of learning, implying that information about a specific individual can help us to provide an educational treatment that is more appropriate for that individual. It must be admitted that to this point the amount of clear, verified information on the relationship between learning style and educational treatment is scrappy and limited, but the basic notion seems to be a promising and fruitful one and may be expected to produce improvements in individual instructional procedures in the future.

Discovering talent in all segments of the population. One heartening characteristic of tests is that they characterize each person as an *individual*, and not as a member of any group. The test does not know whether the person taking it is black or white, rich or poor, male or female. It has no preconceptions as to who should do well or poorly, and will recognize ability no matter by whom it is displayed. This is more than generally can be claimed for teachers and other human evaluators, who may entertain strong convictions that the poor generally, or minority persons specifically, should not aspire to or be encouraged to pursue higher levels of education or certain types of career.

As we indicated in an earlier section, there are legitimate concerns that the different backgrounds of some groups in our society may tend to hold down the general level of performance of those groups. But *individual* differences still remain, and tests are prepared to recognize individual talent wherever it occurs. Thus test results may serve as a liberating force to open up opportunities to talented individuals who, because of their group membership, would otherwise have been denied them.

Additions to knowledge. A fifth value to which testing can contribute is the store of potentially useful knowledge about individuals. A science of psychology, and a science of education so far as education can be a science, depend upon knowing how human beings develop, how they learn, how they react to stress and crisis, and what factors influence the processes of growth, learning, and response. Science observes relationships, manipulates conditions, and measures outcomes. Measurement is central to the whole scientific enterprise. Psychology and education are no exceptions. If we would study the conditions that favor mental development, we must measure that development—probably by some type of test. If we would map the factors that foster hostility toward other subgroups in our society, we must measure that hostility—probably by some type of attitude scale. With all their shortcomings, tests of one sort or another play a central role in research on human growth and learning.

MAXIMIZING THE POSITIVE

We have tried to make clear in the previous sections that although there are certain legitimate concerns about the uses that have been made or might be made of test results, there are significant positive advantages to be gained from testing. Under what circumstances will we be most likely to get the gains while holding the risks of negative effects to a minimum? The prescription that we offer may well be a counsel of perfection, at best approximated by fallible human beings, but it seems to us to define the goal for which we should strive. We will use test results constructively in decision making to the extent that we do the following things.

Examine and become clear about all the values involved. Most decisions, whether they relate to one single individual or to a whole class or category of individuals, involve a complex of interacting and competing values. The decision to place a pupil in a special class may mean more efficient learning, but may involve a degree of social isolation from the mainstream of the school. The decision of a student to apply for admission to a particular law school may involve such satisfactions as personal prestige and future economic benefits if admitted, but costs of loss of self-esteem if rejected or if the candidate fails to meet the demands of the program. A personnel selection system may achieve values to the employer of money saved in shorter training programs and in reduced personnel turnover, but at a cost to the larger society of reduced employment opportunities for young persons from the inner-city ghettos. Only as the competing values are recognized and weighed can one decide whether or how tests can contribute to better decisions.

Recognize that test scores are only indicators or signs of the underlying reality that one is interested in. Score on a reading test is an indicator of reading ability, not the reading ability itself. Score on a scholastic aptitude test is one partial indicator of readiness to succeed in school learning. The sign is at best an imperfect representation of the reality. But the underlying reality is only accessible to us through the signs that it gives. We become aware of fever through the clinical thermometer, or more crudely through a hot and flushed face. However, when distorting physical, cultural, or social factors intervene, the significance of the indicator may become modified or blurred.

Recognize test results as only *one* type of *descriptive* data. The key words in this statement are *one* and *descriptive*. Thus in relation to any decision there are many other types of information that are relevant in addition to test scores. A *Stanford-Binet* or a *WISC* may provide one item of information useful in prescribing for a poor reader, but an assessment of visual abilities, information about home circumstances, or knowledge about interests and hobbies may provide other equally relevant data. And the ability test score can do no more than *describe* one aspect of the person's current functioning. By itself, it does not tell *why* he performs as he does, nor make clear what causal relationships that performance bears, for example, to the difficulties that he is having in reading.

Relate test results to whatever else is known about the person or group. No test score exists in a vacuum. The score gains meaning in proportion as the constellation of information into which it is fitted is complete and comprehensive. This constellation includes information about the cultural context of the individual, family background, personal history, physical and health status, and much, much more. There is a very real question as to how fully and soundly the human mind can synthesize such a complex of information about an individual case. (Eventually computers may do it better.) However, wise decisions will result to the extent that *all* the available evidence can be synthesized, weighted, and digested.

Recognize the possibilities of error in *all* types of descriptive data. Reference has been made repeatedly to the measurement error in test scores. We have even had occasion to point out the possibility of gross error in test administration, scoring, or reporting. The user of test results needs continuously to be aware of the approximate nature of any score, and to bracket the score with a band of uncertainty. But it is equally true, though perhaps less explicitly recognized, that all the other kinds of information we have about a person are also subject to error. The teacher's impression of how well Ellen reads, or how popular she is with her classmates, or how interested her parents are in her school success are all rough and fallible judgments. The physician's appraisal of her health, or the social worker's characterization of her home environment, are both subjective, approximate, and fallible. Our decisions are always arrived at on the basis of partial and fallible information, test scores being fallible along with everything else.

In the light of the above, acknowledge the limits of human wisdom, and maintain tentativeness in decisions, to the extent that to do so is realistically possible. Decisions *do* have to be made. But we make them on the basis of partial and fallible data. We make them as best we can with what wisdom is given to us. Some decisions are tactical day-by-day decisions, as in instructing or guiding a specific child, and the possibility exists of promptly changing direction on the basis of continuous monitoring of progress. Other decisions are instrumental decisions that only partially commit one to the future, as the decision to take mathematics courses because of a tentative commitment to later entering an engineering program. The tentative nature of such decisions can be recognized, and redirection can readily be undertaken in the light of future evidence. With other decisions, reversal is not so easy. But for all decisions, whatever the role that test results may have had in them, let us eternally keep before us the caveat: Maybe we were wrong.

SUGGESTED
ADDITIONAL READING

American Psychological Association. *Ethical standards of psychologists.* Washington, D. C.: American Psychological Association, December 1972.

American Psychological Association, Task Force on Employment Testing of Minority Groups. Job testing and the disadvantaged. *American Psychologist,* 1969, 24, 637-650.

Berdie, Frances S. What test questions are likely to offend the general public. *Journal of Educational Measurement,* 1971, 8, 87-93.

Buchwald, A. M. Values and the use of tests. *Journal of Consulting Psychology,* 1965, 29, 49-54.

Cronbach, Lee J. Five decades of public controversy over mental testing. *American Psychologist,* 1975, 30, 1-14.

Ethical principles in the conduct of research with human participants. Washington, D. C.: American Psychological Association, 1973.

Equal Employment Opportunity Commission (EEOC). Guidelines on employee selection procedures. *Federal Register*, 1970, 35(149), 12333–12336.

Fincher, C. Personnel testing and public policy. *American Psychologist*, 1973, 28, 489–497.

National Council on Measurement in Education. On bias in selection. *Journal of Educational Measurement*, 1976, 13, 1–99.

Privacy and behavioral research. Washington, D. C.: U. S. Government Printing Office, 1967.

Testing and public policy. *American Psychologist*, (Special issue) 1965, 20, 857–992.

The myth of measurability. *The National Elementary Principal*, 54, March/April 1975.

The scoring of children: Standardized testing in America. *The National Elementary Principal*, 54, July/August 1975.

Tittle, Carol Kehr. Sex bias in educational measurement: Fact or fiction? *Measurement and Evaluation in Guidance*, 1974, 6, 219–226.

Tyler, R. W. and R. M. Wolf (Eds.) *Crucial issues in testing.* Berkeley, Calif.: McCutchan, 1974.

PERCENT OF CASES FALLING BELOW SELECTED VALUES ON THE NORMAL CURVE

Deviation in Standard Deviation Units	Percent of Cases Falling Below	Deviation in Standard Deviation Units	Percent of Cases Falling Below
+3.0	99.9	−0.1	46.0
2.9	99.8	−0.2	42.1
2.8	99.7	−0.3	38.2
2.7	99.6	−0.4	34.4
2.6	99.5	−0.5	30.9
2.5	99.4	−0.6	27.4
2.4	99.2	−0.7	24.2
2.3	98.9	−0.8	21.2
2.2	98.6	−0.9	18.4
2.1	98.2	−1.0	15.9
2.0	97.7	−1.1	13.6
1.9	97.1	−1.2	11.5
1.8	96.4	−1.3	9.7
1.7	95.5	−1.4	8.1
1.6	94.5	−1.5	6.7
1.5	93.3	−1.6	5.5
1.4	91.9	−1.7	4.5
1.3	90.3	−1.8	3.6
1.2	88.5	−1.9	2.9
1.1	86.4	−2.0	2.3
1.0	84.1	−2.1	1.8
0.9	81.6	−2.2	1.4
0.8	78.8	−2.3	1.1
0.7	75.8	−2.4	0.8
0.6	72.6	−2.5	0.6
0.5	69.1	−2.6	0.5
0.4	65.6	−2.7	0.4
0.3	61.8	−2.8	0.3
0.2	57.9	−2.9	0.2
0.1	54.0	−3.0	0.1
0.0	50.0		

APPENDIX TWO
CALCULATING THE CORRELATION COEFFICIENT

The correlation coefficient is an index that expresses the extent to which two variables (X and Y) go together. It indicates the extent to which high X scores go with high Y scores, and vice versa. But "high" and "low" must be expressed in some uniform terms from one set of data to another if the index is to have the same meaning for different sets of data. The standard framework for expressing "high" and "low" is the mean and standard deviation of the group. If each X or Y score is expressed as being so many standard deviations above or below the group mean, the product of these X and Y *standard scores* is calculated, and the average of these products is obtained, the result is the *Pearson product-moment* correlation coefficient.

This can be expressed by the following formula:

$$r = \frac{\Sigma z_x z_y}{N}$$

where r is the correlation coefficient.
z_x and z_y are standard scores in X and Y.
N is the number of cases.

This is a *definition* of the correlation coefficient. However it does not provide an efficient routine for calculating the coefficient. In what follows we will illustrate two methods of calculation, one based on hand tallying and one that uses an electronic calculator. We will illustrate each with the data from the reading and arithmetic scores given in Table 2.1.

First we show a procedure for hand tallying and computing the coefficient from a bivariate (two-dimensional) scatter plot.

Step 1. Select class intervals for both of the variables.

In our illustration, both arithmetic and reading scores are grouped by 3's.

Step 2. Prepare a two-dimensional tabulation sheet, indicating class intervals for the X variable on the top and for the Y variable on the left of the chart. Cross-section paper or special tabulating sheets can be used with advantage.

The tabulation sheet is shown in Fig. 1. The X variable is the arithmetic score and the Y variable the reading score.

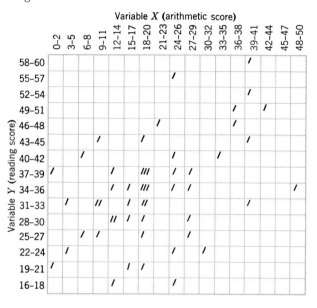

Figure 1

Step 3. Tally the data, entering each score as a tally mark in the cell corresponding to the X and Y score for that case. Count the number of tallies in each cell, and write in the frequency in the upper part of the cell.

Tally marks have been entered in the tabulation sheet in Fig. 1. The frequencies are indicated in Fig. 2 on p. 630.

Step 4. Sum down each column and enter the totals on the bottom edge of the tabulation sheet. Sum across each row and enter on the right. These totals entered in the margin give the simple frequency distribution for X and Y, respectively.

Sums are shown in Fig. 2. The entries across the bottom are for the X (arithmetic) variable and those at the right for the Y (reading) variable.

Step 5. Consider the values entered at the right of the table in step 4. They make up a simple frequency distribution of Y scores. Following Chapter 2 (pp. 42–44), carry out the steps for calculating the standard deviation. Determine N, $\Sigma fy'$ and $\Sigma f(y')^2$.

The values for y', fy', and $f(y')^2$ are shown in the three columns just to the right of the column of frequencies in Fig. 2. For this example, $\Sigma fy' = -7$ and $\Sigma f(y')^2 = 535$. (It may be noted that the Y variable is the reading test, and that these values are identical with the ones calculated for that test in Chapter 2 (p. 43).

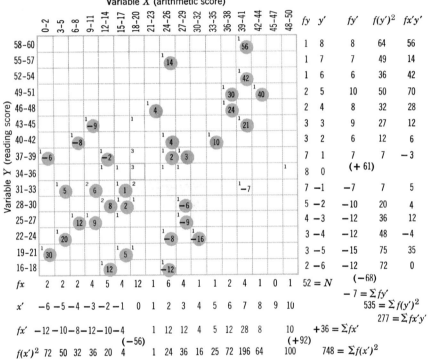

Figure 2

Step 6. Repeat step 5 for the frequencies of the X variable entered at the bottom of the table.

The value of $\Sigma fx'$ is $+36$; $\Sigma f(x')^2$ equals 748.

Step 7. Multiply the frequency in each cell of the two-way tabulation by the x' and the y' values for that cell. Enter this product, i.e., $fx'y'$, in the

These entries have been circled in Fig. 2. Consider the row just above the heavy horizontal rules. Going right from the heavy vertical rules, lower corner of the cell. This procedure will be easier if the column and row chosen for the arbitrary origin are enclosed in heavy rules, to show the zero point for each scale. The frequency in a cell must be multiplied by *both* the x' value for that cell and the y' value.

we come to a frequency of 1 in the second cell. For this cell $f = 1$, $x' = 2$, and $y' = 1$, so the product is $1 \times 2 \times 1 = 2$. For the next cell in the row $f = 1$, $x' = 3$, and $y' = 1$, so the product is $1 \times 3 \times 1 = 3$. Notice that in the upper left and lower right quarters of the table, the products are negative, because either x' or y' is negative. Also notice that all products for cells between the heavy lines are zero.

Step 8. Sum the $fx'y'$ values for all the cells. This gives $\Sigma fx'y'$, the sum of all the products of x' and y' values.

In the example, the values have first been summed across each row, and these sums entered in the column at the far right. This column has then been summed to give $\Sigma fx'y' = 277$.

Step 9. The formula for computing the correlation coefficient is

$$r = \frac{\dfrac{\Sigma fx'y'}{N} - \left(\dfrac{\Sigma fx'}{N}\right)\left(\dfrac{\Sigma fy'}{N}\right)}{\left\{\sqrt{\dfrac{\Sigma f(x')^2}{N} - \left(\dfrac{\Sigma fx'}{N}\right)^2} \times \sqrt{\dfrac{\Sigma f(y')^2}{N} - \left(\dfrac{\Sigma fy'}{N}\right)^2}\right\}}$$

Substitute the proper values in the formula and solve. (It should be noted that the two terms in the denominator are merely the formulas for the standard deviation of X and Y, respectively.

For our example, the solution becomes:

$$r = \frac{\dfrac{277}{52} - \left(\dfrac{36}{52}\right)\left(\dfrac{-7}{52}\right)}{\sqrt{\dfrac{748}{52} - \left(\dfrac{36}{52}\right)^2}}$$
$$\sqrt{\dfrac{535}{52} - \left(\dfrac{-7}{52}\right)^2}$$

$$= \frac{5.33 - (0.692)\,(-0.135)}{\sqrt{14.38 - (0.692)^2}}$$
$$\times \sqrt{10.29 - (-0.135)^2}$$

$$= \frac{5.42}{\sqrt{13.91}\,\sqrt{10.28}}$$

$$= \frac{5.42}{11.90}$$

$$= 0.46$$

With an electronic calculator, one will do one's calculations with the raw (observed) scores. The formula then takes the form:

$$r = \frac{\dfrac{\Sigma XY}{N} - \left(\dfrac{\Sigma X}{N}\right)\left(\dfrac{\Sigma Y}{N}\right)}{\sqrt{\dfrac{\Sigma X^2}{N} - \left(\dfrac{\Sigma X}{N}\right)^2}\sqrt{\dfrac{\Sigma Y^2}{N} - \left(\dfrac{\Sigma Y}{N}\right)^2}}$$

The calculator is used to compute the following sums:

Illustrative Problem

ΣX	1798
ΣY	1086
ΣX^2	66840
ΣY^2	39980
ΣXY	29226

The most efficient way of performing the summations depends on the capabilities of the model of calculator used. Each user will need to learn the capabilities of the calculator available to him.

Substituting the values shown above in the formula we get

$$r = \frac{\dfrac{39980}{52} - \left(\dfrac{1798}{52}\right)\left(\dfrac{1086}{52}\right)}{\sqrt{\dfrac{66840}{52} - \left(\dfrac{1798}{52}\right)^2}\sqrt{\dfrac{29226}{52} - \left(\dfrac{1086}{52}\right)^2}}$$

$$= \frac{768.84 - (34.58)\,(20.88)}{\sqrt{1285.38 - (34.58)^2}\sqrt{562.04 - (20.88)^2}}$$

$$= \frac{768.84 - 722.03}{\sqrt{1285.38 - 1195.78}\sqrt{562.04 - 435.97}}$$

$$= \frac{46.81}{\sqrt{(89.60)\,(126.07)}} =$$

$$= \frac{46.81}{\sqrt{10955.48}}$$

$$= \frac{46.81}{104.67} = 0.45$$

Note that the coefficient calculated from raw scores is not identical with the one calculated from data grouped by class intervals. This will generally be the case, the difference usually being small and of no significance.

SOURCES FOR EDUCATIONAL AND PSYCHOLOGICAL TESTS

There are many agencies that publish one or two tests, questionnaires or other measurement instruments. However, most of the widely used tests are handled by a relatively small group of publishers. The list of publishers that follows includes all those publishing tests that are described in Appendix Four plus one or two others that have a fairly substantial list of titles.

American College Testing Program (ACT)
P. O. Box 168
Iowa City, Iowa 52240

American Guidance Service Inc.
720 Washington Avenue, S. E.
Minneapolis, Minnesota 55414

Bobbs-Merrill Co., Inc.
4300 East 62nd St.
Indianapolis, Indiana 46206

College Entrance Examination Board (CEEB)
Box 592
Princeton, New Jersey 08540

Consulting Psychologists Press, Inc.
577 College Avenue
Palo Alto, California 94306

CTB/McGraw-Hill
Del Monte Research Park
Monterey, California 93940

Educational Testing Service (ETS)
Rosedale Road
Princeton, New Jersey 08540

634
sources for
educational
and
psychological
tests

Harcourt Brace Jovanovich Inc.
757 Third Avenue
New York, New York 10017

Houghton Mifflin Company
One Beacon Street
Boston, Massachusetts 02107

Institute for Personality and Ability Testing
1602 Coronado Drive
Champaign, Illinois 61820

The Psychological Corporation
757 Third Avenue
New York, New York 10017

Psychometric Affiliates
1743 Monterey
Chicago, Illinois 60643

Science Research Associates, Inc.
259 East Erie Street
Chicago, Illinois 60611

Sheridan Psychological Services Inc.
P. O. Box 6101
Orange, California 92667

C. H. Stoelting Co.
424 North Homan Avenue
Chicago, Illinois 60624

Teachers College Press
Teachers College, Columbia University
525 West 120th Street
New York, New York 10027

Western Psychological Services
Box 775
Beverly Hills, California 90213

APPENDIX FOUR
SECTION A

GENERAL ABILITY TESTS

Analysis of Learning Potential

Harcourt Brace Jovanovich   *Testing time:* 50–84 min.
Primary 1, Grade 1; Primary 2, Grades 2–3   depending upon
Elementary, Grades 4–6   level
Advanced I, Grades 7–9; Advanced II, Grades 10–12

Test provides for complete test option, yielding two total scores—learning potential score based on comparisons with examinee's own age group and general composite score based on comparisons with examinee's grade group. In grades 4–12 a reading-mathematics difference score, called "reading-mathematics composite prognostic differential" is also reported. It is also possible to obtain a reading composite prognostic score and a mathematics composite prognostic score. The two total scores are reported as standard scores with a mean of 50 and a standard deviation of 15. Alternate-form reliabilities are quite adequate clustering around .90. Concurrent correlations with achievement batteries range from the .50's to the .70's. The tests are well-normed.

California Short Form Test of Mental Maturity, 1963 Revision (CTMM)

California Test Bureau   *Testing time:* 40–45 min.
Kindergarten–1.5, Grades 1–3, 3–4, 4–6, 6–7, 7–9, 9–12, 12–16

The *CTMM* yields three scores: (1) language IQ, (2) nonlanguage IQ, and (3) total IQ. Only one form of the test is available at each level. Some information is given in this edition of the nature of the

635

factor scores. However, the factor scores are based on a relatively small number of items. The reliability of the nonlanguage subtest tends to be low. The artwork in the nonlanguage section is poor. The language portion of the test has a heavy emphasis on vocabulary. Predictive validity data are not given in the technical supplement but the language IQ and total IQ should have adequate correlations with academic achievement for the higher grades.

Cognitive Abilities Tests (CAT)

Houghton Mifflin Company　　*Testing time:* Primary—40–50 min.
Primary Kindergarten–3　　　　Multilevel—45
Multilevel, 3–13　　　　　　　　for each section

See text pp. 298–301. Nonreading primary test in two levels. Multilevel at eight levels of difficulty. Multilevel provides separate scores for Verbal, Quantitative and Nonverbal sections. Jointly normed with *Iowa Tests of Basic Skills* and *Tests of Academic Progress.* Results reported as Standard Age Scores (Mean = 100, S.D. = 16) and as Grade Percentiles. Reliabilities (Coefficient alpha) range from .89 to .90 for Primary, .91 to .94 for Verbal, .87 to .91 for Quantitative, .90 to .93 for Nonverbal. Three sections show intercorrelations of .65 to .70.

Columbia Mental Maturity Scale: Third Edition

The Psychological Corporation　　*Testing time:* Untimed, usually
Ages 3½–10 years　　　　　　　　requires 15–20 min.

The CMMS is an individually administered mental ability test that requires no verbal response and a minimum of motor response on the part of the examinees. The scale consists of 92 items arranged in eight overlapping levels, with the level to be administered determined by the examinee's chronological age. Each item is printed on a card 6 by 19 inches and requires the examinee to select from a series of drawings the one that does not belong. Raw scores can be converted to age deviation scores, percentile ranks, stanines and maturity index. Reliability and validity data on the revised form (1972) are limited. Young children (4 years of age and below), deaf children and mentally handicapped children tend to have difficulty understanding the oral instructions for the items. The Guide for Administering and Interpreting includes directions in Spanish.

Cooperative School and College Ability Tests (SCAT)

Cooperative Test Division　　　　　　　　*Testing time:* 60–75 min.
Educational Testing Service
Grades 4–6, 6–8, 8–10, 10–12, 12–14

SCAT yields three scores: (1) verbal, (2) quantitative, and (3) total. Manuals and interpretative materials accompanying the tests are excellent. Reliability coefficients are reported for only one form. The total score correlates well with measures of school success, but there is little evidence for differential prediction from the verbal and quantitative scores. Percentile and standard score norms are provided.

Culture Fair Intelligence Tests

Institute for Personality and   *Testing time:* Scale 1, 22 min.
  Ability Testing   Scale 2 and 3, 15 min.
Scale 1, ages 4–8 and older retardates
Scale 2, ages 8–14 and average adults
Scale 3, senior high and college students and adults of superior intelligence.

Scale 1 consists of eight subtests, four of which must be administered individually. Scales 2 and 3 contain four subtests, involving different perceptual tasks, completing progressive series, classifying, solving incomplete designs and evaluating conditions. Raw scores on Scale 1 are converted to mental ages and IQ's; on Scales 2 and 3, they are converted to percentile ranks by age and IQ's. Spanish editions of Scales 2 and 3 are available.

Goodenough-Harris Drawing Test

The Psychological Corporation   *Testing time:* Untimed,
Ages 3–15   usually 10–15 min.

A nonverbal test of mental ability, suitable for use as either a group or an individual test. A 1963 revision of original Draw-a-Man test. Subject is required to draw a picture of a man, draw a picture of a woman and draw a picture of himself. Prospective users of the test should have a copy of Harris's book, *Children's Drawing as a Measure of Intellectual Maturity,* in addition to an examiner's kit. The test was standardized on 2975 children representative of the occupational distribution of the United States in 1950. Raw scores are converted to standard scores with a mean of 100 and a standard deviation of 15. A table is provided for converting standard scores into percentiles. Most of the reliability and validity data reported for the 1963 version apply to the original 1926 test. Within homogeneous age groups, the correlations reported between the 1926 version and the 1963 revision range from .91 to .98. For the 1926 scale, test-retest reliabilities range from .60 to .70; interscorer reliabilities are on the order of .80 to .96 and correlations with the Stanford-Binet range from .36 to .65. No correlations with academic achievement are presented for either the 1926 or 1963 scales.

Henmon-Nelson Tests of Mental Ability, Revised Edition

Houghton Mifflin Company   *Testing time:* 30–45 min.
Grades 3–6, 6–9, 9–12, 13–14

The tests designed for elementary and secondary schools yield a single overall score; the college-level test yields three scores: (1) verbal, (2) quantitative, and (3) total. The total score correlates well with other group tests of intelligence, with teachers' grades and with achievement test results. Reliability coefficients estimated by use of parallel forms range from .87 to .94 for the total score. Normative data for the elementary and secondary school levels and college freshmen are good but norms are lacking for other levels of the college edition. Only percentile norms are presented for the college edition.

Kuhlmann-Anderson Intelligence Tests, Seventh Edition (K-A)

Personnel Press, Inc. *Testing time:* 25-60 min.
Kindergarten; 1, 2, 3-4, 4-5, 5-7, 7-9, 9-12

The *K-A* consists of eight subtests at all levels. The lower levels yield a single overall score; the higher levels yield three scores: (1) verbal, (2) quantitative, and (3) total. Percentile norms and standard score norms (deviation IQ's) are available for each level. Reliability coefficients are generally satisfactory. The difference score between the verbal and quantitative subtests does not appear to have high enough reliability to be used. Data on concurrent validity are satisfactory, but there are few predictive validity coefficients reported in the technical manual. The subtests have very short time limits and, therefore, place heavy demands on the examinees for fast work and on the examiner for accurate timing.

McCarthy Scales of Children's Abilities

The Psychological Corporation *Testing time:* Varies
Ages 2½ through 8½

The scale consists of 18 tests grouped into six overlapping scales: Verbal, Perceptual-Performance, Quantitative, General Cognitive, Memory and Motor. The scale yields scores on each scale that are reported as normalized standard scores with a mean of 50 and a standard deviation of 10. It also yields a General Cognitive score based on 15 of the 18 tests in the battery. Scores on the General Cognitive Scale are reported as a General Cognitive Index (GCI), a normalized standard score with a mean of 100 and a standard deviation of 16. The standardization sample was carefully designed to include equal numbers of males and females and proportional representation by race, geographical region, father's occupational level and urban-rural residence. The median split-half reliability for the General Cognitive Index is about .93 within age levels and ranges from .79 to .88 for the other five scales. Retest reliabilities over a one-month interval for 125 children classified into three age groups was about .90 for GCI and ranged from .69 to .89 for the other scales. Validity data at the present time are somewhat meager.

Harcourt Brace Jovanovich   *Testing time:* 30–50 min.
Kindergarten; 1–1.5; 1.6–3.9; 4.0–6.9; 7.0–9.9; 10.0–12.9

This series is a revision of the *Otis Quick-Scoring Mental Ability Tests* and closely resembles it. It has a spiral omnibus format and yields a total IQ. A very complete technical handbook is provided that describes procedures for constructing the test and gives complete data on validity, reliability, and standardization. Alternate form reliabilities with one or two week intervals range from .81 for age 5 to a high of .94 for age 14 with a median of .92. Split-half and K–R #21 reliability coefficients run slightly higher. Standard errors of measurement are reported for different score levels as well as over-all. Predictive and concurrent validity data are reported and compare favorably with those reported for other instruments. Deviation IQ's, percentile norms, and mental ages are provided.

Peabody Picture Vocabulary Test (PPVT)

American Guidance Service, Inc.   *Testing time:* 15–20 min.
Ages: 2½ years to adult

The PPVT is an individually administered test of vocabulary consisting of a graduated series of 150 plates each containing four pictures. The examiner gives an oral stimulus word and the examinee points to the picture on the plate that best illustrates the meaning of the stimulus word. The PPVT is frequently used as an abbreviated test of general ability. Norms are based on samples of individuals from the age of 2 through 18 years. Raw scores can be converted to three types of derived scores: mental ages, standard score IQ's, and percentiles. Alternate form reliabilities range from .67 to .84 with a median of .77. The median correlation of the PPVT with the Stanford-Binet is .71 and with the Wechsler Scales is .61. The correlations reported between the PPVT and school achievement tend to fall in the .50's.

Raven's Progressive Matrices

The Psychological Corporation   *Testing time:* 30–60 min.
Ages 5 and over

The test is available in a black-and-white and colored form. It represents an attempt to appraise the general ability factor, Spearman's *g*. The tasks consist of designs with missing parts. The examinee chooses from the given options the design that best fits. Although the test is claimed by some to be "culture-fair," there is little evidence to support the claim. There are no time limits. Evidence on the reliability and validity of the test is inconsistent. Test tends to be extremely difficult for young children and reliabilities for the young age groups tend to be low. The manual for the test is inadequate. Normative data at best are sketchy. Most of the norms are based on British samples.

Short Form Test of Academic Aptitude (SFTAA)

CTB/McGraw-Hill   *Testing time:* 31-38 min.
Grades 1.5-12

The *SFTAA* has been designed so that it can be administered in one class period. It is a 1970 revision of the *California Test of Mental Maturity* and yields three scores, Language, Nonlanguage, and Total. It consists of four subtests, Vocabulary, Analogies, Sequences, and Memory. There are five levels of the test that span grades 1.5-12. The *SFTAA* has been concurrently standardized with the *California Achievement Tests,* 1970 Edition and the *Comprehensive Tests of Basic Skills.* Scores are presented in the form of a standard score called the Reference Scale Score with a mean of 100 and standard deviation of 16.

SRA Tests of General Ability (TOGA)

Science Research Associates   *Testing time:* 35-45 min.
Kindergarten-2, 2-4, 4-6, 6-9, 9-12

TOGA attempts to reduce stress on school-learned skills by presenting all test items at all levels in pictorial form. One subtest at each level is supposed to appraise reasoning and the other subtest is supposed to appraise information. Normative samples at all levels are small and *not* representative geographically. The reasoning subtest is claimed to be "culture-fair" but no evidence is presented to support this claim. Concurrent validity data presented indicate that *TOGA* appraises about the same functions as other commonly used intelligence tests and ranks students approximately in the same way. Total score reliability coefficients (split-half) range from .80 to .90 with a median of .87. Directions for administering the test are clear but permit the administrator of the test considerable leeway to alter timing particularly in the information test.

Stanford-Binet Intelligence Scale, Form L-M

Houghton Mifflin Co.   *Testing time:* Varies
Ages 2½ through adult

See pp. 303 to 306 for discussion.

Tests of General Ability: Inter-American Series

Guidance Testing Associates   *Testing time:* 40-60 min.
Preschool; Kindergarten-Grade 1.5;   depending on level.
    Grades 2-3; Grades 4-6; Grades 7-9; Grades 10-13.5

The objective of the author was to produce a series of tests that are parallel in English and Spanish and that yield comparable results when the Spanish edition is administered to Spanish-speaking people and the English edition is administered to English-speaking people. Identical items are used on the two versions. The items are of the type typically found in general ability tests. Norms are presented only for samples drawn entirely from Puerto Rico. Alternate-form reliabilities for the English version total score range from .72 to .90 with a median value of .80 and for the Spanish edition, they range from .59 to .91 with a median value of .88. Concurrent correlations with achievement are reported. The two editions, according to reviewers, are not equivalent and the Spanish edition is not viewed as being equally applicable to all Spanish-speaking minorities on the mainland of the United States.

Wechsler Adult Intelligence Scale

16 years & over

Wechsler Intelligence Scale for Children—Revised

Ages 6½ to 16½

Wechsler Preschool and Primary Scale of Intelligence

Ages 4 to 6½ years

The Psychological Corporation   *Testing time:* Varies

See pp. 306 to 309 for discussion of these tests.

APTITUDE TEST BATTERIES

Differential Aptitude Test Battery

The Psychological Corporation   *Testing time:* 300–330 min.
Grades 8–12

See text, pp. 355–359 for discussion. This is a practical guidance battery for high-school use. It has an extremely full and well-organized manual. Extensive validation data are presented against educational criteria, but little against vocational criteria. Claims for validity are modest and realistic.

Employee Aptitude Survey

Psychological Services, Inc.   *Testing time:* 55 min.
Adult employees, but Grade 9 and above could take

A set of 10 brief tests (9 of 5 min., 1 of 10 min.) designed for use in employee selection. Tests are made short to fit the realities of industrial testing. Occupational norms are provided for 45 groups. Fairly extensive occupational validity data. Good technical manual.

Flanagan Aptitude Classification Tests (FACT)

Science Research Associates   *Testing time:* 210–328 min.
Grades 12–16 and above

This battery consists of nineteen tests and is essentially oriented toward vocational guidance rather than educational guidance. Each test is in a separate booklet and has a self-scoring answer sheet. Construction of test items appears to be very good. Reliability coefficients for separate tests tend to be low, but composite scores have adequate reliability. The greatest weakness in the battery is its lack of validity data to support many of the claims made in the manual and in accompanying materials. Until more validity data are available, it would probably be best to be extremely cautious in interpreting the meaning of the scores.

General Aptitude Test Battery

U. S. Employment Service   *Testing time:* 120–150 min.
Grades 12 and above and adults   for group tests

See text, pp. 359–363, for discussion of this battery. It is available only for use by State Employment Offices.

Nonreading Aptitude Test Battery, 1969 Edition (NATB)

United States Employment Service   *Testing time:* 190 min.
Educationally limited students in grades 9–12 and adults

The battery is an adaptation of GATB (see pp. 359 to 363) designed for high school students and adults with limited reading ability.

SRA Primary Mental Abilities, Revised (PMA)

Science Research Associates   *Testing time:* 65–75 min. (2–4)
Kindergarten–1, Grades 2–4,   50–107 min. (4–6)
  4–6, 6–9, 9–12   35–75 min. (6–9, 9–12)

Although this instrument, yielding 4 subscores as well as a total score (except in the form for grades 4–6, which yields 5 subscores), is promoted in terms of the differential information provided by the part scores, evidence of differential validity is scanty and most data are for the total score. Only one form is available, and for this test-retest reliabilities of total score are in the .80's or low .90's. Data on subtest validities, reliabilities, and norms are meager.

READING TESTS

Davis Reading Test

The Psychological Corporation   *Testing time:* 45–55 min.
Grades 8–11; 11–12

The test yields two scores, (1) level of comprehension, and (2) speed of comprehension. Items on the test are well constructed and measure the subtler aspects of reading comprehension. The equivalent form reliabilities are in the high .70's or low .80's. Correlations between the scores on the reading tests and grades in English average about .50. Standard score norms and percentile norms are provided.

Diagnostic Reading Tests: Survey Section

Science Research Associates   *Testing time:* 60–70 min.
Grades 4–8; Grades 7–13   175–200 min.

The level for grades 4–8 yields 5 scores: (1) word recognition, (2) comprehension, (3) vocabulary, (4) story reading, and (5) total. The level for grades 7–13 also yields 5 scores: (1) rate of reading, (2) story comprehension, (3) vocabulary, (4) comprehension, and (5) total. Manuals accompanying the tests are very difficult to comprehend and contain very little information on reliability and norming procedures. The manuals for administration are somewhat vague about time limits. Normative data are provided on separate mimeographed sheets with no description of the nature of the normative group. Although the tests have some interesting approaches to the appraisal of reading skills, the lack of reliability data, the inadequacy of the normative data, and the poor quality of reproduction would argue against wide use of the tests.

Diagnostic Reading Scales. Revised Edition, 1972

CTB/McGraw-Hill   *Testing time:* Untimed
Grades 1-8 and senior high school students with reading disabilities

The *Diagnostic Reading Scales* consist of an individually administered series of graduated tests containing three word-recognition lists,
22 reading passages, and eight supplementary phonics tests. The
graded word-recognition lists yield a tentative level of performance
that is used to determine the examinee's entry level to the reading
passages. The reading passages are used to establish three reading
levels for the examinee, Instructional Level (oral reading), Independent Level (silent reading), and Potential Level (auditory comprehension). Complete materials include a reusable spiral-bound book
for use by the examinee, an expendable record form for the examiner, and an *Examiner's Manual.*

Doren Diagnostic Reading Test—1973 edition

American Guidance Service, Inc.   *Testing time:* Untimed, 1 to 3 hr
Primary and intermediate grades

The test is limited to word recognition skills in 12 areas, letter
recognition, beginning sounds, whole word recognition, words within
words, speech consonants, ending sounds, blending, rhyming, vowels,
discriminate guessing, spelling, and sight words.

Gates-MacGinitie Readiness Skills Test

Teachers College Press   *Testing time:* Untimed,
Kindergarten-1   approximately 2 hours

The tests consist of seven parts: Listening Comprehension, Auditory Discrimination, Visual Discrimination, Following Direction,
Letter Recognition, Visual-Motor Coordination, Auditory Blending.
An eighth test, Word Recognition, is included as an optional test.
Norms based on two separate standardizations are given for the end
of kindergarten and the beginning of first grade. Stanine scores are
provided for each subtest. Optional weights for the seven subtests
used to predict success in first-grade reading are given. The total
weighted score is easily obtained.

Gates-MacGinitie Reading Tests

Teachers College Press   *Testing time:* 40-50 min.
Primary A-2nd half of Grade 1; Primary B-Grade 2; Primary
C-Grade 3; Primary CS-second half of Grade 2 and Grade 3

Primary A, B, and C each consist of two subtests: Vocabulary and
Comprehension. Primary CS is a separate subtest of speed and accuracy. The vocabulary items in Primary A and B and the early items

in Primary C consist of a picture followed by a choice of four words, one of which is illustrated by the picture. The later items in Primary C consist of a stimulus word followed by a choice of four words, one of which means the same as the stimulus word. The items on Primary A and B Comprehension test consist of a sentence or short paragraph accompanied by a panel of four pictures from which the examinee is to select the one that best illustrates the meaning of the sentence or paragraph. The items in Primary C consist of a short paragraph followed by two questions with a choice of four answers to each question. The Speed and Accuracy test consists of a short paragraph ending in a question or incomplete statement, followed by a choice of four words from which the examinee selects the one word that best completes the statement or answers the question. The tests yield standard scores, percentile scores, and grade scores. Norms are available for beginning, middle, and end of year testing. A revised edition will be available in 1976.

Gates-MacGinitie Reading Tests

Teachers College Press *Testing time:* 45 min.
Survey D–Grades 4,5,6; Survey E, Grades 7,8,9;
   Survey F, Grades 10,11,12

Each battery consists of three subtests: Vocabulary, Comprehension, and Speed and Accuracy. The Vocabulary items consist of a test word followed by a choice of five words, one of which is similar in meaning to the test word. The Comprehension items consist of passages into which blank spaces have been introduced. For each blank space, a choice of five completions is given; the examinee is to choose the one that best conforms to the meaning of the passage. The items on the Speed and Accuracy test consist of a short paragraph ending in a question or incomplete statement, followed by a choice of four words from which the examinee selects the word that best answers the question or completes the statement. Norms are provided for beginning, middle and end-of-year testing. Raw scores can be converted to standard scores, percentiles, stanines or grade scores. A revised edition will be available in 1976.

Gates-McKillop Reading Diagnostic Test

Teachers College Press *Testing time:* Untimed,
All grades about 1 hr

A battery of 17 tests designed to help the reading specialist isolate and analyze specific areas of reading difficulty. The tests are individually administered and the examinee gives his or her responses orally. The following skills and techniques involved in the process of reading are tested: oral reading which yields analyses of 10 different types of error; word perception; phrase preception; blending word parts; giving letter sounds; naming letters; recognizing visual forms of sounds such as nonsense words, initial letters, final letters, and vowels; auditory blending; spelling; oral vocabulary; syllabication; and auditory discrimination. Not all examinees will need to be given all the tests. Two forms of the test are available. Raw scores can be converted to grade scores, age scores or ratings of high, normal or low.

Iowa Silent Reading Tests, 1973 Edition

Harcourt Brace Jovanovich
Level 1, Grades 6-9; Level 2, Grades 9-14;
  Level 3, for academically accelerated
  high school and college students

Testing time: Levels 1 and 2,
  1 hr, 20 min.
  Level 3, 56 min.

All levels of the test appraise vocabulary, reading comprehension and speed of reading with comprehension. Levels 1 and 2 also appraise use of reference materials and skimming and scanning for specific information. Two forms of the tests are available at each level. Raw scores can be converted to standard scores, percentile ranks and stanines. A Reading Efficiency Index, an index of reading speed and accuracy, is also provided.

Metropolitan Readiness Test: 1976 Edition

The Psychological Corporation
Kindergarten-Grade 1

Testing time: 80-90 min.

The 1976 Edition of the MRT has two levels, Level 1 for use with groups judged to be low in skill development and Level II for use with groups judged to be progressing normally in skill objectives. This edition includes a practice booklet as an integral part of both levels of the test. Level I consists of six subtests: 1. Auditory Memory, 2. Rhyming, 3. Letter Recognition, 4. Visual Matching, 5. School Language and Listening, 6. Quantitative Language, and an optional test, Copying. The test yields 10 scores, a score on each subtest and scores for visual area (Tests 3 and 4), language area (Tests 5 and 6) and Prereading Skills Composite (Tests 1-6). Norms are provided for November and for midyear of kindergarten, three levels of performance on each subtest; stanines for two skill area scores (visual, language); stanines and percentile ranks for the Prereading Skills Composite and five quality levels for Copying. Special norms are available for large-city school systems.

Level II consists of six prereading subtests: 1. Beginning Consonants, 2. Sound-Letter Correspondence, 3. Visual Matching, 4. Finding Patterns, 5. School Language, 6. Listening and two optional quantitative tests, 7. Quantitative Concepts and 8. Quantitative operations and an optional test, Copying. Level II yields eight subtest scores, auditory area score (Tests 1 and 2); visual area score (Tests 3 and 4); language area score (Tests 5 and 6); quantitative area score (Tests 7 and 8); Prereading Skills Composite (Tests 1 through 6); and Battery Composite (Tests 1 through 8). Norms are available for the end of kindergarten (April) and for the beginning of Grade 1 (September/early October); tables provide stanines for each skill area; stanines and percentile ranks for Prereading Skills Composite (Tests 1 through 6); five quality levels for Copying. National norms for Battery Composite (Tests 1 through 8) and special norms for large-city school systems are available on request.

Nelson Reading Test, Forms 3 and 4

Houghton Mifflin Co.   *Testing time:* 40 min.
Grades 3–5; 5–7; and 7–9

A new form of the Nelson Reading Test that will be available for use in January 1977. Each level consists of a nine-minute vocabulary test and a 25-minute reading comprehension test. An optional 25-minute word parts test for grades 3–5 will contain subtests in sound-symbol correspondence, root words, and syllabication. There will also be an optional brief reading rate test for grades 5–7 and 7–9.

Nelson-Denny Reading Test, Forms C and D

Houghton Mifflin Co.   *Testing time:* 30 min.
Grades 9–12; College; Adult

The 1973 revision, like previous editions, has two parts, vocabulary and reading comprehension. The second part contains a special passage that is used to measure reading rate. Percentile and grade-equivalent norms are available based on regular time limits. Special norms for adults and reduced-time administration are also available.

Primary Reading Profiles

Houghton Mifflin Company   *Testing time:* 70–85 min.
Grades 1.5–2.5, 2.5–3.5

The battery consists of 5 tests: (1) aptitude for reading, (2) auditory association, (3) word recognition, (4) word attack, and (5) reading comprehension. Test 1 is presented as a listening test and is recommended for use to indicate the level of reading achievement that could reasonably be expected from each student. Split-half reliability coefficient for Test 1 is .77 but for the other tests reliability coefficients (split-half) range from .90 to .96. Test 1 has correlations with the other tests of the battery of .45 to .56, and with mental age from the *Stanford-Binet Tests of Intelligence* of .53. Although the value of Test 1 has not been established, the three tests of reading skills appear to be adequate appraisals of reading at this level.

Stanford Diagnostic Reading Test

Harcourt Brace Jovanovich
Grades 2.5–4.5; Grades 4.5–8.5

Testing time: 160–180 min.
110–130 min.

The battery consists of tests of vocabulary, reading comprehension, and word recognition skills. The intercorrelations among the subtests range from .49 to .81 with an average intercorrelation of about .60. Split-half reliabilities average about .94. Standard errors of measurement are not provided by score levels. Data on validity are meager. The test could be useful to a classroom teacher to obtain leads as to the sources of reading difficulties.

Woodcock Reading Mastery Tests

American Guidance Service
Kindergarten through Grade 12

Testing time: 20–30 min.

A battery of five individually administered reading tests; Letter Identification, Word Identification, Word Attack, Word Comprehension, and Passage Comprehension. Two forms of the test battery are available. Both normative and criterion-referenced interpretations are provided. Normative scores include grade scores, age scores, percentile ranks, and standard scores. The criterion-referenced score scale attempts to indicate probable success that the examinee will have with reading tasks at different levels of difficulty. Only split-half reliabilities are reported and only for grades 1, 4 and 10. These tend to be in the high .90's for each test and for the total score. Validity data are lacking.

SECTION
D

ACHIEVEMENT BATTERIES

Adult Basic Learning Examination (ABLE)

The Psychological Corporation   *Testing time:* Levels I and II
Adults   are untimed;
                                                               Level III,
                                                               3 hr, 25 min.

ABLE is a group test designed to measure adult achievement in basic skills using subject matter drawn from adult life. The test provides measures of vocabulary, reading comprehension, spelling, arithmetic computation and problem solving skills. Three levels of the test are available at different levels of difficulty with alternate forms at each level. A short screening test is available for use in determining the appropriate level of test to administer to an examinee. Cassettes are available for test administration. Raw scores can be converted to grade scores at Levels I and II and to percentile ranks and stanines at Level III. Score distributions for Adult reference groups are available for each level.

Boehm Test of Basic Concepts

The Psychological Corporation   *Testing time:* 30–40 min.
Kindergarten–Grade 2

Tests are available in both an English and a Spanish edition. The content of the test consists of concepts considered important for the understanding and following of directions that are commonly given by teachers or appear in curriculum materials at kindergarten or first and second grades. The test items, 50 in total, appear to be too easy to discriminate levels of achievement among first grade children from middle or higher socioeconomic levels or for second grade children at any socioeconomic level. Reported reliability coefficients range from .68 to .90. Only content validity is reported but this is adequate for the purposes intended for the test.

California Achievement Tests, 1970 Edition

CTB/McGraw-Hill
Level 1, 1.5-2; Level 2, 2-4; Level 3, 4-6;
  Level 4, 6-9; Level 5, 9-12

Testing time: 1 hr, 54 min.
          to 2 hr, 33 min.

Two forms of the tests, Form A and Form B, are available. The battery yields scores for Reading, Language and Mathematics at all levels.

Comprehensive Tests of Basic Skills (CTBS), Forms S & T

CTB/McGraw-Hill

Testing time: 2 hr, 24 min.
          to 4 hr, 28 min.

Level A, Kindergarten-1.3; Level B, Kindergarten 6 mos.-1.9; Level C, 1.6-2.9; Level 1, 2.5-4.9; Level 2, 4.5-6.9; Level 3, 6.5-8.9; Level 4, 8.5-12.9

CTBS, Form S contains seven levels, A–C, 1–4, spanning grades K–12. The Alternate form T contains four levels, 1–4, spanning grades 2.5-12. Level A is considered to be a preinstructional or "readiness' instrument. The total Prereading score for Level A is derived from seven tests, Letter Forms, Letter Names, Listening for Information, Letter Sounds, Visual Discrimination, Language, and Sound Matching. It also includes a mathematics score. Level B has been designed for students who have received one year of instruction and yields four scores, a Total Reading Score, a Total Language Score, a Total Mathematics Score, and a Total Battery Score. Levels C, 1,2,3, and 4 are composed of 10 separate subtests that yield scores in Total Reading, Total Language, Total Mathematics, Reference Skills (except at Level C), Science, and Social Studies. The Total Reading, Total Language and Total Mathematics scores are combined to yield a Total Battery Score. Booklets at Levels A, B, C and 1 are available for machine scoring or hand scoring. Booklets at Levels 2, 3, and 4 are all reusable since separate answer sheets are used.

Content Evaluation Series

Houghton Mifflin Co.
Grades 7-12

Testing time: Varies

The *Content Evaluation Series* consists of a group of standardized end-of-year tests designed to assess student status in specific subject matter areas. Tests are available in the following areas: Language Art (Language Ability, Composition, Literature), Mathematics, Science, Modern Algebra, Agribusiness, Modern Geometry, Economics, and Office Information and Skills. The tests can be bought separately.

Educational Skills Tests, College Edition

CTB/McGraw-Hill
Entering college students

Testing time: English, 1 hr, 45 min.
Mathematics, 45 min.

These tests, one for English and one for Mathematics, are designed for placement of entering college students. The subtests of the English tests are Sounds, Comprehension I, Comprehension II, Organization of Ideas, and Mechanics of Writing. The subtests of the Mathematics test are Basic Information, Computation, and Problem Analysis.

Iowa Tests of Basic Skills, Primary Battery, Forms 5 and 6

Houghton Mifflin Co.
Level 7, Grades 1.7–2.5
Level 8, Grades 2.6–3.5

Testing time: Standard edition,
3 hr, 32 min.
Basic edition,
1 hr, 53 min.

The primary battery is a downward extension of the *Iowa Tests of Basic Skills.* Two editions are available; the Basic Edition consists of six subtests: Vocabulary, Word Analysis, Reading Comprehension, Spelling, Mathematics Concepts, and Mathematics Problems. The Standard Edition consists of these same six subtests plus Listening, Capitalization, Punctuation, Usage, Maps, Graphs and Tables, and References. Most subtests in the Primary Battery are administered orally to separate reading skills from those functions not related directly to reading. The tests are untimed. Two types of norms are available, percentile ranks and grade equivalents. Special percentile norms for large city and Catholic schools are available from the publisher. Both editions are available in machine-scorable or hand-scorable booklets.

Iowa Tests of Basic Skills (ITBS)

Houghton Mifflin Company
Grades 3–9

Testing time: 280–335 min.

The *ITBS* uses a multilevel format, with a single spiral-bound reusable test booklet for all grades. Test level is controlled by starting and stopping at different points. The battery yields 15 scores: vocabulary (one score), reading comprehension (one score), language (four subscores and one total score), work-study skills (three subscores and one total score), arithmetic skills (two subscores and one total score), and composite score. The battery emphasizes the appraisal of functional skills needed by the child if he is to make progress in school. Reliabilities of the subtests are adequate and, of the total tests, are high. Procedures for norming the test were excellent. The *ITBS* and the *Cognitive Ability Tests* were normed simultaneously and percentile norms by ability level are provided in a supplementary manual. In addition to general national norms, special percentile norms are provided for building averages, geographical region, large cities, and Catholic schools. The manuals are excellent—particularly the ones for the teacher and for the administrator. A modern mathematics supplement is available for use in addition to or to replace the arithmetic skills tests in the regular battery.

Iowa Tests of Educational Development (ITED)

Science Research Associates   *Testing time:* 330–540 min.
Grades 9–12

The battery consists of 9 subtests: (1) understanding the basic social concepts, (2) general background in the natural sciences, (3) correctness and appropriateness of expression, (4) ability to do quantitative thinking, (5) ability to interpret reading materials in the social studies, (6) ability to interpret reading materials in the natural sciences, (7) ability to interpret literary materials, (8) general vocabulary, and (9) uses of sources of information. The battery yields 10 scores, one for each subtest and a composite total score based on the first 8 subtests. Predictive validity data and concurrent validity data are provided. Correlations between composite scores obtained in grades 10, 11 or 12 and grades in the freshman year of college range from .40 to .71 with a median of approximately .60. Internal consistency reliabilities are satisfactory. Correlations between scores on the third edition and fourth edition taken one year apart are mostly in the .80's. Correlations among subtests tend to be high in the .70's; therefore, the value of the tests as a diagnostic instrument is questionable. Standard scores, percentiles, and percentile bands are provided.

1970 Metropolitan Achievement Tests

Harcourt Brace Jovanovich   *Testing time:* Varies by level
Primer, Grades K.7–1.4;   from 1 hr, 10 min.
  Primary I, grades 1.5–2.4;   to 4 hr, 30 min.
  Primary II, grades 2.5–3.4;
  Elementary, grades 3.5–4.9;
  Intermediate, grades 5.0–6.9;
  Advanced, grades 7.0–9.5

Primer battery consists of three subtests: Listening for Sounds, Reading, and Numbers. Primary I battery consists of five subtests: Word Knowledge, Word Analysis, Reading, Mathematics Computation, and Mathematics Concepts. The Primary II battery has same subtests as Primary I and adds Spelling and Mathematics Problem Solving. All the other batteries consist of seven subtests: Word Knowledge, Reading, Language, Spelling, Mathematics Computation, Mathematics Concepts, and Mathematics Problem Solving. Science and Social Science subtests are also available for the Intermediate and Advanced Batteries. Raw scores can be converted to standard scores, grade equivalents, percentile ranks, and stanines. Norms are available for fall and spring testing. Two forms of the Primer level and three forms of all the other levels are available.

Sequential Tests of Educational Progress (STEP)

Cooperative Test Division   *Testing time:* 450–500 min.
Educational Testing Service
Grades 4–6; 7–9, 10–12, 13–14

The battery consists of six tests: (1) reading, (2) writing, (3) mathematics, (4) science, (5) social studies, and (6) listening. The tests are supposed to provide a continuous standard score scale to appraise growth in achievement from grade 4 through 14. Critics of the test have raised questions about the equivalence of the scale over the different levels. Norms are presented in terms of percentile bands. Manuals and handbooks for the battery are excellent.

SRA Achievement Series

Science Research Associates   *Testing time:* 270–450 min.
Grades 1–2; Grades 2–4; Grades 4–9

The levels of the test designed for use in grades 1–2 and grades 2–4 are published as separate batteries; the one designed for grades 4–9 is published in a multilevel format. Reading and arithmetic skills are appraised at all levels; a subtest in language arts is added at grades 2–4 and all higher levels; and subtests in social studies and science are added at grades 4 and above. A test of work-study skills is provided as a supplement at grades 4 and above. The tests are very attractive and make good use of color. In the multilevel battery, answer sheets for different grades are color coded. The tests in science and social studies tend to emphasize recall of factual information. Vocabulary is appraised only in context of a reading selection. Reliability coefficients (K–R #20) are satisfactory but may be somewhat inflated. Grade equivalent, percentile, and stanine norms are provided at all grade levels. Procedures for norming, establishing the content of the tests, and determining reliability are inadequately reported.

SRA Assessment Survey

Science Research Associates   *Testing time:* Varies with level
Grades 1 through 12

A norm-referenced program service consisting of six overlapping levels: Primary Edition of the SRA Achievement Series, grades 1–4; Multilevel Edition of the SRA Achievement Series, grades 4–9 and the Iowa Test of Educational Development (ITED), grades 9–12. Each level has subtests in reading, language arts and mathematics.

The Multilevel Edition and the ITED also includes tests in social studies, science, and use of reference sources.

1973 Stanford Achievement Test Series

Harcourt Brace Jovanovich
Primary Level I, grades 1.5–2.4;
   Primary Level II, grades 2.5–3.4;
   Primary Level III, grades 3.5–4.4
Intermediate Level I, grades 4.5–5.4;
   Intermediate Level II, grades 5.6–6.9
Advanced, grades 7–9.5

Testing time: Varies by level
   2 hr, 50 min. to
   5 hr, 20 min.

All levels include subtests on reading, mathematics and language arts. Primary Level II and higher batteries also include Social Science and Science and except for the Advanced Level, Listening Comprehension. Tests are available as either a complete battery or basic battery that includes only reading, mathematics and language arts. Raw scores can be converted to grade equivalents, scaled scores, percentile ranks, or stanines. Norms are available for beginning and end-of-year testing at all grade levels and for middle-of-year testing for grades 1 and 2. Practice tests are provided for each subtest in the Primary Level I through the Intermediate Level II Test batteries. Separate practice tests are also available for all batteries except the Advanced test. Two forms of the test are available.

Stanford Early School Achievement Test (SESAT)

Harcourt Brace Jovanovich
Level I, Grades K.1–1.1
Level II, Grades 1.1–1.8

Testing time: Level I, 1 hr 30 min.
   Level II, 2 hr 20 min.

Both Level I and Level II have the following subtests: Environment, Mathematics, Letters and Sounds, and Aural Comprehension. Level II also has two additional subtests, Word Reading and Sentence Reading. Raw scores can be converted to percentile ranks and stanines.

1973 Stanford Test of Academic Skills (TASK)

Harcourt Brace Jovanovich
Level I, Grades 8–10; Level II, Grades 11–12; Level II, College Edition, Grade 13.

Testing time: 1 hr, 20 min.

Each level of the battery contains threee subtests: Reading, English, and Mathematics. Two forms of the tests are available. Raw scores can be converted to scaled scores, percentile ranks and stanines. Norms are available for beginning and end-of-year testing.

Tests of Academic Progress (TAP)

Houghton Mifflin Company   *Testing time:* 330–340 min.
Grades 9–12

The battery consists of four overlapping tests, one for each grade, in the following six areas: (1) social studies, (2) composition, (3) science, (4) reading, (5) mathematics, and (6) literature. The tests are available in a single booklet or as separate booklets. Three types of norms are provided: standard score norms, grade-percentile norms for individual students, and grade-percentile norms for school averages. The tests were standardized in a coordinated program with the *Iowa Tests of Basic Skills* and the *Cognitive Ability Tests.* Split-half reliability coefficients for the different grades are .85 or better except for the science subtest at grade 9 for which it is .83. The majority of the reliability coefficients are .89 or better. Standard errors of measurement are given for each subtest and for each grade for total score and at selected percentile-rank levels. *TAP* is a well-constructed, well-normed battery of tests that should be useful in a wide variety of secondary schools.

Tests of Basic Education (TABE)

CTB/McGraw-Hill   *Testing time:* 1 hr, 34 min.
Adults   to 2 hr, 56 min.

TABE was adapted from the *California Achievement Tests,* 1957 edition. There are three levels classified by difficulty, Level D (Difficult) is adapted from the junior high level of CAT; Level M (Medium) from the upper elementary level, and Level E (Easy) from the upper primary level. The test was designed to be used with out-of-school youth and adults who have limited levels of ability in reading, language, and arithmetic. Separate tests and scores are provided for reading, language, and arithmetic. A Locator Test is provided to determine the appropriate level of the test to be administered. A new edition of TABE that will be equated to the *California Achievement Tests,* 1970 Edition, will be available in 1976.

Tests of Basic Experiences (TOBE)

CTB/McGraw-Hill   *Testing time:* Untimed
Preschool, Kindergarten, Grade 1

TOBE has two overlapping levels, K and L, and consists of five tests, four of which are related to the curricular areas of language, mathematics, science, and social studies. The fifth test is a General Concepts Test that consists of items drawn from the other four tests plus some items developed specifically for this test. It is recommended that children be given either the four separate tests or the General

Concepts Test but not both. Each test item consists of an oral stimulus and four pictorial responses from which the child is to choose one correct answer. Spanish directions are available for the test. Raw scores can be converted to standard scores, percentile ranks, and stanines.

CRITERION-REFERENCED ACHIEVEMENT TESTS

Customized Objective Monitoring Service, Reading and Mathematics

Houghton Mifflin Co.   *Testing time:* No time limits
Reading, Grades 1-6
Mathematics, Grades 1-8

Like the *Individual Monitoring System* from the same publisher, this service provides a tailor-made criterion-referenced assessment program in reading or mathematics for schools. Schools using the service select the objectives to be appraised from the publisher's *Behavioral Objectives Booklets* and supplemental lists available at regional offices of the publisher. The school using the service specifies the number of items to be included for each objective. The tests are then custom-made for the user by drawing pretested items from the item banks. Booklets, answer sheets, hand-scoring aids or machine-scoring services and other reporting materials are developed on a customized basis.

Diagnosis: An instructional aid series—Reading and Mathematics

Science Research Associates, Inc.   *Testing time:* Untimed
Grades 1 through 6

A series of criterion-referenced tests in reading and mathematics called Probes that have been designed to appraise an individual's specific weaknesses in each of these skill areas. A survey test is provided which is to be used to direct the individual to the Probes needed to give more detailed data on concept and skill deficiencies. The tests are cross-referenced to the SRA individualized instructional programs in reading and mathematics.

Diagnostic Mathematics Inventory

CTB/McGraw-Hill   *Testing time:* Untimed
Grades 1.5–7.5, and students in higher grades needing remedial help

This is a series of criterion-referenced tests designed to appraise 325 behavioral objectives in traditional and contemporary mathematics. The series is divided into seven levels which overlap in terms of the objectives that they measure. Classroom kits are available for each level except Level G. Each kit contains Interim Tests covering 2 to 7 objectives each; an Interim Test Manual; a Learning Activities Guide; a Teacher's Guide; a Guide to Ancillary Materials; a Class Summary Sheet; a Product Overview, and a reorder form. Test results are reported in a number of different ways: Premastery Analysis, Objectives Mastery Report—a class record and an Individual Diagnostic Report.

Everyday Skills Tests

CTB/McGraw-Hill   *Testing time:* Form A, untimed
Grades 6–12   Form B, Reading 30 min.;
                                              Mathematics, 38 min.

These tests have been designed for use as minimum competency tests in reading and mathematics. The *Everyday Skills Tests* are published in separate test books for reading and mathematics. Both the reading and mathematics tests consist of two parts: Part A is a criterion-referenced test and Part B is a norm referenced test. The Reading Test, Part A, appraises 15 objectives with each objective measured by three items. Test B, Reading, is a norm-referenced test of study skills taken from the *Comprehensive Tests of Basic Skills, Form R,* Level 3 (grades 6–8). The Mathematics test, Part A, measures nine behavioral objectives with three items per objective. Test B, Mathematics Computation, is also from CTBS, Form R, Level 3, and consists of 12 items each in addition, subtraction, multiplication, and division.

Individual Pupil Monitoring Systems, Mathematics and Reading

Houghton Mifflin Co.   *Testing time:* No time limit
Mathematics: Grades 1–8
Reading: Grades 1–6

These systems provide criterion-referenced tests in mathematics and in reading. Each set is available in two forms. The Mathematics tests are divided into eight levels; each level assesses performance on 48 to 64 behavioral objectives. The Reading tests are divided into six levels, each containing 43 to 63 behavioral objectives. All items have been tried out on a national sample. Items are related to objectives and not to grades specifically.

The Mathematics objectives at each level are divided among three assessment modules, A–Fall, B–Winter, C–Spring, that correspond to the curriculum typically covered within one-third of a school year. In the Reading series each level has three test booklets designed for three broad categories of skills: Word Attack, Vocabulary and Comprehension, and Discrimination/Study Skills. The system provides for each set of tests, test booklets, Pupil Progress Records, Teacher's Guide, Behavioral Objectives Booklet, the Objectives Cross-reference Booklet and the Teacher's Objective Management Record. Test Booklets for Levels 1 through 3 are consumable whereas all others are either consumable or reusable at the user's discretion. Two types of separate answer sheets are available, insta-mark or hand-scorable. The insta-mark answer sheets are self-correcting but require the use of a special crayon.

Mastery: An evaluation tool

Science Research Associates, Inc.   *Testing time:* Untimed
Kindergarten through Grade 9

This is a criterion-referenced test service in reading and mathematics. Schools and school districts may select objectives to be measured from the publisher's objectives catalogs or may select appropriate levels of catalog tests in reading or mathematics that appraise preselected objectives. The publisher provides scoring services and individual and group reports.

Objectives-Referenced Bank of Items and Tests

CTB/McGraw-Hill   *Testing time:* Untimed
Grades Kindergarten–12

This is a custom service that permits a school or school system to identify the objectives in Mathematics and Reading and Communication that it wishes to appraise and then provides four pretested items per objective for a custom-made criterion-referenced test. The system offers 335 objectives in Reading and Communication Skills and 506 objectives in Mathematics from which customers can choose those most appropriate for their own instruction. The system also provides for scoring services.

Prescriptive Mathematics Inventory

CTB/McGraw-Hill   *Testing time:* Untimed
Grades 4–8

The *Prescriptive Mathematics Inventory* (PMI) is a series of criterion-referenced tests designed to appraise mathematics objectives commonly taught in grades 4 through 8. It is divided into four levels, A,B,C, and D. The four levels cover 351 instructional objectives in traditional and contemporary mathematics. Students record their answers in a machine-scorable answer grid that causes many students difficulty. Five scoring reports are provided: the Individual Diagnostic Matrix, the Individual Study Guide, the Class Diagnostic Matrix, the Class Grouping Report, and the Objective Mastery Report.

Prescriptive Reading Inventory

CTB/McGraw-Hill   *Testing time:* Untimed
Grades 1.5-6.5

The *Prescriptive Reading Inventory* is a series of criterion-referenced tests designed to appraise student achievement of reading objectives that are commonly taught in grades 1.5 through 6.5. It is divided into four levels, A, B, C, and D. The 90 objectives are classified under seven process groups: Recognition of Sound and Symbol, Phonic Analysis, Structural Analysis, Translation, Literal Comprehension, Interpretive Comprehension, and Critical Comprehension. On the average, there are 3 or 4 items per objective. Machine scoring is recommended for all levels because the process of hand-scoring is lengthy and cumbersome. Five scoring reports are available, the Objective Mastery Report, the Individual Diagnostic Map, the Class Diagnostic Map, the Class Grouping Report, and the Individual Study Guide, In addition to the five scoring reports, Program Reference Guides (PRG) are available for each of the reading programs keyed to the *Prescriptive Reading Inventory.* The PRG lists, for all levels, the pages in the textbooks, teacher's editions and workbooks where each objective measured by the PRI is taught. The Interpretive Handbook lists the objectives measured by PRI, provides information on interpreting the reports, and gives suggestions for classroom activities keyed to the objectives.

Sober Español

Science Research Associates, Inc.   *Testing time:* Untimed
Kindergarten through Grade 3

A criterion-referenced test service in reading for Spanish-speaking students. A school or school district can select from 200 objectives in reading those that it wishes to evaluate. A minimum of 10 objectives and a maximum of 30 objectives are recommended by the publisher for each test. The publisher provides custom test booklets and examiner's manuals for each test. All instructions and test items are in Spanish.

INTEREST INVENTORIES

Kuder Form DD Occupational Interest Survey

Science Research Associates, Inc. *Testing time:* Untimed, 30–40 min.
Grades 11–12 and adult

See pp. 411 to 413. The instrument consists of 100 triads. In each triad, the examinee selects one activity that is most liked and one that is least liked. The instrument yields 114 occupational scores and 48 college major scores. Separate scores are reported on female and male occupational and male and female college majors. Scores are reported in terms of the relationship between the examinee's responses and those of successful and satisfied groups in the occupations and the college majors. Answer sheets must be machine scored, but scoring services are quick and efficient.

Kuder Preference Record—Vocational

Science Research Associates   *Testing time:* 40–50 min.
Grades 9–16 and adults

See discussion in text, pp. 410–411.

Kuder Form E General Interest Survey

Science Research Associates, Inc. *Testing time:* Untimed, 30–40 min.
Grades 6 through 12

Similar to Kuder Preference Record—Vocational, the instrument measures the individual's relative preference for activities in 10 job-family groups: outdoor, mechanical, scientific, computational, persuasive, artistic, literary, musical, social service, and clerical. Percentile scores for four norm groups, male and female in grades 6 through 8, and male and female for grades 9 through 12. Booklets can be hand-scored or machine scored.

Minnesota Vocational Interest Inventory (MVII)

The Psychological Corporation *Testing time:* 40-45 min.
High school and adult males

The *MVII* is an empirically-keyed inventory designed to appraise interests in non-professional occupations. It has been designed for use with noncollege-bound high school male students or young adults who have had limited education or had a technical-vocational education. The inventory consists of 158 triads of brief statements describing the tasks or activities in a variety of trades and nonprofessional occupations. It yields scores for 21 occupational scales and 9 area scales that show the examinee's likes and dislikes for activities common to several occupations. Test-retest reliability coefficients for the occupational scales over a 30-day interval range from .64 to .88 with a median reliability of about .82. Validity data reported in the manual consists of differences in mean scores between "satisfied workers" and "dissatisfied workers" and the "percentage of overlap" between the criterion occupation and tradesmen-in-general. The inventory was published in 1965; therefore, it has not been as thoroughly researched and studied as have the *Kuder* and the *Strong*. However, the inventory serves the very important function of providing an interest measure suitable for use with noncollege-bound high school students and similar groups.

Ohio Vocational Interest Survey (OVIS)

Harcourt Brace Jovanovich *Testing time:* Untimed,
Grades 8-13 approximately 80 min.

The instrument is divided into two sections, Student Information Questionnaire and Interest Inventory. The Student Information Questionnaire gathers information about the examinee's occupational plans, school subject preferences, curriculum plans, post-high school plans and vocational course interests. The Interest Inventory consists of 280 work activity items. Scores are given for 24 occupational scales. There is also a score called scale clarity index, which is supposed to reflect the carefulness and consistency of the examinee's answer choices. Raw scores are converted to percentile ranks and stanines by grade and sex.

Strong-Campbell Interest Inventory (SCII)

The Psychological Corporation
Grades 11–12, college, adult

Testing time: Untimed,
approximately 35 min.

See discussion on pp. 405 to 410. The *SCII* Form T325 is a single booklet used for both men and women. Efforts have been made to reduce or remove sex bias in item content and in reporting scores.

Strong Vocational Interest Blank for Men, Revised (SVIB)

Consulting Psychologists Press, Inc.
Ages 17 and over

Testing time: 30–60 min.

Old version of what is now the Strong-Campbell Interest Inventory.

Strong Vocational Interest Blank for Women, Revised (SVIB)

Consulting Psychologists Press, Inc.
Ages 17 and over

Testing time: 36–60 min.

The *SVIB* for women is similar to the blank for men. This version has not been as thoroughly studied as the men's blank, nor does it seem to be as effective as the men's blank.

Vocational Preference Inventory (VPI)

Consulting Psychologists Press,
Grades 12–16 and adults

Testing time: Untimed,
approximately 30 min.

The *VPI* consists of 160 occupational titles to which the examinee indicates like or dislike. The inventory yields 11 scores, 6 of which can be used as vocational interest type scales: realistic, intellectual, social, conventional, enterprising, and artistic. The remaining 5 scales are personality scales: self-control, masculinity, status, infrequency, and acquiescence. The inventory is probably most useful as a vocational interest inventory. The inventory is based on Holland's theory of six personality types. Many reviewers consider the VPI as the best instrument for vocational counseling or research.

SECTION G

The Adjective Check List

Consulting Psychologists Press, Inc.
Grades 9–16 and adults

Testing time: Untimed,
approximately
15-20 min.

The *Adjective Check List* is an alphabetic list of adjectives from "absent-minded" to "zany." The examinee responds by marking the adjectives that are self-descriptive. The instrument can be scored for 24 variables that include 15 needs, measures of personal adjustments, counseling readiness, self-confidence, self-control, and lability. Scoring is complicated because different norm tables are required depending on the number of items checked. Validity data are rather meager; therefore, the instrument is most appropriate for research purposes.

California Psychological Inventory (CPI)

Consulting Psychologists Press, Inc.
Ages 13 and over

Testing time: 45–60 min.

The *CPI* has been developed for use with normal populations. It consists of 480 times to be answered "true" or "false." About one-half of the items on the *CPI* have been taken from the *MMPI*. The *CPI* yields 18 scores, three of which are check scales to determine test-taking attitudes. Items on 11 of the 15 scales were selected on their ability to discriminate contrasting groups. Test-retest reliabilities for high school groups over a year interval averaged .65 for males and .68 for females. Retest reliabilities for an adult group over a one- to three-week interval averaged about .80. Intercorrelations among the scores tend to be high, indicating that the scores are not as independent as the manual tends to imply. Separate norms are provided by sex for high school and college samples. Some of the validity data based on differences between extreme groups are questionable.

Children's Embedded Figure Test (CEFT)

Consulting Psychologists Press, Inc.   *Testing time:* Approximately
Ages 5–12   20 min.

The *CEFT* consists of a series of items that require the examinee to find a simple form in a complex one. The test appraises the dimension called by Witkin field dependence-independence and more recently by others as psychological differentiation. At the present time, the instrument is most appropriate for research.

Edwards Personal Preference Schedule

The Psychological Corporation   *Testing time:* 40–55 min.
College and adults

This test has been designed to assess the relative strengths of 15 manifest needs selected from Murray's need system. Each need is represented by nine statements. The statements representing each need are presented in forced choice format paired with a statement representing another need. The pairs of statements are supposed to be controlled for social desirability. Norms are provided for male and female college students and an adult sample. The representativeness of the adult sample is questionable.

Internal consistency reliability coefficients reported in the manual range from .60 to .87 with a median of .78, and one-week retest reliability coefficients range from .74 to .87 with a median of .83. The *Schedule* has been used extensively in research but consistent validity data are rather meager.

Eysenck Personality Inventory (EPI)

Educational and Industrial Testing Service *Testing time:* 10–15 min.
Grades 9–16 and adults

The *EPI* yields three scores: extroversion, neuroticism and lie. Two forms are available and the author recommends administration of both forms to obtain adequate reliability for individual measurement. The items require a yes-no response. Each form consists of a 24-item extraversion (E) scale, a 24-item neuroticism (N) scale, and a 9 item lie scale. Norms are not differentiated by sex and norm groups are inadequately described.

The FIRO Scales

Consulting Psychologists Press, Inc.

Grades 9–16 and Adults

Testing time: Untimed, approximately 120 min. for all scales.

The *FIRO* Scales are self-report questionnaires designed to assess a person's need for inclusion, control and affection in various aspects of interpersonal situations. There are six scales, each of which focuses on a different interpersonal situation: behavior toward others, feelings toward others, retrospective childhood relationships with parents, coping operations preference enquiry, marital attitudes evaluation, and educational values. In all questionnaires except for coping operations preference enquiry (COPE), the subscales contain nine single-statement items each of which is to be answered on a 6-point scale. The COPE scale is an ipsative scale in which the examinee rank orders the defense mechanisms that s/he uses for each interpersonal situation. Only the behavior towards others scale, FIRO-B, is well enough developed to be used for other than exploratory studies.

Gordon Personal Inventory

Harcourt Brace Jovanovich

Grades 8–16 and adults

Testing time: 15–20 min.

This inventory and the *Gordon Personal Profile* use the same format. Items are arranged in sets of four statements, two favorable and two unfavorable, from which the examinee is to select the one statement that is "most" like him and the one statement that is "least" like him. The inventory yields four scores: cautiousness, original thinking, personal relations, and vigor. Internal consistency reliability coefficients (split-half) of the four scales range from .77 to .84. Validity data consist primarily of correlations between scores on the subtests and performance criteria. However, since there is no theoretical basis for predicting either the direction or magnitude of the correlations, these data must be viewed somewhat skeptically unless they appear for several groups. Percentile norms are provided by sex for high school and college groups and for some occupational groups. The usefulness of the inventory is limited because of the lack of validity data.

Gordon Personal Profile

Harcourt Brace Jovanovich

Grades 9–16 and adults

Testing time: 15–20 min.

The *Profile* yields four scores: (1) ascendancy—A, (2) responsibility—R, (3) emotional stability—E, and (4) sociability—S. Although the four traits were selected as being independent, the correlations between the A and S scales and between the R and E scales are .60

or higher. Reliability is adequate. Validity data reported in the manual include correlations between scores and peer ratings and counselor's trait ratings for college groups. Additional validity data are presented for groups in industrial and training situations. Percentile norms are provided for high school and college students, low and middle level employees, managers, salesmen, and foremen.

Guilford-Zimmerman Temperament Survey

Sheridan Psychological Services, Inc.   *Testing time:* 50-60 min.
Grades 9-16 and adults

See text, pp. 419-423. One of the best inventories for describing aspects of normal personality. Experience is needed to determine whether the dimensions are of practical importance for personal or vocational counseling.

The IPAT Anxiety Scale

Institute for Personality and Ability Testing   *Testing time:* 5-10 min.
Ages 14 and over

The *Scale* consists of 40 items that yield five part scores and a total score. In addition, the 40 items yield separate "covert" and "overt" anxiety scores. Construction of the *Anxiety Scale* was based on extensive factor analytic studies. The validity of the *Scale* is based on the factor analytic studies and external criteria. External validity is based on correlations of total scores with psychiatric ratings (range .30 to .40 uncorrected for attenuation); differences in mean scores between anxiety neurotics and the standardization population; and differences in mean scores among other clinically diagnosed groups.

Reliability coefficients for the part scores, based on subtests with as few as four items and a maximum of 12 items, are too low to justify the use of part scores with individuals. The *Scale* is probably most useful as a quick screening device for literate adults and as a research instrument.

Minnesota Multiphasic Personality Inventory (MMPI)

The Psychological Corporation   *Testing time:* 30-90 min.
Age 16 and over

For discussion see text, pp. 424-426. This instrument is oriented towards abnormal rather than normal groups, and is designed to differentiate between them. There seems to be some doubt that it does this very effectively. It is rather lengthy to use as a screening test. However, the profile based on the separate scale scores provides a good deal of material for interpretation by the sophisticated counselor or clinical psychologist. A Spanish translation of the test is available.

Mooney Problem Check List

The Psychological Corporation   *Testing time:* 20–40 min.
Grades 7–9, 9–12, 13–16, and adults

These check lists provide a systematic coverage of problems often reported or judged significant at the different age levels. Though the items are grouped by areas (health and physical development; courtship, sex, and marriage, home and family; etc.) and a count can be made of items marked in each area, emphasis is placed on using the individual responses as leads and openings for an interview. This instrument does not claim to be a test and the use proposed for it is the type that is probably most justifiable for a self-report instrument.

Myers-Briggs Type Indicator (MBTI)

Educational Testing Service   *Testing time:* Untimed,
Grades 9–16 and adults   approximately 55 min.

The *MBTI* is a forced-choice, self-report inventory that is based on a modification of the Jungian theory of type. It yields four scores: extraversion versus introversion; sensation versus intuition, thinking versus feeling, judgment versus perception. The instrument was originally developed more than 30 years ago and has undergone a number of revisions. It has been most extensively used in counseling and research.

Omnibus Personality Inventory (OPI)

The Psychological Corporation   *Testing time:* 50–70 min.
College students

The majority of the items on the *OPI* have been drawn from other personality inventories, mainly the *MMPI, VC Attitude Inventory, Minnesota T-S-E Inventory,* and the *CPI.* The *OPI* was developed to assess the personality characteristics of college students, especially those who are intellectually superior. The inventory yields 14 scores. Internal consistency reliability coefficients (K–R 21) range from .67 to .89 for the separate subscores. Test-retest reliabilities with a three- or four-week interval range from .79 to .94 for 67 women at three colleges and from .84 to .93 for 71 upper-classmen at one college. Validity data consist primarily of correlations with other inventories and with ratings of various academic groups. Norms for the scales are based on 7283 college freshmen from 37 institutions. At its present stage of development, the *OPI* should be used primarily for research purposes.

Personality Research Form

Research Psychologists Press Inc.   *Testing time:* Untimed;
College students   standard form, approximately 40 min.;
long form, approximately 70 min.

A self-report personality inventory available in a standard edition that yields 15 scores and a long edition that yields 22 scores. Both the standard and long edition yield scores for achievement, affiliation, aggression, autonomy, dominance, endurance, exhibition, harm avoidance, impulsivity, nurturance, order, play, social recognition, understanding and infrequency. The long edition also yields scores on abasement, change, cognitive structure, defendence, sentience, succorance and desirability. The infrequency scale and desirability scale are types of validity scales. Scores are expressed as T scores that are based on samples of 1000 males and 1000 females from more than 30 colleges and universities. The inventory has superior technical sophistication and reviewers consider it to be one of the most promising personality inventories. At its present stage of development, it should be used primarily for research.

Sixteen Personality Factor Questionnaire (16 PF)

Institute for Personality and   *Testing time:* 45–60 min.
   Ability Testing
Age 17 and over

The *16 PF* has been developed to appraise a comprehensive range of traits. The construction of the instrument was based on extensive factor analytic studies and other research. The parent *16 PF* instrument has led to the development of inventories for younger age groups (*High School Personality Questionnaire, Children's Personality Questionnaire, Early School Personality Questionnaire*). The inventory yields 16 scores on primary factors and 4 second order factor scores. Split-half reliabilities of single factor scores from one form of the inventory tend to be low but the split-half reliabilities of the factor scores from pooling two forms of the test (Form A and Form B) are adequate. Norms are provided for college students and adults but normative samples are inadequately described. The *16 PF* is an interesting instrument that is potentiallly useful, but at the present time should be viewed primarily as a research instrument.

Study of Values, Third Edition

Houghton Mifflin   *Testing time:* 20 min.
Grades 13 and over

The *Study of Values,* originally published in 1931, was designed to measure Spranger's six "value types": theoretical, economic, aesthetic, social, political, and religious. The second edition published in

1951 redefined the social value and added more discriminating items. The third edition, 1960, differs from the second edition only in providing more normative data. The median reliability coefficients for different subscales are .82 (split-half) and .88 for test-retest with a one- or two-month interval. Split-half reliabilities are based on groups of 100 subjects and test-retest on groups of 34 and 53 subjects. Validity data presented in the manual consist primarily of demonstrating that the value patterns of various educational and occupational groups differ in the predicted ways. Norms are provided for college groups and for occupational groups that usually require some college education. The instrument has been criticized for lack of evidence on the unidimensionality of the scales, the problem of ipsative scoring, and the lack of generality beyond the college population.

Survey of Personal Values (SPV)

Science Research Associates, Inc.   *Testing time:* Untimed,
Grades 11–16 and adults   approximately 20 min.

The *SPV* yields six scores: practical mindedness, achievement, variety, decisiveness, orderliness, goal orientation. The SPV consists of 30 triads from each of which the examinee selects one that is most important and one that is least important for him or for her. Raw scores are converted to percentile ranks. Norms are provided for college males, college females, high school males and high school females. The high school normative sample is geographically restricted. At its present stage of development, the SPI is primarily useful for research.

Tennessee Self Concept Scale (TSCS)

Counselor Recordings and Tests   *Testing time:* Untimed,
Ages 12 and over   approximately 20 min.

The *TSCS* is a self-administering instrument consisting of 100 statements with five response options ranging from completely false to completely true. Two forms, the Counseling Form and the Clinical and Research Form, are available but the two forms contain the same items and differ only in methods of scoring. The Counseling Form yields 14 scores and the Clinical and Research Form yields 30 scores. Items were constructed to appraise the following aspects of the self: Identity, Self-Satisfaction, Behavior, Physical Self, Social Self, Moral-Ethical Self, Personal Self, Family Self. In addition, three derived scores are provided: Total Positive Score, reflecting overall level of esteem; Variability Score, reflecting the amount of consistency among areas of self; and Distribution Score, reflecting tendency to use extreme response ratings. Scoring is tedious. The manual for the test is incomplete and lacks much essential information. At its present stage of development it is most suitable for research.

Thorndike Dimensions of Temperament (TDOT)

The Psychological Corporation
Grade 11 and above

Testing time: 30–45 min.

For discussion see text, pp. 429–430.

REFERENCES

American Psychological Association. *Standards for educational and psychological tests and manuals.* Washington, D. C.: American Psychological Association, 1974.

Ammons, R. B., & Ammons, H. S. *Full-Range Picture Vocabulary Test.* Missoula, Montana: Psychological Test Specialists, 1948.

Anderson, J. E. The limitations of infant and preschool tests in the measurement of intelligence. *Journal of Psychology,* 1939, **8,** 351–379.

Army Air Force Aviation Psychology Program Research Reports. Report #16, *Psychological research on operational training in the continental air forces.* Washington, D. C.: U. S. Government Printing Office, 1947, pp. 101–105.

Arthur, G. *A point scale of performance tests* (2nd ed.). New York: Commonwealth Fund, 1943.

Assessment Staff, U. S. Office of Strategic Services. *Assessment of men.* New York: Rinehart, 1948.

Baird, L., & Feister, W. J. Grading standards: the relation of changes in average student ability to the average grades awarded. *American Educational Research Journal,* 1972, **9,** 431–442.

Barrett, H. O. An examination of certain standardized art tests to determine their relation to classroom achievement and to intelligence. *Journal of Educational Research,* 1949, **42,** 398–400.

Barrett, R. S. The influence of supervisor's requirements on ratings. *Personnel Psychology,* 1966, **19,** 375–388.

Bayley, N. *Bayley Scales of Infant Development.* New York: Psychological Corporation, 1969.

Bayley, N. Consistency and variability in the growth of intelligence from birth to eighteen years. *Journal of Genetic Psychology,* 1949, **75,** 165–196.

Berdie, R. F. *Strong Vocational Interest* scores of high school seniors and their later occupational entry. *Journal of Applied Psychology,* 1965, **49,** 188–193.

Birns, B. Individual differences in human neonates' responses to stimulation. *Child Development,* 1965, **36,** 249–256.

673

Blatchford, C. H. *Experimental steps to ascertain reliability of diagnostic tests in English as a second language.* Unpublished Ph.D dissertation. New York: Teachers College, Columbia University, 1970.

Bloom, B. (Ed.) *Taxonomy of educational objectives, Handbook I: Cognitive domain.* New York: Longmans, Green & Co., 1956.

Bloom, B. S. *Stability and change in human characteristics.* New York: Wiley, 1964.

Blumberg, H. H., De Soto, C. B., & Kuethe, J. L. Evaluation of rating scale formats. *Personal Psychology,* 1966, **19,** 243–260.

Boynton, B. The physical growth of girls. *University of Iowa Studies in Child Welfare,* 1936, **12,** No. 4.

Boynton, M. Inclusion of "None of These" makes spelling items more difficult. *Educational and Psychological Measurement,* 1950, **10,** 431–432.

Bradway, K. P., & Thompson, C. W. Intelligence at adulthood: A twenty-five year follow-up. *Journal of Educational Psychology,* 1962, **53,** 1–14.

Bray, D. W., Campbell, R. J., & Grant, D. L. *Formative years in business: A long-term AT&T study of managerial lives.* New York: Wiley, 1974.

Brookover, W. B. Person-person interaction between teachers and pupils and teaching effectiveness. *Journal of Educational Research,* 1940, **34,** 272–287.

Buel, W. D. Voluntary female clerical turnover: The concurrent and predictive validity of a weighted application blank. *Journal of Applied Psychology,* 1964, **48,** 180–182.

Buel, W. D., Albright, L. E., & Glennon, J. R. A note on the generality and cross-validity of personal history for identifying creative research scientists. *Journal of Applied Psychology,* 1966, **50,** 217–219.

Buhler, R. A. *Flicker fusion threshold and anxiety level.* Unpublished doctoral dissertation, New York: Columbia University, 1953.

Buros, O. K. Educational, psychological, and personality tests of 1933, 1934, and 1935, *Rutgers University Bulletin,* **13,** No. 1, *Studies in Education, No. 9.* New Brunswick, N. J.: School of Education, Rutgers University, 1936.

Buros, O. K. Educational, psychological, and personality tests of 1936, *Rutgers University Bulletin,* **14,** No. 2A, *Studies in Education, No. 11.* New Brunswick, N. J.: School of Education, Rutgers University, 1937.

Buros, O. K. *The 1938 mental measurements yearbook.* New Brunswick, N. J.: Rutgers University Press, 1938.

Buros, O. K. *The 1940 mental measurements yearbook.* Highland Park, N. J.: The Mental Measurements Yearbook, 1941.

Buros, O. K. *The third mental measurements yearbook.* New Brunswick, N. J.: Rutgers University Press, 1949.

Buros, O. K. *The fourth mental measurements yearbook.* Highland Park, N. J.: Gryphon Press, 1953.

Buros, O. K. *The fifth mental measurements yearbook.* Highland Park, N. J.: Gryphon Press, 1959.

Buros, O. K. *Tests in print.* Highland Park, N. J.: Gryphon Press, 1961.

Buros, O. K. *The sixth mental measurements yearbook.* Highland Park, N. J.: Gryphon Press, 1965.

Buros, O. K. *Reading tests and reviews.* Highland Park, N. J.: Gryphon Press, 1968.

Buros, O. K. *Personality tests and reviews.* Highland Park, N. J.: Gryphon, 1970.

Buros, O. K. *The seventh mental measurements yearbook.* Highland Park, N. J. : Gryphon Press, 1972.

Buros, O. K. *Tests in print II.* Highland Park, N. J.: Gryphon Press, 1974.

Buros, O. K. *Foreign Language: tests and reviews.* Highland Park, N. J.: Gryphon Press, 1975a.

Buros, O. K. *English: tests and reviews.* Highland Park, N. J.: Gryphon Press, 1975b.

Buros, O. K. *Intelligence: tests and reviews.* Highland Park, N. J.: Gryphon Press, 1975c.

Buros, O. K. *Mathematics: tests and reviews.* Highland Park, N. J.: Gryphon Press, 1975d.

Buros, O. K. *Reading: tests and reviews.* Highland Park, N. J.: Gryphon Press, 1975e.

Buros, O. K. *Social Studies: tests and reviews.* Highland Park, N. J.: Gryphon Press, 1975f.

Buros, O. K. *Science: tests and reviews.* Highland Park, N. J.: Gryphon Press, 1975g.

Buros, O. K. *Vocational: tests and reviews.* Highland Park, N. J.: Gryphon Press, 1975h.

Buros, O. K. *Personality: titles and reviews II.* Highland Park, N. J.: Gryphon Press, 1975i.

Campbell, J. P., Dunnette, M. D., Arvey, R. D., & Hellervik, L. V. The development and evaluation of behaviorally based rating scales. *Journal of Applied Psychology,* 1973, **57,** 15–22.

Carroll, J. B., & Sapon, S. M. *Modern Language Aptitude Test.* New York: The Psychological Corporation, 1958.

Cattell, P. *Cattell Infant Intelligence Scale.* New York: The Psychological Corporation, 1960.

Cattell, R. B., Eber, H. W., & Tatsuoka, M. M. *Handbook for the Sixteen Personality Factor Questionnaire (16 PF).* Champaign, Ill.: Institute for Personality and Ability Testing, 1970.

Cattell, R. B., et al. *Objective personality and motivation tests: A theoretical introduction and practical compendium.* Urbana, Ill.: University of Illinois Press, 1967.

Chaney, F. B., & Owens, W. A. Life history antecedents of sales research and general engineering interests. *Journal of Applied Psychology,* 1964, **48,** 101–105.

Chase, C. I. Relative length of options and response set in multiple-choice items. *Journal of Educational Measurement,* 1964, **1,** 38.

Chun, K., Cobb, S., & French, J. R. P., Jr. *Measures for psychological assessment.* Ann Arbor, Mich.: Institute for Social Research, The University of Michigan, 1975.

Clark, C. A. The use of separate answer sheets in testing slow-learning pupils. *Journal of Educational Measurement,* 1968, **5,** 61–64.

Cleary, T. A. Test bias: Prediction of grades of Negro and white students in integrated colleges. *Journal of Educational Measurement,* 1968, **5,** 115–124.

Cleary, T. A. Test bias: Validity of the *Scholastic Aptitude Test* for Negro and white students. *College Entrance Examination Board Research Bulletin,* June 1966.

Coleman, J. S., et al. *Equality of educational opportunity.* Washington, D. C.: U. S. Government Printing Office, 1966.

College Entrance Examination Board. *Effects of coaching on Scholastic Aptitude Test scores.* Princeton, N. J.: College Entrance Examination Board, 1968.

Cook, W., & Leeds, C. H. Measuring the teaching personality. *Educational and Psychological Measurement*, 1947, **7**, 399–410.

Cooley, W. W., & Lohnes, P. R. *Predicting development of young adults.* Palo Alto, Calif.: American Institute for Reserch, 1968.

Coombs, C. H., Milholland, J. E. & Womer, F. B. The assessment of partial knowledge. *Educational and Psychological Measurement*, 1955, **16**, 13–37.

Cronbach, L. J. *Essentials of psychological testing* (3rd ed.). New York: Harper & Row, 1970.

Davis, F. B. Estimation and use of scoring weights for each choice in multiple-choice test items. *Educational and Psychological Measurement*, 1959, **19**, 291–298.

Dizney, H. F., Merrifield, P. R., & Davis, O. L., Jr. Effects of answer-sheet format on arithmetic test scores. *Educational and Psychological Measurement*, 1966, **26**, 491–493.

Doll, E. A. *Measurement of social competance.* Minneapolis, Minn.: Educational Test Bureau, Educational Publishers, 1953.

Doll, E. A. *Vineland Social Maturity Scale.* Minneapolis, Minn.: American Guidance Service, Inc., 1965.

Doppelt, J. Estimating full-scale score on the *Wechsler Adult Intelligence Scale* from scores on four subtests. *Journal of Consulting Psychology*, 1956, **20**, 63–66.

DuBois, P. (Ed.). *The classification program, Army Air Forces Aviation Psychology Program Report No. 2.* Washington, D. C.: U. S. Government Printing Office, 1947.

Dunn, L.M. *Peabody Picture Vocabulary Test.* Minneapolis, Minn.: American Guidance Services, 1959.

Dunn, T. F., & Goldstein, L. G. Test difficulty, validity, and reliability as functions of selective multiple-choice item construction principles. *Educational and Psychological Measurement*, 1959, **19**, 171–179.

Ebel, R. L. Confidence weighting and test reliability. *Journal of Educational Measurement*, 1965, **2**, 49–57.

Ebert, E., & Simmons, K. The Brush Foundation study of child growth and development. I: Psychometric tests. *Monograph of the Society for Research in Child Development*, 1943, **8**, No. 2.

Educational Testing Service, Test Development Division. *Multiple-choice questions: A close look.* Princeton, N. J.: Educational Testing Service, 1963.

Ellis, A. Recent research with personality inventories. *Journal of Consulting Psychology*, 1953, **17**, 45–49.

Ellis, A. The validity of personality questionnaires. *Psychological Bulletin*, 1946, **43**, 385–440.

Ellis, A., & Conrad, H. S. The validity of personality inventories in military practice. *Psychological Bulletin*, 1948, **45**, 385–426.

England, G. W. *Development and use of weighted application blanks.* Dubuque, Iowa: William C. Brown, 1961.

Exner, John E., Jr. *The Rorschach Systems.* New York: Grune and Stratton, 1969.

Eysenck, H. J. *The scientific study of personality.* New York: Macmillan, 1952.

Feldhusen, J. F. An evaluation of college students' reactions to open book examinations. *Educational and Psychological Measurement,* 1961, **21,** 637–646.

Findley, W. G. and Bryan, M. M. Ability grouping: 1970 Status, impact and alternatives. Athens, Ga: Center for Educational Improvement, University of Georgia, 1971.

Fivars, G., & Gosnell, D. *Nursing evaluation: The problem and the process.* New York: Macmillan, 1966, Chapter 9.

Flanagan, J. C., & Cooley, W. W. *Project Talent: One-year follow-up studies.* Pittsburgh, Pa.: University of Pittsburgh School of Education, 1966.

Flanagan, J. C., Tiedman, D. V., Willis, M. B., & McLaughlin, D. H. *The Career Data Book: results from Project Talent's five-year follow-up study.* Palo Alto, Calif.: American Institutes for Research, 1973.

Flanders, N. A. Teacher influence, pupil attitudes, and achievement. *U.S. Office of Education Cooperative Research Monograph.* Washington, D. C.: U. S. Government Printing Office, 1965, No. 12.

French, J. W. The description of aptitude and achievement tests in terms of rotated factors. *Psychometric Monographs,* 1951, No. 5.

French, J. W. The effect of anxiety on verbal and mathematical examination scores. *Educational and Psychological Measurement,* 1962, **22,** 553–564.

Gardner, E. F., & Thompson, G. G. *Syracuse Scales of Social Relations.* New York: Harcourt, Brace & World, 1958.

Garry, R. Individual differences in ability to fake vocational interests. *Journal of Applied Psychology,* 1953, **37,** 33–37.

Gerberich, J. R. *Specimen objective test items: A guide to achievement test construction.* New York: Longmans, Green and Co. (David McKay), 1956.

Gesell, A., et al. *The first five years of life: A guide to the study of the preschool child.* New York: Harper, 1940.

Ghiselli, E. E. The validity of aptitude tests in personnel selection. *Personnel Psychology,* 1973, **26,** 461–477.

Ghiselli, E. E. *The validity of occupational aptitude tests.* New York: Wiley, 1966.

Ghiselli, E. E., & Barthol, R. P. The validity of personality inventories in the selection of employees. *Journal of Applied Psychology,* 1953, **37,** 18–20.

Goodenough, F. L., & Maurer, K. M. The mental growth of children from two to fourteen years: A study of the predictive value of the *Minnesota Preschool Scales. University of Minnesota Institute of Child Welfare Monograph,* 1942, No. 19.

Goodenough, F. L., Maurer, K. M., & Van Wagenen, M. J. *Minnesota Preschool Scales: Manual of instructions.* Minneapolis, Minn.: Educational Test Bureau, 1940.

Gordon, E. *Musical Aptitude Profile.* Boston, Mass.: Houghton Mifflin, 1965.

Gordon, E. *A three-year longitudinal predictive validity study of the Musical Aptitude Profile.* Iowa City, Iowa: University of Iowa Press, 1967.

Goslin, D. A. *Teachers and testing.* New York: Russell Sage Foundation, 1967, pp. 25–33.

Grimsley, G., Ruch, F. L., Warren, N. D., & Ford, J. S. *Employee Aptitude Survey,* Los Angeles, Calif.: Psychological Services, 1963.

Gronlund, N. E. *Sociometry in the class-room.* New York: Harper, 1959, pp. 164–166.

Guilford, J. P. *The nature of human intelligence.* New York: McGraw-Hill, 1967.

Halliwell, J. W. The relationship of certain factors to marking practices in individualized reporting programs. *Journal of Educational Research,* 1960, **54,** 76–78.

Harari, O., & Zedeck, S. Development of behaviorally anchored scales for the evaluation of faculty teaching. *Journal of Applied Psychology,* 1973, **58,** 261–265.

Harrington, W. Recommendation quality and placement success. *Psychological Monographs,* 1943, No. 252.

Harris, D. B. *Children's drawings as measures of intellectual maturity.* New York: Harcourt, Brace & World, 1963.

Harris, D. B., & Pinder, G. D. *The Goodenough-Harris Drawing Test as a measure of intellectual maturity of youths.* Rockville, Md.: National Center for Health Statistics, *DHEW Publication No. (HRA) 74-1620,* 1974.

Hartshorne, H., & May, M. A. *Studies in deceit.* New York: Macmillan, 1928.

Hayward, P. A comparison of test performance on three answer-sheet formats. *Educational and Psychological Measurement,* 1967, **27,** 997–1004.

Highland, R. W., & Berkshire, J. R. *A methodological study of forced choice performance rating.* San Antonio, Tex.: Human Resources Research Center, Lackland Air Force Base, May 1951. *(Research Bulletin 51-9.)*

Hobbs, N. (Ed.) *Issues in the classification of children.* San Francisco: Jossey-Bass, 1975.

Holland, J. L. *The psychology of vocational choice.* Waltham, Mass.: Blaisdell, 1966.

Honzik, M. P., McFarlane, J. W., & Allen, L. The stability of mental test performance between two and eighteen years. *Journal of Experimental Education,* 1948, **17,** 309–324.

Hopkins, K. D., Lefever, D. W., & Hopkins, B. R. TV versus teacher administration of standardized tests: Comparability of scores. *Journal of Educational Measurement,* 1967, **4,** 35–40.

Horn, C. A., & Smith, L. F. The *Horn Art Aptitude Inventory. Journal of Applied Psychology,* 1945, **29,** 350–355.

Hoyt, D. P., & Munday, L. Academic description and prediction in junior colleges. *American College Testing Program Research Reports 1966 No. 10.* Iowa City, Iowa: American College Testing Program, 1966.

Huck, J. R. Assessment centers: A review of the external and internal validities. *Personal Psychology,* 1973, **26,** 2, 191–212.

Hughes, H. II. & Trimble, W. E. The use of complex alternatives in multiple-choice items. *Educational and Psychological Measurement,* 1965, **25,** 117–126.

Judy, C. J. A comparison of peer and supervisory rankings as criteria of aircraft maintenance proficiency. Ed.D. project report. New York: Teachers College, Columbia University, 1952.

Kaufman, A. S. Comparison of the *WPPSI, Stanford-Binet* and *McCarthy* scales as predictors of first-grade achievement. *Perceptual and Motor Skills,* 1973, **36,** 67–73.

Kerlinger, F. N., & Pedhazur, E. J. *Multiple regression in behavioral re-*

search. New York: Holt, Rinehart & Winston, 1973.

Klores, M. S. Rater bias in forced-distribution performance ratings. *Personnel Psychology,* 1966, **19,** 411-421.

Knobloch, H., & Passamanick, B. Prediction from the assessment of neuromotor and intellectual status in infancy. In J. Zubin & G. A. Jervis (Eds.), *Psychopathology of mental development.* New York: Grune & Stratton, 1967.

Krathwohl, D. R., Bloom, B. S., & Masia, B. B. *Taxonomy of educational objectives, the classification of educational goals, Handbook II: Affective domain.* New York: David McKay, 1964.

Lamb, G. S. Teacher verbal cues and pupil performance on a group reading test. *Journal of Educational Psychology,* 1967, **58,** 332-336.

Lesser, G. S., Fifer, G., & Clark, D. H. Mental abilities of children from different social-class and cultural groups. *Monographs of the Society for Research in Child Development,* 1965, **30,** No. 4.

Lewis, L. S. On the genesis of gray-flanneled Puritans. *American Association of University Professors Bulletin,* 1972, **58,** 21-29.

Lins, L. J. The prediction of teaching efficiency. *Journal of Experimental Education,* 1946, **15,** 2-60.

Loehlin, H. C., Lindzey, G., & Spuhler, J. N. *Race differences in intelligence.* San Francisco, Calif.: W. H. Freeman, 1975.

Longstaff, H. P. Fakability of the *Strong Interest Blank* and the *Kuder Preference Record. Journal of Applied Psychology,* 1948, **32,** 360-369.

Lord, F. M. The relation of the reliability of multiple-choice tests to the distribution of item difficulties. *Psychometrika,* **17,** 181-194.

Loughmiller, G. C., Ellison, R. L., Taylor, C. W., & Price, P. B. Predicting career performance of physicians using the biographical inventory approach. *Journal of Vocational Behavior,* 1973, **3,** 269-278.

McCarthy, D. *McCarthy Scales of Children's Abilities.* New York: The Psychological Corporation, 1972.

McClelland, D., et al. *The achievement motive.* New York: Appleton-Century-Crofts, 1953.

McCully, C. H. *The validity of the Kuder Preference Record.* Ed.D. dissertation. Washington D. C.: George Washington University, 1954.

McGrath, J. J. Improving credit evaluation with a weighted application blank. *Journal of Applied Psychology,* 1960, **44,** 325-328.

Mallinson, G. G., & Crumrine, W. M. An investigation of the stability of interests of high school students. *Journal of Educational Research,* 1952, **45,** 369-383.

Miller, D. C. *Handbook of research design and social measurement.* New York: McKay, 1964.

Miller, I. A note on the evaluation of a new answer form. *Journal of Applied Psychology,* 1965, **49,** 199-201.

Mitchell, B. C. Predictive validity of the *Metropolitan Readiness Tests and Murphy-Durrell Reading Readiness Tests* for white and Negro students. *Educational and Psychological Measurement,* 1967, **27,** 1047-1054.

Mogul, S., & Satz, P. Abbreviation of the *WAIS* for clinical use: An attempt at validation. *Journal of Clinical Psychology,* 1963, **19,** 298-300.

Moses, J. L. The development of an assessment center for the early identification of supervisory potential. *Personnel Journal,* 1973, **26,** 4, 569-580.

Munday, L. Predicting college grades in predominantly Negro colleges. *Journal of Educational Measurement*, 1965, **2**, 157–160.

Murray, H. A., et al. *Explorations in personality.* New York: Oxford University Press, 1938.

National Education Association. Reports to parents. *NEA Research Bulletin*, 1967, **45**, 51–53.

Neville, D. The relationship between reading skills and intelligence test scores. *The Reading Teacher*, 1965, **18**, 257–262.

Olson, W. C. The measurement of nervous habits in normal children. *University of Minnesota Institute of Child Welfare Monograph*, 1929, No. 3.

Orleans, J. B., & Hanna, G. S. *Orleans-Hanna Geometry Prognosis Test.* New York: Harcourt Brace Jovanovich, 1968.

Orleans, J. B., & Hanna, G. S. *Orleans-Hanna Algebra Prognosis Test.* New York: Harcourt Brace Jovanovich, 1969.

Osgood, C. E., Suci, G. J., & Tannenbaum, P. H. *The measurement of meaning.* Urbana: University of Illinois Press, 1957.

Owens, W. A., Jr. The retest consistency of *Army Alpha* after 30 years. *Journal of Applied Psychology*, 1954, **38**, 154.

Peres, S. H., & Garcia, J. R. Validity and dimensions of descriptive adjectives used in reference letters for engineering applicants. *Personnel Psychology*, 1962, **15**, 279–286.

Personnel Research Section, AGO. *Analysis of an Officer Efficiency Report (WD AGO Form 67-1) using multiple raters.* Washington, D. C.: Adjutant General's Office, 1952a *(PRS Report 817)*.

Personnel Research Section, AGO. *A study of officer rating methodology,* *validity and reliability of ratings by single raters and multiple raters.* Washington, D. C.: Adjutant General's Office, 1952b *(PRS Report 904)*.

Personnel Research Section, AGO. *Survey of the aptitude for service rating system at the U. S. Military Academy, West Point, New York.* Washington, D. C.: Adjutant General's Office, 1953.

Pimsleur, P. *Pimsleur Language Aptitude Battery.* New York: Harcourt, Brace & Jovanovich, 1966.

Pinchak, B. M., & Breland, H. M. Grading practices in American high schools: National longitudinal study of the high school class of 1972. *Education Digest*, 1974, **39**, 21–3.

Preston, H. O. *The development of a procedure for evaluating officers in the United States Air Force.* Pittsburgh, Pa.: American Institute for Research, 1948.

Raven, J. C. *Progressive Matrices.* London: H. K. Lewis, 1956 (U. S. Distributor: The Psychological Corporation).

Reed, H. J. An investigation of the relationship between teaching effectiveness and the teacher's attitude of acceptance. *Journal of Experimental Education*, 1953, **21**, 277–325.

Remmers, H. H., Shock, N. W., & Kelly, E. L. An empirical study of the validity of the Spearman Brown formula as applied to the Purdue Rating Scale. *Journal of Educational Psychology*, 1927, **18**, 187–195.

Richardson, M. W., & Kuder, G. F. Making a rating scale that measures. *Personnel Journal*, 1933, **12**, 36–40.

Rimland, B. The effects of varying time limits and of using right answer not given in experimental forms of the U. S. Navy Arithmetic Test. *Educational and Psychological Measurement,* 1960, **20,** 533–539.

Robinson, J. P. & Shaver, P. R. *Measures of social psychological attitudes* (Revised Ed.). Ann Arbor, Mich.: Institute for Social Research, The University of Michigan, 1973.

Rollins, H. A., McCandless, B. R., Thompson, M., & Brassell, W. R. Project success environment: an extended application of contingency management in inner-city schools. *Journal of Educational Psychology,* 1974, **66,** 2, 167–178.

Rosenbaum, B. L. *An empirical study of attitude toward invasion of privacy as it relates to personnel selection.* New York: Teachers College, Columbia University. Unpublished Ed.D. dissertation, 1971.

Ross, A. O., Lacey, H. M., & Parton, D. A. The development of a behavior checklist for boys. *Child Development,* 1965, **36,** 1013–1027.

Ruch, F. L., et al. *Employee Aptitude Survey.* Los Angeles: Psychological Services, Inc., 1965.

Sarason, I. G. Test anxiety and the intellectual performance of college students. *Journal of Educational Psychology,* 1961, **52,** 201–206.

Sarason, S. B., et al. *Anxiety in elementary school children.* New York: Wiley, 1960.

Schaefer, C. E., & Anastasi, A. A. Biographical Inventory for identifying creativity in adolescent boys. *Journal of Applied Psychology,* 1968, **52,** 42–48.

Scott, R. D., & Johnson, R. W. Use of the weighted application blank in selecting unskilled employees. *Journal of Applied Psychology,* 1967, **51,** 393–395.

Sears, R. R., Rau, L., & Alpert, R. *Identification and child rearing.* Stanford, Calif.: Stanford University Press, 1965.

Shaw, M. E., & Wright, J. M. *Scales for the measurement of attitudes.* New York: McGraw-Hill, 1967.

Siskind, G. "Mine eyes have seen a host of angels." *American Psychologist,* 1966, **21,** 804–806.

Slater, R. D. The equivalency of IBM mark-sense answer cards and IBM answer sheets when used as answer formats for a precisely timed test of mental ability. *Journal of Educational Research,* 1964, **57,** 545–547.

Slosson, R. L. *Slosson Intelligence Test.* East Aurora, N. Y.: Slosson Educational Publications, 1963.

Smith, P. C. & Kendall, L. M. Retranslation of expectations: An approach to the construction of unambiguous anchors for rating scales. *Journal of Applied Psychology,* 1963, **47,** 149–155.

St. John, C. W. Educational achievement in relation to intelligence as shown by teachers' marks, promotions and scores in standard tests in certain elementary grades. *Harvard University Studies in Education,* 1930, **15.**

Stanley, J. C., & Porter, A. C. Correlation of scholastic aptitude test score with college grades for Negroes versus whites. *Journal of Educational Measurement,* 1967, **4,** 199–218.

Strong, E. K. *Vocational interests of men and women.* Stanford, Calif.: Stanford University Press, 1943.

Strong, E. K. Interest scores while in college of occupations engaged in twenty years later. *Educational and Psychological Measurement,* 1951a, **11,** 335–348.

Strong, E. K. Permanence of interest scores over twenty-two years.

Journal of Applied Psychology, 1951b, **35,** 89–91.

Strong, E. K. Nineteen-year follow-up of engineer interests. *Journal of Applied Psychology,* 1952, **36,** 65–74.

Stutsman, R. *Mental measurement of pre-school children, with a guide for the administration of the Merrill-Palmer Scale of mental tests.* Yonkers, N. Y.: World Book, 1931.

Super, D. E. The *Bernreuter Personality Inventory:* A review of research. *Psychological Bulletin,* 1942, **39,** 94–125.

Symonds, P. M. *Diagnosing personality and conduct.* New York: Century, 1931.

Terman, L. M., & Merrill, M. A. *Stanford-Binet Intelligence Scale: Manual for third revision.* Boston, Mass.: Houghton Mifflin, 1973.

Thorndike, R. L. The prediction of intelligence at college entrance from earlier tests. *Journal of Educational Psychology,* 1947, **38,** 129–148.

Thorndike, R. L. A Verification Key for the *Thorndike Dimensions of Temperament. Journal of Educational Measurement,* 1968, 5, 331–32.

Thorndike, R. L., & Hagen, E. P. *10,000 Careers.* New York: Wiley, 1959.

Thorndike, R. L., Hagen, E. P., & Lorge, I. D. *Lorge-Thorndike Intelligence Tests, Multilevel Edition.* Boston, Mass.: Houghton Mifflin, 1966.

Thorndike, R. L., Hagen, E. P., & Lorge, I. D. *Cognitive Abilities Test, Primary Battery.* Boston, Mass.: Houghton Mifflin, 1968.

Thorndike, R. L., Hagen, E. P., & Lorge, I. D. *Cognitive Abilities Test, Multilevel Edition.* Boston, Mass.: Houghton Mifflin, 1972.

Thurstone, L. L. Primary mental abilities. *Psychometric Monographs,* 1938, No. 1.

Torrance, E. P. *Torrance Tests of Creative Thinking.* Princeton, N. J.: Personnel Press, 1966.

Tuddenham, R. D. Soldier intelligence in World Wars I and II. *American Psychologist,* 1948, **3,** 54–56.

United States Employment Service. *Manual for the General Aptitude Test Battery, Section III: Development.* Washington, D. C.: United States Department of Labor, 1967.

Vernon, P. E. *The structure of human abilities* (rev. ed.). London: Methuen, 1960.

Vernon, P. R. The distinctiveness of field independence. *Journal of Personality,* 1972, **40,** 3, 366–391.

Wahlstrom, M., & Boersma, F. J. The influence of test-wiseness upon achievement. *Educational and Psychological Measurement,* 1968, **28,** 413–420.

Wason, P. Response to affirmative and negative binary statements. *British Journal of Psychology,* 1961, **52,** 133–142.

Waters, L. K. Effect of perceived scoring formula on some aspects of test performance. *Educational and Psychological Measurement,* 1967, **27,** 1005–1010.

Webb, J., Campbell, D. T., Schwartz, R. D., & Sechrest, L. *Unobtrusive measures: Nonreactive research in the social sciences.* Chicago: Rand McNally & Co., 1966.

Wechsler, D. *Wechsler Adult Intelligence Scale.* New York: The Psychological Corporation, 1955.

Wechsler, D. *Wechsler Intelligence Scale for Children—Revised Manual.* New York: The Psychological Corporation, 1974.

Wechsler, D. *Wechsler Preschool and Primary Scale of Intelligence*. New York: The Psychological Corporation, 1967.

Wesman, A. G., & Bennett, G. K. The use of "None of These" as an option in test construction. *Journal of Educational Psychology*, 1946, **37**, 533–539.

Wheeler, L. R. A comparative study of the intelligence of east Tennessee mountain children. *Journal of Educational Psychology*, 1942, **33**, 321–334.

White, M. A., & Boehm, A. Child's world of learning: Written workload of pupils. *Psychology in the Schools*, 1967, **6**, 70–73.

Witkin, H. A., et al. *Psychological differentiation*. New York: Wiley, 1962.

Yamamoto, K., & Dizney, H. F. Effects of three sets of test instructions on scores on an intelligence scale. *Educational and Psychological Measurement*, 1965, **25**, 87–94.

Yonge, G. D., & Heist, P. A. The influence of suggested content on faking a personality test. *American Educational Research Journal*, 1965, **2**, 137–144.

Zern, D. Effects of variations in question phrasing on true-false answers by grade-school children. *Psychological Reports*, 1967, **20** (2), 527–533.

INDEX